MINUTES

OF THE

Eleventh Biennial Convention

OF

The United Lutheran Church in America

Baltimore, Maryland

October 5-12, 1938

THE UNITED LUTHERAN PUBLICATION HOUSE
PHILADELPHIA, PA.

THE UNITED LUTHERAN CHURCH IN AMERICA

CALENDAR, 1938-1940

OFFICERS

President—REV. F. H. KNUBEL, D.D., LL.D., S.T.D., Litt.D.
39 East 35th Street, New York, N. Y.

Secretary—REV. W. H. GREEVER, D.D., LL.D.
39 East 35th Street, New York, N. Y.

Treasurer—E. CLARENCE MILLER, LL.D.
1508 Walnut Street, Philadelphia, Pa.

EXECUTIVE BOARD

Term Expires 1942

Rev. Henry H. Bagger, D.D., 1205 Law and Finance Bldg., 429 Fourth Ave., Pittsburgh, Pa.
Rev. Alvin E. Bell, D.D., 2263 Maplewood Ave., Toledo, Ohio.
Rev. Paul H. Krauss, D.D., 405 W. Wayne St., Fort Wayne, Ind.
Mr. J. K. Jensen, Janesville, Wis.
James C. Kinard, LL.D., Newberry College, Newberry, S. C.
Hon. Claude T. Reno, 719 Hamilton St., Allentown, Pa.

Term Expires 1940

Rev. E. B. Burgess, D.D., LL.D., 39 East 35th St., New York, N. Y.
Rev. H. W. A. Hanson, D.D., LL.D., Gettysburg, Pa.
Rev. E. P. Pfatteicher, Ph.D., D.D., LL.D., 1228 Spruce St., Philadelphia, Pa.
Mr. Robert F. Bowe, 981 Kimball Ave., Bronxville, N. Y.
Robbin B. Wolf, LL.D., 711 Plaza Bldg., Pittsburgh, Pa.
Hon. John L. Zimmerman, LL.D., Springfield, Ohio.

Members Ex-Officio

Rev. F. H. Knubel, President
Rev. W. H. Greever, Secretary
Mr. E. Clarence Miller, Treasurer

Place of next Convention—Omaha, Nebraska

Minutes of the Eleventh Biennial Convention of The United Lutheran Church in America

THE SERVICE—INTRODUCTORY

TRINITY LUTHERAN CHURCH
Baltimore, Maryland
Wednesday, October 5, 1938, 7.30 P. M.

The Opening Service of the Eleventh Biennial Convention was held in Trinity Lutheran Church, 2100 W. Baltimore Street, Baltimore, Md., the Rev. P. S. Baringer, Pastor, beginning at 7.30 P. M., on October 5, 1938.

The Service was conducted by the Secretary, including the Order for Public Confession and the Administration of the Lord's Supper. There were 475 communicants. The Sermon was preached by the President, the Rev. F. H. Knubel, from the text, Matthew 18: 20. The theme, developed with reference to the twentieth anniversary of the organization of The United Lutheran Church in America, was "Gathered Together." The Secretary was assisted in the administration of the Lord's Supper by President Gerberding of the Synod of the Northwest, President Pugh of the Florida Synod, President Lesher of the Iowa Synod, and President Kern of the Texas Synod.

FIRST SESSION

LORD BALTIMORE HOTEL
Baltimore, Maryland
Thursday, October 6, 1938, 8.45 A. M.

Matins were conducted by the Rev. B. H. Pershing

The President called the Convention to order, and, after the use of the Order for the Opening of Synods, declared the Eleventh Biennial Convention of The United Lutheran Church in America open for business.

By general consent the report of the completed roll of delegates was deferred.

The roll, as established at noon, Friday, October 7th, follows: (For attendance, see p. 387.)

ROLL OF DELEGATES BY SYNODS

1. Ministerium of Pennsylvania

Organized August 15, 1748

Clerical	Lay
Pfatteicher. E. P., Ph.D., D.D., LL.D.	Tyson, Levering, Litt.D.
Melhorn, N. R., D.D., Litt.D., LL.D.	Miller, E. Clarence, LL.D.
	Osterlund, Otto W., P.D., P.H.M.
Wilker, Conrad, D.D.	Greiner, John, Jr.
Bechtold, G. H., D.D.	Shimer, J. Myron
Kidd, Harvey S.	Hager, William H.
Offermann, H., D.D.	Keller, Judge Hiram H
Gehr, G. Franklin, D.D.	Jones, George M.
Fretz, Franklin K., Ph.D., D.D.	Billig, Clarence C., O.D.
Keiter, A. Charles R., D.D.	Hagan, Peter P.
Weber, Emil W., D.D.	Deck, J. Milton
Stough, William L., D.D.	Walker, H. Torrey
Henry, J. O., D.D.	Bader, Earle W.
Kinard, G. Harold, D.D.	Yost, Daniel F.
Fischer, Emil E., D.D.	Wenrich, George M., M.D. (a)
Herrmann, William F., S.T.M.	Hodges, Harry
Bachmann, E. F., D.D.	Vickers, Ross M.
MacIntosh, Aden B., D.D.	Mearig, William M.
Mattes, John C., D.D.	Jacobs, Henry S.
Houser, J. Ray	Harr, Luther A.
Krouse, Walter R.	Esser, Charles H.
Reed, Luther D., D.D., A.E.D.	Walborn, Maurice D.
Esterly, Franklin T., D.D.	Sowers, Harry
Urich, Frank M., D.D.	Angerhofer, Fred
Weaver, William M., S.T.D.	Mauch, Russell C.
Huyett, Paul P., S.T.M.	Maberry, Albert
Kressley, G. Smith, Litt.D.	Raeder, Robert D.
Wuchter, M. LeRoy	Wenzel, Theodore
Knudsen, Gunnar	Williams, Gordon
Waidelich, John H., D.D.	Schaumburg, Paul J.
Frankenfield, Ira F.	Woltersdorf, Otto
Miller, Hermann F., D.D.	Ely, William
Atkinson, Thomas	Ganser, W. R.
Ulrich, L. Domer, D.D.	Reitz, D. M.
Cornehlsen, Henry C., Jr., S.T.M.	Kersteen, H. C.
Hauser, Walter K.	McCloughan, Russell
Trexler, Mark K.	Haag, George W.
Kramer, R. E.	Stiles, John
Mann, Horace S.	Wissler, Clarence R.
Wohlsen, Peter N.	

2. United Synod of New York
*October 23, 1786

Clerical	Lay
Burgess, Ellis B., D.D., LL.D.	Dahmer, Charles H.
White, Paul C., Ph.D.	Hartwig, Wilmer H.
Noeldeke, Frederick	Stoughton, C. C.
Eichner, Clifford E.	Beisler, Henry
Keller, Arnold F.	Edelmann, Otto K.
Werner, Oscar V.	Buhl, Paul C.
Tamke, George R. F.	Pfeil, Henry G.
Weidt, William C. J.	Eck, William
Bosch, Herbert A.	Nuss, G. Peter
McKnight, Henry T.	Neumann, Martin
Jaxheimer, David G.	Rabenold, Ellwood M.
Dillenbeck, Andrew L., D.D.	Telleen, S. Frederick
Knubel, Frederick H., D.D., S.T.D., LL.D., Litt.D.	Logan, Howard L.
	Lutz, Jacob
Knubel, F. R., D.D.	Wilke, Louis A.
Kirsch, Paul Andrew	Miller, Ellsworth
Pflum, Henry J., D.D.	Nutzhorn, Adolph
Nutzhorn, Carl W.	Kiesel, Frederick
Scherer, Paul E., D.D., LL.D., Litt.D.	Reisch, Otto
	Lotsch, Joseph M.
Krumwiede, Walter, S.T.D.	Doell, Raymond
Wahl, H. H.	Weller, Walter W.
Krumbholz, Clarence E., D.D.	Smith, Ross E.
Tappert, C. Reinhold, D.D.	Flathmann, J. H.
Hirzel, Carl H.	Van Hoesen, U. Grant
Van Deusen, Robert J.	Brandenberger, O. R.
Brandt, Yost	Bahrenburg, John H.
Meyer, J. Henry	Ehrhardt, Herman T.
Lorenz, Martin J.	Holzkamp, John
Sunday, William F., Ph.D.	Wiegand, Frank
Gerhart, Luther F.	Stewart, Harold I.
Sprock, John H.	Ketterer, Philip H.
Krahmer, J. Christian	Blohm, William, Jr.
Wallick, Cyrus M.	Reed, James A.
Vesper, Herman F.	Schaefer, Fred C.
Miller, Carl H.	Mayer, John
Fritts, Dorr E.	Schubert, Ehrhardt
Wasmund, Henry C., D.D.	Lang, Henry
Gold, Howard R., D.D.	
Steimle, Edmund A.	

* Date of organization of the Ministerium of New York and Adjacent States and Countries which, on June 5, 1929, merged with the Evangelical Lutheran Synod of New York (organized 1830, see Minutes U. L. C. A., 1926, p. 8) and the Evangelical Lutheran Synod of New York and New England (organized in 1902), to form The United Lutheran Synod of New York.

3. United Synod of North Carolina
May 2, 1803

Clerical	Lay
Morgan, J. L., D.D.	Fisher, J. L.
Conrad, F. L.	Fisher, Prof. H. A.
Stirewalt, M. L., D.D.	Capps, Hon. Bismarck
Monroe, P. E., D.D.	Yoder, Prof. M. C.
Petrea, B. E.	Mauney, W. K.
Rhodes, George H.	Sigmon, Hon. J. C.
Lingle, G. H. L.	Monroe, P. E.
Brown, B. S.	Stevens, Dr. M. L.
Fisher, C. P.	Rhyne, T. P.
Fulenwider, E., D.D.	Rudisill, C. A.

* Date of organization of the Evangelical Lutheran Synod and Ministerium of North Carolina, which on March 2, 1921, with the Evangelical Lutheran Tennessee Synod (organized July 17, 1820) merged into the United Evangelical Lutheran Synod of North Carolina under an amended charter of the former of the two synods which merged.

4. Maryland Synod
Organized October 11, 1820

Clerical	Lay
Rasmussen, Carl C., D.D.	Alden, L. Russell
Traver, Amos John, D.D.	Fogle, Harry B.
Fife, J. Frank	Orth, Charles E.
Blackwelder, Oscar F., D.D.	Doub, Virgil W.
Huffman, Paul E.	Renn, John S.
Clare, R. D., D.D.	Frick, J. Henry
Tabor, L. Ralph	Fuss, Merwyn C.
Sloop, Roy L.	Kakel, F. W.
Weidley, Paul A., D.D.	Cooper, A. M.
Wade, William A., D.D.	Weitzel, George R.

5. Synod of South Carolina
Organized January 14, 1824

Clerical	Lay
Pence, E. Z.	Kinard, James C., LL.D.
Brown, P. D., D.D.	Counts, R. C.
Kinard, Karl W.	Torrence, R.
Greever, W. H., D.D., LL.D.	Hare, B. B.
Hiers, W. F.	Yoder. R. A.
Suber, T. F.	Ballentine, J. B.
Davis, W. C., D.D.	Schroeder, Julius A.

6. Central Pennsylvania Synod
*September 5, 1825

Clerical	Lay
Putman, D. F.	Menges, Franklin
Sternat, H. W., S.T.M.	Black, George P.
Lucas, Paul B.	Hershey, W. K. S.
Lind, R. W.	Holtzapple, George E., M.D.
Sammel, W. Raymond	Menges, W. H.
Gresh, R. R.	Nissly, Alvin R.
Stock, H. B., D.D.	Tilberg, W. E., Ph.D.
Hollinger, A. M.	Varner, Charles H.
Alleman, H. C., D.D., LL.D.	Frey, Edward
Hamsher, M. R., D.D.	King, W. H.
Grove, E. Martin, D.D.	Hoover, E. G.
Herman, S. W., D.D.	Frankenfield, O. Roy
Greiss, G. A., D.D.	Emhardt, William H.
Krout, J. D., D.D.	Kurzenknabe, John George
Billheimer, S., D.D.	Deatrick, David P., D.D.S.
Hanson, H. W. A., D.D., LL.D.	Durboraw, A. H.
Ney, W. C., D.D.	Snyder, Ivan J.
Baughman, H. F., D.D.	Gerberich, E. S.
Swank, C. P., D.D.	Boyer, C. H.
Simonton, C. S., D.D.	Shoop, Walter M.
Wunder, F. C., Ph.D.	Daugherty, Roy C.
Yost, H. E.	Slifer, Belding B.
Swoope, W. E.	Biggard, Alfred H.
Kanzinger, A. C., S.T.M.	Miller, I. W.
Sassaman, I. S., D.D.	Hafer, George W.
Foelsch, C. B., Ph.D.	Minnich, A. B.
Rearick, W. M., D.D.	Schnure, W. M.
Brown, W. E.	Steele, Charles
Foulke, Glenn W.	Spigelmyer, W. W., Ph.D.
Janson, J. M.	Holman, Major Edward L.
Stuempfle, H. G.	Wintersteen, A. J.
Hauser, E. Roy	Wilson, John W.
Windman, E. P.	Troutman, S. U.
Shaffer, D. L.	Woods, C. W.
Sigler, S. D.	Weaver, G. E.
Manges, E. L., D.D.	Lansberry, Thomas F.
Shannon, J. S.	Brothers, A. C.
Knoebel, R. P.	Reiter, Frank P.

* Date of organization of the Synod of West Pennsylvania, which, on June 8, 1938, was merged with the East Pennsylvania Synod (organized May 2, 1842), the Alleghany Synod (organized September 9, 1842), and the Susquehanna Synod (formed, on May 22, 1924, by the merger of the Synod of Central Pennsylvania, organized February 21, 1855, and the Susquehanna Synod, organized November 5, 1867, under the name of the Susquehanna Synod of Central Pennsylvania, the name being changed to Susquehanna Synod on April 11, 1932).

7. Synod of Virginia
August 10, 1829

Clerical	Lay
Scherer, J. J., Jr., D.D.	Almond, Judge J. L.
Anderson, R. Homer, D.D.	Mapes, R. E.
Rhyne, Hugh J.	Stauffer, W. T.
Huffman, A. M.	Ahalt, Prof. H. C.
Hewitt, A. K.	Bonham, J. B.
Wertz, L. A.	Speese, C. M.
Minnick, M. L.	Blosser, Gabriel
Strickler, L. W., D.D.	Copenhaver, B. E.

* Date of organization of the Evangelical Lutheran Synod and Ministerium of Virginia which, on March 17, 1922, with the Evangelical Lutheran Synod and Ministerium of Southwestern Virginia (composed of the former Evangelical Lutheran Synod and Ministerium of Southwestern Virginia, organized September 20, 1842, and the Evangelical Lutheran Holston Synod, organized September 29, 1860), merged into the Lutheran Synod of Virginia.

8. Synod of Ohio
November 7, 1836

Clerical	Lay
Sittler, Joseph, Sr., D.D.	Keyser, Dorner L.
Frease, Joseph W.	Shatzer, C. G.
Fry, Franklin Clark	Rinderknecht, Edward
Herman, Earl Cameron, D.D.	Hess, Harry L.
Bell, Alvin E., D.D.	Myers, Dean A.
Miley, George W.	Gump, W. C.
Brandt, Walter M.	Gleeson, T. M.
Kelly, Paul Snowden	Finefrock, H. C.
Young, D. Bruce, D.D.	Goschke, Charles
Getter, Herman C., D.D.	Renz, W. F.
Sittler, Joseph, Jr.	Mellinger, I. F.
Himes, A. M., D.D.	Arnold, H. J., Ph.D.
Moore, Chalmers E., S.T.M.	Zimmerman, Judge Charles B.
Pershing, Benjamin H., Ph.D., D.D.	Bischoff, N. E.
Uhl, B. B.	Melching, Rue
Berger, John W.	Homrighaus, A. H.
Schofer, John A.	Schiewetz, H. J., D.D.S.
Ebert, Walter W.	Maurer, G. C.
Hackenberg, W. M., D.D.	Lutz, Lon C.

* Date of organization of East Ohio Synod which, on November 3, 1920, with the Synod of Miami (organized October 16, 1844), Wittenberg Synod (organized June 8, 1847) and the District Synod of Ohio (organized August 26, 1857) merged into the Synod of Ohio of The United Lutheran Church in America.

9. Pittsburgh Synod
Organized January 15, 1845

Clerical
Bagger, H. H., D.D.
Will, Herman H.
Carlson, Oscar W.
Nicholas, J. R.
Pfeifer, Wm. F.
Myers, John J., D.D.
Fry, G. Arthur, D.D.
Steinfurth, A. W., D.D.
Frey, W. E., D.D.
Stump, A. M.
Fisher, Frank P., D.D.
Scarpitti, Fortunato
Keyser, Paul E.
Hanks, Edgar B.
Himmelman, George L.
Fetterly, Bernard
Shaffer, Bruce R.
Schnur, Paul N.
Schnur, George H., D.D.
Dozer, Charles E.
Fritsch, L. A., D.D.

Lay
Wolf, Robbin B., LL.D.
Gregg, James
Goodman, C. C.
Schnur, Carl E.
Slonaker, N. H.
Hill, D. C.
Reiber, Hon. A. E.
Houser, W. P.
Hartzell, A. M.
Miller, Dr. C. E.
Lehmann, Robert J.
Fox, H. W.
McGraw, Fred W.
Wulfetange, J. F.
Crouse, George
Pebly, H. E.
Smith, William M.
Riggle, A. J.
Krause, Albert
Furgeson, W. B.
Durst, C. J.

10. Indiana Synod
*October 28, 1848

Clerical
Turney, H. E., D.D., S.T.M.
Goering, G. Charles
Keck, Albert H., D.D.
Krauss, Paul H., D.D.
Koch, C. Franklin, D.D.
Hanes, F. M.
Stolldorf, H. C.

Lay
Jensen, Otto K.
Fisher, George A., Sc.D.
Schrope, W. D.
Lantz, J. P.
Kantz, C. W.
Olson, R. E.
Fetta, Oliver C. C.

* Date of organization of the Olive Branch Synod which, on June 24, 1920, with portions of the Chicago Synod (organized in 1871), united to form the Indiana Synod of The United Lutheran Church in America.

11. Illinois Synod
*September 8, 1851

Clerical
Keck, Albert H., Jr.
Bernhard, Harold E.
Uber, T. B., D.D.
Grimes, L. H.
Johnson, Edwin J.
Weng, Armin G., Ph.D.
Spangler, Walter D., D.D.
Hurst, Kenneth A.
Cooper, G. Herman, S.T.M.
Curran, George J.
Kabele, David R.
Schreckenberg, F. L.

Lay
Powers, Gerald S.
Diestlemeier, Dr. A. E
Korte, William H.
Schuermann, John F.
Woltmann, Louis W.
Krause, William
Roth, Lorin J.
Schulz, Carl
List, Erwin H.
Swanson, C. G.
Trapp, Carl
Jensen, Nels

* Date of organization of the Northern Illinois Synod which, on June 10, 1920, with the Southern Illinois (organized 1856), the Central Illinois (organized 1862), and portions of the Chicago (organized 1896) Synods, formed the Illinois Synod of The United Lutheran Church in America.

12. Texas Synod
Organized November 10, 1851

Clerical	*Lay*
Kern, Fred W.	Rapp, W. S.
Bechter, Paul	Zirjacks, Charles C.

13. Mississippi Synod
Organized July 25, 1855

Clerical	*Lay*
Mangum, John W.	Dubard, E. A. (a)

14. Synod of Iowa
Organized September 3, 1855

Clerical	*Lay*
Lesher, Leland H.	Gardner, H. C.
Livers, R. W., D.D.	Lillick, Carl
Schwertz, A. B.	Lowe, George H.

15. Georgia-Alabama Synod
Organized July 20, 1860

Clerical	*Lay*
Black, H. J., D.D.	Wilson, D. E.
Reiser, W. A.	Usina, C. T.

16. Synod of Canada
*July 21, 1861

Clerical	*Lay*
Reble, J. H., D.D.	Christiansen, E. B.
Lotz, Albert W.	Weber, C. N.
Mehlenbacher, W. A.	Brennan, L. H.
Clausen, F. B., D.D.	Preuter, E.
Binhammer, H. K. F.	Schmidt, Ed.
Gomann, E. A., S.T.M.	Johnson, H. (a)
Howald, F. L., S.T.M.	Vogt, W. (a)

* Date of organization of the Evangelical Lutheran Synod of Canada with which, on June 12, 1925, the Synod of Central Canada (organized November 11, 1908) united.

17. Synod of Kansas
Organized November 5, 1868

Clerical	*Lay*
Puls, Charles A.	Easterday, Wayne
McGuire, H. J.	Olson, A. T.
McCulloch, J. A., D.D.	Harkness, Charles A., Jr.
Whittecar, George R.	Simmons, H. W.

18. Synod of Nebraska
Organized September 1, 1871

Clerical	*Lay*
Hershey, J. C., D.D.	Ahrens, Emil
Rinde, Thomas D.	McGrew, Palmer
Frederick, P. W. H., D.D.	Fahrenbruch, H. R.
Young, A. W.	Kuenning, W. W.
Dumler, Henry	Christensen, Marius

19. Wartburg Synod
Organized 1875

Clerical	Lay
Belter, R. R.	Schafer, J.
Neumann, A. M.	Lauterbach, H. (a)
Kaitschuk, Walter E.	Rinne, C. A.
Goeken, J. A.	Ruppel, A. J.
Morack, E.	Heitman, R. W.

20. Synod in the Midwest*
Organized July 24, 1890

Clerical	Lay
Nolte, F. W., D.D.	Boxberger, Fred
Lentz, A. B. J.	Jenny, Wilbur
Hansen, E. C.	Windhusen, J. H.
Koolen, M., D.D.	Dietz, Henry
Schuldt, F. C., D.D.	Rippe, Herman
Goede, Hermann	Laumann, Charles

* German Synod of Nebraska, prior to June 14, 1937.

21. Synod of California
Organized April 2, 1891

Clerical	Lay
Anspach, Howard A.	Noel, Fritz C.
Huber, David R., D.D.	Scheehl, William B.
Trabert, Earnest A., D.D.	Bedau, H. A.
Opperman, Henry W.	Kautz, Roy M.

22. Rocky Mountain Synod
Organized May 6, 1891

Clerical	Lay
Bream, Charles S.	Hiller, John N.
Harner, Elmer W., D.D.	Rights, E. H.

23. Synod of the Northwest
Organized September 23, 1891

Clerical	Lay
Gerberding, R. H., D.D.	Downing, Dr. L. V.
Bartsch, Carl H.	Gottschalk, Charles A.
Genszler, George W., D.D.	Jensen, J. K.
Meck, John I.	Jouno, J. W.
Reed, H. B., D.D.	Mueller, Fred C.
Roth, Paul W., D.D.	Olsen, Harold G.
Streich, A. G.	Wuerthner, Hon. Julius J.
Zinck, A. A., D.D., S.T.M.	Cornelius, B. F.
Grant, Charles L., D.D.	Brann, L. W. (a)

24. Manitoba Synod
Organized July 16, 1897

Clerical	Lay
Hartig, Thomas, D.D.	
Willison, N., Litt.D.	
Heimann, G. A.	
Goos, A.	

25. Pacific Synod
Organized September 26, 1901

Clerical	*Lay*
Kunzmann, Paul L.	Johnson, Marvin C.
Simundsson, K.	Sylliaasen, M. O.
Allen, Harry R.	Reck, John

26. Nova Scotia Synod
Organized July 10, 1903

Clerical	*Lay*
Lossing, H. N.	Hirtle, Jessen

27. Synod of West Virginia
Organized April 17, 1912

Clerical	*Lay*
Portz, C. A.	Smith, L. A.
Roof, E. F. K.	Jones, A. M. (a)

28. Slovak Lutheran "Zion" Synod
Organized June 10, 1919

Clerical	*Lay*
Bella, J. Igor	
Billy, George	

29. Michigan Synod
*June 10, 1920

Clerical	*Lay*
Stickles, C. F.	Buergin, Fred E.
Schildroth, H. E.	Bingaman, C. C.
Rockey, C. J., D.D.	Stratton, Robert

* Date on which churches of the Northern Indiana Synod and of the Chicago Synod organized to form the Michigan Synod of The United Lutheran Church in America.

30. Synod of Florida
Organized September 24, 1928

Clerical	*Lay*
Pugh, W. E., D.D.	Brubaker, C. M.

31. Kentucky-Tennessee Synod
Organized June 6, 1934

Clerical	*Lay*
Funk, David M.	Speckman, Lawrence F.
Robertson, Clayton A.	Wood, James M.

(Associated Synods)
The Andhra Evangelical Lutheran Church, India
Clerical
Neudoerffer, Ernst, D.D.
Swavely, Clarence H.

The Evangelical Lutheran Church in Japan
Clerical
Kawagiri, Shinichi
Thorlaksson, S. O. (Visitor)

(a)—Absent.

On motion the reports, as printed in the Bulletin, were received. By common consent it was decided that reports shall not be adopted as a whole, action being taken only upon resolutions and recommendations.

On motion the order of business was adopted as follows:

PROGRAM OF THE CONVENTION

All meetings will be held in the convention hall at the hotel, excepting as indicated in this program.

The offerings at all evening services will be applied to the Anniversary Appeal of the Board of American Missions.

WEDNESDAY, OCTOBER 5—Night, 7:30 o'clock.

At Trinity Church, 2100 W. Baltimore Street.
The Service. President's Sermon. Sacrament of the Altar.

THURSDAY, OCTOBER 6—Morning, 8:45 to 12 o'clock.

1. Devotions. (Matins will be used. The Committee on Devotions will appoint those who are to conduct all devotions.)
2. Formal Opening of the Convention.
3. Organization of the Convention—Roll. Receipt of reports as printed in the Bulletin. Order of Business. General rules of procedure. Appointment of special committees.
4. Approval of Minutes of last Convention.
5. Reports of the President and of the Secretary.
6. Election of the President and of the Secretary.
7. Treasurer's Report, with audit.
8. Election of the Treasurer.
9. Report of the Executive Board.

    Actions at this and succeeding sessions to be taken on the following items from the report. Any delegate may call up for consideration or question other items not included in the following, which are given in the order in which they are found in the report:

    Consolidation of periodicals.

    Amendment to the Constitution.

    Advanced Age Retirement Limit for Pastors.

    Theological Education under U. L. C. A. control.

    Call to the Ministry.

    Calendar of Special Days and Seasons.

    Central Pennsylvania Synod.

Change of name of German Synod of Nebraska.
Amendments to By-laws.
Merger of Agencies.
Constitution of the Board of Foreign Missions.
Co-operation with American Lutheran Church in India.
Budget.
National Lutheran Council's new Department of Welfare.
World Conference on Faith and Order.
World Council of Churches.
Social Security for Church Workers.

THURSDAY, OCTOBER 6—Afternoon, 2 to 5 o'clock.
1. Devotions.
2. Continuation of action of the Executive Board's report.

THURSDAY, OCTOBER 6—Evening, 6:30 o'clock.
Banquet at the Lord Baltimore Hotel, arranged by the Laymen's Movement. Full particulars will be announced.

FRIDAY, OCTOBER 7—Morning, 8:45 to 12 o'clock.
(Before the opening of the morning session, each delegate must procure his own ballots at the Registration Desk for those elections which are to be held this day at noon.)
1. Devotions. Memorial Service. Necrologist's Obituary Record.
2. Reports of Nominating Committees as to members of the Executive Board, of the Commission of Adjudication, of the Committee on Church Papers, and of the Executive Committee of the Laymen's Movement.
3. Board of Foreign Missions.
4. Committee on Centennial in India.
5. Commission of Adjudication.
6. Unfinished Business.
(Immediately after the close of the session, the election will be held for membership on the Executive Board, the Commission of Adjudication, the Committee on Church Papers, and the Executive Committee of the Laymen's Movement. Polls close at 2 o'clock.)

FRIDAY, OCTOBER 7—Afternoon, 2 to 5 o'clock.
1. Devotions.
2. Minutes.
3. Representatives and General Resolutions. (As arranged by the Committee of Reference and Counsel for this place and for stated places on following days.)
4. Board of American Missions.

5. Committee on Evangelism.
6. Commission on Investments.
7. Committee on Church Papers.
8. Unfinished Business.

FRIDAY, OCTOBER 7—Night, 8 o'clock.

Anniversary Pageant: "God in the Midst of Her," arranged by the Board of American Missions.

SATURDAY, OCTOBER 8—Morning, 8:45 to 12 o'clock.

(Before the opening of the morning session each delegate must procure his own ballots for today's elections.)
1. Devotions.
2. Report of Nominating Committee for today's elections.
3. Report of tellers upon Friday's elections.
4. Parish and Church School Board.
5. Board of Education.
6. Unfinished Business.
(Immediately after adjournment the election will be held for membership on all Boards and Elective Committees not included in the Friday election.)

SATURDAY, OCTOBER 8—Afternoon.

The Baltimore Committee will make special announcement of provisions for this afternoon at Annapolis or for a trip on the Bay.

SATURDAY, OCTOBER 8—Night, 8 o'clock.

Festival of Lutheran music, arranged by the Baltimore Committee, at Peabody Institute. Five Lutheran college choirs. National broadcast.

SUNDAY, OCTOBER 9.

The Baltimore Committee has arranged and will announce the preachers at church services this morning and evening.

Afternoon—3:30 to 4:30—Lutheran Rally at Luther Monument, Druid Park Terrace. Addresses by Pastor Carl Heminghaus (American Lutheran Church), President of the Baltimore Lutheran Ministerial Association; and by Dr. Paul Scherer.

MONDAY, OCTOBER 10—Morning, 8:45 to 12 o'clock.

1. Devotions.
2. Report of tellers upon Saturday's elections.
3. Board of Publication.

4. Board of Deaconess Work.
5. Inner Mission Board.
6. Unfinished Business.

MONDAY, OCTOBER 10—Afternoon, 2 to 5 o'clock.
1. Devotions.
2. Minutes.
3. Representatives and General Resolutions.
4. Board of Ministerial Pensions and Relief.
5. Committee on New Pension Plan.
6. Laymen's Movement.
7. Committee on Memorials from Constituent Synods.
8. Committee on Moral and Social Welfare.
9. Unfinished Business.

MONDAY, OCTOBER 10—Night, 8 o'clock.
Celebration of the Fiftieth Anniversary of the Common Service.
    Convention Hall.

TUESDAY, OCTOBER 11—Morning, 8:45 to 12 o'clock.
1. Devotions.
2. Lutheran Brotherhood.
3. Women's Missionary Society.
4. Luther League of America.
5. Commission concerning title of "Bishop."
6. Unfinished Business.

TUESDAY, OCTOBER 11—Afternoon, 2 to 5 o'clock.
1. Devotions.
2. Minutes.
3. Representatives and General Resolutions.
4. Report of Representative in the Advisory Council of the American Bible Society.
5. Commission on Relationships to American Lutheran Church Bodies.
6. Commissioners to the National Lutheran Council.
7. Executive Committee of the Lutheran World Convention.
8. Unfinished Business.

WEDNESDAY, OCTOBER 12—Morning, 8:45 to 12 o'clock, and afternoon if necessary.
    (Portions of the program for this day may be advanced to Tuesday night, if the convention decides to hold a session that night.)
1. Devotions.
2. Minutes.

3. Committee on President's Report.
4. Committee on Common Service Book.
5. Committee on Church Music.
6. Committee on Church Architecture.
7. Statistical and Church Year Book Committee.
8. Committee on German Interests.
9. Committee on Publicity.
10. Committee on Church and State.
11. Committee on Transportation.
12. Archivist.
13. Lutheran Laymen's Radio Committee.
14. Committee on Army and Navy Work.
15. Committee on Place of Next Convention.
16. Committee on Leave of Absence.
17. Lutheran Historical Society.
18. Lutheran Church Book and Literature Society.
19. Unfinished Business.
20. Printing of Minutes.
21. Final Minutes.
22. Formal Close of the Convention.

The President presented the following rules of procedure which were adopted by the Convention:

1. That any delegate may, from the floor, move a resolution which fits perfectly to any report coming before the convention, but that resolutions of a general character must be handed to the Committee of Reference and Counsel, with whom the mover may confer.

2. That in discussion, the time of speakers be limited to five minutes.

3. That the privilege of the floor be granted to members of the Executive Board, to all members of the Commission of Adjudication, and to officers of other boards, when their reports are before the convention.

4. That in all elections of Boards, Elective Commissions and Committees, the first ballot be considered as a nominating ballot in cases where election does not result, and that the nominees receiving the high vote be declared the nominees on the second ballot, to the number of two nominees for each vacancy, and that voting be limited to those so nominated. In cases of ties, the number of nominees for each vacancy would be increased as necessary on account of the votes.

5. That twelve noon of the third day of the convention (Friday) be designated for the closing of the registration of delegates. (No changes whatsoever can be made in the roll of delegates as it appears at the hour designated for the closing of registration.)

There being no objection, the President ruled that special committees stand as appointed and announced.

SPECIAL COMMITTEES

COMMITTEE OF REFERENCE AND COUNSEL

This Committee is appointed to consider all general resolutions before they are submitted to the Convention; to arrange with the president for the hearing of representatives sent to the Convention; generally to assist the president in the daily program.

Clergymen	Laymen
Mattes, John C., Chairman	Rabenold, Ellwood M.
Suber, T. F.	Orth, Charles E.
Krumwiede, Walter	Copenhaver, B. E.
Frease, Joseph W.	Hagan, Peter P.
Rhodes, George H.	Zimmerman, Charles B
Livers, R. W.	Hoover, E. G.
Reiser, W. A.	Lansberry, Thomas F.
Schuldt, F. C.	Schuermann, John F.
Zinck, A. A.	McGrew, Palmer
Funk, David M.	Buergin, Fred E.
Sunday, William F.	Woods, C. W.
Kinard, G. Harold	

COMMITTEE ON PRESIDENT'S REPORT

Clergymen	Laymen
Krout, J. D., Chairman	Hager, William H.
Keiter, A. Charles R.	Beisler, Henry
Bosch, Herbert A.	Fisher, J. L.
Strickler, L. W.	Almond, J. L.
Simonton, C. S.	Miller, C. E.
Fisher, Frank P.	Powers, Gerald S.
Krauss, Paul H.	Spigelmyer, W. W.
Foelsch, C. B.	Gardner, H. C.
Trabert, Earnest A.	Rights, E. H.
Meck, John I.	Hirtle, Jessen
Schildroth, H. E.	Tyson, Levering
Rearick, W. M.	
Young, D. Bruce	
Carlson, Oscar W.	

COMMITTEE ON LEAVE OF ABSENCE

Clergymen	Laymen
Sittler, Joseph, Jr., Chairman	Easterday, Wayne
Bechter, Paul	Weitzell, George R.
Whittecar, George R.	Black, George P.
Young, A. W.	Olson, R. E.
Simundsson, K.	Swanson, C. G.
Johnson, Edwin J.	Weber, C. N.
Hansen, E. C.	Heitman, R. W.
Petrea, B. E.	Windhusen, J. H.
Wertz, L. A.	Bingaman, C. C.
Sigler, Samuel D.	
Stump, A. M.	

COMMITTEE ON MEMORIALS FROM CONSTITUENT SYNODS

Clergymen	Laymen
Brown, P. D., Chairman	Harr, Luther A.
Miller, Hermann F.	Lotsch, Joseph M.
Hirzel, Carl H.	Tilberg, W. E.
Fife, J. Frank	Kurzenknabe, John George
Shaffer, D. L.	Reiter, Frank P.
Schnur, Paul N.	Fetta, Oliver C. C.
Curran, George J.	Holman, Edward L.
Morack, E.	Simmons, H. W.
Kunzman, Paul L.	Noel, Fritz C.
Pugh, W. E.	Wuerthner, Julius J.
Swoope, W. E.	Capps, Bismarck
Berger, John W.	
Roof, E. F. K.	

COMMITTEE TO NOMINATE EXECUTIVE COMMITTEE OF LAYMEN'S MOVEMENT

Clergymen	Laymen
Keck, Albert H., Chairman	Dubard, E. A.
Hiers, W. F.	Brennan, L. H.
Sternat, H. W.	Rudisill, C. A.
	Durst, C. J.

COMMITTEE TO NOMINATE MEMBERS OF EXECUTIVE BOARD, COMMISSION OF ADJUDICATION, AND CHURCH PAPERS COMMITTEE

Clergymen	Laymen
Tamke, George R. F., Chairman	Counts, R. C.
Conrad, F. L.	Rapp, W. S.
Stock, H. B.	Steele, Charles
Will, Herman H.	Fahrenbruch, Harry
McGuire, H. J.	Sylliaasen, M. O.
Koolen, M.	Brubaker, C. M.
Harner, Elmer W.	Wood, James M.
Lossing, H. N.	Weller, Walter W.
Rockey, C. J.	Mellinger, I. F.

COMMITTEE TO NOMINATE MEMBERS OF ALL OTHER BOARDS

Clergymen	Laymen
Anderson, R. Homer, Chairman	Maurer, G. C.
Cornehlsen, Henry C., Jr.	Deatrick, David P.
Tabor, L. Ralph	Lillick, Carl
Manges, Edmund L.	Usina, C. T.
Spangler, Walter D.	Brann, L. W.
Neumann, A. M.	Goodman, C. C.
Huber, David R.	Jones, George M.
Goos, A.	Pfeil, Henry G.
Billy, George	Smith, L. A.

COMMITTEE ON DEVOTIONAL SERVICES

Clergymen	*Laymen*
Frey, W. E., Chairman	Vickers, Ross M.
Wasmund, Henry C.	Walborn, Maurice D.
McCulloch, J. A.	Fisher, H. A.
Bartsch, Carl H.	Ballentine, J. B.
Weidley, Paul A.	Hiller, John N.
Lotz, Albert W.	Yoder, M. C.
Robertson, Clayton A.	Boyer, C. H.
Minnick, M. L.	Rippe, Herman
Brown, W. E.	
Weidt, William C. J.	

COMMITTEE OF TELLERS No. 1

To conduct the election of the president and of the secretary, and also the Friday elections.

Laymen

Menges, W. H., Chairman	Renn, John S.
Hill, D. C.	Yoder, R. A.
Roth, Lorin J.	Snyder, Ivan J.
Harkness, Charles A., Jr.	Slonaker, N. H.
Hartwig, Wilmer H.	Schrope, W. D.
Lowe, George H.	Christiansen, E. B.
Scheehl, William B.	Schafer, J.
Gottschalk, Charles A.	Johnson, Marvin C.
Eck, William	Schnure, W. M.

COMMITTEE OF TELLERS No. 2

To conduct the election of the treasurer and also the Saturday elections.

Laymen

Nissly, Alvin R., Chairman	Wilson, John S.
Keyser, Dorner L.	Wilson, D. E.
Ganser, W. R.	Kuenning, W. W.
Mayer, John	Jenny, Wilbur
Frick, J. Henry	Bedau, H. A.
Bonham, J. B.	Olsen, Harold G.
Bischoff, N. E.	Lutz, Jacob
Hafer, George W.	Schroeder, Julius E.
McGraw, Fred W.	Lantz, J. P.

Three additional special committees were reported as having been appointed by the President, as follows, and his action was approved:

SPECIAL COMMITTEE ON MINUTES

Clergymen

Frankenfield, Ira F., Chairman	Swank, C. P.
Goering, G. Charles	Grant, Charles L.

COMMITTEE ON PLACE OF NEXT CONVENTION

The chairman of all synodical delegations, with Rev. I. S. Sassaman as chairman.

COMMITTEE ON REPORT OF COMMISSION ON RELATIONS TO AMERICAN
LUTHERAN CHURCH BODIES

All theological professors who are delegates to the convention, namely:

Offermann, H.
Alleman, H. C.
Clausen, F. B.
Fischer, Emil E.
Frederick, P. W. H.
Pershing, Benjamin H.

Reed, H. B.
Reed, Luther D.
Rinde, Thomas D.
Stirewalt, M. L.
Willison, N.

A printed copy of the Minutes of the Columbus Convention, 1936, certified by F. H. Knubel as President and W. H. Greever as Secretary, under seal, was submitted and approved. The President thereupon declared that copy of the Minutes to be the official protocol of the proceedings of the Tenth Biennial Convention of The United Lutheran Church in America. A motion was carried instructing the officers to certify a duplicate copy to be preserved as protocol.

The Rev. Lloyd M. Keller, General Chairman of the Baltimore Committee on Entertainment, was introduced, who, after cordial words of greeting and welcome, presented Dr. John W. Harms, Executive Secretary of the Baltimore Council of Churches and of Christian Education of Maryland and Delaware. Dr. Harms extended a welcome in the name of the churches of Baltimore and spoke at some length concerning the co-operation of the Lutheran Church in connection with his official duties.

Pastor Keller then introduced the Rev. F. O. Evers, pastor of Zion Lutheran Church of Baltimore, who presented a reproduction of the portrait of John Daniel Kurtz, with interesting historical references. Suitable response was made by the President of the Church.

Pastor Keller then introduced the Rev. C. C. Rasmussen, President of the Maryland Synod, who presented a gavel to the convention, which gavel bore the following inscription:

Presented to the U. L. C. A.
Baltimore, October 6, 1938
Wood from the Ev. Lutheran
Church, Frederick, Md.
Founded in 1738

The President accepted the gavel with expression of appreciation of its historical significance.

A greeting from Governor Harry W. Nice, expressing his interest in the proceedings of the convention and expressing regret that he could not be present, was read by Pastor Keller, who then introduced the Hon. Howard W. Jackson, Mayor of the City of Baltimore. Mayor Jackson spoke with understanding and appreciation of the work of the Church and his address was responded to, most fittingly, by President C. C. Stoughton of Wagner College.

The President presented his report as printed in the Bulletin and it was referred to the Committee on President's Report. (For Committee's report, and action thereon, see pp. 494, 495.)

REPORT OF THE PRESIDENT

This tenth biennial report is different. All previous reports aimed definitely, in accordance with a requirement in the By-laws, to "summarize the general conditions in the Church." They were analytical studies, based upon various principles of Church life, and sought to test our actual condition by the principles.

Of necessity this report follows another method. At our last convention a large and new responsibility was laid upon the president—for promotion. He must give an account of it to the Church, especially because no other report will furnish a full accounting of that work. This convention may then decide upon its continuance. Let it be said in advance that although the task was burdensome and although the president felt (if a dignified report may descend to humorous slang) that it was a case of "letting George do it," nevertheless the work has been full of joy, chiefly because of the thrilling assistance from literally the whole Church. This co-operative spirit clearly pervades all that is to be reported.

Several controlling ideas were given full authority in the plans. First of all, we must not expect by one big, driving, excited, unanimous push to put the ball over the goal line. Promotion has gone mad in these times. It is almost amusing to watch occasionally the rather frantic efforts of staid conservatives, even Church bodies, to secure "a place in the sun." So far as we are concerned, promotion was carried on by us, often effectively, before our last convention. We are seeking now merely to put it all in order, to improve it, and to give it patient persistence.

As a mere deduction from that first idea comes the second. We are not setting up a new department in the Church. Everything that has been and will be undertaken is conducted by the departments that now exist. The Church wishes no more machinery, and every plan devised during the biennium was found to fit somewhat remarkably into well-understood agencies we now possess. As a glad result we have come to understand the agencies better, they have come to understand one another better, and have even come to understand themselves better. We must never allow ourselves to be tempted into an assumption that a highly organized Church with intricate machinery means better Christianity. That would mean dependence upon what man does instead of upon what God does. We are dependent upon the Holy Ghost. "I believe that I cannot by my own reason or *strength* believe in Jesus Christ, my Lord, or come to Him; but the Holy Ghost has called me through the Gospel, enlightened me by His gifts, and sanctified and preserved me in the true faith; in like manner as He calls, gathers, enlightens, and sanctifies the whole Christian Church on earth, and preserves it in union with Jesus Christ in the true faith."

The third idea develops from the two preceding ones. The aim has been to unify the working operations of the Church. We have many agencies and each has its specific task. A separate agency is to be encouraged only when it possesses a specific task of true magnitude. Each agency is under constant obligation to justify its existence by its worthwhile performance. While, however, a division of our work is necessary and possible, nevertheless the division is merely theoretical and partial. An absolute division cannot be attained because the work of the Church is essentially one. The agencies we possess constantly cross one another, as could be illustrated by a hundred examples. They must understand, respect, and be mindful of one another. Their operations must be unified. In this respect definite advances were made during the biennium, as this report reveals. The resolutions adopted two years ago prescribed that in the event of disagreements on plans, recourse might be taken to the Church's Executive Board for a decision. There has not been a single instance where this was necessary. The workers forgot there was such a prescription.

This unity of the Church's working operations finds its best expression in its primary objective: strengthening the congregations under the leadership of their pastors. The entire machinery of the Church is most effective only when it is unitedly concentrated upon this purpose. The synods exist chiefly to assist the congregations, and all of the Church's agencies must co-operate with the synods to the same end. This necessity of operation through the synods may seem at times to hamper the agencies, but in reality strengthens them. A Church is well organized and is strong only when it forcefully helps the congregations and their pastors. The congregation is the place where primarily and constantly (1) the Church serves the individual; (2) the individual serves the Church; (3) the Church serves the world; (4) the Church worships God and administers the means of grace. The promotional plans have sought to develop this unity of our working operations in their concentrated objective—the congregations.

Were the controlling ideas above mentioned satisfactory ones? Were they faithfully followed? The convention should answer frankly when it now studies an account of what was done, stated as briefly as possible.

The first step was taken with the seven boards which we commonly call the apportionment boards of the Church. They receive about ninety-five cents from every dollar of the apportionment, and are the Foreign, American, and Inner Mission Boards, the Education and Parish School Boards, the Deaconess and Pension Boards. It must not be regarded as derogatory to other agencies nor does it establish these boards as the primary agencies of the Church when it is now said that there is a sense in which all other agencies are auxiliary to these seven, helping them. That is true even of the Executive Board. These seven embody vividly the great passions of the Church, the passions that must come to possess the soul of every Christian—the evangelistic, educational, and merciful passions. Even that division of three passions, though scriptural, is theoretical and partial because the soul of the educational and merciful passions is also evangelistic. Evangelism can be assigned to no single agency because it belongs to all that the Church does. The promotional plan sought first of all to unify and strengthen the missionary passion of the Church in the congregations.

The executive secretaries of the seven boards were gathered for a meeting. With them was the executive secretary of the Laymen's Movement because through all its years that agency has been at work promoting stewardship in the Church, also stimulating practically and intensively the apportionment. The president was there and was made chairman. Later the secretary of the U. L. C. A. added his wise and vigorous help to the plans. A dozen times that committee has met during the biennium, generally for almost a full day. In the interims individuals worked many days. Ten alert men, giving their best, rejoicing in this practically new fellowship of combined service, each serving the better his own special responsibility. No circle in the Church has ever known more satisfying experiences. Many plans were discussed, many remain undeveloped at present. Three chief projects were accomplished.

First, an annual Pastor's Plan Book was devised. It cannot be described fully here, but is crowded with helps for pastors month by month through the year, and gives information regarding the Church at appropriate seasons. Synodical and congregational information may be readily added by the pastor on its calendar. The second edition, for the year 1938-1939, has just appeared. At the secretaries' request the Board of Publication (not represented on this committee) undertook at its own expense the entire responsibility and has furnished a copy free to every pastor in the U. L. C. A. and to seniors in theological seminaries. The book seems to meet with universal favor. This is probably the first information that many of the laity possess regarding this annual publication.

Second, special days and seasons throughout the year have long existed as occasions when these boards could educate the people of the Church concerning their work. Any financial purposes connected therewith have always been secondary in character. The secretaries realized that this opportunity is more valuable than had ever been conceived. The seasons are now being stressed far more emphatically. Improved literature has been used. An important development is that the season for each board now receives in various ways the support of all other boards. A revised calendar for these seasons was planned by the Committee of Executive Secretaries and was recommended to the Executive Board, which has included the same in its report to this convention. The ideal towards which we are moving is a profitable study by all our people, season by season, of the great causes embodied in the existence of the boards. Even now many more congregations than ever before make use of the special literature.

Third, group meetings. In the fall of 1937 hundreds of group meetings were held within the bounds of all synods, attended by officials from thousands of congregations, who then in their home congregations personally distributed millions of pieces of literature dealing with the passions of the Church, the special seasons, the organization of the Church, etc. The Laymen's Movement merged its entire "every member visitation" plan with this endeavor, giving its executive secretary's full time to set up the group meetings and contributing liberally for the literature. The executive secretaries and many other speakers freely gave time and effort to attend these meetings everywhere. It is to be noted that the aim was to reach all our people by personal contact through the official leaders in their congregations. It was a first effort, was not everywhere successful, but unquestionably sowed many productive seeds.

Group meetings are planned for this fall also but they will be for pastors only. They are to be institutes, conferential in character, and are again being worked out by all the executive secretaries, by the bestowed time of the executive secretary of the Laymen's Movement with the assistance of the secretary of the U. L. C. A., by special leaders for each institute, etc.

What was the cost for a year of this entire work of the Committee of Executive Secretaries? Between $10,000 and $11,000, in addition to the cost of the Pastor's Plan Book which was assumed by the Board of Publication. $4,000 was contributed proportionately by the seven boards; $5,000 by the Laymen's Movement; and $1,000 from the Executive Board's treasury. By no means was all of this amount a new expense. The seven boards had saved much on traveling expense to synodical meetings by their secretaries, which was assumed this year (as explained below) by the Executive Board. The Laymen's Movement would in any event have spent a considerable sum for its regular "every member visitation." All contributions were gladly made and are being repeated in somewhat similar manner for the second year.

We turn now from the seven apportionment boards to the Board of Publication. Some will recall that at the last convention the decision regarding promotion had not reached full clarity so far as this board was concerned. It has developed that this was a blessing because better things were in store. The Board of Publication has been given a separate place in our promotional plans because its sphere is a distinct one. Nor have we covered its distinctiveness when we say merely that it is not an apportionment board. Its influence as an agency of the Church is recognized only when we consider the extent to which its official literature permeates and guides the entire work of congregations. Their constant worship, their schools of every type, their teachers and leaders and pastors are supplied with necessary publications from this board. What would happen to congregational activity if this board were not pouring in supplies? In a sense it is primarily a promotional agency, existing to promote, especially through literature, the faith and the work and the purposes of the Church. During the biennium frequent conferences were held with the board and its committees and officials, in the desire to reach mutual clarity regarding the promotional possibilities of this agency.

Some of the decisions reached were put into immediate operation. Mention has been made, for instance, of the issuance by this board of the Pastor's Plan Book, now going out for the second year. Then also various publications of the board, including notably our official Church papers, have given constant and sturdy support to all promotional efforts which went into effect during the biennium. The best activity, however, still remains in its beginnings, although fully decided. The influence, the possibilities thereof, can be known only in the future. They will result from two definite plans.

First, a new man is entering into the active operations of this board. He will be known, at least for the present, as promotional editor. No attempt has been made as yet to define too exactly his sphere of work. His own initiative will be given true opportunity to develop itself, although full guidance and necessary decisions will be provided by the board and its business manager and also by the president of the Church. The choice of this man, called as one chosen also by the Lord, led finally to the Rev. F. Eppling Reinartz who entered upon this work under date of September 1st.

The second plan contemplates that twenty-five per cent of the so-called profits of the board in one fiscal year may be used during the following year for promotional purposes. Decisions regarding expenditures, subject where necessary to the board's consent, will be made by the promotional editor, the business manager, and the president of the Church.

Clearly the promotional plans of the Board of Publication remain partially incomplete as the biennium closes. This is even truer as we now turn to consider the Church's auxiliaries. It has been impossible to hope that within two years wise and promising plans could be developed for all of the Church's operations, especially because of the three controlling ideas stipulated near the beginning of this report. We are not in this effort running a race with anybody or attempting a performance of stunts. Some showy suggestions have been considered, especially by the executive secretaries, and may be used; but in general "patient persistence" has been our motto. If the Church wishes more speed it must provide extra gasoline and occasionally relief drivers. Even so, "more haste, less speed."

As for the auxiliaries, we have long given to the Luther League of America, the Women's Missionary Society, and the Lutheran Brotherhood full recognition as agencies of the U. L. C. A. Recently we even removed from existence former committees through which they reported to our conventions. They report directly to us, as is proper. They are not received now as being in a sense outside organizations, to whose greetings the convention listens appreciatively and then responds flatteringly through an appointed speaker. They are our own men and women and young people. They are, however, auxiliary agencies, auxiliary to our boards and synods and congregations. This position of theirs was fully elaborated and approved as far back as our convention of 1920. That convention emphasized furthermore that their value as auxiliaries "does not consist primarily in their existence as great general and national bodies, but in their efforts to render the congregations more efficient." The promotional plans being devised with representatives of the auxiliaries contemplate an increased emphasis upon this value of theirs to the individual congregation. It is hoped that their present congregational units will become more effective than ever and that congregations where such units do not exist will gladly open their doors to them. The plans will be developed in full co-operation with the synods and the individual pastors.

In attaining these ends the aim is to reveal their centripetal and centrifugal blessings to a congregation. Centripetal—that is, the auxiliary serves the congregation and is not served by it. It is not a congregational burden but a congregational burden-bearer. Young people, for instance, must not seek to be pampered by a congregation, but must seek ways to contribute their youthful Christian energy to the congregation's strength. Centrifugal—that is, the auxiliary by its educational and other methods will above all else seek to strengthen in the congregation the central Christian passion of evangelism. That is the truest service it can perform—to strengthen the congregation's will to face outward (centrifugal) towards the world of men for whom Christ died. No true congregation has its face turned inward. Practically the auxiliary will help the congregation raise its apportionment and observe the special days and seasons. Then the auxiliary will ask the congregation's help for its own missionary specials. These are the present promotional plans of the auxiliaries in their beginnings.

The story is not quite complete. The Executive Board of the Church also gave serious heed to the resolutions on promotion adopted two years ago. As stated above, it made a financial contribution to the plans of the Committee of Executive Secretaries. It also answered affirmatively the specific resolution addressed to it. During the past two years a special representative of the Church as a whole was present at every meeting of a constituent synod. In all but a few unavoidable instances, he was a member of the Executive Board. This took the place of previous methods, which had proved unsatisfactory both to synods and boards, whereby all of the boards arranged visits of their secretaries to those meetings. Members of the Executive Board gladly assumed the responsibility, often at great personal sacrifice. The entire expense was covered from the Executive Board's treasury. The aim was to have the representative remain as nearly as possible throughout a synod's meeting, and give any desired assistance or advice. Each representative made a written report of his visits, with observations. The reactions from the synods themselves varied but were prevailingly enthusiastic. It may perhaps be said in general that the smaller the synod the greater the enthusiasm. It is for the convention to decide if this procedure is to be repeated or if some other plan is to be followed. Presumably all desire that the interests of the Church as a whole be voiced in some specific and significant manner at every synodical meeting.

Finally, the loyal and unreserved support of every synod to every effort must be mentioned. It has been the inspiration of the host of workers, in addition to their conviction that they were doing a Christian service. The presidents and other officers of synods were themselves quite commonly members of that host of workers. Never has the Church undertaken a task where greater unanimity of hearts and minds and hands was sustained for a period of two years.

In order that the convention may express its will, certain resolutions are presented. Of course the entire plan of promotion or any of its parts may be discontinued. Some of them will in any event continue because they have been fitted into our regular operations and because the Church always has carried on promotional work and always will. (For action, see pp. 494, 495.)

1. Resolved, that this convention express its thankful joy over the unanimous co-operation which has characterized the promotional efforts of the past biennium.

2. Resolved, that this convention approve in general the ideas and plans described in this report and direct that they be continued in harmony with the arrangements adopted at the convention of 1936.

3. Resolved, that the Executive Board be directed to continue the plans whereby it will send to each synodical meeting one representative of the Church as a whole, with all its causes.

4. Resolved, that in repeating our recognition of the Luther League of America, the Women's Missionary Society, and the Lutheran Brotherhood as official auxiliaries of the Church, we request all congregations to consider the desirability of establishing congregational units of these auxiliaries within the congregational operations.

A few items of official action during the biennium must be included in this report since they are not reported elsewhere.

Immediately after the last convention all special responsibilities from that convention were carried out. All commissions and committees were also appointed. The following were not named until after the minutes were printed and are therefore reported now.

Committee on Organized Work with Children: Member of Executive Board—Rev. W. H. Greever, Chairman; Pastor—Rev. A. Steimle; appointed by Women's Missionary Society—Mrs. A. J. Fenner; appointed by Luther League—Rev. P. M. Kinports; appointed by Parish and Church School Board—Rev. S. White Rhyne.

Commission on Work Among Negroes in the South: Representative from Board of Education—Rev. H. H. Bagger; from Inner Mission Board —Rev. P. D. Brown; from Board of American Missions—Rev. Z. M. Corbe; representative from Memorializing Synod—Rev. C. A. Linn.

Commission Concerning Title of "Bishop": Rev. R. E. Tulloss, Convener; Rev. H. J. Pflum, Rev. A. G. Weng, Rev. H. E. Turney, Rev. W. C. Waltemyer, Mr. Harry Hodges, Mr. Carl Distler; Corresponding Member —President of the Texas Synod.

Committee on Centennial in India: Rev. George A. Rupley, Convener; Rev. Fred J. Fiedler, Rev. E. J. Mollenauer, Mr. M. P. Möller, Jr., Mr. Carl Schulz.

Committee on New Pension Plan: Dr. E. Clarence Miller, Convener; Rev. J. Sittler, Rev. Wm. F. Buch, Rev. W. E. Frey, Rev. Jacob Diehl, Mr. B. B. Slifer, Mr. Arthur P. Black

Because of the death of Rev. A. Steimle, Rev. Paul Scherer was appointed a member of the Common Service Book Committee, Rev. Paul Hoh a consultative member of the Federal Council of Churches' Executive Committee, Rev. W. H. Greever a consultative member of the Radio Commission, and Rev. C. S. Simonton a member of the Committee on Organized Work with Children. Because of the death of Rev. E H. Klotsche, Rev. W. D. Allbeck was appointed a member of the Common Service Book Committee. Because of the deaths of Rev. J. A. W. Haas and Rev. Paul W. Koller, Rev. R. E. Tulloss and Rev. A. G. Weng were appointed on the Commission to the National Lutheran Council.

A few elections in 1936 required that the individuals concerned, because of our constitutional requirements, withdraw from certain agencies. Rev. J. Aberly chose to remain a member of the Board of Publication. Rev. H. F. Baughman chose to accept membership on the Board of Publication and the Church Papers Committee. Mr. C. M. Distler chose to remain a member of the Inner Mission Board.

Many anniversaries are being celebrated in addition to our completion of our twentieth year. It is fifteen years since the first meeting of the Lutheran World Convention, twenty since the organization of the National Lutheran Council. The Common Service is fifty years old, an event which is to be celebrated on the Monday evening of our convention. The Missouri Synod has celebrated the centennial of the first arrivals in America of those who founded the Synod. The United Lutheran Church of Australia celebrates its centennial this fall. The Augustana Synod celebrated, in co-operation with the Pennsylvania Ministerium and the East Pennsylvania Synod, the tercentenary of the landing of the first Swedes in America.

By personal privilege, the Secretary introduced Treasurer E. Clarence Miller, to whom he paid a tribute for faithful and efficient service as Treasurer for twenty years, and Treasurer Miller, with similar expression of appreciation of the services of the President, for the full period of the existence of the United Lutheran Church, presented a portrait of the President, executed by New York artists, as the gift of members of the Executive Board, the Executive Secretaries of the serving Boards, and the Presidents of Constituent Synods, as the expression of appreciation of the whole Church. Dr. Miller announced that a companion portrait was also presented to the Church for permanent preservation in the Lutheran Church House at New York. Dr. Knubel accepted the gift and in a most impressive way voiced his love for the Church and his appreciation of the loyalty of all of its members.

The Secretary presented his report as printed in the Bulletin, which report was accepted after reference was made to the fact that the action of the thirty-four Constituent Synods of The United Lutheran Church in America was unanimous in the approval of the amendment to the Constitution submitted by the action of the 1936 convention. This amendment is to Article XIII, Section 2, of the Constitution regarding membership on Boards.

REPORT OF THE SECRETARY

1. Regular Duties:

The biennium has been characterized by expansion in every direction. Great advance has been made in the perfecting of records and directories and very considerable improvement has been achieved in general cooperation from synods and pastors. Conferences, correspondence and special meetings have been multiplied. Items for special information are as follows:

(a) *Amendment to the Constitution.* The amendment to Article XIII, section 2, of the Constitution, regarding membership on boards, was duly submitted to all of the constituent synods and reports have been filed showing that the amendment was approved by thirty-four synods, making it unanimous.

(b) *Memorials.* The following memorials have been received, with such material as has been submitted for interpretation, and they have been placed in the hands of the Chairman of the Committee on Memorials. Mimeographed copies have been prepared for distribution to delegates in the convention.

(1) From the Nova Scotia Synod pertaining to a special edition of the Common Service Book to be sold at a more popular price.

(2) From the Synod of Ohio pertaining to the publication of materials for student group study.

(3) From the Pittsburgh Synod (a) pertaining to missionary agencies and the unification of their educational and administrative programs. (b) Pertaining to the creation of a board of co-ordination. (c) Pertaining to the relationship between Church and State.

(4) From the West Pennsylvania Synod pertaining to salaries and perquisites administered by boards and auxiliaries of the Church.

(c) *Records.* Very great advance has been made during this biennium toward the completion of full and accurate records. The clerical directory is approaching an accuracy which has not previously been achieved, and this directory is now classified so as to make its use immediately available for almost any purpose needed in the work of the Church.

(d) *Comprehensive Index.* The comprehensive index has been brought to the point where assurance of early publication is warranted. This index will be of constant service to those who are interested in the developing life of the Church. This Index will cover all Minutes of the U. L. C. A. to date and include the Minutes of this Convention.

(e) *Convention Bulletin.* Copy was prepared and arrangements were made for the publication of one thousand copies of the Bulletin for this Convention, by instructions from the Executive Board.

2. Special Assignments:

(a) *Statistics.* The statistics for the U. L. C. A. have been compiled for publication in the Church Year Book for 1938 and 1939, and for publication in the Minutes of this Convention. (See report of Statistical and Church Year Book Committee.)

(b) *Church Year Book.* The material for the 1939 Year Book is all in the hands of the printer except such material as must be prepared after the conclusion of this Convention. As in the case of previous conventions, the editorial space will be devoted, in the 1939 Year Book, to the account of action taken by this Convention.

(c) *Publicity.* A definite beginning has been made looking toward church-wide organization for a definite program of publicity, and such efforts as are proposed to the Church will require full co-operation. An appropriation of $1,000 was made by the Executive Board for the publicity service of this Convention. (See report of the Publicity Committee.)

(d) *Transportation.* No report.

(e) *Management of the Lutheran Church House.* The Lutheran Church House has required only ordinary attention to renovations and repairs, and has had no change in occupancy. The occupants have been given the benefit of four months of maintenance within the biennium, and it has been possible to add to the Depreciation Reserve Fund, the amount of $3,000, bringing the total of that fund now up to $8,000. The report as Treasurer, as submitted by the auditors, is an item in the report of the Executive Board.

3. Miscellaneous:

This biennium has offered opportunities for many additional activities in connection with the promotional plan, especially regional meetings and pastors' institutes, and there have been numerous calls for preparation of special statements, to all of which time and energy have been dedicated gladly.

W. H. GREEVER, *Secretary.*

On the basis of this report, the President referred to By-law V, B, 4, second portion, and announced the following ruling: "I therefore now rule that this particular item of the By-law is null and void and is stricken also from the By-laws, as being in conflict with the Constitution as amended."

The President then referred to the fact that at the present time seven individuals held membership in more than one board and, concerning the application of this amendment to them, announced the following ruling: "I must rule that although all elections at this convention are under the control of the Constitution as now amended, we are not empowered to break the contract which the Church made with these seven individual men at previous elections, having elected them definitely for terms of years as specified on ballots cast on those occasions. These individuals, even though the Constitution has been amended, may continue the privilege of serving on two boards until the expiration of the terms for which they have been elected."

These rulings of the President were sustained by the Convention.

The Convention proceeded to the election of a President under Committee of Tellers No. 1.

The Treasurer presented his report with oral explanations and the Convention accepted the auditors' report.

REPORT OF TREASURER OF THE UNITED LUTHERAN CHURCH IN AMERICA

EXECUTIVE BOARD OF THE UNITED LUTHERAN CHURCH IN AMERICA
STATEMENT OF RECEIPTS AND DISBURSEMENTS ON ACCOUNT OF APPORTIONMENT
July 1, 1936 *to June* 30, 1937

Balance in Apportionment Fund—July 1, 1936............................ $ 2,135.37

RECEIPTS

Ministerium of Pennsylvania	$183,883.99
United Synod of New York	96,466.00
North Carolina Synod	23,847.59
Maryland Synod	68,029.28
South Carolina Synod	20,700.00
West Pennsylvania Synod	82,030.00
Virginia Synod	15,333.25
Ohio Synod	83,750.47
East Pennsylvania Synod	69,363.00
Alleghany Synod	39,624.00
Pittsburgh Synod	77,270.72
Indiana Synod	17,990.73
Illinois Synod	35,000.00
Texas Synod	2,678.97
Susquehanna Synod	37,056.30
Mississippi Synod	417.47
Iowa Synod	7,150.00
Michigan Synod	8,697.00
Georgia-Alabama Synod	6,614.14
Canada Synod	3,969.11
Kansas Synod	8,800.00
Nebraska Synod	8,855.12
Wartburg Synod	3,900.00
German Synod of Nebraska (Midwest)	2,482.72
California Synod	6,308.09
Rocky Mountain Synod	4,033.43
Synod of the Northwest	33,271.47
Manitoba Synod	1,100.00
Pacific Synod	3,324.12
Nova Scotia Synod	956.69
West Virginia Synod	4,800.00

Slovak Zion Synod	593.65	
Florida Synod	2,006.37	
Kentucky-Tennessee Synod	7,743.25	
Miscellaneous	160.00	
Total Receipts		968,206.93
		$970,342.30

DISBURSEMENTS

Board of American Missions	$366,415.00	
Board of Foreign Missions	285,000.00	
Board of Inner Missions	16,150.00	
Board of Ministerial Pensions and Relief	111,625.00	
Board of Education	85,500.00	
Board of Deaconess Work	19,000.00	
Parish and Church School Board	10,450.00	
National Lutheran Council	10,925.00	
Tabitha Home	1,900.00	
Lowman Home	380.00	
American Bible Society	2,375.00	
General Fund—United Lutheran Church Treasury	40,280.00	
Total Disbursements		950,000.00
Balance in Apportionment Fund, June 30, 1937		$ 20,342.30

DISTRIBUTION BY MONTHS

August, 1936	$100,000.00
September, 1936	40,000.00
October, 1936	60,000.00
November, 1936	60,000.00
December, 1936	90,000.00
January, 1937	220,000.00
February, 1937	91,000.00
March, 1937	59,000.00
April, 1937	70,000.00
May, 1937	80,000.00
June, 1937	80,000.00
Total	$950,000.00

STATEMENT OF RECEIPTS AND DISBURSEMENTS ON ACCOUNT OF SPECIALS

July 1, 1936 to June 30, 1937

Balance in Specials Fund—July 1, 1936	$ 1,174.55

RECEIPTS

Ministerium of Pennsylvania	$ 29,255.37
United Synod of New York	13,175.99

North Carolina Synod	2,210.88
Maryland Synod	5,371.60
South Carolina Synod	2,545.34
West Pennsylvania Synod	11,483.52
Virginia Synod	3,716.35
Ohio Synod	12,559.68
East Pennsylvania Synod	14,226.00
Alleghany Synod	2,745.64
Pittsburgh Synod	13,428.90
Indiana Synod	4,523.57
Illinois Synod	6,331.10
Texas Synod	980.06
Susquehanna Synod	2,471.07
Mississippi Synod	17.20
Iowa Synod	947.52
Michigan Synod	1,430.53
Georgia-Alabama Synod	627.96
Canada Synod	3,518.23
Kansas Synod	1,069.90
Nebraska Synod	1,703.46
Wartburg Synod	2,093.58
German Synod of Nebraska (Midwest)	2,013.35
California Synod	1,596.82
Rocky Mountain Synod	504.87
Synod of the Northwest	5,600.83
Manitoba Synod	676.62
Pacific Synod	961.42
Nova Scotia Synod	274.08
West Virginia Synod	147.17
Slovak Zion Synod	1,036.41
Florida Synod	385.12
Kentucky-Tennessee Synod	852.89
United Lutheran Publication House	100,000.00
Miscellaneous	3,557.30
Women's Missionary Society	282,573.30
Income in Trust Funds (Designated)	1,320.00

Total Receipts	$537,933.63
	$539,108.18

DISBURSEMENTS

Board of American Missions	$130,855.91
Board of Foreign Missions	288,676.84
Board of Inner Missions	1,945.20
Board of Ministerial Pensions and Relief	20,238.36
Board of Education	11,991.86
Board of Deaconess Work	2,143.70
Parish and Church School Board	1,168.72
National Lutheran Council	875.80
Tabitha Home	140.84
American Bible Society	26.20
Grace College	200.00
Saskatoon College and Seminary	42.27
Midland College	359.96
Carthage College	12.35

Philadelphia Lutheran Seminary	10.00
Nachusa Orphanage	610.97
Tressler Orphans' Home	18.52
Orphans' Home of the South	129.17
Inner Mission Society, Brooklyn	66.67
Red Cross	6.00
Seamen's Mission	10.00
Breklum Missions Haus	2.00
Dr. Bodel Schwingh	11.25
American Mission to Lepers	27.25
Bethesda Leper Home Colony	20.00
Lutheran Orient Mission	30.00
Luther League of America	5.00
Women's Missionary Society	37.69
Radio Commission	8.00
Flood Relief (Inner Missions)	40,517.50

Total Disbursements 500,188.03

Balance in Specials Fund, June 30, 1937 .... $ 38,920.15

SUNDRY FUNDS AND ACCOUNTS

Balance on Hand—July 1, 1936, Virginia Synod .... $ 294.97

Receipts:

Synodical Home Missions, Virginia Synod ....$ 3,494.90	
Synodical Home Missions, United Synod of New York	5,755.67
Payments on account of Church Extension Loans	85.00

     9,335.57

$ 9,630.54

Disbursements: Board of American Missions .... $ 9,630.54

RECONCILIATION OF CASH
July 1, 1936 *to June* 30, 1937

	General Fund United Lutheran Church Treasury	Apportionment Fund	Specials Fund	Trust Funds	Totals
Balance— July 1, 1936	$ 1,864.35	$ 2,135.37	$ 1,469.52	$ 7,520.10	$ 12,989.34
Receipts for Year....	65,674.19	968,206.93	547,269.20	17,426.39	1,598,576.71
	$67,538.54	$970,342.30	$548,738.72	$24,946.49	$1,611,566.05
Disbursed in Year	52,469.76	950,000.00	509,818.57	11,374.19	1,523,662.52
Balance— June 30, 1937	$15,068.78	$20,342.30	$38,920.15	$13,572.30	$87,903.53

STATEMENT OF RECEIPTS AND DISBURSEMENTS ON ACCOUNT OF APPORTIONMENT
July 1, 1937 *to June* 30, 1938

Balance in Apportionment Fund, July 1, 1937 .... $ 20,342.30

RECEIPTS

Ministerium of Pennsylvania	$177,805.83
United Synod of New York	100,655.92
North Carolina Synod	23,171.46
Maryland Synod	66,221.52
South Carolina Synod	23,850.00
West Pennsylvania Synod	82,530.00
Virginia Synod	16,049.37
Ohio Synod	90,944.87
East Pennsylvania Synod	72,050.00
Alleghany Synod	30,952.00
Pittsburgh Synod	82,495.10
Indiana Synod	18,059.79
Illinois Synod	42,500.00
Texas Synod	2,991.52
Susquehanna Synod	39,794.53
Mississippi Synod	397.40
Iowa Synod	9,100.00
Michigan Synod	8,311.00
Georgia-Alabama Synod	6,170.56
Canada Synod	4,981.27
Kansas Synod	11,434.00
Nebraska Synod	9,833.78
Wartburg Synod	3,700.00
German Synod of Nebraska (Midwest)	2,303.50
California Synod	8,556.00
Rocky Mountain Synod	2,823.38
Synod of the Northwest	35,431.26
Manitoba Synod	1,200.00
Pacific Synod	4,036.52
Nova Scotia Synod	828.09
West Virginia Synod	3,800.00
Slovak Zion Synod	750.00
Florida Synod	2,189.47
Kentucky-Tennessee Synod	8,568.34
Miscellaneous	204.40

Total Receipts 994,690.88

$1,015,033.18

DISBURSEMENTS

Board of American Missions	$389,557.00
Board of Foreign Missions	303,000.00
Board of Inner Missions	17,170.00
Board of Ministerial Pensions and Relief	118,675.00
Board of Education	90,900.00
Board of Deaconess Work	20,200.00
Parish and Church School Board	11,830.00
National Lutheran Council	11,615.00
Tabitha Home	1,420.00

Lowman Home 284.00
American Bible Society 2,525.00
General Fund—United Lutheran Church Treasury 42,824.00

Total Disbursements $1,010,000.00

Balance in Apportionment Fund, June 30, 1938 .... $5,033.18

DISTRIBUTION BY MONTHS

August, 1937 .... $110,000.00
September, 1937 .... 50,000.00
October, 1937 .... 70,000.00
November, 1937 .... 80,000.00
December, 1937 .... 100,000.00
January, 1938 .... 230,000.00
February, 1938 .... 90,000.00
March, 1938 .... 50,000.00
April, 1938 .... 70,000.00
May, 1938 .... 70,000.00
June, 1938 .... 90,000.00

Total $1,010,000.00

STATEMENT OF RECEIPTS AND DISBURSEMENTS ON ACCOUNT OF SPECIALS
July 1, 1937 *to June* 30, 1938

Balance in Specials Fund, July 1, 1937 .... $ 38,920.15

RECEIPTS

Ministerium of Pennsylvania ....$ 12,181.41
United Synod of New York 7,723.37
North Carolina Synod 1,138.62
Maryland Synod 1,330.54
South Carolina Synod 2,823.63
West Pennsylvania Synod 9,055.95
Virginia Synod 1,580.49
Ohio Synod 7,420.91
East Pennsylvania Synod 9,916.00
Alleghany Synod 1,670.89
Pittsburgh Synod 8,225.96
Indiana Synod 906.46
Illinois Synod 2,543.06
Texas Synod 786.83
Susquehanna Synod 906.10
Mississippi Synod 6.35
Iowa Synod 509.25
Michigan Synod 209.97
Georgia-Alabama Synod 236.41
Canada Synod 1,123.16
Kansas Synod 353.06
Nebraska Synod 1,054.90
Wartburg Synod 628.57
German Synod of Nebraska (Midwest)...................... 1,694.87

California Synod	165.13
Rocky Mountain Synod	152.22
Synod of the Northwest	4,648.36
Manitoba Synod	293.96
Pacific Synod	361.73
Nova Scotia Synod	50.37
Slovak Zion Synod	100.00
Florida Synod	136.17
Kentucky-Tennessee Synod	473.69
Miscellaneous	65.15
Women's Missionary Society	273,249.16
Income in Trust Funds (Designated)	1,305.89

Total Receipts	355,028.59	
		$393,948.74

DISBURSEMENTS

Board of American Missions	$ 77,787.18
Board of Foreign Missions	260,730.31
Board of Inner Missions	1,391.99
Board of Ministerial Pensions and Relief	8,201.52
Board of Education	2,435.25
Board of Deaconess Work	55.76
Parish and Church School Board	111.55
National Lutheran Council	1,113.91
Tabitha Home	334.76
American Bible Society	87.40
Grace College	299.00
Saskatoon College and Seminary	32.95
Midland College	396.87
Philadelphia Lutheran Seminary	54.17
Chicago Seminary	38.25
Gettysburg Seminary	10.00
Philadelphia Motherhouse of Deaconesses	100.00
Nachusa Orphanage	712.87
Good Shepherd Home	16.94
National Home Finding Society	10.00
Orphans' Home of the South	129.17
Inner Mission Society, Brooklyn	77.22
Dr. Bodel Schwingh	11.25
American Mission to Lepers	17.55
Lutheran Orient Mission	30.00
Bowery Mission	3.00
Women's Missionary Society	48.88
Radio Commission	5.50
Flood Relief (Inner Missions)	26,000.00
The "Gideons"	5.00
Christian Witness to a World at War	5.00
Syrian Orphanage (Jerusalem)	20.71
Federal Council of Churches	5.00

Total Disbursements	380,278.96
Balance in Specials Fund, June 30, 1938	$ 13,669.78

SUNDRY FUNDS AND ACCOUNTS

Receipts:
Synodical Home Missions, Virginia Synod .... $ 3,363.96
Synodical Home Missions, United Synod of New York 5,762.88
Payments on Account of Church Extension Loans 88.00

                                                              $ 9,214.84

Disbursements:
Board of American Missions .... $ 9,214.84

RECONCILIATION OF CASH
July 1, 1937 *to June* 30, 1938

	General Fund United Lutheran Church Treasury	Apportion- ment Fund	Specials Fund	Trust Funds	Totals
Balance— July 1, 1937	$ 15,068.78	$ 20,342.30	$ 38,920.15	$13,572.30	$ 87,903.53
Receipts for fiscal year ended June 30, 1938	95,730.79	994,690.88	364,155.43	7,581.31	1,462,158.41
	$110,799.57	$1,015,033.18	$403,075.58	$21,153.61	$1,550,061.94
Disburse- ments during fiscal year	85,881.10	1,010,000.00	389,405.80	16,708.36	1,501,995.26
Cash Balance— June 30, 1938	$ 24,918.47	$ 5,033.18	$ 13,669.78	$ 4,445.25	$ 48,066.68

STATEMENT OF RECEIPTS AND DISBURSEMENTS—GENERAL FUND
July 1, 1936 *to June* 30, 1937

Balance—July 1, 1936... $ 1,864.35

RECEIPTS

Proportion of Apportionment $40,280.00
Contribution, Board of Publication 25,000.00
Refund, Board of Publication re: Daily Lutheran....   394.19

Total Receipts 65,674.19

                                                                     $67,538.54

DISBURSEMENTS

Salaries:
President ....$ 6,400.00
Secretary 5,220.00
Clerks 3,723.98

Travel Expense:

President	374.92
Secretary	265.20
Expense, Executive Board	1,113.87
Maintenance, Lutheran Church House	2,040.00
General Expense, New York	1,050.61
Stationery, Printing, etc.—New York	539.02
Postage, Telegrams, etc.—New York	284.64
Telephone—New York	111.72
Treasurer's Expense — Accounting, Stationery and Bond	1,359.50
Auditing Expense: Tait, Weller and Baker	231.50
Publicity, General	76.13

United Lutheran Church in America—Convention, Columbus, Ohio:

Publicity, National Lutheran Council..	$ 1,000.00	
Delegates' Travel Expense	13,390.85	
Bulletin and Minutes	3,553.92	
Sundry Expense	471.14	
		18,415.91
Appropriation to Luther League		6,000.00
Appropriation to Federal Council of Churches		2,000.00
Appropriation to World Conference on Faith and Order		100.00
Travel Allowance, Delegates to World Conference on Faith and Order		800.00

Expenses of Committees:

Committee of Adjudication	$	142.47
Committee on Church Papers		82.30
Committee on Common Service Book		346.81
Committee on Church Architecture		94.28
Committee on German Interests		66.08
Committee on Social and Moral Welfare		71.00
Committee on Lutheran Relations		339.38
Committee on Children's Work		84.36
Committee on Negro Work		63.20
Committee of the Call		108.45
Special Committees		55.55
Expense, Commission on Investments		72.14
Expense attending Synod Conventions		446.61
Statistical and Year Book Committee		45.60
Transportation Committee		19.53
Necrologist		325.00

Total Disbursements	$52,469.76
Balance in United Lutheran Church—General Fund, June 30, 1937	$ 15,068.78

STATEMENT OF RECEIPTS AND DISBURSEMENTS—GENERAL FUND
July 1, 1937 *to June* 30, 1938

Balance, July 1, 1937	$ 15,068.78

RECEIPTS

Proportion of Apportionment		$42,824.00
California Synod, Account Promotion		7.25
Refund, Account Promotion		140.66

Funds for Transmission, Anniversary Appeal:

Alleghany Synod	$ 510.00	
California Synod	805.85	
Canada Synod	154.00	
Florida Synod	25.75	
Georgia-Alabama Synod	33.00	
German Nebraska Synod (Midwest)	20.55	
Maryland Synod	7,029.24	
United Synod of New York	817.11	
Synod of the Northwest	53.32	
Ohio Synod	708.85	
Pacific Synod	745.48	
East Pennsylvania Synod	198.00	
West Pennsylvania Synod	4,609.27	
Ministerium of Pennsylvania	16,536.75	
Pittsburgh Synod	98.50	
Rocky Mountain Synod	526.90	
Susquehanna Synod	23.21	
Texas Synod	5.06	
Virginia Synod	10,593.42	
Wartburg Synod	49.78	
		43,544.04
Synodical Home Missions Support		9,126.84
Payments on Account of Church Extension Loans..		88.00

Total Receipts	95,730.79
	$110,799.57

DISBURSEMENTS

Salaries:	
President	$ 6,399.98
Secretary	5,220.00
Clerks	4,537.49
Travel Expense:	
President	550.44
Secretary	120.49
Expense, Executive Board	980.33
Maintenance, Lutheran Church Home	2,244.00
General Expenses, New York City	205.53
Stationery, Printing, etc.—New York City	391.62
Postage, Telegrams, etc., New York City	559.93
Telephone—New York City	110.50
Treasurer's Expense — Accounting, Stationery and Bond	1,356.70
Auditing Expense, Tait, Weller and Baker	230.00
Promotion Expense, Committee of Executive Secretaries	1,000.00
Appropriation to Luther League	6,000.00
Expenses of Committees:	
Committee of Adjudication	304.38

Committee on Army and Navy Work 18.00
Committee on Church Architecture 125.91
Committee on Faith and Order 271.40
Committee on Publicity 26.45
Committee on Transportation 14.15
Committee on German Interests 46.00
Committee on Church Music 16.00
Committee on Common Service Book 242.16
Committee on Lutheran Relationships 308.90
Special Committees 671.33
Expense, Commission on Investments 41.00
Expense, Attending Synodical Conventions 1,089.48
Expense, Account—Convention, Baltimore 40.05
Transmission of Funds, Board of American Missions 52,758.88

Total Disbursements 85,881.10

Balance in United Lutheran Church—General
Fund—June 30, 1938 .... $ 24,918.47

TRUST FUND ACCOUNTS
June 30, 1938

	Real Estate and Equipment	Cash on Hand	Investments Cost or Book Value	Investments Market Values June 30, 1938	Principal
Emma K. Sotter Trust:					$ 9,808.25
$1,800 Altoona and Logan Valley Electric Railway Company, 1st Lien and Collateral Trust 4% due 1/1/54			$ 2,940.00	$ 1,560.00	
12 shares Voting Trust Certificate, Common Stock, Altoona and Logan Valley Railway Company...					
$3,000 Appalachian Electric Power, 1st 4% due 1963			2,962.50	3,176.25	
$3,000 Georgia Power Company, 1st Refunding 5% due 1967			2,983.50	2,752.50	
		$ 922.25P	$ 8,886.00	$ 7,488.75	
M. S. Hottenstein Trust:					1,000.00
$1,000 Certificate of Deposit, Hotel Chelsea Corporation, 1st 6% due 1945			$ 1,000.00	$ 190.00	
W. P. Huffman Trust:					7,500.00
$2,500 First Mortgage, 5407 Vine St., Phila., Pa...			$ 2,500.00	$ 2,500.00	
$3,000 Georgia Power Co., 1st Refunding 5% due 1967			3,000.00	2,752.50	
$2,000 American Gas and Electric, 5% due 2028...			2,000.00	2,170.00	
			$ 7,500.00	$ 7,422.50	
C. Pflaum, Jr. Trust:					5,000.00
$5,000 Times Square and 46th St. Building, New York City, First Mortgage 6% 1953 (Stamped Bonds)			$ 5,000.00	$ 50.00	
Rev. R. A. Hafer Trust:					5,040.00
40 shares Northern Pacific Railroad Co., common..			$ 3,780.00	$ 420.00	

	Real Estate and Equipment	Cash on Hand	Investments Cost or Book Value	Investments Market Values June 30, 1938	Principal
10 shares Public Service Corp., New Jersey, 7% preferred			1,260.00	1,170.00	
			$ 5,040.00	$ 1,590.00	6,472.25
Oscar S. Grim Trust:					
$5,000 Detroit Edison General, 4½% due 1961......			$ 4,787.72	$ 5,675.00	
$1,000 Montana Power Company, 1st 3¾% due 1966			910.00	936.25	
		774.53P	$ 5,697.72	$ 6,611.25	
Oscar V. Haubner Trust:					
$5,000 Pennsylvania Co. secured 4% due 1963			$ 5,000.00	$ 4,450.00	7,987.90
$1,000 Montana Power Co., 1st 3¾% due 1966			910.00	936.25	
$2,000 Ohio Public Service, 1st 4% due 1962			1,950.00	2,045.00	
		127.90P	$ 7,860.00	$ 7,431.25	
General Trust Funds:					
Dr. W. W. Buck					$ 2,600.00
M. E. Smith					505.86
Estate John S. Drew					202.34
Bertha Kreugel					991.49
Naomi Smoots					903.18
William H. Hildebrand					202.34
Lewis Stemple					450.00
Alice M. Roller					1,175.68
					$ 7,030.89

Securities in Above Trusts:

$3,000 Montana Power Co., 1st 3¾% due 1966	$ 2,730.00	$ 2,808.75	
$3,000 Ohio Public Service, 1st 4% due 1962	2,925.00	3,067.50	
	$ 5,655.00	$ 5,876.25	$ 8,540.53

Depreciation Account:

Lutheran Church House, 39 East 35th St., New York City, New York			
$5,000 Monongahela and West Penn Public Service, 1st Mortgage 4½% due 1960	$ 5,125.00	$ 5,287.50	
$5,000 Hudson and Manhattan Railroad, 1st Refunding Mortgage "A" 5% due 1957	2,575.00	2,350.00	
	$ 7,700.00	$ 7,637.50	

$1,375.89P
123.73I

840.53P

Lutheran Church House, 39 East 35th St., New York City, New York			$193,413.44
Real Estate at Wisner, Nebraska: Farm held in Schmauk Trust (Value not determined).			

280.42I

Totals	$54,338.72	$44,297.50	$251,793.26
	$193,413.44		$193,413.44

P — Principal $4,041.10
I — Income 404.15
$4,445.25

$4,445.25

We have audited the accounts of the Treasurer and examined the securities of the Executive Board of the United Lutheran Church in America for the biennium beginning July 1, 1936, and ending June 30, 1938, and we hereby certify that in our opinion the foregoing statements of:

Receipts and Disbursements on Account of Apportionment for the years July 1, 1936 to June 30, 1937 and July 1, 1937 to June 30, 1938

Receipts and Disbursements on Account of Specials for the years July 1, 1936 to June 30 ,1937 and July 1, 1937 to June 30, 1938

Receipts and Disbursements on Account of Executive Board Expenses for the year July 1, 1936 to June 30, 1937

Receipts and Disbursements—General Fund, July 1, 1937 to June 30, 1938

Reconciliation of Cash for the years July 1, 1936 to June 30, 1937 and July 1, 1937 to June 30, 1938

Trust Fund Accounts as of June 30, 1938

are in agreement with the books of account and are true and correct.

TAIT, WELLER AND BAKER,
Accountants and Auditors.

The Convention proceeded to the election of a Treasurer under Committee of Tellers No. 2.

The report of the Executive Board was taken up for consideration in the order of the items presented for action.

REPORT OF THE EXECUTIVE BOARD

I. CONCERNING THE EXECUTIVE BOARD

1. **Members:**

Ex-Officio: Rev. F. H. Knubel, Rev. W. H. Greever, E. Clarence Miller.

Term Expires 1940: Rev. E. B. Burgess, Rev. H. W. A. Hanson, Rev. E. P. Pfatteicher, Robert F. Bowe, Robbin B. Wolf, John L. Zimmerman.

Term Expires 1938: Rev. A. E. Bell, Rev. J. L. Morgan, Rev. R. E. Tulloss, J. K. Jensen, James C. Kinard, Claude T. Reno.

2. **Committees of the Executive Board:**

At the beginning of the biennium the following committees were appointed by the President:

Committee on Constituent Synods

Rev. A. E. Bell   Rev. J. L. Morgan
                    Rev. R. E. Tulloss

Committee on Boards and Committees

Rev. E. B. Burgess   Rev. E. P. Pfatteicher
Rev. H. W. A. Hanson   James C. Kinard

Finance Committee

E. Clarence Miller   Robert F. Bowe
                        J. K. Jensen

Legal Committee

Robbin B. Wolf   Claude T. Reno
                     John L. Zimmerman

Committee on Special Board Pensions and on Pensions to all Church Workers

E. Clarence Miller   J. K. Jensen
Robert F. Bowe   James C. Kinard
                     Robbin B. Wolf

3. Vacancy filled:

The resignation of Mr. Carl M. Distler was presented to the Executive Board at its meeting on January 14, 1937, and was accepted. Mr. Robert F. Bowe, of the United Lutheran Synod of New York, was elected to fill the vacancy caused by the resignation of Mr. Distler, term expiring 1940.

4. Nominations to fill Vacancies:

To fill vacancies occurring at this convention, the Board places the following in nomination for the term expiring 1942: Rev. A. E. Bell, Rev. Henry H. Bagger, Rev. J. J. Scherer, Rev. Paul H. Krauss, Rev. P. D. Brown, Rev. John L. Deaton, J. K. Jensen, James C. Kinard, Claude T. Reno, John Greiner, Jr., George Hemsing, Bismarck Capps.

5. Report of the Executive Board:

The Board instructed the Secretary to prepare the report of the Board for its presentation to the convention, and instructed him to prepare and publish the Bulletin in an edition of 1,000 copies.

II. MATTERS REFERRED

1. Minutes: (Minutes U. L. C. A., 1936, p. 471)

On October 21, 1936, the Committee on Minutes, at a regular meeting, reviewed and approved the Minutes of the Eleventh Session, as authorized by the convention.

At the meeting of the Executive Board, January 14, 1937, the Secretary reported that he had carried out instructions and had placed an order, with the United Lutheran Publication House, for the publication of 4,500 copies of the Convention Minutes and had arranged for their proper distribution.

After consultation with the President, and in view of the many changes made, from time to time, since the publication of the Constitution and By-laws of the Church in 1925, it was decided to publish the Constitution and By-laws, revised to date, as an appendix to the 1936 Minutes.

2. **Change in Place of 1938 Convention if Necessary:** (Minutes U. L. C. A., 1936, p. 467)

See XI of this report.

3. **Commission on Work Among Negroes in the South:** (Minutes U. L. C. A., 1936, pp. 358, 359, 360)

The Commission on Work Among Negroes in the South presented the following report to the Executive Board, at its meeting on April 7, 1938:

The Commission consists of the following members:

Rev. H. H. Bagger, D.D., representing the Board of Education Convener
Rev. P. D. Brown, D.D., representing the Inner Mission Board
Rev. Z. M. Corbe, D.D., representing the Board of American Missions
Rev. C. A. Linn, Ph.D., representing the memorializing synod, the Georgia-Alabama Synod

The Commission would report that it has held two meetings, on January 25, 1937, and on January 27, 1938, respectively. Both were held in Washington, D. C., and all members were present at both meetings from beginning to end. At the first meeting, Dr. H. H. Bagger was elected as Chairman and Dr. C. A. Linn as Secretary.

As a background for its study the Commission took into consideration the following:

previous expressions on the subject as reported in the earlier Minutes of the U. L. C. A. (Buffalo, pp. 452, 456; Chicago, p. 74; Richmond, p. 572; Columbus, p. 165, and the preamble to the memorial of the Georgia-Alabama Synod, p. 358);

the work at present engaged in among negroes in the South by both Protestant and Catholic agencies and more particularly the work being done under the auspices of the American Lutheran Church and, to a much greater extent, of the Synodical Conference;

the needs of the negroes in the South as compared to the needs of other groups more closely related to us or among whom we are already working;

the particular adaptability of our Church to the negro temperament as revealed in our former service to the negroes and in our present modest work among negroes in other areas than the South;

the financial resources that would be needed and the financial resources that are or might be made available;

the considerations that would have to be borne in mind in the conduct of negro work according to the judgment of the agencies represented by the personnel of the Commission;

the availability of our several seminaries for the training of colored ministers;

the judgments of leaders or experienced workers, Lutheran and otherwise, Northern and Southern, white and colored;

the general plan presented by the Georgia-Alabama Synod and the particular opportunity offered by the Sparta Agricultural and Industrial Institute (of Sparta, Georgia), readily available to us as a starting point.

The conclusions and recommendations of the Commission are as follows:

With regard to "B" and "C" of the memorial under consideration the Commission is of the opinion that the establishment of the Lutheran Church among Southern negroes by the United Lutheran Church, in accordance with any comprehensive plan or on the basis of any really adequate program, would involve a large annual and very long-continued appropriation. In the light of available resources of the Church, and our present commitments to work of many sorts, all too inadequately supported, and of the necessity of a realistic facing of the facts, we do not feel that it is financially possible to proceed to carry out "B" and "C."

With regard to "D," the Commission would express appreciation of the genuine Christian spirit that has moved the Georgia-Alabama Synod to draw up the plan which it submitted for consideration and commends the sensitive conscience of that body in the face of the needs it sees 'round about it. The Commission finds itself forced to the conclusion, however, that here, too, the funds that would be necessary are not available.

On the other hand, because the Commission feels that the Church rightly adopted "A" of the memorial and because the adoption of that statement of responsibility demands that something of a concrete character be done by the Church toward the fulfillment of that responsibility, the Commission recommends:

(1) (a) That the Inner Mission Board be instructed to study the question of promoting specific Inner Mission projects in behalf of the negroes in strategic centers of the South;

(b) And that, when in its judgment a beginning of such work should be made, the Inner Mission Board be authorized to proceed in a manner commensurate with its resources;

(2) (a) That the Board of American Missions, having already engaged in some negro work in a number of centers, increase its activities along those same general lines as finances may make possible;

(b) That the Board make a study, in conference with pastors of our Church in the South, of the possibility of subsidizing chapels for colored people under the administration and direction of our white congregations and their pastors;

(c) And that, if deemed feasible, the Board actually enter upon such a program by way of experiment in a typical center or two;

(3)   That, to whatever degree any of these projects may involve the interests of the Board of Education, the standards of that Board shall be observed and that, in turn, the Board of Education shall give its co-operation and support;

(4)   That the United Lutheran Church instruct the Executive Board to make available from the United Lutheran Church Treasury an outright grant of $2,000 a year to the Synodical Conference for the aid of its work among the negroes in the South.

(Signed)   P. D. Brown,
Z. M. Corbe,
C. A. Linn,
H. H. Bagger, Chairman.

At the meeting of the Executive Board, July 14, 1938, the following action was taken concerning this report:

"Moved and carried that the report of this Commission, with its recommendations, be referred to the Committee on Boards and Committees for conference with the Boards concerned, and report back to the Executive Board."

4. Committee on Organized Work with Children: (Minutes U. L. C. A., 1936, pp. 54, 89)

The Committee on Organized Work with Children presented a report, as instructed, to the Executive Board at its meeting on April 8, 1937. After lengthy discussion, the report was returned to the Committee for restudy.

At the meeting of the Executive Board, January 13, 1938, the following report was submitted and was adopted by the Executive Board:

The Committee has held two meetings since the meeting of the Executive Board in October. It now submits the following as the result of review and re-consideration of all phases of the matters involved, and by unanimous action, on January 4, 1938, recommends approval by the Executive Board:

(a)   That the present work of the Light Brigade and the Junior Luther League and the further extension of organized work with children shall be conducted under the name, *The Children of the Church.*

(b)   That the aim shall be: To help the children grow in Christian faith and love, and to express the same through joyful and effective participation in all phases of the life and work of the Church at home and abroad.

(c)   That membership in this special group shall be: All children from birth through eleven years of age, inclusive.

(d)   That the Women's Missionary Society be designated as the agency to carry on this work in all congregations of the Church.

(e)   That a special committee, to build and project the program for the children of the Church, be constituted as follows:

Three representatives appointed by the Women's Missionary Society
Three representatives appointed by the Luther League of America
Three representatives appointed by the Parish and Church School Board

That this commitee be instructed to begin building and projecting this program immediately, and report to The United Lutheran Church in America in 1940.

That during this formative period this committee be under the general direction of the Parish and Church School Board.

5. Approval of Decisions of Commission on Investments of an Annuity Conference: (Minutes U. L. C. A., 1936, pp. 422, 423)

The work of the Commission on Investments, with special reference to an Annuity Conference, is incomplete.

6. Appeal to the Commission of Adjudication: (Minutes U. L. C. A., 1936, pp. 418, 432, 433)

At the meeting of the Executive Board, January 14, 1937, the formulation of an appeal to the Commission of Adjudication, concerning the convention's decisions regarding women as congregational representatives, was submitted by the Legal Committee and was adopted to be transmitted, by the officers of the Church, to the Commission of Adjudication.

Before

THE COMMISSION OF ADJUDICATION

of

THE UNITED LUTHERAN CHURCH IN AMERICA

In the matter of the Reference by The United Lutheran Church in America in Tenth Convention assembled of the action of the Convention upon the report of the "Committee on Women as Congregational Representatives."

THE REFERENCE

To the Commission of Adjudication of the United Lutheran Church in America:

The United Lutheran Church in America, acting by and through the Executive Board thereof, specially authorized thereto by The United Lutheran Church in America in the Tenth Convention thereof assembled in

Columbus, Ohio, on October 21, 1936, respectfully presents this Reference to the Commission of Adjudication and in support thereof (a) states the following facts and (b) prays the judgment of the Commission upon the questions herein stated.

I

STATEMENT OF THE FACTS

1. To the Seventh Convention of the United Lutheran Church assembled at Milwaukee, Wisconsin, October 7 to 14, 1930, there were presented (Minutes, page 142) the following memorials from the Texas Synod:

> (a) "That we memorialize The United Lutheran Church in America in the matter of women delegates to synod, to determine whether or not such procedure is unscriptural."
>
> (b) "Dass wir, die Texas Synode, der Vereinigte Lutherische Kirche von Amerika, ersuchen, ein Gutachten ueber diese Frage zu geben: Ist die Gemeindevertretung seitens der Frauen der Gemeinde Schriftwidrig?"

Whereupon the said convention resolved (Minutes, pages 143, 145) that a special committee be appointed to prepare a statement on the subject for the consideration of the next convention.

2. The "Committee on Women as Congregational Representatives," presented majority and minority reports to the Eighth Convention assembled at Philadelphia, Pennsylvania, October 12 to 19, 1932, which, by said convention, were referred to a new committee to be appointed by the President to study the matter further and report to the next convention. (Minutes, pages 426-430.)

3. The "Committee on Women as Congregational Representatives," appointed pursuant to the action of the Eighth Convention, presented majority and minority reports to the Ninth Convention assembled at Savannah, Georgia, October 17 to 24, 1934, and decision thereon was postponed until the next convention. (Minutes, pages 456-466, 524.)

4. The said majority and minority reports of the "Committee on Women as Congregational Representatives" were presented to the Tenth Convention assembled at Columbus, Ohio, October 14 to 21, 1936 (Minutes, pages 58, 397, 408, 418, 432, 433) and the recommendations contained in the majority report, as follows, were adopted:

> (a) "That the reply of the United Lutheran Church to the Texas Synod be as follows: That the election of women delegates to meetings of synod is not unscriptural in the sense that it is not contrary to or forbidden by the Scriptures."
>
> (b) "That this action shall be understood as applying to any similar question that may hereafter arise concerning the

eligibility of women for membership in church councils, or in general conventions, boards or committees of the Church."

(c) "The conception of spiritual equality in Christ does not alter the fact that, by divine appointment, certain spheres of Christian service are more natural or normal to men, while other types of service can best be performed by women. Since the Church deeply deplores those social, industrial, and economic conditions which oppose the Christian home, the glory of motherhood, and the rearing of children in the nurture and admonition of the Lord, it should encourage the fulfillment of those duties by the exercising of care in the organization and assignment of its work."

5. Subsequent to the adoption of the foregoing recommendations, representatives of the minority of the said Convention dissented from its action, and the attention of the Convention was brought to the Constitution of The United Lutheran Church in America which provides:

ARTICLE VIII

"Section 5. *As to Doctrine and Conscience.* All matters of doctrine and conscience shall be decided according to the Word of God alone. If on grounds of doctrine or conscience the question be raised as to the binding character of any action, the said question shall be referred to the Commission of Adjudication. Under no circumstances shall the right of a minority be disregarded or the right to record an individual protest on the ground of conscience be refused."

Whereupon, the President, having ruled that References can be made to the Commission of Adjudication only by a Convention of the United Lutheran Church or by a constituent synod thereof, "It was moved and carried that the Convention instruct the Executive Board to be its agent in formulating an appeal to the Commission of Adjudication concerning the binding character of the action which adopted the recommendations of the 'Committee on Women as Congregational Representatives.'" (Minutes, page 433.)

6. This Reference has been formulated by the Executive Board pursuant to said action and on behalf of The United Lutheran Church in America and the facts herein stated are true.

7. By reference thereto, all the reports to the United Lutheran Church in relation to this matter and its actions thereon are made a part hereof with like force and effect as though fully and at large recited herein; and the record thus presented is correct.

II

THE STATEMENT OF QUESTIONS INVOLVED

In view of the provisions of Article VIII, Section 5 of the Constitution of The United Lutheran Church in America, providing that questions on grounds of doctrine or conscience as to the binding character of any action shall be referred to the Commission of Adjudication, and such question having been raised on the adoption of the recommendations of the majority report of the "Committee on Women as Congregational Representatives," hereinabove recited, and said question was asserted as a matter of conscience, and in view of the dispute as to whether those portions of the Scripture cited in the majority report and in the minority report of the Committee were involved in the action taken:

1. Is the matter upon which the Convention acted a "matter of conscience"?

2. If the answer to number one is "yea," did the Convention follow the required method and make its decision "according to the Word of God alone"?

3. Does the action of the Convention in adopting the recommendations of the majority report bindingly decide the meaning of and the extent of the authority of certain passages of Scripture?

4. Does the action of the Convention in adopting the majority report bind the consciences of members of The United Lutheran Church in America?

THE UNITED LUTHERAN CHURCH IN AMERICA

Seal

BY:

PRESIDENT

SECRETARY

7. **Committee on the New Pension Plan:** (Minutes U. L. C. A., 1936, pp. 338, 355)

The following were appointed as a special committee on this subject:

E. Clarence Miller, Chairman
Rev. J. Sittler
Rev. Wm. F. Buch
Rev. W. E. Frey
Rev. Jacob Diehl
Mr. B. B. Slifer
Mr. Arthur P. Black

8. **Change in Form of Presenting Budget:** (Minutes U. L. C. A., 1936, pp. 54, 89)

See V, 3, of this Report.

9. **Merger of Agencies:** (Minutes U. L. C. A., 1936, pp. 65, 89, 421)

See IV, A, 2, of this Report.

10. Literature Dealing with the Liquor Traffic: (Minutes U. L. C. A., 1936, pp. 371, 374, 378)

With reference to the publication and distribution of literature on temperance, the Executive Board passed the following resolution at its meeting on January 13, 1938:

> That the Inner Mission Board be requested to co-operate with the Parish and Church School Board and the Board of Publication in carrying out the recommendation of the Columbus Convention of the Church in regard to the preparation and publication of literature on temperance.

11. Representation at Conventions of Constituent Synods: (Minutes U. L. C. A., 1936, pp. 34, 419, 431)

The Executive Board, at its meeting on January 14, 1937, approved the following recommendation from the Officers:

> It is recommended that the Executive Board hereafter arrange to send a representative of the Church to the annual meetings of the constituent synods. The expense is to be carried by the Treasury of the Executive Board. Detailed arrangements are to be made by the officers. In accordance with the authorization of the Columbus Convention, all previous arrangements for the visitation of synods, upon the Minutes of the U. L. C. A., are now rescinded.

This arrangement was put into immediate effect and the Church was represented at the 1937 and 1938 conventions of the constituent synods as here recorded:

1937 Conventions of Synods

Dr. A. E. Bell	Manitoba Synod
	Ohio Synod
	West Pennsylvania
	    Synod
		Dr. F. H. Knubel	Iowa Synod
			Nebraska Synod
			Kansas Synod
			Nova Scotia
			    Synod

Dr. E. B. Burgess	Alleghany Synod		Pennsylvania Ministerium
Dr. W. H. Greever	California Synod German Nebraska Synod		Texas Synod
	Pacific Synod	Dr. E. C. Miller	Pittsburgh Synod
	Rocky Mountain Synod	Dr. J. L. Morgan	Illinois Synod Indiana Synod
	Wartburg Synod		Mississippi Synod
Dr. H. W. A. Hanson	West Virginia Synod	Dr. E. P. Pfatteicher	Michigan Synod New York Synod
Mr. J. K. Jensen	Canada Synod		

	Kentucky-Tennessee
	    Synod
		Dr. R. E. Tulloss	North Carolina
			    Synod

			Northwest Synod
Dr. J. C. Kinard	East Pennsylvania Synod		
	Florida Synod	Dr. R. B. Wolf	Maryland Synod
			Susquehanna
Dr. E. E. Fischer	Slovak Zion Synod		Synod

1938 Conventions of Synods

Dr. A. E. Bell	Iowa Synod Kansas Synod Midwest Synod Nebraska Synod	Dr. F. H. Knubel	Georgia-Alabama Synod South Carolina Synod Virginia Synod
Dr. E. B. Burgess	Alleghany Synod East Pennsylvania Synod	Dr. E. C. Miller	North Carolina Synod
	Susquehanna Synod West Pennsylvania Synod	Dr. J. L. Morgan	California Synod Florida Synod Pacific Synod Rocky Mountain Synod
Dr. W. H. Greever	Canada Synod Illinois Synod Maryland Synod Michigan Synod	Dr. E. P. Pfatteicher Dr. H. B. Schaeffer Dr. R. E. Tulloss	Northwest Synod Mississippi Synod Kentucky-Ten- nessee Synod
Dr. H. W. A. Hanson	New York Synod Pittsburgh Synod		Pennsylvania Ministerium
Mr. J. K. Jensen	Indiana Synod		Wartburg Synod
Dr. J. C. Kinard	Nova Scotia Synod Texas Synod	Mr. H. T. Walker	Slovak Zion Synod
		Dr. R. B. Wolf	Ohio Synod West Virginia Synod

12. **Promotional Plans in Regard to Pastors:** (Minutes U. L. C. A., 1936, pp. 34, 419, 431)

With the approval of the Executive Board, the item referred by the Columbus Convention to the Executive Board, pertaining to the relation of pastors to the promotional plan, has been provided for through the Committee of Executive Secretaries. A church-wide schedule of Pastors' Institutes has been arranged for the latter part of 1938.

*13. **Consolidation of Periodicals:** (Minutes U. L. C. A., 1936, pp. 55, 89, 259, 261, 357, 359, 432)   (For action on this item, see pp. 103, 231, 232, 235, 238.)

As an item in the general plan of promotion, this matter was referred, for investigation, study and recommendations, to the Committee of Executive Secretaries. The report of a sub-committee of that body was transmitted to the Executive Board at its meeting on July 14, 1938, and the Executive Board voted to submit this recommendation to the Baltimore Convention for approval:

> That there shall be three general publications; a weekly paper stressing news and general information of the Church; a monthly for Lutheran workers on methods, study courses, etc.; and a quarterly magazine for pastors to contain theological and practical material.

*14. **Amendments to Constitution:** (Minutes U. L. C. A., 1936, pp. 307, 309, 360)   (Amendments rejected, see p. 107.)

The Executive Board, at its meeting April 7, 1938, adopted the following as a formulation of the motion made at the Columbus Convention for a change of the Constitution pertaining to the term of service for officers, and hereby submits the same for the consideration of the convention:

ARTICLE IX

Section 1. The officers of The United Lutheran Church in America shall be a President, a Secretary and a Treasurer. The President shall be an ordained minister of the Church. The officers shall be elected by ballot at a regular convention, for a term of six years in each case, except that at the first elections following the adoption of this provision, the President shall be elected for six years, the Secretary for four years, and the Treasurer for two years. The assumption of office shall not take place until the first day of the third month after election.

Section 5. In the event of the death, resignation or incapacity of any officer, in the interim between conventions, the Executive Board shall fill the vacancy until the next convention, at which time the convention shall elect for the unexpired term.

*15. Advanced Age Retirement Limit for Pastors: (Minutes U. L. C. A., 1936, pp. 356, 359) (For action on this item, see p. 107.)

At its meeting July 14, 1938, the Executive Board adopted the following as the reply, which it recommends for adoption by the convention, to the memorial from the Ministerium of Pennsylvania to the Columbus Convention:

That the Executive Board reply to this memorial stating that, in view of our Lutheran polity relating to congregations and their relations with their respective pastors, a general rule prescribing a retirement age for pastors is inadvisable, and that accordingly, this matter be left to the mutual desires of the respective pastors and congregations, to be decided in the light of the facts and circumstances involved in each individual case.

*16. Theological Education under U. L. C. A. Control: (Minutes U. L. C. A., 1936, pp. 356, 357, 359) (For action on this item, see pp. 107, 184, 464, 465, 483, 484; and for substitute report as finally adopted, see p. 483.)

At its meeting, January 14, 1937, the Executive Board appointed a special committee of five to whom the memorials on this subject were referred. Members of the committee were: Rev. F. H. Knubel, Rev. W. H. Greever, Rev. A. E. Bell, James C. Kinard, Claude T. Reno. The commiteee made its first report on April 7, 1938, and a second report on July 14, 1938. The Executive Board formulated the following statements, on the basis of the committee's report, to be submitted to this convention as an answer to the memorials in question:

Since the Constitution of the U. L. C. A., as adopted at the time of the organization of the Body, did not provide for the control of theological education by the U. L. C. A.; and

Since the Commission of Adjudication has given an opinion on the subject to the effect that the U. L. C. A. cannot exercise control over theological education under its present Constitution; and

Since it is a fact there was a distinct agreement in the Ways and Means Committee prior to the adoption of the Constitution that theological seminaries and colleges should remain under the control of constituent synods; and

Since real responsibilities in this field were committed to the Church by the language of its Constitution in Article VI, Section 4, "To awaken, co-ordinate and effectively direct the energies of the Church in such operations as the following: (a) The training of ministers and teachers to be witnesses of the Word"; and

Further, in Article VI, Sections 1 and 2, "To preserve and extend the pure teaching of the Gospel and the right administration of the Sacraments. (Eph. 4: 5, 6; the Augsburg Confession, Article VII.) To conserve the unity of the true faith (Eph. 4: 3-16; I Cor. 1: 10), to guard against any departure therefrom (Rom 16: 17), and to strengthen the Church in faith and confession,"

It is recommended, (a) That the answer of the convention to the two memorials on this subject be: That no amendment be made at this time to the Constitution of the U. L. C. A. giving it authority to "establish, control and maintain theological seminaries." (For substitute, see pp. 465, 483.)

(b) That the Executive Board of the U. L. C. A. shall appoint, from the Church at large, a commission of seven members on theological education.

III. SYNODS

A. In General

1. Apportionment to Synods, 1938 and 1939:

The budget of $2,000,000, adopted at the Columbus Convention for the years 1938 and 1939, was apportioned among the constituent synods as follows:

Synod	1938 Communing Members	Apportion- ment	1939 Communing Members	Apportion- ment
Alleghany	20,741	$ 56,034	20,955	$ 55,671
California	4,168	11,260	4,265	11,331
Canada	16,162	43,663	16,273	43,232
East Pennsylvania	35,101	94,829	35,227	93,588
Florida	1,104	2,983	1,194	3,172
Georgia-Alabama	3,027	8,178	3,099	8,233
Illinois	31,544	85,219	32,400	86,077
Indiana	11,900	32,149	12,298	32,672
Iowa	8,385	22,653	8,633	22,935
Kansas	5,657	15,283	5,857	15,560
Kentucky-Tennessee	3,863	10,436	4,107	10,911

Manitoba	6,762	18,268	7,241	19,237
Maryland	32,344	87,381	32,646	86,731
Michigan	4,530	12,238	4,764	12,657
Midwest	10,411	28,126	10,670	28,347
Mississippi	378	1,021	316	840
Nebraska	11,630	31,420	11,622	30,876
New York	108,932	294,291	109,233	290,200
North Carolina	20,463	55,283	20,523	54,524
Northwest	29,801	80,510	31,887	84,714
Nova Scotia	2,250	6,079	2,186	5,808
Ohio	49,970	135,000	50,627	134,501
Pacific	2,166	5,852	2,243	5,959
Pennsylvania Ministerium..	148,989	402,509	151,116	401,471
Pittsburgh	55,625	150,277	57,300	152,229
Rocky Mountain	1,761	4,758	1,825	4,848
Slovak Zion	4,474	12,087	4,394	11,674
South Carolina	15,801	42,688	16,261	43,201
Susquehanna	25,418	68,669	25,786	68,506
Texas	3,513	9,491	3,597	9,556
Virginia	13,307	35,950	13,082	34,755
Wartburg	10,870	29,366	11,560	30,712
West Pennsylvania	35,779	96,661	35,994	95,625
West Virginia	3,475	9,388	3,631	9,647
	740,301	$2,000,000	752,812	$2,000,000

2. Apportionment Receipts, 1929 to 1938:

The following was submitted by the Treasurer of the Church for information:

APPORTIONMENT RECEIPTS FOR FISCAL YEARS 1929 TO 1938

Synods	Year Ending June 30, 1929	Year Ending June 30, 1930	Year Ending June 30, 1931	Year Ending June 30, 1932	Year Ending June 30, 1933	Year Ending June 30, 1934	Year Ending June 30, 1935	Year Ending June 30, 1936	Year Ending June 30, 1937	Year Ending June 30, 1938
Alleghany	$61,264.00	$55,099.00	$58,412.00	$46,471.00	$28,441.00	$39,204.00	$34,377.00	$37,006.00	$39,624.00	$30,952.00
California	10,261.55	9,693.55	7,869.40	6,512.51	4,282.75	4,309.13	5,525.65	5,095.07	6,308.09	8,556.00
Canada	6,195.13	6,395.73	6,505.17	5,514.54	5,163.15	4,402.81	4,545.74	4,766.24	3,969.11	4,981.27
East Penna.	103,825.00	92,375.00	101,763.00	87,784.00	69,638.00	70,760.00	64,886.00	65,094.00	69,363.00	72,050.00
Florida	415.66	2,790.17	2,182.65	1,813.77	1,351.79	1,714.67	1,508.10	1,515.96	2,006.37	2,189.47
Georgia-Ala.	7,970.91	8,945.21	6,179.67	5,724.41	4,302.38	5,353.63	5,083.39	5,373.97	6,614.14	6,170.56
Illinois	61,000.00	70,000.00	61,000.00	54,500.00	19,500.00	34,629.61	31,000.30	27,500.00	35,000.00	42,500.00
Indiana	22,858.80	24,332.41	22,583.38	22,779.22	17,339.98	15,139.37	17,724.40	16,503.63	17,990.73	18,059.79
Iowa	7,200.00	10,100.00	7,900.00	9,450.00	5,350.00	8,382.46	6,950.00	7,000.00	7,150.00	9,100.00
Kansas	11,745.13	13,220.00	11,000.00	10,701.00	7,218.86	7,329.36	8,823.24	8,110.00	8,800.00	11,434.00
Kentucky-Tenn.								7,699.94	7,743.25	8,568.34
Manitoba	1,400.00	1,300.00	1,550.00	1,050.00	507.07	1,275.30	948.16	864.00	1,100.00	1,200.00
Maryland	61,529.94	87,994.04	96,747.12	86,794.97	70,799.99	64,865.25	71,680.63	69,867.79	68,029.28	66,221.52
Michigan	21,799.94	20,857.87	20,325.06	19,182.20	12,395.32	13,722.18	6,406.21	6,867.00	8,697.00	8,311.00
Midwest	2,570.00	3,330.00	2,600.00	1,700.00	1,050.00	2,031.86	1,865.55	2,054.46	2,482.72	2,303.50
Mississippi	585.07	755.38	415.47	428.80	466.76	331.85	351.18	369.32	417.47	397.40
Nebraska	23,258.10	20,040.52	21,629.31	18,733.78	12,921.02	11,959.82	7,930.57	7,296.43	8,855.12	9,833.78
New York	167,058.06	148,842.33	150,900.00	117,400.00	100,400.00	88,288.00	85,125.00	93,520.00	96,466.00	100,655.92
North Carolina	30,906.18	34,927.03	25,915.13	23,502.13	12,601.89	16,091.79	18,830.39	18,050.06	23,847.59	23,171.46
Northwest	34,527.86	40,159.48	39,298.30	33,447.58	27,147.19	30,111.25	30,134.43	29,235.58	33,271.47	35,431.26
Nova Scotia	1,722.57	1,937.17	1,722.99	1,987.39	1,267.00	1,191.24	760.07	663.05	956.69	828.09
Ohio	121,000.00	123,000.00	119,000.00	95,000.00	69,614.33	71,275.91	69,109.87	81,935.16	83,750.47	90,944.87
Pacific	7,892.00	6,506.00	4,000.00	3,600.00	2,500.00	3,253.75	3,172.08	3,352.16	3,324.12	4,036.52
Penna. Minis.	257,418.91	270,962.19	256,105.06	222,206.47	166,985.86	172,013.43	163,933.14	161,837.51	183,883.99	177,805.83
Pittsburgh	128,956.84	136,834.83	135,029.69	108,029.64	74,429.14	68,604.42	68,442.70	69,314.63	77,270.72	82,495.10
Rocky Mountain	4,002.26	3,575.78	3,507.35	2,968.53	2,845.30	2,994.65	2,532.66	3,178.00	4,033.43	2,823.38
Slovak Zion	200.00	350.00	500.00		148.06	497.25	99.83	38.60	593.65	750.00
South Carolina	23,550.00	18,129.60	25,206.43	14,275.00	12,050.00	17,200.00	15,950.00	17,750.00	20,700.00	23,850.00
Susquehanna	68,715.51	72,909.14	65,065.95	51,332.71	38,218.76	33,382.00	31,976.45	34,533.00	37,056.30	39,794.53
Texas	2,906.98	3,150.12	3,196.73	1,974.13	1,935.31	3,327.81	2,350.18	2,483.29	2,678.97	2,991.52
Virginia	17,329.55	19,167.38	16,713.83	15,658.24	11,787.00	12,992.88	12,136.32	14,481.46	15,333.25	16,049.37
Wartburg	3,000.00	5,100.00	5,200.00	5,000.00	2,700.00	3,730.00	2,800.00	3,100.00	3,900.00	3,700.00
West Penna.	93,545.59	102,279.17	97,303.00	87,770.00	78,050.00	69,405.00	71,825.00	76,090.00	82,030.00	82,530.00
West Virginia	5,000.00	7,700.00	5,500.00	3,700.00	2,800.00	4,567.75	4,600.00	4,350.00	4,800.00	3,800.00
Miscellaneous		180.00	510.00	180.00	330.00	722.18	476.28	255.00	160.00	204.40
Luth. Pub. House				10,000.00		60,000.00	40,000.00	30,000.00		
Total	$1,371,611.54	$1,422,919.10	$1,383,336.69	$1,177,172.17	$866,537.91	$945,060.61	$900,575.06	$917,151.31	$968,206.93	$994,690.88

3. Conference of Presidents:

At the meeting of the Executive Board, June 25, 1937, authority was given to the President to arrange for a Conference of Presidents of Synods, at such time and place as circumstances should indicate. The President arranged for such a conference, which was held at Harrisburg, Pa., December 9 and 10, 1937. The program for the Conference provided for the discussion of such questions as "external relationships," "Anniversary Appeal of the Board of American Missions," "call and recall of pastors" and other matters of a practical nature. These conferences have been called "clearing houses of common synodical problems."

*4. Call to the Ministry: (For action on this item, see pp. 103, 105, 106.)

The committee for the study of the subject and the preparation of a statement on the "Call to the Ministry" was continued by the 1936 convention for the present biennium. At the meeting of the Executive Board, April 7, 1938, the following report was submitted, was approved by the Executive Board as a guide on the subject of the "Call to the Ministry" and is herewith submitted to the convention with the recommendation that this action of the Executive Board be approved:

CALL TO THE MINISTRY

The committee appointed by President Knubel to study "The Call" consists of the following: Drs. H. F. Baughman, C. K. Bell, E. E. Flack, R. D. Snyder, and E. P. Pfatteicher—one pastor, three seminary professors and one synodical president. The report herewith presented is the product of the labors of the entire committee.

ORIGIN OF THE COMMITTEE

A number of inquiries concerning the Lutheran conception of the call reached the President of the United Lutheran Church. They were addressed to him by presidents of constituent synods. Impressed by the importance of these queries and the need for a carefully planned pronouncement, President Knubel asked the Conference of Presidents of Constituent Synods, assembled in the Deshler-Wallick Hotel at Columbus, Ohio, on January 7 and 8, 1936, under his leadership, to discuss the question. The President of the Ministerium of Pennsylvania, in whose synod situations had arisen which led to some of these queries, was assigned this subject and, after consultation with several theologians of the Church, presented theses which were earnestly discussed. The President of the Church was petitioned by the Conference to present the subject to the Executive Board and to ask said Board that a committee be appointed to formulate a "statement on the doctrine of the call which could be accepted for guidance with reference to practical present-day problems, particularly the right of a congregation to terminate a call to a pastor or to limit the term of service under the call."

The investigations of your committee have brought to their attention various practices which tend to produce a lowered conception of the holy office of the ministry, and to create administrative problems for the Church. These vary from minor irregularities to gross violations of the principles of the Church. They are found to arise chiefly, from failure clearly to understand the meaning of the call, from lack of sound constitutional practice by congregations, from absence of synodical supervision and discipline, or from failure to appreciate the sacred character and obligations of the ministerial office.

Some of the typical situations that have created the problems presented to this committee are:

The request for ordination by candidates not called to a specific ministry of the Word and the Sacraments, not called by a properly authorized agency of the Church, or called with a definite limitation of time stipulated in the terms of employment.

The admission to synods of the United Lutheran Church of ministers from non-Lutheran communions who, through lack of thorough understanding and appreciation of the genius and polity of the Lutheran Church become involved in pastoral difficulties.

The proposal by some congregations to conduct annual elections for the re-employment of pastors.

The continuation by pastors in congregations in which their ministry is detrimental to the life of the Church, with no apparent recourse by the congregations, thus raising the question of a possible recall.

The refusal of men who have demitted, or have been deposed from, the ministry to surrender their ordination papers.

THE TASK OF THE COMMITTEE

The Committee does not feel itself called upon to undertake a restatement of the doctrine of the call to the ministry. We have the doctrine; most of the difficulties grow either out of failure to apply the doctrine or out of problems inherent in local situations. We are convinced that many of these difficulties would never arise if certain basic principles were to receive a far more vigorous emphasis in the teaching of the Church.

We believe that the call that makes one a pastor comes from God, through the Church, to a particular congregation or agency of the Church. It is not independent of the means of grace and is to be distinguished from the merely individual persuasion of a call. In this sense it may be said that the call has three distinct phases:

1. *It is a call from God.* In Christ we have been called to become to God "what his own hand is to man" (Theologia Deutsch). Any attitude or policy that is not in harmony with the will of God as it is expressed in His Word, or that fails to promote that will, is incompatible with the ministry. This call from God comes through the Church, therefore,

2. *It is a call from the Church.* In the New Testament the Church is described as the Body of Christ (cf. I Cor. 12: 21ff) and the life of the Church is viewed as a continuation of the life of Christ (cf. Acts 1: 1ff). The pastor is not an isolated individual whom God has lifted out from the masses to become His spokesman; he is a member of a living organism, the Body of Christ, in which believers are members one of another. Anarchy and rampant individualism have no place in a church so

conceived. Any attitude or policy that is not in harmony with this corporate conception of the Church is incompatible with the ministry.

3. *It is a call from a local congregation or a duly authorized agency of the Church* (See Article III, Section 5, Constitution of U. L. C. A.). The action of the congregation in a regularly called meeting and not only the action of the church council is necessary to give validity to the call. The pastor is not at liberty to select his field of labor as he would select a suit of clothes. The congregation is not a field which he has chosen or to which he has been assigned; much less is it a vineyard that has been awarded to him, a garden which he is at liberty to exploit for personal gain. It is a community of believers that has chosen him. It is a porch of Bethesda that beckons him. Any attitude or policy that is not in harmony with this conviction is incompatible with the ministry.

THE COMMITTEE'S DEFINITION OF THE CALL

The Committee distinguishes between the *gospel call* which is the universal invitation of God to all who have sinned and the *call to the gospel ministry* as the specific invitation of God through the Christian Church to teach in the Church and administer the Sacraments.

"Of ecclesiastical order they teach that no one should publicly teach in the Church or administer the Sacraments, unless he be regularly called" (Augsburg Confession, Article 14; see also Apology of the Augsburg Confession and Article 28 of the Augsburg Confession).

It may be well here to note certain general deductions:

1. "It is true that all Christians are priests but they are not all ministers. For beyond being a Christian and a priest, he must have an office and officially assigned task. The vocation and mandate make ministers and preachers." (Luther—see II Peter 1: 21; Jeremiah 23: 21.)

2. The "substantia ecclesiae" is however not a matter of individual believers but of Word and Sacraments. (Elert, Morphologie des Luthertums I, p. 301.)

3. On the basis of what has been said, we see that both the ministry and the means of grace are inherent in the Gospel. The ministry is not a separate entity or priesthood in the sense of the priesthood of the Old Testament or the priesthood of the Greek and Roman Catholic Church. (See Apology of Augsburg Confession, Chapter 7; Article 13, pp. 214-5, Jacobs.)

4. We distinguish between the universal priesthood of believers as a common vocation (Stand) and the ministry as an office (Amt). We must therefore emphasize the distinction between the spiritual priesthood of all believers and the office of the ministry. (Elert.)

5. Out of the Church of Jesus Christ and from among those approved by the Church must come men for the ministry.

NOTE: Chemnitz would have young men apply these tests—Isaiah 49: 2; 51: 16; Luke 1: 76; I Timothy 4: 16; I Corinthians 15: 58; I Corinthians 16: 9; II Corinthians 2: 12; John 10: 3.

We, therefore, conceive of the call to the gospel ministry as the inclusive invitation of the triune God, the Church and the congregation, or authorized agency of the Church, to a member of the Church to feed the flock of God through teaching the Word and administering the Sacraments.

POLICIES RECOMMENDED

On the basis of what has been said the committee recommends the following policies for the guidance of the Church.

A. Concerning Candidates

We recommend a more careful selection and nurture of candidates for theological education.

1. By pastors and congregations

Rivalries engendered by pride in the statistical column, "Students for the Ministry," have often resulted in an emphasis upon numbers rather than quality.

We, therefore, recommend careful selection of candidates and suggest that church councils place their stamp of approval on them as they enter college or the seminary. We also recommend that pastors report at least annually to church councils the progress or lack of progress of their candidates for the ministry and that church councils provide, not merely financial, but particularly, spiritual encouragement and nurture.

2. By synodical committees

Heretofore synodical committees on ministerial education have confined themselves too exclusively, even in synods with broader constitutional prerogatives, to the supervision and nurture of those receiving financial aid.

We recommend that synodical committees on ministerial education avail themselves of constitutional provisions in existence or propose constitutional amendments looking toward the supervision and nurture of all students for the ministry coming from within the bounds of their synods.

3. By seminary faculties

The seminary and the synod must both recognize that the seminary is more than an academic institution; it is a training school for ministers. Therefore, far more than a college or a university, it must be concerned with underlying motives, character standards, personal fitness and aptitudes and faith values.

We recommend that seminary faculties provide personal counselors whereby a closer and more constant contact can be sustained between the Christian teacher and the Christian student.

B. Concerning Ordination

We recommend that the constituent synods pursue a uniform policy of ordination, namely, that only those who are regularly called, in accordance with the statement of the call, to preach the Word and administer the Sacraments be ordained. This call must come through a properly authorized channel of the Church to a specific ministry of the Church and shall not carry a limitation of time.

The practice of Licensure in the Lutheran Church was introduced in our country many years ago as a then necessary expedient without biblical or confessional background or warrant. These biblical passages are worthy of study: Num. 27: 18-20; Gen. 48: 14; Matt. 19: 13-15; Acts

6: 6; II Tim. 1: 6; Titus 1: 5; I Tim. 4: 14; 5: 22. The confessional passages are Aug. Conf. Art. 14, the article on "The Power and Jurisdiction of Bishops" in the Smalcald Articles, and the Apology of the Aug. Conf. Art. 7: 12. Ordination loses its proper dignity in the eyes of the Church, if it simply confirms rights already enjoyed.

The practice of admitting candidates to the office of the ministry by the act of licensure carries with it explicitly a time limit. Where licensure is granted without a preceding call, the personal qualifications of the candidate are made to be determinative of the right to the office.

Induction into the office *sine titulo* makes the ministry more or less assume the character of an order, and there is nothing in Scripture or the teaching of the Church to warrant the conferring of the office with a time limit, but rather the opposite (I Peter 5: 1-4, compare Luke 9: 62). If God has not attached a time limit to the exercise of the office of the ministry neither should the Church except upon grounds warranted by Scripture, and definitely formulated in her disciplinary procedure.

Provisions which seem warranted and even necessary in the missionary or pioneer stage of the Church's development should be abandoned as the practice of normal organization can be more consistently applied.

We, therefore, recommend that the practice of licensure be discontinued as a policy of the Church, and we further recommend that Article 9, Section II, in the suggested constitution for constituent synods be omitted from future printings of said model constitution.

The question of the reordination of ordained men coming from non-Lutheran communions has been projected into our deliberations by the fact that many abnormal situations arise from this source. Some of these men have come into our synods because they believed there were certain material advantages to be gained. They have sought the transfer from lower motives. Others whose motives were entirely worthy have come with their whole attitude, practice and bearing predisposed by a training and experience entirely different from that of the Lutheran Church. They have entered a different atmosphere and have not been able to acclimate themselves.

The suggestion that these candidates be reordained does not imply any question of the validity of a previous ordination. It does not propose to set up an exclusive ministry. It aims to deal with a practical question, and is wholly of an administrative character. It is not an indictment of a Church's ministry but only the recognition of a fact to say that ministerial courtesy can be abused.

When a candidate is ordained in the Lutheran Church he is examined in the doctrine and polity of that Church. He is asked, "Will you preach and teach the pure Word of God in accord with the Confession of the Evangelical Lutheran Church?" That means that he is ordained to the ministry of the Lutheran Church. Similarly, it is assumed that the ordinand in any other communion is ordained to the ministry of that particular communion. He is presumed to be schooled in its doctrine and polity and in accord with its entire system of administration. It is, therefore, not a denial of the validity of his ordination or an assertion of the superiority of the Lutheran ministry to ask that one who transfers from a non-Lutheran communion give positive affirmation of his acceptance of the doctrine and polity of the Lutheran Church. Such affirmation presumes a more than casual understanding of the Lutheran practice as well as a deliberate choice of and whole-hearted committal to it.

We, therefore, recommend that all synods of the United Lutheran Church require applicants for admission from other communions to appear before the Examining Committee of the Synod for examination and counsel, with special emphasis upon the teachings and polity of the Lutheran Church, and

We recommend the preparation of a speci l form for use by synods in receiving such applicants from other communions. Said form to emphasize the candidate's acceptance of the Lutheran position concerning the Word and Sacraments. (Amended, see p. 106.)

We further suggest that the desirability of reordination, from the standpoint of corporate fellowship, be pointed out to the candidate.

To clarify and amplify the recommendations concerning ordination, we offer these further statements and recommendations relating to synodical and congregational practice:

1. The call to a particular field of labor normally carries no time limit. In the case of men already ordained, calls to positions of administration in the Church may carry the condition of limited terms of service. In cases necessitating the limitation of time as long a period as is consistent with the best interests of the Church should be indicated. Those holding office in the work of the Church-at-large elected for longer or shorter terms are not, according to the Lutheran point of view, called repeatedly to one and the same office. The thing that happens, after the first election, is the exercise by the electoral body of its constitutional privilege of recall. Congregational constitutions do not and should not carry such a provision for their call is specifically one to administer the Word and Sacraments in a definite parish. The congregational call, as a contractual relationship, can be terminated only when one or the other party fails to live up to its implications. (Amended, see p. 106.)

Since there is no provision in the Model Constitution for Synods clarifying the call to ordained men to administrative positions which carry a limitation of time, we recommend that such provision be made. (Stricken from the report, see p. 106.)

2. It is well known that some of our congregations do not have a church constitution. Others have antiquated or inadequate documents. Much of our lack of efficiency in congregational life may be due to this deficiency in local organization. Constitutions not only guarantee rights; they also define duties. It seems to us to be a most desirable thing that a larger measure of uniformity be sought in this matter, for the sake of both congregations and synodical officers.

We recommend a general and vigorous movement for the adoption by congregations of a uniform constitution, such as that recommended by the Executive Board of the United Lutheran Church.

3. As a practical expression of the principles involved in the statement of the call and to make effective these policies we offer:

In the election of a pastor, it is highly important that a local congregation observe strictly the approved regulations and mode of election provided in the above-suggested constitution. In the interest of congregational harmony and the general welfare of the Church, every precaution should be taken to avoid any irregularity or harmful procedure. To this end—

We recommend that the meeting of a congregation for the election of a pastor be presided over or attended by the president of the synod or his clerical representative.

4. The wording of a call to a parish commonly in use does not differ materially, whether addressed to a candidate for ordination or to one already in the office of the ministry. In either case the call may be valid though it be extended by the laity alone, that is, originating in a congregational meeting attended only by the lay members of the congregation. However, "that mode of extending the call is best where provision is made for the participation of both ministers and laymen" (Summary of Christian Faith, p. 429), the ministry being best fitted by training and experience, for judging the qualifications of the candidate.

In order to bring the form of the call into harmony with our prevailing synodical practice, and to guard against a misconception of the call,—

We recommend the official adoption and use of the call-form published by the United Lutheran Publication House, with the insertion in it of the words "upon the condition of your approval by the synod" following "we, the undersigned, do hereby now extend you a formal call . ."

5. Inasmuch as there are three interests involved in the relationship of a pastorate, the Church-at-large, the congregation and the pastor,

We recommend that a contemplated change of pastorate should be made only after consultation, on the part of the pastor, with the president of the synod, and, upon his advice, with trusted and judicious leaders of the congregation, care being taken not to create restlessness in the congregation and to avoid the appearance of self-interest.

6. Induction into the office of the ministry does not confer an "indelible character" upon the incumbent.

The ordination certificate is a certification of both the act of ordination and of the call upon which that act is based.*

Ordination, as an act, bestows formally and publicly a privilege which may be revoked if it is not used or if it is abused. "He who does not minister is no minister. This ministry must be always one of the Word and Sacraments." (Summary Christian Faith, p. 431, Q. 30.)

---

* The committee recommends the formulation of a uniform ordination certificate to be authorized by the United Lutheran Church and to be commended to the Constituent Synods. We submit the following form:

> This certifies that ....
> was duly set apart by the ....
> Synod of The United Lutheran Church in America
> to the holy Office of the Ministry of the Evangelical Lutheran Church by the rite of ordination
> according to the Order of the Church on the ....
> day of ...., ...A. D.
> In testimony whereof we have hereto set our hands
> and affixed the Seal of the ....
> Synod.
>
>   ....
>   ....

In the removal of names of ministers from the synodical roll, synods are bound by constitutional provisions. Special regulations may be made by a synod determining the circumstances or conditions under which persons may be permitted or required, temporarily or permanently, to demit the office of the ministry (*e. g.*, Article IX, Section I, 7, of a Suggested Constitution for Synods).

To guard the official integrity of the work of the ministry, and in harmony with the action of the U. L. C. A. (Washington, 1920, p. 203),—

We recommend as a policy the adoption by synods of a uniform practice regarding the surrender of ordination certificates.

7. It is the usual and correct practice that every minister received into a synod and every ordinand be required to sign the constitution of synod prior to his enrollment into membership. In order to facilitate the enforcement of the preceding recommendation, and to strengthen the moral right of a synod to demand the return of an ordination certificate in case of engaging in secular pursuits or other violations of the provisions of the synodical constitution, open abuse of the privileges of the ministerial office, or "imposition upon the public in the name of the Church,"—(See report of the Commission of Adjudication, Minutes of the Columbus Convention, 1936, p. 192):—

We recommend that synodical constitutions include a provision explicitly obligating each signer to relinquish his ordination certificate when requested to do so by action of the synod. (Such obligation may be inserted in Article VIII, Section 1, 2, of Suggested Constitution for Synods.)

8. Inasmuch as the privileges of the office of the ministry include the performance of certain acts in which the State also is concerned, especially marriage,—

We recommend to the Presidents of Constituent Synods the practice of reporting to local civil authorities the status of men newly admitted to the ministry and of men who have demitted or who have been deposed from the ministry.

C. Concerning the Question of Recall

In accordance with Article VI, Section 6, of the Constitution for Congregations, approved by the Executive Board, the call to the ministry may be terminated by a synod when certain charges brought against a minister shall have been duly substantiated. It is recognized also that situations arise in which it is desirable and necessary, from the standpoint of congregational and synodical welfare, to terminate the contractual, pastoral relationship without thereby terminating the call to the ministry. (See Zollman, American Church Law, p. 442.)

We, therefore, recommend the formulation and insertion into the Model Constitution for Congregations of a provision specifying the causes and procedure under which such action may be taken. Said causes to be false doctrine, immoral conduct and neglect of duty. Neglect of duty may be defined as including incapacity, infidelity and slothfulness.
(Stricken from the report, see p. 106.)

We recommend that it shall be the policy of the Church to recognize this right of the congregation and that a provision for this be inserted in the Model Constitution for Congregations.

We further recommend that the congregation's right of termination of the contractual relationship shall be exercised only after consultation with the Executive Board or Committee of the synod and after the same prayerful consideration has been used that was invoked at the issuance of the original call, and that it shall become effective by a two-thirds majority of all the votes cast at a duly called congregational meeting.
(Amended, see p. 106.)

D. Concerning Retirements

A factor which has a practical bearing upon the problems presented to this committee is that of the retirement of pastors. The normal movement of men into the pastorate is retarded by the unwillingness or inability of older men to retire. The whole process is being held back by this situation. Many pastors who recognize that they are no longer able to labor effectively in their parishes and who would choose retirement are unable to retire because of the wholly inadequate pension provision of the Church. Many of the distressing difficulties that perplex us arise from this condition. It has a very definite bearing upon the restlessness of congregations, the sordid regard of the office by some youthful candidates, the competition among some pastors for fields, and the sharp bargaining methods of some congregations.

In view of the fact that a contributory system of pensions is a distant possibility for our Church, and as a realistic contribution to a vital problem,

We recommend that the United Lutheran Church take such steps as are necessary to increase ministerial pensions sufficiently to provide a more adequate retirement allowance.

The Board of Publication has been asked to publish an edition of 2,000 copies of this report and to offer the same for general use at a reasonable price.

5. Ecclesiastical Vestments:

In response to requests addressed to the President, for guidance in the adoption and use of proper vestments, the Executive Board, at its meeting April 7, 1938, authorized that a request be made to the Common Service Book Committee for authoritative information. The Common Service Book Committee presented a report on the subject to the Executive Board, at its meeting July 14, 1938, and, by action of the Board, the subject, with the report of the Common Service Book Committee, was recommended as a proper topic for consideration by the Conference of Presidents.

*6. Calendar of Special Days and Seasons: (For action on this item, see p. 107.)

In order to secure conformity in the progressive steps of the Plan of Promotion, the Committee of Executive Secretaries submitted proposed revisions in the Calendar of Special Days and Seasons, and the Committee on Boards and Committees of the Executive Board submitted the following revised calendar at the meeting of the Board, on July 14, 1938, which the Board approved, subject to adoption by the convention.

CALENDAR OF SPECIAL DAYS AND SEASONS
IN
THE UNITED LUTHERAN CHURCH IN AMERICA
(Effective January 1, 1940)

MONTH OR DAY	CAUSE	BOARD OR AGENCY
September	Parish Education	Parish and Church School Board
October	Social Missions	Board of Social Missions
November	Stewardship	Lutheran Laymen's Movement
December	Christian Ministry,	Board of Ministerial Pensions and Relief
January	Foreign Missions	Board of Foreign Missions
February	American Missions	Board of American Missions
Septuagesima	Deaconess Work	Board of Deaconess Work
April	Christian Higher Education	Board of Education
May	World Lutheranism	Lutheran World Convention

a. *The Parish and Church School Board* shall use the month of September to promote parish education, but gather no offerings.

b. *The Board of Social Missions* shall use the month of October to promote the causes of Evangelism, Moral and Social Welfare, and the Inner Mission throughout the Church. Constituent synods shall have the right to gather special offerings from the congregations and Sunday schools for the support of institutions of mercy for which they are directly responsible.

c. *The Lutheran Laymen's Movement* shall use the month of November to further the cause of Christian Stewardship in all the congregations through the circulation of literature and the promotion of the Every Member Visitation.

d. *The Board of Ministerial Pensions and Relief* shall use the month of December to inform the Church of its work, and solicit individuals for the work of special relief, but take no general offerings.

e. *The Board of Foreign Missions* shall use the month of January to promote the cause of foreign missions throughout the Church, and furnish envelopes for the gathering of offerings from the Sunday schools on the last Sunday of the month.

f. *The Board of American Missions* shall use the month of February to promote the work of home missions and church extension throughout the Church, and furnish envelopes for the gathering of offerings from the Sunday schools on Easter Sunday if desired.

g. *The Board of Deaconess Work* shall use Septuagesima Sunday as a recruiting day for deaconess work throughout the Church, but shall gather no offerings.

h. *The Board of Education* shall use the month of April to promote the cause of higher Christian education throughout the

Church; and constituent synods may use the same month to inform their congregations concerning their educational institutions, and furnish envelopes for the gathering of special offerings from congregations and Sunday schools on any Sunday of the month except Easter Sunday.

i. *The Lutheran World Convention* shall use the month of May to inform the congregations of its work, and gather offerings for Lutheran World Service.

j. All special offerings, marked special, shall be sent through the regular channels of congregational and synodical treasurers.

k. Constituent synods are rquested to place this Calendar of Special Days and Seasons in their annual Minutes.

At the meeting of the Executive Board, on October 5, 1938, a change in the name of the Calendar of Special Days and Seasons was suggested, considered and referred to the Committee on Boards and Committees for a later report.

7. General German Conference:

At its meeting, April 8, 1937, the Executive Board authorized the Committee on German Interests to arrange for a General German Conference at Edmonton, Alberta, Canada, for the last week of July 1937; and at its meeting, April 7, 1938, authority was given for a similar conference to be held in October of 1939.

8. Synodical Alignment in the Midwest:

At the meeting of the Executive Board, on January 13, 1938, the Committee on Constituent Synods recommended that a conference be held with representatives of the Executive Committees of the Midwest, Nebraska, Kansas and Iowa Synods relating to synodical alignment in the Midwest. The conference was held on February 3, 1938, at Omaha, Nebr., Dr. A. E. Bell representing the Executive Board and acting as convener.

On July 14, 1938, Dr. Bell reported to the Executive Board, through the Committee on Constituent Synods, that each of the above-named Synods, in their 1938 conventions, voted to appoint three representatives on a joint commission, one of whom is to be a layman, to act as a Committee on Ways and Means to draft a constitution to be submitted to the Synods at their next annual conventions.

9. Finnish Conference:

The Executive Board approved the holding of a Finnish Conference which met in September, 1938.

B. In Particular

*1. The Central Pennsylvania Synod: (For action on this item, see p. 107.)

At the meeting of the Executive Board, April 7, 1938, it received official notice of the proposed merger of the Synod of West Pennsylvania, the East Pennsylvania Synod, the Alleghany Synod and the Susquehanna Synod, and, in connection with this movement, the Executive Board received also a protest from the Executive Board of the Ministerium of Pennsylvania pertaining to problems arising out of overlapping territory with the proposed new synod.

All matters pertaining to the formation of the Central Pennsylvania Synod, including the protest from the Executive Board of the Ministerium of Pennsylvania, were placed in the hands of the Committee on Constituent Synods. That Committee presented the following recommendation, which was adopted by the Executive Board, and Dr. A. E. Bell, Dr. J. L. Morgan and Dr. R. E. Tulloss were appointed as representatives of the Executive Board on the commission as proposed:

"That, in the interest of arriving at a desirable solution of the whole problem of synodical alignments in the State of Pennsylvania, a commission of eleven members be created which shall be charged with the task of studying this entire matter with a view to arriving at an amicable and satisfactory definition of spheres of activity in harmony with the best interests of the whole Church and in accord with the Will of God;

"That said commission of eleven shall be constituted of three members of the Executive Board of the U. L. C. A., four members whose appointment we request the Executive Board of the Ministerium of Pennsylvania to make as its representatives, and four members, one each of whom we request the Executive Boards of the Synods of East Pennsylvania, West Pennsylvania, Alleghany and Susquehanna, respectively, to appoint to represent each of the said four Synods, said commission to report its findings and actions to the Executive Board through its representatives thereon."

At the meeting of the Executive Board, on July 14, 1938, the Committee on Constituent Synods reported that its representatives had had successful meetings with representatives of the above-named Pennsylvania Synods and that agreements had been reached for the continuation of a Commission of Eleven for the further consideration of questions involved after the proposed merger was in effect. The Executive Board authorized the representation requested, namely, three members on the Commission of Eleven, and the three members of the Executive Board, previously appointed, were continued as representatives on that Commission.

The Committee on Constituent Synods reported that it was presenting officially signed and sealed documents of the Central Pennsylvania

Synod, namely, a copy of the Constitution, duly certified by the Secretary, and the official application for the admission of the Synod in the United Lutheran Church. The Committee reported further that they found the Constitution of the new Synod in harmony with the Constitution recommended by the U. L. C. A. for its constituent synods, and recommended the approval of the same, calling attention, however, to certain terminology in two items of the By-laws, upon which they recommended that the Synod be requested to make substitutions which would bring them in harmony with the terminology used by the U. L. C. A.

Upon the report of the Committee, and following the recommendation which it submitted, the Executive Board recommends the following:

> That The Central Pennsylvania Synod of The United Lutheran Church in America be received into The United Lutheran Church in America, and that certification having been made to the Secretary of the United Lutheran Church of a list of delegates and alternates, elected by the merging synods, equalling in their total number, the number of delegates to which the new synod is entitled as a constituent synod of The United Lutheran Church in America, these delegates be recognized as members of the Convention, representing The Central Pennsylvania Synod.

> That the new synod be given the position among the constituent synods of the United Lutheran Church to which it is entitled by reason of the date of organization of the oldest of the merging synods, viz., the West Pennsylvania Synod, organized September 5, 1825.

2. German Synod of Nebraska: (For action on this item, see p. 108.)

*(a) *Change of Name.* At the meeting of the Executive Board, April 7, 1938, approval was given to the action whereby the name of the German Synod of Nebraska was changed to *"The Synod in the Midwest of The United Lutheran Church in America."*

(b) *Budget.* At its meeting, July 14, 1938, the Executive Board approved the request of the Synod in the Midwest to add an item to its synodical budget for the support of a synodical missionary to operate under the direction of the Board of American Missions.

3. Synod of the Northwest:

Budget. At the meeting of the Executive Board, October 14, 1937, a request from the Synod of the Northwest, for permission to make a temporary addition to its budget for the benefit of Carthage College, was approved.

4. Ohio Synod:

Revised Constitution. A copy of an amended Constitution of the Synod of Ohio was submitted to the Executive Board at its meeting, October 14, 1937. The Board adopted the report of its Committee on Constituent Synods concerning this Constitution, which report included several suggestions and one recommendation.

5. South Carolina Synod:

Upon satisfactory information, that the organization was pledged to refrain from legislation and political action, the Synod of South Carolina was granted permission to affiliate itself with the State Council on Alcoholic Education. This action was taken at the meeting held July 14, 1938.

IV. BOARDS, COMMITTEES AND COMMISSIONS

A. in General

*1. Amendments to By-laws: (For action on this item, see pp. 108, 115.)

The Executive Board recommends the following amendments to the By-laws:

(a) Strike out Section V, B, Items 9, (1) and (2)—items pertaining to standing committees on young people's and brotherhood work.

(b) Amend Section VII, A, 3, so as to read "Committee on Memorials from Constituent Synods."

(c) Further amend Section VII, A, by adding item "9. Committee on Place of Next Convention" and item "10. Convention Committee on Daily Minutes."

*2. Merger of Agencies: (For action on this item, see p. 108.)

The Executive Board has had the matter of merging the Inner Mission Board, the Committee on Moral and Social Welfare and the Committee on Evangelism before it throughout the biennium. The details of the plan, whereby a merger could be satisfactorily accomplished, were in the hands of the Committee on Boards and Committees. The outcome of many conferences and discussions was presented to the Executive Board in two successive meetings.

At the meeting of the Executive Board, on April 7, 1938, recommendations were adopted to the effect:

(a) That the present Charter of the Inner Mission Board of The United Lutheran Church in America, Incorporated, be so amended as to become a proper Charter for the new Board, and that the present Inner Mission Board be directed to effect the necessary changes in the Charter as soon as possible.

(b) That the new Board prepare By-laws in harmony with the provision of its Constitution.

(c) That all legal matters, pertaining to the Inner Mission Board, its obligations and property, be referred to the Legal Committee of the Executive Board.

A tentative constitution was submitted and action on it was postponed.

At the meeting of the Executive Board on July 14, 1938, the following Constitution was presented and adopted:

CONSTITUTION
OF THE
BOARD OF SOCIAL MISSIONS
OF
THE UNITED LUTHERAN CHURCH IN AMERICA

ARTICLE I

NAME

Section 1. This board, established under the Constitution of The United Lutheran Church in America, Article XIII, shall be known under the name and title of THE BOARD OF SOCIAL MISSIONS OF THE UNITED LUTHERAN CHURCH IN AMERICA.

Section 2. This board shall be incorporated.

Section 3. This board shall be the legal successor to all the rights and properties of the Inner Mission Board of The United Lutheran Church in America, Inc., the Committee on Evangelism, and the Committee on Moral and Social Welfare, and shall perpetuate, carry on, expand, develop and further any and all of the purposes, objectives and work embraced in or carried on by the said board and committees, and with all the powers, duties and prerogatives committed or given to said board and committees respectively.

ARTICLE II

OBJECT

The object of this board shall be to promote the causes of evangelism, inner mission, and social welfare in the name of The United Lutheran Church in America, and in accordance with the constitution, acts and rulings of The United Lutheran Church in America.

ARTICLE III

DUTIES, POWERS, AND FUNCTIONS OF THE BOARD

Subject to the constitution of The United Lutheran Church in America or its resolutions, this board shall have full power to do its work in the following fields.

1. Evangelism. To stimulate the synods and congregations of The United Lutheran Church in America in the application of the Gospel to win, conserve and reclaim souls for Christ through His Church.

2. Inner Missions. To further the cause of the ministry of Christian love in any and all ways.

3. Social Welfare. To study the moral and social welfare of humanity in the light of Christian principles and to counsel the Church in the Christian solution of the problems of society.

4. To do such other things, under the authority of The United Lutheran Church in America, as are in harmony with the duties, powers and functions described in this article.

ARTICLE IV
MEMBERSHIP

Section 1. This board shall consist of twenty-one members— twelve ministers and nine laymen.

Section 2. No one shall be a member of this board who is not a member in good standing in a congregation in full synodical relations with The United Lutheran Church in America; nor shall any salaried officer or employee of this board, be a member of this board.

Section 3. The members of this board shall be elected by The United Lutheran Church in America at a regular convention according to its established rules for a term not longer than six years. At the first election after this constitution is in force, one-third of the members shall be elected for two years, one-third for four years, and one-third for six years.

ARTICLE V
QUORUM

A majority of the members of this board present at a regularly called meeting of this board shall constitute a quorum.

ARTICLE VI
MEETINGS

Following its first meeting to be held as soon as convenient after its first election, which meeting shall be at the call of a convener appointed by The United Lutheran Church in America, regular meetings for the transaction of business shall be held at such times and places as the board may determine, unless otherwise provided by charter stipulation or by action of The United Lutheran Church in America.

ARTICLE VII
OFFICERS

Section 1. The officers of the board shall be a president, a vice-president, a recording secretary, and a treasurer, to be elected by this board, for a term of two (2) years and to serve until their successors are duly elected and qualified.

Section 2. All the officers, except the treasurer, shall be elected from the membership of this board. The treasurer may or may not be a member of the board.

ARTICLE VIII
DUTIES OF OFFICERS

The duties of the several officers shall be those usually pertaining to their respective offices, or as this board may from time to time determine.

ARTICLE IX
COMMITTEES

There shall be such committees provided for in the by-laws as shall be found necessary for the efficient operation of the board through its basic departments.

ARTICLE X
BY-LAWS

This board shall adopt such by-laws as may be necessary, provided they are not in conflict with this constitution, or with the constitution and by-laws of The United Lutheran Church in America, or with the laws of the State, under which this board shall be incorporated.

ARTICLE XI
AMENDMENTS

All amendments to this constitution must be presented to this board in writing at a regular meeting thereof at least two months before final consideration, must be approved by this board by a two-thirds vote of the members present, and shall not be effective until approved by The United Lutheran Church in America, or its Executive Board.

With reference to procedure, the Executive Board, at its meeting, July 14, 1938, adopted the following recommendations:

That the Executive Board request the officers of the Inner Mission Board to secure the resignations of all present members of that Board, effective on the date of the organization of the Board of Social Missions, and place the same in the hands of the Secretary of the United Lutheran Church.

That the Executive Board direct the Committee on Nominations to present nominations for all members of the new Board of Social Missions, as provided in its constitution, and to recognize the desirability of nominating all present members of the three merging agencies.

3. Secretaries' Conference:

On account of the arrangement, under the promotional plan, by which the Executive Secretaries of the Boards of the Church became members of a special promotional committee under the chairmanship of the President of the Church, the occasion for meetings of the former Secretaries' Conference was minimized. Therefore, the Executive Board, at its meeting on April 8, 1937, adopted the following recommendation from the report of the Officers:

"That for the present, the Secretaries' Conference be placed in the same position as the Conference of Synodical Presidents and of all other conferences in the Church's life."

4. Board of Publication and Parish and Church School Board:

At its meeting, July 14, 1938, the Officers, who had been instructed to confer with representatives of the Board of Publication and the Parish and Church School Board, concerning an agreement that would adjust difficulties between them in their common responsibilities, reported that such an agreement had been reached and had been approved by both Boards and that a copy of the agreement had been placed on file.

5. Appropriation to Boards:

An appropriation of $100,000, made by the Board of Publication to the U. L. C. A., was designated by the Executive Board, at its meeting April 8, 1937, for distribution to the following Boards of the Church according to the proportion for each as indicated in the budget:

> Board of Foreign Missions
> Board of American Missions
> Board of Education
> Parish and Church School Board
> Inner Mission Board
> Board of Ministerial Pensions and Relief
> Board of Deaconess Work

The provision was made that the amount received by each Board should be applied against its deficit, where one existed; that in the case of the Board of American Missions, its portion be added to their campaign fund for Church Extension; and in other cases, the amounts be used for special undertakings.

At the meeting of the Executive Board, October 5, 1938, the Treasurer was instructed to distribute a special contribution to the general treasury of the Church, in the amount of $100,000, by the Board of Publication, as follows:

One-half to the Board of American Missions for the Twentieth Anniversary Appeal Fund; and the other half to the Board of Ministerial Pensions and Relief to be applied against its deficit.

6. China Relief:

At the meeting of the Executive Board, October 5, 1938, the President presented a plan for relief of suffering in China, involving co-operation with other agencies. The particular form of co-operation proposed is that of work through what is known as the Church Committee on China Relief. The plan has been approved by various Churches and by the Board of Foreign Missions of the United Lutheran Church, and authority was given by the Executive Board to the use of the name of the President of the Church and of representatives of the Board of Foreign Missions in the Church Committee.

B. In Particular

1. Commission of Adjudication:

Vacancies filled. At the meeting of the Executive Board, January 13, 1938, the following were elected to fill vacancies in the Commission of Adjudication:

Dr. B. H. Pershing vice Dr. John Aberly, resigned, term expiring 1938.

Dr. Charles M. Jacobs vice Dr. J. A. W. Haas, deceased, term expiring 1940.

2. Board of Foreign Missions:

(a) *Appeal for India Mission.* On January 14, 1937, the Executive Board granted permission to the Board of Foreign Missions to make an appeal in the Church papers in behalf of needs occasioned in India by a destructive cyclone. On the same account, at the same time, the Executive Board authorized that a portion of all income from trust funds during the biennium, not otherwise designated, be given to the Board of Foreign Missions.

(b) *Andhra Christian College.* At the meeting of the Executive Board, October 14, 1937, the following action, taken by the Board of Foreign Missions, was submitted to the Executive Board and approved:

(1) That any contributing group shall not have more than one missionary professor on the College Council, except the C. M. S., who may have two, inasmuch as they are co-operating in a special way by giving up their college classes in Noble College. All other groups are permitted to have only one each.

(2) That the College Council shall not co-opt any members.

(3) That at all times the mission and the college must see to it that the governing Board of the College maintains a majority of those who are members of The United Lutheran Church in America.

(4) That the entire plan for co-operation of missionary groups with Andhra Christian College be presented to the Executive Board of The United Lutheran Church in America for approval.

*(c) *Amendments to the Constitution.* At the meeting of the Executive Board, April 7, 1938, it approved amendments to the Constitution of the Board of Foreign Missions, as follows, for submission to this Convention for its approval: (For action on this item, see p. 184.)

Strike out Section 3 of Article III, and insert the following:

Section 3. Other Lutheran Bodies may, with the approval of the United Lutheran Church in America, co-operate with the Board and severally appoint one representative and one alternate, under the following conditions:

a. These representatives and alternates shall be nominated by the Board of Foreign Missions, and elected by The United Lutheran Church in America in convention assembled, or by the Executive Board of the Church in the interim between conventions.

b. Their number shall not be included in the twenty-one members of the Board, as provided in Section 1 of this Article.

c. The number of such representatives, excluding alternates, shall not exceed five at any one time; and their right to vote shall be limited to questions that concern the use of contributions of their respective bodies to specific fields of the Board.

d. This representation shall in no wise, now or hereafter, entitle their respective bodies to any claim upon the property, real, personal or mixed, held by or in the name of the Board.

*(d) *Co-operation with American Lutheran Church in India.* A statement of the terms of a new external relationship between the United Lutheran Church and the American Lutheran Church, in India, was submitted to the Executive Board, through its Committee on Boards and Committees, July 14, 1938, and was approved by the Executive Board as follows: (For action on this item, see p. 184.)

"Rev. M. H. Schramm took up residence at Luthergiri, Rajahmundry, on November 3, 1937, and was installed on November 7. The following is the agreement of the Joint Committee of our own and of the American Lutheran Mission:

"(1) That Mr. Schramm should be a member of the Religious Education Committee of the Andhra Evangelical Lutheran Church, with voice and vote.

(2) That Mr. Schramm be a member of the faculty at Luthergiri, with voice and vote.

(3) That Mr. Schramm should occupy the north end of Luthergiri bungalow, have use of the heavy furniture there, and that necessary repairs should be made by him in consultation with the U. L. C. missionary in charge, and the expense be borne by the A. L. C. Mission.

(4) That Mr. Schramm's personal budget be provided by the A. L. C. Mission.

(5) That rent as agreed upon should be paid by the A. L. C. Mission for their students occupying mission houses.

(6) That stipends, books, travel, etc., for the A. L. C. Mission students shall be supplied by their Mission.

(7) That a two-years' class would be opened in the Junior Bible Class, beginning July 1937.

"VOTED, That the Executive Board of The United Lutheran Church in America be requested to sanction this co-operation of the India Mission of the American Lutheran Church in the Luthergiri, Rajahmundry, Theological Seminary and Biblical Institute for the education of India pastors and evangelists, with the following additional terms of agreement.

"(1) The American Lutheran Church Mission shall appoint and support one ordained missionary as a teacher, and provide for him suitable accommodations.

"(2) The American Lutheran Church Mission shall contribute for the running expenses of this institution a fixed sum each year, to be determined by agreement between its Board of Foreign Missions and our Board of Foreign Missions in consultation with their respective missions in India."

The Executive Board asks this Convention to approve its action.

(e) *Vacancies filled.* On June 25, 1937, the Executive Board elected Mr. Warren M. Koons vice Mr. Ralph H. Schatz, deceased, as a member of the Board of Foreign Missions, term expiring 1942.

At the meeting of the Executive Board, April 7, 1938, the following elections, to fill vacancies in the Board of Foreign Missions were made:

Rev. Fred J. Fiedler vice Rev. C. M. Snyder, deceased, term expiring 1942.
Rev. Edgar E. Snyder vice Rev. H. C. Brillhart, resigned, term expiring 1940.
Mr. Isaac C. Bucher vice Mr. Frank Howard, resigned, term expiring 1942.

3. Board of American Missions:

(a) *Income from trust funds:* January 14, 1937, the Executive Board authorized the appropriation of a portion of income from trust funds, during the biennium, not otherwise designated, to the Board of American Missions for the increase of its funds for Church Extension.

(b) *Offerings at the Baltimore Convention.* On the same account, the offerings, at the Baltimore Convention, were designated for the benefit of the Anniversary Appeal of the Board of American Missions.

4. Inner Mission Board:

(a) *Disaster Relief Fund.* At the meeting of the Executive Board, April 8, 1937, the Inner Mission Board was authorized to appeal to the Church for relief on account of the disastrous floods in different parts of the United States.

At the meeting, October 14, 1937, the Treasurer reported to the Executive Board that a total of $78,398.34 had been received in response to the special appeal and that there was, at that time, a balance of $19,380.84 to the credit of that fund. The Executive Board passed the following resolution:

> "Resolved, that it is the judgment of the Executive Board that balances in the Disaster Relief Fund remain in the custody of the Treasurer of The United Lutheran Church in America until appropriated by the Inner Mission Board for relief in cases of specific disaster."

At the end of the fiscal year, June 30, 1938, the balance was $13,649.78.

(b) *Vacancy filled.* At the meeting of the Executive Board, July 14, 1938, Mr. Carl H. Lammers was elected as a member of the Inner Mission Board vice Mr. Peter P. Hagan, resigned, term expiring 1942.

5. Board of Ministerial Pensions and Relief:

(a) *Changes in Rules.* On October 14, 1937, the Executive Board approved the following addition to item 3 of the Rules of the Board of Ministerial Pensions and Relief: "No widow shall be entitled to a pension who is engaged in full-time, gainful employment."

On January 13, 1938, the Executive Board approved the change in Rule 4 to make it read as follows: "Children under sixteen years of age of deceased, retired or disabled ministers may be granted $50.00 annually. In cases where physical or mental condition make it impossible for them to earn a livelihood, the age limit may be withdrawn by action of the Executive Committee; but no child, born after the parent becomes a beneficiary of this Board, may qualify for a grant."

(b) *Vacancies filled.* On January 14, 1937, the Executive Board elected Mr. Edward Schoeppe as a member of the Board of Ministerial Pensions and Relief vice Hon. Henry W. Harter, deceased, term expiring 1940.

On October 14, 1937, the Executive Board elected Mr. J. Henry Frick as a member of the Board of Ministerial Pensions and Relief vice Mr. M. P. Moller, Sr., deceased, term expiring 1940.

6. Board of Publication:

Vacancy filled. On April 7, 1938, the Executive Board elected Mr. William H. Menges as a member of the Board of Publication vice George E. Neff, Esq., deceased, term expiring 1940.

7. Board of Deaconess Work:

Vacancies filled. On January 14, 1937, the Executive Board elected Rev. J. J. Schindel as a member of the Board of Deaconess Work vice Rev. H. F. Baughman, resigned, term expiring 1942.

On October 14, 1937, the Executive Board elected Mr. C. C. Stoughton as a member of the Board of Deaconess Work vice Mr. Fred H. Wefer, deceased, term expiring 1940.

On January 13, 1938, the Executive Board elected Mrs. O. A. Sardeson as a member of the Board of Deaconess Work vice Mr. I. Searles Runyon, deceased, term expiring 1938, and the Rev. P. S. Baringer as a member of the Board of Deaconess Work vice Rev. W. A. Wade, resigned, term expiring 1938.

8. Laymen's Movement:

Administrative Committee. On January 14, 1937, the Executive Board elected Dr. James C. Kinard and Dr. Robbin B. Wolf as members of the Administrative Committee of the Laymen's Movement.

C. Standing Committees and Auxiliaries

1. Commission on Investments:

Vacancies filled. On January 14, 1937, Dr. Robbin B. Wolf was re-elected a member of the Commission on Investments for the term expiring 1942.

On January 13, 1938, Dr. R. E. Tulloss was re-elected a member of the Commission on Investments for the term expiring 1943.

2. Luther League:

(a) *Appropriation.* The Executive Board appropriated $6,000 for the work of the Luther League for each of the years of the biennium.

(b) *Missionary Objective.* The request of the Luther League, for the approval of an objective of $10,000 to be made a part of the campaign for Church Extension during the year 1938, under the Board of American Missions, was granted.

(c) *Representatives to meet with Youth Groups of American Lutheran Conference.* Permission was granted to the Luther League to send representatives to meet with duly appointed representatives of youth groups of the constituents of the American Lutheran Conference, the purpose being to discuss closer co-operation.

3. Women's Missionary Society:

On April 7, 1938, the request of the Executive Board of the Women's Missionary Society, for definite statement concerning the age at which it, as an organization, might legitimately promote the cause of missions among young women, was considered. The Executive Board authorized the consideration of this request by a special committee and the President appointed the Committee on Organized Work with Children to serve in this capacity.

4. Lutheran Brotherhood:

Constitution and By-laws: The Executive Board approved the Constitution and By-laws for the Lutheran Brotherhood of The United Lutheran Church in America as presented by that Body.

V. FINANCE

1. Apportionment for 1938 and 1939:

See III, A, 1 of this report.

*2. Budget of The United Lutheran Church in America: (For action on this item, see pp. 386, 481, 482.)

On July 14, 1938, the following recommendation from the Finance Committee was approved for recommendation to the convention, fixing the budget of the U. L. C. A. for 1940 and 1941:

	Amount	Percentage
Board of Foreign Missions	$ 600,000	30.00
Board of American Missions	771,400	38.57
Board of Education	180,000	9.00
Board of Social Missions	36,400	1.82
Board of Ministerial Pensions and Relief	235,000	11.75
Board of Deaconess Work	40,000	2.00
Parish and Church School Board	24,400	1.22
National Lutheran Council	23,000	1.15
American Bible Society	5,000	.25
United Lutheran Church Treasury	84,800	4.24
	$2,000,000	100.00

3. Budgets of the Auxiliaries of the Church:

It has not been possible to consummate the plan completely, whereby the budgets of the Women's Missionary Society, the Luther League, and the Lutheran Brotherhood would be stated as supplementary to the budget of the United Lutheran Church. (Minutes Columbus Convention, 1936, pp. 54, 89.) Following is the budget of the Women's Missionary Society for the present biennium:

Total to Board of Foreign Missions	$162,325.00
Total to Board of American Missions	71,639.00
Total to Board of Education	2,250.00
Total to Board of Ministerial Pensions and Relief	3,990.00
Total to Inner Mission Board	1,000.00
Total to Parish and Church School Board	100.00
Interdenominational Boards and Committees	3,506.35
Special Appropriations	34,622.00
Administration	38,703.80
Emergencies	10,000.00
GRAND TOTAL	$328,136.15

4. Bond of the Treasurer:

The bond of the Treasurer, with the United States Fidelity and Guaranty Company, has been regularly renewed for the biennium.

5. Auditors Appointed:

On January 14, 1937, the firm of Tait, Weller and Baker was appointed auditors for the current biennium.

VI. LUTHERAN CHURCH HOUSE

1. Management and Maintenance:

See report of the Secretary.

2. Auditors' Report:

We herewith present the Auditors' Report for July 1, 1936 to June 30, 1938, which exhibits itemized statements of the Manager and Treasurer.

LUTHERAN CHURCH HOUSE
CASH RECEIPTS
July 1, 1936 to June 30, 1937

	Maintenance	Telephone and Telegrams	Miscellaneous	Total
Executive Board of the United Lutheran Church in America	$2,040.00	$ 152.71	$332.00	$2,524.71
Board of American Missions	1,480.00	110.59		1,590.59
Inner Mission Board	656.16	133.75		789.91
National Lutheran Council	2,475.00	165.64		2,640.64
New York Synod	1,207.50	104.39		1,311.89
Miscellaneous		28.82		28.82
Boston Campaign	253.33	417.24		670.57
Totals	$8,111.99	$1,113.14	$332.00	$9,557.13

CASH DISBURSEMENTS
July 1, 1936 to June 30, 1937

Salaries	$2,851.75
Telephone	1,147.50
Telegrams	268.17
Gas, Electric, Steam	1,612.05
Repairs, Painting, etc.	283.90
Services	518.20
Insurance	139.14
Supplies and Miscellaneous	373.51
Addressograph and Supplies	1,340.03
Furniture and Equipment	564.50
Miscellaneous Exchanges	332.00
Total	$9,430.75

SUMMARY OF CASH
July 1, 1936 to June 30, 1937

Balance—July 1, 1936	$ 9,591.54
RECEIPTS	9,557.13
	$19,148.67
DISBURSEMENTS	9,430.75
Balance—June 30, 1937	$ 9,717.92

CASH RECEIPTS
July 1, 1937 to June 30, 1938

	Maintenance	Telephone and Telegrams	Miscellaneous	Total
Executive Board of the United Lutheran Church in America	$2,244.00	$163.35	$ 15.26	$ 2,422.61
Board of American Missions	1,628.00	160.13	81.66	1,869.79
Inner Mission Board	1,024.76	94.32	50.44	1,169.52
National Lutheran Council	3,025.00	165.29		3,190.29
New York Synod	1,328.25	123.20		1,451.45
Miscellaneous		21.89	128.28	150.17
Totals	$9,250.01	$728.18	$275.64	$10,253.83

CASH DISBURSEMENTS
July 1, 1937 to June 30, 1938

Salaries	$2,938.15
Telephone	903.21
Telegrams	144.17
Gas, Electric, Steam, Water	1,740.83
Repairs, Painting, etc.	529.42
Services	518.20
Insurance	150.66
Supplies and Miscellaneous	373.20
Addressograph	125.41
Furniture and Equipment	137.15
	$7,560.40

SUMMARY OF CASH
July 1, 1937 to June 30, 1938

Balance, July 1, 1937...	$ 9,717.92
RECEIPTS (Exhibit "B")..	10,253.83
	$19,971.75
DISBURSEMENTS (Exhibit "C")...	7,560.40
	$12,411.35
Cash in Bank in New York City...	$ 4,411.35
Cash with E. C. Miller, Depreciation Reserve Fund........................	8,000.00
	$12,411.35

Respectfully submitted,
W. H. GREEVER, *Manager and Treasurer.*

We have audited the accounts of the Lutheran Church House for the biennium beginning July 1, 1936 and ending June 30, 1938. We hereby certify that in our opinion the Statements of Cash Receipts and Disbursements for the two years under audit, as submitted by the Treasurer, are true and correct.

TAIT, WELLER AND BAKER,
Accountants and Auditors.

VII. NATIONAL LUTHERAN COUNCIL

*Department of National Lutheran Welfare: (For action on this item, see p. 482.)

At the meeting of the Executive Board, July 14, 1938, the Committee on Boards and Committees presented the following action of the Executive Committee of the National Lutheran Council of April 19, 1938.

> "The ministry of mercy of the Lutheran Church in its varied forms is a genuine spiritual service, rendered in the name and Spirit of Christ. The motive of this ministry begins in the love of God as revealed in Jesus Christ, and its objective is to seek and promote the highest temporal and spiritual interests of men.

> "Believing that a greater efficiency and a wider service can be accomplished through a more united effort, therefore be it

> "Resolved, That a Department of National Lutheran Welfare be set up by the National Lutheran Council. This department shall not be administrative in function, but shall seek to further the development of real Christian welfare service through the churches, and to co-ordinate the inner mission, charitable, and social welfare work of the constituent bodies."

The Executive Board presents this action of the National Lutheran Council to the convention for its approval, including the expression of the hope that a more descriptive name will be adopted for this department of work at the next meeting of the National Lutheran Council.

VIII. LUTHERAN WORLD CONVENTION

1. 1940 Convention:

The Finance Committee, on April 7, 1938, presented a statement from the American members of the Executive Committee of the Lutheran World Convention, indicating the amount of money that will be necessary to finance the 1940 Convention in Philadelphia, and recommended that the United Lutheran Church guarantee as much of its allotment as is not provided for by special solicitation. The allotment to the U. L. C. A. is $7,600 as its part of a total of $15,500. The Executive Board approved the recommendation of the Finance Committee.

2. Budget:

On October 14, 1937, the Executive Board approved the budget of the Lutheran World Convention as the basis for the appeal in May, 1938, which included $20,000 for the American share of a total of $51,000.

IX. FEDERAL COUNCIL OF CHURCHES OF CHRIST IN AMERICA

1. Appropriation:

On January 14, 1937, an appropriation of $2,000 for the fiscal year was made to the Federal Council of Churches.

At the meeting of the Executive Board on October 5, 1938, the Treasurer was authorized to remit a contribution of $2,000 to the Federal Council of Churches.

2. Report of Consultative Representatives:

The representatives of the various departments of the Federal Council submitted such data as they had to Dr. Corbe, representative on the Executive Committee of the Federal Council, through whom the following inclusive report has been submitted:

Since the last report, the biennial meeting of the Federal Council was held in Asbury Park, N. J. The high point of this convention was the report of the Preaching Mission which had attracted nation-wide attention and in which a number of well-known preachers of the United Lutheran Church had an active part.

The address of the retiring President, dealing chiefly with church unity, received marked attention and gave impetus to the Council's effort to secure a closer approach of the various Christian bodies. A more conservative spirit was noticeable in this convention and an encouraging emphasis was placed on the fundamental doctrines of the Scriptures.

Your representatives on the Executive Committee were able to attend the meetings regularly. Dr. Steimle's death was noted at the December meeting, 1937, and the resolutions adopted were indicative of the high esteem in which Dr. Steimle was held. The Rev. Professor Paul J. Hoh was appointed to fill the vacancy.

During the period covered by this report, many subjects were presented and acted upon, of which only few of special interest are reported.

1. The success of the first Preaching Mission was such that the Council authorized an additional Mission to cover sections of the country not reached in the first effort. This was followed by Preaching Missions to the great educational centers, which also in many cases reached the public school system. So marked were the results, that the Council is now looking forward to a world-wide Preaching Mission in 1940.

2. *Radio and Moving Pictures.* These Departments have made rapid advancement during the biennium. In the development of the radio ministry the United Lutheran Church has had an unusually prominent part. The full details of this participation will be found in the report of the Laymen's Committee. Encouraged by the success of the Roman movement for a reform in the moving picture productions, the Department of Moving Pictures has made great progress in securing a unified Christian approach to this very serious problem of modern life.

3. *Church Unity.* The Federal Council, having as its chief object the closer approach of all Protestant churches, is naturally greatly interested in the world-wide movements that have characterized the life of the churches in recent years. The Council has co-operated most enthusiastically, so much so that some of the efforts might seem to give the impression that the Council wishes to be a controlling factor in a movement, the success of which depends upon securing the authorized representation of the organized Christian Churches of the world.

4. *Social Welfare and International Relations.* These subjects have occupied the greater part of the time of the Federal Council during the past two years. The social unrest and deplorable economic conditions in America and the international situations arising from armed conflicts in other parts of the earth, have brought forth pronouncements both on legislation before Congress and on international affairs in which our Church could take no part. It is gratifying, however, to note the growing Scriptural approach to these great questions. There still remains much in the viewpoint of the Federal Council which effectually prevents the United Lutheran Church from holding any closer relationship than is sustained at present.

5. *Army and Navy Chaplains* At the biennial convention of the Council as well as at the meetings of the Executive Committee pacifistic extremes have been greatly modified. Nevertheless, our Church's participation in this Department of the Council, which has always been more or less unsatisfactory, has been growing increasingly so in recent years and the U. L. C. A. Committee on Army and Navy work will present a recommendation to the convention.

6. The affiliation of State and Local Councils with the Federal Council is one of the most important phases of development in the Council in recent years. The seriousness of the question is shown by the preface to the action taken by the Council in the following quotation:

"The relationship between the Federal Council of the Churches of Christ in America and the councils of churches which exist on the state and local levels has during the last few years become so important that the former dependence upon informal and unofficial co-operation is no longer adequate. A more integral relationship between the various sections of the federative structure—national, state and local—is called for. Two reasons among others make a closer tie necessary The first is the need for local and state councils to avoid isolation from other sectors of the co-operative movement. The second is the vital necessity of the Federal Council's having the kind of contact with state and local councils which will result in their becoming more effective centers for furthering the Federal Council's programs in all parts of the country.

"Any plan for such affiliation should preserve the official character of the Federal Council as directly representing the national denominations and at the same time secure the practical advantages of a well-coordinated structure covering the local, the state and the national experience and outlook."

While an earnest effort is being made to safeguard the relationships of all general bodies organized like the United Lutheran Church, nevertheless the consequences of this closer affiliation will give rise to complications which will compel the United Lutheran Church to review in the near future the entire subject of its relationship to the Federal Council.

7. *Worship.* Dr. Reed reports that the meetings of the Committee on Worship have featured papers and discussions on the broader aspects of public worship and its importance in all the Churches. The papers were frequently presented by outstanding authorities in special fields. There was evidenced a real appreciation of the classic expressions of Christian worship in the historic liturgies, and a desire to promote and recognize the importance of public worship throughout the Protestant Churches.

A sub-committee, of which the United Lutheran Church's representative was a member, published its studies on the Christian Year in pamphlet form, and is now engaged in preparation of a Lectionary for use by the Churches who may desire it. This will contain selections from the Old Testament, the Epistles and the Gospels for each Sunday of the year. The Lessons for the historic Seasons and Festivals will conform as closely as possible to the Lessons in the liturgical Churches.

The work of the committee is undoubtedly of real educational value, particularly among the free Churches. Its studies and recommendations so far have been definitely in the direction of a fuller understanding of the principles and forms of the historic liturgical Churches.

ZENAN M. CORBE,
Representative of the U. L. C. A.

X. ECUMENICAL MOVEMENTS

A. Universal Christian Conference on Life and Work

On January 14, 1937, the following recommendation, from the report of the Officers, with reference to the Universal Christian Conference on Life and Work, was approved:

"It is recommended that the U. L. C. A be not represented at the meeting of the Universal Christian Conference on Life and Work, the chief reason being that the membership of the Conference includes a large proportion of co-opted individuals. The Conference thus ceases to be effectively a Conference of the Churches."

This Conference was held in Oxford, England, August, 1937.

B. World Conference on Faith and Order

1. Appropriation:

On January 14, 1937, the Executive Board authorized an appropriation of $100 for the support of the World Conference on Faith and Order.

2. Delegates to the World Conference on Faith and Order:

Four of the seven commissioners on the World Conference on Faith and Order were authorized to attend the 1937 convention at Edinburgh, Scotland, with the other three as alternates. Those who were able to attend were, Dr. A. Steimle, Dr. A R. Wentz and Dr. E. E. Flack.

*3. Report of the Commissioners: (For action on this item, see p. 482.)

At the meeting of the Executive Board, July 14, 1938, a very comprehensive and scholarly report was presented, pertaining to the discussions and conclusions on doctrine and polity, with reference to the documents of the World Conference on Faith and Order. This report was received as information by the Executive Board and the secretary was instructed to file the same for future reference as our own Commission, or others, may have need for. Along with this report, with its many documentary references, the official reports of the Conference itself will be placed on file.

In connection with this report, the Commission presented the following recommendation, which was approved by the Executive Board for presentation to the convention:

That, pending further developments in the organization of the World Council of Churches, the United Lutheran Church continue its relationship with and participation in the World Conference on Faith and Order and that it authorize the Executive Board to appoint a commission, not exceeding seven members, for that purpose.

C. World Council of Churches

1. Organization:

On January 13, 1938, a preliminary report was made by our entire Commission, which referred particularly to the matters in the Edinburgh

Conference Report which called for definite action. These principal items are as follows:

> That part of the Report which deals with the Church's Unity in Life and Worship gives chief consideration to ways in which the spirit of Unity may be cultivated and expressed. In the opinion of our Commission, the most important of these is the cultivation of the spirit of Unity (No. 3), for where the will to Unity exists, expressions of it will naturally follow.

> The Report leads up to and concludes with a recommendation that a Council of Churches be formed   The broad lines on which it is to be constituted were drawn by a Committee of Thirty-five, representing the Conferences on Life and Work, and Faith and Order, and their proposals regarding steps to be taken for the formation of such a council were adopted by the Edinburgh Conference with only one dissenting vote. A detailed plan is to be worked out by a Committee of Fourteen, one-half to represent Life and Work, the other half, Faith and Order. Dr. A. R. Wentz has been appointed one of the alternate representatives by the Conference on Faith and Order.

> Our Commission recognizes that at present there are urgent matters on which such a Council could and should speak for the Churches unitedly. The way in which our Church's testimony has influenced the Report of the Edinburgh Conference, the fact that this World Council of Churches is to be representative of the Churches, as also the fact that it is not to be empowered to legislate for the Churches, leads the Commission to

> Recommend, (1) That the U. L. C. A. co-operate in the formation of the proposed World Council of Churches, such co-operation to be not independent of but along with the other Lutheran Churches represented in the World Conference on Faith and Order, and on the basis formulated by the Executive Committee of the Lutheran World Convention at its session in Amsterdam, in August, 1937.

> We further recommend, (2) That the Executive Board be asked to authorize an appropriation that will cover a quota of the total expenses of the proposed World Council of Churches that will be adequate to our proportional strength in that body.

Recommendation (1) was adopted and recommendation (2) was referred to the Finance Committee.

At the meeting of the Executive Board, October 5, 1938, the following recommendation from the Finance Committee was approved by the Executive Board:

> "The Joint Executive Committee of the American Sections of the Life and Work and Faith and Order Movements ask for an appropriation to their budget looking forward to our membership in the World Council of Churches, suggesting that the amount based on congregational expenses be $1,060. We recommend that

the officers be authorized to make such a payment in amount as
they may determine but not to exceed $600."

The question of new relationships between ecumenical movements was
profoundly before the Oxford Conference on Life and Work and the
Edinburgh Conference on Faith and Order. The delegates to the Edinburgh Conference, from the U. L. C. A., found it necessary to represent
the U. L. C. A. in the discussion of those questions. The following statement, presented for the three delegates by Dr. Wentz, was before the
Executive Board at its meeting, October 14, 1937:

One item in the work of the Edinburgh Conference, because it probably does call for action on the part of the Executive Board at this time,
should be brought to the attention of the Executive Board at the earliest
possible moment. I refer to the action at Edinburgh which will probably lead to a new organization of the movement in the form of a combination with the Universal Council on Life and Work.

It seems very clear that the action of your Board in declining to
send delegates to the Oxford Conference on Life and Work had a most
salutary effect in making Oxford and particularly Edinburgh Church-
conscious. When, therefore, the Edinburgh Conference considered the
proposal of a merger between Faith-and-Order and Life-and-Work,
special pains were taken to guard the ecclesiastical character of the proposed new organization, which is to be called the World Council of
Churches. Under these circumstances, all of your delegates at Edinburgh voted in favor of the proposed merger of the two ecumenical
movements.

The status of the proceedings in the direction of a World Council of
Churches is this: Edinburgh appointed a Committee of Fourteen (seven
Primarii and seven Alternates) who are to co-operate with a similar
committee appointed by Oxford, and this joint committee is to devise
ways and means for effecting the new organization. On this joint committee there are five Lutherans, two as Primarii and three as Alternates.
The joint committee met in London, August 19th, and decided to invite
the *Churches* to send delegates to a "Preliminary Conference" in Holland
next May to prepare a constitution which in turn is to be submitted to
all Churches for their ratification. Of the delegates to this Preliminary
Conference it is planned that twelve shall be representatives of the
Churches in America. On September 30th there was held in New York
a joint meeting of the American Section of the Continuation Committee
of the World Conference on Faith and Order with the American Section
of the Continuation Committee of the Universal Christian Council on
Life and Work, and with reference to the Preliminary Conference (of
sixty delegates) next May in Holland, it was decided to ask all the
Communions in America to send representatives to an "Electoral Conference" in New York before the end of the present year in order to
select twelve delegates (from America) to the Preliminary Conference
(Constitutional Convention) in Holland next May.

It may be stated that in a general way the idea of the Joint Committee of twenty-eight concerning the Proposed World Council of
Churches is that there shall be a *general assembly* of the Churches meeting every five years and numbering about 200 members, that there shall
be a *Central Committee* meeting annually and numbering about sixty

members, and that there shall be two *commissions,* one for Faith and Order and one on Life and Work. In several quarters the strong hope is held that representation both in the Central Committee and in the large General Assembly will be on Confessional and ecclesiastical rather than on geographical, territorial, or national basis. Perhaps with this information the Executive Board will want to prepare to answer the invitation from the joint Executive Committee of the American sections of the ecumenical movements, asking the United Lutheran Church, either for herself or in combination with other Lutheran bodies, to appoint a delegate to the "Electoral Conference" which is to select one or more Lutheran representatives to the Constitutional Convention next May. It will be possible for this Lutheran delegate to the Electoral Convention to go with instructions from his Communion, that is, with instructions as to a nomination or nominations for the Constitutional Convention.

Dr. W. H. Greever was named as the representative of the U. L C. A. to attend the Electoral Conference which was appointed to meet in Washington, D. C., in January, 1938, and he was instructed to place the name of Dr. F. H. Knubel in nomination as the Lutheran representative among the ten American delegates to the Constitutional Convention, Utrecht, Holland.

At the meeting of the Executive Board on January 13, 1938, Dr. Greever reported that he had attended the meeting of the Electoral Conference, held in Washington, D. C., on January 10, 1938, and that, upon the submission of the name of Dr. F. H. Knubel, as a nominee to represent the Lutherans of America, he was unanimously elected as one of the ten delegates to the Constitutional Convention.

*2. Report of Delegate to Constitutional Convention: (For action on this item, see p. 483.)

The following report was submitted by Dr. Knubel to the Executive Board, at its meeting on July 14, 1938, and the resolution attached thereto was approved by the Executive Board for submission to this convention:

Two ecumenical meetings were held in Europe during the month of May. Both were important, although both were without final authority. The one in Utrecht was a representative gathering of almost all Christians in the world, with the exception of R o m a n Catholics. It planned a constitution for a proposed World Council of Churches. This will be submitted to all Churches which will be invited to send official representatives to a General Assembly two or more years hence. Then a final constitution will be adopted and the organization will come into existence. At Uppsala a regular meeting of the Executive Committee of the Lutheran World Convention was held. It took specific action upon the Utrecht proceedings.

It must be remembered that a number of ecumenical or world organizations of Christians have existed and have of late grown so numerous that insistent calls for their combination have been voiced. In the summer of 1937 two of them, commonly called "Faith and Order" and "Life and Work," met in Great Britain. There the plans for their amalgamation were proposed, and Utrecht was the result. The adopted constitution would practically merge these two but would also open the way for a consultative relationship to the new organization on the part of still other movements like the International Missionary Council, the World Alliance for International Friendship, several youth movements, world confessional associations, etc.

Some forty to fifty official representatives were in attendance, including nine Lutherans (of whom two were from America). Others present were the Joint Committee of Fourteen from the two meetings in 1937, who planned for Utrecht, and representatives of the other movements above mentioned. The languages used were English, an almost equal amount of German, and occasionally French. The Lutherans held two separate conferences to consider their special interest in the outcome.

According to the proposed constitution, a doctrinal basis exists stating that only such Churches are eligible to participate as accept our Lord Jesus Christ as God and Saviour. This was vigorously debated, but was finally adopted by a unanimous vote. The purposes prescribed are the continuation of the work of "Faith and Order" and "Life and Work," the facilitation of common action by the Churches, the promotion of cooperation in study, the promotion of ecumenical consciousness among Christians, the establishment of relations with denominational federations of world-wide scope and with other ecumenical movements, the calling of world conferences on specific subjects as occasion may require. The World Council, however, shall not legislate for the Churches and may act only to offer counsel and to provide opportunity of united action in matters of common interest.

There is to be a General Assembly, meeting every five years, constituted of not more than 450 members, all of whom are to be official representatives of Churches. In the interim a Central Committee of 90 shall meet ordinarily every year. In both, an effort is to be made whereby approximately one-third will be from the laity, both male and female. Some consultative representatives from ecumenical organizations may be designated by the Central Committee, the organizations and the number of their representatives being decided by that committee. The allocation of members is as follows for the Central Committee of 90 (with five times each amount for the General Assembly of 450): 17 from the Orthodox Churches; 22 from the Continent of Europe; 12 from Great Britain and Ireland; 18 from the United States of America and Canada; 10 from Asia, Africa, Latin America, and the Pacific Islands; five from South Africa, Australia, etc.; six representing ecclesiastical minorities not otherwise granted adequate representation above.

Considerable discussion took place concerning particularly this method of allocation. It is to be noted that the Orthodox Churches are admitted as a denominational, a confessional group, but in practically all other respects the allocation is a territorial one. This is true, even though the Churches themselves in each territory mentioned are to arrange for a division of the assigned number. The danger was stressed that a World Council grouped largely on national and territorial lines easily tends to purely secular or political considerations.

The Lutherans took active part in this debate particularly because the Executive Committee of the Lutheran World Convention at its meeting in Amsterdam last August had declared against a territorial allocation for the proposed World Council. As a result a sentence was introduced into the constitution which contemplates a possible change in the present arrangement. It should also be mentioned that throughout the meeting sincere regard was manifested for the world confessional associations,—namely, Lutheran, Presbyterian and Reformed, Baptist, etc.

A committee of twenty-eight members was named to work out details until the first meeting of a General Assembly is held. It consists of the original Committee of Fourteen appointed last summer with the fourteen alternates appointed also at that time. Five Lutherans are included. The Churches everywhere will receive the proposed constitution officially and will be invited to participate in the first General Assembly.

Turning to Uppsala, the Executive Committee of the Lutheran World Convention discussed all of the above facts at length and finally adopted the following statement which will be sent to all Lutheran Churches identified with the Lutheran World Convention. It will also be sent officially to the Committee of 28:

> "The Executive Committee has heard the report of two of its members who participated in the ecumenical meeting at Utrecht from the 9th to the 13th of May, and records with satisfaction that the confession of our Lord Jesus Christ as God and Saviour was unanimously adopted as the basis of the proposed World Council of Churches. We would emphatically state that thereby agreement in faith was acknowledged as the unavoidable requirement for a true unification of the Churches. If Jesus Christ is confessed in the fullest sense as our God and Saviour, it involves that He is the only mediator between God and man and that we are justified before God only through faith in Him, the crucified and risen One. Only where the gospel of Jesus Christ is rightly and purely taught and the Sacraments are administered according to the institution of Jesus Christ will true Church unity be obtained, according to the testimony of the New Testament as confessed by our Church.

> "In the organization of the World Council this principle was practically applied in the case of the Orthodox Church which as such is to have special representation in the proposed new organization. This corresponds factually with the principle of confessional representation expressed in our Amsterdam resolution of 1937. Although this principle was not carried through at Utrecht in the further arrangements for representation, we welcome the fact that the constitution provides for a possible change of the present territorial representation, and regard the present arrangement as only a temporary one, leading to such a change. The Lutheran World Convention believes that only on a confessional basis will participation in the work possess permanent and hopeful prospect."

The official invitation to The United Lutheran Church in America will arrive in September. A copy of the proposed constitution is attached to this report. It is to be noted that the constitution does not become effective until the first General Assembly meets and approves it. I suggest that the Executive Board propose the following resolution to the Baltimore Convention:

The United Lutheran Church in America is willing to co-operate for the present with the proposed World Council of Churches and authorizes the Executive Board to arrange for representation as necessary so long as the Executive Board deems it advisable. We express at the same time our entire agreement with the statement of the Executive Committee of the Lutheran World Convention and emphasize the concluding words, "that only on a confessional basis will participation in the work possess permanent and hopeful prospect."

XI. MISCELLANEOUS

*1. **Social Security for Church Workers:** (For action on this item, see p. 483.)

At the meeting of the Executive Board, June 25, 1937, the matter of social security for Church workers was referred to the officers of the Church.

The following report of the Finance Committee, presented at the meeting of the Executive Board on October 5, 1938, was adopted for presentation to this convention with the recommendation for favorable action:

"Your Committee appointed to consider the pensioning of U. L. C. A. employees not covered by the proposed contributory plan which is to be presented to the Convention, would report as follows:

"They find that those who are included in the stated category consist of clergymen who are not officially connected with any congregation and all others who are engaged or employed by any of the Boards of our Church receiving a regular, specified salary.

"We have been advised that the Social Security Act does not cover any Church employees and we do not believe it advisable at this time for our Church to make an application to the Government that Church workers and employees should be included. We recommend that the protection desired be made in the following way:

"1. *As to Deaconesses:* Inasmuch as they are not on a stated salary and under their life service are cared for by the Board of Deaconess Work or one of the Motherhouses, we do not believe that any additional provision should be made.

"2. *As to missionaries in the foreign field,* they are at present given retirement and pension considerations by the Board of Foreign Missions and we believe that this responsibility should continue with that Board and he handled in such a way and on such a basis as it deems proper and right.

"3. *As to all other employees of Boards,* we believe that when, as and if the proposed contributory pension plan, to be presented at the Baltimore Convention, shall be adopted and put in operation, all of said employees of our Boards should be invited to participate on the same basis as arranged for clergymen with the provision that the Boards shall take the part of the congregation and make one-half contribution of ten per cent of salaries provided for in said plan, when and as the employee shall contribute the five per cent of salary as provided.

"We recommend that the proposed addition to the contributory pension plan proposed in this report be submitted to the convention for its approval and be made operative when the plan itself has been declared in operation by the Board of Ministerial Pensions and Relief."

2. Special Board Pensions and Pensions to all Church Workers:

The Finance Committee of the Executive Board, at the meeting held January 13, 1938, recommended the appointment of a committee to make inquiry of all boards concerning any action with regard to pensions, which has been proposed or is under consideration, and a statement as to the number and character of their employees, and whether any pensions are now in operation, said committee to study conditions and report recommendations to the Executive Board.   This recommendation was adopted by the Executive Board and the president appointed the following committee: Dr. E. Clarence Miller, Mr. Robert F. Bowe, Mr. J. K. Jensen, Dr. James C. Kinard, Dr. Robbin B. Wolf.

The Committee has not yet completed its work.

3. 1938 Convention:

At the meeting of the Executive Board, January 14, 1937, information concerning hotel accommodations and other conditions at Baltimore, Md., was submitted and the Executive Board resolved that the convention should meet in that city, opening October 5, 1938, and that the Lord Baltimore Hotel should be designated as convention headquarters.

4. Convention Reports:

At the meeting of the Executive Board, October 5, 1938, the following action was taken pertaining to convention reports:

(a) That a special committee be established within the Executive Board whose duty it shall be to budget the space for reports to be submitted through the Bulletin to subsequent conventions of the Church and therefore for the Minutes.

(b) That all agencies of the Church include audited financial statements in connection with their reports for the conventions.

Respectfully submitted,
F. H. KNUBEL, *President.*
W. H. GREEVER, *Secretary*
E. CLARENCE MILLER, *Treasurer.*

II, 13, Consolidation of Periodicals, page 60. It was moved and seconded that the recommendation of the Executive Board be adopted.

A motion was made and seconded that this matter be referred to the Committee on Church Papers for report to the Church at the next Convention.

It was moved and carried that consideration of this matter be postponed until the report of the Committee on Church Papers is before the Convention. (For further action, see pp. 231, 232, 235, 238.)

Committee of Tellers No. 1 reported that the Rev. F. H. Knubel, having received 459 votes out of 478, had received the required number for election on the first ballot, whereupon the Secretary declared the Rev. F. H. Knubel elected President of The United Lutheran Church in America for the next biennium.

The President ordered that the Convention proceed to the election of a Secretary under Committee of Tellers No. 1.

Committee of Tellers No. 2 reported that Dr. E. Clarence Miller, having received 411 votes out of 419, had received the required number for election and the President declared Dr. E. Clarence Miller elected Treasurer of The United Lutheran Church in America for the next biennium.

By general consent, Item III, A, 4, Call to the Ministry, was taken up for consideration. (See p. 65.)

It was moved and seconded that the statement be accepted as a guide to the Church.

The hour of adjournment being near, consideration of this statement was suspended. (For further action on this item, see pp. 105, 106.)

Committee of Tellers No. 1 reported that the Rev. W. H. Greever, having received 444 votes out of 456, had received the required number for election and the President declared the Rev. W. H. Greever elected Secretary of The United Lutheran Church in America for the next biennium.

At twelve o'clock the Convention adjourned with prayer by the Rev. Paul H. Krauss.

SECOND SESSION

LORD BALTIMORE HOTEL
Baltimore, Maryland
Thursday, October 6, 1938, 2.00 P. M.

Devotions were conducted by the Rev. Kenneth A. Hurst, and the President called the Convention to order.

The President recognized the Rev. John C. Mattes, Chairman of the Committee of Reference and Counsel, who presented the following report:

REPORT OF COMMITTEE OF REFERENCE AND COUNSEL

1. The Rev. W. E. Schuette, President of the Eastern Conference of the American Lutheran Church, is present as the official representative from the American Lutheran Church. We recommend that Dr. Schuette be heard immediately after the close of this report.

2. Whereas great unrest has troubled the world both at home and abroad, as wars and rumors of wars have disturbed the nations, and because the Church has suffered persecution and oppression in many places, be it

Resolved, That all the pastors of the Church be urged to remind their people continually that God is ever the Author of peace and the Lover of concord, and that it is always the bounden duty of all who call themselves Christians to seek peace and ensue it; and be it

Resolved, That, on the twenty-third Sunday after Trinity, special supplications be offered for the peace of the world and also, being mindful of the special bonds of the Communion of Saints, intercessions be made for those who must bear the Cross for His Name's sake, that they may be comforted and strengthened by His grace, that they may remain steadfast in the one true faith, and that the enemies of the Gospel may be brought to confusion.

The following collects are suggested as especially appropriate:

O God, Who art the Author of peace and Lover of concord, in knowledge of Whom standeth our eternal life, Whose service is perfect freedom: Defend us, Thy humble servants, in all assaults of our enemies; that we, surely trusting in Thy defence, may not fear the power of any adversaries; through Jesus Christ, Thy Son our Lord. Amen.

O Lord, favorably receive the prayers of Thy Church, that, being delivered from all adversity and error, it may serve Thee in safety and freedom; and grant us Thy peace in our time; through Jesus Christ, Thy Son our Lord. Amen.

O God, from Whom all holy desires, all good counsels and all just works do proceed; Give unto Thy servants that peace, which the world cannot give, that our hearts may be set to obey Thy commandments, and also that by Thee, we being defended from the fear of our enemies, may pass our time in rest and quietness; through the merits of Jesus Christ, our Saviour, Who liveth and reigneth with Thee, and the Holy Ghost, ever one God, world without end. Amen.

3. Resolved, That the Convention express its sympathy to those who have been prevented from attending its sessions by infirmity or illness and also for those who have had to bear the cross of separation from those they love, and that it likewise especially commemorate before God those four delegates, who have been called to rest eternal, by rising for prayer while the following intercessions and commemorations are offered by the President:

O Lord, look down from heaven, behold, visit and relieve Thy servants, for whom we offer our supplications; look upon them with the eyes of Thy mercy; give them comfort and sure confidence in Thee; defend them from the danger of the enemy, and keep them in perpetual peace and safety; through Jesus Christ, Thy Son, our Lord. Amen.

O Heavenly Father, Whose blessed Son, Jesus Christ, did weep at the grave of Lazarus, His friend; look, we beseech Thee, with compassion upon those who are now in sorrow and affliction: comfort them, O Lord, with Thy gracious consolations; make them to know that all things work together for good to them that love Thee; and grant them evermore sure trust and confidence in Thy fatherly care; through the same, Jesus Christ, our Lord. Amen.

Almighty God, with Whom do live the spirits of those who depart hence in the Lord, and with Whom the souls of the faithful, after they are delivered from the burden of the flesh, are in joy and felicity: we give Thee hearty thanks for Thy grace bestowed upon Thy servants, who having finished their course in faith do now rest from their labors; and we beseech Thee, that we, with all who have departed in the true faith of Thy Holy Name may have our perfect consummation and bliss, both in body and soul, in Thy eternal glory; through Jesus Christ, Thy Son, our Lord. Amen.

1. Adopted.

2. Adopted.

3. Adopted by a rising vote, and the President offered special prayer in accordance with the resolution.

The Chairman of the Committee of Reference and Counsel introduced Dr. W. E. Schuette, who addressed the Convention as the representative from the American Lutheran Church, and, at the request of the President, the Rev. N. R. Melhorn made an appropriate response.

The consideration of the **Report of the Executive Board,** Item III, A, 4, Call to the Ministry, was resumed. (For other references, see pp. 65, 103.)

Upon motion, an amendment was adopted to the second recommendation on page 70, of these Minutes, by the addition of the words "in cases where Lutheran ordination is not constitutionally required" at the end of the first sentence. The recommendation would then read:

> We recommend the preparation of a special form for use by synods in receiving such applicants from other communions, in cases where Lutheran ordination is not constitutionally required. Said form to emphasize the candidate's acceptance of the Lutheran position concerning the Word and Sacraments.

Motion was made and carried to amend Section "1" on page 70, by striking out all that follows the first three sentences. The section would then read:

> 1. The call to a particular field of labor normally carries no time limit. In the case of men already ordained, calls to positions of administration in the Church may carry the condition of limited terms of service. In cases necessitating the limitation of time as long a period as is consistent with the best interests of the Church should be indicated.

By motion the first recommendation under "C. Concerning the Question of Recall," on page 72, was stricken from the statement.

By motion the third recommendation under "C. Concerning the Question of Recall," on page 73, was amended by substituting the word "President" in the place of "Executive Board or Committee." The recommendation would then read as follows:

> We further recommend that the congregation's right of termination of the contractual relationship shall be exercised only after consultation with the President of the synod and after the same prayerful consideration has been used that was invoked at the issuance of the original call, and that it shall become effective by a two-thirds majority of all the votes cast at a duly called congregational meeting.

The statement on the Call to the Ministry, as amended, was, on motion, accepted as a guide to the Church.

It was moved and carried that the President be authorized to appoint a committee to be instructed to use this statement for the formulation of definite articles to be recommended for insertion into the Model Constitution for Congregations and the Model Constitution for Constituent Synods.

Item II, 14, Amendments to the Constitution, page 60, pertaining to terms of service for the officers and procedure of elections, was next taken up for consideration. The motion to refer to the constituent synods for approval was lost, and the amendments voted down.

Item II, 16, Concerning Theological Education under U. L. C. A. Control, page 61, was considered. Motion was made and seconded to adopt the recommendations of the Executive Board.

The Rev. F. R. Knubel proposed the original memorial from the New York Synod as a substitute for the report submitted by the Executive Board.

A motion was made and carried to refer the substitute proposed, the report of the Executive Board on this matter, and the memorial from the Synod in the Midwest, to a special committee of nine, to be appointed by the President, for consideration and report to this Convention.   (For further action, see pp. 184, 464, 465, 483, 484.)

Item II, 15, Advanced Age Retirement Limit for Pastors, page 61. The recommendation of the Executive Board was adopted.

Item III, A, 6, Calendar of Special Days and Seasons, page 73, was adopted.

Item III, B, 1, The Central Pennsylvania Synod, page 76. The recommendations of the Executive Board, concerning the reception of The Central Pennsylvania Synod, were adopted. Following this action the President declared the following ruling: That, in the order of the constituent synods of The United Lutheran Church in America, this Central Pennsylvania Synod takes the place of four synods and is now established as a constituent synod of The United Lutheran Church in America. Its roll of delegates has been filed with the Secretary

of the Church and they now become the accredited delegates of
The Central Pennsylvania Synod.

The President then called upon the President of the new
synod, the Rev. M. R. Hamsher, for a brief address concerning
the work of The Central Pennsylvania Synod.

Item III, B, 2, (a) Change of name of German Synod of
Nebraska, page 77, was approved.

Item IV, A, 1, Amendments to the By-laws, page 78. Notice
was given of amendments to By-laws and the President
announced that action would be taken on Friday, October 7.
(For action, see p. 115.)

Item IV, A, 2, Merger of Agencies, page 78. Motion was
made and seconded that the name "Inner Mission Board" be
substituted for "Board of Social Missions" as the general title
of the new Board and to be inserted at all points where the
name of the Board is used. After long discussion, motion was
made and carried to extend the time of the session for the
completion of this item.

After the extension of discussion until 5.30 P. M., the
previous question was called, and the proposed amendment
was *lost*.

By motion the Convention then approved the action of
the Executive Board.

The Convention adjourned at 5.34 P. M. Prayer led by the
Rev. F. W. Kern.

Thursday Evening

The biennial banquet of the Laymen's Movement was held
in the Lord Baltimore Hotel with an inspiring program and
an attendance which approached a maximum. A feature of
the banquet was the presentation of a gold cross to Dr. F. H.
Knubel as a token of appreciation for his twenty years' service
as President of The United Lutheran Church in America.

THIRD SESSION

Lord Baltimore Hotel

Baltimore, Maryland

Friday, October 7, 1938, 8.45 A. M.

Matins were conducted by the Rev. R. D. Clare, pastor of St. Mark's Lutheran Church, Baltimore, Md. The service was designated as the memorial service of the Convention. All hymns, Scripture Lessons and prayers referred to the Christian view of death and eternal life. Dr. Clare read the names of the 115 deceased ministers of the United Lutheran Church, who died within the biennium, together with the names of 28 lay men and women. This list was read with impressive reverence, the Convention standing in tribute.

NECROLOGY REPORT

At this time we present records of 115 deceased ministers, 18 outstanding laymen, seven laywomen, and four deaconesses.

A summary of records of deceased members of the United Lutheran Church in America, since the merger, totals 1,017 ministers, 144 laymen, and 74 laywomen (including 11 deaconesses). This means that during the first score years the Church lost nearly one-third of its clerical members by death.

Of the deceased ministers about one-half were active pastors when their call came. One-third had retired before their demise. The balance, or one-sixth of the total number, were in official positions.

The average age limit of ministers was 69 years. Although a few men were spared long enough to serve the Church for three score years, the average tenure of office is 36 years.

The biennial report to the Church, and the annual lists of deceased ministers for the Year Book, claim constant probing and careful tabulating. We humbly beg to thank necrologists of synods for their ready and courteous replies to our many letters.

Name	Born Where	Born When	Ordained	Synod at Death	Died Where	Died When	Where Buried	Age Y.	M.	D.	Years of Service
Ahrens, Ernst Theo.	Teistungen, Germany	July 27, 1869	1903	Pg	Chicago, Ill.	Nov. 18, 1936	Chicago, Ill.	67	3	21	32
Armstrong, Charles H.	Nr. Newark, O.	Dec. 2, 1869	1896	KT	Nr. Shelbyville, Tenn.	June 20, 1937	Shelbyville, Tenn.	67	6	18	41
Bahr, August	Geyerswalde, Germany	Aug. 6, 1866	1899	Cf	Fresno, Calif.	Dec. 22, 1937	Fresno, Calif.	71	4	16	18
Bahr, Frederick, D.D.	Hannover, Germany	Oct. 3, 1863	1889	Nb	Fort Collins, Colo.	Sept. 6, 1936	Lamar, Colo.	72	11	3	42
Bielinski, Reinhold C. G.	Berlin, Germany	Aug. 27, 1871	1893	PM	Riverside, N. J.	May 25, 1937	Hainesport, N. J.	65	8	28	26
Birch, Thomas, B., Ph.D., D.D., LL.D.	Bloomsburg, Pa.	Sept. 11, 1866	1894	O	Springfield, O.	Dec. 20, 1937	Springfield, O.	71	3	9	43
Bressler, J. Walter	York Co., Pa.	July 20, 1876	1908	O	Parma, O.	Feb. 20, 1937	Niles, O.	60	7	0	28
Brown, William R.	Wythe Co., Va.	Aug. 9, 1859	1886	Va	Abingdon, Va.	Dec. 29, 1937	Kimberlin, Va.	78	4	20	14
Cassell, Charles W.	Rural Retreat, Va.	Mar. 25, 1871	1896	Va	Abingdon, Va.	Apr. 14, 1937	Kimberlin, Va.	66	0	19	38
Catlin, Roy G., D.D.	Erie Co., Pa.	May 26, 1883	1908	Il	Maywood, Ill.	Sept. 17, 1937	Erie, Pa.	54	3	21	29
Christ, Fred V.	Peabody, Kan.	June 27, 1878	1908	NY	New Rochelle, N. Y.	July 8, 1937	Peabody, Kan.	59	0	11	29
Deibert, Willis F.	Lehighton, Pa.	Mar. 15, 1883	1910	PM	Geigertown, Pa.	Dec. 18, 1937	Geigertown, Pa.	54	10	23	15
Deitzler, Martin L.	Bernville, Pa.	Feb. 2, 1851	1882	EP	Harrisburg, Pa.	Sept. 27, 1937	Annville, Pa.	86	10	16	25
Derrick, Ira M.	Center Brunswick, N. Y.	May 2, 1858	1884	NY	Rensselaer, N. Y.	Jan. 2, 1937	Troy, N. Y.	79	4	25	27
Dickey, Ephraim F.	Nr. Berlin, Pa.	July 4, 1848	1880	Pg	Derry, Pa.	Jan. 29, 1938	Berlin, Pa.	88	9	28	46
Dieterly, Erwin	Springtown, Pa.	Apr. 30, 1868	1896	EP	Sellersville, Pa.	Jan. 12, 1938	Springfield, Pa.	69	8	29	
Dittmar, Alfred E.	Amanda, O.	Mar. 24, 1910	1936	O	Steubenville, O.	Sept. 2, 1937	Lewisburg, O.	27	5	9	2
Dozer, Clement L. V.	Nr. Zanesville, O.	Apr. 25, 1864	1895	Pg	Geneva, O.	Jan. 12, 1938	Duncan Falls, O.	73	8	18	35
Drach, William C.	Greenport, L. I., N. Y.	Oct. 30, 1874	1898	NY	Rochester, N. Y.	Mar. 15, 1937	Syracuse, N. Y.	52	4	15	39
Dunn, Jesse	Marion Co., Ind.	Aug. 11, 1850	1884	Pg	Stahlstown, Pa.	Mar. 21, 1938	Benton, Ind.	87	7	10	48
Englar, George W., Ph.D., D.D.	Nr. Uniontown, Md.	Mar. 9, 1875	1900	Pg	Pittsburgh, Pa.	Dec. 7, 1937	Uniontown, Md.	62	8	28	37
Estell, Thomas ..., B.D.	Nr. Columbus, Ind.	Dec. 31, 1856	1895	Cf	Los Angeles, Calif.	Jan. 22, 1938	Los Angeles, Calif.	81	0	21	35
Fetter, Clinton R.	Bedminster, Pa.	Feb. 22, 1863	1891	PM	Telford, Pa.	Nov. 25, 1936	Telford, Pa.	73	9	3	45
Fischer, William E., D.D.	Berlin, Pa.	Oct. 6, 1849	1875	Sq	Shamokin, Pa.	Aug. 10, 1936	Berlin, Pa.	86	10	4	61
Fleck, E. Lee	Sinking Valley, Pa.	Sept. 8, 1856	1887	Nb	Lincoln, Nebr.	May 18, 1937	Hamilton, Ill.	80	8	10	22
Flick, Herman H.	Lavansville, Pa.	Feb. 13, 1881	1913	Pg	Wilkinsburg, Pa.	May 8, 1938	Allegheny Co., Pa.	57	2	25	25
Freed, Charles A., D.D.	Waynesboro, Va.	Aug. 23, 1868	1893	SC	Columbia, S. C.	Apr. 6, 1938	Columbia, S. C.	69	7	13	45
Freudenreich, Christel.	Germany	Nov. 19, 1850		NY	Bremen, Germany	Dec. 10, 1936	Brinkum, Germany	74	1	5	
Fricke, H. W.	Hannover, Germany	Oct. 21, 1858	1881	GN	Madison, Nebr.	Apr. 24, 1938	Madison, Nebr.	87	5	5	46
Fry, Charles L., D.D.	Carlisle, Pa.	Nov. 6, 1893	1881	PM	Philadelphia, Pa.	Mar. 19, 1937	Old Trapp Ch., Pa.	78	4	28	45
Gartung, Stanley W. M.	New Hamburg, Ont., Can.	Mar. 29, 1886	1921	Cn	Kingston, Can.	Oct. 12, 1937	Kitchener, Ont., Can.	43	6	6	16
Gent, John J.	LaGrange, Mo.		1918	Il	Nokomis, Ill.	Oct. 3, 1936	Nokomis, Ill.	50	6	4	18
Grommisch, William T.	Stolp, Germany	Oct. 6, 1859	1884	Mh	Detroit, Mich.	Jan. 21, 1937	Detroit, Mich.	77	3	15	45
Grubb, Joel E.	Perry Valley, Pa.	Aug. 18, 1880	1908	Md	Baltimore, Md.	Jan. 10, 1938	Newport, Pa.	57	5	22	30
Haas, John A. W., D.D., LL.D., L.H.D.	Philadelphia, Pa.	Aug. 31, 1862	1887	O	Minnewaska, N. Y.	July 22, 1937	New York, N. Y.	74	10	21	50
Hamfeldt, Hugo C., D.D.	Schleswig, Germany	May 12, 1867	1891	O	Toledo, O.	Nov. 23, 1937	Toledo, O.	70	6	11	46
Hamm, George L., Ph.D.	Fay, Pa.	Oct. 14, 1858	1888	Pg	West Palm Beach, Fla.	Mar. 4, 1938	Slippery Rock, Pa.	79	4	20	41
Hausman, Oscar P.	Meerane, Germany	Nov. 11, 1878	1907	GN	Grand Island, Nebr.	July 5, 1938	Grand Island, Nebr.	57	7	17	29
Heil, Oliver R., B.D.	Williamsport, Md.	July 30, 1903	1930	Pg	Zelienople, Pa.	Feb. 27, 1938	Hagerstown, Md.	34	6	27	7
Hiden, Gustave A.	Sweden			Pf	Oakland, Calif.	July 17, 1937	Olympia, Wash.	74			
Hingkeldey, Ernst F.	Pappenheim, Germany	Sept. 17, 1875	1902	NY	Middletown, Conn.	Jan. 11, 1937	Middletown, Conn.	61	6	3	35
Hogshead, Luther, D.D.	Staunton, Va.	Aug. 13, 1868	1897	Il	Chicago, Ill.	Mar. 20, 1937	Staunton, Va.	68	8	28	40
Holloway, Clayton L.	Athol, Pa.	Dec. 5, 1853	1884	PM	Long Beach, Calif.	Aug. 16, 1937	Long Beach, Calif.	83	11	10	17
Jacobs, Charles M., D.D., LL.D., L.H.D.	Gettysburg, Pa.	Oct. 9, 1875	1899	PM	Philadelphia, Pa.	Mar. 30, 1938	Whitemarsh, Pa.	62	5	25	39
Jeffcoat, Herbert W.	Goshen Hill, Ala.		1894	NC	Boone, N. C.		Columbia, S. C.			26	35
Karg, Charles M., D.D.	Pine Lake, N. Y.	Oct. 27, 1876	1903	NY	Dansville, N. Y.	Apr. 6, 1937	Dansville, N. Y.	60	5	9	34
Kercher, George A.	Nr. Fogelsville, Pa.	Apr. 17, 1874	1896	PM	Mt. Joy, Pa.	July 9, 1937	Old Trapp Ch., Pa.	63	2	22	41
Keyser, Leander S., B.D., D.D.	Shanesville, O.	Mar. 13, 1856	1879	Mh	Springfield, O.	Oct. 18, 1937	Springfield, O.	81	7	5	53

Name	Born Where	Born When	Ordained	Synod at Death	Died Where	Died When	Where Buried	Age Y.	Age M.	Age D.	Years of Service
Kiefer, George L., D.D., Litt.D.	Nr. Millersburg, Pa.	Nov. 25, 1883	1916	NY	Rosedale, L. I., N. Y.	Apr. 25, 1937	Millersburg, Pa.	53	5	0	21
King, Cleason B., D.D.	Abbottstown, Pa.	Jan. 23, 1858	1883	Pg	Bellevue, Pa.	Mar. 11, 1937	Uniondale, Pa.	79	1	17	52
Kirschke, George A.	Berlin, Germany	Sept. 3, 1869	1905	Ks	Little Rock, Ark.	Apr. 13, 1938	Little Rock, Ark.	68	7	10	33
Kistler, Henry A., Ph.D.	Lincoln Co., N. C.	Dec. 30, 1879	1924	NC	Cleveland, N. C.	May 7, 1938	Daniels Ch., N. C.	58	4	7	13
Kline, Raymond A.	Nr. Myerstown, Pa.	Feb. 4, 1897	1931	PM	Tremont, Pa.	Apr. 5, 1937	Myerstown, Pa.	40	2	1	5
Klingbeil, Ludwig	New Sawatka, Poland	June 18, 1887	1900	Mn	Barrhead, Alberta, Can.	Sept. 26, 1936	Meadowview, Alberta.	49	3	8	37
Klotsch, Ernst H., Ph.D., D.D.	Elstra, Germany	Aug. 7, 1875	1881	Wg	Chicago, Ill.	Feb. 11, 1937	Chicago, Ill.	61	6	4	55
Kohler, Frederick W., D.D.	New Holland, Pa.	Sept. 8, 1856	1897	Pg	Rochester, Pa.	Aug. 15, 1937	Rochester, Pa.	80	11	4	40
Koller, Paul W., D.D.	Glenrock, Pa.	July 1, 1872	1916	O	Baltimore, Md.	Nov. 11, 1937	Baltimore, Md.	65	4	10	21
Krauleidis, Wilhelm G.	Ostpreussen, Germany	Dec. 6, 1889	1913	Nb	Salina, Kan.	June 16, 1937	Nr. Perry, Okla.	47	6	10	40
Kuhlman, Luther, D.D.	New Centerville, Pa.	Nov. 8, 1851	1882	WP	Gettysburg, Pa.	Oct. 18, 1936	Gettysburg, Pa.	84	1	10	54
Kunzendorf, Robert	Berlin, Germany	Jan. 22, 1889	1894	GN	Lincoln, Nebr.	Nov. 16, 1937	Emerald, Nebr.	48	9	24	41
Lau, Jeremiah B.	York Co., Pa.	Mar. 8, 1868	1924	WP	East Berlin, Pa.	Feb. 4, 1937	East Berlin, Pa.	68	0	6	13
Lauver, Orville B.	Juniata Co., Pa.	Feb. 12, 1889	1892	O	Newark, O.	Dec. 3, 1937	Springfield, O.	48	9	21	39
Leopold, Elmer O.	Nr. Allentown, Pa.	Mar. 24, 1870	1895	PM	Johnson City, N. Y.	Oct. 21, 1936	Allentown, Pa.	66	6	27	38
Lesher, Samuel M., D.D.	McConnelsburg, Pa.	Aug. 16, 1864	1891	Ia	Rockford, Ill.	June 19, 1936	Burlington, Ia.	71	10	3	45
Lohr, Luther L., D.D.	Lutheolnton, N. C.	Oct. 1, 1860	1878	NC	Lincolnton, N. C.	Aug. 24, 1937	Lincolnton, N. C.	76	10	23	40
Lowe, James A., Ph.D.	Smicksburg, Ind.	Oct. 22, 1851	1874	Nb	Omaha, Nebr.	Apr. 29, 1938	Beatrice, Nebr.	86	6	7	25
Martinis, Alfred	Nr. Hampton, N. J.	Dec. 20, 1843	1911	Il	Newport, Ky.	Nov. 26, 1936	Newport, Ky.	92	11	6	25
Masser, William J.	Nr. Sinking Springs, Pa.	May 8, 1881	1892	PM	Germansville, Pa.	Nov. 30, 1936	Orwigsburg, Pa.	55	9	22	45
McDowell, Samuel J., D.D.	Dallastown, Pa.	Aug. 29, 1863	1882	Md	Baltimore, Md.	Jan. 9, 1937	Baltimore, Md.	73	4	10	45
McSherry, George W.	East Berlin, Pa.	Dec. 10, 1854	1887	Sq	New Berlin, Pa.	Sept. 16, 1937	New Berlin, Pa.	82	9	6	44
Miller, Charles B.	Rowan Co., N. C.	Mar. 24, 1861	1875	NC	China Grove, N. C.	Oct. 1, 1936	Charlotte, N. C.	75	6	7	44
Neudoerffer, Ernst	Malbach, Germany	Mar. 19, 1849	1875	PM	Philadelphia, Pa.	Aug. 26, 1936	Hainesport, N. J.	87	5	7	43
Nicholas, William H., D.D.	Nr. York, Pa.	Feb. 5, 1867	1895	Il	Narberth, Pa.	Jan. 25, 1938	Springfield, Ill.	70	8	20	39
Nideeker, Johannes E., D.D.	Basel, Switzerland	Sept. 19, 1861	1886	SZ	Hillside, N. J.	May 30, 1937	Philadelphia, Pa.	77	8	11	44
Novomesky, Ludwig	Senitz, Hungary	Feb. 28, 1861	1899	GN	New York, N. Y.	Mar. 13, 1938	Hillside, N. J.	77	0	15	37
Nussbaum, George P. E. von	Eberswalde, Germany	Dec. 16, 1877	1892	NY	Manly, Ia.	July 9, 1937	Hastings, Nebr.	59	6	23	45
Oberlander, Fridolin, E. F., D.D.	Covington, Ky.	Jan. 27, 1866	1910	Ia	Jersey City, N. J.	Dec. 5, 1937	Syracuse, N. Y.	71	9	8	27
Parker, George G.	Venlo, Holland	Mar. 19, 1881	1907	NY	Topeka, Kan.	June 10, 1937	Fairfield, Ia.	56	2	21	30
Poensgen, Carl E.	Knox Co., O.	Feb. 17, 1877	1881	Il	Glendale, N. Y.	Oct. 14, 1937	Jersey City, N. J.	60	4	27	48
Porch, Francis M., D.D.	Duennow, Germany	Feb. 16, 1851	1895	NY	Lebanon, Pa.	May 5, 1937	Springfield, O.	85	4	18	42
Preuss, George P. U. J.	Philadelphia, Pa.	Aug. 19, 1868	1895	PM	Kannapolis, N. C.	Feb. 20, 1937	Amityville, L. I.	68	6	1	43
Richards, H. Branson	Nr. Concord, N. C.	Feb. 5, 1873	1909	NC	Thomasville, N. C.	Mar. 7, 1938	Reading, Pa.	65	1	2	28
Reidenhour, Martin L.	Cabarrus Co., N. C.	Oct. 10, 1880	1913	NC	Greenville, Pa.	May 10, 1937	Nr. Concord, N. C.	50	7	0	24
Ritchie, Grover O.	Prospect, Pa.	Feb. 12, 1886	1878	Pg	Minneapolis, Minn.	Feb. 8, 1937	Barrus Co., N. C.	84	9	26	51
Roth, Theophilus B., D.D.	Cogan Station, Pa.	Feb. 9, 1853	1880	Nw	Philadelphia, Pa.	Nov. 10, 1937	Greenville, Pa.	87	6	7	44
Sander, John, L.H.D.	Uebigen, Germany	Nov. 3, 1850	1890	PM	Baldwin, N. Y.	Nov. 10, 1937	St. Peter, Minn.	67	0	28	46
Schmidt, Richard O., D.D.	Flushing, N. Y.	Jan. 10, 1870	1918	NY	Pearl City, Ill.	Sept. 12, 1937	Washington, D. C.	42	11	22	19
Schrothenner, John W., Ph.D.	Nr. St. Mary's, O.	Sept. 20, 1894	1922	Il	Pasadena, Calif.	July 4, 1937	New Ringgold, Pa.	45	0	7	15
Schroer, Frank H.	Hagerstown, Md.	June 27, 1892	1897	Cf	Springfield, Ill.	Feb. 8, 1937	Kent, Ill.	68	9	28	37
Schueler, Edward P., D.D.	Wiedersdorf, Germany	Apr. 11, 1868	1880	Wg	Elkhart, Ind.	Nov. 8, 1937	Glendale, Calif.	83	6	0	57
Schulzke, William, D.D.	Chemnitz, Germany	May 8, 1854	1898	Id	Springfield, O.	Nov. 9, 1938	Springfield, Ill.	64	0	16	40
Schutes, George F., LL.D.	Loogootee, Ill.	Jan. 23, 1874	1878	O	Homestead, Pa.	Apr. 29, 1938	Elkhart, Ind.	85	0	1	37
Schwarm, Samuel, D.D., Ph.D.	Hynemansville, Pa.	Apr. 28, 1853	1902	Pg	Somerset, Pa.	Dec. 20, 1937	Springfield, O.	60	1	17	35
Seiberling, William J., D.D.	Sipesville, Pa.	Nov. 3, 1877	1893	Pg	Tybee, Ga.	Mar. 4, 1938	Seiberlingsville, Pa.	75	10	3	16
Shaulis, Samuel A.	Nr. Leesville, S. C.	May 31, 1862	1897	GA		July 10, 1936	Bakersville, Pa.	74	10	4	39
Shealy, Tillman W., D.D.		Sept. 6, 1861					Nr. Springfield, Ga.				

Name	Born (Where)	Born (When)	Ordained	Synod at Death	Died (Where)	Died (When)	Where Buried	Age Y.	M.	D.	Years of Service
Shriver, Pearl J.	Greenmount, Pa.	Sept. 30, 1875	1901	EP	Clayton, N. J.	Dec. 28, 1936	Philadelphia, Pa.	61	2	28	17
Snyder, Clarence M.	Sellersville, Pa.	Mar. 1, 1888	1915	PM	Norristown, Pa.	Oct. 4, 1937	Norristown, Pa.	49	7	3	22
Steckel, Lloyd W., D.D.	Mulberry, Ind.	Mar. 8, 1879	1904	Nw	Milwaukee, Wis.	Mar. 20, 1938	Mulberry, Ind.	59	0	12	34
Steimle, Augustus, D.D.	Brooklyn, N. Y.	July 23, 1870	1891	NY	New York, N. Y.	Sept. 30, 1937	New York, N. Y.	67	2	7	46
Sterner, Leidy B.	Oakland Co., Pa.	Oct. 31, 1877	1909	PM	Reading, Pa.	Feb. 6, 1937	Richlandtown, Pa.	60	3	8	11
Trowbridge, Charles R., D.D.	Baltimore, Md.	Nov. 1, 1859	1885	EP	Easton, Pa.	Jan. 6, 1937	Kensico, N. Y.	77	2	5	26
Turkle, Alonzo J., D.D.	Fairview, O.	Aug. 6, 1859	1886	Pg	Pittsburgh, Pa.	Oct. 14, 1937	Pittsburgh, Pa.	78	0	13	51
Voskamp, Carl J., D.D.	Antwerp, Belgium	Sept. 18, 1859	1884	CM	Tsingtao, China	Sept. 20, 1937	Tsingtao, China	78	0	2	45
Wagner, Alpheus E., D.D., Ph.D.	Washingtonville, O.		1882	Wp	York, Pa.	July 3, 1936	Hellam, Pa.	80	7	18	46
Wagner, Martin L., D.D.	Wayne Co., Ind.	June 4, 1857	1884	O	Dayton, O.	Jan. 22, 1938	Pershing, Ind.	79	7	6	53
Weaver, John H., D.D.	Elizaville, N. Y.	Oct. 25, 1857	1885	NY	Poughkeepsie, N. Y.	June 1, 1937	Elizaville, N. Y.	78	2	14	29
Weigand, Hermann A. F. L.	Halberstadt, Germany	Dec. 7, 1858	1888	Cn	Jersey City, N. J.	Feb. 22, 1937	Jersey City, N. J.	74	1	11	35
Wenrich, John M.	Reinhold's, Pa.	June 17, 1863	1891	Cf	Stoutsville, O.	Jan. 1, 1938	Stoutsville, O.	63	2	20	46
Wiemken, Henry W.	Oldenburg, Germany	May 26, 1851	1903	Pg	Oakland, Calif.	Mar. 23, 1938	Oakland, Calif.	86	7	14	23
Yeisley, Wilson	Nr. Stroudsburg, Pa.	Feb. 13, 1875	1890	PM	Greenville, Pa.	Aug. 16, 1937	Greenville, Pa.	46	10	9	36
Yiengst, Levi W.	Mt. Zion, Pa.	Jan. 8, 1872	1898	O	Scranton, Pa.	May 16, 1937	Lebanon, Pa.	66	2	21	19
Ziegler, Ben W., D.D.	West Liberty, O.	Jan. 8, 1872	1898	O	Findlay, O.	Nov. 17, 1937	Springfield, O.	88	9	22	34
Zimmerman, Jeremiah, D.D., LL.D., L.H.D.	Wheeling, W. Va. / Snydersburg, Md.	Mar. 8, 1849 / Apr. 26, 1848	1877 / 1876	RM / NY	Evans, Colo. / Syracuse, N. Y.	May 29, 1937 / Feb. 18, 1937	Evans, Colo. / Syracuse, N. Y.	88	9	22	31 / 61

LAYMEN

Name	Born (Where)	Born (When)	Synod at Death	Died (Where)	Died (When)	Where Buried	Age Y.	M.	D.
Abendroth, Harry G.	Milwaukee, Wis.	July 24, 1888	Nw	Milwaukee, Wis.	Nov. 13, 1936	Milwaukee, Wis.	48	3	28
Ackerman, Charles W.	Murphysboro, Ill.	Oct. 17, 1864	NY	Long Beach, L.I., N.Y.	May 9, 1938	New York, N. Y.	73		
Fasig, Prof. Albert C. H.	Reading, Pa.	Sept. 18, 1913	WP	Gettysburg, Pa.	Mar. 3, 1938	Gettysburg, Pa.	24	4	16
Barkley, Daniel L.	Newberry Co., S. C.	Sept. 1, 1887	PM	Allentown, Pa.	Jan. 20, 1938	Reading, Pa.	50	4	4
Kohn, Arthur H.	Cherryville, N. C.	Apr. 6, 1864	SC	Columbia, S. C.	Feb. 6, 1937	Columbia, S. C.	73	5	7
Mauney, Jacob S.	Mt. Pleasant, N. C.	Feb. 18, 1846	NC	Kings Mountain, N. C.	Nov. 13, 1936	Kings Mountain, N. C.	90	7	0
McAllister, Col. George F., M.A., P.D.	Double Pipe Creek, Md.	Sept. 25, 1874	NC	Mt. Pleasant, N. C.	Oct. 18, 1937	Mt. Pleasant, N. C.	63	11	0
Miller, Harvey C.	Mt. Morris, Ill.	July 29, 1862	EP	Philadelphia, Pa.	July 24, 1936	Philadelphia, Pa.	73	11	25
Miller, Walter B.	Mt. Morris, Ill.	Sept. 25, 1861	Al	Altoona, Pa.	July 23, 1937	Shrewsbury, Pa.	75	9	28
Moller, Mathias P.	Bornholm, Denmark	Sept. 29, 1854	Md	Hagerstown, Md.	Apr. 13, 1937	Hagerstown, Md.	82	6	14
Neff, George E., Esq.	York, Pa.	Aug. 12, 1860	WP	York, Pa.	Aug. 16, 1937	York, Pa.	77	0	4
Runyon, Ide S.	Long Valley, N. J.	Jan. 21, 1869	NY	New York, N. Y.	Aug. 3, 1937	Budd Lake, N. J.	68	6	12
Sandt, Benjamin F.	Stockertown, Pa.	May 9, 1861	PM	Easton, Pa.	June 30, 1937	Easton, Pa.	76	1	21
Schatz, Ralph H., Esq.	Spring Valley, Pa.	June 13, 1887	PM	Allentown, Pa.	Feb. 12, 1937	Allentown, Pa.	49	7	29
Schlobohm, Frederick H.	Minneapolis, Minn.	May 30, 1878	NY	Jamaica, N. Y.	Mar. 30, 1936	Baldwin, N. Y.	48	10	0
Sende, Jonas A.	Brooklyn, N. Y.	Nov. 18, 1887	Cf	Altadena, Calif.	June 15, 1936	Los Angeles, Calif.	48	6	27
Van Gilluwe, F. Louis	New York, N. Y.	Jan. 27, 1849	NY	Asbury Park, N. J.	Mar. 10, 1937	Long Beach, N. J.	88	1	13
Wefer, Frederick H.	New York, N. Y.	Aug. 30, 1868	NY	New York, N. Y.	Aug. 6, 1936	Westchester, N. Y.	67	11	6

LAYWOMEN

Name	Born (Where)	Born (When)	Synod at Death	Died (Where)	Died (When)	Where Buried	Age Y.	M.	D.
Berkemeier, Susette	Gumuenden, Germany	Sept. 18, 1856	NY	Narrowsburg, N. Y.	July 3, 1937	New York, N. Y.	80	9	15
Einspruch, Jacoba G.	Chicago, Ill.	Feb. 3, 1896	Md	Baltimore, Md.	Jan. 10, 1937	Baltimore, Md.	40	11	7

Name	Born		Ordained	Synod at Death	Died		Where Buried	Age			Years of Service
	Where	When			Where	When		Y.	M.	D.	
Curran, Sarah S.	Ft. Washington, Pa.	Apr. 2, 1887		Afr	Liberia, Africa.	Aug. 9, 1937	Zorzor, Liberia, Africa.	50	4	7	
Gesler, Anna, M.D.	Southwest, Pa.	Mar. 29, 1896		Ind	Guntur, India.	Mar. 13, 1937	Guntur, India.	41	11	14	
Jacobs, Laura H.	Baltimore, Md.	Nov. 21, 1852		PM	Ithaca, N. Y.	Nov. 9, 1936	Gettysburg, Pa.	83	11	18	
Kreps, Nannie B.	Fincastle, Va.	Sept. 27, 1861		SC	Columbia, S. C.	Aug. 13, 1936	Columbia, S. C.	74	10	16	
Kunzmann, Anna C.	Greenville, Pa.	May 16, 1856		Pf	Seattle, Wash.	Mar. 16, 1937	Seattle, Wash.	80	10	0	
DEACONESSES											
Eich, Sister Veronica.	Germany.	Sept. 6, 1857	1891	PM	Philadelphia, Pa.	Aug. 23, 1937	Philadelphia, Pa.	79	11	17	
Haltiwanger, Sister Juliet M.	Columbia, S. C.	Apr. 7, 1870	1910	Md	Baltimore, Md.	June 15, 1937	Columbia, S. C.	67	2	8	
Heinzmann, Sister Anna.	New Britain, Conn.	Feb. 22, 1899	1922	NY	Grand Canyon, Ariz.	May 12, 1937	Philadelphia, Pa.	38	2	20	
Jaborg, Sister Christine.	Bremenhaven, Germany.	Sept. 28, 1882	1919	Md	Baltimore, Md.	Jan. 17, 1938	Stapleton, Staten Isl.	55	3	19	

Faithfully submitted,

JAMES F. LAMBERT, Necrologist

The Rev. G. F. R. Tamke, Chairman of the Nominating Committee, presented nominations as follows:

For the *Executive Board:*

Term expiring 1942. Rev. Henry H. Bagger; Rev. Alvin E. Bell; Rev. P. D. Brown; Rev. John L. Deaton; Rev. Paul H. Krauss; Rev. J. J. Scherer, Jr.; Rev. Ezra E. Stauffer; Rev. Armin G. Weng; Rev. E. Clyde Xander; Bismarck Capps; John Greiner, Jr.; George Hemsing; J. K. Jensen; James C. Kinard; Claude T. Reno; Charles Gottschalk; Lawrence F. Speckman; C. C. Zirjacks.

The President called for nominations from the floor and declared the nominations closed.

For the *Commission of Adjudication:*

Term expiring 1944. Rev. P. W. H. Frederick; Rev. B. H. Pershing; Rev. G. Keller Rubrecht; Rev. Homer E. Turney; Rev. John C. Mattes; Rev. Charles J. Smith; F. W. Cappelmann; F. H. Horlbeck; John F. Reinhardt.
Term expiring 1940. Rev. Paul J. Hoh; Rev. Charles W. Leitzell; Rev. Samuel Trexler.

The President called for nominations from the floor and declared the nominations closed.

For the *Committee on Church Papers:*

Term expiring 1944. Rev. Ralph D. Heim; Rev. Hermann F. Miller; Rev. Elwood S. Falkenstein; Rev. John W. Horine; Rev. T. Benton Peery; Rev. William F. Sunday; E. E. Croll; E. F. Eilert; Clarence C. Stoughton.

The President called for nominations from the floor and declared the nominations closed.

The Rev. A. H. Keck, Chairman of the Nominating Committee, presented the following nominations for the *Executive Committee of the Laymen's Movement:*

Term expiring 1940. H. J. Albrecht; Henry Beisler; J. L. Clark; P. A. Elsesser; E. S. Gerberich; P. H. Glatfelter; Peter P. Hagan; W. H. Hager; Thomas P. Hickman; Harry Hodges; E. G. Hoover; J. K. Jensen; Henry May; E. Clarence Miller; E. Harry Schirmer; I. A. Shaffer, Jr.; B. B. Slifer; Charles Steele; S. Frederick Telleen; Charles B. Zimmerman; Charles E. Esser; Frederick Henrich; John A. Hoober; Nels Jensen; Edward E. Long; I. T. Mellinger; M. P. Möller, Jr.; Peter G. Schafer; Henry H. Wiegand; H. T. Wentz.

The President called for nominations from the floor and declared the nominations closed.

Item IV, A, 1, Amendments to By-laws, from the report of the Executive Board, was considered, having been presented regularly at yesterday's session, and all amendments were adopted. (For other references, see pp. 78, 108.)

The Rev. S. W. Herman, President, presented the report of the Board of Foreign Missions, making special reference to the late Executive Secretary, Dr. Paul W. Koller. He requested that the Convention precede its consideration of the report by special prayer. The prayer was led by Dr. Herman.

REPORT OF THE BOARD OF FOREIGN MISSIONS

(For action on the recommendations in this report, see p. 168.)

Our Harvest Fields Abroad

"They joy before thee according to the joy in harvest." Isaiah 9, 3.

Our foreign mission fields are harvest fields. Our joy as the Board of Foreign Missions is the joy of harvest time. Souls are being won for Christ, and His Church is being extended by the consecrated work of our foreign missionaries, national ordained pastors and workers. Not only has the number of baptized Christians increased in all our fields abroad since we last reported to the United Lutheran Church, but the indigenous churches have grown in their Christian faith and in their consciousness of responsibility as living active forces for the further and fuller Christianization of their respective areas and countries. This is as it should be. The churches in the mission fields in the very nature of the case must become increasingly missionary in their life and activity. Our organized churches in India and Japan, represented at this Convention by appointed delegates, are growing stronger and more vigorous. Similar church organization in our other fields is our hope and expectation.

The unfinished task of Foreign Missions calls for more and not less foreign mission effort on the part of the parent church. Professor Dr. H. Kraemer in his recent book, "The Christian Message in a Non-Christian World," written to serve as material for the World Missionary Conference in Madras, India, December 10 to 30, 1938, writes:

"The Christian Church is not at the end of its missionary enterprise in the non-Chrisitan world, but just at its beginning. The independence and autonomy of the daughter churches in the non-Christian world does not mean a gradual withdrawal of the missionary activity of the parent churches. On the contrary, the fact that the Christian Church actually has become a world-wide community, the responsibility this involves, and the solidarity in faith and love and hope in which the older and younger churches have been thereby bound together, point to the obligation of renewed missionary consecration and activity."

Our Twentieth Anniversary Joy

Our joy is the joy of harvest in all our foreign fields also on account of the splendid progress made during the past twenty years. At the time of the merger in 1918 the United Lutheran Church had four foreign fields: India, Liberia, Japan and British Guiana. Argentina was added immediately after the merger, and China in 1925, so that we now have six fields abroad.

At the close of the first biennium in 1920, the number of baptized Christians in all fields was 98,284. Now it is 193,000. The largest increase has been in India, where there were 91,764 in 1920, and now the established Andhra Evangelical Lutheran Church has 181,378.

Other evidences of progress will appear in the rest of our report under the heads of the six fields and of the Home Base.

We have still another reason to begin our report with a note of exultant joy. The debt of the Board is gone. At the time of the merger in 1918 the three merging Boards of Foreign Missions were in debt to the amount of $29,453; and the Board never was out of debt until this year. Now we may look forward to another period of missionary advance all along the line at home and abroad; but the Board will go ahead wisely and carefully because it is determined never again to have expenditures exceed income.

Board Members

Someone said that the membership of our Board is exceptionally high in consecration and ability. We wish to confirm this statement. We are thinking not of a comparison with other Boards of our Church, which would not be gracious, but of the faithful attendance of our Board members, of their keen interest in the business of the Board and of their wisdom and courage in facing the problems which constantly test our faith and judgment. We rejoice over the merited recognition of two of our members, Mr. M. P. Moller, Jr., who was elected treasurer of the Foreign Missions Conference of North America, and Mr. S. Frederick Telleen, treasurer of the International Missionary Council.

We wish to record our appreciation of the services of Rev. Stewart W. Herman, D.D., who has been president of our Board since 1930 and a member since 1926; Rev. Samuel T. Nicholas, D.D., a member since 1928; and Mr. Charles H. Dahmer, a member since 1926. These three men are ineligible for re-election. New members elected by the Executive Board ad interim since the last biennial convention of the United Lutheran

Church are: Rev. Fred J. Fiedler to succeed Rev. C. M. Snyder, deceased; Rev. Edgar E. Snyder, D.D., to succeed Rev. H. C. Brillhart, D.D., resigned; Mr. Warren M. Koons of Philadelphia to succeed Mr. Ralph H. Schatz, deceased; and Mr. Isaac C. Bucher of Gettysburg, Pa., to succeed Mr. Frank Howard, resigned. At the close of our report we present as usual a list of all officers and members and make our required nominations.

Deaths

A number of missionaries have died in our service and will be remembered under the head of the foreign fields in which they served.

The Board of Foreign Missions lost a faithful and valuable member when Rev. Clarence M. Snyder died on October 4, 1937. He had served since 1930. Mr. Ralph H. Schatz of Allentown, Penna., who had been a member of the Board from 1936 to the time of his death, was called to his eternal home on February 12, 1937.

Rev. Augustus Steimle, D.D., who died on September 30, 1937, ceased to be a member of the Board of Foreign Missions in 1928, having served since 1916. For twelve years he devoted his many talents and much time and energy without reservation to the cause of foreign missions.

Mr. Mathias Peter Moller, of Hagerstown, Md., was not a member of the Board when he died on April 13, 1937, in his eighty-second year, but he had served with so much interest and consecration both as a member of the Board of Foreign Missions of the General Synod from 1913 to the time of the merger in 1918, and then as a member of the Board of Foreign Missions of the United Lutheran Church until 1928, that we wish to honor his memory in this report.

We wish to record also our appreciation of the services of Rev. Reinhold C. G. Bielinski, who died on May 25, 1937. He was first elected a member of the Board of Foreign Missions of the General Council in 1901 and served continuously for nearly thirty years until 1930. For twenty-five years he was editor of Der Missionsbote, through which, as well as through German pamphlets and articles, he exerted a wide influence for the cause of foreign missions.

On November 11, 1937, God took from us our Executive Secretary, Rev. Paul W. Koller, D.D. After he had served as a member of the Board from 1922 to 1928, he was elected Executive Secretary, took charge of this office in December, 1928, and served nearly nine years with zeal and fidelity throughout a difficult period of depression and indebtedness, the cancellation of which is due to his untiring efforts in conjunction with those of our treasurer, Mr. George R. Weitzel, the Board's efficient finance committee, and a special effort under the direction of General Secretary Dr. M. Edwin Thomas.

Staff Reorganization

After the death of Dr. Koller the Board decided to continue the administration of the work under the direction of Rev. Dr. George Drach and Rev. Dr. M. Edwin Thomas as General Secretaries, and Mr. George R. Weitzel as treasurer, with assigned duties for each member of this staff, which functions as a Council of Secretaries, with Dr. Drach as chairman, through which the Board's business is passed to its regular tri-monthly meetings.

The Board has decided to call a third General Secretary and a special committee has been elected to define his duties, fix his salary and make nominations to the Board. The Board believes it to be essential for this third general secretary first of all to become acquainted with our work of Foreign Missions both in the fields abroad and at the home base, in order that he may enter into his larger work as a recognized leader in the future enterprise of definite and planned advance in Foreign Missions.

Auxiliary Societies and Cooperating Synods

We rejoice over the continued and happy cooperation of the Women's Missionary Society, which supports all women missionaries and their work in our foreign fields.

An agreement with this Society, adopted by the Board of Foreign Missions and the Executive Board of the society, clarifies and fixes more definitely their relations in regard to actions taken by either which concern women's work, in regard to correspondence with the foreign fields, women missionaries on furlough and candidates. Miss Nona M. Diehl, the Executive Secretary of the Women's Missionary Society, has shown a fine spirit of willingness to make the new relations as pleasant and efficient as possible.

We look forward with joyful anticipation to the next missionary objective of the Luther League of America, which we hope will be for some urgent need for buildings in one of our foreign fields, probably India or Africa, to supplement the gift for Andhra Christian College in India, the Educational Building in Buenos Aires, Argentina, the Tokyo Theological Seminary main building and the Tai Tung Chen church, parish house and dispensary in Tsingtao, China, the erection of which unfortunately has been postponed on account of the war in China.

The continued co-operation of the Augustana Synod in our India mission and of the United Danish Church and the Icelandic Synod in Japan, adds another note of joy to our report. The relationship of these co-operating synods to the Board of Foreign Missions has been carefully studied and an amendment to the Board's Constitution, Article III, Membership, Section 3, has been prepared, which will be presented by the Executive Board for adoption at this convention, after which the details of the new arrangement can be worked out.

Foreign Missions Conferences

There are two annual conferences of representatives of Foreign Mission Boards to which we send delegates. One is the Lutheran Foreign Missions Conference of representatives of all Lutheran Boards in America. At its last convention in Chicago, an amendment was adopted giving the Women's Missionary Societies one delegate each. General Secretary George Drach is Vice-President of this conference.

Another annual Conference is the Foreign Missions Conference of North America, composed of representatives of all Protestant Foreign Mission Boards and Societies in the United States and Canada. Mr. M. P. Moller, Jr., and Miss A. Barbara Wiegand are members of its executive committee, which is called the Committee of Reference and Counsel. We rejoice in the selection by this committee of Rev. Prof. Dr. A. R. Wentz of Gettysburg Theological Seminary as a delegate at the Madras convention of the World Missionary Conference in December, 1938. The Board of Foreign Missions has appointed him its special representative to our missions in Japan, China and India, which he will visit on his way to Madras. Mrs. Wentz will accompany her husband, and Mrs. O. A. Sardeson, of Chicago, has been selected to be one of a delegation of fifteen women from America to attend the Madras convention. The Women's Missionary Society has appointed her to be its special representative when she visits our own mission fields. She will be accompanied by her husband.

Foreign Mission Time

Although the whole year round is foreign mission time, our church has set aside the Epiphany season for the more intense and direct cultivation of the foreign missionary interest and activity of our congregations and Sunday schools. The offerings in the schools this year were devoted to the emergency relief, needs and opportunities in China. The report of the treasurer shows the amount received for this purpose and sent to our China mission.

The literature used this year for free distribution during foreign mission time included a leaflet on "Foreign Mission Time," a folder, "Why Foreign Missions?", a brief Sunday school service, an attractive poster, a congregational bulletin and offering envelopes. All pastors and a selected list of laymen and women received by mail a copy of the 1936 Annual Report of our Foreign Missions.

We plead for a more extensive use of this season. Every Sunday school should have at least a foreign mission service on some Sunday in January. The children of the church need to be educated in their privilege and responsibility as servants of the Lord Jesus Christ who has commanded all of his followers, young and old, to make disciples of all nations.

During Foreign Mission Time in January, 1939, the Board will give all Sunday schools an opportunity to take special offerings for some outstanding need in one of our foreign fields and will prepare and distribute the Foreign Mission Time literature as usual.

TREASURER'S STATEMENT

The Board of Foreign Missions is thankful to report that it has not only balanced the budget in this biennium, but that the deficit which was $107,637.75 at the last Convention, of the United Lutheran Church, is eliminated.

Deficit: For ten years we have kept working away at it, and now our ambitions are realized. When one stops to think that it is the first time in the history of this Board that it had no deficit, because at the time of the merger a deficit was established, you can readily see why the Board is thankful.

Yes, this Board was incorporated with a deficit which gradually grew until it reached a peak of $443,119.81. While this was the book deficit, it was not the *true* deficit, because one month's outstanding drafts and other open liabilities were not recorded to an amount of approximately $50,000, so the Board has in addition to eliminating this deficit from the records, also brought its books up-to-date so that the statement as submitted to this Convention dated June 30, 1938, includes all unpaid drafts to that date.

The question is frequently asked how this was accomplished. This was accomplished by making appeals to the Church in the Epiphany Season, which amounted to $253,452.74, a special cleanup drive was conducted by the Board's Department of Special Gifts in the last calendar year amounting to $19,427.01, and the balance by careful budgeting and watching of expenditures by the Board.

The Board is indeed thankful that during these depression years it has been able successfully to place the Board in this financial condition, and wishes to further report to the Convention that it has been gradually stepping up the field budgets in accord with the gradual increase in receipts. The following figures illustrate—

Budget—1934-35	$336,139.00
1935-36	341,887.00
1936-37	352,410.00
1937-38	374,730.00

The policy of the Board is determined by the support of the Church. If contributions increase the budget goes up, if they decrease the budget must be cut. The Board hopes by this policy to never come to the Church again with a deficit.

Apportionment represents 75 per cent of our General Fund Income. This has been on the up-grade for the past four years. Continue this gradual raise and the Board can answer appeals from our foreign fields, which come in regularly for new missionaries, new stations, native workers and other needs.

The Board also wishes to report the completion of the payment for the China Mission. This was purchased at a price of $185,000, and with the exception of $35,000 from the Women's Missionary Society, was paid from Land and Building Fund, which income comes from undesignated legacies. The Board has been fortunate in not only being able to pay this, but also grant and pay for land and buildings to other fields from this fund.

The Board really is happy to present these Financial Statements of 1936-38 to the Convention, and report that the Board has a credit balance of $4,607.48.

Home Base

According to the By-Laws of the Board "the Home Base Department shall have charge of the effective cultivation of the Home Church through education, financial appeals, and deputation work by foreign missionaries. It shall have charge of all missionaries on furlough." Recently an agreement was reached by the Board with the Executive Board of the Women's Missionary Society wherein the latter for the present should have direction of the use of the furloughs of women missionaries in regard to study, deputation work and rest. Reference will be made briefly to the various activities of this department.

Education of the Home Church

This has been attempted through the Synodical Foreign Mission committees, distribution of literature, deputation work of missionaries and visitation of churches by secretaries.

The Foreign Mission Committees of Synods have given fine co-operation particularly during the Epiphany Seasons. They have been unusually helpful in the preparation and dispatch of letters to local pastors drawing attention to the season's appeal, the Board's needs, and available literature. Chairmen of two Synodical Foreign Mission Committees prepare monthly letters, copies of which are sent to every pastor of their respective synods. These letters are being accorded a very fine reception. Recently another foreign mission committee obtained permission from its Synod to send out such a letter to the pastors of the Synod. An amount was appropriated by this Synod for expense of printing and postage. It is hoped that this practice will be adopted by other committees with the approval of their respective synods.

The deputation work of missionaries deserves special mention. Congregations and particularly pastors recognize the value of having missionaries visit and address their people on foreign missions. This is particularly true during the Epiphany Seasons. During January, 1938, every missionary on furlough was extremely busy filling engagements. Foreign Mission Committees as a rule arranged the itineraries. So many were the calls and so few the number of available missionaries that all engagements could not be met in spite of the very helpful assistance of the women missionaries, with the permission of the Executive Secretary of the Women's Missionary Society. The call for speakers does not end with the Epiphany Season. Our missionaries are in great demand throughout most of the year. The Home Base department in general directs these itineraries.

A word should be said about caring for the health of missionaries. Shortly after arrival each missionary on furlough is given a thorough physical examination at some recognized clinic. These medical reports are submitted to the Board's advisory physicians. Their recommendations are required to be followed by the missionaries. A re-examination has recently been ordered by the Board for each missionary just prior to return to the field. These precautionary measures in many cases prolong the service of a missionary.

The Home Base Department is greatly interested in the projected trip of Rev. Prof. Dr. A. R. Wentz to Japan, China and India this coming fall and winter, culminating in the decennial meeting of the International Missionary Council at Madras, India, to which Dr. Wentz is a delegate. It is hoped that there will be many requests for his service as a speaker after his return early in 1939.

The Home Base Department is also greatly interested in the Post Madras meeting which will be held in thirty or thirty-five centers throughout the United States and Canada. These meetings are being set up by the Foreign Missions Conference of North America for February and March, 1939. Representatives, six in number from the younger churches, will be brought to America. They are to interpret conditions in their own countries in the light of the Madras Conference. One of the outstanding leaders in India, Dr. Rajah Manikam, will be a member of the delegation. The Board of Foreign Missions and the Women's Missionary Society are co-operating in underwriting the expenses of these meetings.

The Home Base Department now conducts the official correspondence with the Executive Board of the Women's Missionary Society.

Candidates

Up until April, 1937, this department had very little work for six or eight years. New missionaries could be sent only as replacements due to the financial condition of both church and state. At the April, 1937, Board meeting it was voted to call, appoint and commission one new or replacement missionary for each of the six fields. The following men were sent during the past two years.

Rev. Herman Hammer, Argentina, South America.

Rev. W. Theodore Benze, India.

Rev. Dr. Paul O. Machetzki, British Guiana, South America.

Rev. Louis T. Bowers, Africa.

Rev. J. Christian Port, Argentina, South America.

Rev. Howard A. Alsdorf, Japan.

At the January, 1938, Board meeting Rev. Mr. Bowers was transferred from China to Africa due to a refusal of the United States Government to issue passports to new missionaries because of war conditions in China. At the April, 1938, Board meeting Rev. George R. Flora was called to serve in Liberia, Africa.

It is gratifying to record the receipt of numerous applications from young men in our theological seminaries. One young man, a junior in a seminary, made a special trip to the office of the Board to inquire when he should submit his application to be sent as a missionary to Africa. With the manifestation of such a missionary spirit the Church need not fear a lack of candidate material. The problem is not men but money.

During the biennium the Board called and commissioned the following women missionaries, upon recommendation of the Executive Board of the Women's Missionary Society:

Miss Myrtle A. Onsrud, India

Miss Virginia Aderholt, Japan

Miss Selma M. Bergner, Japan

Mrs. J. W. Miller, Liberia

Miss Elsie Otto, Liberia

Mrs. J. W. Miller (nee Miriam Treon) had served as a missionary in Liberia prior to her marriage in 1926 to Mr. J. W. Miller. After his death she reapplied and was returned to this mission field.

Miss Elsie Otto was reappointed to Liberia after spending five years in America.

Special Gifts

In spite of financial depressions the loyalty of supporters of Specials has remained unabated. The reasons for this are not only that the patrons' contributions supplement the apportionment, but also that contact with the mission field through letters stimulates missionary interest and enthusiasm.

Forty congregations, organizations or individuals are now supporting men missionaries as against thirty-seven at the end of the last biennium. The amount contributed for their support for the fiscal year 1937-38 is included in the Treasurer's Report.

Parishes Abroad

At the close of the last biennium 195 patrons were supporting parishes abroad. At the end of this biennium there are 212 supporters or a net increase of 17. There have been quite a number of cancellations due chiefly to shortage of funds or a desire on the part of churches to first meet their apportionment. It is encouraging to observe that there were others who came forward to take the responsibility of "carrying on." The missionaries in all fields have as a general rule been most diligent in supplying patrons with up-to-date information of their parishes.

Proteges

The number of proteges, both workers and students has decreased during the biennium from 324 to 309. There was a time when twice as many students were supported. Chairmen of several Synodical Foreign Mission Committees are co-operating with the Board in distributing appropriate literature to Sunday schools and other organizations.

CONGREGATIONS AND INDIVIDUALS SUPPORTING MISSIONARIES

Supporters	Pastors	Missionary	Field
Allentown, Pa. Christ's	G. H. Kinard	H. H. Moyer	India
Ashland, O. Trinity	A. H. Smith	J. M. Armbruster	Argentina
Baltimore, Md. 2d English		L. W. Slifer	India
Baltimore, Md. St. Mark's	R. D. Clare	I. Cannaday	India
Baltimore, Md. St. Paul's	J. B. Rupley	J. Jensen, M.D.	Africa
Boyerstown, Pa. St. John's	D. F. Longacre	C. H. Swavely	India
Brooklyn, N. Y. Redeemer	H. T. Weiskotten	A. Neudoerffer	India
Buffalo, N. Y. Holy Trinity	H. J. Pflum	E. Neudoerffer	India
Charleston, S. C.			
St. Andrew's	C. K. Derrick	C. K. Lippard	Japan
Dayton, Ohio. First	D. H. Johnson	V. McCauley	India
Fort Wayne, Ind. Trinity	P. H. Krauss	L. A. Gotwald	India
Gettysburg, Pa. St. James	S. W. Aungst	L. T. Bowers	Africa
Greensburg, Pa. Zion	J. P. Harman	A. Schmitthenner	India
Greensburg, Pa. First	C. W. Shindler	G. K. Gesler	India
Hanover, Pa. St. Matthew's	H. H. Beidleman	J. C. Perry, Jr.	India
Harrisburg, Pa. Christ's	J. E. Rudisill	J. C. Port	Argentina
Harrisburg, Pa. Memorial	L. C. Manges	G. Schillinger	Japan
Harrisburg, Pa. Zion	S. W. Herman	J. K. Linn	Japan
Harrisburg, Pa. Zion	S. W. Herman	L. G. Cooper	China
Harrisburg, Pa. Zion	S. W. Herman	R. Dunkelberger	India
Hummelstown, Pa. Zion	C. G. Leatherman	F. L. Coleman	India
Johnstown, Pa. First	G. W. Nicely	A. J. Stirewalt	Japan
Lititz, Pa. St. Paul's	E. P. Truchses	G. G. Parker	Africa
Mansfield, O. First	G. E. Swoyer	J. C. Finefrock	India
Perkasie, Pa. Hilltown	A. T. Smith	C. Reinbrecht	China
Philadelphia, Pa. Nativity	J. C. Fisher	H. H. Sipes	India
Phila., Pa. Tabernacle	W. J. Miller	M. L. Dolbeer	India
Philadelphia, Pa. Temple	W. G. Boomhower	J. K. Donat	Africa
Reading, Pa. Trinity	H. F. Miller	E. T. Horn	Japan
Rochester, Pa. Grace	H. R. Shepfer	E. G. Wood	India
Rockford, Ill. Trinity	H. M. Bannen	C. W. Hepner	Japan
Shelby, Ohio, First	D. B. Young	P. P. Anspach	China
Shippensburg, Pa.			
Memorial	W. W. Barkley	J. R. Strock	India
Stromsburg, Neb.	Mary and		
	Alfred Augustine	Theo. Scholz	China
Toledo, O. Glenwood	A. E. Bell	V. E. Zigler	India
Washington, D. C.			
Keller Mem.	J. H. Mumper	S. C. Burger	India

Wilmington, Del.
    Holy Trinity ....J. F. Kelly ....J. E. Graefe ....India
    Winchester, Va. Grace ....C. W. Lowe ....L. S. G. Miller ....Japan
    York, Pa. St. Matthew's......J. B. Baker ....H. Heilman ....Africa
    York, Pa. Zion ....W. R. Sammel ....J. R. Fink ....India

CONGREGATIONS SUPPORTING MISSIONARIES UNDER THE WOMEN'S MISSIONARY SOCIETY

Williamsport, Pa., Messiah ....Marie Jensen .... Africa
Milwaukee, Wis., Epiphany ....Lydia Reich .... China
Carlisle, Pa., St. Paul's ....Clara Leaman .... India
Milwaukee, Wis., Redeemer ....Myrtle Onsrud .... India
Souderton, Pa., Emmanuel ....Hilda Kaercher .... India
Omaha, Neb., Kountze Mem. ....Mette Blair .... India
Brooklyn, N. Y., Good Shepherd ....Alice Nickel .... India

LITERATURE

Magazines.—*The Foreign Missionary* is the official English monthly magazine of the Board of Foreign Missions. It has been published regularly for fifty-eight years and meets a real need for our foreign missionaries, our Board's promotional work and for all in our Church who want to keep in touch with all our foreign work and workers. It has a circulation of over 4,500 every month. Dr. George Drach has edited this magazine for thirty years.

Der Missionsbote, edited by Rev. Paul C. Burgdorf, Ph.D., issued monthly, serves a limited constituency of members and women's societies in German congregations. It is the joint publication of the Board of Foreign Missions and the Women's Missionary Society.

Annual Report.—Every year the Board publishes a report written by the missionaries in their respective fields. This year's report has been distributed by mail to all pastors before the biennial convention of our Church. Lay delegates to the convention may get copies either at the office of the Board at 18 East Mount Vernon Place, or in the exhibit room of the convention.

Occasional Literature.—During the past biennium the Board has published a widely used study pamphlet entitled, "In Seven Nations," which briefly describes our work in all six foreign fields and at the home base. Leaflets for free distribution, still available are: "Liberia and the Mission Path," by Dr. Paul W. Koller, "Why Foreign Missions?" by Dr. George Drach, which was used during the Epiphany season in 1938, and "Can You Answer These Questions on Our India Mission?" by Dr. M. L. Dolbeer, intended especially for distribution by India missionaries on furlough.

Motion Pictures and Stereopticon Slides.—The use of visual education in foreign missions has become quite extensive in our churches, schools and societies. The Board of Foreign Missions has sets of slides with lectures on all our fields and five very good general lectures with slides. It also has sets of 16 mm. motion picture reels on all the fields except British Guiana. Slides and reels are sent out without a rental charge but transportation must be paid both ways.

FOREIGN FIELDS
INDIA
MISSIONARIES

Name	Residence	Arrival
Rev. L. L. Uhl, D.D.	Emeritus	1873
Miss Agnes I. Schade	Emeritus	1890
Rev. J. George W. Albrecht, Ph.D.	Emeritus	1892
Miss Katherine Fahs	Emeritus	1894
Miss Mary Baer, M.D.	Emeritus	1895
Miss Anna E. Sanford	Tenali	1895
Rev. Dr. S. C. Burger	Dowlaishwaram	1898
Rev. Dr. and Mrs. V. McCauley	Repalle	1898
Rev. Dr. and Mrs. E. Neudoerffer	Furlough	1900
Miss Emilie L. Weiskotten	Rajahmundry	1900
Rev. Dr. and Mrs. I. Cannaday	Guntur	1902
Rev. Dr. and Mrs. J. Roy Strock	Guntur	1908
Miss Jessie S. Thomas	Furlough	1908
Miss Betty A. Nilsson, M.D.	Bhimawaram	1908
Rev. Dr. and Mrs. R. M. Dunkelberger	Tenali	1909
Rev. Dr. and Mrs. J. C. Finefrock	Tarlupad	1911
Rev. and Mrs. A. F. A. Neudoerffer	Bhimawaram	1912
Miss Mary S. Borthwick	Bhimawaram	1912
Miss Florence M. Welty	Emeritus	1912
Rev. Dr. and Mrs. H. H. Sipes	Guntur	1913
Miss Louise A. Miller	Samulkot	1913
Rev. Dr. and Mrs. Fred L. Coleman	Luthergiri, Rajahmundry	1914
Rev. Dr. and Mrs. J. E. Graefe	Furlough	1915
Miss Charlotte B. Hollerbach	Rajahmundry	1915
Miss Hilma Levine, R.N.	Rentichintala	1915
Miss Agnes Christenson	Rajahmundry	1915
Miss Emma K. Baer	Rentichintala	1919
Rev. Dr. and Mrs. J. R. Fink	Rentichintala	1921
Rev. and Mrs. H. H. Moyer	Furlough	1921
Rev. and Mrs. A. F. Schmitthenner	Furlough	1921
Rev. and Mrs. L. A. Gotwald	Furlough	1921
Rev. and Mrs. M. L. Dolbeer	Furlough	1921
Miss Lilith Schwab	Repalle	1921
Miss Alice J. Nickel	Narasaravupet	1921
Miss Mette K. Blair, R.N.	Rajahmundry	1921
Miss Maida S. Meissner, R.N.	Bhimawaram	1921
Miss Edna Engle	Guntur	1922
Rev. and Mrs. Leon E. L. Irschick	Tanuku	1922
Rev. and Mrs. C. H. Swavely	Furlough	1922
Miss Clara Leaman	Guntur	1923
Miss Verna Lofgren, R.N.	Rajahmundry	1923
Miss Lottie Martin, R.N.	Rentichintala	1923
Miss Ruth H. Swanson	Furlough	1924
Miss Edith Eykamp	Furlough	1924
Miss Emma Johnson	Furlough	1924
Rev. and Mrs. L. W. Slifer	Guntur	1925
Rev. and Mrs. R. L. Cunningham	Sattenapalli	1925

Name	Residence	Arrival
Rev. and Mrs. W. Theo. Benze	Peddapur	1925
Miss Arlene Beal, M.D.	Furlough	1925
Dr. and Mrs. Virgil E. Zigler	Rentichintala	1928
Miss Grace L. Moyer, M.D.	Rajahmundry	1928
Miss Mabel H. Meyer, R.N.	Chirala	1928
Miss Hilda M. Kaercher	Rajahmundry	1929
Rev. and Mrs. E. G. Wood	Chirala	1929
Miss Christie Zimmerman	Guntur	1930
Miss Jessie Mae Cronk	Rajahmundry	1930
Rev. and Mrs. J. C. Peery, Jr.	Furlough	1931
Miss Barbara De Remer, M.D.	Furlough	1932
Miss Amelia L. Brosius, R.N.	Furlough	1932
Miss Nanna Lindahl, R.N.	Guntur	1934
Miss Susan Glatz	Guntur	1935
Miss Gladys Morgan, M.D.	Guntur	1935
Rev. and Mrs. G. K. Gesler	Rajahmundry	1936
Rev. and Mrs. R. S. Oberly	Rajahmundry	1936
Miss Theodora K. Neudoerffer	Guntur	1936
Miss Myrtle A. Onsrud	Rajahmundry	1936

Ordained men in our field number twenty-six, unordained one, wives twenty-five, and single women thirty-three, a total of eighty-four. In September, 1937, Rev. and Mrs. W. Theodore Benze rejoined the staff of India missionaries after a lapse of five years. This fall a new woman missionary leaves for India, Miss Hazel E. Naugle. Rev. J. E. Graefe, Th.D., and Arlene Beal, M.D., having resigned on furlough, will not return. There are also two retired men, Dr. L. L. Uhl and Dr. George Albrecht, and four retired single women, the Misses Agnes I. Schade, Katherine Fahs, Mary Baer, M.D., and Florence Welty.

Under appointment, Rev. and Mrs. Paul Harold Gleichman.

THE APPROACHING CENTENARY

Joy fills our hearts whenever we think of our India mission with its gratifying missionary results, its large and increasing number of Christians, its penetration from the low and outcaste groups into the higher caste Sudra circles, and its established and maturing Andhra Evangelical Lutheran Church. It has appointed Rev. Ernst Neudoerffer, D.D., and Rev. Clarence E. Swavely as its delegates to this biennial convention.

But most of all we do rejoice in anticipation of the celebration of one hundred years of foreign mission work by the Lutheran Church in America. During the year 1942 when we celebrate this centenary our minds will be fixed primarily on our India field, but we must also include in our prayers and songs of missionary thanksgiving the work and achievements in our other five foreign fields. Moreover, we would like all Lutheran Church bodies and congregations to join in this celebration, for after all, it is the centenary of the beginning of the foreign mission effort of the Lutheran Church in America. Father Heyer belongs to the whole Lutheran Church in America. We would like also to have the centenary celebration issue in a permanent memorial to Father Heyer in India. We present a set of resolutions concerning the approaching centenary. (See Recommendation 1.)

CYCLONE DAMAGE AND RELIEF

We cannot of course in such a brief report as this one recount all the events and achievements of the work of our India mission. We must confine ourselves to a limited number of the outstanding features.

We think, first of all, of the terrific cyclone which swept over a part of our field in a riot of destruction on October 28, 1936. The Chirala, Guntur and Narsaravupet areas were mostly affected and when the final reports of property damage were received, the total amounted to $30,000, not including the destruction and damage of many small churches and schools. We made a special appeal for relief and reconstruction with the permission of the Executive Board of the U. L. C. A. and sent to India $14,547, including $5,000 from the Women's Missionary Society, which was not nearly enough. Fortunately the loss of life was small, but the harrowing experience of the missionaries and Christians will never be forgotten by them.

MISSION DEFICITS

We cannot overlook the fact that our India mission has been running a deficit, and that old building debts have been a grievous burden; but the heroic measures taken last year by the mission with the financial help of the Board, promise to get the mission out of debt in a few years. The budget granted by the Board for the next year has been slightly increased and provision in its budget has been made for the restoration of 50 per cent of the cut in native workers' salaries.

SICKNESS, DEATHS AND RESIGNATIONS

On the whole the health of our missionaries has been good. We now have an annual physical examination of all missionaries by the mission doctors. Several of our missionaries have suffered from protracted illness, not however due to the climate. Mrs. Anna John Gesler died after an operation in the Kugler Hospital, Guntur, on March 13, 1937.

As an additional precaution to insure good health and vigorous activity despite the tropical climate, the rules demand that every missionary shall take a vacation of six weeks at one of the hill resorts, preference being given to Kodaikanal and Kotagiri, where we have mission-owned property and bungalows.

We regret, that on account of health, Arlene Beal, M.D., felt obliged to resign, to take effect at the end of her furlough in October, 1938. She spent thirteen years as a medical missionary in India, largely at the

Kugler Hospital in Guntur. Health conditions in his family also caused the resignation of Rev. J. E. Graefe, Th.D., D.D., who spent twenty-three years as an educational missionary in India with special reference during the latter part of his service to theological education at Madras and Guntur in the Joint Lutheran Theological College.

MEDICAL WORK POLICY

Medical mission work in India is undergoing changes, which we must be prepared to meet. First of all there is the drift toward making the hospitals for women and children, general hospitals by adding men's wards with men doctors. For the time being Indian doctors are being employed but in the very near future such hospitals as the Kugler hospital in Guntur and the Rajahmundry hospital will call for American men doctors. In the second place, difficulties are being multiplied in securing recognition for American doctors, which may mean that all doctors for service in India will have to take degrees from Canadian or English medical colleges, or at least supplement their American studies and training by courses in medical schools in England or Canada.

The retirement of Dr. Mary Baer, the resignation of Dr. Arlene Beal, the protracted illness of Dr. Grace Moyer and the marriage of Dr. Gladys Morgan leave the hospital and medical work in a condition which requires immediate replacement. Dr. Virgil Zigler is the only man doctor in India. He is located at the Rentichintala Hospital. A second man doctor as well as two women doctors are needed.

The hospital equipment has been improved everywhere except at Rentichintala, which calls for more and larger buildings, and at Nidadovol, where Dr. Samuel John has continued his splendid work. The new buildings for the Bhimawaram Hospital for which funds were provided by the Women's Missionary Society of the Augustana Synod, make a fine appearance and fill a great need, but with Dr. Betty Nilsson's return to Rajahmundry no American doctor became available for Bhimawaram. Gradually better hospital buildings are being provided for the Tuberculosis Sanatorium at Visrantipuram near Rajahmundry, including an attractive Selma Anderson Memorial Chapel. This Sanatorium is under the direction of Andhra Evangelical Lutheran Church, because it is intended to be an indigenous institution in its support and conduct. The only missionary at work there is Miss Mette K. Blair.

EVANGELISTIC EFFORT

Sudra Movement.—While the work among the outcastes continues unabated, the Sudra movement is becoming both more extensive and intensive in our mission field in India. The following paragraphs are quoted from an article by Dr. Isaac Cannaday:

"In the early days in this part of the country evangelism among the Sudras was almost entirely confined to street or bazaar preaching, and in many cases when a missionary visited a village he gave his time and attention almost exclusively to the Christians and others among the untouchables; only incidentally did Sudras get a chance to hear the message. Then gradually it became the custom to hold special evangelistic services or street meetings for the Sudras in their part of the villages. Still later forms of evangelism were employed and a more active campaign was conducted. Not only street meetings but house meetings were held and house-to-house visits were made, literature was distributed, personal work was done and musical or lyrical evangelism became the vogue, with processions of singing bands of men and women through the village streets and with special 'musicals' conducted by trained men and women at convenient places. Still later what is now called a 'Sudra Camp' came to be one of the best methods of evangelism. After a suitable time and place have been arranged the missionary in charge will summon to his side such help as he can secure not only from his own field but also from other fields. All the pastors, evangelists and other Christian workers in that area will be in attendance and actively engage in the common effort, also one or more doctors with nurses with an ambulance and they will hold daily clinics. All forces are coordinated and concentrated and directed toward one end: evangelism.

Work will be done in all surrounding villages. In this way during the time of one camp many hundreds and it may be thousands will hear the gospel, some of them for the first time. A number will become seriously interested and will give in their names as inquirers to be instructed more perfectly in the Way.

"At the end of 1934 in the mission field as a whole there were 8,154 baptized Sudra Christians. In 1935 as many as 846 were baptized. At the end of 1935 there were 2,471 inquirers. More than 95 per cent of these Sudra Christians were in the Guntur district. Now a good beginning has been made in nearly every part of the field. The practical question remains: How can the Sudra converts be welded into a harmonious group with older Christians who are mostly from the untouchables?"

EDUCATIONAL INSTITUTIONS

Andhra Christian College.—At last we have at Guntur a real joint Christian college. The Church Missionary Society of England through its Telugu mission began active co-operation in July, 1937, by sending one missionary professor, Rev. A. Bagshaw, two Indian lecturers and two classes of students to Andhra Christian College at Guntur. In July, 1938, the other two classes were brought over and so Noble College, Masulipatam, became wholly u n i t e d with our Guntur College in Andhra Christian College. Others who desire to unite and have said so are the

American Baptist and the American Lutheran Missions and their Home Boards, the only hindrance at present being financial.

One result of this co-operation has been an increase in the number of Christians enrolled. There are now 156 Christian students out of a total of 554. Next year the proportion of Christians will be still larger.

From Andhra Christian College funds a site of six acres near the present campus, called the Munsiff Court Site, was purchased for $26,500 on April 30, 1937, and a dormitory building called Noble Hall is being erected at an initial cost of $17,000. Another dormitory in the church compound, called Heyer Hall, is also under construction at a similar expenditure.

For the running expenses of the college the Board is granting all the interest of the Andhra Christian College Fund from year to year. As money is withdrawn from this fund for the erection of buildings, the interest decreases, but it still amounts to about $10,000 a year. One of the urgent questions to be decided soon is how large an endowment fund should be held in reserve. The fund now amounts to $310,252.04.

One of the interesting developments is the increase of the number of girl students. In 1937 thirty-three attended and all but four were Christians. The housing of the girl students requires a dormitory for them which the mission plans to erect on the compound of the Stall High School for Girls. The Women's Missionary Society has been requested to help finance the erection of the first section of this girls' dormitory, estimated to cost $15,000.

Andhra Christian college is affiliated with the Andhra University which is located at Vizagapatam. Hindu Colleges also affiliated with this university have been established in Guntur and Bezwada. Principal Strock writes: "This competition means that our strength will gradually decrease and the decrease in enrollment means more financial problems, since in India all colleges are to a great extent dependent on the fees of the students for their support. On the other hand, it must not be overlooked that the decrease in Hindu students means a larger proportion of Christian students and consequently more preponderant Christian life and influence in the college.

THEOLOGICAL EDUCATION

Luthergiri.—The theological school which has produced the greatest number of ordained pastors in India is the Theological Seminary and Bible Training Institute at Luthergiri near Rajahmundry. The students in the theological department for the most part are high school graduates. Instruction is largely in Telugu. A class is given a continuous course of three years, graduated, and then another class is brought in for a similar course of three years. The graduates are given a year or so of probation in practical work as assistants in parishes before ordination. The total number of ordained men now is one hundred.

Sometimes, as during the year April, 1937, to April, 1938, the theological class is discontinued and a series of Refresher Courses for pastors in active service is carried out.

Another department of this school is called the Junior Bible Class. It is conducted as a two years' course in Telugu. The students in this class are of lower than high school grade and are trained for service as lay evangelists, catechists and teachers. In this department the American Lutheran Church Mission now co-operates. Ten students from this mission were entered in July, 1937, and Rev. Milton H. Schramm, a missionary of the American Lutheran Church, was made a member of the faculty. The other professors are Rev. E. Neudoerffer, D.D., Rev. Fred L. Coleman, D.D., Rev. Pantagani Paradesi, B.D., and Rev. P. B. Paul. The total number of students now in this department is eighty-five.

A third department consists of a course of Bible study for the wives of the students in both of the other departments, taught by a woman missionary or a qualified Indian Christian woman. This course is intended to help the Indian wives of workers to become more efficient co-laborers of their husbands in the villages.

Joint Theological College.—Dr. J. E. Graefe, Principal of the Theological Department of Andhra Christian College, writes as follows: "The Federation of Lutheran Churches in India has long contemplated a Joint Lutheran Theological College. The purpose, aside from joining forces to a common end, was two-fold: (1) The raising of the standard of ministerial education, and (2) the establishment of a center where special attention could be given to scholarly research. The first of these purposes was to be in a position to command the intellectual respect of the more enlightened classes and to influence leadership; and the second was aimed towards bringing about a better understanding of the essence of Christianity in the Indian cultural environment. The students of this college were to be men who had completed their academic education and had obtained their B.A. degrees. Such an entrance requirement was necessary for another consideration. Since the various Lutheran bodies work in different language areas it was necessary that the medium of instruction by the English language, and students with less than a complete college education are scarcely sufficiently proficient in the use of this language to comprehend theological literature. The religious and theological literature available in the various vernaculars of India is exceedingly limited and, on the whole, poor in quality. This is a recognized fact. It is therefore almost impossible to give anything like a thorough training in Christian thought, particularly in reference to the meaning of Christian terms in contrast with those of the pantheistic vocabulary which must necessarily be used to convey religious ideas in translations, when one is confined to the vernacular.

"Heretofore the great drawback to the establishment of a Joint Theological College has been mainly the lack of college graduates in sufficient numbers to justify its operation. However in the last decade Christian College graduates have been appearing in larger numbers. Consequently a beginning of the college was made.in 1931 in Madras, with a class of twelve members, five of which were from the Andhra Evangelical Lutheran Church and the other seven from the Leipzig, Swedish and Danish Missions and from the Tamil Evangelical Lutheran Church. This first class finished its course in April, 1934.

"Largely because of the excessive expense of conducting the Theological College with only one class as an independent institution in Madras, it was transferred in July, 1934, to Guntur, to be operated in conjunction with the Andhra Christian College. Here a class of ten members was enrolled, seven from the Andhra Evangelical Lutheran Church, one from the Gossner Autonomous Evangelical Lutheran Church, one from the Swedish National Lutheran Church Mission of Stockholm in Central India, and one special student from the Swedish Mission in Abyssinia. Of this class there were graduated, in March, 1937, eight members, six of which were from the Andhra Evangelical Lutheran Church. The members of the Faculty of the Andhra Christian College who participated in instructing this class were Dr. J. E. Graefe, Dr. H. H. Sipes, Dr. J. R. Strock, Dr. R. Manikam, Rev. C. H. Swavely, Mr. D. Moses and the pastor of St. Matthew's congregation, Rev. E. Prakasam.

"Since its establishment in 1931 at Madras the Joint Theological College has been affiliated with the Lutheran Theological Seminary in Gettysburg, Penna. Preliminary examinations for candidature for the B.D. degree have been conducted under the auspices of this institution, and degrees finally conferred by it.

"One of the great difficulties of operating the Joint Theological College has been the maintenance of an adequate staff. With furloughs of missionaries and resignations breaking in, and with the transference of men such as Dr. R. Manikam to other fields of work, this difficulty has, at times, become very serious. It is for this reason that the Theological College has had since July, 1937, to be temporarily held in suspension. It is expected that it will soon again begin operations."

The Federation of Lutheran Churches and Missions in India, under whose auspices the Joint Theological College at Madras and at Guntur was conducted, has reaffirmed "The need for a common permanent higher-grade theological college," and has tentatively sanctioned its location at Guntur as a temporary measure. Because we wish our Mission and Church in India to be in a position to join in this college-grade theological seminary when it is reopened in 1940 or 1942, either at Guntur or elsewhere, we present a set of resolutions for adoption at this convention of The United Lutheran Church in America. (See Recommendation 2.)

Other Developments

Other developments in the educational institutions, medical and merciful work and evangelistic efforts increase our joy over the results accomplished for our Lord Jesus Christ and His Church. The Women's Missionary Society will report more in detail concerning the missionaries and work which it supports, over which also we greatly rejoice. Our joy over the India mission surely is the joy of harvest for our Lord and His Church. We look forward to the centenary celebrations in 1942 with happy anticipation both here in the Parent Church and over there in the daughter church in India. We are proud of our daughter church in India. May she always remain beautiful and strong and active, and ever display our family likeness as she develops into her full maturity.

Statistics

The report of our India mission for the year 1937 contains the following statistics: The number of baptized members has risen to 181,378, of whom 85,817 are communicants. The increase over the previous year is 4,962. Of the 9,137 persons baptized 4,604 are from Christian families and 4,533 from non-Christian families. The villages in which there are Christians or inquirers number 2,026 and the congregations 1,820. In 1,033 mission schools there are 24,003 Christian and 4,165 non-Christian boys and girls. The number of native workers is as follows: Pastors 99, other evangelistic workers 536, school teachers 1,878, other workers 444, a grand total of 2,957.

Support received from America in 1937 amounted to $108,000 (Rs. 285,680) funds raised in India including government grants and fees from students and patients $240,000 (Rs. 632,417). The following table shows the financial trend, all figures given in rupees:

TOTAL RECEIPTS

General Work, Not Including Women's Work

Year	From America	From India	Tota.
1933	366855	457802	824657
1934	274524	434858	709382
1935	283235	422176	705411
1936	282577	571666	854243
1937	285680	632417	918097

The total received from America for General and Women's Work in 1937, including buildings, amounted to about $300,000 (Rs. 727,340).

Another interesting table shows the membership increase during the past five years.

MEMBERSHIP

At the end of	Baptized members	Gain over previous year	Per cent gain
1933	163955	2945	1.8
1934	168013	4058	2.4
1935	171812	3799	2.2
1936	176416	4604	2.6
1937	181378	4962	2.7

LIBERIA, AFRICA
MISSIONARIES

Name	Residence	Arrival
Miss Laura E. Gilliland, R.N.	Phebe Hospital, Main Station	1915
Mrs. C. E. Buschman	Zorzor	1915
Miss Bertha Koenig	Kpaiye	1916
Miss Mabel A. Dysinger	E. V. Day Girls' School, Main Station	1917
Mrs. J. W. Miller	Muhlenberg Boys' School, Main Station	1924
Rev. and Mrs. Harry H. Heilman	Furlough	1927
Jacob R. Jensen, M.D.	Zorzor	1927
Miss K. Marie Jensen, R.N.	Sanoyea	1928
Dr. and Mrs. George K. Gulck	Phebe Hospital, Main Station	1929
Rev. and Mrs. J. K. Donat	Sanoyea	1935
Rev. and Mrs. G. Gordon Parker	Zorzor	1936
Miss Elsie Otto	Main Station	1924
Rev. and Mrs. Louis T. Bowers	Sanoyea	1938
Rev. and Mrs. George R. Flora		1938

The ordained men number five, unordained men two, single women seven, wives six, a total of twenty.

Miss Hazel Biederbeck under appointment.

Depleted Staff

During the biennium this Mission has been handicapped by the very limited number of ordained men missionaries. At no time were there more than three. This number was reduced to two when Rev. Harry Heilman, the president of the Mission, left on furlough, August, 1937. Had it not been for the very faithful services of all missionaries on the field, including doctors, single women and wives the work would not be in as good condition as it now is. Reports indicate that progress has been made in each district and station. A few of the outstanding accomplishments are:

Licensure of John B. Clinton

On November 25, 1937, Mr. John Clinton was licensed by Rev. J. K. Donat under authorization of the East Pennsylvania Synod. The event received wide publicity in the mission field since this was the first service of this kind ever to be performed. Mr. Clinton is a product of the mission having graduated from Muhlenberg School and later from the Bible Training School. In addition, he was given a special course in Lutheran theology and church polity. As to character he has been a man of good report among missionaries, fellow-workers and others. Since his licensure, Rev. Mr. Clinton has been installed as pastor of Day Memorial Church, Main Station. His achievement is an incentive to other deserving men, and at the same time an inspiration to the local members as they seek to establish an indigenous church.

Growth in Church Members

One of the most encouraging features of the work in Liberia is the increase in baptisms. During 1936 there were 421 accessions and in 1937 there were 254. In these two years the total church membership increased from 1,055 to 1,730. During the same period almost 300 were confirmed and thus received into full church membership. At the end of 1937 the mission reports that there are 900 inquirers in preparation for baptism. Practically all of the increase has come from the tribal people in the hinterland. Results have amply proven the wisdom of opening and continuing work in the interior. Encouragement comes just from reading the names of villages where congregations have been newly established during the past biennium.

Progress in the Medical Department

The results of this work at the three stations have been very gratifying. At Sanoyea a dispensary has been maintained by Miss K. Marie Jensen. During 1937 she alone gave more than 16,000 treatments. At Zorzor, which is almost 200 miles from the Muhlenberg Main Station, the doctor and his assistants were kept so busy that they had little or no time for other official duties. The dispensary attendance reached its peak one day numbering 190. Surgical work grew so that it was necessary for the doctor to operate four times a week. Doctor Jensen reported that he did as much work in six months during 1937 as he did during the whole year in 1936. In addition to routine hospital work there were several smallpox epidemics when he was called upon by the Liberian Government to vaccinate thousands of people.

New Recruits

The mission rejoices in the sending of new missionaries to the field. Rev. and Mrs. Louis T. Bowers arrived on the field in June, 1938. They were under appointment for China, but transferred to Liberia in January, 1938, due to the undeclared war in China. Rev. George R. Flora and Dr. Paul J. Pauliny are under appointment. Miss Elsie Otto has returned to the field after spending five years in the homeland. She will fill a great need as treasurer and business manager. When all these new recruits reach the field our mission will be well equipped to carry forward the Church's task in Liberia.

Death of Mrs. J. D. Curran

After Dr. Curran's death eight years ago Mrs. Curran was called to serve as a commissioned missionary. During these years she labored faithfully and efficiently, serving principally the women and children at Zorzor. On August 9, 1937, she was called home. Of her it can truly be said, "Well done good and faithful servant."

Statistics

The following is a summary of the statistics of the Africa Mission for the year 1937: Missionaries in active service, 15; national pastor, one; other workers, 42; baptized members, 1,730; baptisms, 254; confirmed, 130; communicants, 514; inquirers, 900; congregations, 32; total school enrolment, 366; field contributions, $1,007.

JAPAN
MISSIONARIES

Name	Residence	Arrival
Rev. and Mrs. J. M. T. Winther	Fukuoka	1898
Rev. Dr. and Mrs. C. K. Lippard	Osaka	1900
Rev. Dr. and Mrs. A. J. Stirewalt	Tokyo	1905
Rev. Dr. and Mrs. L. S. G. Miller	Kumamoto (Kyushu Gakuin)	1907
Rev. Dr. and Mrs. E. T. Horn	Tokyo (Theol. Sem.)	1912
Rev. Dr. and Mrs. C. W. Hepner	Tokyo (Theol. Sem.)	1912
Miss Martha B. Akard	Kumamoto (Kyushu Jogakuin)	1913
Rev. and Mrs. John K. Linn	Tokyo (Theol. Sem.)	1915
Rev. and Mrs. S. O. Thorlaksson	Furlough	1916
Rev. and Mrs. D. G. M. Bach	Kumamoto	1916
Miss Maude O. Powlas	Tokyo (Bethany Home)	1919
Rev. Dr. and Mrs. G. W. Schillinger	Kumamoto (Kyushu Gakuin)	1920
Rev. and Mrs. A. C. Knudten	Nagoya	1920
Miss Marion E. Potts	Kumamoto (Kyushu Jogakuin)	1921
Miss Helen M. Shirk	Fukuoka	1922
Miss Faith Lippard	Osaka	1925
Miss Mary E. Heltibridle	Osaka	1927
Miss Maya Winther	Ogi, Saga	1927
Miss Helen H. Harder	Fukuoka	1927
Miss Virginia Aderholdt	Kumamoto (Kyushu Jogakuin)	1936
Miss Selma R. Bergner	Tokyo	1937
Rev. Howard A. Alsdorf	Tokyo	1938

There are twelve ordained men, eleven wives and eleven single women at work as our missionaries in Japan.

Nothing has happened during the past few years which has given our mission in Japan more real encouragement than the call, commissioning and sending out of a new ordained missionary in the person of Rev. Howard A. Alsdorf, who reached Japan this fall.

Despite the sending of Japanese troops to the war areas in China the work has been going on in the usual way in the hope of richer harvests to come as a result of increasing evangelistic zeal among the Christians in Japan.

A new church building was erected in East Kobe, another in Yawata, and an adequate building on a new site was provided for the Old People's Home in Tokyo.

New work among women and children has been started in Osaka, where Miss Faith Lippard and Miss Mary Heltibridle have been stationed. The result will be new Kindergartens and social service work.

Rural work has been carried on around Kumamoto on the island of Kyushu, at Koromo near Nagoya, on the island of Hondo, and a Wajiro near Fukuoka on the island of Kyushu.

The newspaper evangelism at Fukuoka is being carried on hopefully with a restricted budget.

The educational work in the theological seminary at Tokyo, in the Academy for boys at Kumamoto, called Kyushu Gakuin, in the Janice James School for girls, Kumamoto, called Kyushu Jogakuin, and in the sixteen Kindergartens, shows encouraging progress. The enrolment this year in the Kumamoto schools for boys and girls has been better than ever before.

Social service work at the Colony of Mercy, Kumamoto, called Jiaien, and in Tokyo at the Bethany Home for mothers and their children, and at the Old People's Home, makes a strong appeal to the Japanese, as an evidence of the merciful service of Christian love, and government grants are received for the conduct of all these inner mission institutions.

Japanese Students in America

The Board of Foreign Missions has a plan for foreign students in America under which two may come at a time from India and one from each of the other fields. The expenses are handled under the respective mission budget. During the past two years Rev. T. Fukuyama took a special course at the Lutheran Theological Seminary in Philadelphia followed in the fall of 1937 by Rev. Shinichi Kawagiri, who is the official delegate of the Lutheran Church in Japan to this convention. Other Japanese students are attending various schools at their own expense.

Statistics

The report of the Japan mission shows a total of 43 congregations and preaching places, of which seven are listed as self-supporting, 19 as aided and 17 as unorganized. They have a total baptized membership of 4,815, of whom 1,662 are adult communicants. The net gain in baptized membership in 1937 was 185. In the 43 Sunday schools are 288 teachers and

3,462 pupils. The contributions of the churches in 1937 amounted to about $6,500 (Yen 22,616).

The statistics for the mission institutions are as follows:

1. Theological Seminary, Tokyo, 5 professors, 14 students; Kyushu Gakuin, Kumamoto, 33 teachers, 800 students; K y u s h u Jogakuin, 25 teachers, 330 students.

2. Kindergartens 16, with 33 teachers and 640 pupils.

3. Inner Mission Institutions — For Children: The Konodai or "Get Well" Home, Tokyo, with two workers and 10 children; the Honjo Baby Nursery, Tokyo, with one worker and five children; the Jiaien Orphanage, Kumamoto, with 13 workers and 52 children.

For Children and Mothers: "Bethany Home," Tokyo, two workers and 75 inmates; Jiaien Boshi Home, Kumamoto, one worker and 14 inmates.

For Old People: Tokyo Old People's Home with one worker and 20 inmates; Jiaien Old People's Home with one worker and 32 inmates.

CHINA
MISSIONARIES

Name	Residence	Arrival
Rev. and Mrs. Theodore Scholz	Furlough	1904
Miss Freida Strecker	Kiachow	1908
Mrs. W. Matzat	Tsingtao	1922
Rev. and Mrs. P. P. Anspach	Tsingtao	1925
Miss Erva Moody	Tsingtao	1925
Miss Elvira Strunk	Furlough	1925
Miss Lydia Reich, R.N.	Tsingtao	1927
Rev. and Mrs. L. Grady Cooper, Ph.D.	Tsimo	1928
Rev. and Mrs. Charles H. Reinbrecht	Kiaochow	1928
Miss M. Clara Sullivan	Tsimo	1929
Rev. and Mrs. R. W. Sell	Furlough	1931
Miss Mae L. Rohlfs, R.N.	Peiping	1932

The missionaries in active service number five ordained men, five wives and seven unmarried women. Miss Kate Voget is living in Germany as a retired missionary.

Contributions for Relief, Needs and Opportunities in China

The Epiphany Season Foreign Mission Time appeal was for the immediate relief, needs and opportunities of our mission in China. The treasurer's report shows that up to July 1, 1938, $7,500 was sent to the China mission for this purpose and an additional $3,043 was forwarded later. Acting according to the instructions of the Board of Foreign Missions the China mission adopted the following plan for the allocation of relief funds:

1. The mission will take over the operation of porridge kitchens already established at Tai Tung Chen and Tsang Kou Church compounds,

if and when funds from Tsingtao Relief Association are no longer available.

2. Work projects, such as building of roads connecting Tsimo compounds, and other improvements where unskilled labor may be used are to be undertaken.

3. Appropriations to relief work of other Lutheran missions and the National Christian Council are to be deferred until we know more about the needs of our own field and until we have specific information from these two groups.

4. The Executive Committee will determine all appropriations and projects with the concurrence of the mission body.

5. In special individual cases requiring immediate action the missionary in concurrence with one other missionary may make appropriations up to $10.00.

Fortunately our mission field in the Shantung province with its main stations at Tsingtao, Tsimo and Kiaohsien (Kiaochow), was not in an active war zone. Japanese naval forces occupied Tsingtao in January, 1938, and since that time things have been quiet and our missionaries have been working in safety along all available lines with some curtailment in the district evangelistic and in the educational work but with considerable activity in the hospital and dispensary work at Tsingtao.

Missionaries

Rev. Luther Grady Cooper, Ph.D., and his wife were detained in India on their way to China. They spent several months in visiting our India field and sight-seeing in North India. A baby was born to them at the Kugler Hospital, Guntur, on January 17, 1938, and received the name of Kathryn Anne Cooper. When the way opened for them to leave India for China, they sailed without danger or disturbance and reached Tsingtao April 15, 1938. Mrs. W. Matzat from Germany with her two younger sons and Miss Erva Moody from America had no difficulty in returning to the field. Rev. and Mrs. Theodore Scholz and Miss Elvira Strunk left the field in July on regular furlough. Rev. and Mrs. Ralph W. Sell with their two children, despite difficulties of travel in China, were able to leave Hankow. Mrs. Sell and the children came to America in November, 1937, and Rev. Mr. Sell followed in April, 1938. The Board of Foreign Missions has included in its annual budget a new missionary this year, either a doctor or an ordained man. Rev. C. J. Voskamp, D.D., died at Tsingtao on September 20, 1937, at the ripe old age of 78 years after having served as a missionary in China for fifty-three years, since 1925 under our Board and before that under the Berlin Mission Society. He was a missionary pathfinder in China, and deserves to rank with its outstanding Christian missionary leaders. During the last eight years he lived in retirement at Tsingtao. His widow expects to return to Germany with their son next year.

Tai Tung Chen

On account of the disturbed conditions in China the Board of Foreign Missions instructed the mission to postpone all building operations. Unfortunately this order affected in particular the Luther League project at Tai Tung Chen, but we hope that in the near future the money which the Luther League of America holds for this purpose can be used for the erection of a church, parish house and dispensary building at Tai Tung Chen.

The Situation in General

A brief survey of conditions at present indicates that the work at the Lutheran Hospital in Tsingtao is somewhat increased, the enrollment at the Women's Bible Institute continues about the same, the Middle School at Tsimo, a co-educational institution, is functioning with a reduced number of students, in the evangelistic district work it has not been possible to carry on tent meetings as formerly; but everywhere the attitude of the people towards the missionaries is exceptionally friendly. The feeding of refugees and other needy Chinese at the porridge kitchens in Tsingtao and the workers' camps at Tsimo and Kiaohsien (Kiaochow) offer evangelistic opportunities, and the return of those who fled from the cities to the country has made the church attendance at the main stations almost normal again.

In expressing its gratitude to the United Lutheran Church for designating the 1938 Epiphany season appeal for relief, needs and opportunities in China, our mission declares that by this action the Mother Church greatly heartens the young Daughter Church, which is being sorely tried.

Fortieth Anniversary

On April 15, 1938, our mission in China held services to commemorate the fortieth anniversary of the founding of the mission at Tsingtao. Other services were held elsewhere and especially in connection with the Annual Assembly of missionaries, pastors and workers in August, 1938, when another Chinese was ordained by Rev. Dr. L. Grady Cooper, under the authorization of the North Carolina Synod to which he belongs. Rev. Wang Yung Sheng is the fourth Chinese evangelist to be ordained, the others being Rev. Yang Kwang En, Rev. Chang Sung San and Rev. David Hang. These men were given a theological training at the Joint Lutheran Theological Seminary at Shekow, which is located about twenty miles north of Hankow.

The Lutheran Church in China

Besides supporting the Shekow Theological Seminary, the Lutheran missions in China unite in the Lutheran Board of Publication at Hankow, of which Rev. Ralph W. Sell had temporary charge for about a year. Most of the other Lutheran missions are located within reasonable reach of Hankow in the Honan, Hopeh and Hunan provinces. In all these are eleven American and European Lutheran missions in China, including Manchukuo. Ten of them have joined to form the organized Lutheran Church in China, which held a regular meeting in Loyang in July, 1937. The president and secretary under date of February 14th, sent official greetings to the officers of the Lutheran World Convention, to the Mother Churches in America and Europe and to the Boards of Foreign Missions, which contained the following sentences:

"What the future has in store for our nation and for our beloved Lutheran Church in China is hid from our eyes. Large sections of our land have been laid waste. As a church and a nation we need to humble ourselves before God in deep contrition. It is of the Lord's mercies that we are not consumed. God grant that the terrible suffering which the Chinese people are enduring may not be borne in vain. On behalf of our people we want to thank you all for what you are doing for the suffering people of China, for supplying mission funds so that we may continue the work of the Gospel and keep our schools and hospitals going as far as possible. We cease not to give thanks for you, making mention of you in our prayers."

Statistics

Seventeen missionaries are at work in our China field, and 125 national workers. The baptized membership is 3,800, of whom 1,550 are communicants. In 1936 the mission reported 527 accessions and 450 inquirers. In Sunday schools about 1,000 are instructed and in mission schools 995. The Tsingtao Lutheran hospital and dispensary treated 714 in-patients and 3,172 out-patients. The field contributions amount to about $4,000 annually.

SOUTH AMERICA
ARGENTINE
MISSIONARIES

Name	Residence	Arrival
Rev. and Mrs. John M. Armbruster	Buenos Aires	1924
Miss Myrtle Wilke	Buenos Aires	1927
Rev. and Mrs. Herman Hammer	Eldorado	1936
Rev. and Mrs. J. Christian Port	Buenos Aires	1938

There has been comparatively little change in the work in the Mission during the past two years. The missionaries and six national pastors have been sowing the seed of the Word of God and here and there reaping the harvest. There are, however, a number of items which deserve special reference.

New Congregations

On May 13th, 1937, a congregation was organized at Villa Ballester with forty-one charter members. Later nine more persons were added bringing the total by the end of the year to fifty. Pastor Gusman has been transferred from the Church of the Redeemer, Villa del Parque, to this new congregation. This addition makes a total of six congregations in and around Buenos Aires.

Additional Buildings

The Mission is gradually assembling in one center in Villa del Parque a very fine piece of property. In addition to owning the church buildings, the manse, school building and land on which they stand, it is adding through monthly payments in lieu of rent two more adjoining properties, Massotta and Lohfeldt. The former is a large building which houses two departments of the school on the first floor and a missionary family on the second floor. The Lohfeldt property lies back of the church and is used as a boarding school for girls and the residence of the woman missionary. In addition to these properties the Mission with the aid of the Board has paid for the church building at Caseros. From July, 1938, the Mission will carry without further help from the Board the purchasing of the land in connection with the church plant at Villa Progresso. With these new acquisitions the United Lutheran Church Mission in the Argentine has property valued at about $200,000.

Misiones Territory

The Argentine Mission is divided into two distinct sections. The older portion is in and around Buenos Aires. The younger part, Misiones, is located 650 miles north of the capital city on the Parana river. Here German, Dane and Polish immigrants have settled. In the fall of 1936, Rev. and Mrs. Herman Hammer were sent by the Board to succeed Dr. Paul O. Machetzki, resigned. The w o r k in the Misiones territory is pioneer work and corresponds with work done in the United States during the period of colonization. Missionary Hammer has found the situation quite discouraging at times, particularly among some of the Germans. He says that greater loyalty has been shown by the people on the national frontier than on the Christian frontier. In many cases they have been forced to make a decision between their church and "national loyalty." For awhile the latter had been dominant but with the ban placed on meetings of the German Bund by the Argentine government the situation has improved. The work among the Danes and Poles is very encouraging.

The Mission maintains a central school in the Misiones. As far as the enrollment is concerned this is larger than it was formerly. However, the same difficulties which have been encountered with the church work among some of the Germans has affected the school. The Government recently has also forbidden the continuation of the German Bund schools. Spite of all discouragements the missionary and national pastors are remaining at their posts of duty and much good work is being accomplished.

Ordination

In April, 1937, Rev. Mauritz Priebe was ordained to the gospel ministry and given work in the Misiones among the Polish immigrants. He is pastor of the congregation which has erected their own building and called it "Peace." The members have taken such an interest in the adorning of their church edifice that it stands as the pride of all the Mission's church buildings in the Misiones. Pastor Priebe served this congregation prior to his ordination.

New Missionaries

Rev. Herman Hammer was sent to the Argentine at the beginning of the biennium. At its close another ordained man, in the person of Rev. J. Christian Port was called, commissioned and sent to the field. He and family arrived on the 27th of April, 1938. Missionary Port had a limited knowledge of Spanish before he left America. As a result he is assisting in the active work of the mission in addition to studying the language. This mission is better equipped both in personnel and buildings, than any time in its history. The prospects for the immediate future are very promising.

Statistics

The following is a summary of the statistics of the Argentine field: Missionaries in active service, seven; national workers, 30; congregations, 12; baptized membership, 1,559; communicant membership, 1,028; Sunday school scholars, 280; day schools, seven; number of students, 668; income of schools, $16,540; income of boarding schools, $5,666; income of congregations, $3,660.

SOUTH AMERICA
BRITISH GUIANA
MISSIONARIES

Rev. Dr. and Mrs. Paul O. Machetzki..1937

The history of this field for the biennium naturally divides itself into three periods.

The first is the ministry of Rev. and Mrs. W. Theodore Benze. Rev. Mr. Benze served until December 28, 1936, when he was compelled to return to the U. S. A., due to ill health. Both he and his wife contracted malaria fever from which they were unable to secure relief until after leaving the field. While in charge of British Guiana these missionaries rendered faithful and efficient service.

The second is the ministry of Rev. Aubrey Bowen. When Rev. and Mrs. Benze left the field, the work was tentatively turned over to Rev. Aubrey Bowen. The Rev. Mr. Bowen received his education both in college and seminary at Wittenberg, Springfield, Ohio. He was ordained on November 1, 1936, by Rev. Mr. Benze under the authorization of the Ministerium of Pennsylvania of which Missionary Benze was a member. Rev. Mr. Bowen carried the responsibility of the entire mission until October 3, 1937. In addition to acting as pastor of the church at New Amsterdam he had the oversight of five congregations and four schools. Two of the congregations are located among East Indian settlements and three along the Berbice river. One of these, Ituni, is composed of South American Indians. He was able to maintain the work until the Board could secure and send a missionary.

The third is the ministry of Rev. Dr. Paul O. Machetzki. On October 3, 1937, Dr. Machetzki and family arrived on the field. He had been a missionary for years in the Argentine field. With this experience he was able to begin work at once. He is in general charge of the Mission and pastor of Ebenezer Church at New Amsterdam. The Board has adopted some general rules for the conduct of the Mission. It will not be long until the field will have two national pastors with the return of Rev. Patrick Magalee, just recently graduated from Northwestern Theological Seminary.

Outlook

In a recent letter received from the field, Dr. Machetzki writes with much enthusiasm. He reports that he confirmed forty-one and received sixteen by letter of transfer and profession of faith at Ebenezer Church, New Amsterdam. Up to Easter-time including these fifty-seven he has received into this one congregation one hundred and two. With the two national pastors cooperating with the missionaries, for Mrs. Machetzki does much and efficient work, the future growth on this field is more encouraging.

Statistics

The following is a summary of the statistics of the British Guiana Mission on January 1, 1937: Missionaries in active service, two; national pastors, two; other workers, 12; communicants, 304; additions, 34; baptized members, 665; Sunday school scholars, 381; elementary schools, 4; number of pupils, 125; field contributions, $1,748.

STATISTICAL SUMMARY OF THE FOREIGN MISSIONS OF THE UNITED LUTHERAN CHURCH IN AMERICA
January 1, 1938

Missions	Year Established	Missionaries	National Workers	Congregations	Membership				Sunday School Pupils	Mission Schools		Field Contributions (1937)	Hospitals		Dispensaries	
					Baptized	Communicants	Accessions (1937)	Inquirers (1937)		No. of Schools	Pupils		Number	In-Patients	Number	Out-Patients
India	1842	83	2957	1820	181,378	85,817	4,962	18,658	55,617	1,033	48,168	$239,000	7	7799	8	35,103
Liberia	1860	15	43	32	1,730	514	254	900	250	5	366	1,007	2	448	3	4,449
Japan	1892	33	170	43	4,815	1,662	185	200	759	19	1,719	7,000			1	3,172
China	1898	17	125	40	3,767	1,546	527	449	1,000	21	995	4,000	1	714		
British Guiana	1889	2	13	6	665	304	34	27	381	4	125	1,748				
Argentina	1908	5	30	12	1,559	1,028	50	......	280	7	668	2,900				
Totals		155	3338	1953	193,914	90,871	6,012	20,234	58,287	1,089	52,041	$255,655	10	8961	12	42,724

BOARD OFFICERS AND MEMBERS

The list of the officers, secretaries and members, as now constituted, is as follows:

President: Rev. Stewart W. Herman, D.D., 121 State St., Harrisburg, Pa.
Vice-President: Rev. George A. Greiss, D.D., 38 S. 8th St., Allentown, Pa.
Recording Secretary: Rev. George Drach, D.D., 18 East Mount Vernon Place, Baltimore, Maryland.
Treasurer: Mr. George R. Weitzel, 18 East Mount Vernon Place, Baltimore, Maryland.

THE STAFF

Board office: 18 East Mount Vernon Place, Baltimore, Maryland.
Rev. George Drach, D.D., General Secretary.
Rev. M. Edwin Thomas, D.D., General Secretary.
Mr. George R. Weitzel, Treasurer.

ADVISERS

Medical Advisers: Dr. George A. Stewart, Baltimore; Mrs. Dr. George A. Stewart, Baltimore.
Legal Adviser: George S. Yost, Esq., Baltimore.

OFFICIAL REPRESENTATIVES AT PORTS

New York: Rev. Samuel Trexler, D.D., 1170 Fifth Ave., New York, N. Y.
San Francisco: Rev. E. A. Trabert, D.D., 2516 Ashby Ave., Berkeley, Calif.
Seattle: Rev. O. A. Bremer, D.D., 5018 16th Ave., N. E., Seattle. Wash.

MEMBERS OF THE BOARD

Terms Expire in 1938

Rev. Stewart W. Herman, D.D., 121 State St., Harrisburg, Pa.
Rev. Samuel T. Nicholas, D.D., 7527 Parkview Rd., Upper Darby, Pa.
Rev. F. Eppling Reinartz, 1228 Spruce St., Philadelphia, Pa.
Rev. Robert D. Clare, D.D., 1900 St. Paul St., Baltimore, Md.
Mr. Charles H. Dahmer, 530 Fifth Ave., New York, N. Y.
Mr. Claude L. Peterman, 253 Springettsbury Ave., York, Pa.
Mr. George S. Yost, Esq., 215 Chancery Road, Baltimore, Md.

Terms Expire in 1940

Rev. Louis C. Manges, D.D., 1431 Walnut St., Harrisburg, Pa.
Rev. George A. Greiss, D.D., 38 S. 8th St., Allentown, Penna.
Rev. Edgar E. Snyder, D.D., 320 N. Jefferson St., Van Wert, Ohio.
Rev. Samuel G. Trexler, D.D., 1170 Fifth Ave., New York, N. Y.
Mr. S. Frederick Telleen, 722 Upper Blvd., Ridgewood, N. J.
Mr. W. A. Rast, Cameron, S. C.
Mr. Mathias P. Moller, Jr., Hagerstown, Maryland.

Terms Expire in 1942

Rev. P. E. Monroe, D.D., Lenoir Rhyne College, Hickory, N. C.
Rev. Prof. Emil E. Fischer, D.D., 7322 Boyer St., Mt. Airy, Phila., Pa.
Rev. P. O Bersell, D.D., 415 Harvard St., S. E., Minneapolis, Minn.
Rev. Fred J. Fiedler, 145 S. Spruce St., Birdsboro, Pa.
Rev. Harry H. Beidleman, D.D., 55 Frederick St., Hanover, Pa.
Mr. Warren M. Koons, 805 West Erie Ave., Philadelphia, Pa.
Mr. Isaac C. Bucher, Gettysburg, Pa.

NOMINATIONS FOR BOARD MEMBERSHIP

Rev. F. Eppling Reinartz (Eligible for re-election), 1228 Spruce St., Philadelphia, Pa.

Rev. Robert D. Clare (Eligible for re-election), 1900 St. Paul Street, Baltimore, Md.

Rev. Joseph B. Baker, D.D., 839 W. Market St., York, Pa.

Rev. J. Harold Mumper, S.T.M., 907 Maryland Ave., N. E., Washington, D. C.

Mr. Claude L Peterman (Eligible for re-election), 253 Springettsbury Ave., York, Pa.

Mr. George S. Yost, Esq. (Eligible for re-election), 1101 Longwood St., Baltimore, Md.

Mr. John C. Korn, 137 Mortimer Ave., Rutherford, N. J.

RECOMMENDATIONS

(For action, see p. 168.)

The Board of Foreign Missions presents to this convention the following recommendations for its adoption:

1. *Our Centenary Celebration of Foreign Missions—*

Resolved (1) that the pastors, congregations, schools and societies of our Church be encouraged and urged to observe the year 1942 as the one hundredth anniversary of our foreign mission enterprise, begun by Father Heyer when he founded our India mission at Guntur.

Resolved (2) that special anniversary services be held throughout our Church on Sunday, July 26th, the Sunday preceding July 31st, which is the date on which Father Heyer reached Guntur, and that the Board of Foreign Missions publish an anniversary service for that day in the year 1942.

Resolved (3) that the Board of Foreign Missions be authorized to secure special contributions during Foreign Mission time in January, 1942, for a Father Heyer Memorial in India, the exact nature of which is to be determined by the Board of Foreign Missions in consultation with our India mission.

Resolved (4) that the Board of Foreign Missions and the Women's Missionary Society be authorized to co-operate in the preparation and distribution of a foreign mission study book for use throughout the Church in 1942, with special reference to our Foreign Mission Centenary, to be published under a joint imprint.

Resolved (5) that the Board of Foreign Missions be authorized to appoint such sub-committees as it may deem helpful to enable it to make this celebration of church-wide significance, and that these sub-committees may consist of members of the Board or such other members of the United Lutheran Church as the Board may designate.

2. *Joint Lutheran Theological Seminary in India—*

Resolved (1) that the United Lutheran Church in America in principle approve the establishment of a joint Lutheran theological seminary in India for college graduates.

Resolved (2) that the details of the co-operation of our India Mission and Church in such a Joint Lutheran Theological Seminary at Guntur, Madras, or elsewhere, be referred for further consideration to the Board of Foreign Missions and for final decision by the Executive Board of The United Lutheran Church in America.

3. Additional resolution inserted by the convention, see p. 168.

Respectfully submitted,

STEWART W. HERMAN, *President.*

GEORGE DRACH, *Recording Secretary.*

REPORT OF THE TREASURER OF THE BOARD OF FOREIGN MISSIONS

BALANCE SHEET
June 30, 1937

ASSETS

Cash in Banks:

General Fund		$124,266.57	
Investment Fund	$ 55,329.60		
Investment Fund Savings Account..	10,217.28		
		65,546.88	
			$189,813.45

Investments at Book Value:

Bonds and Stocks	$339,822.61*		
Certificates of Participation	819.00		
		$340,641.61	
Ground Rents, Mortgages and Notes Receivable		12,504.55	
Real Estate		47,508.94	
Total Investments at Book Values			400,655.10

Other Assets:

Loans and Accounts Receivable	$ 5,226.10		
Women's Missionary Society	1,724.45		
		6,950.55	
Total Assets			$597,419.10

LIABILITIES

Unpaid drafts for June, 1937	$ 33,707.06		
Accounts Payable	10,728.36		
		$ 44,435.42	
Reserve for Contingencies		5,000.00	
Total Liabilities			49,435.42
Net Assets			$547,983.68

FUNDS

Trust Funds	$209,874.77
Annuity Funds	94,450.00
Andhra Christian College Fund	260,663.67
Pohlman Fund	1,600.00
Anstadt Miller Memorial Fund	1,038.00
Reformation Diamond Jubilee Advance Fund	12,840.64
Land and Building Fund	9,097.82
Total Funds	$589,564.90
Less: Overdraft General Fund	41,581.22**
Total Net Funds	$547,983.68

NOTE: This statement does not include as assets, investments in foreign fields, nor does it include liabilities incurred in the purchase of such properties.

* Market Value of Bonds and Stocks at June 30, 1937, $302,223.87.
** Overdraft.

BALANCE SHEET
June 30, 1938
ASSETS

Cash in Banks:

General Fund		$ 80,675.79
Investment Fund	$ 7,081.85	
Investment Fund Savings Account..	20,593.88	
		27,675.73
Total Cash		$108,351.52

Investments at Book Value:

Government and Municipal Issues..	$187,965.18	
Corporate Bonds	265,866.65	
Total Book Value of Bonds		$453,831.83*
Ground Rents Receivable	$12,568.34	
Mortgages	2,500.00	
Notes Receivable	5,181.00	
	$ 20,249.34	
Stocks	4,176.00	
Certificates of Participation	819.00	
Real Estate	45,168.86	
Total Book Value of Other Investments....	70,413.20**	
Total Investment at Book Values		524,245.03

Other Assets:

Loans and Accounts Receivable	5,148.08
Total Assets	$637,744.63

LIABILITIES

Unpaid Drafts for June, 1938	$ 44,923.23	
Accounts Payable	11,200.50	
Accounts Payable — Women's Mis- sionary Society	9,244.54	
	$ 65,368.27	
Reserve for Contingencies	7,500.00	
Total Liabilities		72,868.27
Net Assets		$564,876.36

FUNDS

Trust Funds	$155,174.77	
Annuity Funds	82,550.00	
Andhra Christian College Fund	310,252.04	
Pohlman Fund	600.00	
Anstadt Miller Memorial Fund	238.00	
Land and Building Fund	11,454.07	
Total Funds		$560,268.88

General Fund (Surplus) 4,607.48

      Grand Total of All Funds $564,876.36

* Market Value of Bonds, June 30, 1938, $394,547.56.
** Market and Appraised Values, June 30, 1938, $67,292.17.

NOTE: This statement does not include as assets, investments in foreign fields, nor does it include liabilities incurred in the purchase of such properties.

GENERAL FUND—INCOME
July 1, 1936 to June 30, 1937

Apportionment		$285,000.00
Parishes Abroad		19,368.10
Missionaries' Salaries		35,427.39
Proteges		11,365.58
Interest on Investments:		
Income from Securities, Notes, Ground Rents		
and Mortgages	$ 5,305.84	
Rents Received from Real Estate (net).............	511.52	
		5,817.36
Co-operating Synod:		
Augustana Synod	$ 3,745.00	
Danish Synod	4,405.83	
Proteges-Danish Synod	1,155.65	
		9,306.48
Contributions		17,562.68
Interest, Andhra Christian College		12,246.80
Epiphany Appeal		10,310.54
Slides		18.50
Magazines		2,290.63
Gifts to Missionaries		1,268.00
Mission Study		9.39
Profit on Sale of Securities		1,251.05
Mamie Telleen Memorial India Scholarship		25.00
Special Contributions for Board's Debt:		
United Lutheran Church in America		31,874.20
Other Contributions		5,835.00
Total Income—General Fund		$448,976.70

GENERAL FUND—DISBURSEMENTS
July 1, 1936 to June 30, 1937

Fields:	
Budgets Paid to Missions	$181,560.52
Salaries Paid to Missionaries	102,780.22
Traveling Expenses of Missionaries to and from fields	28,966.74
New Missionaries	600.00
General Work	1,543.08
Literature Department:	
Annual Report	521.68
Occasional Pamphlets	265.42
Magazines and Publicity	3,866.14

Motion Pictures and Stereopticons		123.53

Finance Department:

Auditing		700.00
Interest on Uninvested Funds, Andhra Christian College....		3,415.45
Interest on Annuities		5,770.74

Home Base:

Interboard Activities		1,050.00

Salaries—Secretaries and Treasurer:

Paul A. Koller, D.D.	$5,100.00	
George Drach, D.D.	3,825.00	
E. R. Thomas, D.D.	3,825.00	
George R. Weitzel	3,825.00	
		16,575.00
Office Salaries		5,295.20

Expenses—Secretaries, Treasurer and Board Members:

Secretaries and Treasurer	$1,051.92	
Board Members	1,154.35	
		2,206.27
Special Allowances and Pensions		5,513.85

Expenses of Maintaining "Baltimore Mission House and the "Brown House":

Repairs	$ 131.42	
Janitor	514.80	
Miscellaneous Expense	18.00	
Taxes	12.95	
Interest	60.00	
Coal	238.50	
Insurance	85.12	
		1,060.79
Expense—Missionaries in preparation and on furlough		6,655.26

General Expenses:

Telephone, Telegraph and Cables	$ 468.99	
Postage and Express	766.81	
Gas, Electricity and Water	156.98	
Office Supplies and Expenses	321.61	
Premium on Officers' Bonds	90.00	
Supplies and Miscellaneous Expenses	995.41	
		2,799.80

Specials—General Fund:

Gifts to Fields and Missionaries		1,212.75
Expenses re: Contributions to Board's Debt		465.51
Expenses re: Epiphany Appeal		1,091.61
Adjustment of Women's Missionary Society Balance due Board as of July 1, 1936		8,880.61
Total Disbursements—General Fund		$382,920.17

SUMMARY OF INCOME AND DISBURSEMENTS—VARIOUS FUNDS
July 1, 1936 to June 30, 1937

Trust Funds:

Balance, July 1, 1936	$207,430.18	
Contributions to Trust Funds:		
Anna M. Sterling	2,444.59	
Balance—June 30, 1937		$209,874.77

Annuity Fund:
Balance, July 1, 1936 .... $ 97,950.00
Annuities Issued 2,500.00

$100,450.00

Less Annuities Cancelled by Death and Trans-
ferred to General Fund 6,000.00

Balance, June 30, 1937 .... 94,450.00

Andhra Christian College Fund:
Balance, July 1, 1936 .... $285,850.13
Income for Year:
Interest on Uninvested Funds........ $ 3,415.45
Interest on Invested Funds 8,831.35

$12,246.80
Less Transferred to General Fund.... 12,246.80

Profit on Sale of Securities 1,313.54

$287,163.67
Less Remittances to Field 26,500.00

Balance, June 30, 1937 .... 260,663.67

Pohlman Fund:
Balance, July 1, 1936 .... $ 1,600.00
Balance, June 30, 1937 .... 1,600.00

Anstadt Miller Memorial Fund:
Balance, July 1, 1936 .... $ 457.00
Contributions Received 581.00

Balance, June 30, 1937 .... 1,038.00

Reformation Diamond Jubilee:
(Advance Fund):
Balance, July 1, 1936 .... $ 17,840.64
Less Transferred to Land and Building Fund 5,000.00

Balance, June 30, 1937 .... 12,840.64

Land and Building Fund:
Balance, July 1, 1936 .... $ 149.48
Donations 15,798.34

$ 15,947.82
Less Disbursements:
Buenos Aires Property .... $ 1,850.00
India Property 5,000.00 6,850.00

Balance, June 30, 1937................. 9,097.82

General Fund:
Overdraft, July 1, 1936 .... $107,637.75*
Operating Surplus for year ended June 30,
1937 .... $74,937.14
Less Adjustments re: Women's Mis-
sionary Society balance 8,880.61

Net Decrease in General Fund Overdraft
for year ended June 30, 1937................... 66,056.53

Overdraft, June 30, 1937 .... 41,581.22*

Total of all Funds (Net) $547,983.68

* Overdraft.

SUMMARY OF CASH RECEIPTS AND DISBURSEMENTS
July 1, 1936 *to June* 30, 1937

Cash Balance, July 1, 1936 .... $ 97,132.46
Receipts:
General Fund Income $448,976.70
Less:
Transferred from Annuity Fund.... $ 6,000.00
$3,801.22 Unsecured Note of York
Ice Machinery Corporation 1.00   6,001.00

Cash Received for General Fund $442,975.70
Sale of Stock and Bonds 80,243,08
Payments made on Account of Mortgage 500.00
Payments made on Account of Loans and Ac-
counts Receivable 9,781.90
Women's Missionary Society 227,038.90
Accounts Payable 18,085.51
Trust Funds 2,444.59
Annuities Sold 2,500.00
Andhra Christian College Fund 13,560.34
Land and Building Fund 10,798.34
Anstadt Miller Memorial Fund 581.00

Total Cash Receipts for Year $808.509.36

Disbursements:
General Fund $382,920.17
Less Unpaid Drafts for June, 1937,
charged in disbursements but not
paid until July, 1937 .... 33,707.06

Cash Disbursed from General
Fund $349,213.11
Securities Purchased 69,714.01
Loans and Accounts Receivable
Advanced 3,532.84
Women's Missionary Society 217,850.74
Outstanding Drafts, July 1, 1936.... 12,508.57
Accounts Payable 17,412.30

Andhra Christian College 38,746.80
Land and Building Fund 6,850.00

Total Cash Disbursements for year 715,828.37

Excess of Cash Receipts over Disburse-
ments 92,680.99

Cash Balance, June 30, 1937 .... $189,813.45

GENERAL FUND—INCOME
July 1, 1937 to June 30, 1938

Apportionment $303,000.00
Parishes Abroad 20,450.56
Missionaries' Salaries 34,280.32
Proteges 11,693.72
Interest on Investments:
Income from Securities, Notes, Ground Rents and Mort-
gages, Rents Received from Real Estate (Net) 8,402.48
Co-operating Synods:
Augustana Synod .... $ 4,390.00
Danish Synod 3,275.18
Icelandic Synod 400.00
                                                                              ————   8,065.18
Danish Synod (Specials) 1,199.60
Contributions 21,831.37
Interest, Andhra Christian College (Budgeted) 9,000.00
India Cyclone Relief .... $ 26.78
Slides 9.20
Magazines 2,144.21
Gifts to Missionaries 1,241.76
Specials for Fields 4,480.29
Occasional Pamphlets 3.25
Mamie Telleen Memorial India Scholarship 25.00
In Seven Nations 33.42
Epiphany Appeal $15,184.73
Remittances to Field and Expenses
Incurred $12,141.66
To be sent to Field 3,043.07
                                                          ————   15,184.73

Andhra Christian College Interest Received in Ex-
cess of Budget Item 3,390.74
Contributions for Board Debt 13,592.01
                                                                              ————   24,946.66

Total Income, General Fund $442,869.89

GENERAL FUND—DISBURSEMENTS
July 1, 1937 to June 30, 1938
Fields:
General Work $178,774.52
Salaries and Children's Allowances 103,353.52

Traveling Expenses of Missionaries	26,779.65
New Missionaries	6,852.11
Literature Department:	
Annual Report	565.99
Occasional Pamphlets	678.11
Magazines and Publicity	4,101.95
Motion Pictures and Stereopticons	238.93
Finance Department:	
Auditing	700.00
Interest on Uninvested Funds, Andhra Christian College....	1,225.44
Interest on Annuities	5,147.87
Home Base:	
Interboard Activities	1,843.00
Salaries—Secretaries and Treasurer:	
Paul A. Koller, D.D.	3,800.00
George Drach, D.D.	4,275.00
E. R. Thomas, D.D.	4,275.00
George R. Weitzel	4,275.00
Office Salaries	5,401.03
Expense—Secretaries, Treasurer and Board Members:	
Secretaries and Treasurer	1,334.67
Board Members	1,297.96
Special Allowances and Pensions	6,369.34
Expenses of Maintaining "Baltimore Mission House" and the "Brown House":	
Repairs	1,824.65
Janitor	514.80
Taxes	11.30
Interest	60.00
Coal	243.00
Insurance	58.15
Expense, Missionaries in Preparation and on Furlough	6,601.34
General Expenses:	
Telephone, Telegraph and Cables	3,103.26
Postage and Express	804.45
Gas, Electricity and Water	108.25
Reserve for Contingencies	2,500.00
Specials—General Fund:	
Loss on Sale of Investments	4,048.53
Specials to Fields	3,757.27
Interest Andhra Christian College	3,390.74
Expenses re: Contributions to Board's Debt	249.00
Gifts to Missionaries	1,138.52
Committee of Executive Secretaries	1,274.97
Brooklyn Inner Mission House	100.00
Foreign Mission Conference of North America	300.00
Repairs and Improvements, etc. re: Baltimore Mission House	4,763.92
Funeral and Medical Expenses	539.95
Total Disbursements—General Fund	$396,681.19

SUMMARY OF INCOME AND DISBURSEMENTS—VARIOUS FUNDS
July 1, 1937 to June 30, 1938

Trust Funds:
Balance, July 1, 1937 .... $209,874.77

Contributions to Trust Funds:
Sarah Curran .... $ 3,400.00
W. L. Gladfelder Estate................... 27,900.00   31,300.00

                                                          $241,174.77

Less Transfers:
Andhra Christian College Endow-
  ment Fund $83,000.00
Real Estate Investment,
  (Elizabeth Quist) 3,000.00   86,000.00

Balance, June 30, 1938 .... $155,174.77

Annuity Funds:
Balance, July 1, 1937 .... $ 94,450.00
Annuities Issued 2,300.00

                                                         $ 96,750.00

Less Annuities Cancelled by Death and Gift,
  and Transferred to General Fund.. $10,800.00
Transferred to Trust Funds
  (Sarah J. Curran) 3,400.00   14,200.00

Balance, June 30, 1938 ....   82,550.00

Andhra Christian College Fund:
Principal Account:
Balance, July 1, 1937 .... $260,597.04
  Donations for year ended June 30, 1938 ....   655.00
  Transferred from Trust Funds 83,000.00

                                                         $344,252.04
  Less Remittances to Field 34,000.00

Balance, June 30, 1938 ....   310,252.04
Interest Account:
Balance, July 1, 1937 .... $ 66.63
Interest on Invested and Uninvested Funds,
  year ended June 30, 1938 .... 12,390.74

                                                         $ 12,457.37
Less Remittances to Field .... $ 9,000.00
Transferred to Accounts Pay-
  able for remittance to field 3,457.37   12,457.37

Balance, June 30, 1938 ....   ——

Pohlman Fund:
Balance, July 1, 1937 .... $ 1,600.00
Less Remittance to Zor Zor, Africa, for
  Dispensary 1,000.00

Balance, June 30, 1938 ....   600.00

Anstadt Miller Memorial Fund:
Balance, July 1, 1937 .... $ 1,038.00

Less Remittance to Zor Zor, Africa, for Bungalow	800.00	
Balance, June 30, 1938		238.00

Reformation Diamond Jubilee:
(Advance Fund):

Balance, July 1, 1937	$ 12,840.64	
Less Transferred to Land and Building Fund..	12,840.64	
Balance, June 30, 1938	—	

Land and Building Fund:

Balance, July 1, 1937		$ 9,097.82
Donations	$ 3,579.61	
Transferred from Reformation Diamond Jubilee (Advance Fund)	12,840.64	16,420.25
		$ 25,518.07

Less Remittances to Fields:

India Field	$ 5,000.00	
Africa Field	400.00	
British Guiana Field	1,629.00	
Buenos Aires Field	4,535.00	
India Field	2,500.00	
		14,064.00
Balance, June 30, 1938		11,454.07

General Fund:

Overdraft, June 30, 1938	$ 41,581.22*	
Operating Surplus for year ended June 30, 1938	46,188.70	
Balance, June 30, 1938 (Surplus)		4,607.48
Total of All Funds		$564,876.36

* Overdraft.

SUMMARY OF CASH RECEIPTS AND DISBURSEMENTS
July 1, 1937 *to June* 30, 1938

Cash Balance, July 1, 1937		$189,813.45
Receipts:		
General Fund Income	$442,869.89	
Less:		
Transferred from Annuity Fund	10,800.00	
Cash Received from General Fund	$432,069.89	
Sale of Stocks and Bonds	$59,192.29	
Payments made on Mortgages	1,500.00	
	60,692.29	
Payments made on account of Loans and Accounts Receivable	7,858.98	
Women's Missionary Society	198,900.37	

Accounts Payable	5,188.02
Annuities Sold	2,300.00
Andhra Christian College Fund	13,045.74
Land and Building Fund	2,753.84

Total Cash Receipts for year ended June
30, 1938.. $722,809.13

Disbursements:

General Fund $396,681.19

Less:

Reserve for Contin-
gencies .... $ 2,500.00
Unpaid Drafts for June,
1938, charged in Dis-
bursements but not
paid until July, 1938.. 44,923.23
_____ 47,423.23

Cash Disbursed from General Fund	$349,257.96
Securities Purchased	158,556.45
Loans and Accounts Receivable Advanced......	7,780.96
Women's Missionary Society	187,931.38
Outstanding Drafts, July 1, 1937	33,707.06
Accounts Payable	8,173.25
Andhra Christian College	43,000.00
Land and Building Fund	14,064.00
Pohlman Fund	1,000.00
Anstadt Miller Memorial Fund	800.00

Total Cash Disbursements for year ended
June 30, 1938 .... $804,271.06

Excess of Disbursements over Receipts for
year ended June 30, 1938 .... 81,461.93

Cash Balance, June 30, 1938 .... $108,351.52

RECONCILIATION OF ACCOUNTS
July 1, 1936, to June 30, 1937

ASSETS	Balance July 1, 1936	Cash Receipts	Cash Disbursements	Non-Cash Items Debit	Non-Cash Items Credit	Balance June 30, 193;
Cash	$ 97,132.46	$808,509.36	$715,828.37			$189,813.45
Investments:						
Stocks, Bonds and Certificates of Participation	351,170.68	$ 80,243.08	$ 69,714.01			340,641.61
Ground Rents and Mortgages	7,823.55	500.00				7,323.55
Notes Receivable	5,180.00			$ 1.00		5,181.00
Real Estate	47,508.94					47,508.94
Other Assets:						
Loans and Accounts Receivable	11,475.16	9,781.90	3,532.84			5,226.10
Women's Missionary Society	10,912.61	227,038.90	217,850.74			1,724.45
Total Assets	$531,203.40					$597,419.10
LIABILITIES						
Due on Unpaid Drafts	$ 12,508.57		12,508.57		$ 33,707.06	$ 33,707.06
Accounts Payable	10,512.15	18,085.51	17,412.30	457.00		10,728.36
Total Liabilities	$ 23,020.72					$44,435.42
RESERVES						
Reserve for Contingencies	$ 5,000.00					$ 5,000.00
Net Assets	$503,182.68					$547,983.68

FUNDS					
Trust Funds	$207,430.18	2,444.59			$209,874.77
Annuity Funds	97,950.00	2,500.00		6,000.00	94,450.00
Andhra Christian College Fund	285,850.13	13,560.34	38,746.80		260,663.67
Land and Building Fund	149.48	10,798.34	6,850.00	5,000.00	9,097.82
Reformation Diamond Jubilee Fund	17,840.64			5,000.00	12,840.64
Pohlman Fund	1,600.00				1,600.00
Anstadt Miller Memorial Fund		581.00		457.00	1,038.00
	$610,820.43	442,975.70	349,213.11	6,001.00	$589,564.90
Less Overdraft—General Fund	107,637.75*		33,707.06		41,581.22
Total Funds	$503,182.68	$808,509.36	$715,828.37	$45,165.06	$547,983.68
			$45,165.06		

* Overdraft.

RECONCILIATION OF ACCOUNTS
July 1, 1937 to June 30, 1938

	Balance July 1, 1937	Cash Receipts	Cash Disbursements	Non-Cash Items Debit	Non-Cash Items Credit	Balance June 30, 1938
ASSETS						
Cash	$189,813.45	$722,809.13	$804,271.06			$108,351.52
Investments:	400,655.10	$ 60,692.29	$158,556.45	$ 28,725.77	$ 3,000.00	524,245.03
Other Assets:						
Loans and Accounts Receivable	5,226.10	7,858.98	7,780.96			5,148.08
Women's Missionary Society	1,724.45	198,900.37	187,931.38			9,244.54*
	$597,419.10					$628,500.09
LIABILITIES						
Due on Unpaid Drafts	$ 33,707.06		33,707.06		44,923.23	$ 44,923.23
Accounts Payable	10,728.36	5,188.02	8,173.25		3,457.37	11,200.50
	$ 44,435.42					$ 56,123.73
RESERVES						
Reserve for Contingencies	$ 5,000.00				2,500.00	$ 7,500.00
Net Assets	$547,983.68					$564,876.36
FUNDS						
Trust Funds	$209,874.77			86,000.00	31,300.00	$155,174.77
Annuity Funds	94,450.00	2,300.00		14,200.00		82,550.00
Andhra Christian College Fund	260,663.67	13,045.74	43,000.00	3,457.37	83,000.00	310,252.04
Land and Building Fund	9,097.82	2,753.84	14,064.00		13,666.41	11,454.07
Reformation Diamond Jubilee Fund	12,840.64			12,840.64		
Pohlman Fund	1,600.00		1,000.00			600.00
Anstadt Miller Memorial Fund	1,038.00		800.00			238.00
	$589,564.90					
Less Overdraft—General Fund	41,581.22**	432,069.89	349,257.96	47,423.23	10,800.00	4,607.48***
Total Funds	$547,983.68	$722,809.13	$804,271.06	$192,647.01	$192,647.01	$564,876.36

* Deficit.
** Overdraft.
*** Surplus.

SCHEDULE OF INVESTMENTS
June 30, 1938
Government and Municipal

Par Value	Bonds	Value Carried on Books June 30, 1938	Market Value June 30, 1938
$ 3,620	British Guiana Government Church Endowment 5% 1946	$ 3,620.00	$ 3,620.00
1,500	City of Coral Gables, Florida Refunding Preferred Average 3½% 1977	630.00	720.00
2,779.05	City of Coral Gables, Florida Tax Participation Certificates Issued January 1, 1937	125.77	166.74
3,000	Denmark (Kingdom of), 3½% 30 years External 1955	2,985.00	3,030.00
20,000	Federal Farm Mortgage 2¾% 1947/42	20,250.00	21,018.75
80,000	Home Owners' Loan Corporation Series "B" 2¾% 1949/39	80,911.96	82,300.00
400	United States Government Treasury Certificates 3⅛% 1946/49	392.38	433.62
8,500	United States Treasury Notes Series "D" 1⅜% 9/15/39	8,500.00	8,651.41
50,000	United States Treasury Bills due 7/1/38	50,000.00	50,000.00
20,000	City of Yonkers, Series "2" General 4% 1942	20,550.07	20,100.00
		$187,965.18	$190,040.52

Corporate

Par Value	Bonds	Value Carried on Books	Market Value
$ 5,000	Adams Express Company 50 years, Collateral Trust 4% 1948	$ 4,658.75	$ 4,650.00
3,000	American and Foreign Power Company, Incorporated, Debenture 5% 2030	2,692.50	1,687.50
6,000	Associated Electric Company 4½% 1953	5,655.00	2,542.50
5,000	Atlantic Coast Line Railroad Company L. & N. Division Collateral, 4% 1952	4,293.75	2,925.00
4,000	Baltimore and Ohio Railroad Company First 4% 1948	3,050.00	1,640.00
9,500	The Baltimore Transit Company Series "A" First 5% Regular Debenture 1975	9,500.00	1,710.00
4,000	The Baltimore Transit Company Series "A" First 4% Regular Debenture 1975	4,000.00	680.00
10,000	Canadian Pacific Railway Company, Convertible Collateral 6% 1942	10,573.80	10,125.00
5,000	Canadian Pacific Railway Company, Collateral Trust 4½% 1960	5,000.00	4,568.75
4,000	Central Illinois Public Service Company, First 4½% Series "F" 1967	3,790.00	3,830.00
3,000	Central Illinois Public Service Company, First 5% Series "G" 1968	2,925.00	3,000.00

Par Value	Bonds	Value Carried on Books June 30, 1938	Market Value June 30, 1938
1,000	Central Indiana Power Company Collateral and Refunding 6% 1947	1,000.00	870.00
5,000	Central States Electric Corp. Convertible Debenture 5% 1948	4,825.00	1,731.25
1,000	Cespedes Sugar Company, First Sinking Fund 7½% 1939	1,000.00	72.50
10,000	Chicago and Western Indiana Railroad Company, Consolidated 4% 1952........	9,900.93	8,550.00
1,000	Cities Service Company, Convertible Debenture 5% 1950	1,000.00	650.00
5,000	Commonwealth Edison Company Series "F" First 4% 1981	4,725.00	5,412.50
2,000	Consolidated Cities Light, Power and Traction Company First 5% 1962	1,659.90	1,480.00
2,000	Continental Investment Bond Corporation, Guaranteed and Collateral Trust Bond I. Average 3½% 1953....	2,000.00	1,545.00
30,000	Commercial Credit Company Debenture 2¾% 1942	29,812.50	30,600.00
500	Columbia Holding Company First Sinking Fund Average 4¼% 1947	500.00	170.00
750	Duquesne Natural Gas Company General and Refunding Mortgage 7% 1948	750.00	510.00
3,000	Electric Power and Light Corp. Debenture 5% 2030	2,790.00	2,175.00
5,000	Federated Utilities, Incorporated First Lien Collateral Trust 5½% 1957	4,737.50	3,325.00
5,000	Florida East Coast Railway Company First 4½% 1959	3,950.00	2,900.00
4,000	Florida Power and Light Company First 5% 1954	3,814.00	3,620.00
3,000	Forty Wall Street Corporation (Manhattan Company Building) First Mortgage Leasehold Sinking Fund 6% 1958	2,940.00	1,215.00
3,000	Gary Electric and Gas Company (Stamped) Series "A" First Lien Collateral 5% 1944	2,932.50	2,700.00
2,000	Greenwich Water and Gas Company Series "A" Collateral Trust 5% 1952	1,820.00	1,990.00
21.02	Hotel St. George Corporation Scrip Certificate	1.00	9.04
3,400	Hotel St. George Corporation First Mortgage Sinking Fund 4% 1950........	944.00	1,496.00
5,000	Illinois Central Railroad Company 4¾% 1966	4,825.00	1,900.00
2,000	Illinois Power and Light Company First and Refunding Series "C" 5% 1956	1,960.00	1,800.00
2,000	Indiana Ice and Fuel Company First Mortgage 6½% Series "A" 1947	2,000.00	1,150.00
4,000	Interstate Power Company First Mortgage 5% 1957	3,900.00	2,080.00

Par Value	Bonds	Value Carried on Books June 30, 1938	Market Value June 30, 1938
3,000	Kentucky Utilities Company First Mortgage 5% series "H" 1961	3,000.00	2,430.00
1,000	Lehigh Valley Railroad Company General Consolidated Mortgage 4% 2003	1,000.00	210.00
500	Nassau and Suffolk Lighting Company First 5% 30 years Sinking Fund 1945	500.00	410.00
5,000	National Union Mortgage Company Series "B" Collateral Trust Average 3½% 1954	5,000.00	3,700.00
3,000	New England Gas and Electric Association Convert. Debenture 5% 1950	2,677.50	1,612.50
3,000	New York Central Railroad Company Equipment Trust 4½% 1942	2,871.36	3,090.00
3,000	New York Central Railroad Company Series "A" Refunding and Improving 4½% 2013	2,992.50	1,653.75
5,000	New York Central Railroad Company Secured Sinking Fund 3¾% 1946	4,938.15	3,625.00
3,000	North American Company Debenture 5% 1961	2,902.50	3,150.00
1,000	North Carolina Gas Company Trustee Certificate First Mortgage Sinking Fund 6% 1948	970.00	15.00
5,000	Penn Central Light and Power Company First 4½% 1977	4,725.00	4,162.50
2,000	Pennsylvania Electric Company Series "F" First Refunding 4% 1971	1,827.50	1,765.00
3,000	Peoples Gas, Light and Coke Company First and Refunding Series "B" 4% 1981	2,820.00	2,685.00
8,000	Potomac Bond Corporation Guaranteed Collateral Trust Average 3½% 1953	8,000.00	6,000.00
3,000	Public Service Company of Northern Illinois Series "F" First and Refunding 4½% 1981	2,925.00	3,127.50
2,000	Puget Sound Power and Light Company Series "A" First and Refunding 5½% 1949	1,340.00	1,460.00
1,000	St. Louis County Gas Company First 5% 1951	1,000.00	1,055.00
900	Scranton Transit Co. First Mortgage Sinking Fund Series "B" 4% 1959	1,000.00	405.00
200	Scranton Transit Co. 2nd Mortgage and Collateral Cumulative Income 3% 1959		29.50
3,000	Seaboard and Roanoke Railroad Co. Certificate of Deposit First 5% 1931	3,022.50	1,140.00
4,000	Seaboard Airline Railway Certificate of Deposit First 4% 1950	3,392.61	465.00
1,000	Seventy-nine Realty Corporation Maximum Refund Bond 5% Interest paid as earned	979.00	105.00
4,000	South West Missouri Railroad Company, General Refunding 5% 1931	4,080.00	40.00
5,000	Southern Pacific Railroad Company 4% 1955	4,731.25	3,012.50

Par Value Bonds	Value Carried on Books June 30, 1938	Market Value June 30, 1938
3,000 Southern Pacific Company 4½% 1968	2,992.50	1,342.50
5,000 Southern Pacific Company Secured 3¾% 1946	4,738.15	2,693.75
1,500 Standard Power and Light Co. Debenture 6% 1957	1,492.50	772.50
2,000 Texarkana and Fort Smith Railway Co., Series "A" Guaranteed First Mortgage 5½% 1950	2,010.00	1,640.00
10,000 Union Electric Company of Missouri Notes 3% 1942	10,112.50	10,400.00
30,000 York Ice Machinery Corporation 6% 1947	27,900.00	27,000.00
	$265,866.65	$204,507.04

Ground Rents, Mortgages and Notes Receivable

	Value Carried on Books June 30, 1938	Appraisal Value June 30, 1938
Ground Rents on properties located at:		
924, 1040, 1042 W. Fayette St., Baltimore, Md.	$ 3,323.55	$ 1,950.00
1635 E. 25th St., Baltimore, Md., face value $1,000	1,078.12	1,000.00
3818 Beech Ave., Baltimore, Md.	1,666.67	1,666.67
3824 Beech Ave., Baltimore, Md.	2,000.00	2,000.00
601 W. 39th St., Baltimore, Md.	1,500.00	1,500.00
605 W. 39th St., Baltimore, Md.	1,500.00	1,500.00
609 W. 39th St., Baltimore, Md.	1,500.00	1,500.00
First Mortgage on 5716 Hagerman St., Philadelphia, Pennsylvania 5½%	2,500.00	2,500.00
Notes of Chas. R. Fisher 6% Guaranteed by G. B. Morehead, in hands of attorney due April 10, 1936, September 10, 1929, September 30, 1930; extended indefinitely	5,180.00	3,875.00
Unsecured Note of York Ice Machinery Corporation dated April 10, 1936, due December 1, 1944, 3% face value $3,801.22	1.00	3,420.00
	$20,249.34	$20,911.67

No. of Shares Stocks:		
6 Altoona and Logan Valley Common		$ 180.00
1 American Telephone and Telegraph Co. Common	$ 113.00	142.00
$2,500 Electric and Peoples Traction Co. Stock Trust Certificate 4% 1945	2,500.00	150.00
14 The Elk Horn Coal Corporation Second Preferred	1,000.00	42.00
2 Easton National Bank, Easton, Pa.	70.00	60.00
10 Seventy-nine Realty Corporation Voting Trust Certificate		
17 Pennsylvania Railroad Co. Common	493.00	331.50
	$4,176.00	$ 905.50

	Value Carried on Books June 30, 1938	Appraisal Value June 30, 1938
Certificates of Participation		
$3,500 Federal Mortgage Co. Series "J" Asheville, North Carolina	$ 819.00	Not Ascertainable
Real Estate		
Equity in Property located at 2900 Woodland Ave., Baltimore, Maryland	$ 10,057.22	$ 6,375.00
Property located at 18 E. Mt. Vernon Place, Baltimore, Md.	16,000.00	16,000.00
Property located at Kodiakanal, India	13,000.00	13,000.00
Property located at 1019 S. Randolph St., Philadelphia, Pa.	1,610.64	400.00
Property located at 5849 Woodcrest Ave., Philadelphia, Pa.	4,500.00	4,200.00
Farm located at Roosevelt, Oklahoma, 160 acres..	1.00	5,500.00
	$ 45,168.86	$ 45,475.00

Summary of Investments:		
Government and Municipal Bonds	$187,965.18	$190,040.52
Corporate Bonds	265,866.65	204,507.04
Ground Rents, Mortgages and Notes Receivable	20,249.34	20,911.67
Stocks	4,176.00	905.50
Certificates of Participation	819.00	
Real Estate	45,168.86	45,475.00
	$524,245.03	$461,839.73

Respectfully submitted,
GEORGE R. WEITZEL, *Treasurer.*

We have audited the books of account of the Treasurer, and examined the securities of the Board of Foreign Missions of the United Lutheran Church in America for the biennium beginning July 1, 1936 and ending June 30, 1938, and we hereby certify, that in our opinion, the foregoing statements of Income and Expense, together with the Balance Sheet and other pertinent schedules, are in agreement with the books of account, and are true and correct.

TAIT, WELLER AND BAKER,
Accountants and Auditors.

Dr. Herman introduced the Rev. George Drach, General Secretary, who spoke of present conditions in the various fields where the Board is operating.

Mr. George R. Weitzel was next introduced by Dr. Herman, and, as Treasurer of the Board, Mr. Weitzel spoke especially of the cancellation of all of the Board's indebtedness.

Dr. Herman then introduced the Rev. M. E. Thomas, General Secretary, who spoke of the workers in the field. Dr.

Thomas in turn presented the following missionaries from the foreign fields: From *Africa:* Miss Laura Gilliland; Dr. Jacob Jensen; Rev. J. K. Donat. From *China:* Rev. and Mrs. Ralph W. Sell; Miss Elvira Strunk; Miss Charlotte Kao. From *India:* Rev. and Mrs. Paul H. Gleichman; Rev. and Mrs. C. H. Swavely; Rev. and Mrs. J. C. Peery, Jr.; Rev. H. H. Moyer; Miss Amelia Brosius; Dr. Barbara De Remer; Miss Edna Engle. From *Japan:* Rev. Shinichi Kawagiri; Rev. S. O. Thorlaksson.

The following was offered by Dr. Pfatteicher to follow the recommendations submitted by the Board:

> Resolved, That the Convention express its respect and regard for the work that the President of the Board has done in his conduct of the work of that Board.

The resolution was adopted.

The recommendations of the Board of Foreign Missions were considered:

Recommendations 1, (1), (2), (3), (4), (5), and 2, (1), (2), were adopted.

Moved and carried that a telegram of congratulations and of love be sent to Dr. L. L. Uhl, the oldest living missionary of The United Lutheran Church in America.

Dr. Drach presented Mr. M. P. Moller, Jr., member of the Board and Treasurer of the Foreign Missions Conference, and Mr. S. F. Telleen, member of the Board and Treasurer of the International Missionary Conference, both of whom addressed the Convention.

The following greetings from the foreign fields were read by Dr. Drach who requested that Dr. L. B. Wolf, who served fifty-five years in the work, stand by his side as he read the greetings.

> "The Council of the India Mission sends greetings to the Convention of the United Lutheran Church and prays for God's guidance and blessing in its deliberations."

> "Greetings from the Andhra Evangelical Lutheran Church in Convention. We have you in our mind and prayers, and confidently ask for your prayers for and interest in the plans which we are making for the

worthy celebration of our Centenary, 1942-43. Please keep this request of ours in your mind and convey the same to your own congregations with our greetings."

"Conference and missionaries of African Mission send greetings and prayers U. L. C. A. Convention."

"The China Mission wishes to express to the church at home by means of this statement addressed to the Eleventh Biennial Convention of the United Lutheran Church assembled at Baltimore its great thanks for gifts that have been sent to be used for relief and emergency work in this stricken country. The mission also appreciates the continued concern of our brethren at home for us and our work.

"We wish to tell friends at home that we count it a high privilege to stand by our Christian Chinese brethren in their time of difficulty and anxiety. We repoice in celebrating this year the fortieth anniversary of the founding of this mission. Previous critical and trying periods have been experienced and have confirmed the truth that God does not desert His own. There have been losses to our people and to our work, but there have also been great blessings. The bravery and faith of our people have been an inspiration.

"As a mission and individually we send you our greetings. During the past year we have consciously sensed your love for us in Christ, our glorious Lord. We have felt the sustaining strength coming from your prayers. In genuine appreciation, we implore our Heavenly Father to bless you richly in life and work. Our Chinese brethren join us wholeheartedly in these expressions. Their gratitude to you is deep and sincere."

"The Council of Missionaries of the United Lutheran Church in Argentina, speaking on behalf of the missionaries, pastors, national workers and laymen of our great Church in this Republic, expresses to the mother Church in convention assembled, its gratitude for the prayerful support received from the beginning of work on this field to the present day and prays God's most abundant blessing on you all, and His guidance in your deliberations.

"At the same time, be assured of our deep interest in the work of the Church at large, and of our persevering loyalty to the Cause of the Kingdom. May the work of the Church be ever increasingly extended in the home land and in all mission fields, that His name may be glorified on earth as in Heaven."

It was moved and carried that the Secretary be instructed to send appropriate answers to these greetings.

The Rev. E. Neudoerffer brought the greetings from India, as did the Rev. C. H. Swavely who brought greetings from the Andhra Evangelical Lutheran Church.

The Rev. Shinichi Kawagiri presented the greetings of the Evangelical Lutheran Church in Japan.

On motion the report of the auditors was accepted.

In view of the expiration of the terms for which he was eligible as a member of the Board, Dr. Herman expressed his appreciation of the privilege of serving the Church through the Foreign Mission Board.

By general consent, the President recognized the Chairman of the Committee of Reference and Counsel, the Rev. John C. Mattes, who presented the Rev. S. O. Sigmond who, by commission from the President of his body, presented the greetings of the Norwegian Lutheran Church of America.

At the request of the President, the Rev. Joseph Sittler, President of the Synod of Ohio, responded to the greetings from the Norwegian Lutheran Church.

Mr. Carl Schulz, a member of the Committee, presented the Report of the Committee on Centennial in India.

REPORT OF THE COMMITTEE ON CENTENNIAL IN INDIA

(For action on the recommendations in this report, see p. 173)

The committee was appointed in accordance with the terms of a resolution adopted at the Convention of 1936 (Minutes, page 398), which reads:

Resolved, that a Committee of Five be appointed by the President to consider and to report at the next convention, concerning the feasibility of planning a tour to India in 1942 to attend the centennial celebration of the founding of our mission work in India.

The committee corresponded with officials of the Church, the Board of Foreign Missions, the India Mission, and with missionaries. It submits the following conclusions.

I. TIME FACTORS

The climate of India determines the time of the celebration there. The months of November, December, January and part of February are much like our northern May. The rest of the year is hot and dry, or rainy. The India Mission therefore plans to have its chief celebration in these pleasant months in 1942-43. Dating of the celebrations in India would carefully provide for previous attendance at the 1942 Convention of the United Lutheran Church.

There are two principal centers, Guntur and Rajahmundry, about one hundred miles apart, with many outlying stations in each area. It would take a number of weeks to visit every local division. The program therefore will be determined, not by what is to be seen, but by the amount of time American visitors can spend in India. President Knubel suggests May 25, 1938—"the best that can be expected is a stay of two to three weeks on the mission fields." He and Mrs. Knubel, with Treasurer Miller and Mrs. Miller, spent about that much time there in 1928, and visited a number of centers and met many people. Arrangements would gladly be made by the missionaries for any visitors who could remain longer.

To spend three weeks on the mission fields would mean close to thirty days between arrival at a port in India, and sailing from a port. The voyage to India via Europe, with a few days of sightseeing, would require about thirty days. A relatively unhurried but direct trip would therefore need about ninety days. A trip around the world (see next section) would need one hundred and twenty days. If pressed for time, one could hasten there and return, via Europe without stopover, in a total absence from Eastern America of about nine weeks, and spend two of the nine weeks on the fields.

II. Cost Factors

The 1938 price of a round-the-world trip by the Dollar Line is $930.00, first class. On some of their ships there is also tourist class, $590.00, which is very comfortable. It is quite possible and pleasant to travel on other lines at slightly lower rates. These inclusive prices provide all the sea-going transportation. The Dollar ships sail every two weeks, and stop-overs are allowed between ships in as many ports as one desires, provided the whole voyage is completed within two years. That is, one could stay two, four or six weeks in India, or any other multiple of two weeks.

The Dollar Line vessels all sail in the one direction, west. Their ports of call are New York, Havana, Panama, Los Angeles, San Francisco, Honolulu, Kobe, Shanghai, Hong Kong, Manila, Singapore, Penang, Colombo, Bombay, Suez (Cairo), Naples, Genoa, Marseilles, Gibraltar, New York. The continuous trip on the same vessel, with one to three days in each port of call, takes 104 days. Twenty days of this are used between New York and San Francisco. One could use the railway at a small additional cost and save fourteen days, making the trip itself ninety days. The stay in India of thirty days would make the total absence one hundred and twenty days.

If one went and returned by the more direct European routes the cost would be a little less than by the round-the-world trip.

As to expense of thirty days in India, the missionaries would arrange at cost for food and for any extra lodging needed beyond the capacity of their bungalows, perhaps $2.00 a day. There would be about 2,000 miles of rail travel from and to the ports, Colombo and Bombay, and on the mission fields. First class rail with meals would be about

$100.00, and second class, quite satisfactory, about $50.00. There are no extra charges for sleeping accommodations.

The necessary expenses for the direct trip from American ports if made in 1938 would be fully covered by the following schedule. No one can predict 1942 rates at the present time. The travel from one's home to the American port used, and return, would be additional. Whatever one chooses to spend in seeing the ports of call would be additional, but it need not be large to see much. The ship would be the hotel in most instances, and included in the total rate.

	First	Tourist and Second
Dollar Line Round-the-World	$930.00	$590.00
Railway Fare in India	100.00	50.00
Food and Lodging in India, 30 days	60.00	60.00
Add for passports, visas, baggage transfer, steamer and other tips, and general "leakage of travel—"	100.00	100.00
Total	$1190.00	$800.00

The committe, having considered the time and cost factors, report that they find the tour feasible, and desirable.
(See Recommendation No. 1.)

III. RELATIONSHIP TO A TOTAL PLAN

The committee believes that this proposed tour should not be an isolated adventure. It can be used to unite the celebrations of our Church in America and our Mission and Church in India. A group of visitors can carry to India a sense of the deep interest and continued backing of the home Church, and they can bring from India fresh and vivid impressions of what they have actually seen and heard.

The best modern forms of reporting can be used, in printed matter with illustrations in the present attractive fashion, in new slides and moving pictures, and in phonographic records of characteristic matters, all with a view to convey the true meaning of the century of work in India, its great expansion in recent years, and the still scarcely touched opportunities for further work among the middle classes. But no form of report excels the personal description of eye-witnesses in conveying the reality of the trust God has given to our Church in its India fields.

This tour can therefore become a true agency of the Lord in furthering among our American congregations better knowledge of their work in India.

(See Recommendation No. 2.)

IV. METHOD OF CONTINUED PLANNING

To promote such a tour, and to obtain for our Church in India and in America the useful results inherent in it, much work will be required in the next four years and longer. This committee therefore recommends that a new committee, of seven members, representative of the interests concerned, have charge of the formulation and execution of the necessary plans. This recommendation is agreed to by the Board of Foreign Missions.

(See Recommendation No. 3.)

With this report the committee has completed its work.

(See Recommendation No. 4.)

RECOMMENDATIONS

(For action see p. 173)

1. That a planned tour to India in the cold season of 1942-43, November to February, to attend the centennial celebration of the founding of our mission work in India, is feasible and desirable.

2. That this planned tour be made a part of a comprehensive program for the centennial celebration in the United Lutheran Church in America in 1942-43.

3. That a committee of the United Lutheran Church in America, of seven members, be appointed by the President to formulate and carry out plans for this Centennial Tour to India in co-operation with the Board of Foreign Missions, the Women's Missionary Society, and the India Mission and Church.

4. That this committee be discharged.

Signed: FRED J. FIEDLER,
E. J. MOLLENAUER,
M. P. MOLLER, JR.,
G. A. RUPLEY,
CARL SCHULZ,
Committee.

Recommendations 1, 2, and 3 were adopted. The President stated that, without special action (recommendation 4) the committee was discharged with thanks.

The Rev. W. F. Rangeler, President, presented the report of the Commission of Adjudication and a Supplementary Report of the Commission of Adjudication.

REPORT OF THE COMMISSION OF ADJUDICATION

After the elections were held at the Columbus Convention the membership of the Commission of Adjudication was oomposed of the following named persons:

Term expiring in 1938,

Rev. John Aberly, D.D., LL.D.;

Rev. W. F. Rangeler, D.D.;

Hon. C. M. Efird, LL.D.

Term expiring in 1940,

Rev. George J. Gongaware, D.D., LL.D.;

Rev. J. A. W. Haas, D.D., LL.D.;

Hon. John F. Kramer.

Term expiring in 1942,

Rev. W. E. Frey, D.D.;

Rev. L. Franklin Gruber, D.D., LL.D.;

Hon. James F. Henninger.

Just prior to the Columbus Convention, Rev. Luther Kuhlman, D.D., then president of the Commission, had tendered his resignation from the Commission to the President of the United Lutheran Church on account of his failing health. In the providence of God, Dr. Kuhlman died while the Columbus Convention was in session. Dr. W. F. Rangeler was asked by the Commission to prepare a note on the death of Dr. Kuhlman, to be spread upon the minutes, and presented the following:

MINUTE ON THE DEATH OF REV. LUTHER KUHLMAN, D.D.

When the United Lutheran Church in America was assembled in convention at Columbus, Ohio, announcement came of the death of Dr. Luther Kuhlman, then president of the Commission of Adjudication. He passed to his eternal rest on October 18, 1936, at his home in Gettysburg, Pennsylvania, at the advanced age of eighty-five years.

Dr. Kuhlman was elected to the Commission in 1926, at Richmond, Virginia, and was re-elected at Philadelphia, Pennsylvania, in 1932, and at the organization of the Commisison for 1932 he was elected President and retained that office until the time of his death. As president of the Commission he followed the late Dr. A. G. Voigt of Columbia, South Carolina, and as president read the report of the Commission at the Savannah Convention in 1934.

Dr. Kuhlman was a very faithful member of the Commission of Adjudication, and his capable mind and large acquaintance with the Church and experience in its work made him very efficient in the services he rendered to the Church. At the time of his death the papers which he was preparing for the report of the Commission to the Columbus Convention were lying on his desk.

The various other capacities in which he served his Church through the years, as a pastor, as a professor for thirteen years in Gettysburg Theological Seminary, member of the Board of Foreign Missions for thirty-two years, for nineteen of which years he was President of the Board, and for three years its field secretary, and many other lines of service marked Dr. Kuhlman as an outstanding servant of the Church.

The Commission of Adjudication hereby records its high appreciation of his devoted service and of the gracious Christian spirit always manifested in the inspiring fellowship it enjoyed with him. It would also hereby express the deep sense of loss it has felt at his removal from our midst and its heartfelt sympathy to the Church and to the many personal friends and relatives of Dr. Kuhlman.

Respectfully submitted for record by

W. F. RANGELER.

As we enter upon the report to be presented at the Twentieth Anniversary of the United Lutheran Church in America, may we give a brief paragraph or two in reflection?

The first Commission of Adjudication constituted at the merger convention in 1918 was made up of the following named persons:

Rev. H. E. Jacobs, D.D., LL.D., President.

Rev. D. H. Bauslin, D.D., LL.D., Vice-President.

Rev. Holmes Dysinger, D.D., LL.D., Secretary.

Hon. E. K. Strong, Clerk.

Hon. Henry Harter, Hon. Aaron E. Reiber, Rev. L. A. Fox, D.D., LL.D., Rev. J. A. W. Haas, D.D., LL.D., and Rev. A. G. Voigt, D.D., LL.D

Now, of the laymen of this original group so far as we know, the only survivor is the Hon. Aaron E. Reiber, and of the clerical members, the only survivor is the Rev. Holmes Dysinger, D.D., LL.D., at present professor emeritus of systematic Theology in Western Theological Seminary. The present incumbent, Dr. Rangeler, is the only survivor of those who have served in the office of President of the Commission. Those who have served in this capacity since the merger were Rev. Henry E. Jacobs, D.D., LL.D., Rev. A. G. Voigt, D.D., LL.D., Rev. Luther Kuhlman, D.D., and the present incumbent in the office.

Since the merger quite a number of major questions have come before the Commission for opinion and decision as may be seen by a reference to the printed minutes of the United Lutheran Church conventions from time to time, opinions and decisions that have been far reaching in the life and practice of the church. It has fully demonstrated the wisdom of the church in providing in its constitution for such a Commission of Adjudication and in giving it judicial authority.

At the conclusion of the elections at the Columbus Convention in 1936 there was no quorum of the Commission present, so that a reorganization of the Commission could not be effected at that time, and it went into the present biennium, with Rev. W. F. Rangeler, D.D., the Vice-President, acting as president; Rev. George J. Gongaware, D.D., LL.D., secretary, and the other offices vacant.

Rev. John Aberly, D.D., LL.D., who had been elected to fill the un-expired term of Dr. Kuhlman, declined to serve as he had been elected to the Board of Publication. The Executive Board, on the recommendation of the Commission, appointed Rev. B. H. Pershing, Ph.D., of Hamma Divinity School, to take Dr. Aberly's place on the Commission, the term expiring in 1938.

The first meeting of the Biennium was called at Springfield, Ohio, July 7, 1937. Only four regular members attended together with Dr. Knubel, President of The United Lutheran Church in America as ex-officio member. They were Drs. Frey and Rangeler, and Hons. Henninger and Kramer. There being no quorum no official business was transacted, but those present spent the day in studying and discussing the question referred to the Commission by the Columbus Convention through the Executive Board. A tentative outline of opinion was agreed upon and the Hon. James F. Henninger appointed to draft an opinion to be acted upon, and adjournment taken to January 11, 1938, at Harrisburg, Pa., when a quorum was present. At this meeting the regular reorganization of the Commission was had, resulting in the election of Rev. W. F. Rangeler, D.D., President; Rev. L. Franklin Gruber, D.D., LL.D., Vice-President; Rev. George J. Gongaware, D.D., LL.D., Secretary, and Hon. James F. Henninger, Clerk.

In the meantime death had entered the ranks of the Commission and taken away one of its able members in the person of Rev. John A. W. Haas, D.D., LL.D., L.H.D., and to succeed to his place on the Commission, Rev. C. M. Jacobs, D.D., LL.D., was recommended to the Executive Board and appointed. As the church is well aware death came also to Dr. Jacobs before there was any opportunity for him to function as a member and, therefore, the vacancy remains on the Commission of Adjudication, as no subsequent meeting has been held at which a nomination could be made.

Action was taken at the Harrisburg meeting requesting the secretary, Dr. Gongaware, to prepare an appreciation of the services of Dr. Haas with the request that it be made a part of this report. It follows herewith:

1862—THE REVEREND JOHN A. W. HAAS, D.D., LL.D., L.H.D.—1937

Through Church Academy, State University and Theological Seminary in Philadelphia, and through Leipsic University in Germany, Dr. Haas came to New York in 1888, where he took his vows of Ordination to the Office of the Ministry of the Gospel. In this metropolitan center he served Grace Church until 1895 and then St. Paul's Church until he was called to the presidency of Muhlenberg College in 1904. Resigning his office in 1936 he was made President Emeritus, and he continued his active interest in the cause of Christian Education until the close of his fruitful life on July 22, 1937.

A child of sturdy stock, endowed richly in mind and heart, a graduate of high-grade institutions, an independent thinker and an indefatigable worker, he went far into the fields of theological, philosophical, ethical and economic truth, and, as a master bulider and a discriminating judge, he gathered choice materials and builded them into helpful books, such as, "Trends of Thought and Christian Truths," "Freedom and Christian Conduct," "Unity of Faith and Knowledge," "Christian Truths," "What I Ought to Believe," "The Christian Way of Liberty," and "Christianity and Its Contrasts," with an eighth manuscript, lacking only its title, ready for the press when death stilled his voice and stopped his facile pen.

Dr. Haas' vivid personality and his kindly concern for mankind led him into varied avenues for investigation and counsel and service, but his consuming passion was for the Church and for her educational system. He must have sensed the mind of the Church and known surely his own strength when he decided to give himself, as he approached the peak of his powers, to the presidency of Muhlenberg College. This institution is, for the day, his material memorial, but his enduring tribute will be made vocal by the lips and will become increasingly eloquent in the lives of his beloved "Boys" to the third and fourth generation of their children.

Dr. Haas was an understanding friend, a wise counselor and a discriminating judge in a day when fellowship and justice and judgment were much needed.

He was a devoted churchman and loyal parishioner, a fearless prophet, and a great preacher of a great Gospel in a time when constancy and courage and conviction were demanded.

He was a valuable member of our Commission of Adjudication, and we are very deeply conscious of a sense of loss, even while we rejoice at his release into the very fullness of life in the presence of God, and we hereby bear to this body, The United Lutheran Church in America, our sincere tribute of affectionate and grateful esteem for his rare ministry in the general field of human affairs, but, chiefly, for his illustrious career as a scholar, preacher, educator, author, and executive.

Signed: GEORGE J. GONGAWARE,
For the Commission of Adjudication.

The following additional actions taken at the Harrisburg meeting of the Commission should be reported:

1. The Clerk of the Commission was requested to prepare an historical narrative of the office of Clerk of the Commission from the beginning of the life of the Commission.

2. The Secretary was authorized to have published a new edition of the "Synopsis" of the Constitutional Provisions creating and governing the Commission and its rules of procedure as adopted and amended by the United Lutheran Church to the present time. This has been done, and the supply is in the custody of the Secretary of the Commission.

3. At the Baltimore Convention the terms of Dr. Pershing, Dr. Rangeler, and Hon. C. M. Efird expire, the latter two being ineligible to re-election by reason of having served the constitutional limit of

twelve years. The following nominations were therefore made for the Baltimore election:

As successor to himself, Rev. B. H. Pershing, Ph.D., Hamma Divinity School, Springfield, Ohio;

As successor to Hon. C. M. Efird, F. W. Cappelmann, Columbia, S. C.

As successor to Dr. Rangeler, The Rev. P. W. H. Frederick, D.D., Western Theological Seminary, Fremont, Nebraska.

The death of Dr. Jacobs occurred since these nominations were made. The Commission therefore has sought permission of the Executive Board to present additional nominations in a supplemental report prior to the appointment of the nominating committees at Baltimore.

The major action at the Harrisburg meeting was the rendering of an opinion on the question of reference of the Columbus Convention. It has been certified to the Executive Board and is as follows:

Before

THE COMMISSION OF ADJUDICATION

of

The United Lutheran Church in America

In the matter of the Reference by The United Lutheran Church in America, in Tenth Convention assembled, of the action of the Convention upon the report of the "Committee on Women as Congregational Representatives."

THE REFERENCE

This matter came before the Commission of Adjudication by reference from The United Lutheran Church in America pursuant to the terms of a resolution passed at its Tenth Convention at Columbus, Ohio, on October 2, 1936 (Minutes, page 433) as follows:

"It was moved and carried that the convention instruct the Executive Board to be its agent in formulating an appeal to the Commission of Adjudication concerning the binding character of the action which adopted the recommendation of the 'Committee on Women as Congregational Representatives.'"

The Executive Board thereupon formulated a reference, stating the facts leading to the action of the convention and giving a statement of the questions involved. In accordance with Rule 3 of the Commission of Adjudication, under Practice as to Resolutions for submission, the reference was in the form of four questions answerable "yes" or "no" as follows:

1. Is the matter upon which the convention acted a "matter of conscience"?

2. If the answer to number one is "yes," did the convention follow the required method and make its decision, "according to the Word of God alone"?

3. Does the action of the convention in adopting the recommendations of the majority report bindingly decide the meaning of and the extent of the authority of certain passages of Scripture?

4. Does the action of the convention in adopting the majority report bind the conscience of members of The United Lutheran Church in America?

The matter referred is properly before the Commission (See Article VIII, Section 5, and Article XII, Section 1 of the Constitution of The United Lutheran Church in America, providing for reference to the Commission of Adjudication by resolution of the U. L. C. A.)

THE PROBLEM

The matter arises out of memorials from the Texas Synod to The United Lutheran Church in America, submitted to its Seventh Convention at Milwaukee, Wisconsin, in 1930 (Minutes, page 142), to determine whether or not the election or seating of women as representatives to synod is unscriptural.. A special committee was appointed to consider these memorials (Minutes, pages 143-145) which presented majority and minority reports to the Eighth Convention in Philadelphia, Pennsylvania, in 1932. Thereupon a new committee was appointed to reconsider the matter (Minutes, pages 426 to 430) and this committee reported again with majority and minority reports at the Ninth Convention at Savannah, Georgia, in 1934 (Minutes, pages 456 to 466, 524). Action was postponed until the Tenth Convention at Columbus, Ohio, in 1936, at which the following recommendations contained in the majority report were adopted:

(a) That the reply of The United Lutheran Church in America to the Texas Synod be as follows: That the election of women delegates to meetings of Synod is not unscriptural in the sense that it is not contrary to or forbidden by the Scriptures.

(b) That this action shall be understood as applying to any similar question that may hereafter arise concerning the eligibility of women for membership in Church Councils, or in general conventions, boards or committees of the Church.

(c) The conception of spiritual equality in Christ does not alter the fact that, by divine appointment, certain spheres of Christian service are more natural or normal to men, while other types of service can best be performed by women. Since the Church deeply deplores those social, industrial, and economic conditions which oppose the Christian home, the glory of motherhood, and the rearing of children in the nurture and admonition of the Lord, it should encourage the fulfillment of those duties by the exercising of care in the organization and assignment of its work (Minutes, pages 58, 397, 408, 418, 432, 433).

The Commission has concluded that the matter was referred to it solely as a question of conscience and of church polity. The holding of the Lutheran Church, however, that the canonical Scriptures of the Old and New Testament are the inspired Word of God and the only infallible rule and standard of faith and practice (Formula of Concord, Introduction, Part I, Par. 1, and Part II, Par. 1, Jacobs' Book of Concord, Ed. 1911, pages 491 and 535, Mueller paging pages 517 and 569) renders any unscriptural procedure contrary also to its doctrine. We find no pronouncement in our Church controlling this question and, therefore, it follows that, if representation by women is not unscriptural it is permissible in Lutheran Church polity. The decision of the main question, therefore, will resolve any point of doctrine and polity as well as of conscience that may be involved.

THE ANSWER

The Commission has deemed it advisable to state certain principles which will answer the questions presented to it, in preference to replying categorically to each question.

I. The Propriety of the Convention's Action

We take it that, in the absence of a pronouncement upon the subject in her symbols and confessions, the Church may adopt any desirable (to her) practice or usage, which is not contrary or forbidden by the Scriptures. (Formula of Concord, Part I, Chapter X, Par. 4, Jacobs, page 523, Mueller, page 552.) While this section speaks of rites and ceremonies, the principle would apply as well to Church administration. As the diaconate seems to have been set up for the sake of expediency and apparently in the absence of specific Divine command or direction, so it is sufficient justification for administrative policy in the Church today that it is expedient, desirable and not contrary to nor forbidden by the Scriptures.

It is not the function of this Commission to determine whether the attitude of the Church as expressed in its adoption of the recommendations of the Majority Report is either expedient or desirable. Nor is it our function to restudy the original problem and to formulate an independent opinion of our own either in conformity with or contrary to the opinion of the Majority Report on the main question as to whether or not representation of women is unscriptural. Our sole function, in the first place, is to determine whether or not the decision in the Majority Report and in the action of the Convention was based "on the Word of God alone."

We note that nowhere does the Committee or the Convention intimate that its action is based upon expediency alone. In fact, the third recommendation indicates reluctance in acceding to the right of women to act as representatives. Therefore, we do not have a situation in which an unscriptural action is urged, because of expediency, in which case we could readily say that the decision was not based "on the Word of God alone."

Nor would we be bound by any statement of the committee that it is deciding solely on Scriptural grounds, if the contrary were apparent. "When under the title and pretext of external adiaphora, such things are proposed, as (although painted another color) are in fact contrary to God's Word, these are not to be regarded adiaphora, but should be avoided as things prohibited by God." (Formula of Concord, Part II, Chapter X, Par. 5, Jacobs, page 644, Mueller, page 698.)

It is our duty, however, to assume that the majority of the committee were sincere in their opinion that the proposed procedure was not forbidden by nor contrary to the Scriptures, unless we are inevitably forced to a contrary conclusion. This obligation to assume sincerity becomes still more pressing when formal action is taken by a deliberative body such as The United Lutheran Church in America in convention assembled. Furthermore, we note that the minority members of the committee do not question the sincerity of the majority nor their exegetical methods, but question simply their conclusion as to the meaning of the passages of Scripture studied. That other sincere scholars arrive at a different conclusion does not destroy the validity of the Majority Report.

We conclude, therefore, that the Majority Report, as adopted by the Convention, is based, not upon a denial of the validity or binding force of any Scriptural provisions, but upon a sincere and considered belief that those provisions advanced by the minority as forbidding women representatives do not apply and were not intended to apply to the part women are permitted to take in the deliberative, administrative bodies of the Church, and that they found no other Scriptural provisions applicable, and that the proposed action is not forbidden by nor contrary to the Scriptures and is, therefore, not unscriptural. The Majority Report, therefore, and the action of the Convention is based "on the Word of God alone" as that expression is understood in the Lutheran Church and does not violate the standards of The United Lutheran Church in America for the determination of its problems.

II. THE DOCTRINAL EFFECT OF SUCH ACTION

If the problems under discussion were dealt with in any of the confessions or symbols of the Lutheran Church, one who claimed membership in that Church could be expected to adhere to its pronouncement upon the subject. It is admitted, however, that no such pronouncement exists. If The United Lutheran Church in America were to attempt to deviate from its historical doctrines, it could not do so by vote of its conventions. Therefore, the action of the Tenth Convention in taking a position upon the matter before it, did not add any tenet to its doctrinal basis. It follows, then, that the doctrinal conformity of its members cannot be tested by adherence or non-adherence to the position taken by the convention on this problem.

That the Tenth Convention in answering the Texas Synod Memorial did adopt an interpretation of Holy Scriptures cannot be denied. The fact that it had no authority to write this interpretation into the doctrinal basis of the Church did not prevent it from making such interpretation for its own guidance in solving the immediate problem before it.

To give this the effect of an authoritative interpretation would be contrary to the first principle of Lutheran doctrine that the Scriptures are the only infallible standard of faith and doctrine (Formula of Concord, Introduction, Part I, Par. 1, Jacobs page 491, Mueller page 517) and that the writings of no man may take precedence over the very Scriptures themselves but must be subordinated thereto. (Formula of Concord, Introduction, Part II, Par. 9, Jacobs page 537, Mueller page 571.)

Since, then, the action of the Tenth Convention did not become a part of the doctrine of the Church nor establish an authoritative interpretation of the Scriptures, such action is not binding upon the conscience of any individual member of The United Lutheran Church in America.

III. THE PRACTICAL EFFECT OF SUCH ACTION

The question as presented in the Memorials from the Texas Synod was in reality an academic question, no instance having been given in which any woman had presented credentials to be seated as a representative to a synod. To declare it a moot question, however, would be to refuse to face a problem of imminent importance. We have, therefore, given careful consideration to the practical effect of the action of the Tenth Convention in adopting the resolutions contained in the Majority Report.

First, the Convention answered a particular memorial; next, it declared that its answer would be the same to any other synods making the same inquiry; then, it held that the answer applied not only to women as representatives to synod, but to women as members of Church Councils, Church Conventions, and Boards and Committees of the Church. These decisions became the settled policy of the Church, using the word settled not in the sense that the policy is irrevocable or infallible, but in the sense that it will continue indefinitely until the Church may see fit to reverse or modify it.

Meanwhile, all persons in office amenable to the authority of The United Lutheran Church in America are in duty bound in their official capacity to recognize this policy. So the President of The United Lutheran Church in America would be bound to seat women delegates with proper credentials; a synodical secretary or president would be bound to certify a woman as a delegate to The United Lutheran Church in America Conventions if otherwise eligible; a Board or Committee Chairman of The United Lutheran Church in America would be compelled to recognize a woman appointed to such Board or Committee; The United Lutheran Church in America in any controversy would recognize a woman as a proper member of any of the bodies mentioned.

The action of the convention does not in itself make women eligible for any such positions. It simply prevents any objection on the ground that the recognition of women in such capacities would be contrary to or forbidden by Scriptures. Any existing constitutional provisions forbidding women such authority are not affected by the action of the convention.

Furthermore, the action of the convention would not prevent any synod from duly making proper constitutional provision that women shall not be eligible as representatives to its synods or as one of its delegates to The United Lutheran Church in America conventions. Nor would it prevent a congregation from taking similar action as to its Church Council or its representatives in synod.

Conclusion

We feel that the above fully disposes of the problem presented to the Commission for what has been said covers all the points in the reference to this Commission. To be more explicit would entail a most injudicious anticipation of future situations without a complete statement of the issues that might be involved.

Consented to at Harrisburg, Pa., January 11, 1938, at a regularly called meeting of the Commission of Adjudication,

By W. F. Rangeler, *President,*
L. Franklin Gruber, *Vice-President,*
George J. Gongaware, *Secretary,*
W. E. Frey,
John F. Kramer,
James F. Henninger.
All of whom were present at the meeting.

Two members were absent on account of illness, Judge C. M. Efird and Dr. B. H. Pershing. One vacany existed on the Commission, caused by the death of Dr. J. A. W. Haas. There was no dissenting voice to the opinion.

Appreciations are due to The Honorable Judge James F. Henninger of Allentown, Pa., who was entrusted by the Commission with the work of giving proper formulation to the opinion, and who did the work in such excellent manner.

It was voted at the Harrisburg meeting that unless further business should arise to make an earlier meeting necessary, the Commission would hold its next meeting at Baltimore preliminary to the opening of the United Lutheran Church convention.

By action of the Commission at Harrisburg the president of the Commission was authorized to prepare this report and to present the report of the Commission at the Baltimore Convention.

Respectfully submitted by the Commission of Adjudication of The United Lutheran Church in America.

Signed: GEORGE J. GONGAWARE, Secretary,
W. F. RANGELER, President.

SUPPLEMENTARY REPORT OF THE COMMISSION OF ADJUDICATION

The Commission of Adjudication met in regularly called session in the Lord Baltimore Hotel, Baltimore, Maryland, October 5, 1938, and completed its business for the biennium with reference to the following items:

1. Nominations were completed and certified to the Committee on Nominations for the election to membership on the Commission of Adjudication as follows:

For the term expiring in 1944, Rev. Benjamin H. Pershing, Ph. D., Synod of Ohio (eligible to re-election); Rev. P. W. H. Frederick, D.D., Nebraska Synod; Rev. H. E. Turney, S.T.M., D.D., Indiana Synod; Rev. G. Keller Rubrecht, D.D., Nebraska Synod; Hon. F. W. Cappelmann, Columbia, S. C.; Hon. F. H. Horlbeck, Charleston, S. C.

For the term expiring in 1940 (made vacant first by the death of Rev. J. A. W. Haas, D.D., LL.D., L.H.D., and again by the death of Rev. C. M. Jacobs, D.D., LL.D.), Rev. Paul J. Hoh, S.T.M., Pennsylvania Ministerium, Rev. C. W. Leitzell, D.D., New York Synod.

2. The Commission completed its work on the matter of Reference by The United Lutheran Church in America and delivered the officially signed copy of its opinion to the Secretary of The United Lutheran Church in America, the opinion being officially signed by the eight members of the Commission now in office.

3. Two matters of importance to which the Commission was asked to give attention at this meeting had to be refused consideration because they were not brought through the proper sources, and therefore did not come within its jurisdiction.

In this connection pastors and others should be reminded that appeals can regularly be brought to the Commission of Adjudication only from three sources, namely, by resolution of a constituent Synod, by resolution of the United Lutheran Church in convention assembled, or by resolution of the Executive Board of the United Lutheran Church in the interim between conventions. (See Rules of Practice and Procedure, page 10, Item 1.)

4. Provision was made for an item to be recorded in the minutes of the Commission touching the death of Dr. C. M. Jacobs.

5. In closing this report we should like to make mention of our deep gratitude to the Honorable Judge C. M. Efird, LL.D., of Lexington, S. C., and Dr. W. F. Rangeler of Fremont, Nebr., for their efficient and faithful services as members of this Commission for the past twelve years and whose services now cease through constitutional limitations.

Physical infirmities have prevented Judge Efird from being present at this convention. We therefore record our sympathy with him and our earnest prayers for his restored and continued health.

Respectfully submitted by

THE COMMISSION OF ADJUDICATION,

GEORGE J. GONGAWARE, Sec.

W. F. RANGELER, Pres.

The President declared that the decision of the Commission of Adjudication on "the binding character of the action of the Convention on the status of women in the Church," is the decision of the Church.

Consideration of the report of the Executive Board was taken up as an item of unfinished business.

Item IV, B (c), Amendments to the Constitution of the Board of Foreign Missions, page 84. The amendments were approved.

Item IV, B (d), Co-operation with the American Lutheran Church in India, page 84. This item was approved.

The President reported that he had appointed the following as the Committee of Nine to which was referred Item II, 16, of the report of the Executive Board and the memorial from the New York Synod, etc.: (For other references to this item, see pp. 61, 107, 464, 465, 483.)

Rev. A. E. Bell, Chairman	Rev. R. H. Gerberding
Rev. F. R. Knubel	Rev. A. J. Traver
Rev. L. W. Strickler	Rev. H. J. Pflum
Rev. F. W. Kern	Mr. W. H. Hager

Mr. W. H. Menges

At twelve o'clock the Convention adjourned with prayer by the Rev. R. W. Livers.

FOURTH SESSION

LORD BALTIMORE HOTEL

Baltimore, Maryland

Friday, October 7, 1938, 2.00 P. M.

Devotions were conducted by the Rev. H. J. Black, and the President called the Convention to order.

The Special Committee on Minutes reported that they had examined the Minutes of the first and second sessions and, finding them correct, moved their approval. The motion was carried and the President declared the Minutes approved.

The Rev. H. J. Pflum, President, presented the report of the Board of American Missions.

REPORT OF THE BOARD OF AMERICAN MISSIONS

The re-thinking of missions by the earnest men and women of our churches appears to have crystallized during the past biennium into certain conclusions.

A conviction has grown and is finding audible expression that all too frequently the primary objective of home missions, the winning of souls for Christ and His Church, has seemed to be overshadowed by a desire to add congregations to a Synodical roll or to erect buildings to impress a community.

Generous supporters of the cause of missions have openly given as their mature conviction that benevolence money was being mis-used when spent on fields that were organized with more zeal than knowledge.

Others whose heart and soul are devoted to the cause of missions, have felt that the home mission enterprise should mean more than the mere gathering together and the housing of little groups of our own faith. There is a growing conviction among them that something must also be done to provide the socially and spiritually under-privileged and neglected areas of life with the enriching ministry of the Gospel of Christ. Numbers of them have further expressed their judgment that this could in many instances be accomplished more successfully through the general board co-operating with established congregations rather than by inaugurating new enterprises.

A reflection of this changed attitude will be evident in portions of this report. During the coming years the ideals which guide the Board of American Missions we trust will become still more manifest and in ever-increasing measure will satisfy the longing of many hearts for the dawn of a new day in home missions.

DIVISION OF SURVEY AND RESEARCH

This enlarged vision of the Home Mission enterprise inevitably imposes an increased "stewardship of spending" on your Board of American Missions. It was that which lay behind the establishment of its Division of Survey and Research, after the Columbus Convention formally authorized it. Through that Division an orderly progress in opening new fields has been made financially possible, as well as a similar service for strengthening existing, strategically located congregations.

In November, 1936, the board stated the general purpose of this new Division as follows:

"This Division is charged with the duty of a constant study of all mission stations under the board's jurisdiction. It shall seek especially for additional methods by which missions m a y be m o r e thoroughly equipped for their task and assisted to earlier self-support. Under the direction of this committee periodic studies of the trends of population and changing social conditions which affect the board's work shall be conducted."

"In the study of the missions of the Church, this Division shall:

1. Conduct re-surveys of existing mission fields and as far as funds and personnel permit, conduct a re-survey of each field once in three years.

2. Supervise all original surveys, whether conducted by synodical or board personnel.

3. Collate, analyze, and prepare reports with all pertinent information on surveys and re-surveys for submission through the Executive Secretary to the proper synodical authorities.

4. Prepare analytical reports of economic conditions and other data which will be of assistance to the board in making decisions concerning the administration of the Home Mission enterprise.

"The activities of this Division are not at any time to be administrative, and its activities are to be confined to fact-finding for the information of the board and its administrative agencies."

The Division of Research and Survey has, since its organization, conducted 162 surveys of prospective fields and 46 re-surveys of fields in which the board was already interested. Of the 162 original surveys, the Division has recommended 35 fields for starting work, 30 fields for subsequent review, and has rejected 97 fields as containing no field, at present, for the Lutheran Church. To do this work personal calls have been made upon 147,000 families in the prospective fields and 73,000 in the fields re-surveyed. Allowing that the average family contains four members, the board's canvassers have compiled data on the church membership of 880,000 people in over 200 fields. The Division has worked on the territory of twenty-five of the constituent synods of the U. L. C. A.

This Division has produced facts that powerfully confirm what was formerly only a conviction of home mission leaders; namely, that at the present time there are opportunities for the inauguration of successful missions such as would require resources in men and money four times greater than are now available.

So heavily does this matter weigh upon the board members that a study has been ordered of all fields now receiving support from the board in the expectation and resolve that within the next biennium the care of the more backward fields will be provided for without draining the mission funds of the church. The men and money so released will then be used in the more hopeful fields constantly being discovered by the Division of Survey and Research.

DIVISION OF LINGUISTIC INTERESTS

An Account of Opportunities

Dr. Tappert, Secretary of the Division of Linguistic Interests, writes: "Man's extremity is not only God's opportunity, it is also man's opportunity. It presents a challenge which must drive a Christian to greater exertion, to more persistent effort. A few comparatively prosperous months moved upward the receipts on apportionment and hope was revived. Then came a recession that brought despair to the business world, but even this did not daunt the spirit of our bi-lingual missionaries. Even though a large part of the linguistic fields suffered an additional calamity through the severe drought, which extended over a period of from three to five years, nevertheless, the mission work goes on. Again man's extremity became man's opportunity. Those who were directly touched by this widespread calamity were spurred by necessity to greater efforts while their more fortunate brethren here found their opportunity to show Christian love in extensive relief of the distressed and the needy. This in return released spiritual forces in those who were benefitted and the result will be greater loyalty to the Lord Who gives and the church which serves Him in the least of His brethren.

Sincere appreciation is due to the Board of Inner Missions for the very valuable assistance which has been rendered in these critical situations.

OPPORTUNITIES IN WESTERN CANADA.—Experience has demonstrated over and over again that a mission congregation seldom feels a sense of permanency until it possesses a church property. Conditions in the Western Canada field make efforts in this direction imperative. In the newly settled districts there are no buildings of sufficient size in which a congregation can gather for worship. Even schoolhouses are scarce and small, while the shacks of the settlers are in most cases totally inadequate. The absence of material possessions outside of the land makes it impossible for these pioneers to finance the most modest church buildings. This extremity became the opportunity for many mission-minded friends who supplied amounts, in most cases not exceeding a few hundred dollars, but sufficient to aid these people in the construction of church and parsonage buildings. The understanding is that the cash is to pay for items which the people cannot manufacture themselves, and that the members of the congregation must do all the required labor free of charge. The first church building was erected at Hines Creek in the Peace River District, under direction of former field missionary A. Goos. The money, $200, was given by an aged brother and sister, members of St. Paul's Church, The Bronx, N. Y. When the neat little building was completed an accounting of the cost was given. It amounted to $199.50. Since then a great many buildings have been erected so that every parish has at least some of its congregations provided with a place of worship, and almost all our missionaries are housed. At this writing forty-two church buildings have thus been aided, thirty-seven of which are completed, and eighteen parsonages. Gifts have come from a great many individuals in amounts of $1.00 up, also from Sunday schools and church societies. A few larger amounts came to us through bequests. Many of the structures are built of logs; others are frame. Some of the churches are quite large and beautiful, like the one in Barrhead, Alberta, into which went a $450 bequest from a lady in Johnstown, Pa., or like the one in Patience, Alberta, for which a gentleman in Philadelphia had made provision. In one case, at The Pas, Manitoba, the hall of the Canadian Legion was purchased and re-modeled into a church and parsonage; in another, at S t o n y Plain, Alberta, the Anglican church building was bought for $300, provided by a Sunday school in Waterloo, Ontario. This building program has tremendously aided our mission activities. We have no complete figures to make comparisons with other church bodies with regard to the number of mission churches, but in thirty missions we have twenty-six parsonages, while another synod on the same territory has only eight parsonages in thirty-nine missions. We have no doubt that about the same percentage prevails with regard to church buildings. Since the establishing of new parishes and the organizing of new congregations must continually go on, there will be need of more church buildings and parsonages.

In addition to providing mission parishes with buildings an attempt has been made to safeguard the future of some of the more isolated missions by endowing them with a homestead, the receipts from which will help them to attain self-support in the shortest possible time. Thus a 160-acre farm for the Woodhill, Saskatchewan, Parish has been secured, and another for the Northmark, Alberta, Parish, both financed through the generous gifts of a lady in Chicago, as well as one at Hines Creek, Alberta, for which a lady in Johnstown, Pa., provided the funds. With land prices as cheap as they are at present it would be helpful to endow all our country parishes in this practical way.

DIVIDING PARISHES FOR MORE EFFECTIVE WORK—One of our most pressing problems is the necessity of reducing the size of large mission parishes for more effective work. Due to the shortage of men and the scarcity of means, some of our missionaries must serve a field altogether too large for one man to care for properly. A parish in Saskatchewan still has twelve preaching places, in spite of the fact that it has been divided three times and three parishes have come out of it. In Alberta there are three parishes which should be divided; one has eight, one seven and one five congregations. What that means to the missionary no one can comprehend unless he knows the magnificent distances that separate these points. It stands to reason that with so many congregations so far apart there cannot be a service every Sunday at all the points, nor can proper attention be given to the training of the young when the pastor must continually rush from one place to another. More pastors of the pioneer type are sadly needed. What is more, the men can be secured, if the c h u r c h will supply the funds for their training.

OPPORTUNITIES THROUGH SASKATOON SEMINARY—At the beginning the supply of missionaries for both Eastern and Western Canada came from the Fatherland. The World War cut off this supply. For the Manitoba Synod especially this produced an extremity, yea, a calamity, but it also proved the opportunity for Saskatoon Seminary. Through its establishment shortly before the war, as things turned out, the Manitoba Synod had unwittingly saved its own life. For twenty-five years now this seminary has rendered the greatest service to the mission field, until today about half of the pastorates there are filled with its graduates. But still greater things are expected from it in the future. Strategically located as it is, it is capable of wider service. In order to speed this day this lone seminary covering a territory of more than a million square miles, should be strengthened in its teaching force as well as in its physical equipment. It is true that buildings do not make a great seminary; but it is likewise true that the lack of proper equipment is a great handicap. May the day soon come when Saskatoon Seminary will receive what is needed to make it the training ground of missionaries for the entire Lutheran constituency of Western Canada!

FINNISH OPPORTUNITIES IN CANADA—Our Finnish field in Canada extends from Quebec in the East to Vancouver in the West. In Vancouver our Finnish Lutherans are being supplied by the pastor of our English church, who is of Finnish extraction. In the Prairie Provinces the situation in the Finnish settlements is very much the same as in the German and Scandinavian districts. In the main, they have their churches and their parsonages, but both the Alberta and the Saskatchewan parishes have been vacant most of the time. We have a Finnish student in Saskatoon who gives occasional care, but there is no immediate prospect of having them permanently supplied. The Finnish field is too young, and has not as yet produced the material from which we could train native Finnish pastors. In the industrial and mining districts of Quebec and Ontario the situation is a little more favorable. Here we have a more recent immigration which in case of need can be served by men imported from Finland. In Montreal we have a flourishing congregation but no building; in Toronto a building was acquired but the congregation must wait for funds before it can be remodeled. In the great nickel center at Sudbury a chapel has been erected and a parsonage is ardently desired. In the Timmins-South Porcupine Parish a building is contemplated this summer. In Kirkland Lake, in the gold land, the congregation is worshiping in its recently completed church building. During this summer it is planned to enter the largest Finnish settlement in Ontario.

OPPORTUNITIES IN EASTERN CANADA—Our German opportunities in Eastern Canada are somewhat limited. Ontario, which used to be an important German mission field, has only six German-English missions, three of them classified as sustentation points. In Nova Scotia and New Brunswick, we have a missionary working among the newly arrived settlers in widely scattered colonies. The success of this work largely depends on increasing immigration. Smaller groups, such as Hungarian and Slovak, are to be found in Montreal, Toronto, Hamilton and Windsor. Only the Hungarian group in Windsor, Ont., is properly housed. Their progress is exceedingly slow.

LINGUISTIC OPPORTUNITIES IN THE UNITED STATES—German missions in the United States total thirteen; one in the Midwest Synod, three in the Ministerium of Pennsylvania, three in the Pittsburgh, one in the Texas, three in the New York, and two in the Wartburg Synod. The East and the West are still full of Germans who are unchurched. A mission is greatly needed among the post-war Germans in the New York area. The Germans in the East, however, can still find many churches in which there is some German preaching. The church, however, should be aroused about the plight of our German Lutherans in the West. While our Lutheran Church is hardly doing anything, the Congregational Church is making rapid progress among the German Lutherans of the West; yea, they have become so encouraged by these successes that they have extended their work to the German Lutherans in Brazil, for whom we are doing nothing. There they work with such persuasion that in January of this year the Evangelical Lutheran Confessional Synod merged with them at a conference held at New Wuertemberg, Brazil. They have a Seminary at Yankton, S.D., with three professors and sixteen students, in which they train their men specifically for service among the German Lutherans from Russia who in some counties of the Dakotas have appropriated almost every farm in the county. They use Luther's Catechism and pretend to be Lutherans; that may be true for the present generation; but in the next generation these congregations will not be Lutheran but Congregational. Repeated attention has been drawn to these conditions but apparently without success. Synods with such large foreign-speaking groups on their territory should carefully investigate the possibilities.

Of Slovak missions we have one in Pennsylvania, one in New York, one in Ohio, and one in the Slovak Synod. The mission in Lorain, Ohio, was recently taken over. It was salvaged from the financial rocks by Pastor Vojtko of Akron, Ohio, and reorganized. A number of Slovak fields are without pastors, and while we have a number of students in preparation, none is immediately available. All these fields are in need of men who can make effective use of the English language since there is no longer any Slovak immigration and the hope of these churches rests upon their English-speaking youth.

Of Hungarian missions, we have one in the Pennsylvania, three in the New York, one in the Pittsburgh, and one in the Ohio Synods. All are making progress. The new mission on Cleveland's West Side is particularly promising. The Wendish mission at Newark, N. J., has been made a part of an English-speaking parish.

Our Lettish, Estonian and Lithuanian groups are dormant at this time. Off and on they show signs of life but they are waiting for better times before they can become active again.

Our Spanish work in New York is progressing steadily in spite of all handicaps. The Bronx group shows the more rapid growth. The hope and future of this work rests in a building in which they can be housed. The Presbyterians have recently turned a church building in the Bronx over to their Spanish mission; if we could do the same, our Spanish work would grow by leaps and bounds.

The Italian work has been rather stationary. In New York good progress has been made financially. The congregation is contributing a considerable amount toward the pastor's salary, largely due to the efforts of Dr. Gregorius, member of Holy Trinity Church, who has volunteered to watch over their finances. The Philadelphia mission also shows slight improvement along these lines. The Erie mission has not improved financially but has a promising English work.

There remains one more item to report, our Jewish work. Our Baltimore mission has greatly expanded its publicity and literature work; our Pittsburgh mission has established a free clinic in the charge of the missionary's wife, who is herself a licensed physician; our Philadelphia mission has extended its influence into the State of New York and our Toledo mission has done the same with Indiana, Illinois and Michigan. It is slow and hard work, the fruits of which are not always apparent.

In this connection we will briefly touch on a serious problem which has arisen only lately in consequence of the so-called Nuremberg laws, which have expatriated not only the Jews but also Jewish Christians in

Germany. It is estimated that for every Jew there are two Christians that fall under this ban. Among the unfortunate victims are many Lutheran pastors and theological students who, since they cannot serve in the Lutheran Church of Germany, must seek openings in other countries. Naturally the eyes of many are turned to America, but the difference in language makes the employment of any large number of them in our American church work impossible. Only a small number of carefully selected men who have linguistic ability and an acceptable personality can be absorbed by our church. We have been constrained to limit it so far and these are given a thorough training in American church methods in our seminaries in the United States and Canada. We are sure that our church will be enriched by the influx of these men. The Jews have been advertising the fate of their kin all over the country and they are raising a great amount of money for their support, but there seems to be little effort on the part of the Lutheran Church to relieve the distress of these Lutherans of Jewish ancestry who are members of the Body of Christ and who have a right to expect the helping hand of fellowship of their brethren in the faith.

For record it is reported that during the biennium the mission church at Sutton, Nebr., became self-supporting, as well as St. John's, Farrell, Pa., and the Slovak Church at Northampton, Pa. A number of new parishes were formed out of the very large fields being cared for by the missionaries and there were restored to the mission roll the congregations at Arnprior-Northcote, Ont., Canada, and the Slovak congregation at Lorain, Ohio. A new congregation was organized among the Hungarians in the West Side, Cleveland, Ohio.

It is also our sad duty to record the death of our senior missionary among the Jews, Rev. Paul I. Morentz, who departed this life on the 16th of July, 1938. His unwavering testimony for the faith will be sorely missed and his place will be hard to fill.

We also pay tribute to Missionary Ludwig Klingbeil, who served so faithfully as a pioneer in the fields of Manitoba, departing this life on September 26, 1936."

DIVISION OF ENGLISH MISSIONS

On November 1, 1936, the Rev. Dr. Arthur M. Knudsen, President of the Pacific Synod and missionary pastor at Longview, Washington, took up the duties of Divisional Secretary of English Missions with residence and office in Chicago, Illinois. Dr. Knudsen is a native of Minnesota and received his education there in the public schools, is a graduate of business college and an alumnus of St. Olaf College, Northfield, Minn., and of Luther Seminary, St. Paul, Minn. His ministry having been spent chiefly in mission fields, his report eloquently reflects his past experiences as a missionary.

"Our first impulse is one of profound gratitude to the great Head of the Church for His manifest blessing upon the work of our missions during the past years. Without His Divine enabling there would be little to record in the way of accomplishment. Our second word is one of deep appreciation to the missionary pastors for their splendid, consecrated service, and to the synodical officers and home mission committees for their generous support and co-operation. There is no finer group of Christian workers than our home mission force. And the men who constitute the synodical home mission committees and boards are among our most dependable co-workers.

Part of this report includes the administrative service of the venerable missionary leader, Dr. John F. Seibert, whose continued interest and counsel in his position of Assistant General Superintendent have been most helpful.

At the beginning of the biennium two hundred and ninety-eight English missions were receiving aid on pastor's salary from the board. If the attainment of self-support by our missions is an index of progress then there is much to encourage us in the achievements of the past two years. The following thirty-three missions in thirteen Synods, scattered from coast to coast, reached this goal during the biennium.

California Synod: Fresno, First Church; *Georgia-Alabama Synod:* Cullman, Christ; *Illinois Synod:* Chicago, Reformation, St. Andrew's, St. Mark's; *Maryland Synod:* Baltimore, All Saints', St. John's; Sparrows Point, St. John's; *Nebraska Synod:* South Sioux City, Nebr., First; *New York Synod:* Babylon, L. I., First; Bellerose, L. I., Holy Trinity; Flatbush, Holy Trinity; Great Kills, S. I., Christ; Hillside, N. J., Calvary; Maywood, N. J., Redeemer; Richmond Hill South, St. Matthew's; Leesville-Sharon Parish; East Taghkanic; *North Carolina Synod:* Bessemer City, Grace; Liberty Parish; Mt. Pleasant-Boone Parish; Lebanon Parish; Thomasville, Grace; *Northwest Synod:* Billings, Mont., First; Jefferson, Wis., St. Mark's, Waukesha, Wis., St. Luke's; West Allis, Wis., First; White Bear Lake, St. Andrew's; *Ohio Synod:* Marion, St. Paul's; *Pacific Synod:* Seattle, St. Paul's; *Rocky Mountain Synod:* El Paso, Texas, St. Paul's; *South Carolina Synod:* Columbia, S. C., St. Luke's; *Texas Synod:* Houston, Grace.

The pressure of economic conditions has made itself felt in all of our churches, and it is a tribute to our mission congregations that they have weathered so well the storms of these uncertain days. A few missions have been closed. Because of unsatisfactory progress and prospects in the fields and the limited funds at our disposal it was necessary to withdraw board assistance. Several missions have merged with nearby congregations to form self-supporting parishes. In some instances the congregations simply agreed to disband.

During the biennium there have been added or restored to the roll of English missions the following mission churches: *Kentucky-Tennessee Synod:* Nashville, White's Creek Pike; *Ministerium of Pennsylvania:* Hightstown, N. J., St. Paul's; New Williams, St. John's; Summit Lawn, St. Andrew's; *Mississippi Synod:* Craigs Springs, Church of the Redeemer; *Nebraska Synod:* Omaha (Dundee), Luther Memorial; *New York Synod:* St. Albans, L. I., Prince of Peace; *North Carolina Synod:* Kannapolis, Blackwelder Park Church; *Northwest Synod:* Milwaukee, St. Peter's; Polar, Wis., St. John's; *Texas Synod:* Austin, First.   There were restored to the mission roll: *California Synod:* Gardena, St. John's; Santa Monica, St. Paul's; *Florida Synod:* Lakeland, Grace; *Iowa Synod:* Iowa Falls, English; *Kansas Synod:* Hutchinson, Zion; *Ministerium of Pennsylvania:* West Chester, Calvary; *Northwest Synod:* Madison, Wis., Luther Memorial; *Pittsburgh Synod:* Pittsburgh, Mount Lebanon; *Rocky Mountain Synod:* Laramie, Wyo., Trinity.

One of the features of the work of the biennium has been the rehabilitation of several distressed missions in strategic centers. In this work extensive use has been made of the board missionaries, and they have proved themselves most effective in saving seemingly hopeless situations. Emergency grants have been required in several places to tide struggling congregations over their crises. And in a few instances temporary aid has been given to downtown city churches to help them recover from depression and despair. Helpfulness of this character does not appear in recorded statistics, but it has nevertheless been a distinct contribution to the work of the church in these difficult days.

For several years in the Middle West drought followed drought with such deadly monotony that it came to be regarded as almost a permanent condition. Congregations in the stricken areas were unable to pay their pastors, and pastors serving heroically as long as it was possible to live finally had to leave the parishes shepherdless. Deeply stirred by the plight of our afflicted brethren our board has s o u g h t to bring some measure of relief through emergency appropriations to these needy fields.

The board has endeavored to maintain the highest possible ideals of church life and work. With a view to the constant elevation of church standards everything of a doubtful character has been discouraged, notably all questionable or positively unscriptural methods of raising money. The board's position on commercialism in the church has aided many pastors in their battle with this condition in their congregations. A very noticeable improvement in the financial set-up of our missions is discernible. An increasing number of missions is operating on budgets. There is careful scrutiny of income, and an equally careful supervision of expenditure.

Our missions are participating in the general work of the Church.

Their benevolent contributions are generally most encouraging. Evangelism is stressed. Unchurched Lutherans are gathered into the congregations, and hosts of unsaved people are won to Christ. Indeed, the numerical growth of some synods is due chiefly to the development of the mission congregation.

It is gratifying to report that the majority of our missions are moving steadily toward self-support. Many pastors gratefully testify to the help rendered them by the ten-year rule, or the designation of a date for self-support. They find it easier to encourage their congregations to assume each year a larger share of the pastor's salary. Obviously it is only in this way that funds may be released for new work. And with the great opportunities beckoning us in every part of the country, that is increasingly important.

We are far from having reached the saturation point in evangelizing America, with half the population still outside the church, and no small portion of those nominally within the church needing evangelization. In every part of the country industries are moving and populations are shifting, and it becomes necessary to watch the openings and opportunities that occur in newly developing sections of long established communities as well as in the more recently settled areas of our country.

In the last analysis, the success of our mission work depends under God upon the missionary. The home mission churches are demanding our finest, most capable men. It has been our constant aim to secure properly qualified pastors to take charge of the mission congregations. And we have endeavored to help the mission pastors to become more efficient and effective workers through the summer schools, the loan library, the provision of literature, and the circulation of the board's "Ecclesia Plantanda," and through personal visitation of the staff. Faithfully our mission pastors serve, doing much pioneer work. They deserve the gratitude of the entire church as they build and battle for God.

The Church and our board have suffered the loss of a number of successful missionaries during the biennium. Death claimed five of our workers: Pastor G. O. Ritchie, Thomasville, N. C., on February 8, 1937; Pastor J. W. Bressler of Redeemer Church, Parma, Cleveland, Ohio, on February 20, 1937; Pastor John W. Schmitthenner, Ph.D., on September 12, 1937; Pastor Alfred E. Dittmar, Steubenville, Ohio, on January 12, 1938; and Pastor H. H. Flick of Trafford City, Pa., on May 8, 1938, and as this report was being written news came of the death of our veteran missionary at Missouri Valley, Iowa, the Rev. J. M. Herbst, D.D. "Being dead they yet speak, 'and their works do follow them.' "

SOUTHERN MOUNTAIN WORK

On recommendations of the Joint Commission on Mountain Work that the administration of this work be placed under one board, the Executive

Board of the United Lutheran Church voted to assign this work to the Board of American Missions. No date was given when the transfer was to become effective nor did the action either of the Joint Commission or the Executive Board propose any methods of procedure. The only condition added to the transfer was "that regular reports of inner mission activities at the Konnarock Training School aid the Iron Mountain School be sent to the Inner Mission Board."

At the January, 1936, meeting of the Board of American Missions willingness was expressed to accept this task or any other that the United Lutheran Church may assign. The staff of the board was instructed to arrange the details for the transfer of this work by May 1st.

Conferences were held with the executive secretary of the United Lutheran Church Brotherhood in regard to the financial aspects of the Iron Mountain School.

Since the property at Konnarock Training School for Girls was held in the name of the Inner Mission Board, for the sake of a transfer of title the Board of American Missions had to be domesticated in the State of Virginia. In making arrangements for the transfer of the work at Konnarock Training School for Girls and Iron Mountain School for Boys the board took over the direct supervision of the work of the institutions.

The property of the Iron Mountain School for Boys was held by a corporation under the direction of the Brotherhood and meetings were arranged between the representatives of the Brotherhood and the board's Committee on Mountain Work.

In order to meet commitments already made by the Brotherhood and to maintain the institution as originally planned, the Brotherhood made special request of the Executive Board of the United Lutheran Church that permission be granted to solicit special offerings. This permission was granted with the limitation "that the appeal is to be made only to the Brotherhood and similar men's groups." In the meantime the board authorized its treasurer to advance funds for necessary expenses in operating the school and was instructed to secure additional notes from the Iron Mountain School Board for money so advanced.

On February 4, 1937, the board was domesticated in the State of Virginia, Dr. J. J. Scherer being elected as the representative of the board within the State of Virginia.

Regular budgets were set up for the missionary work in the southern mountains and an effort is being conscientiously made to live within the generous amount thus appropriated out of the funds of the Board of American Missions.

Great encouragement was given to the work by the action of the Luther League of America to take part in the special Anniversary Appeal effort in 1938 by choosing as their missionary objective and special project for 1938 a medical center at Konnarock.

All contracts with the present teachers at the K. T. S. were renewed pending the result of a current study to ascertain the possibility of reorganizing the work so as to accomplish more fully the objectives for which the mountain mission was organized. Some changes have nevertheless occurred, among which we report the resignation of Miss Helen Dyer, Principal, and Miss Alice Baumgarner, teacher in the upper grades, effective July 1, 1938, and Miss Eleanor Nelson, nurse at the Helton Health Center.

New helpers called into the field were: Rev. John W. Gable, Director of Religious Education; Licentiate Theodore H. Zimmerman, Assistant to Missionary Killinger; Mr. F. W. Kirsch, headmaster at Iron Mountain School; Miss Katrina Umberger is to be Acting Principal at Konnarock Training School.

One of the mountain boys, J. Bruce Weaver, has been assisted in his preparation for the Gospel ministry.

Satisfactory progress has been made in an effort to co-ordinate the work on the farms of both schools.

Members of the staff have made frequent visits to the fields and have attended regularly the Mountain Workers' Conferences, three of which were held in 1937 and four in 1938.

SCHOOLS FOR MISSIONARIES

A general and widespread sentiment has obtained that the Board of American Missions should provide additional training for home missionaries. For the present at least, that need is being met by summer schools with a center selected in each great area for the men of that section. An experimental effort was undertaken at Massanetta Springs, Virginia, in connection with the regular Summer School of the Synod of Virginia, July 20-26, 1936, and scholarships were provided for qualified missionaries who were desirous to take advantage of this offer. Fifty-five from thirteen synods were enrolled. Four periods were given daily and in addition to the courses offered, the advantages of the general assembly periods of the Summer School were enjoyed. It was evident both from the reports and opinions of the missionaries in attendance that the experiment was a success and that its value to the mission work would justify its continuation.

The Board's Summer School Committee under the chairmanship of Pastor Franklin Clark Fry, gave continued painstaking study and as a result of the reports thus submitted from time to time to the board, plans were made for two schools to be conducted in 1937. One was held at Long Lake, Illinois, July 25-31, the other at Massanetta, Virginia, August 2-8. At Long Lake a staff of fourteen instructors and speakers served the forty-nine missionaries from thirteen synods in attendance. At Massanetta ten instructors served on the faculty and sixty missionaries from seventeen synods were in attendance. In these two schools, twenty-three of the thirty-four synods in the U. L. C. A. were represented.

In planning for 1938 it was decided to add a third school, which is to vary in location from year to year so as to take in the far west and Canadian Northwest. It was also decided to make specific request of all home mission congregations not to consider the home missionary's absence in attendance at the training school as part of his vacation, but that it be considered an essential part of his work. By special request it was voted to provide activities for the wives and children of home missionaries at the training schools; and a plan for the equalization of expenses for the missionaries attending the schools from a distance beyond three hundred miles was approved.

The enrollment at the 1938 schools was one hundred and forty-four and within this group twenty-three of the thirty-one synods in the U. L. C. A. were represented.

We record with grateful appreciation the names of the instructors who assisted in making the schools of such lasting help.

In 1936: Pastor Franklin Clark Fry, Dr. John C. Mattes, Dr. S. White Rhyne, in addition to members of the staff.

In 1937: Pastor Franklin Clark Fry, Pastor Ernest H. J. Hoh, Dr. Paul J. Hoh, Dr. Clarence E. Krumbholz, Dr. Henry J. Pflum, Jr., Dr. Emil W. Weber, Dr. H. M. Bannen, Dr. O. Garfield Beckstrand, Pastor John I. Meck, Dr. Edwin Moll, Pastor Oliver W. Powers, Dr. Martin Schroeder. Dr. Frederick J. Weertz.

In 1938: Dr. J. Hamilton Dawson, Dr. Walton H. Greever, Dr. Edwin Moll, Mrs. Virgil B. Sease, Litt.D., Dr. R. Homer Anderson, Dr. O. Garfield Beckstrand, Dr. Albert H. Keck, Rev. Arthur M. Huffman, Dr. George W. Miley, Rev. L. H. Steinhoff, Dr. Paul J. Hoh, Rev. Carl F. Yaeger.

LATIN AMERICA

Since the last convention the mission fields in the West Indies have enjoyed the most satisfactory period of their history. Under the efficient guidance of the board's representative, the Rev. William G. Arbaugh, there has been substantial development in every phase of the work.

CHANGES IN PERSONNEL—Following the plan of an annual "interneship" in the islands, the Rev. Elmer H. Ganskopp has served most acceptably in the only English Lutheran Church in Puerto Rico. Each year for the past two years, there has been a candidate from our Puerto Rican field who has entered the ministry, having graduated from the University of Puerto Rico and Mount Airy Theological Seminary. Rev. Francisco Agostini, ordained in 1937, is now serving the Dorado Parish, and the Rev. Francisco Molina, ordained in 1938, will, after supplying for Pastor Roig, now on furlough, enter upon the new work which is being undertaken at Hato Rey. Both pastors were ordained by the United Lutheran Synod of New York, which had generously aided in their support both in college and seminary.

Rev. John Pettit of the Indiana Synod, accepted the board's call to the West Indies field and entered upon his work in May of 1938. Pastor Pettit and wife are valuable additions to our staff. Mrs. Pettit, having taught in Spanish America for several years, will be able immediately to become an active factor in the life of the community.

To the working force there has also been added Mr. Evaristo Falco, formerly canon in the cathedral at Barquisimeto, Venezuela, South America. Having accepted the Evangelical faith by conviction, this highly educated and cultured man, recognized as an orator, joined the Protestant Church and attended services for almost a year before accepting a position as lay-worker. During the past year he has served most acceptably under the direction of our pastors in Puerto Rico and at the same time pursued a special course of studies in Lutheran polity and doctrines. He successfully passed his examination and was ordained by the authority of the East Pennsylvania Synod. Pastor Falco now serves San Pablo Church, Puerta de Tierra.

Thus, for the first time since Lutheran work was undertaken in Puerto Rico, there is at present a full staff of workers which will enable us to enter new fields.

In the Virgin Islands, only one c h a n g e has occurred. When Mrs. Mengers, wife of the pastor at Christiansted, St. Croix, could not return to the field on account of health, Pastor Mengers resigned but loyally remained at his post until a successor could be secured. The Rev. Hans Naether of Borna bei Leipzig, Germany, formerly in charge of the Lutheran School for Negroes at Greensboro, North Carolina, has been called and will take up the work as soon as he can secure his release from his large parish in Germany. Both Pastor Naether and wife were successful missionaries in our Puerto Rico field before their marriage.

WORKS OF MERCY—There has been no change either in the personnel or the extent of this work, which reaches out to assist the poor and distressed in the communities in which our mission stations are located. Sister Maren Knudsen, through the gracious permission of the Motherhouse in Copenhagen, Denmark, continues her loving service among the sick and neglected in St. Croix, ever endeavoring to fulfill the hopes of the band of Christian women of Denmark who established the Queen Louise Homes for Sick and Neglected Babies in the West Indies under the patronage of the Royal House. In the Orphanage for Girls, our only colored deaconesses, Sister Emma Francis and Sister Edith Prince, are carrying on until the present objectives of the home can be better accomplished through a home-finding organization. Sister Edith is developing a very successful kindergarten in Frederiksted and is giving much time to work among children in the parish.

In Puerto Rico, Miss Frieda M. Hoh, R.N., continues most energetically her ministry of mercy to the hosts of under-privileged women and children living in the cities where our missions are located. Under Miss Carmen Villarini, Director of Religious Education, the standard of the teaching staff in this field has been raised and the religious education in the parishes greatly extended.

During the biennium, the Women's Missionary Society of the United Lutheran Church decided to discontinue the sale of products from this field in line with the board's preference for a complete abolition of all commercialism in the church auxiliaries. To achieve this end the board hopes that the society may successfully end the sale of all products. The accounts of the Calada Fund have not yet been closed but a good balance will be left for the Women's Missionary Society to allocate for work in Puerto Rico. The society has asked the Spanish Conference to choose a suitable objective in harmony with the intentions of those who organized the fund.

SPANISH CHURCH IN NEW YORK—Closely connected with the work in Latin America are the congregations in New York City under the care of Pastor Soler, who with his talented wife has become an important factor in Spanish Protestantism in the great metropolis. This work is still severely handicapped by lack of proper housing. One of the congregations must worship far from its center in our West Indies Church in Harlem. The congregation in the Bronx fares much better through the kindness of the Rev. G. H. Tappert, in whose church services are being held. This church, however, is also at a far edge of the Spanish settlement.

WORK AMONG NEGROES—Our negro congregations, because of their origin, are also associated with the West Indies. The two congregations in New York are making substantial progress even though economic conditions bear heavily upon the members of this race. Missionary Routte, assisted by his brother, who is also a graduate of Augustana College and recently of Hartwick Lutheran Seminary, and who is now awaiting a call, has met with encouraging response in the Jamaica, L. I., field. Transfiguration Church in Harlem, under Pastor West, continues its upward course. For several years each Palm Sunday has witnessed the confirmation of a catechetical class of more than forty members. For this service St. Paul's (German) Church is graciously loaned to the congregation each year and invariably it is taxed to the limit to accommodate the membership of over one thousand. On every one of these occasions this large church is filled to the last pew and the spacious gallery crowded. A liberal response in the Anniversary Appeal would enable the board to make great headway among the negroes of America.

AMERICAN INDIAN—The work at the Rocky Boy reservation has made no spectacular growth but it has nevertheless ranked high among the mission fields of the Protestant churches. Present social and economic disturbances have added to the difficulties of the mission. The post office, located at the mission since its establishment and forming an important point of contact, has been removed, resulting in a loss in salary to the missionary and to the interpreter, Malcolm Mitchell. This will make several readjustments necessary.

WORK AMONG ORIENTALS—For some years the Mission Committee of the California Synod has been asking for the inauguration of work among the Japanese. A preliminary study was made by the board, some time ago, but the work was delayed because of unfavorable financial conditions. However, on an appeal from the Japan Lutheran Church, formally adopted at its annual convention and forwarded through the Board of Foreign Missions, the board has ordered an immediate investigation of the possibilities in this field. This situation, unique as it is in the history of mission work, should rebuke us and stir us to action. A native church, only recently evangelized, has had to call the attention of the mother church to the spiritual needs of its nationals in our own country!

CHURCH EXTENSION

During the biennium, the Department of Church Extension has continued to assist, within the limitations imposed by the funds available, in the erection of new church buildings for mission congregations and also in refinancing and readjusting indebtedness. In this period, forty-seven loans have been granted from the funds of the board. Fifteen of these were made for the purpose of assisting in the refinancing of the property of mission congregations. These, when further analyzed, show that the board was able to reduce the interest paid. Specifically,

a. Seven congregations were assisted in the reduction of their senior financing.
b. Five congregations were granted loans from the investment funds of the board (at 4% interest) to effect a reduction of 50% or more of their first mortgage indebtedness.
c. In the adjustment of the affairs of three congregations, all in strategic locations, the board purchased the properties involved. They were: Luther Memorial, Madison, Wisconsin; St. Paul, Spokane, Washington; St. Paul, Santa Monica, California.

During this biennium, we regret to report, the following congregations suffered the loss of their church buildings by completed foreclosures: Christ Church, Fort Wayne, Indiana; Trinity (Barnitz Memorial), Denver, Colorado; First, Palmyra, New Jersey; and Wilmette, Ill. The combined Church Extension loans lost through these foreclosures total $39,975.

of which $15,000 was from the loan funds of the Women's Missionary Society.

In addition to these, University, Seattle, Washington (Church Extension loan, $19,400); Hope, Detroit, Michigan (Church Extension loan, $6,711.68) and Luther Memorial, Detroit, Michigan (Church Extension loan, $7,000) are involved in foreclosure proceedings that are not entirely hopeless as yet.

It is interesting to note that the loans granted during the last biennium were made on the territories of seventeen of the constituent synods and that the average construction loan (excluding Manitoba Synod, where the loans are unusually small), was $4,120.

Because, in some instances, congregations cannot find a source for senior financing, the board adopted (June, 1938) the following rules for the lending of funds in which the board is completely financing construction above the equity furnished by the congregation:

"1. That such loans shall be considered only after careful inquiry has been made by the Department of Church Extension as to reported inability of the congregation to secure first mortgage funds locally.

2. That loans of this nature shall be divided into a first mortgage loan and a second, or Church Extension loan. The principal sum of the first mortgage loan shall be two-thirds of the total sum granted, and the remaining one-third shall be a second mortgage loan.

3. The first mortgage loan is to be made for a term not to exceed five years bearing interest at 4% and the second mortgage loan shall be for a period not to exceed five years without interest.

4. When the loan is made, the Department of Church Extension is to include in the mortgages, or as a separate agreement with the congregation, a definite plan of amortization, which plan is to arrange that repayments are to begin immediately — first on the Church Extension loan, with no application on principal of first mortgage loan until the Church Extension loan shall have been completely repaid."

"Further, the Department of Church Extension shall include in the contract with the congregation, a provision as to the amount which is to be paid monthly, such monthly payments to include the interest due on the first mortgage and the payments on account of principal to be applied as indicated previously."

The principal problems of the biennium arose from the number of debt situations reaching crises, the mounting labor costs in construction in certain areas, the difficulties experienced in finding sources for first mortgages and last but not least, the difficulty encountered in convincing congregations considering construction, that any debt created must be within the ability of the congregation to pay.

INVESTMENTS AND FINANCES

During this biennium the Finance Committee of the Board has continued its careful supervision of the annual budgets. The increased drain on available funds as a result of the discovery of new and promising Home Mission fields through the Division of Survey and Research, in the face of no large increase in the sums received from the apportionment, has demanded a rigid scrutiny of all appropriations for salary aid.

The Finance Committee has spent many hours during this biennium in the exercise of a true "stewardship of spending" that every dollar might count effectively for the extension of the Kingdom.

The policy by which a portion of the funds available for investment has been invested in first mortgages on mission churches, under the terms of rigid rules adopted by the Board, has been continued. Twenty-five thousand dollars has been thus invested during the biennium. The total amount now so invested is $45,844.26. The interest on these loans is being met promptly by all except one congregation and this one is not over six months in arrears as to interest at the time this report is written.

In an effort to increase the income from our investments, a portion of the board's funds has been invested in selected first mortgages on homes. At the recommendation of the Finance Committee rules governing the investment of these funds were adopted by the board limiting the amount to be invested in any one community to $15,000 and limiting the amount of any one loan to $5,000, such loans to be made to individual home owners. The sum of $17,520 has been invested.

The financial statements included with this report indicate the financial progress during the last two years and the position of the board as of June 30, 1938.

The situation as to synodical budgets for objects for which the United Lutheran Church has laid an apportionment still continues without change since the action taken at Savannah. The United Synod of New York and the Synod of Virginia shortly after the Savannah Convention asked the board to undertake the direction of all mission activities on their territory and to the present date have continued the arrangement as one that has proved mutually beneficial. Realizing, naturally, that the board would not be in a position to carry this extra cost, these two synods have paid monthly into the board's treasury as a "special" the amounts required for the work transferred. No other plan seems possible until the general subject has been determined finally by the United Lutheran Church as a whole. Other synods have been inclined to make a like agreement but the board has been reluctant to engage a staff large enough to care for the increased work that would be entailed. The board's chief concern, as always, is with results not methods, and every effort will be made to reach as many souls as our resources of men and money will permit.

THE ANNIVERSARY APPEAL

The Convention of the United Lutheran Church in America, Columbus, Ohio, in October, 1936, determined that the year 1938 should be used as a year of "special effort" by the Board of American Missions for the cause of Church Extension.

At the time, many delegates to the convention signified that in their opinion any "high pressure campaign" for funds would meet with disapproval all over the Church.

In fitting celebration of the twentieth anniversary of the United Lutheran Church, the board early determined to term this "special effort" the Anniversary Appeal.

Nearly a year was spent in conference and board meetings in evolving the program of the appeal. Two principles were uppermost in the minds of the members of the board; namely:

1. The Appeal must be something of lasting value to the Church;
2. The Appeal must be an "appeal" for the urgent needs of the Church—that we prove worthy of the cause of our Lord and Master in these times.

Therefore the three objectives:

Objective 1. That the United Lutheran Church gather its forces for an aggressive action—

(a) to win those who are unwon.
(b) to return as many as possible of those who, having been confirmed, have forgotten their altar-made covenants and who now form the non-communing group of our confirmed membership. To attain this objective a well-defined program of personal evangelism was developed with aids and suggestions.

In spite of the evident limitations of the emphasis on Evangelism in the Anniversary Appeal, there has been a real and encouraging response on the part of the pastors and lay folk of our church. This, we believe, is due to the fact that as a united church we are now courageously attempting to face the challenge and opportunity that goes out to all in the name of our Lord and Saviour, Jesus Christ.

By way of resumé:

1. Over 736 congregations contacted to date of this report and over 7,500 lay representatives.
2. New impulse and impetus has been provided for existing Synodical, Conference and Congregational programs on Evangelism.
3. As the various educational forces of the Anniversary Appeal touch individuals w i t h i n the congregations of our church, we were enabled to lay the challenge of serving Christ more directly upon their hearts and consciences. The emphasis on Evangelism in the program of the Anniversary Appeal is assisting, we believe, in

breaking down the inferiority complex or hesitancy on the part
of the average Christian to bear witness. It is aiding the pastor in
clearing the way for action by helping him lay plans within his
congregation to do this Christ-commanded witnessing.

4. We are able to suggest, where a beginning has not already been
made, a simple plan of procedure, emphasizing that the only way
to begin, after a preliminary period of study, is to learn by doing.
Splendid reports have come in on the work being done and on
plans for the future. Let us pray that God may richly bless this
primary objective of the Anniversary Appeal.

Objective 2. That the United Lutheran Church be urged to strengthen
its inner loyalties that Lutheranism keep its proper place in American
Protestantism by—

(a) A demonstration of the tremendous unapplied potential of the
present membership.

(b) A reiteration of the peculiar strength and timeliness of the Lutheran approach to this age.

To attain this objective the following program was developed:

The first of these was the sound film, "The Thunder of the Sea." This,
incidentally, we believe, is the first sound motion picture presentation
to be prepared by any branch of the Christian Church.

During the first six months of 1938, 3,048 congregations have viewed
this picture. With thirty-three projectors the route operators of the
board have carried the "Thunder of the Sea" to over 350,000 of our
people. Voluminous correspondence from pastors and laity alike, testi-
fied to a favorable response to its message and a creditable reaching of
this objective.

As this report is written, the picture has yet to be presented to twelve
synods in the central western portion of the United States, and the territory of the Canada and Manitoba Synods. In order to take the picture
to the rural areas in America and Canada, a station wagon with a motor
generator is now touring these areas.

The newspaper publicity attendant on the Anniversary Appeal has
been a potent force in arousing the interest of the membership of the
church generally. Those who are familiar with church publicity assure
us that the space received throughout the Appeal is by far the high-
water-mark in space devoted to the activities of the United Lutheran
Church. The 3,199 clippings received in the office up to the end of June,
1938, total 19,812 column inches. Inasmuch as only a minor fraction of
the publicity items printed everywhere would find their way into the
office of the Anniversary Appeal, it is estimated conservatively in excess
of 12,500 separate stories were published, representing five hundred
eight-column pages.

The board takes this opportunity to thank *The Lutheran*, as well as synodical and congregational publications for their generous attention to the Anniversary Appeal.

Beginning in the Fall of 1937, the four-page *Ecclesia Plantanda* was expanded to a sixteen-page monthly in order to carry up-to-the-minute news of the Anniversary Appeal, as well as information of a practical character, to aid every active pastor in planning his congregational program.

On January 1, 1938, the National Broadcasting Company extended to us the use of its entire facilities without charge for a coast-to-coast hook-up for a program inaugurating the Anniversary Appeal. The appearance of Dr. F. H. Knubel on this program vitalized its message to the membership of the United Lutheran Church. Many local stations have co-operated by carrying addresses, sermons, rallies and pageants. It should be reported that the United Synod of New York paused in its deliberations long enough to hear an Appeal broadcast from a station in Rochester, New York.

In addition, a series of Anniversary Rallies has been held throughout the areas covered. Fifty-eight of these have been conducted as of July 1, 1938. In each of these rallies the need for evangelical Christianity in the world today; the peculiar responsibility resting on the United Lutheran Church in this age, and the necessity of advancing the Kingdom through adequate financial support were stressed by the speakers.

It is a matter of record that 21,950 of our membership had attended the Rallies held up to July 1, 1938.

All sections of the Church were called upon to provide the speakers for the rallies. The board wishes to record its appreciation of those who left their parishes or other duties in order to assist in this work. Those who thus assisted in the Anniversary Appeal (to July 1, 1938) were:

The Rev. F. H. Knubel, D.D., LL.D., S.T.D., Litt.D.
"   "   W. H. Greever, D.D., LL.D.
"   "   W. C. Davis, D.D.
"   "   John L. Deaton, D.D.
"   "   Hugo L. Dressler
"   "   Charles B. Foelsch, D.D., Ph.D.
"   "   Franklin Clark Fry
"   "   H. W. A. Hanson, D.D., LL.D.
"   "   J. Edward Harms, D.D.
"   "   Paul J. Hoh, S.T.M., D.D.
"   "   A. J. Holl, D.D.
"   "   Park W. Huntington, S.T.M.
"   "   Paul Andrew Kirsch
"   "   A. M. Knudsen, D.D.
"   "   Sam H. Kornmann
"   "   C. E. Krumbholz, D.D.
"   "   Hermann F. Miller, D.D.
"   "   Edwin Moll, D.D.

The Rev. Harmon J. McGuire
"   "   John W. Ott, D.D.
"   "   E. P. Pfatteicher, D.D., Ph.D., LL.D.
"   "   H. J. Pflum, Jr., D.D.
"   "   Charles A. Puls
"   "   W. C. Schaeffer, D.D.
"   "   Wilfrid A. Schmidt
"   "   C. S. Simonton, D.D.
"   "   L. H. Steinhoff
"   "   Ross H. Stover, D.D.
"   "   L. Ralph Tabor
"   "   Emil W. Weber, D.D.
"   "   Raymond D. Wood
"   "   A. A. Zinck, D.D.
E. Clarence Miller, LL.D.
James C. Kinard, LL.D., Ph.D.
Heiby W. Ungerer, Esq.

As a supplemental part of this program, a series of pageants, three for congregational use and one for one or more congregations, has been distributed as the various areas were reached. These have won wide acceptance and have contributed in arousing the interest of many in the whole program of the whole church.

Objective 3. To finance the cause of Church Extension by meeting the needs listed below with emphasis on the first three. These were stated in the printed material as follows:

a. Urgently needed to continue present program.

   I. Eighty-five home mission congregations now worshiping in storerooms and lodge halls, and serving unchurched territory will have to disband unless they can borrow money for building the houses of worship imperatively needed. Loans for single purpose structure—which of course includes mission churches—cannot be obtained through commercial borrowing channels. The Church must establish its own loan fund for this purpose.

   II. Our Church must go to the aid of Home Mission congregations who are compelled to refinance existing mortgage debts or lose their property through foreclosure.

   III. Critical as are the needs set forth in the two preceding items, the immediate future, the next five years—will bring us face to face with additional responsibilities. The least we can do is to provide for the planting of new churches, and lending them for building.

b. Needed for the expansion of the existing program.

   I. An advance program is necessary to rehabilitate churches which, due to the trends in rural life, in economic conditions and improved transportation, are unable with their existing equipment to meet present needs.

    II. To supply the physical equipment needed for the important spiritual work of student pastors at our colleges and universities.

    III. To adjust the equipment of Saskatoon Seminary to provide for more workers in the Canadian Northwest, where thousands of Lutherans are shepherdless.

    IV. To complete the fine start at Konnarock Training School and Iron Mountain School in the Southern Mountains.

    V. Expansion of our present work among Negroes.

  c. For a new program which should be begun.

    I. To carry "The Good News" to all—Mexicans and Orientals who have moved into the United States, to migrant workers, to trailer camps, etc.

As of the date of this report 984 congregations are known to have actively participated financially, 455 others have indicated that they will endeavor to meet their financial objectives this fall. During the fall months of 1938, the Anniversary Appeal will be under way in the 926 additional congregations on the territories of the following synods: Indiana, Kentucky-Tennessee, Mississippi, Illinois, Wartburg, Northwest, Kansas, Iowa, Nebraska, Midwest, Texas, Manitoba, Canada and Nova Scotia.

Thus far we have still no report from 1,580 congregations in the areas in which the program has already been conducted. However, only twenty-four congregations in the same areas are known to have failed to participate at all in the financial phase of the Appeal because of peculiar local conditions. Gifts reported thus far total $321,548. Because the program will continue throughout the year 1938 by action of the Columbus Convention, it is obviously not possible to make a complete report to this Convention.

The testimony of the leaders of the Church to the valuable contribution which the Anniversary Appeal has made in arousing interest in Personal Evangelism and to heightening morale, and the hope of ultimately removing many barriers between the Word and the unchurched, have brought encouragement to the board and have evidently justified the months of planning and effort.

TRIBUTES—The Rev. Lloyd W. Steckel, D.D., had been a member of the Board of American Missions for eight years when he was called to his eternal reward on March 20, 1938. Dr. Steckel was deeply interested in home missions, having served as a home missionary himself for many years. His experience in the large city parish which he was serving at the time of his death gave him a sympathetic understanding of the many problems confronting the board. Dr. Steckel filled many offices of trust during his active ministry but none was prized more highly than his membership in the Board of American Missions.

The board also records its appreciation of two leaders who during their lifetime gave liberally of their talents for the advancement of the causes represented by the Board of American Missions.

George E. Neff, Esq., of York, Pa., who for more than two generations took a prominent part in the development of the Lutheran Church, serving on important boards of the church before and after the merger for which he labored effectually. For a quarter of a century he acted as attorney for our Home Mission Boards, cheerfully donating his services as needed.

The Rev. Charles A. Freed, President of our Southern Seminary, was a member of the Board of American Missions and its predecessor, the Board of West Indies Missions, for sixteen years. At the time his term expired he was vice-president of the Board of American Missions.

MEMBERS RETIRING THROUGH LIMITATION OF SERVICE—The board takes this opportunity to express its sincere appreciation of the service rendered by the retiring members who having served two terms are not eligible for re-election.

Mr. Henry F. Heuer has served on this board, on the Joint Commission for the reorganization of the home mission work, and on the predecessor Board of West Indies Missions, on the Jewish Committee and on the Virgin Islands Board of the General Council for a period of more than twenty-five years. During all these years with the exception of two, he was the able and efficient secretary. There is probably no layman in the church so well informed concerning the details of the work of our home mission activities and his loss will be keenly felt.

The other members whose years of service have made them invaluable in the work of the board are: the Rev. Fritz O. Evers, who as a member of the Jewish Committee, the Joint Commission and the Board of American Missions, has served for twenty years; Dr. L. H. Larimer has been a member of the Jewish Committee, the Board of American Missions for almost as many years; and Messrs. Bikle and Hoober have served two terms on the Board of American Missions. The faithful service of these brethren will always be an inspiring memory to those who will continue to carry on the task.

THE WOMEN'S MISSIONARY SOCIETY—Without the very generous and helpful support given the Board of American Missions by the Women's Missionary Society of the United Lutheran Church, it would be necessary to abandon ten per cent of the work now being done. The very regular attendance of their representatives on the board, Mrs. J. M. Cook and Mrs. Oscar Schmidt, has been most helpful.

ORGANIZATION

The organization of the board for the biennium was: President—Rev. Henry J. Pflum, Jr., D.D.; Vice-President—Rev. J. J. Scherer, Jr., D.D.; Secretary — Mr. Henry F. Heuer; Treasurer — Mr. H. Torrey Walker; Executive Secretary—Rev. Zenan M. Corbe, D.D.; Assistant Executive Secretary—Rev. Paul Andrew Kirsch; Divisional Secretary of English Missions—Rev. Arthur M. Knudsen, D.D.; Assistant General Superintendent—Rev. John F. Seibert, D.D.; Divisional Secretary of Linguistic Interests—Rev. Ernst A. Tappert, D.D.; Departmental Secretary of Church Extension, Finance, Survey and Research—Mr. H. Torrey Walker; Term expires 1942—Alexander S. Bauer, Esq.; Mr. Louis Hanson; Rev. A. J. Holl, D.D.; Rev. John Schmieder; Rev. Chester S. Simonton, D.D.; Heiby W. Ungerer, Esq; Rev. Emil W. Weber, D.D.; Term expires 1940—Rev. O. G. Beckstrand, D.D.; Rev. Franklin Clark Fry; Rev. J. E. Harms, D.D.; Rev. J. J. Scherer, Jr., D.D.; Mr. Henry Beisler; Mr. A. H. Durboraw; Mr. Wm. Eck; Term expires 1938—Rev. F. O. Evers; Rev. L. H. Larimer, D.D.; Rev. H. J. Pflum, D.D.; †Rev. L. W. Steckel, D.D.; Mr. Horace W. Bikle; Mr. Henry F. Heuer; John A. Hoober, Esq.

Divisional Committees: English Missions—Rev. J. Edward Harms, D.D., Chairman; Rev. O. G. Beckstrand, Mr. Horace W. Bikle, Rev. A. J. Holl, D.D. Church Extension—Rev. Emil W. Weber, D.D., Chairman; A. S. Bauer, Esq., Heiby W. Ungerer, Esq., Mr. Louis Hanson. Linguistic Interests—Mr. Wm. Eck, Chairman; Rev. F. O. Evers, Rev. John Schmieder, †Rev. L. W. Steckel, D.D. Latin America—Rev. Franklin Clark Fry, Chairman; Rev. C. S. Simonton, D.D., Rev. L. H. Larimer, D.D., Mr. A. H. Durboraw. Finance—Mr. Henry F. Heuer, Chairman; Mr. Henry Beisler, John A. Hoober, Esq., Rev. J. J. Scherer, Jr., D.D. Research and Survey—Rev. J. J. Scherer, Jr., D.D., Chairman; Rev. L. H. Larimer, D.D., Mr. Henry Beisler, Mr. A. H. Durboraw.

HENRY J. PFLUM, *President.*
H. F. HEUER, *Secretary.*
ZENAN M. CORBE, *Executive Secretary.*

APPENDIX I
BOARD OF AMERICAN MISSIONS

Synods	No. of Parishes	No. of Congregations	No. of Missionaries and Workers	Membership		Appropriations By The Board			Value of Property	Indebtedness	No. of Parsonages	Contributions	
				Confirmed	Sunday School	Salaries and Expenses	Interest	Loans Church Extension				*Local Expense	Benevolence
Alleghany	9	9	8	1,042	759	$3,690		$15,755	$138,400	$33,713	2	$17,425	$1,746
California	22	36	20	3,055	1,262	12,770		33,016	192,200	75,197	13	30,802	2,347
Canada	16	16	14	3,783	3,423	7,487		49,310	623,892	306,796	13	65,492	5,867
East Pennsylvania	17	17	7	886	474	5,630		39,328	137,600	42,648	3	14,371	1,986
Florida	5	5	7	522	456	3,900		37,550	108,000	53,842	2	12,068	1,884
Georgia-Alabama	5	3	3	194	106	354		1,108	20,100	9,558	1	1,880	100
Synod in the Midwest	17	17	18	3,424	2,612	10,415	$100	69,913	381,460	219,756	8	41,610	4,748
Illinois	9	9	9	1,267	1,007	3,832	600	41,940	262,100	138,930	1	24,122	2,527
Indiana	4	4	4	718	425	1,105		6,405	66,034	13,067	2	7,166	487
Iowa	3	3	3	542	399	850		20,300	95,915	51,500	2	8,415	2,393
Kansas	6	6	5	684	526	2,100		17,500	58,950	25,152	2	10,435	1,681
Kentucky-Tennessee	31	104	27	4,015	1,125	18,970		27,932	119,450	42,960	21	12,472	1,224
Manitoba	7	7	9	1,902	1,404	5,978		24,879	238,900	115,361	3	26,591	2,269
Maryland	9	9	9	1,495	1,128	5,628		38,232	127,193	89,305	2	16,247	2,825
Michigan	4	8	8	515	216	1,779		1,134	33,100	3,999	3	4,506	652
Mississippi	4	4	3	419	300	1,980		300	7,400	2,517	2	4,134	437
Nebraska	42	47	41	6,375	4,438	24,133	1,403	59,322	504,050	212,053	13	89,574	6,386
New York	16	24	17	2,167	2,244	10,659		22,971	330,350	52,432	7	28,556	3,141
North Carolina	18	22	14	3,937	2,036	10,065		67,888	298,660	188,299	5	40,362	4,588
Northwest	2	2	2	195	50	660		5,000	24,000	14,000	1	3,056	91
Nova Scotia	18	18	15	2,362	1,844	12,180		55,221	314,475	167,838	4	33,379	4,641
Ohio	16	18	16	2,558	1,376	9,240	100	55,858	194,200	89,502	7	26,369	3,237
Pacific	35	43	35	8,450	7,252	20,244		76,460	924,987	475,220	13	113,603	9,080
Pennsylvania Ministerium	28	32	27	4,793	3,496	17,436		60,098	660,886	325,711	17	78,878	6,693
Pittsburgh	7	7	7	1,132	754	2,190		38,901	121,550	70,780	5	16,807	1,959
Rocky Mountain	1	2	1	1,332	96	600		3,000	35,000	15,125		5,107	141
Slovak Zion	8	13	7	736	543	5,405		7,726	96,633	17,060	2	6,676	7,226
South Carolina													
Susquehanna													
Texas	9	12	8	1,061	784	5,269		10,551	62,850	21,642	7	15,479	1,937
Virginia	15	41	12	2,899	2,217	8,950		17,500	300,720	27,179	10	25,175	4,101
Wartburg	6	6	5	1,500	809	3,580		12,164	70,875	29,967	1	16,130	1,370
Puerto Rico	9	14	20	882	2,043	23,632			153,000		10	2,913	366
Virgin Islands	3	5	6	800	340	10,849			156,700		3	4,800	1,000
West Pennsylvania		1	1	125	220	800			11,800			4,903	600
West Virginia													
Rocky Boy Mission	1	1	3	35	95	4,225			13,625		1	1,253	218
Totals	390	555	381	64,806	46,259	$256,585	$2,203	$917,262	$6,821,985	$2,931,109	185	$810,756	$89,948
Loans and Interest Grants— No Salary Aid	173	174	165	53,261	35,552		1,030	753,116	7,651,523	3,138,716	95	774,821	83,451
Grand Totals	563	729	546	118,067	81,811	$256,585	$3,233	$1,670,378	$14,473,508	$6,069,825	280	$1,585,577	$173,399

*Includes both Current and Unusual Expenses.

APPENDIX II

Loans and Investments of Church Extension Funds, classified according to Synod.

Synod	Amount
California	$ 93,851.73
Canada	37,960.50
North Carolina	29,095.75
South Carolina	12,623.75
Florida	53,319.50
Georgia-Alabama	40,650.00
Illinois	150,064.19
Indiana	45,205.00
Iowa	45,972.88
Kansas	40,336.30
Kentucky-Tennessee	18,500.00
Manitoba	39,365.20
Maryland	44,273.08
Michigan	95,340.23
Mississippi	1,043.71
Nebraska	30,365.00
Midwest (German Nebraska)	4,392.50
New York	188,113.45
Northwest	283,339.88
Nova Scotia	5,000.00
Ohio	99,965.96
Pacific	88,742.50
East Pennsylvania	67,973.87
Ministerium of Pennsylvania	104,156.33
Susquehanna	1,000.00
Pittsburgh	81,359.50
Rocky Mountain	30,697.87
Slovak Zion	15,353.95
Texas	14,995.20
Virginia	22,700.00
West Virginia	5,800.00
Wartburg	19,735.46
Investment Notes (United Synod of New York)	177.50

REPORT OF THE TREASURER OF THE BOARD OF AMERICAN MISSIONS

BALANCE SHEET AT June 30, 1937

ASSETS

Cash		$148,250.23
Securities owned at Ledger Values:		
Bonds	$ 321,074.26	
Stock	12,670.89	
Savings Bank Accounts	120,927.44	
Real Estate Mortgages	9,500.00	
		464,172.59
Advanced Expenses		800.00
Advanced a/c Estates		64.18
Advanced a/c 1938 Special Appeal		2,931.92
Advanced a/c Real Estate		55,000.00
Loans to Churches:		
Church Extension Funds	$1,416,114.73	
Investment Funds	27,750.71	
Agency Funds	216,271.23	
Investment Notes	1,847.50	
		1,661,984.17
Real Estate and Buildings:		
Owned and held by Board	377,516.75	
Held as Agent	34,481.78	
		411,998.53
Equipment and Furniture		6,555.88
Accounts Receivable		7,600.00
		$2,759,357.50

LIABILITIES

Loans Payable	$ 13,700.00	
Held for Women's Missionary Society	10,332.48	
		24,032.48
		$2,735,325.02

FUNDS

General Funds:		
Missions	$ 99,979.63	
Church Extension	353,098.88	
		$ 453,078.51
Endowment Funds:		
Missions	48,692.73	
Church Extension	15,408.42	
		64,101.15
Permanent Loan Fund		1,249,776.50
Memorial Loan Fund		169,531.42
Restricted Funds		82,497.97
McMurray Fund		23,655.93

Annuity Funds		50,048.56
Designated Gifts and Special Funds:		
Missions	42,424.82	
Church Extension	192,648.23	
		235,073.05
Reserve for Guaranteed Annual Synodical Budgets		145,462.11
Agency Funds:		
Women's Missionary Society	236,429.82	
Sundry Churches	25,670.00	
		262,099.82
		$2,735,325.02

CONSOLIDATED STATEMENT RECEIPTS AND DISBURSEMENTS
Year ended June 30, 1937
RECEIPTS

United Lutheran Church on Apportionment		$366,415.00
Women's Missionary Society:		
On Budget	$69,639.00	
Designated Gifts	7,193.55	
		76,832.55
Contributions:		
Synodical Missions		12,762.54
Individuals, Congregations, Sunday Schools, etc....................		22,232.07
Bequests		17,707.88
Designated Gifts and Special Funds		6,907.43
Income on Investments		16,720.58
Proceeds Sale of Equipment		50.00
Proceeds Maturity and Sale of Securities		186,795.14
Annuities		5,500.00
Repaid on Church Extension Loans		35,481.54
Interest on Church Extension Loans		2,653.71
Repaid on Class B Securities		994.72
U. L. Publication House for 1938 Special Appeal		40,979.60
Brotherhood of U. L. C. A. for Iron Mountain School		9,000.00
Departmental Transfers		41,443.67
		$842,476.43

DISBURSEMENTS

Loans to Churches	$ 37,180.00
Interest and Special Grants to Churches	9,577.78
Salary—Executive Secretary	4,000.00
Rent and Expense Allowance—Executive Secretary	900.00
Salary—Assistant Executive Secretary	4,000.00
Salary—Secretary of Church Extension and Treasurer...........	4,000.00
Salary—Divisional Secretary of Linguistic Interests...............	4,000.00
Salary—Divisional Secretary of English Missions....................	1,600.00
Rent Allowance—Divisional Secretary of English Missions.	400.00
Salary—Assistant General Superintendent	2,666.67
Salaries to Missionaries and Field Men	277,682.70

Expenses of Missionaries and Field Men	29,793.12
Seminary and Student Aid	2,978.00
Charitable Work in the Virgin Islands	3,250.00
Payments to Annuitants	3,747 00
Interest on Loans and Mortgages	1,289.45
Designated Gifts transmitted	3,786.19
Southern Mountain Schools	22,988.61
Special Work in Canada	5,171.46
Purchase of Equipment	1,620.88
Real Estate Maintenance	539.25
Securities purchased	152,416.83
Invested in Savings Fund accounts	11,883.69
Accrued interest on securities purchased	576.50
Repaid on Loans and Mortgage	21,000.00
Advance a/c Real Estate	55,000.00
Lenten Publicity	2,828.70
Advance a/c 1938 Special Appeal	2,931.92
Refund a/c Bequest	500.00
Officers, Administrative and Office Expense	12,816.94
Departmental Transfers	41,443.67
	$722,569.36

Consolidated Summary

Balance, July 1, 1936	$ 28,343.16
Receipts for year	842,476.43
	870,819.59
Disbursements for year	722,569.36
Balance, June 30, 1937	$148,250.23

H. TORREY WALKER, *Treasurer.*

CERTIFICATE OF AUDIT

We have audited the books of account of The Board of American Missions of the United Lutheran Church in America for the fiscal year beginning July 1, 1936, and ending June 30, 1937. We certify that in our opinion the Balance Scheet at June 30, 1937, hereto attached correctly sets forth the fiscal position of The Board of American Missions on that date: the Consolidated Statement of Receipts and Disbursements for the year under audit, hereto attached, contains all receipts from apportionment, contributions, and other income, as recorded in the books of account, the accounting for these having been duly and properly made, and that all disbursements appearing therein were supported by proper vouchers. All securities on hand at June 30, 1937, were either examined by us or otherwise properly accounted for.

TAIT, WELLER & BAKER,
Accountants and Auditors.

BALANCE SHEET AT June 30, 1938
ASSETS

Cash:		$ 69,529.66
Securities owned at Ledger Values:		
Bonds	393,993.59	
Stocks	12,670.89	
Savings Bank Accounts	123,298.60	
Real Estate Mortgages	17,520.00	
Federal Savings and Loan Associations	5,195.17	
Notes Receivable	3,275.92	
		555,954.17
Advanced Expenses		1,300.00
Advanced a/c Estates		64.18
Advanced from Special Funds		1,408.81
Loans to Churches:		
Church Extension Funds	1,383,156.82	
Investment Funds	45,844.26	
Agency Funds	228,795.71	
Investment Notes	1,807.50	
		1,659,604.29
Real Estate and Buildings:		
Owned and held by Board	536,849.33	
Held as Agent	25,670.00	
		562,519.33
Equipment and Furniture		19,459.47
Accounts Receivable		7,000.00
		$2,876,839.91

LIABILITIES

Loans Payable	$13,700.00	
Held for Women's Missionary Society	11,102.46	
		24,802.46
		$2,852,037.45

FUNDS

General Funds:		
Missions	$67,456.94	
Church Extension	528,229.58	
		595,686.52
Endowment Funds:		
Missions	47,374.68	
Church Extension	15,909.29	
		63,283.97
Permanent Loan Fund		1,205,323.70
Memorial Loan Fund		172,642.01
Restricted Funds		86,569.23
McMurray Fund		23,986.26
Annuity Funds		48,875.22
Designated Gifts and Special Funds:		34,891.72
Missions	22,869.92	
Church Extension	192,905.91	
		215,775.83
Reserve for Guaranteed Annual Synodical Budgets		145,462.11

Agency Funds:
Women's Missionary Society 233,870.88
Sundry Churches 25,670.00
                                                                                                 259,540.88

                                                                                          $2,852,037.45

CONSOLIDATED STATEMENT RECEIPTS AND DISBURSEMENTS
Year Ended June 30, 1938

RECEIPTS

United Lutheran Church on Apportionment .... $ 389,557.00
Women's Missionary Society:
On Budget $68,024.08
Designated Gifts 2,329.00
                                                                                          70,353.08

Contributions:
Synodical Missions 12,190.15
Individuals, Congregations, Sunday Schools, etc.................... 16,236.53
Anniversary Appeal 52,822.45
Bequests 51,426.89
Designated Gifts and Special Funds 3,437.34
Income on Investments 16,652.30
Proceeds Sale of Real Estate 750.00
Proceeds Maturity and Sale of Securities 50,774.21
Maturity Class B Securities 550.00
Return on Advance a/c 5,000.00
Annuities 1,000.00
Repaid on Church Extension Loans 36,239.27
Interest on Church Extension Loans 4,152.46
Repaid on Real Estate Mortgage 180.00
McMurray Fund 425.75
Brotherhood of U. L. C. A. for Iron Mountain School 3,595.00
Departmental Transfers 80,252.46

                                                                                          $795,594.89

DISBURSEMENTS

Loans to Churches .... $ 89,621.89
Interest and Special Grants to Churches 10,334.36
Salary—Executive Secretary 4,600.00
Rent and Expense Allowance—Executive Secretary.............. 900.00
Salary—Assistant Executive Secretary 4,000.00
Rent Allowance—Assistant Executive Secretary..................... 600.00
Salary—Secretary of Church Extension and Treasurer........ 4,000.00
Rent Allowance—Secretary of Church Extension and Treas-
urer 600.00
Salary—Divisional Secretary of Linguistic Interests 4,000.00
Rent Allowance—Divisional Secretary of Linguistic Interests. 600.00
Salary—Divisional Secretary of English Missions.................... 3,300.00
Rent Allowance—Divisional Secretary of English Missions.... 600.00
Salary—Assistant General Superintendent 2,000.00

Salaries to Missionaries and Field Men	290,595.40
Expenses of Missionaries and Field Men	28,914.59
Seminary and Student Aid	2,982.37
Charitable Work in the Virgin Islands	3,326.43
Payments to Annuitants	3,874.50
Interest on Loans	718.50
Designated Gifts transmitted	4,936.64
Southern Mountain Schools	19,483.92
Special Work in Canada	5,616.70
Purchase of Equipment	15,048.59
Real Estate Maintenance	2,755.41
Advances from Special Funds	1,628.81
Securities purchased	128,118.22
Invested in Savings Fund accounts	5,371.16
Accrued interest on securities purchased	813.78
Real Estate Purchases	43,596.80
Invested in Real Estate Mortgages	8,200.00
Notes Receivable	3,275.92
Savings and Loan Associations	2,195.17
Legal and Bank Charges, review and care of securities	810.74
Advances a/c Anniversary Appeal	84,824.75
Officers, Administrative and Office Expenses	11,818.35
Departmental Transfers	80,252.46
	$874,315.46

Consolidated Summary

Balance, July 1, 1937		$148,250.23
Receipts for year		795,594.89
		943,845.12
Disbursements for year		874,315.46
Balance, June 30, 1938		$69,529.66

H. TORREY WALKER, *Treasurer.*

CERTIFICATE OF AUDIT

We have audited the books of account of The Board of American Missions of the United Lutheran Church in America for the fiscal year beginning July 1, 1937, and ending June 30, 1938. We certify that in our opinion the Balance Scheet at June 30, 1938, hereto attached correctly sets forth the fiscal position of The Board of American Missions on that date: the Colsolidated Statement of Receipts and Disbursements for the year under audit, hereto attached, contains all receipts from apportionment, contributions, and other income, as recorded in the books of account, the accounting for these having been duly and properly made, and that all disbursements appearing therein were supported by proper vouchers. All securities on hand at June 30, 1938, were either examined by us or otherwise properly accounted for.

TAIT, WELLER & BAKER,
Accountants and Auditors.

CASH RECEIPTS AND DISBURSEMENTS
July 1, 1937 to June 30, 1938
MISSIONS ACCOUNTS
RECEIPTS

United Lutheran Church on Apportionment		$389,557.00
Women's Missionary Society:		
On Budget	$51,194.08	
Konnarock School	8,550.00	
Designated Gifts	1,643.69	
		61,387.77
Contributions:		
For Synodical Missions		12,190.15
Individuals, Congregations, etc.		13,028.86
Interest and Dividends		7,193.76
Designated Gifts and Specials		3,037.34
Repaid on Special Loan		40.00
Return on Advance a/c		5,000.00
Bequest		10,661.86
Proceeds maturity and sale securities		18,094.31
Total		$520,191.05

DISBURSEMENTS

Missionaries' Salaries		$277,921.77
Missionaries' Expenses:		
General	$11,698.21	
Moving	4,069.32	
Furlough	1,240.00	
		17,007.53
Field Staff Salaries		13,500.00
Clerical Salaries		1,128.00
Field Staff Expenses		3,707.36
Clinical Training:		
Salaries	3,300.00	
Expenses	412.65	
		3,712.65
Seminary Student Aid		2,982.37
Charitable Work in the Virgin Islands		3,326.43
Interest Grants		4,879.34
Special Grants		3,471.35
Designated and Special a/cs:		
General items transmitted		4,886.60
Konnarock Training School		9,335.37
Iron Mountain School		10,148.55
Special Work in Canada		5,616.70
Advances		120.00
Securities purchased		90,561.07
Accrued interest and commission on purchases		742.27
Invested in Savings Fund a/cs.......................................		5,246.44
Real Estate Mortgages		6,100.00
Transfer to Church Extension		80,252.46
Total		$544,646.26

CHURCH EXTENSION ACCOUNTS
RECEIPTS

Bequests	$ 40,765.03
Annuities	1,000.00
Contributions:	
Individuals, Sunday Schools, Congregations	3,777.67
Anniversary Appeal	52,822.45
Women's Missionary Society:	
Budget for Loans	8,280.00
Designated Funds	685.31
Interest and Dividends	9,458.54
Maturity of Class B Securities	550.00
Proceeds Maturity and Sale of Securities	32,679.90
Proceeds Sale of Real Estate	750.00
Interest on Church Extension Loans	4,152.46

Repaid on Principal of Church Extension Loans:

From Loan Funds	$31,532.00	
From Agency Funds	2,165.82	
From Investment Funds	2,501.45	
		36,199.27
McMurray Fund Income		425.75
Brotherhood of U. L. C. A. for Iron Mountain School		3,025.00
Repaid on Real Estate Mortgage		180.00
Advance on Special Funds returned		400.00
Transfer from Missions		80,252.46
		$275,403.84

DISBURSEMENTS

Loans to Churches:		
From Loan Funds	$43,621.89	
From Agency a/c	26,000.00	
From Investment Funds	20,000.00	
		$ 89,621.89
Equipment purchased		15,048.59
Real Estate Maintenance		2,755.41
Special Grants to Churches		1,983.67
Interest on Loans		718.50
Real Estate purchased		43,596.80
Payments to Annuitants		3,874.50
Review and Care of Securities		666.25
Legal and Bank Charges		144.49
Secretary of Church Extension and Treasurer Salary		4,000.00
Secretary of Church Extension and Treasurer, Rent Allowance		600.00
Clerical Salaries		1,882.00
Field Staff Expenses		1,439.69
Contingent Fund		500.00
Special Funds advanced		1,508.81
Special Funds transmitted		50.04
Division of Survey and Research:		
Salaries		8,173.63
Expenses		2,727.41
Debt Reduction Program Expenses		1,309.95
Advanced for Anniversary Appeal Expenses		84,824.75

Invested in Savings Fund a/cs..	124.72
Savings and Loan Associations	2,195.17
Real Estate Mortgages	2,100.00
Notes Receivable	3,275.92
Bonds	37,557.15
Accrued interest and commissions on securities purchased....	71.51
	$310,750.85

ADMINISTRATION

DISBURSEMENTS

Office Supplies	$	264.47
Telephone and Telegraph		169.33
Contribution: Lutheran Church House		1,628.00
Postage, insurance, etc.		763.76
Auditing		500.00
Interdenominational contributions		324.00
Publicity		1,870.21
Salaries: Executive Secretary, salary		4,600.00
Executive Secretary, rent and expense allowance......................		900.00
Assistant		1,600.00
Clerical		2,920.00
Expenses: Executive Officers		90.78
Board and Committee Meetings		3,287.80
		$18,918.35

SUMMARY OF CASH RECEIPTS AND DISBURSEMENTS

July 1, 1937—Balance on hand		$148,250.23
Receipts: Missions $520,191.05		
Church Extension 275,403.84		
		795,594.89
		$943,845.12
Disbursements:		
Missions 544,646.26		
Church Extension 310,750.85		
Administration 18,918.35		
		874,315.46
June 30, 1938—Balance on hand		$ 69,529.66

MISSIONS BALANCE SHEET, June 30, 1938

ASSETS		LIABILITIES AND FUNDS	
Cash in General Fund....$	6,165.07	Designated Gifts and	
Endowment Fund	59.30	Special Funds	$ 22,869.92
Designated Funds	13,613.72	General Fund	67,456.94
Glatfelter Fund	1,287.43	Reserve for Guaranteed	
Harroway Fund	675.64	Annual Synodical	
Kaercher Fund	1,355.42	Budgets	145,462.11
		Endowment Fund	47,374.68
	$ 23,156.58	Glatfelter Fund	10,961.86

Bonds	219,705.86	Harroway Fund	11,292.54
Stocks	3,520.88	Kaercher Fund	12,637.32
Savings Fund Accounts..	70,067.01	Women's Missionary	
Investment Notes	1,807.50	Society	11,102.46
Contingent Funds	800.00		
Real Estate Mortgages....	10,100.00		
	$329,157.83		**$329,157.83**

SECURITIES IN MISSIONS FUND ACCOUNTS

Bonds	Book Value	Market Value 6-30-38
4,000 Lehigh Valley Genl., 4½s 2003	$ 4,000.00	$ 925.00
7,000 Chicago, Burl. and Quincy, 4s, 1958	6,597.50	6,448.75
1,000 Metropolitan Edison, 4½s 1968	1,000.00	1,097.50
2,000 St. Louis County Gas, 1st 5s 1951	2,000.00	2,115.00
2,000 Westchester County, 6s 1950	2,000.00	2,535.00
5,000 U. S. A. Treas. Notes, 4¼s-3¼s 1943-45	5,000.00	5,487.50
13,000 U. S. A. Treas. Bonds, 2¾s 1948-51	13,000.00	13,597.19
14,000 U. S. A. Treas. Bonds, 2¾s 1956-59	14,000.00	14,393.75
15,000 U. S. A. Treas. Bonds, 2½s, 1949-53	15,000.00	15,290.63
500 U. S. A. Treas. Bonds, 2¾s, 1945-47	500.00	531.88
5,000 Great Northern R. R., 4s, 1946	5,037.50	4,000.00
5,000 Consumers' Power Co., 3½s 1970	5,175.00	5,243.75
5,000 Dominion of Canada, 2½s 1945	4,862.50	5,118.75
5,000 Dominion of Canada, 3s 1955	4,937.50	4,900.00
5,000 Pennsylvania R. R. Co., 2¾s 1946	4,976.68	4,900.00
5,000 Atlantic City R. R., 4s 1951	5,047.50	3,250.00
7,000 American Tel. and Tel., 3¼s 1961	7,070.00	7,175.00
4,000 American Tel. and Tel., 3¼s 1966	4,080.00	4,095.00
10,000 Nassau County, N. Y., 2¾s 1948	10,151.00	10,025.00
5,000 City of New York, 3s 1977	4,837.50	4,912.50
10,000 Philadelphia Electric, 3½s 1967	10,250.00	10,850.00
5,000 Consolidated Oil S. F. Deb., 3½s 1951	5,012.50	5,150.00
5,000 No. American Car Corp. Eq., 4½s 1939	5,085.00	4,925.00
10,000 Northwestern Refrig. Eq., 3½s 1944	9,625.00	9,387.50
5,000 Youngstown Sheet and Tube, 4s 1961	4,998.75	5,100.00
5,000 Pa. and N. Y. Canal and R. R., 5s 1939	5,112.50	2,250.00
10,000 City of New York R. T. Rec., 3¼s 1975	10,000.00	9,950.00
5,000 Ohio Edison 1st, 4s 1967	5,000.00	5,075.00
5,000 Central N. Y. Power Genl., 3¾s 1962	4,950.00	5,281.25
10,000 York Ice Mach. Corp. 1st, 6s 1947	9,674.43	9,000.00
10,000 Appalachian Elec. Pr., 4s 1963	9,875.00	10,575.00
5,000 Chicago and Northwestern, 5s 1987	4,950.00	800.00
5,000 Third Avenue Ry. Adj., 5s 1960	4,950.00	337.50
10,000 Mo. Kans and Texas, 4s 1990	9,450.00	5,712.50
1,500 Northern Pacific, 3s 2047	1,500.00	783.75
	$219,705.86	**$201,219.70**

Stocks		
88 Shares York Trust Co.	$ 3,520.88	$ 1,320.00

CHURCH EXTENSION BALANCE SHEET, June 30, 1938

ASSETS		LIABILITIES AND FUNDS	
Cash in General Fund	$4,804.59	Loans Payable ....$	13,700.00
Permanent Loan		General Fund	528,454.58
Fund	4,712.15	Permanent Loan Fund	1,205,098.70
Memorial Loan Fund	11,646.03	Memorial Loan Fund....	172,642.01
Endowment Fund	684.91	Endowment Fund	15,909.29
Restricted Funds	2,268.96	Restricted Funds	86,569.23
McMurray Fund	1,622.01	McMurray Fund	23,986.26
Annuity Funds	837.36	Annuity Funds	48,875.22
Designated Funds	347.86	Designated Funds	347.86
Special Funds	9,711.30	Special Funds	120,729.10
Omnibus Invest. a/c	4,662.74	Omnibus Invest. a/c....	71,828.95
W. M. S. Agency a/c	5,075.17	Agency Funds:	
		Women's Miss. Soc....	233,870.88
	46,373.08	St. Luke's, York, Pa.	25,000.00
Savings Fund a/cs........	53,231.59	Harmony Grove, Pa.	500.00
Bonds	174,287.73	Cly, Pa.	170.00
Stocks	9,150.01		
Loans to Churches:			
Board Funds	1,383,156.82		
Agency Funds	228,795.71		
Investment Funds	45,844.26		
Real Estate and Build-			
ings	536,849.33		
Equipment and			
Furnishings	19,459.47		
Due from Synods	7,000.00		
Advances from Special			
Funds	1,472.99		
Agency Real Estate	25,670.00		
Savings and Loan			
Associations	5,195.17		
Real Estate Mortgages	7,420.00		
Notes Receivable	3,275.92		
Contingent Fund	500.00		
	$2,547,682.08		$2,547,682.08

SECURITIES IN CHURCH EXTENSION FUND ACCOUNTS

Bonds	Book Value	Market Value 6-30-38
11,000 Westchester County, 6s 1950	$11,000.00	$13,942.50
2,000 Westchester County, 6s 1953	2,000.00	2,560.00
5,000 Louisville and Nashville 1st, 4½s 2003	5,100.00	4,137.50
15,000 L. and N. Unified, 4s 1940	14,580.00	15,018.75
5,000 Illinois Central, 4s 1955	4,743.75	2,200.00
5,000 Illinois Central, 4¾s 1966	5,005.00	1,900.00
3,000 Electric and Peoples' Trac., 4s 1945	1,875.00	165.00
1,000 Howard Gas and Coal, 6s 1937	1,000.00	5.00
4,000 Metropolitan Edison, 4½s 1968	4,000.00	4,390.00
10,000 Canadian Pacific Equip., 4½s 1941	9,892.00	10,625.00
6,000 Southern Pacific, 4s 1955	5,692.50	3,570.00

1,000 Jefferson and Placquemines 2-4s 1971	1,000.00	350.00
1,000 City of Cincinnati, Ohio, 4s 1960	1,000.00	1,195.00
5,000 Penna. R. R. Genl. Mtge., 4½s 1965	5,043.75	4,700.00
10,000 Penna. R. R. Genl., 3¾s 1970	9,887.50	8,400.00
1,000 Lehigh Valley R. R. Genl., 4s 2003	1,000.00	220.00
5,000 Dominion of Canada, 2½s 1943	4,775.00	5,100.00
10,000 Dominion of Canada, 3s 1967	9,780.00	9,800.00
5,000 Penn Central Lt. and Pr., 4½s 1977	5,000.00	4,193.75
5,000 Standard Oil of N. J., 3s 1961	4,981.25	5,150.00
10,000 U. S. A. Treas. Notes, 2½s 1949-53	10,084.38	10,193.75
50 U. S. A. Treas. Notes, 3¼s 1943-45	50.00	54.88
500 U. S. A. Treas. Notes, 2¾s 1945-47	516.40	531.88
5,000 Ohio Edison 1st Mtge., 3¾s 1972	5,006.25	4,837.50
70 Unified Debenture Corp., 2-5s 1955	70.00	22.40
10,000 Union Elec. of Mo., 3¾s 1962	10,000.00	10,800.00
25,000 York Ice Mach Corp. 1st, 6s 1947	24,186.07	22,500.00
5,500 Northern Pacific, 3s 2047	5,785.00	2,873.75
1,500 City of Coral Gables, Fla., 2½s-5s 1977.......	152.63	678.75
2,779.05 City of Coral Gables Tax Ant. Cert.	645.00	166.74
5,000 Chicago and N. W. Genl., 5s 1987	5,303.75	800.00
5,000 Ohio Public Service 1st, 4s 1962	5,132.50	5,106.25
	$174,287.73	$156,188.40

Stocks

18 Integrity Trust Co., Phila.	$ 3,520.01	$ 45.00
45 Cincinnati Gas and Elec. 5% A Pref.	4,140.00	4,432.50
6 Dayton and Michigan Ry. 8% Pref.	390.00	468.00
11 Little Miami R. R. Par $50	737.00	957.00
11 Littl Miami Spec. Guar. Bet. Par $50	363.00	440.00
	$9,150.01	$6,342.50

REAL ESTATE OWNED

June 30, 1938

In United States and Canada

Property, 74 West 126th Street, New York, N. Y.	$ 37,000.00
McMurray Estate, Commercial Street, Waterloo, Iowa	18,500.00
Aspen, Colorado	1.00
David City, Nebraska	1.00
Martindale, Nebraska	1.00
Colorado City, Colorado	1.00
Lewisburg, Pennsylvania	3,500.00
York Haven, Pennsylvania	100.00
Sylvan Lake, Alberta, Canada	520.00
Iron Mountain Boys' School, Konnarock, Virginia	16,892.08
Property, Luther Memorial Church, Madison, Wis.	89,361.50
Property, Lincoln Blvd. and Washington Ave., Santa Monica, California	56,600.00
Property, Hamilton and Illinois, Spokane, Washington	5,905.00
	$228,382.58

In the Virgin Islands

* Church at St. Thomas	$ 36,400.00
* Parsonage at St. Thomas	7,400.00
* Parish House at St. Thomas	3,400.00
* Church at Christiansted, St. Croix	36,400.00
* Parsonage at Christiansted	7,400.00
* Administration Buildings and Cottages, Christiansted	1,400.00
† Children's Home, Christiansted	6,600.00
* Church at Frederiksted, St. Croix	22,300.00
* Parsonage, Frederiksted	3,400.00
* Parish House, Frederiksted	3,000.00
† Children's Home, Frederiksted	4,600.00
† Ebenezer Orphanage, Frederiksted	12,600.00
* Church at St. John's	1,200.00
* Church at Kingshill, St. Croix	3,400.00
	$149,500.00

* Property held under protection of Treaty between the United States and Denmark.
† Title held by the West Indies Mission Board.

* In Puerto Rico

Puerta de Tierra—Church and Parsonage	$ 26,200.00
Santurce—Parsonage, Lutz Street	3,500.00
Parsonage, Gertrudis Street	5,000.00
Dorado—Chapel	2,600.00
Parsonage	1,200.00
Bayamon—Church	9,500.00
Sunday School Building	6,000.00
Parsonage	7,000.00
Villa Betania	8,500.00
Comerio Street Church	8,600.00
Comerio Street Sunday School Building	2,400.00
Catano—Church	7,000.00
Sunday School Building	4,200.00
Parsonage	1,000.00
Palo Seco—Church, Parsonage and Lot	3,000.00
Lot	56.75
Monteflores—Chapel, Parsonage, Training School	34,400.00
Monacillo—Church	3,500.00
Maracayo—Chapel	425.00
Gandul—Chapel and Parsonage	2,400.00
Juan Domingo—Church and Lot	810.00
Toa Baja—Church	5,500.00
Parsonage and Lot	3,000.00
Higuillar—Chapel	425.00
	$146,216.75

* All titles held by West Indies Mission Board.

Rocky Boy, Montana

Indian Help House	$ 350.00
Light Plant	750.00
Mission House	5,100.00
Chapel	900.00
Barn and Live Stock	450.00
Parsonage	5,200.00
	$12,750.00

Buildings at Rocky Boy Indian Reservation, erected by Board, revert to the United States Government should work be abandoned.

Total Real Estate

In United States and Canada	$228,382.58
In the Virgin Islands	149,500.00
In Puerto Rico	146,216.75
In Rocky Boy Indian Reservation	12,750.00
	$536,849.33

EQUIPMENT OWNED
June 30, 1938

Philadelphia Offices	$ 234.18
Anniversary Appeal	958.81
New York Offices	1,194.66
Chicago Office	819.47
Merrick Office	200.00
Survey Division	270.00
Konnarock Medical Center	150.00
Iron Mountain School	2,538.53
Lutheran Radio Pictures, Inc.	9,251.04
Puerto Rico Parsonages	1,689.29
Virgin Islands Parsonages	1,403.49
Rocky Boy Mission	750.00
	$19,459.47

LOANS TO CHURCHES

Board Loans:

In Permanent Loan Fund	$1,200,386.55
In Memorial Loan Fund	145,437.08
In Restricted Funds	30,183.19
In Annuity Funds	6,893.55
In Annuity Funds (Interest at 4%)	25,450.71
In Special Funds	20,650.00
In Kaercher Fund (Missions)	250.00
In General Fund (Missions)	1,380.00
In Weiskotten Fund (Missions)	177.50

Agency Loans:
Women's Missionary Society 228,795.71

$1,659,604.29

Real Estate Mortgage Loans

3321 Delaware Avenue, Richmond, Va.	$ 2,000.00
3325 Florida Avenue, Richmond, Va.	2,000.00
625 Haddon Avenue, Collingswood, N. J.	4,000.00
3318 Second Avenue, Richmond, Va.	1,320.00
1209 Warren Avenue, Richmond, Va.	2,600.00
Snead Road, Richmond, Va.	1,500.00
504 North 34th St., Richmond, Va.	600.00
3401 Missouri Avenue, Richmond, Va.	3,500.00

$17,520.00

Dr. Pflum presented the Rev. Z. M. Corbe, Executive Secretary of the Board, who spoke of the causes served by the Board and of the prevailing conditions under which the tasks are being faced.

Dr. Pflum then presented Mr. H. Torrey Walker, Treasurer of the Board and the director of the Anniversary Appeal, who spoke of procedures and achievements, and paid tribute to those whose co-operation and support have brought both tangible and intangible results of great value to the Church.

Moved and carried that this Convention express its appreciation to the leaders and those who have assisted in preparing and presenting this appeal to the Church.

On motion the report of the auditors was accepted.

The Report of the Committee on Evangelism was presented by the Rev. Franklin Clark Fry, a member of the Committee.

REPORT OF COMMITTEE ON EVANGELISM

This is the Committee on Evangelism's valedictory report. Eighteen years ago, when the United Lutheran Church was in session at Washington, its career began. As a promising innovation then, a by-law was adopted creating a distinct agency to lead in the spread and stimulating of evangelism, and high hopes were reposed in it. Now the cycle is complete and this committee's trust is to be absorbed among the functions of a new Board.

Naturally a tinge of regret remains. What aggravates it most in your committee's view is the enforced inactivity to which it has more and more been confined. During the past biennium not even a single meeting has been authorized, with the result that what might have been vigorous life has been reduced to a state of suspended animation.

As individuals, of course, the appointees to the Committee on Evangelism have exerted themselves conscientiously, scattered as they were, to accomplish all they could—but hundreds of other pastors all over the church have, too. It would come with ill grace indeed to try to represent what any of them did, or all of them together, as an adequate substitute for a committee's proper labors.

The only just exception that dare be allowed has to do with our chairman. Dr. Pohlman has continued to itinerate from church to church in behalf of evangelism, principally on the West Coast, almost constantly during these two years. As your committee's unsalaried "special representative," his ministry has been cordially welcomed and certainly blessed.

But if regret cannot be avoided that too much has not been fulfilled that ought to have been, there need be no shame. Your Committee on Evangelism is convinced honestly, and with all due humility, that any derelictions that can be charged against it must fairly be ascribed to frustration rather than to wilful or careless neglect. Throughout its entire existence, it has not only been handicapped with insufficient funds, as is the common complaint of all church agencies. Its financial means not only have not been commensurate with its task. They have been literally non-existent, with no appropriations or apportionments whatever under the committee's own control for the furtherance of its vital duties.

Even the one apparent promise of a better future proved to be more of a phantom than a substantial prospect. At Richmond in 1926, you may recall, a resolution was actually adopted that proposed that the Committee on Evangelism should "employ a full-time secretary as soon as they deem it feasible." Since it was not implemented with any provision for the necessary income, however, and since even in those days of financial flood tide it did not commend itself to our superiors in the church, it has never become effective.

Yet, despite it all, how marvellously God's grace has operated in the sphere of evangelism in these formative eighteen years! Doubtless it is not expedient to glory even in retrospect—above all for a frail committee like this—but the very word "evangelism," which was almost resented as an alien, an intruder, not so long ago in the Lutheran Church is now inscribed on its very heart. It has come to strike the master-chord in all the church's being until it is truthful to assert that there is no acuter sense today in our synods and parishes, among our pastors and hosts of our laity, than this ringing imperative to win, conserve and reclaim souls for Christ. Evangelism has saturated and permeated the United Lutheran Church incomparably more than ever before.

The Committee on Evangelism, with the prospect of its dissolution upon it, pleads and believes that its earnest, sincere efforts to exalt the very essence of the Gospel, lamentably restricted as they have been, have nevertheless not been in vain. May it find its life in losing it to its successor Board!

A. POHLMAN, *Convener,*
R. HOMER ANDERSON,
RUSSELL F. AUMAN,
J. FREDERICK BERMON,
WALTER C. DAVIS,
FRANKLIN CLARK FRY,
G. ARTHUR FRY,
ARNOLD F. KELLER,
G. HAROLD KINARD,
FRED W. OTTERBEIN,
CALVIN F. STICKLES.

The Rev. Hermann F. Miller, Chairman, presented the report of the Committee on Church Papers.

REPORT OF THE COMMITTEE ON CHURCH PAPERS

(For action on the recommendations in this report, see pp. 231, 232, 235, 238.)

Your committee held two meetings during the biennium, and the Executive Committee met twice. The organization resulted in the election of Dr. Hermann F. Miller, Chairman; Dr. H. F. Baughman, Secretary; Dr. M. R. Hamsher as third member of the Executive Committee.

Your committee has been mindful of the resolution of the Savannah Convention to choose an Associate Editor. In order to assist the committee in this assignment the Editor of *The Lutheran* was urged to invite able men to contribute editorials, which was apparently an impossible request in the judgment of the Editor. Furthermore, in view of the election of a Promotional Editor by the Board of Publication, and his probable close co-operation with *The Lutheran* and the *Lutherischer Herold,* it was deemed expedient to postpone the selection of an Associate Editor until the Promotional Program had been organized.

The request of the Columbus Convention for a film estimate service has received attention by the Editor of *The Lutheran,* and some progress has been made, although no special department has been established.

The attention of the Church is called to the improved format of *The*

Lutheran, to the changes of departments, such as the omission of the Daily Devotions, and the addition of the page, "In the World's Eye," by Dr. Seebach, the increased variety of articles and the improvement in the News Letters. The response to the Editor's request for articles by members of the Church, particularly by faculty members of our Colleges and Divinity Schools, has been encouraging and gratifying. About one hundred eighty persons have made special contributions to the columns of our paper. About three hundred fourteen special articles have appeared. The members of the News Letters Staff have in most Synods written regularly and well. However, one large Synod submitted but two such letters from its territory. Meetings, conventions, and special events in the Church have been faithfully reported.

It has been the endeavor of the Editors, and the Committee to increase the so-called "Human Interest" features of *The Lutheran,* and the secretaries of the various Boards of the Church have been asked to use the pages of our paper with such material for the promotion of this work. Not much of such material has been offered. It is hoped that the Promotional Plan will meet that need.

In order to increase the circulation of our official Church papers, it was resolved to participate in a Church Papers Week in October. The attention of pastors and people was thus called to our paper, and special inducements to subscribe were offered. The result was not encouraging. Both editors lament the comparatively small number of subscriptions.

The helpfulness of the Board of Publication must be recognized. Our Church Papers are published at a loss. The Board of Publication meets the deficit. Our official weeklies are in reality being subsidized.

The committee also noted the steady increase of other publications within the United Lutheran Church, which serve special interests and sections, and is of the opinion that a publication policy should be determined.

The present editors—Dr. N. R. Melhorn for *The Lutheran,* and Dr. C. R. Tappert for the *Lutherischer Herold,* are renominated by the committee for the following biennium.

The terms for Dr. Miller, Dr. Hamsher, and Mr. Henry Streibert have ended. Dr. Hamsher is ineligible for re-election, and Mr. Streibert recently resigned from the committee. Your committee places in nomination the following: Rev. Hermann F. Miller, D.D., Rev. Ralph D. Heim, Ph.D., and Mr. E. E. Croll.

The following resolutions are recommended to the Convention: (For action, see pp. 231, 232, 235, 238.)

1. Resolved, that in view of the increasing number of publications within the United Lutheran Church, the Church Papers policy of the United Lutheran Church be clearly defined. (Amended, see p. 231.)

2. Resolved, that the United Lutheran Church, through the Pro-

motional Editor, give first consideration to the official Church Papers as mediums of publicity for the Promotional Plan.
(Amended and then eliminated from the report, see p. 232.)

3. Resolved, that the United Lutheran Church sufficiently subsidize *The Lutheran* and the *Lutherischer Herold,* that the subscription price may be offered for one dollar a year. (Referred, see p. 232.)

Respectfully submitted,
HERMANN F. MILLER, *Chairman,*
H. F. BAUGHMAN, *Secretary.*

Dr. Miller introduced the Rev. N. R. Melhorn, Editor of *The Lutheran,* and the Rev. C. R. Tappert, Editor of the *Lutherischer Herold,* each of whom addressed the Convention.

It was moved and carried that the present editors, the Rev. N. R. Melhorn of *The Lutheran,* and the Rev. C. R. Tappert of the *Lutherischer Herold,* be elected for the next biennium. The President declared them elected for the biennium.

The resolutions of the Committee on Church Papers were presented.

Resolution 1. Motion was made and seconded to amend resolution 1 by adding the words "by the Committee on Church Papers."

An amendment to the amendment was moved and seconded, substituting the words "by a special committee appointed by the President, covering all interests involved" in place of the words "by the Committee on Church Papers." The amendment to the amendment was adopted.

It was moved and seconded that the original recommendation of the Executive Board, concerning consolidation of periodicals, Item II, 13 (page 60), be substituted for Resolution 1. This motion was *lost.*

Resolution 1 as amended was adopted.

The President announced that the motion to refer Item II, 13, Consolidation of Periodicals, to the Committee on Church Papers, was deferred until this time. (For other references, see pp. 60, 103, 232, 235, 238.)

It was moved and carried that the motion to refer be amended by striking out the words "Committee on Church

Papers" and substituting for them the words "the Committee named in resolution 1 of the report of the Committee on Church Papers." The motion as amended was adopted.

Resolution 2. It was moved and carried to strike out the word "first" in Resolution 2.

It was moved and seconded to adopt Resolution 2 as amended. The motion was *lost*. (Resolution 2 is therefore eliminated from the report.)

Resolution 3. It was moved and carried that Resolution 3 be referred to the Committee to Define Church Paper Policy, authorized under Resolution 1.

Moved and carried that the United Lutheran Church express its appreciation of the faithful labors of the Editors of *The Lutheran* and the *Lutherischer Herold*.

Moved and carried that the Committee to Define Church Paper Policy, authorized under Resolution 1 of the report of the Committee on Church Papers, submit its report at the next convention. (For further action, see pp. 235, 238.)

The Report of the Commission on Investments was presented by Mr. S. F. Telleen, a member of the Commission.

REPORT OF THE COMMISSION ON INVESTMENTS

The annuities committee of the Commission has been active during the past biennium. It has sent copies of its report on annuities to all the Boards of the Church, to the Women's Missionary Society and to other organizations and institutions which have expressed any interest.

The committee has also approved a model form of annuity agreement which has been adopted by the Board of Foreign Missions and by the Women's Missionary Society. These organizations have been advised of the practical necessity of obtaining competent assistance in the handling of annuities and their attention has been directed to an annuity service bureau now available to church organizations which appears to fill this need. The Board of Foreign Missions thereupon contracted for the services of this annuity bureau and the Women's Missionary Society decided to do so. The Board of Ministerial Pensions and Relief already had available to it the services of an annuity expert.

An increasing number of states have enacted regulatory legislation and have instituted taxes which make the issuance of agreements and the handling of annuities no simple matter. Your Commission therefore most strongly urges every annuity-issuing organization of the Church, which has not already done so, to familiarize itself with the laws of its own state as to reserves, taxation, etc., and with the laws of other states in which it may have resident annuitants or in which it intends to solicit annuities. The Commission's Committee on Annuities composed of Messrs. S. F. Telleen, B. B. Slifer, and Robbin B. Wolf stands ready to be of any assistance it can.

At the latest convention of the Church the Commission was authorized to arrange a conference between its own committee on annuities and fiscal representatives of the several boards and agencies, for the purpose of reviewing thoroughly all phases of the annuity question. Developments since then have seemed to make such a meeting unnecessary and therefore after consulting officers of the Church the conference was not arranged.

INVESTMENT SERVICES

The Commission has continued to offer investment recommendations whenever requested to do so, each recommendation being first approved by at least three of its members as required by its rules. The chairman of the Commission also continues to furnish investment review service to the Board of Education and the Women's Missionary Society. The other boards of the Church function in investment matters largely through their own finance committees, and the Commission, being satisfied that their investment matters are in competent hands, has avoided all interference and duplication of effort. Some requests for investment advice and information have been received from institutions of the Church other than its own boards and agencies and these have likewise received attention.

The Commission through its chairman maintains a standing record of investments of all of the Boards and requests every Board to keep the chairman promptly advised of changes in its investments and of securities received as gifts and legacies in order that this record may be complete and up-to-date at all times. It is also highly desirable that the chairman be kept advised of changes in investment policy and standing investment resolutions adopted by any board so that the Commission in turn may be kept fully informed at all times.

CONFORMITY WITH RULES

At the latest convention of the Church a resolution was adopted requesting each of the boards and agencies holding endowments to reexamine the existing Rules and Regulations of the Commission with a view to conforming its investment procedure therewith or proposing to the Commission such amendments to the Rules and Regulations as seem to it desirable. The Commission has received no report from any board or agency on this subject nor has it pressed the matter upon the attention of any board. Unless otherwise instructed by the Church the Commission will now proceed to take initiative in this matter and will canvass the finance committees of the several boards and agencies for their suggestions and comments, hoping to develop during the next biennium a procedure for every board in full conformity with the Commission's Rules and Regulations.

The Commission's function can best be described as a reserve agency that can be called into action on short notice if an emergency arises. So long as a Board has well-developed facilities of its own there is no need for the Commission to duplicate those facilities. It is, however, highly desirable that there exist a close co-ordination of effort between the Commission and every Board and Agency, and this should be the well-defined purpose in any revision of the Rules and Regulations.

The Commission invites suggestions and criticisms from any source. It is a volunteer organization with no office or staff. However its membership is composed almost entirely of persons who carry investment responsibility in some form. To the limit of its ability it stands ready to serve the Church and its boards and agencies.

Respectfully submitted,

WILLIAM H. STACKEL, *Chairman.*

The report was received as information.

Mr. W. H. Menges, Chairman of Committee of Tellers No. 1, reported elections as follows:

For the *Executive Board* each of the following received a majority of the votes cast for the term expiring 1942:

Rev. Henry H. Bagger   J. K. Jensen
Rev. Alvin E. Bell   James C. Kinard

The President declared them elected and stated that one clergyman and one layman were yet to be elected.

For the *Commission of Adjudication,* each of the following received a majority of the votes cast:

Term expiring 1944: Rev. B. H. Pershing.
Term expiring 1940: Rev. Paul J. Hoh.

The President declared them elected and stated that one clergyman and one layman were yet to be elected for the term expiring 1944.

For the *Committee on Church Papers,* the Rev. Hermann F. Miller received a majority of the votes cast, term expiring

1944. The President declared him elected and stated that one clergyman and one layman were yet to be elected.

For the *Executive Committee of the Laymen's Movement,* each of the following received a majority of the votes cast for the term expiring 1940:

H. J. Albrecht	W. H. Hager
J. L. Clark	E. Clarence Miller
P. H. Glatfelter	S. F. Telleen
Peter P. Hagan	C. B. Zimmerman

M. P. Moller, Jr.

The President declared them elected and stated that one layman was yet to be elected.

Moved and seconded that action on the motion, instructing the Committee to Define Church Paper Policy to report to the next Convention, be reconsidered. (For other references, see pp. 60, 103, 231, 232, 238.)

A motion to adjourn was carried.

The Convention adjourned at 5.30 P. M. Prayer led by the Rev. E. W. Weber.

Friday Evening

The Board of American Missions presented the work of the Church in its field and relationships through an impressive pageant entitled "God in the Midst of Her." The pageant gave the Lutheran Church its proper historic setting.

FIFTH SESSION
LORD BALTIMORE HOTEL
Baltimore, Maryland
Saturday, October 8, 1938, 8.45 A. M.

Matins were conducted by the Rev. H. J. McGuire.

The President called the Convention to order.

The Rev. R. Homer Anderson, Chairman of the Nominating Committee, presented nominations as follows:

For the *Board of Foreign Missions:*

Term expiring 1944. Rev. Joseph B. Baker; Rev. Robert D. Clare; Rev. J. Harold Mumper; Rev. F. Eppling Reinartz; Rev. Frederick J. Baum;

Rev. Charles G. Beck; Rev. Robert H. Daube; Rev. Albert U. Gesler; Rev. Clarence Hershey; Rev. Robert L. Lang; Rev. Herbert D. Shimer; Rev. Simon Snyder; John C. Korn; Claude L. Peterman; George S. Yost; Virgil W. Doub; Frederick C. Feld; George F. Greiner; Harry C. Hoffman; Addison J. Keim; C. B. Patterson.

The President called for nominations from the floor, and the Rev. George A. Rupley and the Rev. R. H. Gerberding were nominated. There being no further nominations, the President declared the nominations closed.

For the *Board of American Missions* and the *West Indies Mission Board:*

Term expiring 1944. Rev. Robert H. Ischinger; Rev. George W. Miley; Rev. Henry J. Pflum; Rev. A. A. Zinck; Rev. I. J. Bella; Rev. Samuel Boerstler; Rev. Alfred L. Grewe; Rev. Paul J. Hoh; Rev. Edward T. Horn, III; Rev. M. E. Lesher; Rev. Edmund L. Manges; Rev. Charles A. Puls; Philip Glatfelter; J. C. Kinard; Elwood M. Rabenold; J. Chester Crowther; J. Milton Deck; George M. Jones; E. D. Moyer; Charles F. Obenhack; John R. Wald.

The President called for nominations from the floor and declared the nominations closed.

For the *Board of Education:*

Term expiring 1944. Rev. J. L. Deaton; Rev. A. O. Frank; Rev. C. F. Koch; Rev. M. L. Koolen; Rev. D. F. Putman; Rev. C. J. Rockey; Rev. W. H. Traub; Rev. A. R. Wentz; Rev. Fuller Bergstresser; Rev. Wm. E. Eisenberg; Rev. Chalmers E. Frontz; Rev. Charles L. Venable; J. L. Almond, Jr.; H. S. Bechtolt; Charles Bergesen; L. C. Hassinger; Carl Schulz; J. Conrad Seegers; Harry R. Hess; Wm. E. Paul; Levering Tyson.

The President called for nominations from the floor and declared the nominations closed.

For the *Board of Social Missions:*

Term expiring 1944. Rev. Russell F. Auman; Rev. G. H. Bechtold; Rev. J. Frederick Bermon; Rev. H. E. Crowell; Rev. Charles B. Foelsch; Rev. Franklin Clark Fry; Rev. J. Henry Harms; Rev. A. H. Keck; Rev. Harold S. Miller; Rev. J. Luther Sieber; Rev. Henry Cornehlsen, Jr.; Rev. Ira S. Sassaman; Carl M. Distler; W. H. Hager; Harry C. Hoffman; H. C. Ahalt; A. B. Berresford; W. K. Mauney; Alvin R. Nissly; Charles Passavant, III; C. G. Shatzer.

Term expiring 1942. Rev. R. H. Anderson; Rev. Stanley Billheimer; Rev. Herman Brezing; Rev. W. C. Davis; Rev. Frank A. Dressel; Rev. E. E. Flack; Rev. F. K. Fretz; Rev. G. Arthur Fry; Rev. F. W. Otterbein; Rev. August Pohlman; Rev. N. Willison; Rev. Arthur M. Huffman; H. E. Isenhour; L. Henry Lund; J. W. Jouno; A. E. Koch; Howard L. Logan; Oliver C. Riethmiller; Paul J. Schaumberg; John F. Schuermann; M. W. Spigelmyer.

Term expiring 1940. Rev. P. D. Brown; Rev. Paul H. Heisey; Rev. Arnold F. Keller; Rev. R. E. Kern; Rev. G. Harold Kinard; Rev. W. A. Sadtler; Rev. G. Morris Smith; Rev. Calvin F. Stickles; Rev. Wm. C. Zimmann; Rev. F. L. Conrad; Rev. James Oosterling; Rev. I. Hess Wagner; Thomas P. Hickman; Carl H. Lammers; Harry L. Hess; Oscar G. Heyen; Robert Johnson; George E. Kieffner; John G. Kurzenknabe; C. E. Miller; Louis A. Wilke.

The President called for nominations from the floor and declared the nominations closed.

For the *Board of Publication:*

Term expiring 1944. Rev. Harry F. Baughman; Rev. A. H. Holthusen; Rev. Lloyd M. Keller; Rev. Russell D. Snyder; Rev. Harmon McGuire; Rev. J. L. Morgan; Rev. Theodore O. Posselt; Rev. Harry L. Saul; Rev. Joseph Sittler, Sr.; Rev. G. Morris Smith; Rev. A. W. Steinfurth; Rev. Luther W. Strickler; F. Wm. Cappelmann; David P. Deatrick; Henry F. Heuer; D. L. Biemesderfer; Horace Bikle; Clarence C. Dittmer; David F. Fortney; E. H. List; Wm. Patrick.

The President called for nominations from the floor and declared the nominations closed.

For the *Board of Ministerial Pensions and Relief:*

Term expiring 1944. G. Harry Ditter; Francis Seiberling; Belding B. Slifer; Ralph L. Smith; Daniel F. Yost; Frank D. Baker; Harry E. Cope; C. C. Culp; Clyde Gerberich; H. H. Keller; Pallad Krout; J. Ludwig; J. D. Thomas; Henry G. Wollmer; R. A. Yoder.

The President called for nominations from the floor and declared the nominations closed.

For the *Parish and Church School Board:*

Term expiring 1944. Rev. Charles B. Foelsch; Rev. Paul J. Hoh; Rev. Paul H. Krauss; Rev. Paul N. Schnur; Rev. H. T. Weiskotten; Rev. Armin G. Weng; Rev. Earl S. Rudisill; Rev. Carl R. Simon; Rev. Raymond C. Sorrick; Alvin Schaediger; W. E. Tilberg; R. E. Mapes.

The President called for nominations from the floor and declared the nominations closed.

For the *Board of Deaconess Work:*

Term expiring 1944. Rev. P. S. Baringer; Rev. H. H. Hartman; Rev. Lewis A. Speaker; Rev. H. E. Turney; Rev. Theodore Buch; Rev. Ernest H. J. Hoh; Herbert M. Day; Mrs. George H. Haase; Harry R. Hagerty;

Charles E. Orth; Mrs. O. A. Sardeson; Wm. E. Zschiesche; Mrs. W. P. M. Braun; Roy C. Daugherty; Peter P. Hagan.

The President called for nominations from the floor and declared the nominations closed.

The President stated that there was a motion pending, from the close of the Fourth Session, to reconsider the action taken instructing the Committee to Define Church Paper Policy to report to the next convention. The President also stated that a motion to reconsider could be in order only on the same day on which the action is taken, which is to be reconsidered, or on the day following. (For other references, see pp. 60, 103, 231, 232, 235.)

The motion to reconsider was put and carried.

The motion concerning the report of the Committee to Define Church Paper Policy was before the Convention.

Thereupon, the following was adopted as a substitute:

That the special Committee to Define Church Paper Policy shall report its study with recommendations to the Executive Board, during the biennium, for review; and, that the review report of the Executive Board with its recommendations, together with the full report of the special committee with its recommendations, shall be submitted to the next convention.

The Rev. F. R. Knubel, President, presented the report of the Parish and Church School Board.

REPORT OF THE PARISH AND CHURCH SCHOOL BOARD

The Parish and Church School Board herewith submits its regular biennial report to The United Lutheran Church in America.

I. A COMPARATIVE STATEMENT

Since this is the twentieth anniversary of The United Lutheran Church in America, the Board prefaces its report with a comparative statement of its program at the time of the merger and at the present.

Not one of the three general bodies which merged into The United Lutheran Church in America had a Board charged with the responsibilities of developing the educational work of the congregation. Each of the general bodies had committees on Sunday school work, more or less related to their Boards of publication, but no Boards of parish education.

The framers of our Church saw the need of a new Board for that purpose and made provision for it. When the constitution of this new Board was presented to and adopted by the Church in 1920, the Church gave this Board fourteen specific responsibilities. These responsibilities may be summarized in the following five statements:

A. The direction of the activities of the Board.
B. The development of a plan of education for the congregation.
C. The preparation of a literature for the congregation.
D. The development of a leadership in the congregation.
E. The promotion of a wider and more effective use of parish education.

In the beginning, the work of this Board was something new to the whole Church. The only inheritance handed down to the Board was the responsibilities given it by the Church, the three different systems of literature from the three committees on Sunday school work, and an undefined relationship with the new Board of Publication. The Board had to blaze its way in an uncharted field. It was compelled to analyze its own responsibilities, to define its involved relationships, to organize its limited forces, to develop a new program, and to project and promote its varied activities. The Board grasped the nature of its work almost in the very beginning, and although very little material progress was made by 1920, the germ of most of today's program had been planted in the first two years of the Board's existence.

An attempt to compare and contrast the program of 1920, when the constitution was adopted, with that of 1938, is made in the following outline and around the five general objectives of the Board:

A. THE DIRECTION OF THE ACTIVITIES OF THE BOARD

1920

The staff consisted of two members, both editors. These two staff members were also officers, president and secretary, of the Board.

The Board was organized with regular officers, an executive committee, and the following standing committees: Lesson

1938

The staff consists of: three editors (one position now vacant), one assistant editor, two associate secretaries, one for leadership education and one for field work, and an executive secretary.

The Board is organized with regular officers, an executive committee, and a standing committee for each of the following de-

Texts, Libraries and Hymnals, Weekday Christian Training, Christian Kindergarten, and Vacation Bible Schools.

partments of the Board: Literature, Field Work, Finance.

The Board was not placed on the apportionment budget of the Church until the year 1924, and then the amount was 0.55 cents of the apportionment dollar.

The Board now receives 1.22 cents of the apportionment dollar. The editors are paid by the Board of Publication, and $6,000.00 is received from that Board for work to be done in leadership education.

In 1920 all expenses of the Board were paid directly from the treasury of the Church.

The offices of the Board are in Philadelphia, and the field secretary makes his home in Fremont, Nebraska.

The Board of Publication paid the expenses of the editors.

B. The Development of a Plan of Education for the Congregation

1920

No general plan for the educational work of the congregation had been formulated. The following educational agencies were being promoted:
(1) The Sunday school with an enrollment of 514,924;
(2) The weekday church school (including the vacation church school) with a total enrollment of 4,779;
(3) The catechetical class with 36,689 catechumens.

1938

A five-year progressive program of education for the congregation was projected in 1937 through the *Guide and Standards in Parish Education.* It includes the work of the Sunday school with an enrollment of 668,673; the weekday church school (including the vacation church school) with an enrollment of 77,994; the catechetical class with 60,459 catechumens; the leadership training work; and all other educational activities in the congregation. All of these are placed under the direction of the congregation's parish education cabinet, composed of representatives from each educational agency in the congregation.

C. The Preparation of a Literature for the Congregation

1920

Into the merger of the Church, two general bodies brought rather extensive systems of Sunday school literature, including Sunday school papers. The other general body brought a system which was an adaptation of the other two. It was agreed at the merger that there was to be a

1938

The *Augsburg Uniform Series,* improved and graded, is still provided for all age groups with *The Augsburg Teacher* and the *Lesson Commentary* for teachers and leaders. A new graded course, *The Christian Life Course,* has been prepared with lessons for pupils 4-17 years of common literature. Steps toward this were being taken in 1920. The old *Lutheran Graded Course* for pupils 4-17 years of age was continued, but to be revised, and the *Augsburg Uniform Series* was continued, graded, and improved, providing materials for all ages. Several children's story papers had been merged into *Lutheran Boys and Girls* for children, and s e v e r a l young people's papers had been merged into *Lutheran Young Folks* for young people. Three hymnals—all unofficial—were being used. Three teacher training texts were also carried over into the new program.

age, and teachers' books for each age group. A Nursery Packet for parents of pupils under three years of age, and a Nursery Course for pupils three years of age are offered. Seven elective courses, with others in course of preparation, are o f f e r e d for young people, pupils 18-23; and a course for prospective church members, primarily for adults, has just been prepared.

Texts in bound book form for the primary and junior departments of both the weekday and vacation church school are promoted. *The Children's H y m n a l and Service Book* and *The Parish School Hymnal* are the two official hymnals. *Lutheran Boys and Girls* and *Lutheran Young Folks* have been c o n t i n u e d throughout the years. Special services for Christmas, Easter, and Children's Day are prepared. *The Parish School*, a magazine for leaders in parish education, and the *Lutheran Leadership Course* for the training of leaders are made available.

A large volume of promotional literature is prepared in connection with the promotional work of the Board, especially for Parish Education Month.

D. The Development of a Leadership in the Congregation

1920	*1938*
Three textbooks were in use without any official approval, but no system of credits had been developed.	Two series of texts have been developed. In the First Series there are eight texts available, and in the Second Series there are five texts available. Other texts are being prepared in both series.
	Course Cards and Certificates of Progress are issued—C o u r s e Cards on the basis of textbooks completed and Certificates of Progress on the basis of textbooks completed and participation in the life and work of the Church.

The Parish School magazine is a definite leadership training project.

In addition, the Board has prepared special manuals for leaders or teachers of all leadership books and for all Sunday, weekday, and vacation church school units.

One associate secretary and one office secretary give their full time to the promotion of leadership training.

Nawakwa Leadership Training Camp is the model camp of the Board. Summer schools for Church workers, conventions, and institutes are promoted.

E. THE PROMOTION OF A WIDER AND MORE EFFECTIVE USE OF PARISH EDUCATION

1920

In 1920, the Board was using the following means:
1. Publicity through literature.
2. Visitation of congregations and conventions by the staff.
3. Correspondence.

1938

In 1938, the Board is using the following means:
1. A field secretary.
2. Visitation by all members of the staff. In the last biennium the staff touched, through personal visitation, congregations and leaders in all the synods of the Church, approximately three-fourths of the congregations of the Church.
3. An active synodical committee on parish education in every synod reporting to the synods and working in the congregations.
4. Annual regional conferences of the members of these committees.
5. The use of September as Parish Education Month.
6. Publicity through literature.
7. Periodic surveys and reports of findings.
8. Promotional literature.
9. Systematic correspondence.
10. Advice on buildings and equipment.
11. A department of leadership education.

II. Activities of the Past Biennium

The Parish and Church School Board rejoices in the progress and development of the program of the Board during the past twenty years, but it is ever conscious of the many undeveloped and even untouched areas of its work. The Board and the staff pledge their deepest devotion to the further development of the great task which the Church has given them, and pray for the co-operation of every congregation, every synod, and The United Lutheran Church in America. May the God for whom we work grant His blessings upon our endeavors and upon the efforts of the whole Church.

The activities of the Board during the past biennium have been exceedingly fruitful. These activities are presented under the same five headings used in the comparative statement above. These headings describe the five departments of the work of the Board.

A. The Direction of the Activities of the Board
  1. *Organization of the Board:*
    a. The officers of the board are as follows:
       President—Rev. F. R. Knubel, D.D., Rochester, N. Y.
       Vice-President—Rev. W. C. Schaeffer, Jr., D.D., Allentown, Pa.
       Secretary—Rev. D. Burt Smith, D.D., Philadelphia, Pa.
       *Treasurer—Rev. M. Hadwin Fischer, Ph.D., Gettysburg, Pa.
    b. The advisory members of the Board from the Women's Missionary Society are:
       Mrs. W. F. Morehead, Philadelphia, Pa.
       Mrs. J. J. Neudoerffer, West Hazleton, Pa.
    c. The members of the committees of the Board are as follows:
       Executive Committee:
         Rev. F. R. Knubel, D.D., Rochester, N. Y.
         Rev. W. C. Schaeffer, Jr., D.D., Allentown, Pa.
         Rev. M. Hadwin Fischer, Ph.D., Gettysburg, Pa.
         Rev. A. J. Traver, D.D., Frederick, Md.
         Rev. P. D. Brown, D.D., Columbia, S. C.
       Committee on Field Work:
         Rev. P. D. Brown, D.D., Columbia, S. C.
         Rev. C. C. Rasmussen, D.D., Washington, D. C.
         Rev. R. Homer Anderson, D.D., Lynchburg, Va.

---

* As this report was going to print, news came to the Board of the death of Dr. Fischer. Dr. M. Hadwin Fischer gave twelve years of faithful service to the Board. Two of his outstanding accomplishments during that period were the establishment of Camp Nawakwa and the guidance of the money matters of the Board as its treasurer, and chairman of its finance committee. Dr. Fischer combined a deep piety with practical wisdom. He had an abiding enthusiasm that flooded all difficulties somehow out of the way. His open-hearted friendship endeared him to every member. The youth of the Church are his everlasting beneficiaries.

Committee on Literature:
Rev. A. J. Traver, D.D., Frederick, Md.
Rev. Paul H. Heisey, Ph.D., Springfield, Ohio.
Rev. W. C. Schaeffer, Jr., D.D., Allentown, Pa.
Mrs. Virgil B. Sease, Litt.D., New Brunswick, N. J.
Rev. J. D. M. Brown, Litt.D., Allentown, Pa.
Committee on Finance:
Rev. M. Hadwin Fischer, Ph.D., Gettysburg, Pa.
Mr. C. C. Dittmer, Brooklyn, N. Y.
Mr. George M. Jones, Reading, Pa.
D. The present employed personnel of the Board is:
Executive Secretary—Rev. S. White Rhyne, D.D.
Associate Secretaries—Rev. Chas. H. B. Lewis, D.D., Rev. Arthur H. Getz.
Editors—Rev. Chas. P. Wiles, D.D., Rev. D. Burt Smith, D.D.
Assistant Editor—Miss Mabel Elsie Locker.
Rev. Paul J. Hoh, D.D., formerly editor, resigned his position on the staff to accept a call to become professor at the Lutheran Theological Seminary at Philadelphia, Pa., effective September 1, 1937.

2. *Nominations:*
The following four members of the Board whose terms expire at this convention are all ineligible for re-election, having served their full terms:
Rev. J. D. M. Brown, Litt.D., Allentown, Pa.
Rev. M. Hadwin Fischer, Ph.D., Th.D., Gettysburg, Pa.
Rev. F. R. Knubel, D.D., Rochester, N. Y.
Mr. George M. Jones, Reading, Pa.
According to the recommendation of the Executive Board, The Board offers the following two sets of nominees for membership on the Board:
Rev. Paul H. Krauss, D.D., Fort Wayne, Ind.
Rev. Charles B. Foelsch, Ph.D., D.D., Sunbury, Pa.
Rev. Paul J. Hoh, D.D., Philadelphia, Pa.
Mr. Alvin Schaediger, North Bergen, N. J.
Rev. Armin G. Weng, Ph.D., Elgin, Ill.
Rev. Paul N. Schnur, Irwin, Pa.
Rev. H. T. Weiskotten, Ph.D., Brooklyn, N. Y.
Dean W. E. Tilberg, Gettysburg, Pa.

3. *General Conferences:*
Two meetings of the Intersynodical Conference on Elementary Education were held in Chicago, Ill., during the biennium. Drs. Wiles and Smith attended and participated in the 1937 meeting, and Drs. Wiles and Rhyne in the 1938 meeting.
Members of the staff had the privilege of attending the two meetings of the International Council of Religious Education, held in Chicago, Ill., during the biennium.
Miss Locker and Drs. Lewis and Rhyne attended the Quadrennial Convention of the International Council of Religious Education in Columbus. Ohio. during July, 1938.

4. *General Direction of the Committee on Program for the Children of the Church:*

A special committee to build and project the program for the children of the Church, having been authorized and, during the formative years, put under the general direction of the Parish and Church School Board by the action of the Executive Board of the Church in adopting the report of the Committee of Five on Children's Work, the Board has concurred in the following program and plan of the committee:

"PROGRAM AND PLAN OF OPERATION

"I. Name:
    The Children of the Church.

"II. Aim:
    To help the children grow in Christian faith and love, and to express the same through joyful and effective participation in all phases of the life and work of the Church at home and abroad.

"III. Membership:
    All children from birth through eleven years of age, inclusive.

"IV. Program Building and Projecting Agency:
    The Committee on Program for The Children of the Church.

"V. Promotional Agency:
    The Women's Missionary Society.

"VI. Agency of General Direction during Formative Years:
    The Parish and Church School Board.

"VII. Activities:
    Study, worship, planning and reporting (business), service, play.

"VIII. Literature:
    A. General
        The features of a literature perculiar to the needs of this character of work to be so incorporated into the plan for the Weekday Church School materials that there will be one body of materials known as the curriculum of *The Children of the Church,* but adaptable for use in weekday or Sunday sessions comparable to those of Weekday Church Schools, Vacation Church Schools, former Junior Luther Leagues and Light Brigades, or any enriched programs.

    B. Name
        The name of the course to be *The Program for the Children of the Church.*

C. Type of Materials
   1. The curriculum to consist of basic and current materials.
   2. The basic materials to include the leader's texts and pupils' materials.
   3. The current materials to consist of such as the following: Materials for the Calendar of Special Days and Seasons, visual education, missionary emphasis, seasonal, administrative, and promotional suggestions.

D. Organization
   1. Materials to be supplied for at least 52 sessions of 1½ hours each.
      a. Built on the group graded plan for the nursery, beginner, primary, and junior groups.
      b. Following the general outline suggested for the Weekday Church School texts.
      c. Providing for four 10-session units and one 12-session unit, the 12-session unit to be based on the Calendar of Special Days and Seasons, where applicable.
   2. Extra materials to accommodate groups meeting longer than 1½ hours per session to be supplied through:
      a. Suggestions for expanded sessions given in the leader's text for each unit.
      b. Extra units on special subjects.
   3. Related current materials, in packet form, for use in connection with basic materials, to be prepared, consisting of promotional and educational helps, such as:
      a. Calendar of Special Days and Seasons.
      b. Visual education materials.
      c. Source materials.
      d. Missionary materials.
      e. Seasonal materials.
      f. Administrative and promotional materials.

E. Activities
   1. Study.
   2. Worship.
   3. Planning and reporting (business).
   4. Service activities.
   5. Play.

F. Subject Matter
   1. Bible.
   2. Catechism.
   3. The life and work of the Church, such as:
      a. Missions.
      b. Life service and stewardship.
      c. Peace, temperance, citizenship.

G. Preparation of Materials
   1. Preparation of the basic materials to be under the auspices of the Parish and Church School Board.
   2. The current and promotional materials to be prepared and distributed free under the auspices of the Women's Missionary Society.
   3. The Committee on Program for The Children of the Church to co-operate with both agencies in the preparation of these materials.

"IX. Promotion:
   A. To be conducted by the Women's Missionary Society as one of the regular departments of its work.

   B. The head of this department to be a full-time, salaried worker to be known as the Secretary of *The Children of the Church*, and to be appointed by the Women's Missionary Society in consultation with the Committee on Program for The Children of The Church.

   C. This secretary to be paid a salary comparable to the salaries of the other secretaries of the Women's Missionary Society.

   D. The Women's Missionary Society, in carrying on this work, to use as synodical secretaries, leaders to be known as Synodical Secretaries for *The Children of the Church*. These synodical secretaries to be appointed by the Committee on Parish Education of each synod, in consultation with the officers of the synodical Women's Missionary Society and Luther League.

   E. The approach in the congregation to be made to those leaders or groups best qualified to develop the work in each particular local situation.

"X. Finance:
   A. Free-will offerings to be taken at the regular session of the children's groups to help vitalize the educational program and to train in stewardship. Twenty per cent of this may remain in the local children's organization to be used for literature, supplies, or local projects; the remainder to be for The United Lutheran Church in America for its mission work, which shall include the projects at present sustained by the Light Brigade and the Junior Luther League, until such time as other provision may be made for these projects. However, until the Church provides a sufficient annual appropriation for the prosecution and promotion of this work, forty per cent of the funds received from this

source shall be used for expenses involved in carrying on this work.

B. Special offerings may be taken as authorized by this committee. All of the funds received from special offerings shall be used for the causes designated.

C. This committee shall elect a general treasurer, who shall receive and dispense all funds according to the budget arranged by this committee.

D. The synodical secretaries for *The Children of the Church* shall receive the funds from the congregational groups and remit them to the general treasurer of *The Children of the Church*.

"XI. Organization in the Local Congregation:
To be developed later.

"XII. Other Relationships:
To be considered later."

5. *A Program of Work for the Board:*
During the biennium the Board completed work on "A Program of Work" for the Board for the next four or five years. The program includes plans for organization, administration, and literature. In this program, the Board recognizes the following fields of educational work in our parishes:
a. The general congregational field under the special responsibility of the pastor: church services, congregational meetings, and catechetical classes.
b. The church school field: Sunday school, weekday church school, vacation church school.
c. The field of special visitation: Shut-ins, shut-outs, and unreached within the community.
d. The field of leadership, including parent education as well as education of present and prospective church workers.
e. The field of education that is within the province of the recognized auxiliary agencies of the church.
The Board recognizes, further, that in all these fields there are children, young people, and adults, and that each of these divisions needs special educational attention.
To develop these fields, the Board will promote:
a. A Parish Education Cabinet in every congregation.
b. A Workers' Conference in every congregation.
c. Synodical Committees on Parish Education, with annual regional conferences of the members of these committees.
d. Planned field work.
To assist in the development of these, and the already established activities of the Board, a literature program as described in Section C of this report is being projected.

6. *Joint Committee with the Board of Publication:*
   A joint committee with the Board of Publication has been established to handle matters of common interest between the two Boards.

7. *A New Secretary:*
   The Rev. Arthur H. Getz, formerly of Spring City, Pa., was added to the staff in March, 1938, as an associate secretary and was assigned to the administration and promotion of leadership education. At the same time, the Board took action changing the title of Dr. Lewis from that of field secretary to that of associate secretary. Dr. Lewis was assigned to field work.

8. *Finance:*
   During the biennium, the Board received approximately $23,490.00 on apportionment. With these funds the Board must finance all of its executive, field work, and general Board expenses. The ever-enlarging work of the Board is always encumbered by the lack of funds. At the same time, the following projects are being delayed on this account:
   A department of visual education.
   An aggressive program of field work.
   A program for reaching the unreached.
   Office expansion.
   For the first time in the history of the Board, the Board received special contributions from synods through the treasury of The United Lutheran Church in America. These contributions were unsought, but were deeply appreciated. This expression of support from synods seems to denote a growing appreciation of the work of parish education.
   In 1938, the Women's Missionary Society contributed $100.00 to the Board for Camp Nawakwa.

9. *Advisory Members from the Women's Missionary Society:*
   At the last meeting of the Board, the Board received for the first time two advisory members from the Women's Missionary Society. This new relationship bids fair to be of real value to the work of the Board.

B. The Development of a Plan of Education for the Congregation:
   A Guide and Standards in Parish Education
   The Board has developed a five-year program of education for the congregations of the Church. At the present it has been introduced into approximately 1,000 congregations. This plan presents a definite, concrete, workable scheme by which congregations may improve their educational work and make progress in the attainment of their educational goals. A practical guide with a progressive series of standards, set up for achievement over a five-year period, directs the congregation in its educational program. The major factors that need to be developed in an educational program are forwarded through specific goals

which are established for each year. The plan is workable in any type of congregation in the Church.

C. The Preparation of a Literature for the Congregation:

The Board has continued the development of its literature program as follows:

1. Continued preparation and publication of *The Augsburg International Uniform Course,* including *The Augsburg Teacher* and *The Lesson Commentary.*
2. Continued publication of *The Christian Life Course.*
3. Continued preparation and publication of the *Elective Courses for Young People.* During the biennium the following texts have been added in this field: *Worship* by Finck, *The Christian Home* by Brown, *Studies in First Corinthians* by Hoh, *Studies in Life Service* by Traver, *The Minor Prophets and Modern Problems* by Baughman, and *Studies in Social Problems* by Heisey and Traver.
4. Careful study of the whole field of *Elective Courses for Adults,* and possibly, the planning and preparation of a number of such courses.
5. Continued preparation and publication of *The Nursery Packet.*
6. Continued preparation and publication of *The Lutheran Leadership Course,* including necessary blanks, course cards, and certificates; and continued study of the needs in this area with a view to possible expansion of our leadership curriculum.
7. Continued preparation and publication of *The Parish School,* with the continuation of all of its departments, including the one on the workers' conference.
8. Continued preparation and publication of *Lutheran Boys and Girls* and *Lutheran Young Folks.*
9. Continued preparation and publication of *The Beginner-Primary Hymnal* and *Young People's Hymnal.*
10. Continued preparation and publication of the *Christmas, Easter,* and *Children's Day Services.*
11. Continued preparation and publication of a catechetical class for adults, *What a Church Member Should Know.*
12. Continued preparation and publication of *A Handbook for Service Organizations.*
13. Continued preparation and publication of *The Guide and Standards in Parish Education.*
14. Preparation of the basic literature for *The Children of the Church.*
15. Preparation of a new series of *Weekday and Vacation Church School* texts.
16. Continued preparation of the topics for *The Lutheran Brotherhood.*
17. Preparation and publication of *Publicity and Promotional Materials.*
18. Informal and unofficial consultation with the auxiliary agencies of the Church, with a view to securing a more thoroughly integrated literature for our local churches.

The following activities in the preparation of literature are of special interest to the church:

The topics for *The Lutheran Brotherhood* during 1938 have been arranged and prepared under the auspices of the Board.

The basic literature for *The Children of the Church* will be prepared under the auspices of the Board.

The Board is in the process of preparing a young people's hymnal for the Sunday school.

The Augsburg International Uniform Lesson Series has appeared with new covers for the past two years. Considerable improvement has been made in the arrangement and the content of the lesson books; and the preparation of *Little Ones*, the four-page leaflet for the beginner and primary children, is now being made by Miss Locker of the staff. For more than thirty-five years these leaflets had been prepared by Miss Laura Wade Rice of Baltimore, Maryland.

The text for adult catechetical work, *What a Church Member Should Know*, by Dr. A. A. Zinck, has been prepared and is offered to the Church.

D. The Development of a Leadership in the Congregation:

A definite department of leadership education was organized within the Board in March, 1938, and Rev. Arthur H. Getz, of Spring City, Pa., was called to be its director. The Board has always recognized the need and the importance of leadership education and leadership work has always been promoted, but always by members of the staff in connection with their other and primary responsibilities. When the opportunity came to put this important work in a special department with a full-time director, the Board grasped it. In organizing this new department it was necessary for the Board to increase its office space and office secretarial staff. The whole force of the Board is now behind this department and its work and the co-operation of synodical committees, congregations, and pastors is sought.

While a large proportion of leadership work in our church is done on a non-credit basis, the Board urges congregations to work on an accredited basis. The Board is ready and anxious to advise pastors and leaders on the organization and administration of leadership classes, schools, summer schools, and camps.

During the past biennium, standard course cards were issued to workers in our church as follows: First Series—4,871; Second Series—8,639.

Nawakwa Leadership Camp continues to render a real service to the Church in the development of leaders and in guiding other groups in the organization and administration of new camps.

The Board continues to offer its services in developing programs for Summer School for Church Workers. At present there are sixteen such schools in the Church under the auspices of synods and conferences. These schools are rendering an invaluable service. During the past biennium the Board has had representatives at eleven of these schools each year.

E. The Promotion of a Wider and More Effective Use of Parish Education:

The program and literature of the Board must be known, appreciated, and used by the congregations of the church if they are to accomplish their intended purpose. To get this program and literature known, appreciated, and used, the Board must contact and cultivate the field. This department of the Board's work has received special attention in recent years. The following are examples of the type of work done by this department:

1. *Engagements in the Field:*

All members of the staff do some field work, although the field secretary does the major portion. Group meetings of various types are attended and promoted. During the past biennium, the members of the staff attended 603 group meetings, representing 5,040 congregations, and 59,696 individuals.

The different synods and other Church bodies touched, and the number of times each was touched, is shown in the following list:

Alleghany	9
California	15
Canada	16
East Pennsylvania	39
Florida	10
Georgia-Alabama	9
Illinois	15
Indiana	7
Iowa	8
Kansas	17
Kentucky-Tennessee	9
Manitoba	14
Maryland	33
Michigan	5
Midwest	3
Ministerium of Pennsylvania	69
Mississippi	1
Nebraska	36
New York	45
North Carolina	20
Northwest	22
Nova Scotia	11
Ohio	10
Pacific	28
Pittsburgh	31
Rocky Mountain	5
Slovak-Zion	1
South Carolina	7
Susquehanna	17
Texas	9
Virginia	19
Wartburg	4
West Pennsylvania	16
West Virginia	11

Other Lutheran Bodies 2
Interdenominational 22
General 8
                                                                       ———
Total 593

2. *New Field Secretaries:*

Recognizing the need of additional field secretaries, the Board has gone on record that it will place three additional secretaries in the field as soon as finances will allow.

Two synods, New York and Ohio, now have full-time secretaries on religious education and young people's work, and two others are on record desiring them.

3. *Co-operation with Synods:*

Continuing its policy of co-operating with synods in the development of their programs of parish education, the Board has sent its representatives to meetings of synodical committees on parish education on request and has sponsored regional conferences each year in three sections of the church. There are now synodical committees on parish education in each synod and these committees are doing splendid work.

4. *Sunday School Conventions:*

The Board co-operates with synods and conferences in setting up and conducting all types of Sunday School Conventions and Conferences. It prepares and distributes each year a series of suggested themes and programs for such conventions.

5. *Parish Education Month:*

This promotional project grows in use and in effectiveness each year. Each year a special emphasis is chosen and emphasized throughout the Church. In 1937 the emphasis was on Literature for the Congregation with the slogan —*Christian Literature and Christian Living;* the emphasis for 1938 is on power for the Congregation's Educational Program and the slogan is *Christian Worship and Christian Workers.* For the next two years the emphases will be upon Leaders for the Congregation's Educational Program and Expansion for the Congregation's Education Program.

6. *Can You Answer These:*

A little eight-page folder on the work of the Board, "Can You Answer These?" was prepared and distributed free to every pastor and to every Sunday school officer and teacher in the Church.

7. *The Parish School Magazine:*

This magazine increases in popularity each year, and deserves a place in the reading of every church worker. Many congregations are subscribing to the magazine for all workers in the church school.

8. *Visual Education:*
   The Board recognizes the growing importance of visual education in the congregation's educational program. It has voted an expenditure of $500.00 to begin a department of this work as soon as that amount is available. At the same time the Board is emphasizing, through its magazine and other means, practical suggestions in visual education for the congregation.

9. *Participation in the Promotional Program in The United Lutheran Church in America:*
   In accordance with the action of The United Lutheran Church in America, the Board has participated in the promotional program set up by the committee of executive secretaries of the church.

Christ continues to say to His Church, "Go—teach." The Church continues to say to The Parish and Church School Board, "Plan—prepare—promote." The Board is earnestly and faithfully attempting to carry out this commission of Christ and this authorization of the Church. The splendid co-operation of pastors, congregations, and synods encourages the Board to move forward.

F. R. KNUBEL, *President,*
S. WHITE RHYNE, *Executive Secretary.*

REPORT OF THE TREASURER OF THE PARISH AND CHURCH SCHOOL BOARD

STATEMENT OF CASH RECEIPTS AND DISBURSEMENTS
July 1, 1936 to June 30, 1937

Balance in Bank, July 1, 1936... $1,754.08

RECEIPTS:

United Lutheran Church on Apportionment............	$10,450.00	
Accounts Receivable	1,210.00	
Board of Publication of the United Lutheran Church in America (Special Grant)	1,168.72	
Refund on Expense	36.06	
Sale of Office Machines	80.00	
Liquidating Dividends, Pennsylvania Trust Co., Reading, Pa.	180.13	
Total Receipts		13,124.91
		$14,878.99

DISBURSEMENTS:

Salary, Executive Secretary	$3,850.00	
Salary, Field Secretary	3,300.00	
		$7,150.00
Executive Secretary's Expense:		
Office Secretary	$1,105.50	

Office Supplies 157.74
Telephone and Telegraph 73.15
Traveling Expense 361.73
Postage 156.61

Total Expense $1,854.73
Less: Credits Received from Fields...... 193.42
                                                                          1,661.31

Field Secretary's Expense:
Traveling Expense $594.12
Office Supplies 31.62
Communication 11.80
Clerical Help 17.00

Total Expenses $654.54
Less: Refunds 121.38
                                                                          533.16
Travel and Expenses, Board Meetings 313.60
Travel and Expenses, Committee Meetings 115.20
Travel and Expenses, Editors 179.12
Publicity 431.09
Auditing 25.00
Dues 14.00
Contribution for Maintenance of Muhlenberg
Building 660.00
Premium on Treasurer's Bond 12.50
Insurance 36.00
Nawakwa Leadership Camp 200.00
Furniture and Fixtures 239.70
Rental, Safe Deposit Box 5.50
Miscellaneous 57.97

Total Disbursements $11,634.15

Balance in Bank, June 30, 1937 .... $3,244.84

STATEMENT OF CASH RECEIPTS AND DISBURSEMENTS

July 1, 1937 to June 30, 1938

Balance in Bank, July 1, 1937 .... $3,244.84

RECEIPTS:
United Lutheran Church on Apportionment............ $11,830.00
United Lutheran Church on Account of Specials.... 111.55
Board of Publication of the United Lutheran
Church in America (Leadership Promotion)........ 5,500.00
Donations from the Field 191.73
Liquidating Dividends—Pennsylvania Trust Co.,
Reading, Pa. 180.13
S. W. Rhyne—Revolving Account 100.00
Total Receipts 17,913.41

                                                                                              $21,158.25

DISBURSEMENTS:

Salary, Executive Secretary		$4,200.00
Salary, Associate Secretary Rev. C. H. B. Lewis, D.D.		3,600.00
Salary, Associate Secretary Rev. A. H. Getz		991.66

Executive Secretary's Expense:

Office Secretaries	$2,613.50	
Office Supplies	481.72	
Telephone and Telegraph	93.76	
Traveling Expense	495.65	
Postage	531.47	
Miscellaneous	131.94	
Convention of Young People's Hymnal	127.86	
	$4,475.90	
Less Credits Received from Fields	83.60	
		4,392.30

Associate Secretary's Expense: (Rev. C. H. B. Lewis, D.D.):

Traveling Expense	$353.24	
Office Expense	21.92	
Hotels and Meals	193.28	
Miscellaneous	4.87	
	$573.31	
Less Credits Received from Fields	156.75	
		416.56
Rev. A. H. Getz—Revolving Fund		100.00

Associate Secretary's Expense: (Rev. A. H. Getz):

Transportation	$93.78	
Hotel and Meals	39.80	
Miscellaneous	1.10	
	$134.68	
Less Credits Received from Fields	23.50	
		111.18
Special Books and Postage		428.43
Travel and Expenses, Board Meetings		336.80
Travel and Expenses, Committee Meetings		197.99
Travel and Expenses, Editors		85.60
Publicity		627.13
Auditing		25.00
Dues		25.00
Contribution for Maintenance of Muhlenberg Building		1,060.00
Premium on Treasurer's Bond		12.50
Insurance		127.37
Nawakwa Leadership Camp		300.00
Furniture and Fixtures		997.69
Rental of Safe Deposit Box		5.50
Miscellaneous		79.60
Total Disbursements		18,120.31
Balance in Bank, June 30, 1938		$3,037.94

Respectfully submitted,

M. HADWIN FISCHER, *Treasurer*.

We have audited the books of account of The Parish and Church School Board of the United Lutheran Church in America for the biennium beginning July 1, 1936 and ending June 30, 1938, and we hereby certify that, in our opinion, the foregoing statements of Cash Receipts and Disbursements are in accordance with the books of account, and are true and correct.

TAIT, WELLER AND BAKER,
Accountants and Auditors.

Dr. Knubel presented the Rev. C. P. Wiles, senior editor of the Board, who spoke on the varied types of service performed.

Dr. Knubel next introduced the Rev. S. White Rhyne, Executive Secretary, who spoke more directly concerning the organizational work of the Board.

The Rev. Charles B. Lewis, Field Secretary, and Miss Mabel Elsie Locker, Assistant Editor, were introduced.

Dr. Knubel also introduced the Rev. Arthur H. Getz, Associate Secretary in charge of Leadership Education, and the Rev. Theodore K. Finck, Editor, each of whom addressed the Convention.

The Rev. A. J. Traver presented the following resolution which was adopted: In view of the intelligent and consecrated leadership in Christian education of the retiring President of the Parish and Church School Board, the Rev. F. R. Knubel, resolved, that the Convention record its vote of sincere appreciation.

On motion the report of the auditors was accepted.

The Rev. H. R. Gold, President, presented the report of the Board of Education.

REPORT OF THE BOARD OF EDUCATION

(For action on the recommendations in this report, see p. 329.)

LUTHERAN HIGHER EDUCATION THROUGH THE YEARS

The Church has always been interested in education. Her Founder is known as the world's greatest teacher. Throughout her history, she has been called the handmaid of education and the m o t h e r of schools.

Primarily this interest was due to the necessity of adequately training a clerical leadership. But Martin Luther called attention to the fact that all youth should be properly educated in the significant sentence, "The right instruction of the youth is something in which Christ and all the world are concerned."

In America the interest of the Church has been circumscribed by the policy of separation of church and state which has been interpreted to mean the separation of religion and education and by the consequent establishment of the public school system. Only the Catholic Church is seriously maintaining a complete program of education. In 1930 there were 2,000 academies of which 1,500 were church-related. In 1895 the Catholic Church had 280 academies, while in 1930 it had 1,000. In higher education the Protestant churches are merging and closing colleges while the Catholic Church is increasing the number, developing academies into junior colleges and junior colleges into senior colleges.

The Protestant churches too easily gave up their responsibility in primary and secondary education. They thought the Sunday school and young people's work were sufficient. The interest in higher education—seminaries, colleges, and religious work with students appears to have a deeper rootage.

The Church is in higher education to train its own leaders. "Dreading to leave an illiterate ministry to the churches, when our present ministers shall lie in the dust" is an attitude of the church today as it was of the New England fathers in 1630. A church must train its pastors and leaders according to its own spirit. Colleges and seminaries are established so that adequate instruction may be given in subjects necessary for the full equipment of the Christian leader.

The Church is in higher education to make education effective in character building. Once education was spoken of as the acquisition of information; then as the discipline of the mind; again, as the development and training of skills; more recently, as life adjustments; and finally, as the development of the great appreciations. Because of this uncertainty as to what education is, we find confusion in educational circles. Means have been stressed as though they were ends. Quantity has been glorified with an imitation of the mass production systems of industry. Procedures have been mechanized so that no consideration is given to the growth in moral stature and in spiritual understanding.

The Church contends that education is a means to an end, and that the end is the reconstructive development and enrichment of the student for the sake of himself, the welfare of others, and the glory and honor of God. Education is a transforming power, not a conforming machine. Paul's words are the motto of the Church in her educational program: "Be ye not conformed to this world but be ye transformed by the renewing of your mind so that you may know what is that good, and acceptable and perfect will of God." The Church's activity in the field of education gives education that motivation and purpose which makes it effective in the lives of people.

The Church is in higher education to assure a Christian civilization. Leaders in the Church are not enough. There must be Christian leaders in all walks of life. If modern civilization is to be saved from the revolutionary, destructive forces now at work in the world, the Church will do it through her educational program. The Church can counteract the anti-religious movement working s u b t l y in education and establish through her witness the reality of the living personal God. The Church can contradict a materialistic psychology and indicate the reality of the spiritual. The Church can overcome the moral anarchy of modern life by that Christian ethic which meets human needs and prevents social injustice. Keen observers of the signs of the times are convinced that the Church's educational program is the only effective agent in the maintenance of a desirable civilization and in the conservation of the great values of life.

In higher education, the United Lutheran Church in America is interested. At the time of its organization in 1918 the three merging bodies supported eleven seminaries, twelve colleges, four junior colleges, and six academies. During the past twenty years many changes have been experienced and much progress has been effected. To present a picture of the past, an analysis of the present, and a program for the future is the purpose of this report in fulfilment of the duty of the Board of Education and as a contribution to the twentieth anniversary celebration.

I. LUTHERAN HIGHER EDUCATION THROUGH TWENTY YEARS: 1918-1938

Render therefore to all their dues; tribute to whom tribute is due; custom to whom custom; fear to whom fear; honor to whom honor.   Romans 13:7.

1. The Personnel of the Board of Education

a. Members

Clergy: E. E. Blint*, 1919-22; C. R. Bowers, 1926-30; H. H. Bagger, 1930- ; H. J. Black, 1930- ; S. Billheimer, 1936- ; R. D. Clare, 1918-30; G. M. Diffenderfer, 1926-38; F. K. Fretz, 1930- ; F. G. Gotwald*, 1918-19; L. F. Gruber, 1918-28; G. J. Gongaware, 1918-26; H. R. Gold, 1918-26; 1930- ; W. H. Greever, 1930-32; J. H. Harms, 1918-28; W. F. Hoppe*, 1918-30; W. M. Horn*, 1922-30; A. J. Holl, 1928-30; E. C. Herman, 1928- ; M. J. Kline*, 1918-28; P. H. Krauss, 1926-38; E. P. Pfatteicher, 1918-30; A. Steimle*, 1918-30; M. L. Stirewalt, 1930- ; C. H. Stein, 1931-32; A. J. Turkle*, 1918-26; W. H. Traub, 1932- ; A. R. Wentz, 1932- ; N. Willison, 1934-36; A. A. Zinck, 1928- .

Laity: L. A. Anderson*, 1918-22; F. W. Albrecht*, 1918-28; H. G. Buehler*, 1919-24; Adelaide LeS. Burge, 1928- ; H. W. Bikle, 1930-36; H. S. Bechtolt, 1935- ; O. F. H. Bert, 1936- ; G. M. Cummings, 1920-30; Henry Denhart*, 1918-26; A. S. Downing*, 1919-24; J. H. Dingle*, 1926-32; C. J. Driever*, 1926-35; Frederick Henrich, 1930- ; L. C. Hassinger, 1932- ; R. D. Owen, 1926-38; William Pore*, 1918-19; Flora Prince, 1934- ; F. M. Riter*, 1918-26; J. M. Snyder*, 1918-28; W. H. Stackel, 1918-26; W. T. Stauffer, 1918-26; W. J. Showalter*, 1923-34; R. S. Saby, 1926-36; Chas. Steele, 1928- ; R. J. Seeger, 1936- ; R. B. Wolf, 1918-20; H. C. M. Wendel, 1924-32.

* Deceased.

b. Officers

The Rev. Robert D. Clare, D.D., convened the board and presided at its first meeting, December 17, 1918. The Rev. A. J. Turkle, D.D., was elected president at that meeting and continued until 1926, when the Rev. A. Steimle, D.D., was elected, serving until 1930. The Rev. H. R. Gold, D.D., was elected president in January, 1931.

As vice-presidents, the board elected the Rev. G. J. Gongaware, D.D., 1918-1926; Professor H. C. M. Wendell, Ph.D., 1926-1930, and the Rev. H. H. Bagger, D.D.. since 1930.

The Rev. H. R. Gold, D.D., was the first secretary serving from 1918 to 1926. He was followed by the Rev. W. M. Horn, D.D., from 1926 to June, 1930, when the Rev. Gould Wickey, Ph.D., D.D., the executive secretary, was elected secretary.

From 1918 to June, 1929, the treasurer was J. M. Snyder, who was succeeded by R. D. Owen, Ph.D., serving for one year to June, 1930. At this time, sensing the need for the treasurer to be in close touch with the office, and in accordance with constitutional provision, the board elected Thomas P. Hickman, a non-member of the board, treasurer.

c. Staff

At the first meeting of the board, the Rev. C. S. Bauslin, D.D., the secretary of the Board of Education of the General Synod, was elected secretary and in May, 1919, was designated secretary for Lutheran colleges and recruiting. On February 11, 1919, the Rev. A. J. Turkle, D.D., president of the board, reported to the Executive Committee that the Women's Missionary Society was ready to co-operate with the board in maintaining the office of a woman secretary. Accordingly Miss Mary E. Markley was elected to this secretaryship to serve the interests of both the Missionary Society and the board. This is the first time that a woman representative of a Board of Education combined in one office this double approach to students. As one of the secretaries of the National Lutheran Commission for Soldiers' and Sailors' Welfare, Miss Markley did not start her service until some months later. At the same meeting the Rev.

Paul H. Krauss, D.D., was elected "a secretary of this board with a special view of work among Lutheran students at non-Lutheran institutions of learning." His service was delayed by his chaplaincy in the navy. In May, 1919, the Rev. F. G. Gotwald, D.D., formerly editor of the *Lutheran Observer*, a member of the board, was e l e c t e d executive secretary.

At a meeting in December, 1920, Secretary Krauss resigned, and Miss Mathilde Peper was elected assistant secretary for women students on a part-time basis. The Rev. C. P. Harry, D.D., pastor for students in Philadelphia, was elected secretary for university students in May, 1922. In February, 1926, Executive Secretary Gotwald died and his duties were assigned to Secretary Bauslin. Miss Peper resigned in April, 1928, and Miss Mildred E. Winston was elected on a full time basis, taking office September, 1928. The Rev. Gould Wickey, Ph.D., president of Carthage College, was elected secretary in April, 1929, taking office July 1st. In June, 1930, the resignation of Secretary Bauslin was accepted to be effective September 1, 1930.

2. A Program of Progress

The board was organized "to promote the general educational interests of the Church, to conserve the religious life of the students in the educational institutions of the Church, in state universities, and in other schools; to stimulate the supply of candidates for the ministry; to administer the work of ministerial education for co-operating synods and to render financial aid to educational institutions."

In accordance with this object the chief emphases in the work of the board twenty years ago were: financial grants to institutions, recruiting for the ministry, and work with students. This work was organized under an executive secretary, a c o l l e g e secretary, a secretary for women students, and a secretary for university students.

In 1930 the work was re-organized under an executive secretary and three secretaries for students, the executive secretary functioning also in the special service to colleges and seminaries in administration and promotion. The divisions of the board's work were designated: administration, public relations (promotion), research, students, and institutions.

The emphases in the work today are:

(a) Educational and financial aid to colleges and seminaries.

(b) Intensifying and extending the work with Lutheran students.

(c) Better as well as more men for the ministry through co-operation with synodical committees.

(d) Promotional programs to awaken the membership of the Church to the significance of Christian higher education.

(e) Research on matters of value to the Church and her educational institutions.

(f) Building of funds for more effective work, the income from the apportioned benevolence being wholly inadequate.

In 1926 the first comprehensive survey of church-related colleges in America was initiated and carried through by the Board of Education. The findings were published in 1929 by the Bureau of Publications of Teachers' College of Columbia University in three volumes totaling 1,625 pages under the title: *Survey of Higher Education for the United Lutheran Church in America.* To the institutions this survey gave numerous suggestions for economies, more effective organization, and constructive improvements. Many presidents knew of necessary changes, but the survey emphasized and supported the presidents in appeals to their boards and constituencies. To the Church the survey serves as a means of knowing the nature and quality of the service rendered by any one institution and of knowing in what direction efforts should be expended for the development of the whole educational program.

To the 1932 convention of the Church, the Board of Education in conjunction with the Executive Board and the presidents of the synods presented a significant study of the Church's arrangements for the training of ministers and teachers. Definite suggestions were given as to curriculum, faculty, library, endowment. church constituency, the school year, and the realignment of seminaries. Within eighteen months, or before the end of 1934, three seminaries suspended operations with a saving of more than $16,000 per year to the Church. This study offers the seminaries guiding principles for an effective development of their work.

3. Types of Publications

Going to College: A 96-page book admirably adapted to the needs of every prospective college student, written by *the Staff* and published in 1936.

Study Outline Books: Facing the Faith, Bierstedt; *How,* Harry; *Jesus the Unique, Perennial Problems,* Gearhart. (Out of print.)

Monographs: Truths by Which We Live, Delk; *The Student,* Dysinger; *Religion and the Tendency of Modern Science,* Elson; *The Beginnings of Work Among Lutheran Students,* Gold; *Value of the Observance of the Church Year,* Gotwald; *Christian Theology and Modern Science, Science and Revelation,* Gruber; *Luther's Contribution to Education,* Peery; *Some Chapters in the History of Higher Education for Lutheran Women,* Markley; *Christianity and Education,* Wickey. (Out of print.)

Pageants and Programs for Life Service: The Key, Copenhaver; *The Lost Call, Signal Hill, The Witness,* Piero; *Here Am I; Follow Me; What Shall I Do; Who Follows In Their Train.* (Out of print.)

Vocational Material: Most of it in behalf of the ministry—some for young boys, more for high school students, some adapted to college students. *Mary Slessor of Calabar, Soldiers, The Good Doctor,* Lewars; *Do You Say You Are Not Fitted for Leadership, For Any Father and Mother, You Fathers and You Mothers, Help Us Get Ministers, Leads for Leaders, Profit and Loss in Recruiting, What Shall I Do with My Life, Who Calls,* Bauslin, C. S.; *Is the Ministry an Attractive Vocation,* Bauslin, D. H.; *Why I Entered the Gospel Ministry,* Ard; *The Challenge of the Ministry,* Baker; *Why I Became a Minister,* Blackwelder et al; *The Object of the Christian Ministry,* Englar; *Why I Stay in the Ministry,* Keller; *The Unassisted Triple, Would You Do It Again,* Nicely; *An Open Letter to Open Minded Young Men,* Pfatteicher; *Claims of the Gospel Ministry on College Men,* Stevenson; and *The Present Task of the Ministry,* Woodrow Wilson (Reprints). (Out of print.) *The Ministry —Points, Preparation, Work; Making Life Count,* Harry; *Open Letter on Opening Possibilities, So You Are Going to Be—You, So You Are Going to be—A Teacher. So You Are Going to Be—A Nurse, So You Are A Nurse,* Markley.

Devotional Material: Christ for Others, The Church, Guidance, How to Know God, Living the Life, Personal Work, Reasonableness of Christian Faith, Science, Philosophy and Religion, Sharing the Word, Some Reasons Why, Harry. (Out of print.) *Knowing the Bible,* Winston; *Foundations, Power, Prayer Life, Group Prayer, Lutheran Church and Modern Religious Life, Sacraments,* Harry.

College and University Promotional Material: A Symposium on the Christian College, edited by C. S. Bauslin; *Will It Pay, Why Go to College,* Bauslin; *Going to College, Students Coming and Going, Does It Make Sense,* Markley; *At College,* Dysinger; *Higher Education* (reprint); *After High School What,* Wickey; *I Choose the Church College* (reprint); *The Christ, the Church, the Student* (an illustrated book on the work of the board, 1922); *Do You Know,* Markley; *Like a Mighty Army,* Meade (reprint); *Lutheran Synods in America; Church and Social Problems; Why Lutherans Should Do Religious Work Among Students, The State University—a Challenge to the Church,* Krauss; *Helping the Student, What To Do, Method, Program and Schedule of Student Work,* the Staff; *Introduction, Application* and *Guest Membership Cards.*

Survey of Higher Education for the United Lutheran Church in America: Leonard, Evenden and O'Rear (3 volumes) Bureau of Publications, Teachers College, Columbia University, New York City, 1929. (Out of 216 Surveys this ranked as one of thirty of outstanding value,—one of ten of national scope. *Surveys of American Higher Education,* W. C. Eells, p. 220.)

4. Funds and Finances

When the board was organized it had no funds. Today its capital funds are *General Endowment Fund, Ministerial Education Fund,* and *Scholarship and Loan Fund for Women,* with a total amount of only $90,597. The income from the endowment fund is used for the general work of the board, while the income from the other funds assists young men and women to prepare for full-time Christian life service.

The income of the board for its whole sphere of work is limited to the 9 per cent of the apportionment which amounted to $90,900 for the year 1937-38. In 1919-1920 the income was $97,236, which was 12 per cent of the apportioned benevolence.

After extended study of the problem of expenditures, the board decided to allot as grants-in-aid to institutions 55 per cent of the budget, to student centers 15 per cent, and for all other expenses 30 per cent. With the uncertainty of income since 1932 this plan has tended to stabilize grants-in-aid as well as determine to what extent expenditures could be made for items of administration and promotion.

5. Ministering to Students

Before 1918.

The church for more than a decade prior to 1918 had been pioneering in its ministry to students. In July, 1907, the first Lutheran pastorate at a state university was begun and continued for nine years—the Rev. Howard R. Gold, pastor for students at the University of Wisconsin, Madison. Called by the Home Missions Board of the General Council. Pastor Gold with leaders in the General Council had aroused sufficient interest in the student field to see appointed in 1909 a standing Committee on Student Life in Non-Lutheran Schools, this committee to consist of seven clergy and five laymen. The committee recommended was as follows: Chairman, the Rev. A. J. Reichert; secretary, Erland Lind, Esq.; treasurer, Charles L. Trabert, Esq.; and the Reverends August T. Seashore, Peter Peterson, William K. Frick, Gottfried Nelson, Howard R. Gold, Paul H. Roth. Other lay members of the committee were Charles G. Schultz, superintendent of public instruction of Minnesota, A. A Stomberg, professor of Scandinavian languages at the University of Minnesota, and L. A. Anderson, actuary of the insurance department of the state of Wisconsin.

This committee was "charged with the work of inquiring into the religious conditions of student life in non-Lutheran institutions so far as it applies to the Lutheran Church, and empowered to take such action in the matter as it may deem necessary." The committee was "instructed to seek the co-operation of other Lutheran bodies in this work, upon such terms as may be found possible consistently with the principles and practices of the General Council." The committee assumed supervision of the purely student interests in the congregation organized in 1906 in Madison, Wisconsin and designated Pastor Gold as its representative. Upon his resignation in 1916 the Rev. Howard E. Snyder became pastor and continued the service to students until his resignation in March, 1918, when he took a chaplaincy in the army.

In 1910 the General Council Committee called the Rev. Gustaf Rast, D.D., as pastor for students at the University of Minnesota. After several years of successful pioneer work, Dr. Rast in July, 1914, was succeeded by the Rev. C. A. Wendell. In addition to his work with university students, Pastor Wendell visited state teachers and other colleges in several states in behalf of work among Lutheran students. Dr. Wendell as pastor of Grace Lutheran Church of the Augustana Synod, still continues as student pastor and represents 24 years of unbroken and cumulative service to Lutheran students.

Two notable advances were made about the same time in two other parts of the Church. The Home Mission Board of the General Synod in September, 1911, organized a congregation of thirty-one charter members which held services in University Hall of the University of Illinois in Urbana. From the beginning students have been an important part of the work which was inaugurated and stabilized by the Rev. F. B. Heibert, pastor from 1913 to 1925.

The New York and New England Synod called as Students' Pastor the Rev. Samuel Trexler, who assumed his duties in December, 1912. For two years he traveled among the students in the universities—Cornell, Syracuse, Columbia, Yale, and Harvard—organizing, ministering, and preaching. "After these years of experience it seemed wise to recommend that resident pastors should be called to give continuity to the work. Cornell was selected as the first center. Neighboring pastors served until in 1916 the Reverend Edwin F. Keever, D.D., was called as pastor and served until in 1917 when, as chaplain, he went with the army overseas. In December of the same year the Reverend William M. Horn, D.D., became the pastor for Lutheran students at Cornell and continued until his death in 1932."

A full time pastor for students at Cornell University since 1916, the work supported uninterruptedly by a synod—now the United Lutheran Synod of New York—remains a unique example of what the Church should and could do in ministering to students.

The General Council Committee in 1917, after conference with the University of Pennsylvania administration, with the co-operation of the Ministerium of Pennsylvania, called the Rev. Carolus P. Harry as pastor for students. From 1909 a committee of Philadelphia had promoted the spiritual welfare of Lutheran students at the university. Rev. Harry gave all his time to students, centering worship in local congregations, chiefly the Church of the Holy Communion. On the campus he worked in co-operation with other pastors for students. He also extended his service to other universities and colleges in and near Philadelphia. This student pastorate in Philadelphia continues to be unique in that the pastor with no responsibility for the upbuilding of any congregation can give his undivided ministry to students.

The Committee on Student Life in Non-Lutheran Schools, active since 1909, made its last report to the first convention of the United Lutheran Church in 1918. The balance in the treasury of the committee, $4,199.75, was given to the treasurer of the Board of Education of the United Lutheran Church in America, to which was assigned the work among students. "This work," wrote the chairman, Dr. W. K. Frick, in his last report, "will be one of the crown jewels of the United Church." [Quotations and facts from The Beginnings of Work Among Lutheran Students, Howard R. Gold, D.D. 1936.]

Since 1918.

The Board of Education has carried forward the work handed over to it. At the University of Wisconsin the successive pastors of the Luther Memorial, the Rev. Norman E. Goehring, the Rev. A. J. Soldan, the Rev. C. J. Rockey, were assisted by varying grants-in-aid to work among students. At the University of Minnesota the board has continued its relationship with Rev. C. A. Wendell, D.D., through the co-operation of the Augustana Synod. At the University of Illinois, the Rev. Alfred J. Beil and the Rev. Dwight P. Bair, D.D., since 1931 have devoted much time to student work with the combined help of the board and of the Illinois Synod. In Philadelphia since 1922 the Rev. Robert H. Gearhart, D.D., with the backing of a local committee, the co-operation of the Ministerium of Pennsylvania and the East Pennsylvania Synod and with the salary provided by the board, has developed a far-reaching work on the most important campuses and made his program an integral part of the work of the churches.

University Student Work has been established, stimulated and stabilized by the assistance which the board has given to the local pastors at the State Universities of California—the Rev. E. A. Trabert, D.D., pastor since 1918—Colorado, Iowa, Kansas, Michigan, Washington, and West Virginia. Other state institutions like Purdue in Indiana, Clemson and Winthrop in South Carolina, Polytechnic Institute in Virginia, and Pennsylvania State College, have pastors who are aided to devote rewarding time to ministering to students. At the latter institutions, with about 600 Lutherans, the Rev. John F. Harkins, D.D., pastor since 1919, ministers to the largest group of United Lutheran students at any one institution. At State Teachers' Colleges, especially the thirteen in Pennsylvania, the board through its resident pastors and student secretaries has done pioneer work. The board was the first general Church Board to realize the significance to the church of the thousands of young people preparing to be public school teachers.

Metropolitan Student Centers have been cultivated with most rewarding results. Since 1925 when the Rev. Norman D. Goehring was called to the work, Boston has steadily shown the value of a careful and continuous service to students on the part of the Church. New York City student work for seven years has been directed and correlated by a member of the staff of the Board, Mildred E. Winston. As long ago as 1925 the board established a Fellowship to be granted to a young man student in some metropolitan university in return for part time service to Lutheran students. This position continued from 1925 to 1931 with three incumbents. Between 1933 and 1937 young metropolitan pastors assisted in the work with Columbia students. From 1918 until his death in 1937, the Rev. A. Steimle, D.D., pastor of Advent Church, was not only the designated pastor for Columbia students, but was also the untiring advocate of systematic student work planned for New York City in 1912. The Rev. Paul Scherer, D.D., pastor of Holy Trinity Church, since 1920 has been giving of his best to students in the metropolitan area.

In Baltimore until recently individual pastors like the Rev. R. D. Clare, D.D., have been doing the student work. Now the Ministerial Association composed of both United Lutheran and American Lutheran pastors, as well as a metropolitan student council, are carrying forward. In Washington, under the general direction of the Inner Mission Society, work has been successfully going forward for a number of years on the campuses of George Washington and Maryland Universities. Both cities have had metropolitan and area student conferences.

Chicago pastors, like the Rev. E. C. Paulus, D.D., since 1914, have faithfully worked with students, sometimes with the assistance of the board. The growth in interest has now culminated in a pastor for students, the Rev. Charles W. Kegley, who has no parish responsibility.

Pittsburgh is the metropolitan center where most recently the efforts of interested pastors and laity over a period of years have taken on concrete form in a co-operative work under the leadership of the Rev. Merle R. Kunkelman, the American Lutheran Church and the United Lutheran Church through the local conferences and synods participating.

Milwaukee, too, where the Rev. John F. Fedders, D.D., since 1919 has been an active leader among students, through the Ministerial Association and the Inner Mission Society, gives evidence of the leadership of the board. A vigorous Lutheran Nurses' Guild supplements the campus student associations.

The significant part which the United Lutheran Church has played in the initiation and development of the service of pastors to students is well portrayed in *The Church Follows Its Students* by Clarence Prouty Shedd. This volume of 325 pages published by the Yale University Press in 1938 is a documentary study of a "student ministry, developed first within denominations, and then becoming a significant, self-conscious church movement among students." Mr. Wickey, Miss Markley and Dr. Gold were freely consulted concerning historical data and the preface of the book recognizes with gratitude the assistance of Miss Markley and particularly of Mr. Wickey.

6. Facts from the Seminaries and Colleges

Through the brief history of the United Lutheran Church in America the seminaries and colleges have played an important part. The faculty members have been active on boards and committees determining the policy and progress of the Church. The institutions themselves have experienced growth and progress. The names of those who have served well and sacrificed for the cause of Christian higher education cannot be recounted here, but the following facts do present an interesting picture of names, dates, and events which have been vital in the education of leaders for the Church and the State.

a. The Presidents of Seminaries and Colleges, 1918-38

The Presidents or Deans of Seminaries

Hartwick: Frank Wolford, D.D., 1918-20; 1925-29; A. E. Deitz, D.D., 1920-24; S. M. Paulson, D.D., 1929- .

Gettysburg: J. A. Singmaster, D.D., LL.D., 1906-26; John Aberly, D.D., LL.D., 1926- .

Southern: A. G. Voigt, D.D., LL.D., 1903-33; C. A. Freed, D.D., 1933-38; C. K. Bell, D.D., 1938- (Acting).

Hamma: D. H. Bauslin, D.D., LL.D., 1918-22; V. G. A. Tressler, Ph.D., D.D., 1922-23; L. H. Larimer, D.D., 1923- .

Philadelphia: H. E. Jacobs, D.D., LL.D., 1894-1926; C. M. Jacobs, D.D., LL.D., 1926-38; L. D. Reed, D.D., A.E.D., 1938- (Acting).

Chicago: E. F. Krauss, D.D., 1915-20; and 1925-26 (Acting); J. E. Whitteker, D.D., LL.D., 1920-25; L. F. Gruber, D.D., LL.D., 1927- .

Western: H. Dysinger, D.D., 1910-30; J. J. Raun, Ph.D., 1930-33; W. F. Rangeler, D.D., 1933- .

Canada (Waterloo): C. H. Little, D.D., S.T.D., 1917-20; 1920-27 (Dean); 1929-31 (Acting); A. A. Zinck, D.D., S.T.D., 1925-27; F. B. Clausen, D.D., 1932- .

Saskatoon: J. Goos, D.D., 1913-18; H. W. Harms, 1918-33; W. Magnus, 1932-36 (Acting); N. Willison, Litt.D., 1936- .

Northwestern: J. Stump, D.D., LL.D., L.H.D., 1921-35; P. H. Roth, D.D., 1935- .

The Presidents of Colleges

Gettysburg: W. A. Granville, Ph.D., LL.D., 1910-23; H. W. A. Hanson, D.D., LL.D., 1923- .

Wittenberg: C. G. Heckert, D.D., LL.D., 1903-20; R. E. Tulloss, Ph.D., D.D., LL.D., 1920- .

Roanoke: J. A. Morehead, D.D., LL.D., 1903-20; C. J. Smith, D.D., LL.D., 1920- .

Newberry: S. J. Derrick, LL.D., 1918-30; J. C. Kinard, LL.D., 1930- .

Susquehanna: C. T. Aikens, D.D., 1905-27; J. Diehl, 1927-28 (Acting); G. M. Smith, D.D., 1928- .
Thiel: H W. Elson, Ph.D., Litt.D., 1916-21; E. F. Ritter, D.D., 1921-23 (Acting); C. A. Sundberg, D.D., 1923-25; B. H. Pershing, Ph.D., 1925-26 (Acting); E. C. Xander, D.D., 1926-33; E. S. Rudisill, Ph.D., D.D., 1934- .
Muhlenberg: J. A. W. Haas, D.D., LL.D., L.H.D., 1905-36; R. C. Horn, Ph.D., 1936-37 (Acting); Levering Tyson, Litt.D., LLD.., 1937- .
Carthage: H. D. Hoover, Ph.D., S.T.D., D.D., 1909-26; Gould Wickey, Ph.D., D.D., 1926-29; J. Diehl, D.D., LL.D., 1929-33; I. W. Bingaman, D.D., 1933-35 (Acting); R. G. Schulz, Jr., D.D., 1935- .
Wagner: A. H. Holthusen, D.D., 1918-26; F. Sutter, D.D., 1926-27; 1930-31; 1934-35 (Acting); C. F. Dapp, Ph.D., D.D., 1927-30; H. Brezing, D.D., 1931-34; C. C. Stoughton, A.M., 1935- .
Midland: R. B. Peery, Ph.D., D.D., 1912-19; E. E. Stauffer, D.D., 1919-22; J. F. Krueger, Ph.D., D.D., 1922-25; H. F. Martin, Ph.D., D.D., 1925- .
Lenoir Rhyne: R. L. Fritz, D.D., 1901-20; J. C. Perry, D.D., 1920-25; H. B. Schaeffer, D.D., 1926-34; P. E. Monroe, D.D., 1925-26; 1934- .
Waterloo: E. Hoffman, D.D., 1920-25; A. A. Zinck, D.D., S.T.D., 1925-27; C. H. Little, D.D., S.T.D., 1927-31 (Acting); F. B. Clausen, D.D., 1932- .
Hartwick: (Started 1928), C. R. Myers, D.D., 1928-29; C. W. Leitzell, D.D., 1929-
Marion: C. B. Cox, A.M., 1916-28; E. H. Copenhaver, D.D., 1928-38; H. J. Rhyne, A.M., 1938- .

b. Faculty Members Serving Through 1918-38
Seminaries
Hartwick: Frank Wolford, D.D., 1913- .
Gettysburg: M. Coover, D.D., 1905-26, Emeritus; H. C. Alleman, D.D., LL.D., 1911- ; A. R. Wentz, Ph.D., D.D., 1916- .
Southern: C. K. Bell, D.D., 1918- ; J. W. Horine, D.D., 1918- .
Hamma: L. H. Larimer, D.D., 1908- ; J. L. Neve, D.D., 1909- ; L. S. Keyser, D.D., 1911-1937.
Philadelphia: L. D. Reed, D.D., A.E.D., 1905- ; H. Offermann, D.D., 1910- ; C. M. Jacobs, 1913-38.
Chicago: E. F. Krauss, 1915- .
Western: H. Dysinger, 1905-37, Emeritus.
Waterloo: C. H. Little, D.D., 1917- .
Saskatoon: J. Goos, 1913- .

Colleges
Gettysburg: C. B. Stover, A.M., 1896- ; K. J. Grimm, Ph.D., LL.D., 1906- : C. F. Sanders, D.D., 1906- ; C. P. Cersna, A.M., 1915- ; F. H. Clutz, Ph.D., 1918- .
Wittenberg: A. F. Linn, Ph.D., 1888- , Emeritus; E. O. Weaver, Sc.D., 1889- · J. P. Schneider, Ph.D., 1904- ; C. G. Shatzer, Sc.D., 1901- ; R. H. Hiller, Litt.D., 1911- ; K. F. R. Hochdoerfer, Ph.D., 1891- , Emeritus; Hettie B. Hochdoerfer, A.M., 1907- , Emerita; Alice M. Mower, A.M., 1891- ; Rose Cadwgan, A.M., 1912- ; Grace Prince, A.M., 1892- ; T. B. Birch, Ph.D., LL.D., 1908-1937; J. A. Ness, Ph.D., 1904-1937.
Roanoke: G. G. Perry, A.M., 1905- ; W. E. Mann, A.M., 1910- ; C. R. Brown, Ph.D., 1918- .
Newberry: S. J. Derrick, A.M., 1896- ; E. B. Setzler, Ph.D., Litt.D., 1898- ; J. C. Kinard, LL.D., Litt.D., 1916- .
Susquehanna: J. I. Woodruff, Litt.D., LL.D., 1892- ; G. E. Fisher, Ph.D., 1896- ; E. M. Brungart, A.M., 1905- .
Thiel: N. W. Harter, A.M., 1911- .

Muhlenberg: G. I. Ettinger, Ph.D., Litt.D., 1880- , Emeritus; R. C. Horn, Ph.D., Litt.D., 1904- ; O. F. Bernheim, A.B., 1907- ; R. R. Fritsch, D.D., 1907- ; S. G. Simpson, A.M., 1911- ; J. D. M. Brown, Litt.D. 1912- ; A. C. H. Fasig, M.S., 1913-38; I. M. Wright, Pd.D., 1917-
Carthage: W. C. Spielman, A.M., 1916- ; A. O. Boatman, A.M., 1918-
Wagner: W. R. Ludwig, D.D., 1907-36, Emeritus.
Lenoir Rhyne: R. L. Fritz, D.D., 1901- .
Marion: May Scherer, 1912- .

c. Closed Seminaries and Colleges

Theological Seminaries	*Years of Service*		
Susquehanna	1858-1933	75	(Suspended,
Pacific	1911-1933	22	
Martin Luther	1913-1934	21	

Academies and Colleges			
Hartwick Academy	1815-1934	119	
Gettysburg Academy	1827-1935	108	
Wittenberg Academy	1845-1926	82	
Collegiate Institute	1854-1933	79	
Mont Amoena Seminary	1859-1927	68	
Elizabeth College	1897-1922	25	
Weidner Institute	1902-1930	28	
Summerland College	1912-1930	18	
Saskatoon Academy	1913-1933	20	

To have lived and served is not to have lived in vain. Through these institutions the labors and sacrifices of faithful teachers and the gifts of devoted friends have entered into the building of manhood and woman-hood,—than which there is no nobler human work.

d. Faculties of Seminaries and Colleges

SEMINARY FACULTIES

	1918					1938				
		EARNED DEGREES					EARNED DEGREES			
	Number	A.B. only	A.M. only	B.D. only or S.T.M.	Ph.D.	Number	A.B. only	A.M. only	B.D. or S.T.M.	Ph.D.
Hartwick	4	2	2			6		2		4
Gettysburg	5		4		1	10	1	2	1	6
Southern	3	1	2			4		3		1
Hamma	5	2	1		2	9	1	3		6
Philadelphia	8	1		1		13	7	2	2	2
Chicago	7	2	4	1		7	2	4		1
Western	3	1	2			5		4	1	
Waterloo	3	3				3	2	1		
Saskatoon	2					4	2		2	
Northwestern*	6	1	2	3		6		2	3	1

* Founded 1921.

COLLEGE FACULTIES

	1918						1938					
	Number	Men	Women	A.B. only	A.M. only	Ph.D.	Number	Men	Women	A.B. only	A.M. only	Ph.D.
Gettysburg	23	23		2	11	10	40	40		3	19	18
Wittenberg	19	17	2	1	12	6	83	54	29	17	28	38
Roanoke	16	16		11		4	24	23	1	3	12	9
Newberry	8	8		6	1	1	21	18	3	11	5	5
Susquehanna	21	16	5	9	1	1	35	25	10	11	13	11
Thiel	16	9	7	6	2	4	23	16	7	4	11	8
Muhlenberg	16	16		7	6	3	33	33		5	15	13
Carthage	17	9	8	2	7	2	29	19	10	8	15	6
Wagner	8	8		3	3	2	20	18	2	2	8	10
Midland	14	11	3	1	7		28	21	7	10	14	4
Lenoir Rhyne	15	10	5	4	8		23	18	5	8	9	6
Waterloo	3	3		2			11	8	3	3	7	1
Hartwick	12	9	3	5	4	3	22	15	7	5	6	11
Marion (Junior)	16	1	15	10	1		12	1	11	3	5	

e. TOTAL STUDENT REGISTRATION AT SEMINARIES THROUGH TWENTY YEARS

Seminaries	1918-1919	1919-1920	1920-1921	1921-1922	1922-1923	1923-1924	1924-1925	1925-1926	1926-1927	1927-1928	1928-1929	1929-1930	1930-1931	1931-1932	1932-1933	1933-1934	1934-1935	1935-1936	1936-1937	1937-1938
Hartwick	38	37	41	50	49	No Report	34	52	57	68	71	10		19		26		41		28
Gettysburg	24	23	21	13	11	41	33	33	42	41	41	78	85	92	98	82	90	99	110	94
Southern	30	31	48	50	46	16	79	91	79	79		42	30	29	31	36	36	30	27	26
Hamma	75	83	91	97	89	55	111	111	91	113	53	51	47	56	56	66	67	52	45	44
Philadelphia	106	109	55	91	125	101	119	105	133	109	119	130	163	191	195	176	150	150	158	164
Chicago	14	15	13	14	11	18	14	11	16	12	11	95	75	79	76	71	75	64	63	64
Western	10	9	11	7	10	10	11	12	12	11	11	15	19	19	21	23	15	13	5	8
Waterloo	2	2	2	4	2	2	4	6	8	11	9	13	11	11	9	9	10	13	11	11
Saskatoon				19		19		32		32		10		13		14		9		12
Northwestern												70		39		20		23		32

TOTAL STUDENT REGISTRATION AT COLLEGES THROUGH TWENTY YEARS

Colleges	1918-1919	1919-1920	1920-1921	1921-1922	1922-1923	1923-1924	1924-1925	1925-1926	1926-1927	1927-1928	1928-1929	1929-1930	1930-1931	1931-1932	1932-1933	1933-1934	1934-1935	1935-1936	1936-1937	1937-1938
Gettysburg	500	405	414	425	581	628	668	668	663	663	672	672	635	587	538	515	487	535	635	673
Wittenberg	1023	971	1068	1220	1245	1576	1884	1993	2466	2487	2825	2588	2434	1892	1614	1636	1663	1655	1910	1894
Roanoke	152	164	163	196	201	259	248	257	258	261	250	264	286	335	361	374	371	431	479	501
Newberry	158	218	246	263	301	305	278	304	320	333	316	306	337	379	360	370	354	358	376	577
Susquehanna	390	390	418	450	669	732	761	779	862	896	1263	1168	899	730	590	419	402	381	444	400
Thiel	197	246	269	382	422	478	545	524	545	548	496	453	437	460	422	376	374	323	314	320
Muhlenberg	184	SATC	219	250	272	286	317	361	375	455	470	438	441	454	452	456	417	426	413	436
Carthage	381	305	280	294	350	359	361	421	387	372	349	326	382	297	321	311	323	335	336	328
Wagner	16	29	32	28	27	24	28	35	50	57	76	83	92	99	116	192	278	297	326	350
Midland	201	456	718	715	560	629	731	769	721	600	612	625	848	953	741	629	667	688	622	602
Lenoir Rhyne	262	256	458	562	482	502	526	628	1116	1096	1000	1472	1505	1130	1024	992	697	1135	1355	1411
Waterloo				65		50		74		84		63		74		118		125		72
Hartwick											235	336	394	533	556	501	493	435	338	331
Marion (Junior)	174	154	161	158	156	163	183	183	180	178	148	147	133	120	131	137	134	116	105	123

f. Books by Faculty Members

To the charge that Lutheran pens are not active in the production of books, the following exhibit is an effective answer. The list is undoubtedly incomplete, but it brings together the books, written or translated, during the past twenty years by faculty members of our seminaries and colleges. In addition, hundreds of articles were printed in numerous learned journals and encyclopedias. To the more popular but highgrade magazine our teachers should be frequent contributors.

Seminaries

Gettysburg

Aberly, John—*Acts of the Apostles* (N. T. Commentary), 1936; *Bible Dictionary* (Contributor, 6 vols. in Telugu), 1923-26.

Alleman, H. C.—*Prayers for Boys,* 1919; *Old Testament: A Study,* 1934; *New Testament: A Study,* 1934; *Lutheran Commentary on the New Testament,* editor, 1936; *Hebrew Grammar* (Co-author with H. Creager).

Fischer, M. H.—*Story of Jesus,* 1924.

Stamm, R. T.—*Introductory Article and St. Mark* (N. T. Commentary), 1936.

Wentz, A. R.—*History of the Maryland Synod,* 1920; *When Two Worlds Met,* 1921; *Lutheran Church in America,* 1923, 1933; *History of the Gettysburg Seminary,* 1926; *Fliedner the Faithful,* 1936; *History of the Lutheran Church in Frederick, Md.,* 1938.

Hamma

Allbeck, W. D.—*Revision of Neve's History of the Lutheran Church in America.*

Flack, E. E. — *The Revelation of John* (N. T. Commentary), 1936; *Biblical Criticism* (The Translated Bible, ed. by Norlie), 1934.

Larimer, L. H.—Editor (with Bowers and Seegers), *Gospel Preaching for the Day.* (2 vols.)

Keyser, L. S.—*A System of Natural Theism,* 1917, 1927; *A System of General Ethics,* 1918, 1934; *In the Redeemer's Footsteps,* 1919; *Contending for the Faith,* 1920; *In the Apostles' Footsteps,* 1920; *A System of Christian Evidence,* 1922, 1926, 1930; *Man's First Disobedience,* 1924; *A Handbook of Christian Psychology,* 1926, 1928; *A Manual of Christian Ethics,* 1926; *The Problem of Origins,* 1926; *The Philosophy of Christianity,* 1928; *A Reasonable Faith,* 1933.

Neve, J. L.—*History of the Lutheran Church in America; Introduction to Symbolics; Lutherans in the Movement for Church Union; Story and Significance of the Augsburg Confession.*

Philadelphia

Fischer, E. E.—*Social Problems; Life, Work and Teachings of Jesus* (N. T. Commentary), 1936.

Jacobs, C. M.—*Luther's Work in English,* Vols. III, IV, 1930; V. 1931, VI. 1932 (Co-editor); *The Way—A Little Book of Christian Truth,* 1922; *The Story of the Church,* 1925; *Helps on the Road,* 1933; *An Outline of Christian Doctrine,* 1926 (trans. from German of W. Elert); *The Faith of the Church,* 1938.

Nolde, O. F.—*Luther's Catechism;* Co-author with P. J. Hoh: *My Life,* 1934; *My Pupils,* 1934; *My Bible,* 1935; *My Work,* 1935; *My Preparation,* 1935; *My Materials,* 1935; *My Group Sessions,* 1936; *My Progress,* 1937.

Offermann, H.—*The Jesus of the New Testament* (N. T. Studies); *Introduction to the Epistles and Gospels of the Church Year; What is Lutheranism?* 1930 (Contributor); *Matthew* (N. T. Commentary), 1936; *Life and Work of Paul* (N. T. Commentary), 1936.

Reed, L. D.—*The Philadelphia Seminary Biographical Record*, 1923.

Snyder, R. D.—*First Corinthians* (N. T. Commentary), 1936.

Tappert, T. G.—*H. Sasse's "Here We Stand"* (translator), 1938.

Chicago

Gruber, L. F.—*The First New Testament and Luther*, 1928; *World Book Encyclopedia and Its Annuals* (Contributor).

Klotsche, E. H.—*Outline of the History of Doctrines; Christian Symbolics*.

Krauss, E. F.—*Galatians* (N. T. Commentary), 1936.

Schaeffer, Henry—*Hebrew Tribal Economy*, 1922; *The Call to Prophetic Service*, 1926.

Waterloo

Little, C. H.—*Distinctive Doctrines*, 1936.

Northwestern

Gerberding, G. H.—*Lutheran Fundamentals*, 1925; *Reminiscent Reflections*, 1928.

Stump, Joseph—*Russelism, A Counterfeit Christianity*, 1922; *The Christian Life*, 1930.

Colleges

Gettysburg

Bachman, A.—*Censorship in France from 1715-1750: Voltaire's Opposition*, 1934.

Boughton, J. S.—*The Idea of Progress in Philo Judœus*, 1932.

Cline, T. L.—*Critical Opinion in the Eighteenth Century English Personal Letters*, 1923.

Fortenbaugh, R.—*The Development of the Synodical Polity of the Lutheran Church in America to 1829*, 1926; *A History of Christ's Evangelical Lutheran Congregation*, 1936; Contributor to: *Inland Lutheran Migrations*, 1926; *The History of Gettysburg College*, 1932.

Glenn, J. G.—*Chapters in the Style of the Roman Elegy: the Adjective*, 1936.

Kramer, F. H.—*Experimental Research as a Factor in Commercial Education*, 1920.

Laning, W. A.—*Oscillations in Corona Discharges in Rarified Gases.* (In printer's hands.)

Mason, F. C.—*A Study in Shelley Criticism*, 1937.

Miller, G. R.—*The First Spark Spectrum of Rubidium (Rb. II) and Cœsium (Cs. II)*, 1931.

Ostrom, J. W.—*Controlling Ideas*, 1934.

Sanders, C. F.—*The Taproot of Religion and Its Fruitage*, 1931; *Orientation Syllabus,* 1926, 1936; Translated: *Problems of the Secondary Teacher (Jerusalem)*, 1918; *Introduction to Philosophy (Jerusalem)*, 1910, 1932; *The Mission of Philosophy to the Present Age (Utitz)*, 1937 (Negotiating with publisher); *The Philosophy of Eternal Man (Kraenzlen)*, 1938 (Ready for printer).

Sloat, C. A.—*Laboratory Exercises in General Chemistry; Laboratory Manual of Physical Chemistry*.

Tilberg, W. E.—*The Democrats and the Tariff, 1883-1888*, 1928.

Von Schwerdtner, E. O.—*Fundamental Language Facts*, 1933.
Waltemyer, W. C.—*A Personal God in an Age of Science*, 1929; *First Peter* (N. T. Commentary), 1936.

Wittenberg

Beaver, W. C.—*Bacteria in the Soil*, 1919; *Laboratory Outlines of General Zoology*, 1924; *Thermophilic and Thermotelorant Bacteria*, 1928; *Laboratory Outlines of General Biology*, 1936; *Laboratory Outlines of General Biology*, 1938; *Fundamentals of General Biology* — To be published latter part of 1938.

Birch, T. B.—*The De Sacramento Altaris of William of Ockham* (Edited), 1930.

Bloomhardt, P. F. — *A Short Biography of F. A. Kahler*, 1937; *The Poems of Haggai*, 1928.

Bowman, Leona F.—*Problems in Home Economics Teaching*, 1925; Co-author *Status of Home Economics in American Schools*—University of Chicago Monograph, 1922.

Brees, P. R. and Kelley, G. V.—*Modern Speaking*, 1928. (Three editions since.)

de Boer, Josephine—*Edition Critique de "Chryseide et Arimant" par Jean Mairet* (1625), Paris,—1925. (Co-author); *Mallorcan Moods in Contemporary Art and Literature*, 1938.

Heisey, P. H. — *Lutheran Graded Series of Sunday School Material*, 1926; *Three Essays on Luther*, 1932; *Studies in Social Problems*, 1938.

Hiller, R. H.—*Odyssey of Homer* (Tr. into English Prose), 1928.

Kruger, F. K.—*An undiplomatic Diary by the American member of the inter-allied military mission to Hungary*, 1919-1920 (Columbia University Press, New York, 1935); *Gesichtspunkte, Methoden und Ziele einer Wissenschaftlichen Amerika kunde*, Berlin, 1928; Article "J. H. W. Stuckenberg" in "The Encyclopedia of Social Sciences," Vol. XIV. (In conjunction with Prof. L. L. Bernard); Articles in the "Encyclopedia Americana" on "German Judiciary," "The Imperial German Government," "German Parties."

MacPherson, Georgia and Gianakoulis, T. P.—*Fairy Tales of Modern Greece*, 1930.

Neuberg, M. J.—*Principles and Methods of Vocational Choice*, 1934; *Right Living*, 1925-27; Co-author: *Introduction to Guidance*, Ohio State Board of Education, Bulletin No. 1, 1930; Co-author: *A Guidance Program for Grades Seven to Twelve*, Miami County Board of Education, Ohio, 1931; Co-author: *A Guidance Program and Course of Study of Grades VII-XII*; Montgomery County Board of Education, Ohio, 1932.

Nystrom, Wendell C.—*The Selection and Provision of Textbooks with Special Reference to Kansas*, 1937.

Pershing, B. H.—Contributor to the *Dictionary of American Biography. The Ordinances of 1787; Its Operation and Influence in American History; First Prize Northwest Territory Sesquicentennial*, 1938.

Suhr, E. G.—*Sculptured Portraits of Greek Statesmen with a Special Study of Alexander the Great*, 1931.

Van de Wall, Clara M. and William—*Music in Institutions*, 1937.

Newberry

Aman, J. A.—*Federal Quarantine Administration*, 1935.

Carroll, Ruth—*High School Latin Manual*, 1937.

Ensrud, Paul—*The Lord's Prayer*, 1926; *Triboulet*, 1927; *Practice Hints*, 1928; *The Atonement*, 1929; *We Wait Thy Loving Kindness*, 1929; *The*

Creed, 1931; *Church Year Choral Series*, 1931; *Supplication*, 1932; *Hosanna*, 1932; *Hulder's Song*, 1932.

Epting, T. E.—*La Medecine chez Moliere*, 1931.

Nelson, Erland—*Radical-Conservatism in Student Attitudes*, 1938; *Religion on the Campus* (in hands of printer).

Park, J. G.—*2-p-Cymyl-4-semicarbazide and Certain Derivatives*, 1929.

Setzler, E. B.—*Introduction to Advanced English Syntax*, 1924; *The Anglo-Saxon*, Vol. I and II, 1926-29; 1936; *A Primer of Poetics*, 1936; *Jefferson Anglo-Saxon Grammar and Reader*, 1938 (co-author with H. H. and E. L. Setzler).

Setzler, H. H.—*Different Methods of Teaching Certain Subjects Found Effective in South Carolina High Schools*, 1926; *The Effects of Certain Starches on Unsized Cotton Yarn*, 1931.

Voigt, G. P.—*A History of Ebenezer Lutheran Church; The Religious and Ethical Element in the Major American Poets*, 1925.

Susquehanna

Ahl, A. W.—*Bible Studies in the Light of Recent Research*, 1923.

Thiel

Elson, H. W.—*Modern Times and the Living Past*, 1921.

Muhlenberg

Barba, P. A.—*German Lyrics and Ballads*, 1935 (co-author).

Badger, K. M.—*Verb Finder*, 1937 (co-author).

Brown, J. D. M.—*The Constant Christ*, 1938.

Corbiere, A. S.—*Juan Eugenio Harzenbusch and the French Theatre*, 1937.

Fluck, E. J.—*A Study of Greek Love Names*, 1937 (co-author).

Haas, J. A. W.—*In the Light of Faith*, 1922; *Freedom and Christian Conduct*, 1923; *The Unity of Faith and Knowledge*, 1926; *The Truth of Faith*, 1927; *What Ought I to Believe*, 1929; *The Christian Way of Liberty*, 1930; *Christianity and Its Contrasts*, 1932.

Horn, R. C.—*Followers of the Way*, 1926; *The Use of the Subjunctive and Optative Moods in the Non-Literary Papyri*, 1926.

Swain, J. E.—*Struggle for Control of the Mediterranean; History of World Civilization*, 1938.

Carthage

Arbaugh, Geo.—*Revelation in Mormonism*.

Evjen, J. O.—*Life of J. H. W. Stuckenberg*, 1938; contributor to *What is Lutheranism?* 1930; *The Translated Bible*, 1934; *Dictionary of American Biography*, and *The New Schaff-Herzog Encyclopedia of Religious Knowledge*.

Neumann, R. — *The Book of Job, A Metrical Translation from the Hebrew Text*, 1932; *Essentials of the Word*, 1933; *Modern Medical Missions*, 1934 (co-translator). Ready for publication: *The Gospel Day by Day; Two Worlds and One God; An Evangelical System of Religious Education*.

Wagner

Hefelbower, S. G.—*History of Gettysburg College*, 1932; contributor to *What is Lutheranism?* 1930.

Palleske, Theodore—*Prize Translation of Siegfried* (second act by R. Wagner).

Rodick, B. C.—*Human Nature in American Politics; English Art in the XVIIIth Century* (both in manuscript form, ready for publisher).

Lenoir Rhyne
Keiser, A.— *Lutheran Mission Work Among the American Indians,* 1922; *The Indian in American Literature,* 1933.
Setzler, E. L.—*The Jefferson Anglo-Saxon Grammar and Reader,* 1938 (co-author).

g. Marks of Progress

Besides the increase in faculties and growth in enrolments, noted elsewhere in tables, and the celebration of anniversaries, it is desirable to record the items which indicate progress and high standards.

Seminaries

Gettysburg inaugurated the Gettysburg Seminary Week in 1925 which brings to the institution annually lecturers of national and international reputation—received the Charles and Susan Cronhardt bequest which, although not completed, has now reached a total of $285,000—added a full-time librarian and rebuilded and recatalogued the library according to the system of the Library of Congress—accredited by the American Association of Theological Schools—developed seminary choir.

Hamma installed new pipe organ in chapel, established new courses, introduced seminars for graduate students, received bequests for library and scholarships.

Southern erected the Voigt Administration Building and two houses for professors—secured $38,000 as a Voigt Memorial Fund.

Philadelphia purchased houses for professors a n d Graduate Hall—completed reorganization and expansion of curriculum with the development of a Graduate School with an enrolment of 87, all resident work —established two graduate fellowships—established Practice School for Weekday Religious Education and regular supervision of clinical work of students—was accredited by the American Association of Theological Schools.

Western purchased Nye property.

Waterloo (Canada) enlarged main building—increased financial assets.

Saskatoon erected president's residence—enlarged campus.

Northwestern purchased a building and secured an endowment of $78,000.

Colleges

Gettysburg enlarged campus—erected five new buildings — enlarged and remodeled others—increased endowment—was accredited by the Association of American Universities—admitted women—developed a college choir—installed chapters of honorary scholastic societies.

Wittenberg increased endowment $1,500,000—increased assets $2,700,000 —enlarged campus, erected five new buildings, remodeled and enlarged others—added departments of American literature, art archæology, biography, business administration, comparative literature, health and physical education, home economics, music, public speech, religious education, and sociology—developed extension classes and organized Junior College in Dayton—established offices of Dean of Men, Dean of Women, Business Manager, Controller, Student Counsellor, Director of Religious Activities, and Personnel Director—was accredited by the Association of American Universities and American Association of University Women—installed chapters of honorary scholastic societies for freshmen—developed an excellent college choir.

Roanoke erected gymnasium—increased financial assets $500,000—was accredited by the Southern Association—admitted women.

Newberry e r e c t e d gymnasium and men's dormitory — remodeled women's dormitory—merger of Summerland College with Newberry—increased financial assets—was accredited by the Southern Association—developed an excellent college choir—revised and enlarged curriculum.

Susquehanna enlarged campus by 23 acres—erected three buildings—renovated and remodeled others—increased endowment $50,000—inaugurated retirement system for teachers—established two trustee scholarships for graduate work of $150 each—was accredited by the Middle Atlantic States Association—Motet choir awarded second position by the Columbia Broadcasting Company in its quest for excellent choirs during 1938.

Thiel built gymnasium—was accredited by the Middle Atlantic States Association—established office of personnel director.

Muhlenberg increased the endowment and erected science building, library, and chapel, one of most attractive college chapels in America—revised curriculum—developed an extension school—was accredited by the American Association of Universities—established plan of faculty sabbatical leave—installed chapters of eight scholastic societies—had outstanding success in oratory and debating.

Carthage increased endowment — secured $175,000 from the General Education Board—erected a field house—was accredited by American Association of University Women and the North Central Association—developed an outstanding a capella choir.

Wagner erected administration building—increased assets—revised curriculum—was accredited by Middle Atlantic States Association.

Midland erected a gymnasium—commons building and a girls' dormitory—developed an a capella choir of outstanding merit.

Lenoir Rhyne received most of the $434,000 endowment—erected four buildings and purchased and equipped the Athletic Field — was accredited by the Southern Association of Colleges—had outstanding success in oratory and debating.

Waterloo increased assets—enlarged curriculum.

Hartwick (Founded in 1928) secured financial and property assets valued at $655,000—was accredited by the Regents of New York State—developed a college choir.

II. LUTHERAN HIGHER EDUCATION THROUGH THE BIENNIUM: 1936-1938

"Without it—the church college—the church would become a decadent, antiquated institution, just as medicine would be if colleges and medical institutions did not apply to medicine the rapidly developing body of scientific knowledge. The stagnant college means a stagnant church, and a stagnant church means ultimate death."—J. H. Reynolds, president of Hendrix College.

"Nobody who is in touch with the universities can fail to observe how the young men and women are turning back to seek almost desperately for the secrets of the Christian faith and life. And the tide is coming in fast. But to watch it fills one with hope and fear."—F. R. Barry, The Relevance of the Church, p. 53.

Formed "to promote the general educational interests of the Church," the Board of Education believes this can best be accomplished by keeping Christ in education. Seminaries will be conscious that they are training young men for service to the Church, not merely for a profession. Theological students will have that sacrificial consecration befitting one called into the ministry. Colleges will realize that they are at least church-related, that the atmosphere of the campus, the attitude of the faculty members towards the Church, and even the accounting system, will exhibit the characteristics known as Christian. Students, wherever they are, will be understood and guided in those loyalties and qualities which become a Christian anywhere and any time.

In partial fulfilment of this function during the biennium the staff visited 223 campuses, 47 Lutheran and 176 non-Lutheran, in thirty-one states and three provinces, with a total of 495 visits; attended 1,133 sessions of committees' conferences, boards, and conventions; and had 6,305 personal interviews.

To present an analysis of the present status of higher education in the United Lutheran Church in America and the service of the Board of Education during the biennium is the purpose of this section of this report.

1. COOPERATING WITH THE INSTITUTIONS

To serve the colleges and seminaries so that they may grow in Christian fellowship and their service to the Church may become more effective.

a. The Service of the Board

Advice and Grants-in-Aid

The secretaries take opportunities for extended conferences with the president and members of the faculty, round-table discussions with the faculty, visits to classes, and examination of buildings and grounds. The type of advice sought by the institutions and offered by the secretaries covers general administrative problems, curriculum changes, teaching staff changes, student welfare, promotion, and relations to the alumni and church constituency.

While the advice of the secretaries often results in desirable changes, and appears to be appreciated, the grants-in-aid of the Board are increasingly necessary in order that both the colleges and seminaries may function more effectively. During the biennium the institutions received a total of $100,540, which is $6,190 more than during the previous biennium.

By formal resolution the Board of Education called upon all the colleges and seminaries to engage the services of a certified public accountant to audit accounts at least annually, and requested the colleges to adjust their bookkeeping records and forms in harmony with the suggestions of the National Commission on Standard Reports for Institutions of Higher Education which were approved by the Board several years ago. To assist the colleges in this adjustment, the board has offered the services of the Financial Advisory Service of the American Council on Education. With adjustments made the financial records of our colleges can be compared on a similar basis with more than 600 other colleges.

Contacts and Publicity

During May of 1937 and 1938 secretaries were used by some colleges to speak at meetings set up by the college officials in co-operation with pastors. These meetings gave opportunities for valuable contacts and desirable discussion of the problems of Christian higher education.

Educational News Bulletin

Issued nine times each year, in mimeographed form, this bulletin continues to be of special value in keeping the colleges and seminaries informed of what other schools are doing, in presenting summaries of educational projects being carried on by both Lutheran and non-Lutheran institutions, in giving ideas for more effective and efficient administrative policies, and in bringing the board and the institutions into closer co-operative relationship.

Co-operation with Church Educational Groups

Conference of Theological Professors. The proceedings of the meetings held in June, 1937 and 1938, were mimeographed by the office of the board and distributed to all seminary faculty members. The board agreed to aid teachers in the Canadian seminaries in getting to the conference. The service of the board is greatly appreciated by the seminaries.

National Lutheran Educational Conference. Through the staff the board continues a co-operation that has been uninterrupted since the formation of the Conference in 1913. Mr. Wickey is on the executive committee and Miss Markley is editor of the monthly News Bulletin distributed through the National Lutheran Council. At the meeting in Chicago during January, 1938, the twenty-fifth anniversary was celebrated on the program of which both Miss Markley and Mr. Wickey had prominent parts. The Board of Education renders special service in aiding Lutheran teachers seeking positions on Lutheran college faculties.

Council of Church Boards of Education. Mr. Wickey continued to serve as the General Secretary of the Council of Church Boards of Education, organized in 1911 with Dr. F. G. Gotwald as one of the founders. This service is rendered "without prejudice to the work of the Board of Education." In appreciation of this co-operation the Council of Church Boards of Education shares in travel expenses, pays for the salary of an office secretary who serves our board, and grants an honorarium. Mr. Wickey has been returning to the Board the sum of $600 per year. This arrangement has continued for three years without detriment to the work of our Board; in fact, there has been much assistance to our work. As editor of *Christian Education,* a Journal of Christian Higher Education, Mr. Wickey is exerting a very significant national influence.

Miss Markley has been honored by being elected to the chairmanship of the National Commission on University Work of the Council of Church Boards of Education. This Commission functions as a clearing house for materials and methods in the field of work with students.

b. The Institutions Report

In accordance with the by-laws of the United Lutheran Church in America, the colleges and seminaries report to the Church through the Board of Education. Statistics on finances and enrolments are secured on blanks especially prepared for that purpose. Statements of important events and facts are received from time to time, and are herewith summarized for the information and record of the Church.

Changes in Presidents

Philadelphia Seminary: The Rev. Luther D. Reed, D.D., A.E.D., professor of Liturgics and Church Art, was elected acting president after the death on March 30, 1938, of President Charles M. Jacobs, D.D., L.H.D., LL.D.

Southern Seminary: The Rev. Charles K. Bell, D.D., professor of Practical Theology, was elected acting president after the death on April 6, 1938, of President C. A. Freed, D.D.

Saskatoon Seminary: The Rev. N. Willison, Litt.D., became president on September 1, 1936.

Marion College: The Rev. Hugh Rhyne accepted the call to the presidency upon the resignation of President E. H. Copenhaver, D.D., effective August 1, 1938.

Muhlenberg College: Mr. Levering Tyson, Litt.D., accepted the call to the presidency effective June, 1937.

The Enrolment of Students

On October 1, 1937, the colleges reported a registration of 4,743, which is a 2.6 per cent increase over the figure of 4,619 for October, 1935. This small increase in a two year period, with one-half the colleges having decreases, is an indication of the keen competition for students, in spite of the fact that our colleges are improving their scholastic standards.

The enrolments in the seminaries continue to decrease. In 1934 there were 362 enrolled in the undergraduate courses; in 1935, 345; in 1936, 319; in 1937, 312; and in 1938, 293. Two reasons for this decline are the stricter standards for admission and the fact that synods no longer give financial aid so freely.

The actual figures of students enrolled at each seminary in the undergraduate courses for the past three years are seen in the following tables.

Name of Seminary	1937–38	1936–37	1935–36
Hartwick	16	21	22
Gettysburg	72	78	77
Southern	25	23	27
Hamma	24	35	38
Philadelphia	77	78	72
Chicago	28	27	29
Western	6	5	14
Waterloo	11	11	13
Saskatoon	12	17	10
Northwestern	22	17	17
	293	312	319

The Church Affiliation of Students at the Colleges

For the year 1935-36 the colleges reported 1,923 or 41.6 per cent Lutheran students enrolled out of a total enrolment of 4,619. The first table below shows the church affiliation or preference of students enrolled at our thirteen senior colleges and one junior college for the past two academic years. All denominations and sects having less than one per cent enrolled are placed in "others" item which includes twenty-seven groups, making a total of thirty-seven religious groups represented in the student bodies at our colleges. One Buddhist and one Deist are listed for 1937-38. Ten denominations account for 94.5 per cent of the students. The drop from 96 in 1935-36 to 73 in 1937-38 of students having no religious affiliation is interesting.

Of special interest is the exhibit in the second table indicating the number and percentage of Lutheran students at each of the colleges, not including special schools, during the past two years.

	1936-37		1937-38	
Denomination	No.	%	No.	%
Lutheran	2,017	42.7	2,002	42.2
Methodist	767	16.4	737	15.3
Presbyterian	460	9.8	473	9.9
Baptist	330	7.	350	7.3
Catholic	268	5.7	254	5.4
Reformed	139	2.7	161	3.3
Episcopal	167	3.5	190	4.
Cong.-Christian	158	3.4	97	2.5
Jewish	59	1.3	64	1.
Evangelical	86	1.8	98	2.6
Others	181	3.9	252	5.4
No Affiliation	87	1.8	73	1.1
Totals	4,719	100.0	4,743	100.0

Colleges	Total Enrol.	Lutheran No.	Lutheran %	Total Enrol.	Lutheran No.	Lutheran %
Carthage	292	152	52.1	286	155	46.3
Gettysburg	630	343	54.4	642	360	56.
Hartwick	285	35	12.3	277	29	10.4
Lenoir Rhyne	377	166	44.	445	189	42.5
Marion	76	27	28.1	61	21	34.4
Midland	303	128	42.2	278	115	41.3
Muhlenberg	436	201	46.1	429	181	42.1
Newberry	308	153	46.6	276	136	49.3
Roanoke	363	45	12.4	376	48	12.7
Susquehanna	282	140	50.	307	153	49.8
Thiel	262	105	40.	277	114	41.1
Wagner	207	97	42.	205	92	44.8
Waterloo	70	25	36.7	61	20	32.8
Wittenberg	828	400	48.3	823	389	47.2
Totals	4,719	2,017	42.7	4,743	2,002	42.2

c. Persistent Problems

The Church's Arrangements for the Training of Ministers and Teachers

In January, 1937, the Board of Education directed its executive secretary "to approach the authorities of the four eastern seminaries and of supporting synods with reference to the consideration of Washington as a possible site for a consolidated institution." Investigation and personal conversations revealed considerable sentiment in some sections for this suggestion but strong opposition in other centers. The attitude seems to be "to dig in and stay put," allowing time to be the judge, in spite of growing indebtedness and decreasing enrolments.

In January, 1938, the Board of Education voted to encourage the seminaries "to give favorable and earnest consideration to higher standards as set forth both in the Report of the Church in 1932 on the Church's arrangements for the training of ministers and teachers, and by the American Association of Theological Schools." The standards adopted by this association are lower than those approved by the Church, and yet only two of the four seminaries of our Church which applied for accreditation were accepted.

In light of this total situation the Board of Education at its meeting in June, 1938, voted "to review the 1932 program on the Church's arrangements for the training of ministers and teachers" and to "consider ways and means of having all of the Church's theological seminaries accredited by the American Association of Theological Schools, either by strengthening or by merging institutions." This whole problem must be faced realistically and courageously by the Church and the synods supporting seminaries.   (See Recommendation 2.)

Men for the Ministry

During the biennium members of the staff have met most of the committees on men for the ministry in the synods of the church. Several conferences with committees from synods in adjoining territory were held resulting in better and more uniform arrangements for aiding students financially. The time for beginning aid has been moved in most instances to the sophomore year in college and in some to the beginning of seminary work. We have sought to impress on the Church that the chief function of these committees should be to seek and direct men in preparing for the ministry, rather than to aid financially which should be limited to exceptional cases of great promise and great need.

Two separate studies were made of the Church's need for men for the ministry and the number of unemployed ministers. These studies seem to show that in the operation of the Church at the present time there are approximately one hundred pastors not being used. They show also that there is about the same number of vacant parishes. This rate seems to be somewhat constant. It is not alarming. In any case 3½% is a low unemployment rate as well as a low vacancy rate. Besides many of the unemployed ministers are in poor health or are prevented from an effective ministry for other reasons. Some of the vacant parishes are not able to support a minister. A study of the need of the Church due to retirement and old age shows that the average removal by death is fifty-three each year and the average by retirement is forty-two each year. There is some duplication in these figures. It seems that about eighty men are needed annually to replace ministers who retire or who die.

For the last five years our seminaries have graduated an average of 111; the highest number being 134 in 1934, and the lowest 98 in 1936. This year, 1938, 115 were graduated. Practically all who have graduated have been called into the service of the Church. We are meeting the present needs adequately, so far as numbers are concerned.

Figures from our colleges show men planning to enter our seminaries as follows: 1938—52; 1939—54; 1940—61; 1941—48. It is difficult to estimate the number of men who may come from non-Lutheran colleges and universities during the same period. It seems likely there will be nearly enough. If, however, the Church puts on a program of expansion, we shall not have enough men.

The Church must not relax her vigilance in seeking the best men in the parishes and colleges and in urging them to prepare for her ministry. There is no need for second rate men and no financial help should be given to any except those of unusual qualifications and extremely limited economic resources. The Church should get away from the system of subsidizing men preparing for the ministry. Grants-in-aid should be granted only to exceptionally gifted men whose financial resources are entirely insufficient.

Training of Men for the Bilingual Ministry

Action of the United Lutheran Church in America requires that this board give careful attention to the whole problem of bilingual training for the ministry. Accordingly, grants have been allowed for students to study both in this country and in Germany. For 1936-37, $300 was given to Karl J. Knauff, graduate of Waterloo College and Seminary, to study at the University of Erlangen and to visit inner mission institutions. He is now serving as the assistant pastor to St. Matthew's Lutheran Church, Kitchener, Ont., Canada, where he preaches in German twice a month, directs the work of the German Sunday school, and does much of his pastoral work in the German language. For the year 1937-38 Helmut Lehmann, graduate of the University of Saskatchewan and of the seminary at Saskatoon, was granted the sum of $300. He will continue his studies during 1938-39 with the assistance of the "Martin Luther Bund" at the University of Erlangen. To study at Gettysburg Seminary, $125 was granted Richard Syre, of Silesia, who had studied at the University of Vienna and Biblical Seminary. Of Mr. Syre, the faculty at the Gettysburg Seminary wrote, "We all feel confident that he will prove a useful man in the bilingual ministry of the United Lutheran Church in America." He is now in the service of the Board of American Missions at Gary, Indiana.

d. The Story of Numbers

Statistics tell a story which is interesting if not always revealing of the true status. The figures for our colleges and seminaries show that the total value of their assets is $25,103,838, or $430,069 more than in 1936. The indebtedness is $2,932,777, or $140,447 less than two years ago, but $1,032,292 more than in 1930. The most remarkable fact is seen in the indebtedness of the current funds amounting to only $21,923, which is $13,855 less than in 1936 and $73,525 less than in 1930. The seminaries had deficits amounting to $17,856, while those of the colleges amount to only $4,067.

These figures are encouraging but another aspect of the picture is seen in the requests from the colleges for buildings to cost $2,055,000, for permanent funds to be increased by $5,125,000, for $2,334,700 to pay accumulated and building indebtedness, and for $50,000 to balance current budgets. The seminaries need $425,000 to pay indebtedness and $22,000 to balance budgets. Their needs for buildings and permanent funds are relative to a final merger of institutions and correlation of programs. Thus the immediate needs of the colleges and seminaries amount to more than ten million dollars.

The statistical tables will answer questions of detail concerning the stewardship of the fourteen colleges and the ten seminaries. Totals are not given in connection with the tables, but the following tabulation of summaries of certain items will prove worth while.

SUMMARY OF STATISTICS FOR INSTITUTIONS

Financial	10 Seminaries	14 Colleges	Grand Total
Value of all Property	$2,488,528	$11,860,036	$14,348,564
Value of Fund Assets	2,628,135	8,127,139	10,755,274
Total Value of all Assets	$5,116,663	$19,987,175	$25,103,838
Total Indebtedness	$424,728	$2,518,049	$2,932,777
Current Funds			
Income	$219,898	$2,010,438	$2,230,336
Expenditures	237,754	2,014,505	2,252,259
Total Current Deficits	$17,856	$4,067	$21,923
Libraries			
Total Volumes	138,350	379,730	518,080
Faculties			
Total Faculties	67	410	477
Total Student Enrolment	487	8,092	8,579
Total Alumni	4,928	26,376	31,304

STATISTICAL TABLES—I. THEOLOGICAL SEMINARIES

THE PROPERTY

Index No.	Institution	Founded	Location	President or Dean	Plant — Campus Acres	Plant — Campus Value	Plant — Buildings No.	Plant — Buildings Value	Value of Real Property	Equipment — Library Vol.	Equipment — Library Value	Equipment — Furn. and Fixtures	Value of Equipment	Total Value of Property
1	Hartwick Theo. Seminary	1797	New York, N. Y.	Rev. S. M. Paulson, D.D.						2000	$1500			$1500
2	Luth. Theo. Seminary	1826	Gettysburg, Pa.	Rev. J. Aberly, D.D., LL.D.	40	$47000	9	$215000	$262000	45000	50000	$18000	$68000	330000
3	Luth. Theo. Southern Sem.	1830	Columbia, S. C.	Rev. C. K. Bell, D.D., Acting	6	15000	5	145000	160000	11000	12000	3000	15000	175000
4	Hamma Divinity School	1845	Springfield, Ohio	Rev. R. E. Tulloss, Ph.D., D.D., LL.D.					See Wittenberg College					
5	Luth. Theo. Seminary	1864	Philadelphia, Pa.	Rev. L. D. Reed, D.D., A.E.D., Acting	10	350000	15	745000	1095000	43000	52300	25000	77300	1172300
6	Chicago Luth. Theo. Sem.	1891	Maywood, Ill.	Rev. L. F. Gruber, D.D., LL.D.	15	218250	11	197744	415994	20000	18000	34834	52834	468828
7	Western Theo. Seminary	1893	Fremont, Neb.	Rev. H. F. Martin, Ph.D., D.D.	6	15000	7	20000	35000	5500	3250	5000	8250	43250
8	Luth. Sem. of Canada	1911	Waterloo, Ont., Can.	Rev. F. B. Clausen, D.D.	16	10000	6	165000	175000	3650	3000	1000	4000	179000
9	Lutheran Seminary	1919	Saskatoon, Sask., Can.	Rev. N. Willison, Litt.D.	16	4050	7	56558	60608	4200	2200	1900	4100	64708
10	Northwtn. Luth. Theo. Sem.	1921	Minneapolis, Minn.	Rev. P. H. Roth, D.D.	16		1	34456	34456	4000			19476	53942

NOTE: Cents are omitted. Blanks indicate no report or nothing to report.

THE FUNDS—PERMANENT

Index No.	Productive — Restricted	Productive — Unrestricted	Unproductive — Annuities	Unproductive — Other	Total Endowment	Scholarships	Other Assets — Interest Bearing	Other Assets — Non-Interest Bearing	Total All Funds	Total All Assets Property and Funds	Additions to Capital 1936–37	Additions to Capital 1937–38	Total Indebtedness
1					$38795				$38795	$40295			$32185
2	$345000	$534500	$26500		906000	$69000			975000	$1305000	$19000	$91000	9000
3	73097		7600	$15000	95697		$2969	$3886	102552	277552	23601	5546	14904
4	45000	232414			277414	12500			289914	289914	1950		56950
5	77000	637400			714400				714400	1886700			173950
6		223843	120451		344294				344294	813122			83175
7	1700	37394			39094	6000			45094	88344			None
8	29816				29816				29816	208816		1000	42769
9										64708			11795
10	77875				77875			10395	88270	142212			None

I. THEOLOGICAL SEMINARIES—Continued

THE FUNDS: CURRENT INCOME — CURRENT EXPENDITURES

Index No.	Endowment	Students	The Church — U.L.C.A.	The Church — Synods	The Church — Parishes	The Church — Total	Special Gifts	Miscellaneous	Total Current Income	Administration	Instruction	Books Equipment	Operating	Maintenance	Interest	Loss on Annuities	Miscellaneous	Total Expenditures	Surplus or Deficit
1	$1756	$653				$1561	$3141	$310	$7421	$765	$4125	$1200	$8992	$642	$85		$854	$6472	$949 s
2	26243	2057		$10835		10835	1773	500	41408	8902	22074	700	2130	4709	768		636	41168	240 s
3	2504	600	$3583	5766		9349	4914	1348	18715	204	9945	388	4369			$2700	4471	18592	123 s
4	13156	770		8134		8134	600	420	23081	947	12102		18453		2740		18909	24977	1896 d
5	24959	2707		22447	$10745	33192	3388	3673	67919	6048	30400	600	6200	2042	4340	5678	2251	76550	8631 d
6	16062	95	2750	4166		6916	1000	1284	25262		11750	25	1192	571			60	32861	7599 d
7	1258			1318		1318	48		2719	297	3681							5826	3107 d
8										See Waterloo College	See Waterloo College								
9	3805		9800	1732		11532	1970	227	13729	1326	4595	912	1989		480		4044	13346	383 s
10				14066		14066	549	1223	19944		13457	348	4030			19	108	17962	1682 s

THE FACULTY — THE STUDENTS — College Graduates Enrolled

Index No.	Number Full Time	Number Part Time	Degrees—Earned Only No Degree	A.B.	A.M.	B.D.	S.T.M.	Doctor	Under-Graduates 1st Year	2nd Year	3rd Year	Special	Total	Graduates In Residence	In Correspondence	Total	Total Enrolled	1st Year	2nd Year	3rd Year	Special	Grad. in Residence	Grad. in Corresp.	Total Col. Grad.	Non-Lutheran	Alumni
1	3	3			2			4	3	3	7	5	18	12		12	30	2	2	7	2	9		22		323
2	6	4		1	2	1		6	24	19	28	2	73	21		21	94	24	19	28		21		92	7	1656
3	4	5			3			1	9	8	9		26				26	9	8	9				26		338
4	4	2		7	3	1	1	6	2	10	9	3	24	20	37	17	44	2	10	9	3	20	37	44	17	704
5	11	4		2	4	3		2	21	25	30	1	77	87	2	87	164	21	25	30	1	87	2	164	11	997
6	5				1			1	9	7	11		27			37	64	9	7	11				64		450
7	3	2		2	1	1		1	5	4	3		8			2	10		4	3				6		221
8	3				1				4	4	3		11	1			11			3		1				76
9	2			2		3			7	4	4		12		9	9	12			4			9			35
10	4	2			2			1	7		11		22			10	32			11						128

STATISTICAL TABLES—II. COLLEGES

THE PROPERTY

Index No.	Institution	Founded	Location	President	Type	Accredited by	Campus Acres	Campus Value	Buildings No.	Buildings Value	Value of Real Property	Library Vols.	Library Value	Laboratory and Museum	Furniture, Fixtures, Etc.	Value of Equipment	Total Value of Property
1	Gettysburg	1832	Gettysburg, Pa.	Rev. H. W. A. Hanson, D.D., LL.D.	C	1, 2, 3, 4	96	$161500	16	$1274176	$1435676	60000	$100000	$138357	129581	$238357	$1674000
2	Wittenberg	1845	Springfield, O.	Rev. R. E. Tulloss, Ph.D., D.D., LL.D.	C	1, 2, 3, 4	55	334715	17	1645106	1979822	60630	46960	125500	123870	302040	2281862
3	Roanoke	1853	Salem, Va.	Rev. C. J. Smith, D.D., LL.D.	C	2, 3, 4	20	62746	8	476128	538874	18000	92466	29377		153247	692121
4	Newberry	1856	Newberry, S.C.	J. C. Kinard, Litt.D., LL.D.	C	2, 3, 4	47	12587	12	335249	347836	21000	33000	12000	47581	94581	442417
5	Susquehanna	1858	Selinsgrove, Pa.	Rev. G. M. Smith, D.D.	C	2, 3, 4	62	141154	18	533513	675067	14600	22000	16000	91704	129704	804771
6	Thiel	1866	Greenville, Pa.	Rev. E. S. Rudisill, Ph.D., D.D.	C	2, 3, 4	35	35000	8		353486	17000	15000	16000	36809	67809	456295
7	Muhlenberg	1867	Allentown, Pa.	Levering Tyson, Litt.D., LL.D.	M	1, 2, 3, 4	75	571828	8	1552210	2124038	47500	51000	102657		153657	2277694
8	Carthage	1870	Carthage, Ill.	Rev. R. G. Schulz, D.D.	C	2, 3	38	27808	10	364884	392692	25000	24335	23740	48373	92469	489230
9	Wagner	1885	Staten Is., N.Y.	C. C. Stoughton, A.M.	C	2, 4	50				1077342	15000				79007	1156349
10	Midland	1887	Fremont, Neb.	Rev. H. F. Martin, Ph.D., D.D.	C	3	15		5		337532	15000				28213	365745
11	Lenoir Rhyne	1891	Hickory, N.C.	Rev. P. E. Monroe, D.D.	C	2, 3, 4	37	92332	6	449714	542046	15000	25000	30000	28213	79405	621451
12	Waterloo	1911	Waterloo, Ot., Can.	Rev. F. B. Clausen, D.D.	C						See	Waterloo Seminary			24405		
13	Hartwick	1928	Oneonta, N.Y.	Rev. C. W. Leitzell, D.D.	C	4	75	35000	6	275000	311000	11000	15000	75000	22000	112000	423000
14	Marion (Junior)	1873	Marion, Va.	Rev. E. H. Copenhaver, D.D. (Resigned)	C	5	5	25000	1	125000	150000	7500	8000	1000	16101	25101	175101

Note: Blanks indicate no report or nothing to report.
Code: M—Men. W—Women. C—Coeducational.

Code:
1. Association of American Universities.
2. Regional Accrediting Associations.
3. State University.
4. The Regents (New York).
5. Virginia State Board of Education.

THE FUNDS: PERMANENT / OTHER ASSETS / Inc. for Perm. Assets and Debts—1936-38 / Indebtedness

Index No.	Productive Restricted	Productive Unrestricted	Unproductive Annuities	Unproductive Other	Total Endowment	Scholarships	Loan Funds	Notes Interest Bearing	Notes Non-Int. Bearing	Other Property and Funds	Total Other Assets	Total Funds and Assets	Total Value of All Assets	Inc. Plant and Equip.	Inc. Endowment	Inc. Indebtedness	Indebtedness Bldgs. Equip. Etc.	Cur. Accumulated	Total
1	$96073	$657848	$40000		$795921						$88414	$884335	$2558335						None
2	249765	1274897	384811		1909474	$11699	$80013	$21506	$55076		168294	2077768	4359630		$57571	$883	$659500	$13269	$672769
3		659464	3000		662464		9102			$26030	35132	697596	1389717		5634		71600	50304	121904
4		328157			328157				269654	723	270377	598534	1040951	$5000	4754	3000		53282	53282
5	21656	342254	36300		400210						174654	574864	1379635	3765			98500		98500
6	1271	160881	1800	$7908	171860					2752	2752	174612	630907				160000	64368	224368
7	295754	704243			999997		1988					999997	3277691	2762	3708		573950	49250	623200
8	10610	859574	16400		886584	1000			4640	3400	8040	894624	1383854				128740	17478	146218
9					394717					394	394	395111	1551460						354646
10	32500	95170	5500		133170		1695				1695	134865	500610				72445	24878	97323
11	432491		1750		434241					25782	25782	460023	1081474						None
12						See Waterloo Seminary													
13	72000		1500	3500	77000	23000		12000	120000		155000	232000	655000			2500	81000	4000	85000
14					2810						2810	177911					36700	4139	40839

STATISTICAL TABLES—II. COLLEGES—Continued

THE CURRENT FUNDS—INCOME

Index No.	Students	Educational and General — The Church — Endowment	U.L.C.A.	Synods	Parishes and Individuals	Total	Sales and Services	Miscellaneous Sources	Total	Auxiliary Activities and Enterprises — Dormitories	Dining Halls	Other	Total	Non-Educational Purposes — Invested Funds	Current Gifts	Other	Total	Total Annual Income
1	$242688	15645		$17036		17036		$9701	$258333			$95	$95	$2781			$2781	$258333
2	302981	71523	$1800			1800		3722	401241	$3750	$821		4571	180			180	404117
3	84978	28287	4800	5721		10521		1400	123379	235	913		1148					128130
4	44726	11300	2050	8600	$280	10930			67947	16230	4376	2507	23113					74095
5	88295	21343	4500	26357	209	31066		2301	121978	1284	1500	387	3171	3258		$25	3283	148374
6	67774	5132		18000	4525	22525		14982	106273	6533		4848	11381					109444
7	162435	44678	4000	3183	5268	12451		3008	244626	2852	37473	4216	44542	66			66	256001
8	59144	7546					$177		73339									126756
9								206										112883
10	52429	4192	8400	8117	203	16720			73724	5440	2919	910	9269			472	472	83465
11	81229	11475	2706	4000		6706		317	99410	12377	32223	13451	58051	1298			1298	158759
12	5500	1406	5050	18788	857	24695	1500		31918	350		79	350					31997
13	65782	4291	750	5835	3715	10300		2086	83959	13532		124	13656	1335			1335	85644
14	16456		600	300		900		1021	18444					340			$340	32440

EXPENDITURES

Index No.	General Admin.	Instruction	Organ. Research	Extension Activities	Library	Operation and Maintenance	Total	Dorm. and Res.	Dining Halls	Other	Total	Annuities (Net Loss)	Interest on Loans	Scholarship Student Aid	Other	Total	Plant and Equipment	Indebtedness	Other	Total	Total Expenditures	Surp. or Deficit
1	$87565	$182092		$12522	$9523	$54105	$345807	$4064	$1967	$4422	$10453	$1755	$27660	$29970	$18	$59405					$250695	$7638 s
2	32185	59135			2203	7245	100768			1998	1998	180	5991	11706		17895	$2914			$2914	415644	11527 d
3	11882	44480			2445	3942	62749			4149	4149		2160	760	3575	6495	4088			4088	123375	4555 s
4	26331	64808	$579	2812	2707	24954	115577			4149	4149	2138	5980	16738	607	25463					73332	763 s
5	16550	76967			1907	13320	80036			6792	6792		8058	11880	4074	24012			$3000	3000	148189	185 s
6	38130	41310		26426	4166	28629	174218		1430	13816	15246	1190	30813	35699	6877	74579			500	4932	115772	6328 d
7	18574				573	12510	72967	2782	26060	3804	32647	668	2561	8810	4300	16338		$4432			264043	8042 d
8																		1246	808	4816	126768	12 d
9										4713	4713										112877	6 d
10	21946	40298		2591	1454	9499	75788	4892	29037	20981	54910			3628		3628	7	230		237	84366	901 s
11	13342	56120		928	4572	13063	88024							5231	2895	8126					151060	7699 s
12		25465		25		3032							2336								30855	1139 s
13	19896	51182		619	3470	6374	81541	356	29037	140	5853		3500	2400		5900	1600			2100	89681	4037 d
14	4579	9906			793	1857	17135		5497				2220	580		2800	1857			1857	27645	4795 s

STATISTICAL TABLES—II. COLLEGES—Continued

THE FACULTY · THE STUDENTS

Index No.	M	W	T	Lutheran M	Lutheran W	Lutheran T	No. Degree	A.B. Only	A.M. Only	Doctor	Fresh. M	Fresh. W	Fresh. T	Soph. M	Soph. W	Soph. T	Jun. M	Jun. W	Jun. T	Sen. M	Sen. W	Sen. T	Spec. M	Spec. W	Spec. T	Grad. M	Grad. W	Grad. T
1	44		44	31		31	4	3	19	22	168	31	199	131	57	188	106	33	139	90	13	103	7	8	15			1
2	54	29	83	44	14	59		13	28	38	157	150	307	104	107	211	66	58	124	84	53	137	11	4	15	2	1	7
3	23	1	24	13	1	7		3	12	9	70	41	111	42	25	102	34	26	77	22	23	52			3			
4	18	3	21	16	5	14		11	5	5	54	31	85	56	25	81	27	21	60	28	17	45	7	7	14			
5	24	10	34	10	3	21		10	13	11	56	44	100	35	29	64	27	27	48	34	23	45	10	3	13			
6	16	7	23	19		13		4	11	8	136	37	101	116	33	116	95	17	54	82	25	57	4	5	9			
7	33		23	18	6	19		3	15	15	62	38	106	47	18	80	32	10	95	30	9	82		13	18	14	24	38
8	20	10	30	16		24		11	14	5	68	79	140	36	39	54	33	23	49	19	16	55	5	6	2			
9	21	2	28	18	6	16	1	2	9	11	61	55	125	28	43	67	22	43	43	22	28	28	8	3	14			
10	16	7	28	13	4	24	2	11	14	2	70			56		99	37	29	45	34		38	2		5			
11	16	6	22	6	3	17	2	8	6	6		33	104	39	34	73	22		80	23	25	64	4	4	11			
12	15	4	14	11	2	9		4	6	2	71	46	55	1	28	29		29	51			48	7	9	30			
13		7	22	11	7	13		5	6	11	9												21					
14	1	9	10	1		8	3	7																				

THE STUDENTS—Continued · ALUMNI

Index No.	Total M	Total W	Total T	Lutheran M	Lutheran W	Lutheran T	Acad. M	Acad. W	Acad. T	Spec. Sch. M	Spec. Sch. W	Spec. Sch. T	Summer Sch. M	Summer Sch. W	Summer Sch. T	Ext. M	Ext. W	Ext. T	Grand Total M	Grand Total W	Grand Total T	Graduates	Ex-Students
1	502	143	645	269	91	360				111	146	257	12	61	73	225	370	595	524	149	673	4088	2770
2	424	377	801	206	170	376							279	116	395				788	1106	1894	6439	
3	313	83	396	48	2	50				18	27	45	80	75	155				368	133	501	1167	3700
4	189	146	335	81	86	167							192	50	242				239	338	577	1688	3000
5	175	97	272	85	68	153				44	40	84	39	33	72				215	158	373	3000	700
6	156	128	284	67	51	118				20	11	31	30	36	66				172	148	320	1186	5000
7	429		429	190		190				102	212	314							429		429	2735	2100
8	176	127	303			162				14	69	83	22	11	33				184	144	328	1307	5478
9	158	75	233	57	64	121							178	38	216	63	64	127	221	143	364	517	
10	141	163	304	89	89	178							500	167	667	14	90	104	185	417	602	761	6500
11	199	172	371			20										50	250	300	444	1061	1505	2352	2224
12						30		15													72	125	
13	162	125	287			121							26	21	47		26	29	169	162	331	401	675
14	31	83	114		38	38	1		16	2	11	13				3			14	109	123	610	2106

2. SERVING OUR STUDENTS

To develop and maintain active centers of Christian fellowship for Lutheran students, so that their faith is conserved, their interest in the work of the Church is increased, and their talents directed in Christian service.

The Student Division carries on its work of serving the students of the Church in the seminaries and the colleges of the Church, in church-related colleges, in tax-supported institutions of higher learning, in privately endowed colleges and universities, in professional and technical schools and colleges.

a. Visits of Secretaries

Lutheran Institutions Visited

United Lutheran Colleges: Carthage, Gettysburg, Hartwick, Lenoir Rhyne, Marion, Midland, Muhlenberg, Newberry, Roanoke, Susquehanna, Thiel, Wagner, Waterloo, Wittenberg. *Seminaries:* Chicago, Gettysburg, Hamma, Hartwick, Northwest, Philadelphia, Saskatoon, Southern, Waterloo, Western. *Secondary Schools:* Allentown Preparatory School, Konnarock Training School, Lankenau School for Girls. *Motherhouses:* Baltimore, Philadelphia. *Hospitals:* Lankenau, Manhattan.

Other Lutheran Institutions: Colleges: Augsburg, Capital, Concordia, Gustavus Adolphus, Immanuel, Jon Bjarnason, Luther, Uppsala. *Motherhouses:* Immanuel, Milwaukee, Norwegian. *Hospitals:* Chicago-Augustana, Norwegian; Milwaukee; Brooklyn-Norwegian.

Non-Lutheran Institutions Visited

Colorado: University.

Connecticut: Hartford Seminary Foundation, Wesleyan, Yale.

Delaware: University.

Georgia: Agnes Scott, Emory, Georgia Institute of Technology, Mercer, Oglethorpe, Wesleyan.

Illinois: Aurora, Chicago, Macomb Teachers, National College of Education, Northwestern.

Indiana: Purdue, Rose Polytechnic.

Iowa: University.

Kansas: University, State, Emporia, Hays State Teachers' College.

Maryland and District of Columbia: University, George Washington, Goucher, Hood, Johns Hopkins, Naval Academy.

Massachusetts: Amherst, Boston, Harvard, Massachusetts Institute of Technology, Radcliffe, Simmons, Wellesley.

Michigan: University.

Minnesota: University.

Missouri: Park.
Nebraska: University, Wayne State Teachers' College.
New Hampshire: Dartmouth.
New Jersey: Rutgers, New Jersey, Princeton, Rider. *State Teachers' Colleges:* Newark, Trenton.
New York: Buffalo, Cornell, Rochester, Russell Sage, Syracuse, Vassar, West Point. *State Teachers' Colleges:* Albany, Buffalo. *Metropolitan New York:* Adelphi, Art, Ballard, Barnard, Biblical Seminary, Brooklyn, College of the City of New York, Columbia, Cooper Union, Design, Fine and Applied Arts, Hunter, International House, Julliard, Long Island, Music, New, New York, New York School of Social Work, Packard, Packer, Pratt, St. Joseph, Sarah Lawrence, Teachers, Union Theological Seminary. *Hospitals:* Bellevue, Christ, City, Cornell, Fifth Avenue, Henry Street, Metropolitan, Mt. Sinai, Presbyterian, St. Luke's, Stuyvesant.
North Carolina: University, State, Women's College of the University, Appalachian, Catawba, Duke, Elon, Greensboro, Guilford, Meredith. Peace, St. Mary's.
Ohio: University, State University, Kent, Miami, Oberlin, Toledo, Western Reserve.
Oregon: University, Reed, Williamette.
Pennsylvania: University, Bucknell, L e h i g h, Pittsburgh, Temple, Albright, Beaver, Bryn Mawr, Moravian College, Moravian Seminary, Pennsylvania School of Social Work, Pennsylvania State College, Swarthmore, Ursinus, Wilson. *State Teachers' Colleges:* Bloomsburg, Clarion, East Stroudsburg, Indiana, Kutztown, Lock Haven, Millersville, Shippensburg, West Chester.
Rhode Island: Brown.
South Carolina: University, Clemson, Winthrop. Converse, Furman, Greenville, Wofford.
Tennessee: University, Chattanooga, King, Vanderbilt.
Texas: Rice.
Virginia: University, Polytechnic Institute, Emory and Henry, Intermont, Randolph Macon, Staunton, Sweet Briar, Washington and Lee, William and Mary.
Washington: University.
Wisconsin: University, Beloit, Carroll, Lawrence, Ripon. *State Teachers' Colleges:* LaCrosse, Oshkosh, Platteville.
West Virginia: University, Fairmont.
Canada: Manitoba, Ontario, Saskatchewan, Toronto.

b. Congregations in Educational Centers

A principle of work among students is that the congregation in the college community is responsible for the Christian welfare of students.

The pastors of 250 congregations in the educational centers of the United States and Canada are listed. Most of these pastors are rendering some service to students in universities, colleges, and professional schools. To these pastors the *Board of Education* gives guidance by occasional Service Bulletins, through directions for work, and through printed material for students. Pastors seeking personal assistance are helped by the visits and correspondence of secretaries of the board. To fifteen pastors or congregations in which the financial situation is such that the work with students cannot be carried on without some assistance the Board makes annual grants. For six pastors small expense items have been carried. The board makes possible work among students in metropolitan centers— Boston, New York, Syracuse, Philadelphia, Chicago. But the vast majority of pastors and congregations minister to students as a Christian privilege.

DIRECTORY OF PASTORS IN EDUCATIONAL CENTERS:

Alabama

G. H. C. Park......................Birmingham ....Birmingham Southern College

Arizona

Tucson ....University of Arizona

California

E. A. Trabert......................Berkeley ....University of California
Clifford B. Holand ....Los Angeles ....University of California
John E. Hoick ....Los Angeles ....University of Southern California
Henry Irving Kohler ....Los Angeles ....Junior College
James Beasom ....Glendale ....Glendale Junior College
                                        Fresno ....Fresno State College
F. C. Pryor ....Oakland ....Mills College
George H. Hillerman .....Pasadena ....Institute of Technology
W. C. Miller ....Redlands ....University of Redlands
D. L. Dyreson ....San Diego ....San Diego State College
J. Edward Oslund ....San Francisco ....San Francisco State College
W. E. Crouser ....San Jose ....San Jose State College
E. T. May ....Santa Barbara ....Santa Barbara State College

Colorado

E. E. Habig ....Boulder ....University of Colorado
R. B. Wolf ....Colorado Springs ....Colorado College
E. W. Harner ....Denver ....University of Denver

Connecticut

Herbert D Dichsen ....Hartford ....Hartford Foundation
Robert Heidenreich ....Middletown ....Wesleyan University
F. W. Schaefer ....New Britain ....Teachers of Connecticut
Berhend E. Mehrtens ....New Haven ....Yale University

District of Columbia

Frances Dysinger, Sec.....Washington ....All Universities and Colleges
O. F. Blackwelder ....Washington ....George Washington University
S. H. Kornmann ....Washington ....University of Maryland

Florida

Chauncey R. Botsford ....Deland ....Stetson University
J. C. Derrick ....Lakeland ....Florida Southern College
P. G. McCullough ....Miami ....University of Miami

Theodore K. Finck ....St. Petersburg ....St. Petersburg Junior College
G. F. Snyder ....Tampa ....University of Tampa

Georgia
J. L. Yost ....Atlanta ....Emory University and Other Colleges
H. G. Fisher ....Macon ....Mercer University and Wesleyan

Illinois
Charles Landwere ....Carthage ....Carthage College
Dwight P. Bair ....Champaign ....University of Illinois
Charles W. Kegley, Jr....Chicago ....All Universities and Colleges
C. E. Paulus ....Chicago ....Chicago University
C. A. Naumann ....Evanston ....Northwestern University
I. O. Miller ....Aurora ....Aurora College
C. I. Empson ....Decatur ....James Millikin University
T. B. Hersch ....East St. Louis ....Park Air School
R. R. Frobenius ....Elmhurst ....Elmhurst College
Kenneth Knudsen ....Macomb ....Western Illinois State Teachers
W. L. Wilson ....Peoria ....Bradley Polytechnic Institute
O. G. Beckstrand ....Rockford ....Rockford College
G. J. Curran ....Wheaton ....Wheaton College
D. R. Kabele ....Wilmette ....National College of Education

Indiana
H. C. Stolldorf ....Lafayette ....Purdue University
L. T. Riley ....Evansville ....Evansville College
P. M. Brosy ....Goshen ....Goshen College
A. K. Trout ....Indianapolis ....Butler University
Arthur L. Mahr ....Indianapolis ....Professional Schools
L. H. Wyandt ....Muncie ....Ball State Teachers' College
H. R. Ogle ....North Manchester ....Manchester College
C. F. Koch ....Richmond ....Earlham College
George Aigner ....Terre Haute ....Rose Polytechnic and Teachers
P. W. Schrope ....Valparaiso ....Valparaiso Universty

Iowa
Ralph Krueger ....Iowa City ....State University of Iowa
Henry Scherer ....Cedar Rapids ....Coe College
J. A. Miller ....Davenport ....Palmer School of Osteopathy
F. J. Weertz ....Des Moines ....Drake University
M. E. Lesher ....Dubuque ....University of Dubuque
W. F. Rex ....Fairfield ....Parsons College
A. B. Schwertz ....Sioux City ....Morningside College

Kansas
C. A. Puls ....Lawrence ....University of Kansas
W. E. Wheeler ....Atchison ....St. Benedict's and Other Colleges
O. W. Ebright ....Emporia ....State Teachers' and College of Emporia
W. H. Moeller ....Hays ....Ft. Hays Kansas State
(Augustana) ....Manhattan ....Kansas State College
B. R. Lantz ....Salina ....Kansas Wesleyan University
A. J. Beil ....Topeka ....Washburn College
E. E. Stauffer ....Wichita ....Friends and Municipal Universities

Kentucky
H. C. Lindsay ....Louisville ....University of Louisville

Maryland
Leon N. Zahn ....Baltimore ....Johns Hopkins University
R. D. Clare ....Baltimore ....Goucher College
J. F. Fife ....Baltimore ....State Teachers (Towson)
A. J. Traver ....Frederick ....Hood College

W. V. Simon .... Frostburg .... State Teachers
H. H. Spangler .... Lutherville .... Maryland College
P. W. Quay .... Westminster .... Western Maryland College

Massachusetts

Norman D. Goehring ....Boston .... Harvard and Boston Univer-
                                                                                      sities and Other Colleges

Michigan

H. O. Yoder .... Ann Arbor .... University of Michigan
H. J. Fennig .... Battle Creek .... Battle Creek College
C. J. Rockey .... Detroit .... Wayne University
                                          Detroit .... Other Colleges
R. J. White .... Grand Rapids .... Calvin College
J. F. Eshbaugh .... Hillsdale .... Hillsdale College
C. E. Jensen .... Kalamazoo .... Western State Teachers and
                                                                                      Kalamazoo
Axel Larson .... Lansing .... Michigan State College

Minnesota

C. A. Wendell
   (Augustana) .... Minneapolis .... University of Minnesota
Frank H. Clutz .... St. Paul .... Hamline and Macalester
H. E. Reinhart .... Duluth .... State Teachers College
F. W. Ihlenfeld .... Winona .... State Teachers College

Mississippi

J. W. Mangum .... Jackson .... Bellhaven and Millsaps

Missouri

Andreas Bard .... Kansas City .... University and Other
                                                                                      Colleges
F. F. Mueller .... St. Louis .... Washington University and
                                                                                      Other Colleges
Marvin Reichert .... Cape Giradeau .... Southeast State Teachers

Montana

L. C. Cloninger .... Billings .... Billings Polytechnic
                                                                                      Institute

Nebraska

F. C. Wiegman .... Fremont .... Midland College
R. E. Rangeler .... Lincoln .... University of Nebraska
F. C. Schuldt .... Hastings .... Hastings College
W. H. Traub .... Omaha .... Creighton and Omaha
                                                                                      Universities
W. C. Heidenreich .... Wayne .... Nebraska State Teachers
W. F. Most .... Wayne .... Nebraska State Teachers
Blaine Simon .... York .... York College

New Jersey

A. H. Holthusen .... New Brunswick .... Rutgers University and New
                                                                                      Jersey College for Women
Edmund A. Steimle .... Jersey City .... Normal School and Other
                                                                                      Colleges
Edmund A. Steimle .... Princeton .... Princeton University
P. T. Warfield .... Trenton .... State Teachers and Rider
                                                                                      Colleges

New Mexico

W. F. Martin .... Albuquerque .... University of New Mexico

New York

Frank L. Gollnick .... Oneonta ...,...................... Hartwick College and State
                                                                                      Normal
Frederick Sutter .... Staten Island .... Wagner College
C. E. Frontz .... Albany .... N. Y. State Teachers
P. E. Schmidt .... Brooklyn .... Pratt Institute
H. J. Pflum .... Buffalo .... University of Buffalo and
                                                                                      Other Colleges
C. E. Eichner .... Elmira .... Elmira College
E. T. Horn .... Ithaca .... Cornell University
Mildred E. Winston. Sec..New York City .... All Institutions

R. J. Olson (Counsellor)..New York City, 600 West
                               122d Street ....Columbia University
Wm. H. Davies ....New York City ....New York University
Wm. J. Villaume ....New York City ....Hunter College
F. J. Baum ....Poughkeepsie ....Vassar College
F. R. Knubel ....Rochester ....Rochester University and
                                                                         Other Colleges
H. D. Shimer ....Schenectady ....Union College
Rollin G. Shaffer, Sec.....Syracuse, Hendricks
                                 Chapel ....Syracuse University
L. H. Grandy ....Troy ....Rensselaer Polytechnic and
                                                                         Russell Sage College

North Carolina

J. D. Mauney ....Hickory ....Lenoir Rhyne College
Henry A. Schroder ....Chapel Hill ....University of North
                                                                         Carolina
E. F. Troutman ....Boone ....Appalachian State Teachers
J. F. Crigler ....Charlotte ....Queens-Chicora College
H. A. Schroeder ....Durham ....Duke University
C. E. Fritz ....Greensboro ....Woman's College of U. of
                                                                         North Carolina
F. L. Conrad ....High Point ....High Point College
C. E. Norman ....Raleigh ....State and Meredith Colleges
                                 Salisbury ....Catawba College
S. W. Hahn ....Winston-Salem ....Salem College

Ohio

Carl W. Shanor ....Springfield ....Wittenberg College
E. Clyde Xander ....Springfield ....Wittenberg College
E. R. Walborn ....Columbus ....Ohio State University
G. D. Busch ....Athens ....Ohio University
C. L. Stager ....Ada ....Ohio Northern University
Franklin C. Fry ....Akron ....University of Akron
S. D. Myers ....Alliance ....Mt. Union College
A. H. Smith ....Ashland ....Ashland College
Walter Charlesworth ......Bowling Green ....Bowling Green State
                                                                         University
H. L. Meister ....Cincinnati ....University of Cincinnati
A. M. Lutton ....Cincinnati ....Other Colleges
Joseph Sittler, Jr. ....Cleveland ....Western Reserve and Case
Dana Johnson ....Dayton ....University of Dayton
B. F. Hofer ....Defiance ....Defiance College
John R. Himes ....Marion ....Ohio Wesleyan University
                                                                         (Delaware)
J. L. Urich ....Elyria ....Oberlin College (Oberlin)
H. Ward Grieb ....Findlay ....Findlay College
M. W. Wappner ....Kent ....Kent State University
W. L. Spielman ....Marietta ....Marietta College
W. M. Brandt ....Newark ....Denison University
                                                                         (Granville)
W. O. Kantner ....Tiffin ....Heidelburg College
W. W. Larson ....Toledo ....University of Toledo
P. J. Renz ....West Middletown ....Miami University and
                                                                         Western (Oxford)
P. S. Kelly ....Wooster ....College of Wooster

Oklahoma

                                 Stillwater ....Oklahoma College
F. H. Bloch ....Oklahoma City ....Oklahoma City University
                                 Tulsa ....University of Tulsa

Oregon

F. S. Beistel ....Eugene ....University of Oregon
L. R. Nielson ....LaGrande ....Eastern Oregon Normal
                                                                         School
W. F. Brinkman ....Portland ....Reed College
P. W. Eriksen ....Salem ....Willamette University

Pennsylvania

H. P. C. Cressman ....Allentown ....Muhlenberg College
D. F. Putman ....Gettysburg ....Gettysburg College

W. E. Eisenberg .... Greenville ....Thiel College
D. C. Baer .... Selinsgrove ....Susquehanna University
R. H. Gearhart .... Philadelphia ....University of Pennsylvania
                                                                and Other Colleges
M. R. Kunkelman .... Wilkinsburg ....University of Pittsburgh,
                                                                Carnegie Institute and
                                                                Other Colleges
J. F. Harkins .... State College ....Pennsylvania State College
N. S. Wolf ....Bloomsburg ....State Teachers College
F. C. Snyder .... Clarion ....State Teachers College
A. J. Pfohl .... Indiana ....State Teachers College
Carlton Heckman .... Kutztown ....State Teachers College
C. J. Stein .... Lock Haven ....State Teachers College
Ellerslie A. Lebo .... Millersville ....State Teachers College
W. W. Barkley .... Shippensburg ....State Teachers College
J. S. Kistler .... Stroudsburg ....State Teachers College
J. H. K. Miller .... West Chester ....State Teachers College
J. M. Patterson .... Annville ....Lebanon Valley College
A. C. Kanzinger .... Ardmore ....Haverford College
J. R. Booth .... Beaver Falls ....Geneva College
G. F. Gehr .... Bethlehem ....Moravian Colleges
Corson C. Snyder .... Bethlehem ....Lehigh University
H. B. Stock ...., Carlisle ....Dickinson College
C. A. Neal .... Chambersburg ....Wilson College and Penn
                                                                Hall
H. A. Weaver .... Chester ....Pennsylvania Military
                                                                Academy
W. O. Fegley .... Collegeville ....Ursinus College
                          Easton ....Lafayette College
Frank Croman .... Elizabethtown ....Elizabethtown College
E. L. Manges .... Huntingdon ....Juniata College
Kenneth Otten .... Philadelphia ....Beaver College (Jenkin-
                                                                town)
E. J. Hoh .... Lancaster ....Franklin and Marshall
                                                                College
Vernon D. Naugle .... Lewisburg ....Bucknell University
R. A. Kline .... Meadville ....Allegheny College
L. S. Sweitzer .... Reading ....Albright College
H. B. Ernest .... Washington ....Washington and Jefferson
                                                                College

South Carolina

E. B. Keisler .... Newberry ....Newberry College
Palmer P. Pierce .... Columbia ....University of South
                                                                Carolina
K. W. Kinard .... Columbia ....Columbia College
G. J. Gongaware .... Charleston ....College of Charleston and
                                                                The Citadel
J. E. Stockman .... Greenville ....Furman University and
                                                                Greenville College
H. S. Petrea .... Rock Hill ....Winthrop College
D. B. Wertz .... Spartanburg ....Converse and Wofford
                                                                Colleges
B. M. Clark .... Walhalla ....Clemson College

Tennessee

A. M. Huffman .... Knoxville ....University of Tennessee
H. A. McCullough, Jr.....Chattanooga ....University of Chattanooga
L. A. Wertz .... Greeneville ....Tusculum College
V. D. Derrick .... Memphis ....Southwestern Teachers
I. W. Gernert .... Nashville ....Vanderbilt University, Pea-
                                                                body Teachers and Other
                                                                Colleges
Texas

F. W. Kern .... Austin ....University of Texas
N. H. Kern ....Dallas ....Southern Methodist
                                                                University
A. H. Schnake .... El Paso ....School of Mines
Donald Elder .... Houston ....Rice Institute
J. F. Vorkoper .... San Antonio ....Westmoorland College

Virginia

C. A. Honeycutt .... Marion ....Marion College
                          Salem ....Roanoke College

John Schmidt .... Blacksburg .... Virginia Polytechnic Institute

Bristol .... Sullins and Va. Intermont Colleges

A. J. Shumate .... Harrisonburg .... State Teachers College

R. T. Troutman .... Lexington .... Washington and Lee University and Virginia Military Institute

M. L. Minnich .... Lynchburg .... Randolph Macon, S w e e t Briar and Lynchburg Colleges

C. T. Neas .... Radford .... State Teachers College

J. J. Scherer .... Richmond .... University of Richmond and Other Colleges

J. L. Sieber .... Roanoke .... Hollins College

R. D. Wood .... Staunton .... Staunton Military Academy and Mary Baldwin College

Washington

O. A. Bremer .... Seattle .... University of Washington

Bellingham .... Western Washington College of Education

W. I. Guss .... Spokane .... Whitworth College and Gonzaga

H. N. Svinth .... Tacoma .... College of Puget Sound

West Virginia

W. R. Hashinger .... Morgantown .... West Virginia University

W. P. Cline .... Charleston .... Kanawha and Other Colleges

A. F. Richardson .... Davis .... Davis and Elkin College

H. L. Hahn .... Fairmont .... Fairmont Teachers

Carl R. Plack .... Huntington .... Marshall College

J. H. Fray .... Shepherdstown .... Shepherd State Teachers

Wisconsin

E. J. Blenker .... Madison .... University of Wisconsin

D. E. Bosserman .... Appleton .... Lawrence College

F. A. Berg .... Beloit .... Beloit College

H. N. Stoffel .... LaCrosse .... State Tachers

J. F. Fedders .... Milwaukee .... Milwaukee-Downer and State Teachers

A. A. Zinck .... Milwaukee .... Marquette University

E. R. Wicklund .... Oshkosh .... State Teachers

R. R. Doering .... Platteville .... State Teachers

A. C. Riggle .... Superior .... State Teachers

I. R. Kraemer .... Waukesha .... Carroll College

Wyoming

Leland C. Soker .... Laramie .... University of Wyoming

Canada

Henry Hodel .... Saskatoon, Sask. .... Lutheran College and Seminary

C. S. Roberts .... Waterloo, Ontario .... Waterloo College and Seminary

Reinhold Krisch .... Edmondton, Alberta .... University of Alberta

A. Grunwald .... Toronto, Ontario .... Toronto University and Other Colleges

Winnipeg, Manitoba .... University of Manitoba

In any educational center where there is no United Lutheran pastor, the staff co-operates as far as possible with pastors of other Lutheran Synods.

c. Work in Certain Student Centers

Boston

Since 1925 the Rev. Norman D. Goehring, D.D. has served as pastor for students, now under the joint auspices of the Board of Education of The

United Lutheran Church and the United Lutheran Synod of New York. He ministers to students attending Harvard, Radcliffe, Massachusetts Institute of Technology, Simmons, Wellesley and all the other universities, colleges, and professional schools in the area. His continuous service is exceeded by that of only one other church worker among students in the area.

During the academic year 1936-37 the United Lutheran Synod of New York engaged in the task of raising funds to build a chapel on the valuable property in the heart of the new housing development of Harvard University. Sufficient in cash and pledges was raised to pay the property indebtedness of $42,000, to enlarge and recondition the present Parish House, and to furnish a substantial start for the Chapel.

A congregation of about 150 members, most of them professional people, now stabilizes and strengthens the University Lutheran Association of more than 100 active students. The 250 Lutheran students in the Boston area number many doing graduate work, and represent more states and countries as well as a greater variety of synodical bodies proportionately than any other one student center.

The Lutheran Student Council of students from seven different institutions co-operates closely with the Church Board. This makes the administrative aspect of the Association an important part of the Christian life of the students. One of the results has been most generous financial contributions from the students. A weekly discussion meeting supplements the regular morning service of worship, which more than taxes the limited capacity of the Parish House. A well-balanced program has helped to create a loyalty that continues in the relationships and support of Lutheran alumni.

Numerous invitations f r o m t h e administrations of institutions in Greater Boston and in New England where the Lutheran Church is not known, bring Dr. Goehring before large groups of students. In that way he has become an influence in the Student Christian Movement and has gained for the University Lutheran Student Association a noteworthy significance.

New York City

During the biennium the work in New York City has continued under the direct personal supervision of the staff. This method begun in 1931 is part of Miss Winston's responsibility.

Constant touch has been maintained with forty-one different institutions ranging from universities and colleges to the smaller professional, arts, and vocational schools. On ten campuses there are organized Lutheran Student Associations. The Lutheran S t u d e n t Association of Greater New York, of which Miss Winston is the adviser, unites in fellowship and service the members of these groups, including the Lutheran Nurses' Guild. This makes possible a youth group in the Church with which students on the smaller campuses may become associated. The Lutheran Nurses' Guild is composed of young women from about twenty different hospitals and training schools. The Guild holds a communion service every Ash Wednesday.

The Lutheran Church is the only Protestant Church which has an inclusive program for all students in New York City. This is made possible through the co-operation of several congregations and numerous individuals.

Columbia University. During the first semester of 1936-37 pastoral work with the men students was done by the Rev. R. F. Auman of Scarsdale. In 1937-38 the board re-established its secretary-fellowship for personal and organizational work on the campus. It was held with much success by Mr. Russel J. Olson of Iowa, a graduate of Carthage College and a middler at Union Theological Seminary. By action of the Board of Religious Work of Columbia University in April, 1938, the holder of the secretary-fellowship is known as Associate Counsellor for Protestant Students, to work with the Chaplain of the University through the Counsellor for Protestant Students. Lutheran student life in New York City has suffered a great loss in the death of Dr. A. Steimle. Dr. Steimle, as pastor of the Church of the Advent, was designated by the Board of Education as pastor for students at Columbia University in 1920. Advent Church continues as the student center for Columbia students through the services of worship and the Sunday evening meetings directed by Sister Pearle Lyerly and Mr. Olson.

New York University Lutheran Student Association has been recognized by the student senate of the University. This recognition facilitates the organizational work of the Association and will make possible a greater number of personal contacts. Holy Trinity Church, through the associate pastor, the Rev. W. H. Davies, sponsors the New York University Association.

Hunter College has distinct associations at its three branches. They are sponsored by professors—Miss Dorothea Hess, Dr. Helene Hartung, Miss Henrietta Tichy. The Hunter Lutheran Student Association meets monthly and unites the three branch organizations and the Alumna Club. St. James' Church, Dr. Charles Trexler, pastor, gave the association the use of its edifice for meetings.

Wagner College through its student religious council is active in the Lutheran Student Association. In March, 1938, the campus entertained the Nineteenth Annual Conference of the Lutheran Student Association of the North Atlantic Region. President Stoughton, Professor Hinman, and Mr. Alfred Schroeder, who was also president of the metropolitan association, were the hosts.

The co-operation of various groups is invaluable to the work of the board. *The Board of Education of the United Lutheran Synod of New York* through its student committee has taken a personal interest in student life. *The Women's Missionary Society* of the Synod contributes through the general treasury of the Women's Missionary Society to Miss Winston's salary for work done on its territory. This is in addition to the taking of the census and placing on its synodical, conference, and local programs the presentation of the interests of the board.   The *Lutheran Women's League* assists the local Lutheran Student Association financially. The recently organized *Friends of Lutheran Students* is an independent group composed of pastors and laymen from several synodical bodies. The group co-operates with the Board and with the Lutheran Student Association.

Pioneer work among Lutheran students in New York began in 1912. Since 1918 the board has united the interests of pastors and laymen in working with approximately 2,000 students yearly who come from many foreign countries and from every Lutheran synodical body in America.

Syracuse

A secretary-fellowship was established at Syracuse University in September, 1937, in co-operation with the United Lutheran Synod of New York and the Syracuse Lutheran Ministers' Association. Notice of the fellowship was sent to United Lutheran colleges in the East and to a selected list of other colleges and universities. From the applicants Mr. Rollin Shaffer of St. Mark's Church, Williamsport, Pa., was selected. Mr. Shaffer, a graduate of Muhlenberg College in 1937, is majoring in English. He has charge of the work with 203 Lutheran students on the campus, all of whom he knows. He has conducted Lutheran worship and discussion groups every week in one or another of the Lutheran churches of Syracuse or on the campus. He has appeared in a number of churches and in the university chapel. He co-operates with the campus Christian work under the direction of Dean William H. Powers and is listed as one of the staff with privileges of the university connected with that position. His activity has received favorable comment from the pastors in Syracuse and from the university.   It is expected that Mr. Shaffer will continue in this work for at least another year.

Philadelphia

The Rev. Robert H. Gearhart, D.D., pastor for students in Philadelphia since 1922, has rendered the longest uninterrupted service in the student field of the United Lutheran Church. His work is backed influentially and financially ($3,752 during the biennium) by a local committee of laity and clergy which has functioned since 1908. The Ministerium of

Pennsylvania and the East Pennsylvania Synod some years ago purchased an admirable house for the student pastor's residence and have annually during the biennium given grants of $900 and $500 respectively. The salary of $2,500 is paid by the Board of Education.

The Lutheran student population of Philadelphia is 1,647. Of this number 210 spend the week-ends in their homes and 870 are commuting students. More than 900 students are reached by Dr. Gearhart.

At the University of Pennsylvania Pastor Gearhart is associated with the student pastors of five other communions. The Christian Association building, to which Philadelphia Lutherans made liberal contributions, provides excellent headquarters. In it the fifth and sixth successful annual metropolitan conferences of Lutheran students were held in 1936 and 1937.

On three other campuses Pastor Gearhart has maintained regular hours for counselling. As a partial result nine students were led to seek confirmation in their home congregations.

In discussion groups held on various campuses Dr. Gearhart has presented his own material under the general head—*What Constitutes A Christian?* Three themes have been comprehensively considered: *The Difference Between Christianity and Other Religions, The Positive Program of Jesus, What is the Meaning and Value of the Creeds?* More than one hundred students have been regular in their attendance.

Student deputation groups, forty-two in number, in which thirty-two students participated, have visited churches and young people's societies, speaking to the theme, *What My Faith Means to Me.* The regular Sunday evening group centered their attention on the Sermon on the Mount.

Approximately twenty congregations have co-operated with Dr. Gearhart in his work with students during the past academic year.

At Temple University, in addition to consultation hours and calling, there have been engagements by request of the administration and Holy Communion has been celebrated during Holy Week.

Work among the alumni has resulted in the circulating by Dr. Gearhart of recent books with a religious message. This recently initiated plan has been enjoyed by sixty-three alumni and will be continued and developed.

Chicago

Work among Lutheran students in the Chicago area has been a concern of the Board of Education for fifteen years or more. The board promoted such efforts as the pastors of congregations nearest the great universities could carry on by giving them annually modest grants-in-aid.

In the fall of 1934 the board asked Mr. Charles W. Kegley, then a middler at Chicago Seminary and a graduate student at Northwestern University, to work with students on that campus. Mr. Kegley's interest and contact with students on other campuses grew until in November, 1934, and March, 1935, he helped conduct successful conferences for students. When the Metropolitan Student Council was organized in October, 1935, Mr. Kegley was elected active adviser. Through this Council made up of representatives of graduate and professional schools, universities and colleges, arts and business schools and schools of nursing, Mr. Kegley has been able to reach in one way or another 2,100 registered Lutheran students. The Council holds regular metropolitan conferences and has acted as hosts in November, 1935, and November, 1937, to the Hub Region of the L. S. A. A.

The Rev. Charles W. Kegley at its regular meeting in June, 1938, was designated by the board as the pastor of students in the Chicago area. The Illinois Synod has officially voted its enthusiastic co-operation and financial support by the allocation of $900 per year. The Chicago Conference of the Women's Missionary Society have been helpful in their co-operation. The Friends of Lutheran Students is a fellowship of individuals of various Lutheran bodies who by personal interest and gifts are valuable assistants not only in working with students but in awakening the Church to the needs of students.

The students from all parts of the country and all bodies of the Lutheran Church are registered at 135 institutions including technical schools. An excellent work has been begun among students in schools of nursing, numbering forty-eight. With able leadership provided from Augustana Hospital and the Lutheran Deaconess Hospital, an active Lutheran Nurses' Guild has been functioning for several years. A Lutheran Alumni Association has been formed.

The scattered students are reached by printed material, conferences, and calls. On a number of campuses, notably Northwestern and Chicago Universities, a regular program of meetings for study and fellowship is carried on. At Northwestern and at Chicago Universities Pastor Kegley is a regular member of the Religious Council.

City pastors and students who are local residents help Pastor Kegley find church homes for the students. Concordia Church, the Rev. Carl Lund-Quist, pastor, and Wicker Park Church, the Rev. Charles Leslie Venable, pastor, have held special student vespers.

Pastor Kegley has accepted numbers of invitations from administrative officers and students to speak on local campuses. He has also been the guest speaker at church youth group meetings. He has been called upon to talk over the radio and to arrange for student speakers, two of whom were Lutherans.

The Chicago area with its varied types of institutions, its diversified student groups, its many Lutheran congregations, offers a magnificent opportunity for a co-operative project in student service.

Madison, Wisconsin

The Rev. Edward J. Blenker was called in August, 1937, by the Board of Education as pastor for students at the University of Wisconsin. Mr. Blenker is a graduate of the Northwestern Seminary in 1936. He acted as pastor for Luther Memorial Church between the resignation of the Rev. C. J. Rockey, D.D., in the fall of 1936 and the arrival of the Rev. Edwin Moll, D.D., in the fall of 1937. Rev. Blenker has inaugurated well-planned and intensive work with students under an agreement satisfactory to the pastor and church council of Luther Memorial, to the Board of American Missions and the Board of Education.

Of the 1,700 students registered as Lutheran at the University of Wisconsin, about half are of the Missouri Synod and are well cared for by a pastor with an excellent chapel and student headquarters. The other students belong to American, Augustana, Danish and Norwegian Synod congregations as well as to United Lutheran Church congregations. Pastor Blenker has brought about what promises to be a constructive and creative co-operation with the pastors of these synods in Madison. Of this co-operation an integrated program during the summer session of the University was the first concrete evidence.

The Northwest Synod and the Wisconsin Conference have encouraged the resumption of aggressive work among students by renewed interest and a small grant toward expenses. Rev. Blenker has been invited to present the cause to a number of church groups.

As a member of the University Religious Council, Pastor Blenker had a place in the planning of the Preaching Mission at the University of Wisconsin in February, 1938. The Mission held under the auspices of the Federal Council of Churches and the Council of Church Boards of Education brought to the campus Mary E. Markley, of the staff of the Board of Education and Dr. Conrad Hoffman, of world-wide reputation. once a member and worker with students in Luther Memorial congregation. Both guests were introduced to the Lutheran students in a planned and cumulative program.

The regular procedure of developing a student cabinet or council has been followed with a corresponding emphasis upon student stewardship of service and money. Leadership for the Hub Region of the L. S. A. A. has come from the group and the group will entertain the next regional conference. Sunday evening fellowship hour is followed by a worship and study period. A Lutheran Graduate Club of unusual promise has been formed. Data on alumni and plans for enlisting their active interest and service are being sought. Systematic calling in university and local residences and particularly in the Infirmary have helped bring more than fifty students into guest membership at Luther Memorial. Two students were instructed and confirmed.

The University of Wisconsin enrolls students from every section of the United States and from every body of Lutherans. It offers a great challenge for careful and constructive work with students of our church.

d. Co-operative Activities and Contacts

The Church can minister to students effectively only with the understanding co-operation of auxiliaries, boards, and synods.

With the Synods

Every synod has been requested and urged to have a committee on work with students. With such a committee the staff tries to keep in touch through occasional meetings when visiting on the territory and through correspondence. From year to year more synods see the possibility and necessity for such a committee.

The sense of responsibility toward the student youth of the Church can be noted in the fact that sixteen synods have made grants for work among students on their territory: Illinois, Indiana, Iowa, Michigan, Midwest, Nebraska, New York, North Carolina, Northwest, Ohio, Pacific, Ministerium of Pennsylvania, East Pennsylvania, Susquehanna, South Carolina, Virginia.

With the Augustana Synod

With the formation of the United Lutheran Church the Augustana Synod requested that it "be permitted to continue to assist in the support of religious work among Lutheran students at the different state universities, and that this work at the Minnesota State University be assigned to the Augustana Synod." (Minutes of U. L. C. A., 1918, p. 50.) This request was referred to the Board of Education and was granted.

The Augustana Synod has always had an official representative on the Board of Education, usually the president of the synod. The Rev. G. A. Brandelle, D.D., served for years. President P. O. Bersell is the present representative.

An annual appropriation to the support of work among students has been made by the Augustana Synod. Beginning at $2,000, the maximum of $3,000 was reached in 1926. Since then smaller appropriations were made.

The Augustana Synod has recognized the secretaries of the Board of Education as representing it in work with students and has accorded them every facility and courtesy. The secretaries have served Augustana students in twenty-one centers in thirteen states and the printed material of the board was widely used among Augustana students. The board appreciates the fine spirit of co-operation on the part of the Augustana Synod, both personal and financial, and trusts that it may continue.

With the Luther League

Reports from student pastors show that in a number of places the Luther League is the organization through which work with students is carried on. Much printed material in the field of Christian guidance published by the board has been used by the Luther League. Mr. Harry continues as educational secretary and editor of the *Topics Quarterly* of the Luther League.

With the Women's Missionary Society

Because the Women's Missionary Society in 1918 saw the advantage of doing its promotional work among college women through a secretary for women students on the staff of the Board of Education, The United Lutheran Church has the distinction of being the first church which brings to college women, through one staff agency, the complete challenge of the church.

In 1922 Miss Markley became a member of the candidate committee, and in 1924 the chairman. Until 1938 she remained the chairman of the enlarged personnel committee which is charged with finding young women qualified for specific positions. With Miss Winston she continues a member of the personnel committee which presents to the executive board of the Women's Missionary Society young women fitted for appointments by the Board of American Missions and by the Board of Foreign Missions.

Miss Markley and Miss Winston, through official membership or special appointment in the educational department and sub-committees keep in touch with the executive board of the Women's Missionary Society. As guest speakers at missionary conventions they emphasize the inherent relation of Christian higher education and the progress of the Church at home and abroad.

The direct contact of the board with the Women's Missionary Society is through the two women who are named as advisory members to the Board of Education and who are voting members of its committee on student work. To the Board of Education the Women's Missionary Society has been making an annual grant since 1920. The Women's Missionary Societies of the Synod of New York and of the Ministerium of Pennsylvania provide a share of this grant.

Through a student secretary in every s y n o d i c a l and conference Women's Missionary Society since 1919 an annual census of students has been taken by the board. In the taking of this census a number of the synods now co-operate through the standing committee on students. For the academic year 1937-38, 9,402 students were reported, belonging to 1,682 congregations. These names are valuable to pastors and to the staff in making contact with students. But the most valuable service rendered by the seventy women who act as student secretaries is their part in creating a consciousness and conscience in regard to Christian higher education not only in the home congregation but in the congregation at the student center.

With the Inner Mission Board

The Board of Education has always considered student nurses as part of the general student group and pastors have included them in their work. Inner Mission pastors in some metropolitan centers have ministered to student and graduate nurses as they meet them in institutional activities. A joint committee of the Board of Education and of the Inner Mission Board is working on the responsibility of the Church in this field. Two pieces of printed material in editions of 20,000 have been issued with the joint imprint of the two boards.

A Guild for Lutheran Nurses,—nation-wide, to be open to all nurses of the Lutheran Church,—somewhat on the lines of the Lutheran Student Association of America, is in the forming. Such guilds are now in existence in six metropolitan centers.

With the Board of Deaconess Work

A folder on the diaconate has been published with the joint imprint of the Board of Education.

With the Board of American Missions

The Board of American Missions has direct relationship to many of the congregations through which work with students is being done. In thirty-five such congregations there are church extension loans. To thirty-five additional congregations salary grants are being made.

To twelve of these seventy congregations the Board of Education makes grants-in-aid. The amount varies in relation to size of congregation, number of students, educational strategy, and amount of time devoted to work with students by the pastor. These congregations assisted by one or both boards are situated in the cities and towns where the great state institutions are located:—California, Colorado, Illinois, Indiana, Michigan, Nebraska, North Carolina, Ohio, Oregon, South Carolina, Washington, Wyoming.

The other congregations aided by the Board of American Missions through whom smaller groups of students must be cared for are in Connecticut, Florida, Georgia, Mississippi, Missouri, Montana, Oklahoma, Tennessee, Texas, and Canada.

Obviously congregations must have proper church facilities if the students of the church are to be served. For that reason the Board of American Missions has included in its appeal the need for adequate equipment for congregations in college and university communities. For the same reason at the 1936 Convention the following action was passed:

"That the United Lutheran Church authorize the Board of Education to assist financially in the necessary building programs of parishes doing student work."

The Church has never yet adequately faced the challenge of maintaining adequate parishes in strategic educational centers. A far-reaching policy of establishing and adequately sustaining parishes in educational centers must be worked out and adopted by the Church.

In Educational Centers

At the *University of Michigan* a joint committee consisting of members of the United Lutheran congregation and of the American Lutheran congregation oversees the student work. By agreement the parish house of the American Lutheran congregation is the student center, and the pastor of the United Lutheran congregation directs the student work. Plans are being worked out between the Michigan Synod, the Student Service Commission of the American Lutheran Church, and the Board of Education for a more intensive program.

At the *University of Nebraska* a joint committee, composed of pastors and laymen, uses a local United Lutheran pastor, the Rev. Ralph E. Rangeler, on part time to make initial contacts with students, to link them with the local congregations, and to direct the activities of the Lutheran Student Association. The budget of the committee is balanced by grants from the Nebraska and Midwest Synods of the United Lutheran Church, from the Danish Synod, from the Augustana Synod, from the American Church, and from the Board of Education.

In *Oregon* pastors and laymen form the Oregon Lutheran Student Service Association which provides for individual and group membership. A pastor of the American Lutheran Church, the Rev. Wm. Schoeler, is the secretary and directs work at the State University in Eugene, at the State College in Corvallis, and at the State Teachers College in Monmouth. The Pacific Synod co-operates in this work, as does the Board of Education.

In *Los Angeles* pastors and laymen form the Luther Associates. This organization gathers funds, co-operates with the university religious conference, and through an executive committee carries on work among students. Students and pastors representing different campuses, congregations, and Lutheran bodies coordinate their activities through the Lutheran Student Association. Several successful conferences—regional and area—have been held. Several United Lutheran pastors are active advisers of student groups. The student committee of the California Synod and the Board of Education offer such personal and financial assistance as is possible.

With the Lutheran Student Association in America

This nation-wide association, organized in 1922, with a membership of students from practically every general Lutheran body, has no official affiliation with any synod. The work of the L. S. A. A. is directed by the Lutheran Student Council of America made up of representatives from the nine geographical regions and of elected advisers. Mr. Harry, who has been annually elected by the council as one of its advisers. was in 1935 elected an adviser for life. By invitation all members of the staff have been guest speakers and leaders at various regional conferences during the past biennium. Mr. Harry helped organize and conduct the national conference or Ashram held in Oconomowoc, Wisconsin, August, 1936. All members of the staff participated in the Ashram held August, 1937, at Susquehanna University, Selinsgrove, Pa. Mr. Harry and Mr. Wickey were active participants in the Ashram held at Flathead Lake, Montana, in August, 1938.

The aims of the L. S. A. A. are as follows: On every campus: To stimulate and sustain students in using the Bible privately and in groups, in prayer, in regular church attendance, and in frequent reception of Holy Communion; to encourage students in the study and appreciation of the church's message and in loyal participation in the church's work by personal activities and gifts; to develop healthy social life and strong Christian friendships; to develop a conscious need of Christ in facing modern life and problems. To hold intercollegiate conferences in order to assist students on every campus to accomplish those purposes. To build up a national and international fellowship of Lutheran students.

The L. S. A. A. continues its annual grant-in-aid for graduate study to a student in India. It also continues to assist the National Lutheran Council in its overseas work. No fellowship in the church is doing more constructive work to bring about a better understanding of the Lutheran Church and of its present and future responsibility.

With the Student Commission of the American Lutheran Conference

Since 1935 the staff has been exploring areas of co-operation and co-ordination with the Commission in the field of service to students. A number of joint meetings have been held and general agreements have been reached. The obvious co-operative privileges are in the publishing of literature and in the counselling and encouraging of the L. S. A. A. Further opportunities for co-operative work lie in educational centers where service to Lutheran students is undeveloped.

e. Items of Interest

Publications

The Beginnings of Work Among Lutheran Students by the Rev. Howard R. Gold, D.D., president of the board, is a valuable monograph which during the biennium has been widely distributed.

New Folders covering preparation and work of the ministry have been printed for use by the committees of synods.

Reprints of the most valuable of the folders and other materials used in former years have been furnished upon request to pastors ministering to students. Many other pastors have ordered material especially of the devotional type and have gladly paid the nominal costs.

The Service Bulletin was issued during the academic year 1936-37. During the past academic year its place has been taken by material germane to work with students from various sources which the board has furnished to pastors.

Work Among Alumni

College graduates are potentially the most valuable human asset of the Church. To care for students and to neglect to care for alumni and to build them into the life of the Church would be foolish. Work with alumni has gone on for many years especially through the Cornell Alumni Associations and Boston Alumni groups, which meet at least annually in several centers. There is a news service reaching them through a bulletin from the campus. Penn State has begun the same sort of news service during the biennium looking toward development of Penn State Lutheran Alumni in several centers.

Local alumni associations which include all Lutheran college graduates have been developed especially in Chicago, Milwaukee, and Los Angeles. The idea is spreading and groups are ready to organize in Berkeley, California and in Philadelphia. These groups meet several times a year to discuss problems of Christian education especially as it affects and is affected by our Church.

The Philadelphia alumni have formed a book-reading club to circulate recent books on current religious problems.

The opportunity of home-coming days is utilized by pastors and Lutheran Student Associations to keep alumni informed and interested in the work in which they had part as students. Some groups also use a news letter or a round robin.

The Board of Education has been calling special attention to the importance of work among alumni both to pastors of student groups and to pastors of our larger congregations. They are being urged to hold at least one meeting a year of their college graduates to discuss and act on problems of Christian Education in the parish and the Church especially from the point of view of college people. Several such groups have met during the biennium. The potentiality of such groups is high. College graduates have much to contribute to the local congregation and to the Church's plans for Christian Education.

The Scholarship and Loan Fund for Women

Since its beginning in 1923 the fund has assisted twenty-two young women to the amount of $6,155. Of these seven young women have gone into missionary work abroad and one is devoting herself to church work in this country. The grants-in-aid which they received have therefore been cancelled. Five young women have paid back their loans amounting to $925.00. One of these young women occupies an important position in the Church. Two young women are repaying their loans. One young woman is under appointment by the Board of Foreign Missions. Other outstanding loans are not yet due. Up to the present time all recipients of grants-in-aid from this fund have complied with all requirements.

3. INFORMING THE CHURCH

To keep the Church informed of educational trends and needs, so that the membership may be aroused to a sense of the Church's educational responsibility.

a. The Season for Christian Higher Education

The four Sundays after Easter, assigned by the Church for consideration of the board's work and prayer for seminaries, colleges, universities, students, is being used by a growing number of pastors. For the season of 1938, 1,125 pastors ordered the board's literature which was offered gratis. In addition, some pastors ordered folders through their colleges. The Board of Education appreciates this excellent response and believes that the members of all parishes would like to learn more about the cause of Christian education. There is a direct relation between an uninformed people and the failure of benevolence, the terrible indebtedness on the parishes, and the indifference on the part of the people of which the pastors complain. Interest is largely dependent upon information. (See Recommendation 1.)

b. Articles and Addresses

The promotional efforts of the board are not limited to one season. During the biennium the staff delivered 1,029 addresses; formal and informal, speaking at church services, church schools, Luther Leagues, synodical conferences, synods, conventions, summer assemblies, and student conferences. Every opportunity is taken to show the integration of the work of the Board of Education with the whole program of the whole Church. In addition 143 articles were written which appeared in *The Lutheran, The Parish School, Lutheran Woman's Work, Luther League Review, News Bulletin of the National Lutheran Educational Conference, The American Lutheran Student, The Lutheran Church Quarterly,* and *Christian Education.* The staff is active in securing others to write desirable articles for various papers and journals, and in editing the same.

4. FINDING THE FACTS

To make surveys and investigate phases of education for the information of the Church and as a basis for recommendations to institutions and the Church.

Facts from Figures About Students

Statistics for Lutheran students are no more easily gathered than are statistics for Lutherans in any other category. For that reason especially valuable is *A National Survey of the Religious Preferences of Students in American Colleges and Universities,* 1936-37, made by Dr. Gould Wickey as general secretary of the Council of Church Boards of Education. The Survey is printed in full in the October, 1937, issue of the magazine, *Christian Education.* That Survey has evidence of 7,599 Lutheran students at Lutheran colleges and junior colleges including Missouri Synod institutions as over against 5,502 at other Protestant colleges. In this connection note should be made of the fact that Lutheran students are being educated in Roman Catholic institutions—567 being reported.

This Survey on students has surprised many people and upset some preconceived notions. Of the colleges and universities, 91.9% replied to the inquiries made of them. In 1,171 institutions 730,632 students out of 828,071 expressed a definite religious preference—or 88.3%! Of the others only 5.5% had no preference and the institutions had no information on 6.2%. Commenting editorially on the general figures Dr. Wickey writes: "While we do not know what percentage of the students are actually members of the churches, there is every reason to believe that a large percentage of those expressing a preference are in actual affiliation with some church. On the other hand, the fact that such a large percentage of American students do express a religious preference . . . should awaken all churches to the opportunity which the campus does offer." In the case of Lutherans it is highly probable that practically all are confirmed members of the Church. The obligation of the Church to follow her members is non-debatable.

In Lutheran Institutions. The liberal arts enrolments of October, 1937, showed at fourteen United Lutheran colleges 4,743 students. At the twelve colleges of the American Lutheran Conference similar enrolments totaled 5,392. At the United Lutheran colleges 2,002 students are Lutheran; at the American Lutheran Conference colleges 3,870 students are Lutheran. The percentage of Lutheran students in the first group is forty-two and in the second group seventy-one.

At Tax-Supported Institutions. As over against 17,394 Lutheran students reported attending Independent, Catholic, Lutheran and other Protestant colleges, there are 20,945 Lutherans reported in municipal and state universities and colleges. This is naturally an under-estimate because 19% of the state and municipal institutions answered that they did not have the information on religious preferences of students. The point can be distinctly shown by the Lutheran students reported in tax supported institutions in various states. From Minnesota 3,900 are reported; from New York, 5. In the latter state no data on religious preferences is asked by the institutions. As a matter of interest the figures for Lutherans in the tax supported institutions of the states reporting most are listed: Wisconsin, 2,008; North Dakota, 1,890; Ohio, 1,277; Pennsylvania, 1,216; Michigan, 1,161; Iowa, 1,123; Illinois, 867; Washington, 856; Nebraska, 770; Indiana, 548.

Totals of Church Preference. Of prime importance is the number of students preferring the various churches. First is the Methodist with 156,423 students. The Roman Catholic with 122,786 comes next. After another big gap comes the Baptist with 99,219; Presbyterian with 88,473; Christian-Congregational with 48,354; Protestant Episcopal with 47,729; *Lutheran with 38,339;* Hebrew with 32,405. Of the total number of students covered by the Survey, the Methodists are 18.89%; the Catholic, 14.83%; the Presbyterian, 10.69%; the Lutheran, 4.61%. Dr. Wickey calls attention to the fact that these percentages are not correlated to the numerical strength of the various religious groups in the United States. In order of numbers the church groups are Roman Catholic, Baptist, Methodist, Lutheran, Hebrew, Presbyterian, Protestant Episcopal, Disciples of Christ, Eastern Orthodox, and Christian-Congregational. Instead of ranking *fourth,* the Lutheran student group ranks a poor *seventh* —4.61% against the highest per cent 18.89 Methodist.

Cultural Attitudes. So far as cultural attitudes are dependent upon higher education the Lutheran Church does not rank high. Lutherans and Hebrews (fourth and fifth in numbers) seem to give the same relative importance to higher education, as they stand seventh and eighth in numbers of reported student religious preferences.

The cultural lag in the Lutheran Church might be explained in a number of different ways: economic status, rural membership, nationalistic backgrounds and regard for the education of women. None of these seem at all a satisfying explanation when one compares the figures of Lutheran students with the baptized Lutherans of the various states. We use as our norms the figures compiled by the Rev. Edward Trail Horn III for the Lutheran World Almanac, found on page 87, Volume VIII for 1934-37. The six states (using round figures) first in baptized Lutheran membership are: Pennsylvania, 604,000; Wisconsin, 484,000; Minnesota, 483,000; Illinois, 349,000; New York, 241,000; Ohio, 240,000. By comparing the number of students with baptized membership of the Lutheran Church in these states Minnesota and Ohio have about the same index;

Wisconsin and New York; Illinois and Pennsylvania. Minnesota's ratio of students is almost twice as high as that of Pennsylvania. Obviously the inadequate reporting from a state like New York by tax supported institutions does an injustice to that state.

Comparisons and Contrasts. For the purpose of emphasis we have picked the twelve states which according to the Survey of the Council of Church Boards of Education have eleven hundred (1,100) or more Lutheran students. These students in order number Washington, 1,124; Indiana, 1,138; New York, 1,141; Nebraska, 1,316; Michigan, 1,335; North Dakota, 1,965; Iowa, 2,251; Illinois, 2,458; Wisconsin, 2,746; Ohio, 2,958; Pennsylvania, 4,185; Minnesota, 6,217. On the basis of baptized membership the Lutheran Church ranks *first* among Protestants in Pennsylvania, Wisconsin, Minnesota, Michigan, Nebraska, and North Dakota; it ranks *second* in Illinois, Ohio, Iowa; it ranks *third* in Washington; and *fourth* in New York and Indiana. No correlation is apparent on the basis of relative strength of our church in the various states.

Clearer and juster are the ratios between students and the confirmed membership of our church in the twelve states named above. In Volume VII of The Lutheran World Almanac for 1931-32 on page 383, the tables prepared by Dr. George Linn Kieffer based on the United States Census of religious bodies for 1926 give the necessary information on membership of the confirmed or those thirteen years of age and older in the various states. According to those figures (using round numbers) Pennsylvania, Wisconsin, and Minnesota stand first with 428,000—333,000, and 328,000 confirmed members. At the end of the list stand North Dakota, Indiana, Washington, with 86,000—66,000 and 17,000 confirmed members. Yet according to ratio the state of Washington stands at the top of the scale for Lutheran students. Following in order come North Dakota, Minnesota, Indiana, Iowa, Nebraska, Michigan, Illinois, Pennsylvania, Wisconsin, New York, Ohio. The actual scale ranges from .062 for Washington, .022 for North Dakota, .018 for Minnesota to .0097 for Pennsylvania, .008 for Wisconsin, .007 for New York and .0017 for Ohio. To reach the same ratio which students in the state of Washington bear to the confirmed Lutheran membership, Lutheran students in Ohio would have to be more than tripled. In Pennsylvania multiplying six times and in New York multiplying eight times would not bring the number of Lutheran students up to the ratio of the state of Washington. Even allowing for inaccuracies in the census of students, there emerges an appalling conclusion—in some states where our church is large and well established in tradition there is relatively little interest in higher education.

The incontrovertible evidence of the Survey of the Council of Church Boards of Education—an under-statement of the figures in the liberal arts schools of universities, colleges, and junior colleges—shows how much the *Church* is depending upon the *State* to give higher education to our students. The least the Church can do is to follow these student members wherever they are and to give a mandate to congregations and pastors. In 250 educational centers the United Lutheran Church has at least one congregation where students may worship and have pastoral care. Other Lutheran bodies have congregations in many additional educational centers; at least 155 pastors of other Lutheran bodies are ministering to students. In such congregations the Church has an unrivaled opportunity to make its influence felt. The lack of a congregation at a university center or the presence of a pastor who cannot meet the intellectual and spiritual needs of students, will inevitably weaken a synod and to that extent retard the growth of our church.

5. ADMINISTERING THE WORK

To direct the educational program of the Church economically, efficiently, and effectively.

a. Personnel of the Board

The following constituted the officers and membership of the board for the biennium:

Officers:
President—Rev. H. R. Gold, D.D.
Vice-President—Rev. H. H. Bagger, D.D.
Secretary—Rev. Gould Wickey, Ph.D., D.D.
Treasurer—Thomas P. Hickman.

Staff:
Executive Secretary—Rev. Gould Wickey, Ph.D., D.D.
Secretaries—Mary E. Markley, Litt.D.
        Rev. C. P. Harry, D.D.
        Mildred E. Winston, A.M.

Members:
Terms expiring 1938—Rev. G. M. Diffenderfer, D.D., Howard S. Bechtolt, L. C. Hassinger, Rev. Paul Krauss, D.D., Ralph D. Owen, Ph.D., Ed.D., Rev. W. H. Traub, D.D., LL.D., Rev. A. R. Wentz, Ph.D., D.D.
Terms expiring 1940—Rev. H. H. Bagger, D.D., Adelaide LeS. Burge, Rev. E. C. Herman, D.D., Flora Prince, Charles Steele, Rev. M. L. Stirewalt, D.D., Rev. A. A. Zinck, D.D., S.T.D.
Terms expiring 1942—O. F. H. Bert, Sc.D., Rev. Stanley Billheimer, D.D., Rev. H. J. Black, D.D., Rev. F. K. Fretz, Ph.D., D.D., Rev. H. R. Gold, D.D., Frederick Henrich, R. J. Seeger, Ph.D.

Advisory Members:
The Rev. F. H. Knubel, D.D., LL.D.—Ex-officio president, The United Lutheran Church in America.
Miss Nona Diehl and Mrs. Merle Cain — Representing the Women's Missionary Society of the United Lutheran Church.

The Board of Education expresses its deep appreciation for the services rendered by the Rev. G. M. Diffenderfer, D.D., the Rev. Paul H. Krauss, D.D., and Professor Ralph D. Owen, Ph.D.. Ed.D.. who served for two consecutive terms and are not eligible to re-election. The Church cannot adequately express its thanks to both clergy and laity who give of their time and talent freely for the sake of the work of the Kingdom.

b. Nominations of the Board

The nominations of the board for the terms which expire at this convention are the following:

Clergy	Residence	Synod	Occupation
Rev. J. L. Deaton, D.D.	Baltimore, Md.	Maryland	Ministry
Rev. A. O. Frank, D.D.	York, Pa.	Central of Pa.	Ministry
Rev. C. F. Koch, D.D.	Richmond, Ind.	Indiana	Ministry
Rev. M. L. Koolen, D.D.	Lincoln, Neb.	Midwest	Ministry
Rev. D. F. Putman, D.D.	Gettysburg, Pa.	Central of Pa.	Ministry
Rev. C. J. Rockey, D.D.	Detroit, Mich.	Michigan	Ministry
Rev. W. H. Traub, D.D.*	Omaha, Neb.	Nebraska	Ministry
Rev. A. R. Wentz, Ph.D.*	Gettysburg, Pa.	Maryland	Ministry

Lay			
J. L. Almond, Jr., Esq.	Roanoke, Va.	Virginia	Law
H. S. Bechtolt*	Chicago, Ill.	Illinois	Education
Charles Bergesen	Philadelphia, Pa.	Min. of Penna.	Business
L. C. Hassinger*	Bristol, Va.	Virginia	Business
Carl Schulz	Chicago, Ill.	Illinois	Business
J. Conrad Seegers, Ph.D	Philadelphia, Pa.	Central of Pa.	Education

* Renominations.

c. Finances of the Board

During the biennium through the apportioned benevolence, the board received $176,400, which is $12,220 more than the sum received during the previous biennium, 1934-36, but $18,924 less than the sum received during the period 1919-1921. Since most seminaries, colleges, and student centers are vitally dependent upon the financial assistance given by this board, it is plainly evident that their status and service is determined by the gifts of the Church to the cause of Christian higher education.

About 70% of the board's expenditures are in the form of grants-in-aid to institutions and student centers. During the biennium all the expenditures were distributed as follows: Administration, 5.5%, Promotion and Research, 8.4%, Student Work 27.9%, and Institutions 58.2%. Lack of adequate income is a hindrance to administrative efficiency and to larger progress in the service rendered in student work and to the colleges and seminaries. (See Recommendation 1.)

III. LUTHERAN HIGHER EDUCATION THROUGH THE FUTURE

The Lutheran Church is founded on Jesus Christ, the incarnate Word of God. Her faith, her theology, and her life are Christ-centered. Loyalty to that Word and His Name will determine the strength and power of our Church.

1. Guiding Principles

Christian in philosophy. The faith of the Church will condition the philosophy of the Church. The Christian philosophy of life includes both how to think and what to think. Christian education is more than a program of methodology; there is a body of knowledge which must be conveyed. There is a Christian view of the world: God is active in the universe fulfilling a divine plan. There is a Christian view of man: his inherent sin is acknowledged but he is judged in terms of what he may become when brought under the influence of Christ. There is a Christian view of society: only as individual units within society become changed will society be effectively changed. This philosophy of life must be woven into the warp and woof of the Church's educational program. It is not enough to criticize pagan philosophies. The Church must effectively present her own philosophy.

Personal in purpose. In contrast to the changing goals of secular education, the Lutheran Church believes the individual, child or adult, must be brought into contact with Christ through faith. This requires the response of the individual in all experiences throughout life to Jesus Christ. The development of the intellect cannot be the chief concern of education. The complete realization of personality through faith in Jesus Christ is the objective of Christian higher education.

Individual in method. Much of the mess in education is due to the attempt at mass education. Individual differences must be recognized in both student and teacher. Christian education refuses to be formalized so that the individual is forgotten.

Inclusive in students. Christianity is not conditioned by nationality, race, class, and sex. The universal command, "into all the world," has more than an evangelistic application. Education, teaching, is a prominent part of the program. Christian education must give consideration to the great mass of adults as well as to children. While the Church will offer her educational program to all peoples, she will be selective in seeking to train a leadership adequate for her tasks and responsibilities.

Comprehensive in program. The task of the Church is not to preserve the past. Preserved things are generally dead. While the Church conserves the values of the past, she is charged to deliver her message to the present,—everywhere and under all conditions. Her philosophy, her purpose, her method, her students,—all require a comprehensive program beyond that offered by secular education.

Adequate in support. Religious liberty is purchased at the price required to build a system of education equal in efficiency and more complete in program than that offered by secular education. Throughout the history of the Church it cost much to maintain Christian schools. It will cost much more to establish and maintain an educational system capable

of answering the challenge of a hostile world and responding to the
command of a divine Lord.

2. Parts of a Program

Principles and ideas must be bathed in a bath of application, says an
American philosopher. The field of this report allows for the presenta-
tion of only parts of a program to which the United Lutheran Church in
America should give serious consideration.

*Theological education more closely related to the needs of the whole
Church.* Theological seminaries prepare ministers for the whole Church
and not for any one section of it only. A united church cannot be accomplished by divisive theological factors and competing seminaries. Curricula and methods must meet the demands of the age if the ministry
is to be effective. Too long has the Church neglected to provide adequate
training of teachers, editors, foreign missionaries, home missionaries,
pastors in the rural parish, and workers, lay and clerical, in the field of
social missions. (**See Recommendation 2.**)

College education more closely integrated with the life of the Church.
The purpose of the college program should be in harmony with the life
and work of the Church. Faculty members will be active in local parishes. Teachers will be alert to present and defend the interests of the
Church. Certain departments should be called upon to make special
research of value to the Church and to render special service in the life
and work of the Church. Mention may be made of such departments as
social science, education, dramatic art, and music. (**See Recommendation 4.**)

Students more effectively served. Student work calls for more and better leaders and more adequate equipment. Lutheran students are attracted by the better equipment of other churches. In one great state
university Lutheran students were chairmen of the Methodist and Presbyterian student clubs.

Creative writing encouraged. In the faculties of the seminaries and colleges and among the pastors and church leaders are men and women
who should be encouraged and assisted in writing much needed books,
such as a Christian philosophy of life, a new apologetics and dogmatics,
a history of Lutheran world-wide missions, and the Church and the
State.

Adequate financial support assured. For new buildings, increase in
permanent funds, and payment of indebtedness, the seminaries and colleges need $10,000,000. The scholastic rating of the seminaries and colleges
has been hindered and in cases is today endangered by lack of financial
support. To assist financially in the necessary building programs of par-

ishes doing student work, and in offering more personal counselling to students, $50,000 additional per year should be available.

To carry on this work the Church allots to the Board of Education 9% of the apportioned benevolence. In 1920 it was 12%. To reduce expenditures in higher education is not a foresighted policy. Through a period of seventeen years the whole cause of education received through the unapportioned benevolence only 17.6%. If the apportioned and the unapportioned benevolence were combined, the cause of Christian education would receive about 14%. One Lutheran Church body gives 25% of its benevolence to education. The question arises: Is the United Lutheran Church in America fully conscious of its responsibility in the field of Christian higher education? *If Lutheran higher education is to be effective through the future, a much larger financial support must be assured.*

3. Recommendations
(For action, see p. 329.)

Gratefully acknowledging the help and guidance of the great Head of the Church, we submit the following recommendations for prayerful consideration:

The Necessity of Christian Higher Education

(1) That the United Lutheran Church in America call upon its pastors to keep the cause of Christian higher education ever before the membership of the Church as a vital integrating factor in the whole program of the whole Church.

The Church's Arrangements for the Training of Ministers and Teachers

(2) That the United Lutheran Church in America direct the Board of Education to review the 1932 program on the Church's arrangements for the training of ministers and teachers and consider ways and means of having all the Church's theological seminaries accredited by the American Association of Theological Schools, either by strengthening or merging institutions.

Men for the Ministry

(3) That synodical committees on Men for the Ministry be directed to give attention to the personal qualifications and education of men for the ministry rather than to the financial needs and subsidy.

The Service of Colleges to the Church

(4) That the United Lutheran Church in America call upon the synods to consider procedures by which the colleges may more constructively and co-operatively serve the Church in the field of higher education.

HOWARD R. GOLD, *President.*
GOULD WICKEY, *Secretary.*

IV. REPORT OF THE TREASURER OF THE BOARD OF EDUCATION

RECEIPTS AND DISBURSEMENTS
GENERAL FUND

July 1, 1936 *to June* 30, 1937

Cash in General Fund—July 1, 1936 .... $ 13,562.44

RECEIPTS

Apportionment, United Lutheran Church in America		$85,500.00
Contributions:		
Women's Missionary Society $2,250.00		
Augustana Synod 1,200.00		
Ministerium of Penna., West Chester.... 50.00		
Miscellaneous Parishes 207.50		
Special Contributions:		
United Lutheran Publication House 9,562.27		
From Friends 1,739.30		
	15,009.07	
Refunds	70.24	
		100,579.31
		$114,141.75

DISBURSEMENTS

Seminaries and Colleges—Regular $48,450.00		
Seminaries and Colleges—Special Seminaries 1,001.00		
Seminaries and Colleges—Special Colleges 221.50		
Student Centers 13,341.14		
Salaries—Secretaries 12,125.00		
Salaries—Stenographers 1,639.25		
Service 132.36		
Travel—Secretaries 3,543.46		
Board Members 758.72		
Others 55.89		
Rent—Office 1,200.00		
House 1,200.00		
Furniture and Fixtures 157.18		
Supplies and Stationery 260.09		
Telephone and Telegraph 299.46		
Postage and Mailing 367.72		
Printing and Publications 3,088.04		
"Going to College" 1,231.55		
Auditing 188.50		
Books and Magazines 50.19		
Dues and Fees 549.00		
Insurance 28.80		
		89,888.85

Cash in General Fund—June 30, 1937 .... $ 24,252.90

RECEIPTS AND DISBURSEMENTS
OTHER FUNDS—INCOME ACCOUNTS
July 1, 1936 to June 30, 1937

	Annuity Fund	Endowment Fund	Permanent Ministerial Education Fund	Scholar-ship and Loan Fund for Women
Balance—July 1, 1936			$ 73.14	$ 706.10
Contributions			399.00	185.00
Income on Securities	$2,911.02	$108.12	312.50	246.87
Repayment of Loans				55.00
Transfers	1,232.93			
Totals	$4,143.95	$108.12	$ 784.64	$1,192.97
Paid to Annuitants	$4,142.30			
Paid to Students			$1,061.00	$ 685.00
Transfers		$107.40		
Accrued Interest and Charges on Security Purchases	1.65	.72	14.63	.09
Totals	$4,143.95	$108.12	$1,075.63	$ 685.09
Balance—June 30, 1937			$290.99*	$ 507.88

* Represents Deficit.

ANALYSIS OF FUNDS
July 1, 1936 to June 30, 1937

	General Fund	Annuity Fund	Endowment Fund	Permanent Ministerial Education Fund	Scholar-ship and Loan Fund for Women
Balance—July 1, 1936......	$13,562.44	$63,494.89	$6,868.67	$13,322.55	$7,193.60
Receipts	100,579.31	4,341.79	108.12	824.07	486.87
	$114,141.75	$67,836.68	$6,976.79	$14,146.62	$7,680.47
Disbursements	89,888.85	4,174.16	108.12	1,075.63	685.09
Balance—June 30, 1937....	$24,252.90	$63,662.52	$6,868.67	$13,070.99	$6,995.38

RECEIPTS AND DISBURSEMENTS—GENERAL FUND
July 1, 1937 to June 30, 1938

Cash in General Fund, July 1, 1937 .... $ 24,252.90

RECEIPTS

Apportionment, United Lutheran Church in
America $90,900.00

Contributions:

Women's Missionary Society	$2,250.00	
Augustana Synod	500.00	
New York Synod	100.00	
Slovak Zion Synod	50.00	
Miscellaneous Parishes	109.00	
From Friends	1,009.50	
		4,018.50

Other Receipts:

Refunds ....$ 62.03

Sale of "Going to College"	11.99	
Lutheran Student Association	26.41	
Lutheran Survey	16.00	
	116.43	
		95,034.93
Total Receipts		$119,287.83

DISBURSEMENTS

Grants in Aid to Colleges	$32,890.00
Special Contributions to Colleges	3,012.90
Grants in Aid to Seminaries	19,200.00
Special Contributions to Seminaries	3,582.27
Bi-Lingual Training	600.00
Grants in Aid to Student Centers	15,020.80
Financial Advisory Service	207.04
Salaries, Secretaries	12,400.00
Salaries, Stenographers	1,886.12
Service, Office Equipment	177.30
Travel, Secretaries	3,895.65
Travel, Board Members	1,014.80
Travel, Others	53.00
Rent, Office	1,233.00
Rent, Home	1,200.00
Furniture and Fixtures	499.00
Supplies and Stationery	625.32
Telephone and Telegraph	274.88
Postage and Mailing	858.70
Printing and Publications	3,037.63
Magazines and Books	307.16
Auditing	186.00
Insurance	180.40
Dues and Fees	636.93
Total Disbursements	102,978.90
Cash in General Fund, June 30, 1938	$ 16,308.93

RECEIPTS AND DISBURSEMENTS
OTHER FUNDS—INCOME ACCOUNTS
July 1, 1937 to June 30, 1938

	Annuity Fund	Endowment Fund	Permanent Ministerial Education Fund	Scholarship and Loan Fund for Women
Balance—July 1, 1937			$290.99*	$ 507.88
Receipts:				
Contributions			294.33	280.00
Income on Securities	$3,140.64	$166.47	688.98	378.55
Repayment of Loans				295.00
Transfers	995.25			
Totals	$4,135.89	$166.47	$692.32	$1,461.43

Payments:

Paid to Annuitants	$4,134.24			
Paid to Students			$813.05	$ 600.00
Transfers		$166.14		
Charges on Security Purchases	1.65	.33	.35	.19
Totals	$4,135.89	$166.47	$813.40	$600.19
Balance—June 30, 1938			$121.08*	$861.24

* Represents Deficit.

RECEIPTS AND DISBURSEMENTS BY FUNDS
July 1, 1937 to June 30, 1938

	General Fund	Annuity Fund	Endowment Fund	Permanent Ministerial Education Fund	Scholarship and Loan Fund for Women
Balance—July 1, 1937	$ 24,252.90	$63,662.52	$6,686.67	$13,070.99	$6,995.38
Receipts	95,034.93	3,581.98	171.47	1,033.31	953.55
	$119,287.83	$67,244.50	$7,040.14	$14,104.30	$7,948.93
Disbursements	102,978.90	4,135.89	172.87	813.40	600.19
Balance—June 30, 1938	$16,308.93	$63,108.61	$6,867.27	$13,290.90	$7,348.74

GRANTS IN AID TO STUDENT CENTERS

July 1, 1936 to June 30, 1938

	1936-37	1937-38
University of California	$ 600.00	$ 600.00
University of Colorado	100.00	50.00
University of Illinois	800.00	800.00
Metropolitan Chicago	750.00	1,540.00
Purdue University	150.00	160.00
University of Iowa	450.00	133.33
University of Michigan	550.00	575.00
University of Kansas	50.00	
Nebraska Intersynodical Committee	200.00	200.00
Grace Church	100.00	
Boston Metropolitan Area	2,500.00	2,374.98
New York City Metropolitan Area	412.53	849.38
Duke University	400.00	
Duke University and University of North Carolina		450.00
State College, North Carolina	250.00	250.00
Syracuse University		600.00
Ohio Synod	425.00	425.00
Metropolitan, Philadelphia	2,500.00	2,499.96
Pennsylvania State College	500.00	600.00
West Chester State Teachers College	466.61	
Clemson College, South Carolina	150.00	166.00
Winthrop College, South Carolina	225.00	187.50
Virginia Polytechnic Institute	100.00	25.00
University of Washington	250.00	250.00
University of West Virginia	200.00	200.00
University of Wisconsin	500.00	1,500.00

Special Points	712.00	
District of Columbia		75.00
Ernest Habig, Traveling		30.90
Oregon		225.00
Maryland		14.00
Kansas		50.00
Minneapolis		100.00
Student Conferences		55.00
East St. Louis		25.00
Princeton		9.75

Total Grants to Student Centers $13,341.14 $15,020.80

GRANTS AND SPECIAL CONTRIBUTIONS TO COLLEGES
and SEMINARIES
July 1, 1936 to June 30, 1938

Colleges:	Grants	—1936-37— Special Contributions	Total
Carthage	$ 4,000.00		$ 4,000.00
Hartwick	750.00		750.00
Lenoir Rhyne	2,400.00		2,400.00
Midland	8,400.00		8,400.00
Marion	600.00		600.00
Newberry	4,500.00		4,500.00
Roanoke	1,800.00		1,800.00
Susquehanna	1,800.00		1,800.00
Thiel	4,000.00		4,000.00
Wagner	1,500.00		1,500.00
	$29,750.00		$29,750.00
Seminaries:			
Chicago	$ 2,400.00		$ 2,400.00
Southern	3,500.00		3,500.00
Saskatoon	7,800.00	$1,000.00	8,800.00
Waterloo	5,000.00		5,000.00
Mt Airy		1.00	1.00
	$18,700.00	$1,001.00	$19,701.00
	$48,450.00	$1,001.00	$49,451.00

Colleges:		—1937-38—	
Carthage	$ 4,000.00	$1,012.90	$ 5,012.90
Gettysburg	480.00		480.00
Hartwick	750.00		750.00
Lenoir Rhyne	2,700.00		2,700.00
Midland	8,400.00	2,000.00	10,400.00
Marion	600.00		600.00
Muhlenberg	480.00		480.00
Newberry	4,800.00		4,800.00
Roanoke	1,800.00		1,800.00
Susquehanna	2,100.00		2,100.00

Thiel	4,500.00		4,500.00
Wagner	1,800.00		1,800.00
Wittenberg	480.00		480.00
	$32,890.00	$3,012.90	$35,902.90

Seminaries:

Chicago	$ 2,700.00		$ 2,700.00
Southern	3,600.00		3,600.00
Saskatoon	7,800.00	$3,020.00	10,820.00
Waterloo	5,100.00	562.27	5,662.27
	$19,200.00	$3,582.27	$22,782.27
	$52,090.00	$6,595.17	$58,685.17

SALARIES OF SECRETARIES AND RENT ALLOWANCES

July 1, 1936 to June 30, 1938

	1936–37	1937–38
Gould Wickey	$ 3,900.00	$ 3,900.00
Mary E. Markley	3,000.00	3,000.00
C. P. Harry	3,000.00	3,000.00
Mildred E. Winston	2,225.00	2,500.00
Gould Wickey Rent	1,200.00	1,200.00
	$13,325.00	$13,600.00
Salaries as Shown	$12,125.00	$12,400.00
Rent	1,200.00	1,200.00
	$13,325.00	$13,600.00

BALANCE SHEET
June 30, 1938
ASSETS

Cash in Banks:

General Accounts	$12,667.85	
Office Accounts	1,000.00	
		$ 13,667.85
Stocks, Bonds, Notes and Other Investments at Ledger Values		93.256.60*
Office Furniture and Equipment		2,069.99
Total Assets		$108,994.44

FUNDS

General Fund	$ 18.378.92
Annuity Fund	63.108.61
Endowment Fund	6.867.27

Permanent Ministerial Education Fund		13,290.90
Scholarship and Loan Fund for Women		7,348.74
Total Funds		$108,994.44

* Market Value June 30, 1938, $74,802.86.

INVESTMENTS
June 30, 1938
ANNUITY FUND

Par Value	Book Value	Market Value June 30, 1938
$4,800 Altoona and Logan Valley Electric Railway 4s due 1954	$ 4,800.00	$ 3,408.00
1,000 Associated Gas and Electric Company, 5½s due 1973	1,000.00	635.00
2,000 Atchison, Topeka and Santa Fe, 4s due 1995	2,036.83	2,055.00
2,000 Baltimore and Ohio Railroad, 5s due 1948....	1,975.00	870.00
4,000 Baltimore and Ohio Railroad, 5s due 1950....	4,055.00	1,200.00
6,500 Bell Telephone Co. of Pennsylvania, 5s due 1948	6,395.00	7,629.37
1,000 Burlington Realty Trust (Boston Parcel Post Station)	980.00	90.00
3,000 Georgia Power Company, 5s due 1967...........	2,943.75	2,752.50
2,000 Lackawanna and Wyoming Valley Railroad Company, 5s due 1951	1,935.00	300.00
1,000 Minnesota Power and Light Co., 5s due 1955	1,000.00	1,020.00
5,000 National Dairy Products, 3¾s due 1951........	5,182.52	5,112.50
3,000 Oregon Washington Railroad, 4s due 1961....	2,909.00	2,970.00
1,000 Potomac Edison, 5s due 1956	1,055.21	1,070.00
2,000 Pennsylvania Railroad, 4¼s due 1981	2,075.30	1,780.00
2,000 Pennsylvania Railroad, 4¼s due 1984	1,955.00	1,772.50
4,500 Pacific Gas and Electric, 4s due 1964	4,699.43	4,961.25
3,500 Philadelphia Elec. Power Co., 5½s, due 1972	3,631.25	3,920.00
3,000 Southern Railroad, 5s due 1994......................	3,202.50	1,950.00
4,000 United Post Offices Corporation, Certificates of Deposit	4,000.00	800.00
5,000 United States Treasury, 2½s due 1936-53	5,003.12	5,096.87
500 United States Treasury, 2¾s due 1956-59	513.75	514.06
Total Bonds	$61,347.66	$49,907.05

Shares	Stocks		
32	Altoona and Logan Valley Railroad, common	$ 320.00	$ 960.00
15	District Building and Loan Association Shares	3,000.00	3,000.00
5	Eastern Building and Loan Association Shares	1,000.00	1,000.00
13	Western Union Telegraph Company	1,560.00	378.63
	Total Other Investments	$ 5,880.00	$ 5,338.63
	Total Annuity Fund Investments	$67,227.66	$55,245.68

INVESTMENTS
June 30, 1938
SCHOLARSHIP AND LOAN FUND FOR WOMEN

Par Value		Book Value	Market Value June 30, 1938
$ 500	Associated Gas and Elec. Co., 5½s due 1973	$ 500.00	$ 317.50
1,000	Lackawanna and Wyoming Valley Railroad 5s due 1951	967.50	150.00
3,000	Westmoreland Water Co., 5s due 1952	2,970.00	3,030.00
1,000	United Biscuit Co., 5s due 1950	1,056.40	1,060.00
1,000	United States Treasury Note, 3s due 1946-48	1,034.53	1,077.81
	Total Scholarship and Loan Investment	$ 6,528.43	$ 5,635.31

PERMANENT MINISTERIAL EDUCATION FUND

Par Value		Book Value	Market Value
$1,000	Chelsea Hotel Company, 6s due 1945	$ 1,000.00	$ 180.00
1,000	Illinois Post Office Building, Chicago, Ill., Certificate of Deposit, 5½s due 1932	1,000.00	20.00
2,000	Lackawanna and Wyoming Valley Railroad, 5s due 1951	1,935.00	300.00
500	Pacific Gas and Electric, 4s due 1964	538.82	551.25
1,000	Philadelphia Electric Power Company, 5½s due 1972	1,022.50	1,120.00
1,000	Southern Railroad, 5s due 1994	1,067.50	650.00
4,000	Washington Gas and Light General Mortgage, 5s due 1960	4,283.75	4,650.00
1,000	United States Treasury, 2½s due 1936-53	1,000.63	1,019.37
1,000	United States Treasury, 3¼s due 1946	1,000.00	1,097.50
	Total Permanent Ministerial Education Fund Investments	$12,848.20	$ 9,588.12

ENDOWMENT FUND

Par Value		Book Value	Market Value
$1,000	United Biscuit Co., 5s due 1950	$ 1,072.75	$ 1,060.00
2,059.34	Franklin National Bank Impounded Funds	2,059.34	*
1,000	New York Central Railroad, 3¾ due 1946	982.71	725.00
500	United States Treasury, 3¼s due 1946	537.51	548.75
Shares 10	Eastern Building and Loan Association	2,000.00	2,000.00
	Total Endowment Fund Investments	$ 6.652.31	$ 4.333.75

Respectfully submitted,

* Not Ascertainable.

THOMAS P. HICKMAN, *Treasurer.*

We have audited the books of account of the Treasurer and examined the securities of the Board of Education of The United Lutheran Church in America for the biennium beginning July 1, 1936, and ending June 30, 1938, and we hereby certify that, in our opinion, the foregoing statements of Cash Receipts and Disbursements for the years ending June 30, 1937 and June 30, 1938, the Balance Sheet as of June 30, 1938, and pertinent schedules, are in accordance with the books of account and are true and correct.

TAIT, WELLER AND BAKER,
Accountants and Auditors.

Dr. Gold introduced the Rev. Paul H. Krauss, a retiring member of the Board of Education, who described the service of the Board to students both in Lutheran and non-Lutheran institutions.

The Rev. Gould Wickey, Executive Secretary, was next introduced by Dr. Gold, and Dr. Wickey addressed the Convention.

Dr. James C. Kinard asked the privilege of introducing Congressman B. B. Hare, of South Carolina, who thereupon addressed the Convention on Christian higher education.

The recommendations of the Board of Education were considered.

Recommendation 1 was adopted.

Recommendation 2. It was moved and seconded to adopt the recommendation.

It was moved and seconded to refer this recommendation to the Special Committee of Nine which was appointed to bring in a report on control of theological education. The motion was *lost.*

The original motion to adopt recommendation 2 was carried.

Recommendation 3 was adopted.

Recommendation 4 was adopted.

The Rev. M. L. Stirewalt, speaking as a representative of educational institutions in the United Lutheran Church, presented the following, which was adopted:

> Resolved, that, since this Convention has heard an expression of gratitude for the benefits which our Colleges and Seminaries have received from the Church, through our Board of Education, we call again upon the Church for a continued and increased loyalty that these benefits may become even more effective.

On motion the report of the auditors was accepted.

After announcements by the Local Committee, the Convention adjourned at twelve o'clock with prayer by the Rev. A. M. Neumann.

Saturday Afternoon and Evening

Saturday afternoon was free time in which the delegates to the Convention enjoyed entertainment privileges provided by the hospitable Local Committee.

One of the great features of the 1938 Convention was the musical festival given on Saturday evening in Peabody Hall by the combined choirs of five U. L. C. A. Colleges: Newberry, Gettysburg, Muhlenberg, Susquehanna and Hartwick.

Sunday

Practically all of the Lutheran pulpits in Baltimore and vicinity were occupied by delegates to the Convention, and in the afternoon a most successful open air mass meeting was held at the Luther Monument in Druid Hill Park, with an attendance of about 7,000 people. The meeting was presided over by Dr. F. H. Knubel and addresses were made by the Rev. Carl Heminghaus and the Rev. Franklin Clark Fry.

At five o'clock on Sunday afternoon, Dr. Paul E. Scherer, of New York, gave a special broadcast over the Columbia network, by the arrangement of the chairman of the Broadcasting Committee of the Convention, the Rev. A. R. Naus.

SIXTH SESSION

LORD BALTIMORE HOTEL
Baltimore, Maryland
Monday, October 10, 1938, 8.45 A. M.

Matins were conducted by the Rev. A. W. Steinfurth.

The President called the Convention to order.

Mr. Alvin R. Nissly, Chairman of Committee of Tellers No. 2, reported elections as follows:

For the *Board of Foreign Missions,* each of the following received a majority of the votes cast for the term expiring 1944:

Rev. Joseph B. Baker	Claude L. Peterman
Rev. Robert D. Clare	George S. Yost
Rev. F. Eppling Reinartz	

The President declared them elected and stated that one clergyman and one layman were yet to be elected.

For the *Board of American Missions* and the *West Indies Mission Board,* each of the following received a majority of the votes cast for the term expiring 1944:

Rev. Robert H. Ischinger	Philip Glatfelter
Rev. Henry J. Pflum	James C. Kinard
Rev. A. A. Zinck	Elwood M. Rabenold

The President declared them elected and stated that one clergyman was yet to be elected.

For the *Board of Education,* each of the following received a majority of the votes cast for the term expiring 1944:

Rev. J. L. Deaton	Levering Tyson
Rev. W. H. Traub	
Rev. A. R. Wentz	

The President declared them elected and stated that one clergyman and two laymen were yet to be elected.

For the *Board of Social Missions,* each of the following received a majority of the votes cast:

Term expiring 1944

	Carl M. Distler
Rev. G. H. Bechtold	W. H. Hager

The President declared them elected and stated that three clergymen and one layman were yet to be elected.

Term expiring 1942:

Rev. Herman Brezing	H. E. Isenhour
	L. Henry Lund

The President declared them elected and stated that three clergymen and one layman were yet to be elected.

Term expiring 1940:

Rev. P. D. Brown	Thomas P. Hickman
Rev. Paul H. Heisey	Carl H. Lammers

The President declared them elected and stated that two clergymen and one layman were yet to be elected.

For the *Board of Publication,* each of the following received a majority of the votes cast for the term expiring 1944:

Rev. Harry F. Baughman	F. Wm. Cappelmann
Rev. Lloyd M. Keller	Henry F. Heuer
Rev. Russell D. Snyder	

The President declared them elected and stated that one clergyman and one layman were yet to be elected.

For the *Board of Ministerial Pensions and Relief,* each of the following received a majority of the votes cast for the term expiring 1944:

G. Harry Ditter	Belding B. Slifer
Francis Seiberling	Daniel F. Yost

The President declared them elected and stated that one layman was yet to be elected.

For the *Parish and Church School Board,* each of the following received a majority of the votes cast for the term expiring 1944:

Rev. Paul J. Hoh	
Rev. Paul H. Krauss	

The President declared them elected and stated that one clergyman and one layman were yet to be elected.

For the *Board of Deaconess Work,* each of the following received a majority of the votes cast for the term expiring 1944:

Rev. P. S. Baringer   Harry R. Hagerty
                                       Mrs. O. A. Sardeson

The President declared them elected and stated that one clergyman and one layman were yet to be elected.

Th Rev. S. W. Herman, President, presented the report of the Board of Publication.

REPORT OF THE BOARD OF PUBLICATION

The two decades, which have passed since the publication interests of the Church were merged into the Board of Publication, have been years of accomplishment and progress in the life of the Board of which the Church may well be proud. As this Board's activity is the publication business, it is natural to view results from that standpoint primarily. As a business, the work of the Church's Board has been blessed with success. It has continued unabated; its volume of trade has increased; its accomplishments have been gratifying, nothwithstanding the changing conditions which this period of time has seen.

But the Board's business is to publish in the interests of the Church: its limitations are those strictly of the so-called "denominational" publishing house: not those of a religious press. Success, therefore, must be measured by service, rather than by monetary returns. For this there is an unfailing standard of judgment, namely, the quantity of publications distributed to the individual congregations, and the service of an ever-growing number of individuals. According to this standard it may be said without fear of contradiction, that the Board does serve the Church.

Within a few years after the merger, the new Board erected and occupied its own fine building at Thirteenth and Spruce Streets, Philadelphia. On the street floor is a book room, second to none in the city either in stock or attractiveness. Here also are the shipping rooms and stock rooms. Two floors are occupied by the general business and editorial offices. Three other floors are at the present occupied by other official groups of the Church as their headquarters,—The Ministerium of Pennsylvania, The Philadelphia City Mission, The Synodical Mission Board of East Pennsylvania, The Parish and Church School Board, The Board of Ministerial Pensions and Relief, The Women's

Missionary Society, the Promotion Secretary, and The Luther League of America.

Until 1930 the manufacturing department,—composing room, presses, bindery, etc., occupied two of the floors. In that year, a commodious and thoroughly modern printing plant was erected at Fiftieth and Lancaster Avenue, Philadelphia. Here all the "manufacturing" is now centered under ideal conditions and produced by the most up-to-date equipment. The many magazines, weeklies, quarterlies, etc., are shipped directly from this center. The Board owns and uses in the service of the Church a physical equipment which compares favorably with non-religious publishing houses. This in itself tells the story of success, but it is a success built entirely upon service; for did not the Board meet and satisfy the widely diversified needs of the Church, there would be no necessity for this fine equipment. It is not pride, but plain fact, that among denominational publishing houses, the Board stands as well equipped and as active and successful as any in the country.

It must be recorded, however, that much of this gratifying advance is certainly due to the sagacious and careful direction of the business management. Organization, from manager through every department, has contributed to a well established publishing business.

We doubt whether the Church at large realizes the extent of the publishing activities of this Board. If all of the titles of books, periodicals of various sorts, pamphlets, services, Sunday school literature, etc., published in these two decades by this Board were assembled, the result would be a catalog of astonishing proportions.

It will be interesting to summarize these activities:—Being the Church's publishers, the first group naturally is authorized publications. Since 1918 *The Common Service Book with Hymnal* alone has had a distribution of hundreds of thousands of copies. In the "authorized" group are also *The Occasional Services, The Parish School Hymnal, The Children's Hymnal and Service Book, Collects and Prayers,* The *Kirchenbuch,* and *Sonntag Schul Buch.* These are provided in a variety of editions. Besides, books current at the time of the merger are still stocked; though *The Church Book* has been discontinued.

The next major group is that of Sunday school literature. Here every possible need of church schools is provided for in a number of series of excellent quarterlies and textbooks,—*The Augsburg Series* and the new *Christian Life Course* are prepared for use of both teacher and scholar. A *Lesson Commentary* is an annual issue. Textbooks of some of the old General Council Graded Series are still to be had. In this classification must be included textbooks and other publications and requisites for Daily Vacation Bible Schools.

A third classification of publications includes official journals,—*The Lutheran, Lutherischer Herold, Young Folks, Lutheran Boys and Girls;*

also, *The Parish School* and *Der Jugend Freund.* These run into thousands of copies weekly and monthly.

Another classification includes book and pamphlet publications of a general character. In the course of these twenty years, works, both meritorious and of real worth, have been issued in every branch of the theological science. To enumerate a list of these would include the names of our best writers and in number of titles would be a startling surprise but a real witness of the Board's ideal to build up a literature for the Church which is both worthy and lasting. Outstanding in this classification are the six volume edition of Luther's Works in English and the one volume Commentary on the New Testament, both major and successful undertakings. Translations of important foreign works, books of devotion, sermonic literature and helps also appear in this group. Occasionally fiction also has been added to this list, but this, of course, is entirely in harmony with religious ideals. The range of titles in this particular classification is both numerous and surprising.

A wide and varied line of supplies needed by both church and school is also stocked by the Board. Anything required in church and school equipment is furnished by the House. This may range from a simple card or reward pin, church flag or envelopes or collection plates, to complete furniture equipment for a church or parish building. The Ecclesiastical Goods Department, a development of the past few years and planned strictly for service, maintains a fine showroom where a completely and correctly furnished altar is on display. Here also will be found cases of altar and other brasses and communion ware. A complete service for the making of vestments for both minister and choir is also the work of this department; as well as altar linens, colored stoles, liturgical paraments from the simplest design to the more ornate embroideries.

As a Board we are deeply thankful that we have been privileged to accomplish all this for the Church; and we record with gratitude the loyalty of the churches and schools whose support has contributed so much to the upbuilding of the Board's fine business and the unfailing co-operation of the personnel of our establishment, whose ambition, as is also the Board's, is to be of service to the interests of the Church.

Respectfully submitted,

S. W. HERMAN, *President,*

HENRY W. HARMS, *Secretary.*

NEW BOOKS

The following new books have been published during the biennium ending June 30, 1938:

The Christian Home, Student's Edition; The Christian Home, Leader's Edition—by P. D. Brown.

Studies in First Corinthians, Student's Edition; Studies in First Co-
rinthians, Leader's Edition—by Paul J. Hoh.
Studies in Life Service, Student's edition; Studies in Life Service,
Leader's Edition—by Amos J. Traver.
Worship, Student's Edition; Worship, Leader's Edition—by Theodore
K. Finck.
The Minor Prophets and Modern Problems, Pupil's Edition; The Minor
Prophets and Modern Problems, Leader's Edition—by Harry F. Baugh-
man.
My Group Sessions—by O. Fred Nolde and Paul J. Hoh.
My Progress—by O. Fred Nolde and Paul J. Hoh.
Our Congregation and Its Work—by Paul E. Keyser.
What a Church Member Should Know—by A. A. Zinck.
Lesson Commentary, 1937—by Charles P. Wiles and D. Burt Smith.
Lesson Commentary, 1938—by Charles P. Wiles and D. Burt Smith.
Der Lutherischer Kalender, 1937—C. R. Tappert, Editor.
Der Lutherischer Kalender, 1938—C. R. Tappert, Editor.
The Way of Righteousness—by J. Henry Harms.
Keeping Lent—by J. Henry Harms.
New Testament Commentary—edited by Herbert C. Alleman.
Church Unity—by F. H. Knubel.
Mellow Fruits of Experience—by L. M. Zimmerman.
A Guide to Worship—by Charles Stork Jones.
The Faith of the Church—by Charles M. Jacobs.
Truth and Life—by O. Fred Nolde.
Fliedner the Faithful—by Abdel Ross Wentz.
Pastor's Plan Book.
The Resurrection Truth, Easter Pageant—by Henry W. Snyder.
A Guide and Standards in Parish Education—prepared by the Parish
and Church School Board.
Year Book, 1937—W. H. Greever, Editor.
Year Book, 1938—W. H. Greever, Editor.

NEW PAMPHLETS

During the biennium new pamphlets have been issued as follows:
Our Congregation and Its Work, Leader's Guide—by Paul E. Keyser.
My Group Sessions, Leader's Guide—by O. Fred Nolde and Paul
J. Hoh.
My Progress, Leader's Guide—by O. Fred Nolde and Paul J. Hoh.
Nursery Department Packet.
Church Year Calendar, 1937.
Church Year Calendar, 1938.
Children's Day with Jesus—by Marion Poppen Athy.
O Come Let Us Worship—by Ernest J. and Ruth C. Hoh.
Peace on Earth, Christmas Service—by Carolena Nolde Stoner.
O One with God the Father, Christmas Service—by Sister Lydia
Fischer.
The Resurrection, Easter Service—by William Benbow.
Christ Risen for All—by Theodore and Mary Finck.
Symbols and Terms of the Church—by Howard R. Kunkle.
I Believe in the Resurrection—by Walter C. Davis.
I Was Glad—prepared under auspices of Parish and Church School
Board.
Power—prepared under auspices of Parish and Church School Board.

A Table and a Toiler—prepared under auspices of Parish and Church School Board.

Teach Us To Pray—prepared under auspices of Parish and Church School Board.

CATALOGS

During the biennium we have issued catalogs as follows:

Two Lenten and Easter catalogs, two holiday catalogs, one supply catalog, one Fall catalog, one vacation text and supply catalog.

PERIODICALS

Weekly—The Lutheran, Lutherischer Herold, Lutheran Young Folks, Lutheran Boys and Girls.

Monthly—Augsburg Sunday School Teacher, Little Ones, Senior Lesson Leaves, Jugend Freund, The Parish School, Light for Today.

Quarterly—Home Department Lessons, Adult Lessons, Young People's Lessons, Intermediate-Senior Lessons, Junior Lessons, Bible Lesson Picture Cards, Bible Lesson Picture Charts.

CHRISTIAN LIFE COURSE

Beginners' Department

        Year 1—The Heavenly Father's Little Ones.
        Year 2—The Heavenly Father's Children.

Primary Department

        Course   I—Our Homes.
        Course II—Our World.
        Course III—Our Friends.

Junior Department

        Course IV—God's Heroes.
        Course V—God's Workers.
        Course VI—God's Book.

Intermediate Department

        Course VII—Christian Boys and Girls.
        Course VIII—Men and Women of God.
        Course IX—The Story of God's People.

Senior Department

        Course X—The Christian Church.
        Course XI—The Christian Life.
        Course XII—Life Problems.

In addition the Augsburg Series, referred to under "Periodicals," has been issued regularly.

REPORT OF THE BUSINESS MANAGER AND TREASURER OF THE
BOARD OF PUBLICATION

CONSOLIDATED STATEMENT OF PROFIT AND LOSS

July 1, 1936 to June 30, 1937

SALES $654,568.48
  Less: Returns and Allowances................................... 4,313.84

  Net Sales $650,254.64

COST OF SALES 357,380.64

  Gross Profit $292,874.00

SHIPPING AND DELIVERY EXPENSES:
  Salaries and Wages $8,762.00
  Postage and Supplies 21,266.64
  Freight and Hauling (Outbound) 3,712.56
  Provision for Depreciation, Truck 328.95

    Total Shipping and Delivery Expense $34,070.15

EDITORIAL EXPENSES:
  Salaries, Editors and Office Assistants $45,665.76
  Illustrations 2,792.57
  Dues and Subscriptions 276.30
  Miscellaneous Expense 216.33
  Manuscript Account 200.00
  Contributors 7,489.15

    Total Editorial Expenses $56,640.11

ADMINISTRATIVE AND GENERAL EXPENSES:
  Insurance $373.63
  Telephone 926.30
  Light and Power 995.49
  Expenses—Board Meetings 794.00
  Advertising 8,774.69
  Salaries 67,341.36
  Christmas Bonus to Employees 2,209.00
  Pensions 1,200.00
  Provision for Retirement Pensions 6,124.64
  Library 7.73
  Office and Showroom Rent 22,570.00
  Provision for Depreciation, Furniture, etc. 1,756.86
  Auditing 1,638.40
  Stationery and Supplies 7,465.87
  Miscellaneous Expenses 934.14
  Appropriations—Apportionment 125,000.00
  Appropriations—Lutheran Historical Society.......... 500.00

Traveling and Moving Expense 2,486.57
Taxes 713.62

Total Administrative Expenses $251,812.30

Total Expenses $342,522.56

Net Loss from Operations $49,648.56*

OTHER INCOME:
Interest Earned on Notes Receivable $20.83
Bad Debts Recovered 12.20
Cash Received on Balances in Closed Banks............ 191.73

Total Other Income 224.76

$49,423.80

OTHER DEDUCTIONS:
Bad Accounts Charged Off $1,563.23

Net Loss before Gain from Building Operations..................... $50,987.03

PROFIT FROM BUILDING OPERATIONS: 1,439.94
Net Loss Carried to Surplus $49,547.09*

*Represents Loss.

CONSOLIDATED STATEMENT OF PROFIT AND LOSS

July 1, 1937 to June 30, 1938

SALES $669,226.30
Less: Returns and Allowances 4,263.14

Net Sales $664,963.16

COST OF SALES 373,972.20
Gross Profit $290,990.96

SHIPPING AND DELIVERY EXPENSES:
Salaries and Wages $9,379.67
Postage and Supplies 24,652.53
Freight and Hauling (Outbound)............................... 4,909.29
Provision for Depreciation, Truck 493.42

Total Shipping and Delivery Expense................... $39,434.91

EDITORIAL EXPENSES:
Salaries, Editors and Office Assistants........................ $41,672.22
Illustrations 825.00
Dues and Subscriptions 315.76

Miscellaneous Expense	924.07
Contributors	6,036.31
Total Editorial Expense	$49,773.36

ADMINISTRATIVE AND GENERAL EXPENSES:

Insurance	$621.08
Telephone	1,011.21
Light and Power	1,074.47
Expenses, Board Meetings	603.56
Advertising	10,806.29
Salaries	70,976.36
Christmas Bonus to Employees	1,968.00
Pensions	1,200.00
Provision for Retirement Pensions	6,425.79
Library	2.25
Office and Showroom Rent	22,570.00
Provision for Depreciation, Furniture, etc.	2,044.26
Auditing	1,670.00
Legal Expense	307.50
Stationery and Supplies	5,927.49
Miscellaneous Expenses	1,036.65
Leadership Training	5,500.00
Provision for Promotional Expenses	10,484.24
Traveling and Moving Expenses	3,111.68
Taxes	818.36

Total Administrative Expense	$148,159.19
Total Expenses	$237,367.46
Net Profit from Operations	$53,623.50

OTHER INCOME:

Interest Earned on Notes Receivable	$26.19
Bad Debts Recovered	17.45
Cash Received on Balances in Closed Banks	55.05
Total Other Income	98.69
	$53,722.19

OTHER DEDUCTIONS:

Bad Accounts Charged Off	$206.57
Loss on Sale of Equipment	132.67
Total Other Deductions	339.24
Net Profit before Loss from Building Operations	$53,382.95

LOSS FROM OPERATION OF BUILDINGS 21,930.24

Net Profit to Surplus	$31,452.71

CONSOLIDATED BALANCE SHEET

June 30, 1938

ASSETS

CURRENT ASSETS:
Cash in Banks and on Hand $258,870.28
Notes Receivable $801.97
Accounts Receivable:
Merchandise $132,818.31
Advertising 1,139.71
Unpaid Subscriptions 391.14

$135,151.13
Less Reserve for Doubtful Accounts 25,000.00

Net Accounts and Notes Receivable 110,151.13
Accrued Interest on Investments 3,300.61
Inventories of Books, Publications, Paper Stock, etc............... 210,334.50

Total Current Assets $582,656.52

FIXED ASSETS:
Land $211,859.50
Buildings 629,679.81
Machinery and Equipment 198,544.46

$1,040,083.77
Less Reserve for Depreciation 403,160.02

Net Book Value Fixed Assets $636,923.75

DEPRECIATION RESERVE FUNDS:
Uninvested Cash Balances $51,080.52
Bonds at Market Value 277,792.01

Total Depreciation Reserve Funds 328,872.53

OTHER ASSETS:
Permanent Fund Assets 7,535.44
Prepaid Accounts:
Taxes and Water Rent $2,148.20
Insurance 2,280.49

Total Prepaid Accounts 4,428.69

Total Assets $1,560,416.93

LIABILITIES

CURRENT LIABILITIES:
Accounts Payable $8,160.54
Accrued Royalties Payable 1,252.56
Accrued Printing Expenses 300.00

Total Current Liabilities $9,713.10

DEFERRED INCOME:
Subscriptions to:

"The Lutheran"	$12,076.01
The "Lutherischer Herold"	1,931.76
Periodicals	50,353.09
Total Deferred Income	64,360.86

PERMANENT FUNDS:

John Rung Legacy	$3,000.00
David Beidle Bequest	200.00
Accumulated Profits Appreciation of Securities and Income	4,335.44
Total Permanent Funds	7,535.44

RESERVE FOR RETIREMENT PENSIONS 18,613.14

RESERVE FOR PROMOTIONAL EXPENSES 9,683.76

CAPITAL AND SURPLUS 1,450,510.63

Total Liabilities and Capital $1,560,416.93

DEPRECIATION RESERVE FUND, SECURITIES

July 1, 1937 to June 30, 1938

Par Value	Security	Market Value June 30, 1937	Market Value June 30, 1938
$5,000	Baltimore and Ohio Railroad, First Mortgage, 4s, due 1948	$5,225.00	$2,050.00
4,600	Electric and Peoples Traction Certificates, 4s, due 1945	460.00	264.50
6,000	Lehigh Coal and Navigation Company, 4½s, due 1954	5,700.00	3,300.00
5,000	Lehigh Valley Railroad, General Consolidated, 4s, due 2003	2,531.25	1,100.00
5,000	Reading Company, General and Refunding, 4½s, due 1997	5,325.00	3,462.50
10,000	Baltimore and Ohio, Southwest Division, First 5s, due 1950	10,200.00	3,000.00
5,000	Reading Jersey Central, 4s, due 1951	4,818.75	2,900.00
10,000	Philadelphia Company, 5s, due 1967	9,400.00	9,300.00
5,000	Metropolitan Edison, 4½s, due 1968	5,325.00	5,487.50
10,000	Penn Central Light and Power, First 4½s, due 1977	9,137.50	8,387.50
5,000	Missouri Pacific, First Series "F," 5s, due 1977	1,675.00	975.00
5,000	Illinois Central, 4¾s, due 1966	3,400.00	1,900.00
5,000	New Orleans, Texas and Mexico, First 5s, due 1954	2,400.00	1,650.00

10,000	American Gas and Electric, Debenture, 5s, due 2028	10,675.00	10,850.00
5,000	Central Illinois Public Service, Series "G," 5s, due 1968	5,050.00	5,012.50
5,000	Public Service Company of Northern Illinois, 4½s, due 1978	5,200.00	5,206.25
5,000	Railway Express Agency, 5s, due 1938....	5,300.00	
10,000	Pennsylvania Power and Light, First 4½s, due 1981	10,075.00	9,875.00
5,000	Commonwealth Edison, Series "F," 4s, due 1981	5,206.25	5,418.75
5,000	Consolidated Gas Company of New York, 4½s, due 1951	5,350.00	
10,000	City of Philadelphia, Regular 4s, due 1945	10,400.00	10,650.00
30,000	United States Treasury, 3⅛s, due 1949-52	31,350.00	32,428.13
20,000	United States Treasury, 3s, due 1951-55.	20,500.00	21,256.25
10,000	Pennsylvania Company, 4s, due 1963......	10,200.00	8,900.00
5,000	Republic Steel, 4½s due 1961..................	4,743.75	4,481.25
10,000	Pennsylvania Railroad, 3¾s, due 1970.	9,975.00	8,400.00
5,000	United States Treasury, 2¾s, due 1948, 1951	5,021.88	5,218.75
10,000	Chesapeake and Ohio, 3½s, due 1996.......	9,600.00	9,400.00
10,000	National Dairy Products, 3¾s, due 1951	10,200.00	10,225.00
10,000	Lehigh Valley Harbor Terminal, 5s, due 1954	10,050.00	3,500.00
10,000	Great Northern Railway, 3¾s, due 1967.	9,450.00	7,150.00
30,000	United States Treasury, 2½s, due 1953...	29,315.63	30,581.25
10,000	Altoona and Logan Valley Electric Railway, 4s, due 1954	8,500.00	7,100.00
10,000	Philadelphia Electric, First and Refunding 3½s, due 1967	10,300.00	10,850.00
5,000	Central New York Power, General Mortgage, 3¾s, due 1962		5,268.75
2,000	United States Treasury, 2½s, due 1945....		2,118.13
10,000	New York Connecting Railway, First 4½s, due 1953		9,900.00
10,000	Ohio Edison, 4s, due 1965		10,225.00
	Totals	$292,060.01	$277,792.01

PERMANENT FUNDS
SUMMARY OF CASH ACCOUNT

July 1, 1937 to June 30, 1938

Cash in Bank, July 1, 1937 .... $2,574.01

RECEIPTS:
Income from Investment $278.25
Interest on Balance on Deposit 64.49

Total Receipts 342.74

$2,916.75

DISBURSEMENTS:

Julius F. Seebach, Prize	$500.00	
Mrs. J. R. E. Hunt, Prize	200.00	
Transferred to General Fund for Printing Costs	300.00	
Total Disbursements		1,000.00
Cash in Bank, June 30, 1938		$1,916.75

PERMANENT FUND SURPLUS ANALYSIS

Balance, Permanent Fund Surplus, July 1, 1937		$6,158.64
Add: Income from Investments	$278.25	
Interest on Balance on Deposit	64.49	
Total Additions		342.74
		$6,501.38

Deduct:
Prizes Awarded:

Julius F. Seebach	$500.00		
Mrs. J. R. E. Hunt	200.00		
		$700.00	
Estimated Printing Costs		300.00	
Decrease in Market Value of Securities		1,165.94	
Total Deductions			2,165.94
Balance, Permanent Fund Surplus, June 30, 1938			$4,335.44

PERMANENT FUNDS

BALANCE SHEET

June 30, 1938

ASSETS

Cash in Bank	$1,916.75

Investments (at market value):

Par Value

Par Value		Market Value
$1,000	United States Treasury, 3⅛s, due 1949-52	$1,080.94
1,000	Lehigh Valley Railroad, 4½s, due 2003	231.25
1,000	Pennsylvania Power and Light, 4½s, due 1981	987.50
1,000	Detroit Edison Series "D," 4½s, due 1961	1,135.00
2,400	Altoona and Logan Valley Railroad, 4s, due 1954	1,704.00

Shares
16   Altoona and Logan Valley Railroad, Common   480.00
                                                                  ──────────
                                                                   5,618.69
                                                                  ──────────
              Total Permanent Fund Assets $7,535.44
                                                                  ──────────

FUNDS
Principal:
John Rung Legacy $3,000.00
David W. Beidle Bequest 200.00

Surplus:
Accumulated Interest and Adjustment of Value of Securi-
ties to current market value 4,335.44
                                                                  ──────────
      Total Permanent Funds and Surplus $7,535.44
                                                                  ──────────

Respectfully submitted,
GRANT HULTBERG,
Business Manager and Treasurer.

We have audited the books of account and examined the securities of
the Board of Publication of the United Lutheran Church in America
for the biennium beginning July 1, 1936 and ending June 30, 1938, and
we hereby certify that the foregoing Profit and Loss Statements, setting
forth the result of the operations for the biennium under audit, together
with the Balance Sheet as of June 30, 1938, setting forth the financial
condition at that date, and the Statements of Permanent Funds, are in
our opinion, true and correct.

TAIT, WELLER AND BAKER,
Accountants and Auditors.

Dr. Herman paid tribute to the Rev. C. M. Jacobs, who had
been a member of the Board. He also stated that this is the
first time the Business Manager, Dr. Grant Hultberg, was not
able to attend the Convention. Dr. Herman asked a moment
of prayer for the recovery of Dr. Hultberg, who is now on
extended leave of absence.

Dr. Herman introduced Mrs. M. A. Roberts, cashier of the
Publication House, who is acting as manager during Dr.
Hultberg's absence.

Mr. R. H. Huntington, the Rev. P. Z. Strodach, the Rev. E. O. Armbruster, Mr. E. P. Hoeppner, Mr. Frank Rhode, and the Rev. J. W. Gouker were introduced to the Convention.

On motion the report of the auditors was accepted.

It was moved and carried that the Executive Board be asked to study the relation of the Board of Publication to the Parish and Church School Board, the Committee on Church Papers, the Common Service Book Committee and any other interests that it deems pertinent; and report to the next Convention.

Moved and carried that the Secretary of the United Lutheran Church send a telegram of affection and greetings to Dr. Grant Hultberg.

The Rev. H. D. Hoover, President, presented the report of the Board of Deaconess Work.

REPORT OF THE BOARD OF DEACONESS WORK

The Board of Deaconess Work herewith presents its eleventh biennial report to the United Lutheran Church in America.

To the Board of Deaconess Work the Church has entrusted the training and direction of her deaconesses. These servants of the Church are the spiritual successors of those noble women who ministered to Christ and served the Church with the apostles of old. The deaconesses of the Lutheran Church of America have been called on to adjust themselves to meet calls of many different kinds of service and conditions. We may safely say there is a gradual Americanization of the Diaconate, both in training and in service.

Our Lutheran deaconesses have rendered exceptionally fine service in the parish and in the institutions of the Church. Their ministries of mercy, their teaching and counselling, their evangelistic and missionary efforts, combined with administrative work, have included a wide variety of service in many fields. The deaconess has generally been called upon to serve in our largest and best organized congregations. She has been subjected to the severest tests of situation and service. She has proven herself not only a valuable deaconess, but a person of deep, religious experience and wholeome spirituality.

This report will attempt to give a brief description of deaconess work under three divisions: the work in general, the service of the deaconess during the past twenty years, and a brief of the busy biennium ending 1938.

I. GENERAL

A. The number of Lutheran Motherhouses and deaconesses in the world.

Germany—69 Motherhouses, 27,638 deaconesses; Denmark— 2 Motherhouses, 619 deaconesses; Finland—2 Motherhouses, 457 deaconesses; France—3 Motherhouses, 312 deaconesses; Holland— 10 Motherhouses, 1,188 deaconesses; Norway—3 Motherhouses, 1,534 deaconesses; Austria—2 Motherhouses, 232 deaconesses; Poland—2 Motherhouses, 408 deaconesses; Roumania—1 Mother-house, 35 deaconesses; Sweden—2 Motherhouses, 719 deaconesses; Switzerland—4 Motherhouses, 2,323 deaconesses; Czechoslovakia— 1 Motherhouse, 46 deaconesses. Total Motherhouses 101, deacon-esses 35,511.

B. The number of Lutheran Motherhouses in America.

There are nine Lutheran Motherhouses and 475 deaconesses in America. Two of these, the Philadelphia Motherhouse and the Baltimore Motherhouse, belong to the United Lutheran Church in America, with a total of 195 deaconesses.

Many other communions have developed deaconess training schools and are profiting by their service. Some of these denomi-nations have a very large number of trained deaconesses in the service. From published announcement we note the tendency to raise the standard and efficiency of the preparation of the deaconess for her work.

II. TWENTY FRUITFUL YEARS

During the past twenty years 108 deaconesses were consecrated, 55 at the Baltimore Motherhouse and 53 at the Philadelphia Motherhouse. In 1918 the Baltimore Motherhouse had 49 deaconesses and the Philadelphia Motherhouse 89. There are at present 195 deaconesses in the service of the United Lutheran Church, 73 with the Baltimore Motherhouse and 122 with the Philadelphia Motherhouse. This total of 195 is greater than the clerical membership of the following nine synods: Florida, Georgia-Alabama, Kentucky-Tennessee, Mississippi, Nova Scotia, Pacific, Rocky Mountain, Texas, and West Virginia. These 195 deaconesses are as many as all the ministers of the United Lutheran Church stationed in the following states: Washington, Oregon, California, Montana, Idaho, Nevada, Colorado, Utah, New Mexico, Arizona, Oklahoma, and Texas.

The deaconesses of the United Lutheran Church, during its history of twenty years, have served in 19 of its district synods, in 45 of its institutions or societies, and in 88 parishes. The total baptized member-ship of the parishes served by deaconesses is 112,038. These are distributed in the following synods: Alleghany, East Pennsylvania, Illinois, Kansas, Maryland, Michigan, New York, North Carolina, Northwest, Ohio, Ministerium of Pennsylvania, Pittsburgh, Rocky Mountain, South Carolina, Susquehanna, Virginia, West Pennsylvania, and West Virginia, with a total of 88 parishes and over 120,000 baptized members. This is nearly seven per cent of the baptized membership of the entire United Lutheran Church, and it is more than the total baptized membership of the six synods of Virginia, North Carolina, Georgie-Alabama, Florida, Mississippi, and West Virginia.

The following parishes have been served by deaconesses throughout the entire history of the United Lutheran Church: Philadelphia, Pa.— Zion, Tabor, St. Matthew's; New York, N. Y.—St. Paul's; Canton, Ohio— Trinity; Easton, Pa.—St. John's; Erie, Pa.—St. John's; Syracuse, N. Y.— Zion; Richmond, Va.—First; Hagerstown, Md.—Trinity.

The following institutions have been served by deaconesses throughout the entire existence of the United Lutheran Church: The Mary J. Drexel Home for the Aged, the Mary J. Drexel Children's Hospital, the Mary J. Drexel Kindergarten, the Lankenau Hospital, the Lankenau School for Girls, Kensington Dispensary, River Crest Preventorium, Tabor Orphans' Home, Erie Home for the Aged, The Philadelphia Settlement House, the Baltimore Inner Mission Society, Washington National Home for the Aged, Tabitha Home, Franke Home, Baltimore Motherhouse Kindergarten.

HONOR ROLL

The roll of noble women who have been called home during these twenty years follows: Of the Baltimore Motherhouse—Sisters Regina Bowe, Eleanor Frank, Sarah Anthony, Katherine Aufhammer, Inez Metzger, May Haltiwanger, and Christine Jaborg. Of the Philadelphia Motherhouse—Sisters Martha Frey, Emma Knipscheer, Amalia Hartwig, Anna Marie Enderlein, Marie Sowa, Emily Schwarz, Wilhelmina Dittman, Mary Anna Kraetzer, Lydia Klein, Christine Doerr, Julie Mergner, Else Dodenhoff, Emma Carlson, Helen Kuhn, Elenore Diehl, Marie Koeneke, Flora Mazor, Anna Heinzman, Veronica Eich.

The Rev. Dr. Charles E. Hay, Pastor of the Baltimore Motherhouse for twenty-five years, was called to his eternal reward on November 30, 1934.

III. A BUSY BIENNIUM

Anniversaries.

Several significant anniversaries were celebrated. The Philadelphia Motherhouse and the Mary J. Drexel Home celebrated the fiftieth anniversary in 1938. This institution has been used of God to render remarkable service to the Church as a whole and to a number of institutions of mercy in particular.

Dr. Foster U. Gift, Superintendent of Instruction at the Baltimore Motherhouse, celebrated the fifteenth anniversary of his service in that office. During nine years of this time he also served as pastor. Dr. Gift has been connected with deaconess work in some capacity for the past twenty-five years.

Sister Anna Ebert, Directing Sister of the Philadelphia Motherhouse, completed eight years of service in that office. Sister Edna Hill has been the Training Sister at the Baltimore Motherhouse for fifteen years. Sister Martha Hansen, who served during ten years as Director of the Settlement House in Philadelphia, has been the Directing Sister of the Baltimore Motherhouse six years.

Dr. E. F. Bachmann completes thirty-two years as the pastor of the Philadelphia Motherhouse.

Dr. William A. Wade, who began his work as Executive Secretary of the Board of Deaconess Work, November 1, 1937, completed eleven years as a member of the Board and nine years as President of the Board. His long and faithful service in this office fits him unusually well for his present work.

Anniversaries of Deaconess Service.

Sister Magdalene Von Bracht has been in deaconess work sixty-nine years, and if she lives until next year, she will celebrate the seventieth anniversary of her consecration. Among the Sisters of the Philadelphia Motherhouse there are three who have served fifty and more years, eight who have served forty years and more, and thirteen others who have served over twenty-five years. Among the Sisters of the Baltimore Motherhouse there are seven who have served forty years and more, and fourteen who have served twenty-five years and more.

PUBLICATIONS

Useful folders were sent out to the pastors desiring them to assist congregations properly to present the cause of deaconess work on Septuagesima Sunday. The *Motherhouse Tidings* and the *Deaconess Messenger* were published regularly throughout the year. A new folder, "So You Are Going To Be a Deaconess," by Sister Anna Ebert, has just been issued from the press.

CONFERENCES

At the two Deaconess Conferences held, one in September, 1936, at Omaha, Nebr., and the other in June, 1938, at Philadelphia, Pa., the nine Lutheran Motherhouses in the United States were represented and a fine spirit prevailed. The papers presented and discussed at both conferences indicated that the Diaconate is not only interested in the whole program of the Church, but also is making plans to increase its efficiency so that it may continue to serve the Church in its work of mercy and by winning souls for the Kingdom of God.

The National Inner Mission Conference was held at Philadelphia, June 22-24, 1938, and attended by a goodly number of deaconesses from both Motherhouses, and also representatives from the other Lutheran Motherhouses, whose Conference was held in Philadelphia. Many of our deaconesses are engaged in Inner Mission, institutional, congregational, and community work.

The Parish Workers' Conference of Pennsylvania and Adjacent States was held at Gettysburg Seminary, May 19-20, 1938. This Conference includes a number of our deaconesses who are engaged in parish work. Nearly all of the parish workers connected with the Conference were trained at our Baltimore Motherhouse Training School.

ADVANCE

There are more calls for the service of deaconesses than can now be filled. These calls come from parishes, institutions, social service agencies and missionary societies and synods.

EXECUTIVE SECRETARY

The office of Executive Secretary was created in order to properly promote the work and make the Church aware of the opportunities and needs of deaconess work. The great advance looking toward the promotion of our work in the Church was the selection of the Rev. William A. Wade, D.D., as Executive Secretary of the Board of Deaconess Work. For some time the Board has felt the need of a full-time representative on the field to visit institutions, organizations and congregations to present the work and also to visit the Sisters serving in congregations and institutions of the Church. The Board chose the one who had served for a number of years as a member and President of the Board, and his work began November 1, 1937. Through the office of Executive Secretary literature has been prepared and sent to the congregations throughout the entire territory. 200,000 copies of the special bulletin, together with more than 6,000 copies of other literature, were sent to pastors and congregations on request for use at the Septuagesima season. The cause has been presented in many of our colleges and theological seminaries, and the remaining institutions will be visited in the near future. As a result of this means of publicity many pastors, parents, and young women have written in for further information concerning the training of young women for the Diaconate, and we believe the creation of this new office will fill a long standing need in the work in general.

STANDARDS

The other great step in advance made during this biennium was the serious attempt to fulfill the promises in the report made by the Board two years ago. Definite progress has been made in improving the standard of training. A careful study was made of the curricula of our own and other training schools by members of the Board, and other churchmen, who were asked to co-operate in this attempt to supply a training which would fit the deaconess more adequately for the difficult service she is called upon to render the Church.

Higher standards will be required for candidates for the diaconate. Spirituality is of prime importance. The personality of the candidate must meet carefully administered tests. The educational preparation of the candidate has also been raised from that of high school graduation to a minimum of two years of college work, with the reservation that exceptions may be made by action of the Board. We are looking forward to the time when the preparation of the deaconess will be sufficiently thorough to meet modern standards in similar activities.

Steps are being taken as rapidly as finances will permit to secure additional teachers. The aim will be to obtain spiritually trained and well qualified instructors.

The clinical service of candidates in training will receive very careful attention and supervision. For example, we present here a summary of the clinical work of the deaconesses in training at the Baltimore Motherhouse during the past biennium: 3,648 parish calls made, 1,029 classes taught in Sunday schools and weekday church schools, 6 catechetical classes taught, 58 teacher training classes taught, 7 young people's societies directed, 178 services conducted, 36 educational tours. Institutional internships served at the Norwegian Lutheran Hospital, Brooklyn, the Lankenau Hospital, Philadelphia, the Lutheran Settlement House, Philadelphia.

Provision is made, wherever possible, to give advance training in colleges, universities or special schools to more adequately prepare deaconesses now in service for their particular kind of work.

ADEQUATE SUPPORT

One great hindrance to every effort to advance and improve the work has been the lack of financial resources. The Board has advanced the charge for deaconess service in parishes to $250 per year and in institutions to $300 per year.

The very small rate of apportionment assigned to the deaconess work limits its possibilities. Either there will need to be a more adequate support through the channel of apportionment or the friends of the work must give directly, if the work is to go forward unhindered.

The Church needs this work. The Church is calling for well trained deaconesses.

OUR ANNIVERSARY APPEAL

We pray you enable us to answer these calls for service. Study the report of the work done; over 100,000 personal calls in parish and in institutional work by our deaconesses in the past biennium and then ask yourself whether one cent per member is sufficient contribution to this great work.

ADMINISTRATIVE

Three of the members of the Board, who have served faithfully and well for a number of years, will end their service with this Convention. We appreciate the services of the Rev. George N. Lauffer, D. D., a very faithful member of the Board for the past twelve years. The Board will also miss the presence and splendid work of Edgar W. Young, Esq., who has been a member for the past twelve years, very active, not only in the work of the Board, but also in the administration of the Baltimore Motherhouse. We appreciate very much the gracious service of Mrs. J. L. Morgan, an advisory member, whose deep interest in the work was shown during her membership for the past six years.

ORGANIZATION OF THE BOARD

President—Rev. Harvey D. Hoover, D.D., Ph.D., S.T.D., Litt.D., Gettysburg, Pa.

Vice-President—Rev. Luther A. Thomas, D.D., Lincolnton, N. C.

Executive Secretary—Rev. William A. Wade, D.D., 1905 Thomas Ave., Baltimore, Md.

Treasurer—Frederick J. Singley, Esq., 215 N. Charles Street, Baltimore, Md.

Members of the Board

Terms Expire 1942

Rev. J. J. Schindel, D.D.	Rev. L. A. Thomas, D.D.
Rev. Allen L. Benner, D.D.	Mr. E. S. Gerberich
Frederick J. Singley, Esq.	

Terms Expire 1940

Rev. Harvey D. Hoover, D.D.	Rev. W. C. Schaeffer, Jr, D.D.
Rev. U. S. G. Rupp, D.D.	Mrs. Elsie Singmaster Lewars, Litt.D.
President C. C. Stoughton	

Terms Expire 1938

Rev. P. S. Baringer	Mr. Harry R. Hagerty
Rev. George N. Lauffer, D.D.	Edgar W. Young, Esq.
Mrs. O. A. Sardeson	

Advisory Members

Mrs. W. P. M. Braun	Mrs. John M. Cook

NOMINATIONS FOR BOARD MEMBERSHIP

Rev. Philip S. Baringer (eligible for re-election)..............Maryland Synod
Mr. Harry R. Hagerty (eligible for re-election)...............Maryland Synod
Mrs. O. A. Sardeson (eligible for re-election)............................Illinois Synod
Rev. Lewis A. Speaker, D.D..Ohio Synod
Charles E. Orth, Esq...Maryland Synod
Rev. Herbert H. Hartman...Maryland Synod
Rev. H. E. Turney, D.D...Indiana Synod
Mrs. George H. Haase...Nebraska Synod
Mr. Herbert M. Day..Maryland Synod
Mr. William E. Zschiesche..Maryland Synod

APPRECIATION

We sincerely appreciate the fine Christian service, the deep devotion and unselfish sacrifice made by the deaconesses who have so effectively and faithfully fulfilled their mission.

We are grateful for the publicity given the deaconess work by the publications of the Church: *The Lutheran, The Lutheran Woman's Work, Lutheran Men, The Augsburg Teacher, Lutheran Young People,* etc.

We commend the Women's Missionary Society for its very helpful co-operation in promoting the cause of deaconess work. The use of the deaconess in society conventions, the publication of pamphlets, the helpful support by the general society, and the individual efforts of its many members have rendered a valuable service to the cause of the Church.

The Board appreciates the co-operation of pastors and churches and pleads for a larger support, for a more effective promotion and an understanding appreciation of the Diaconate.

THE BALTIMORE MOTHERHOUSE

William A. Wade

Interest in the cause of deaconess work and the establishment of a Motherhouse within the Lutheran Church of the General Synod began to manifest itself in March, 1883, when the Rev. Dr. F. P. Manhart introduced the subject in the North Branch Conference of the Susquehanna Synod. The matter was seriously considered, and after a full discussion the Conference resolved, "That we believe there is an actual need of an Order of Deaconesses in our Church, and that we ask Synod at her next meeting to consider the matter." At the next meeting of Synod it received favorable consideration, and a special committee was appointed to study the matter further and to report one year later.

Interest in the cause grew and developed, and the General Synod appointed a Board and authorized the establishment of the work. Nine young women made response to the call as early as April, 1891, but it was not until 1893 that there were qualified candidates. The first candidates took some of their training in Europe. In July, 1893, two candidates sailed for Germany to receive training in Kaiserswerth. Several others followed them soon afterwards, and one took her training at the Mary J. Drexel Home at Philadelphia. The first six deaconesses were consecrated in First English Lutheran Church, Baltimore, October 23, 1895. From that small beginning the work has continued to grow and God has richly blessed the efforts of all who labored so faithfully and earnestly, and today the sisters are laboring in many parishes and institutions of the Church.

The present beautiful four-story Motherhouse, constructed of solid granite, 144x72 feet, together with the churchly chapel, was dedicated on June 10, 1911, in the presence of the General Synod Convention, the Rev. Dr. J. B. Remensnyder, President, presiding. At the time of the merger, in 1918, the Baltimore Motherhouse, with all of its property, buildings, and equipment, valued at more than $200,000, was handed over to the United Lutheran Church, free of debt.

OUR SISTERS

At present there are seventy-three sisters, ten of whom are probationers, connected with the Baltimore Motherhouse. Of these twenty-six are serving in parishes and twenty-one in institutions of the Church, ten are doing service in the Motherhouse, eight are retired, and nine are in training. During the biennium two sisters were called to their heavenly home,—Sister May Haltiwanger and Sister Christine Jaborg, and seven probationers were consecrated.

PARISHES AND INSTITUTIONS

Among the parishes in which sisters are serving are: Akron, Ohio; Baltimore, Md.; Canton, Ohio; Columbus, Ohio; Detroit, Mich; Grand Rapids, Mich.; Hagerstown, Md.; Lewistown, Pa.; Milwaukee, Wis.; New York, N. Y.; Omaha, Nebr.; Philadelphia, Pa.; Richmond, Va.; Rochester, N. Y.; Syracuse, N. Y.; Toledo, Ohio; Washington, D. C.; Williamsport, Pa.; Wilmington, Del.

Among the institutions in which sisters are serving are: Inner Mission Society and Girls' Hospice, Baltimore, Md.; Tabitha Home, Lincoln, Nebr.; Lutheran Settlement, Martin Luther Neighborhood House and Haverford Center, Philadelphia, Pa.; Good Shepherd Home, Allentown, Pa.; Home for the Aged, Washington, D. C.; Franke Home, Charleston, S. C.; Tiding Over Home, Brooklyn, N. Y.; Inner Misison Society, Chicago, Ill.; Artman Home, Ambler, Pa.; St. John's Orphan Home, Buffalo, N. Y.; Gettysburg College (Women's Division), Gettysburg, Pa.

In addition to all this, the Motherhouse conducts a Christian kindergarten and a flourishing Weekday Church school, and the students of the Training School engage in the various parish and institutional work in Baltimore.

The Triennial Homecoming

The usual Triennial Homecoming took place, beginning June 8th and concluding June 17th. Practically all of the sisters were in attendance. Matins was used each morning at 8.30, and lecture periods followed throughout the forenoon. The lecturers this year were Miss Grace Sperow, Miss Mabel Locker, Dr. Henry Einspruch, and Dr. H. D. Hoover. A very impressive memorial service was held, with brief talks on the lives of the sisters who had been called into the Church Triumphant, and also on the life of the Rev. Charles E. Hay, former pastor, who was called to his reward November 30, 1934. A white rose was placed on the altar for each of those who had departed, by those who spoke. The Holy Sacrament of the Lord's Supper was administered. In addition to the services and lectures many social affairs were enjoyed and all were delighted with the homecoming.

The Training School

During the biennium forty-five young women were enrolled as students of the Training School. Of this number eleven were candidates for the Diaconate. The others were students in the one and two-year courses offered by the Motherhouse to young women who do not desire to become deaconesses or cannot qualify. Among these students there were several who had college training and others had teaching and practical experience. Ten states and Canada were represented.

With the addition of the departments in Social Service and Sacred Music within the past two years, with the probability of a new teacher in the near future, and with increased interest in the work generally, prospects are bright for the future.

Our Main Purpose

While there are different departments of work in our institution, which are of much importance, the principal purpose of the work of the Motherhouse is that of training young women for the Diaconate. This has always been the policy of the Deaconess Motherhouse, and whatever else we may be able to accomplish, our life purpose centers in the work of the Diaconate.

Surrounded by so much sorrow and suffering in the world, and seeing so many who have experienced the loss of their faith, we desire to be of service to the Church and humanity, and we offer that loving service in the name of our Lord and Saviour, Jesus Christ.

Philadelphia Motherhouse
E. F. Bachmann

Fifty years of service to more than 200,000 patients and many thousands of other persons in distress, is the record of the Philadelphia

Motherhouse. With the Mary J. Drexel Home for the Aged, the Mother-house shares the magnificent building dedicated on December 6, 1888. The work done here for half a century is a testimonial to Christian faith working by love. It has also enabled other institutions of the Church to do their work more effectively and has actually "mothered" a number of important organizations which without this Motherhouse would hardly have been founded or maintained. Twenty years ago at the Merger, the General Council was highly gratified to bring this Motherhouse into the United Lutheran Church as one of the important assets and contributions.

Today the Sisterhood has a membership of 123, of whom ninety-seven are Deaconesses and twenty-six probationers. They serve two *hospitals* with almost 4,000 patients annually, and more than 30,000 visits to the clinics; one *dispensary* for the treatment of about 200 tuberculosis patients; four *Homes* with 260 aged men and women; two *Homes* with over 200 children; one *Preventorium* for about 300 children threatened by tuberculosis; one *Hospice* for sixteen women; two sisters serve in two *Inner Mission Societies*. With only two exceptions our sisters are in charge of these institutions. Six deaconesses are in parish work. Our sisters are also conducting the *Lankenau School for Girls,* admitting day and boarding pupils to elementary and high school grades with college preparatory or general courses. The *Kindergarten* also meets the standards, so that kindergarten students are sent to us by Temple University for practice teaching. We also must add the Orphanage and the Kindergarten in Fredericksted, Virgin Islands, conducted by two native sisters affiliated with the Philadelphia Motherhouse and visited this summer by our assistant, the Rev. August Fisher. Every one of these fields of labor offers wonderful opportunities for Christian influence.

During the past biennium the Lord called two of our sisters from their labors, Sister Anna Heinzmann, on May 12, 1937, after nearly twenty years of service, and Sister Veronica Eich, on August 23, 1937, retired after having rendered valuable service since 1890. By investiture four candidates were admitted as probationers on May 28, 1937, and three on Ascension Day, May 26, 1938. On Pentecost, 1937, four pro-bationers were consecrated as deaconesses.

MOVING FORWARD!

The Philadelphia Motherhouse is preparing for larger and still better service in the second half of its first century. Quite aware of various difficulties and dangers, aggravated by the present serious world con-ditions, we would dedicate ourselves anew to God with a consecration and a pioneering spirit like that of our founders fifty years ago. Under the leadership of John D. Lankenau and his co-laborers, high standards were set up. We of today, charged with the responsibility of carrying on the work begun by them, dare not be content with routine fidelity. Constant watchfulness, larger vision, willing adjustment to ever changing opportunities and requirements, are essential to the further development of deaconess work. While grappling with other serious problems, the following moves have been made toward a greater future:

1. The *Charter has been amended,* enabling the Board of Trustees to be increased from nine to twelve members. Dr. Luther A. Harr, Judge Frank F. Neutze, and Howard R. Detweiler, Esq., have been added to the Board. William P. M. Braun, elected to the Board in 1901 to succeed John D. Lankenau, is serving as President since 1917. The other members are Dr. H. Offermann, Dr. E. P. Pfatteicher, Dr. J. J. Schindel, Herman C. Rumpp, Henry G. Deininger, Ph.D., Oscar C. Schmidt, and John Schnabel. The vacancy left by the death of a faithful member, Louis Sigel, has not yet been filled. Directing Sister Anna Ebert, and the pastor, also belong to the Board. In addition, the Board of Deaconess Work of the U. L. C. is represented on the Board by the Rev. Dr. Allen L. Benner, and the Ministerium of Pennsylvania by its Secretary, the Rev. Dr. W. L. Stough, and by the Rev. William F. Herrmann. At the same time the words "General Council," in Art. I, 1, have been changed to "United Lutheran Church in America."

The new Board has undertaken a revision of the By-laws and a thorough study of the work and the financial situation of the corporation.

2. During the past year *"The Philadelphia Deaconess Association"* has been launched to enlist friends in the direct financial support of our Deaconess Department, and to foster a more personal interest in winning young women for the deaconess work. So far this organization has enrolled fully 500 members who have contributed somewhat over $1,000.00 If this encouraging beginning made on the Philadelphia territory will find also elsewhere the support of pastors and other friends, this association may become an important factor in the advancement of the diaconate.

3. Though all requests to send deaconesses to institutions and congregations had to be declined during the past biennium, we were happy to place three deaconesses into *new work* this summer. Two sisters conducted summer schools in parishes not yet familiar with the diaconate, and the third had charge of a camp organized and maintained by a Philadelphia organization of women interested in combating diabetes. One hundred children were given two weeks each of expert care and scientific study during the two summer months. This is the first attempt of its kind in the Philadelphia territory, and we are pleased that one of our deaconesses, an instructress at the Lankenau Training School for Nurses, was placed in charge after having been given special train-

ing at a New England camp last summer. Other new lines of work can be taken up, when sisters in sufficient number are available.

4. The *new educational standards* for admission to the diaconate are in harmony with the educational policy of the Philadelphia Motherhouse. For more than twenty years we have been appealing to young women with a college degree or with professional training as teachers, nurses or social workers. They could serve the Church along similar lines in the diaconate. Only five of the sixty-one who entered during the past twenty years had such special training. From now on may such respond in larger numbers!

Because our Motherhouse was desperately in need of deaconesses for positions requiring an academic degree, we have at great loss of time and at heavy expense sent sisters selected for such special work, to the University of Pennsylvania, to Temple University, to Drexel Institute, and to the New York School of Social Service. Now they qualify under various professional standards. *Today ten of our deaconesses have college degrees* and are holding important positions with a corresponding strong Christian influence. This year four of our sisters are full-time students. Yet we need more and would be happy to give college graduates and professional women further special training, if necessary, following the two-year course for candidates. The latter course is fundamental and of essential value for its religious studies, its training in practical activities, its adjustment to fellowship, and its spiritual experiences. At the same time, however, the Church cannot insist on making two college years a rigid requirement. Superior intelligence, practical ability, and sound judgment, in the long run may far outweigh scholastic credits, so that any consecrated young woman who has only a high school diploma and meets our other requirements, need not hesitate to offer herself for the diaconate. The sisters of the Philadelphia Motherhouse are engaged in *more than twenty different kinds of work,* requiring a wide range of talents and spiritual gifts, so that every capable young woman can expect finally to be in a position for which she is best fitted, either as an executive or an assistant. The diaconate is a challenge to all young women desiring to enter a life service.

FINANCES

The Motherhouse of Deaconesses is one of three departments conducted in the large building known as the Drexel Home. The others are the Home for Aged and the Children's Hospital. All share in one household and administration, and are included in the treasurer's annual report. Based on careful study, the Motherhouse is chargeable with forty per cent, the Home for Aged with twenty-two per cent, and the Hospital with thirty-eight per cent. From the annual reports of the treasurer as they have appeared in "The Deaconess Messenger," the following summary may serve the present purpose.

EXPENSES

	1936	1937
Deaconess Account	$20,708.00	$20,671.00
Salaries, Pastors, Doctors, etc.	9,016.00	9,145.00
Wages	18,211.00	19,622.00
Household Supplies	22,965.00	22,717.00
Repairs and Improvements	3,396.00	1,807.00
Miscellaneous	12,390.00	15,560.00
	$86,686.00	$89,522.00

RECEIPTS

	1936	1937
From Stations Served by Sisters	$13,872.00	$14,982.00
Entrance Fees to Home	6,956.00	6,013.00
Children's Hospital	17,234.00	19,141.00
Income from Investments	27,983.00	29,791.00
Miscellaneous	1,037.00	4,007.00
	$67,082.00	$73,934.00
Deficit	$19,604.00	$15,588.00

SPECIAL INCOME

	1936	1937
From the United Lutheran Church	$2,303.00	$3,375.00
From the "Friends of Children" for Hospital	863.00	1,308.00
From the Founders' Day Fund	2,490.00	3,177.00
Donations	1,582.00	2,140.00
	$7,238.00	$10,000.00

Ever since this institution "was dropped as a gift from God into the lap of the Church," as the late Prof. Henry E. Jacobs expressed it in an anniversary address, it has constantly rendered various important services to the Church besides the training and maintenance of deaconesses. The total cost of maintenance during the past fifty years is well over $3,500,000.00 The annual deficts incurred during the past biennium were simply unavoidable while fulfilling the charitable trust imposed upon us. The income from the endowment left by John D. Lankenau and the contributions from friends, were insufficient to cover the difference between the expenses and the income for services rendered.

We are grateful for the $5,678.00 received from the United Lutheran Church during the past two years for our Motherhouse department. This is, however, not quite $24.00 a year per each of our sisters, for whose maintenance—including training—in the Motherhouse needed $272.00 a year beyond the income from stations. To continue with assurance the great work of our deaconesses, more funds must soon become available. A special committee has been charged with the study of the entire situation and we look for some constructive recommendations. We need the sympathy, prayers, and support of the whole Church. May God provide beyond our immediate needs!

Our Motherhouse is prepared to stand by the Church facing the challenge of a despairing and yet seeking generation; and we hope and pray that in the future far more than in the past, deaconesses in their ministry of mercy may work effectively alongside of the Ministry of the Word in expressing the redeeming love of God and leading souls into the Kingdom of Christ. His Name alone be praised!

Respectfully submitted,

HARVEY D. HOOVER, *President.*

WILLIAM A. WADE, *Executive Secretary.*

REPORT OF TREASURER OF THE BOARD OF DEACONESS WORK

CASH RECEIPTS AND DISBURSEMENTS—GENERAL FUND

July 1, 1936 *to June* 30, 1937

Cash Balance—July 1, 1936 .... **$6,694.00**

RECEIPTS

United Lutheran Church in America—Apportionment	$19,000.00
Synods	18.75
Stations	10,057.13
Tuition	4,512.50
Kindergarten	367.50
Nursing	230.00
Contributions	1,068.00
Interest on Securities	121.39
Annuity Ground Rents Collected	1,340.23
Discounts Earned	121.91
Rents, 1905 Thomas Avenue (net)	364.59
Miscellaneous, Refunds, etc.	588.99
Music Fund	19.76
Total Receipts	**$37,810.75**
(Forwarded)	**$44,504.75**

DISBURSEMENTS

Books	$427.79
Lectures and Instruction	1,030.13
Board Expenses	466.76
Pastor's Salary—Dr. Gift	2,218.90
Pastor's Travel	193.42
Office Supplies and Expenses	63.72
Clerical Help	529.20
Sisters' Quarterly Allowances	5,095.00
Sisters' Vacation Allowances	1,575.00

Sisters' Travel	249.90
Sisters' Hospital and Medical Expense	2,016.70
Sisters' Wearing Apparel	3,356.88
Telephone and Telegraph	235.67
Printing and Stationery	385.55
Postage	257.34
Audit	118.00
1901 Thomas Avenue, Water Rent	24.00
1905 Thomas Avenue, Water Rent	24.00
Incidentals	704.90
Household Wages	2,102.10
Household Food	4,911.32
Household Furnishings	461.83
Gas and Electric	769.65
Coal	1,150.23
Engineer	750.00
Helper	303.95
Grounds and Property	353.35
Insurance	688.79
Improvements and Repairs	1,034.20
Water Rent	77.10
Miscellaneous	21.80
Mary J. Drexel Home and Philadelphia Motherhouse of Deaconesses	2,375.00
Annuity Bond Interest	1,955.47
Funeral Expenses	150.00
Pageant, Columbus, Ohio	316.77
Clerical Permits	144.00
Pamphlet, "Fliedner the Faithful"	910.00

Total Disbursements	$37,448.42

Cash Balance—June 30, 1937	$7,056.33

CASH RECEIPTS AND DISBURSEMENTS—OTHER FUNDS

July 1, 1936 to June 30, 1937

	New Building Fund	Endowment Fund	Annuity Fund
Cash Balances—July 1, 1936	$1,118.19	$2,520.63	$7,784.13
RECEIPTS			
Interest on Deposits	28.36	63.79	91.60
Distribution in Bank Reorganization	19.78	40.76	
Subscriptions	27.10		
Ground Rent Sold			1,500.00
Annuities Purchased			1,350.00
United Lutheran Publication House		2,124.95	
	$1,193.43	$4,750.13	$10,725.73
Securities Purchased			9,335.76
Cash Balances—June 30, 1937	$1,193.43	$4,750.13	$1,389.97

ANALYSIS OF FUNDS

June 30, 1937

	General Fund	New Building Fund	Endowment Fund	Annuity Fund	Total
Cash	$7,056.33	$1,193.43	$4,750.13	$1,389.97	$14,389.86
Ground Rents				21,333.33	21,333.33
Securities				11,332.63	11,332.63
Real Estate	317,816.15				317,816.15
Burial Plot	600.00				600.00
Dues from General Fund	12,136.38*	6,137.23	2,500.00	3,499.15	
Totals	$313,336.10	$7,330.66	$7,250.13	$37,555.08	$365,471.97

*Represents Deficit.

CASH RECEIPTS AND DISBURSEMENTS—GENERAL FUND

July 1, 1937 to June 30, 1938

Cash Balance, July 1, 1937 .... 7,056.33

RECEIPTS

United Lutheran Church in America—Apportionment	$20,200.00
Synods	55.76
Stations	9,490.15
Tuition	1,335.00
Kindergarten	189.50
Contributions	1,278.74
Interest on Securities	422.50
Annuity Ground Rents Collected	1,319.11
Discounts Earned	113.65
Rents, 1905 Thomas Avenue	128.25
Miscellaneous, Refunds, etc.	657.95
Organ and Music Fund	255.50
Pamphlet, "Fliedner the Faithful"	122.20

Total Receipts $35,568.31

(Forwarded) $42,624.64

DISBURSEMENTS

Books	$290.43
Lectures and Instruction	807.76
Board Expenses	361.24
Pastor's Salary, Dr. Gift	2,314.44
Executive Secretary's Salary, Dr. Wade	1,600.00
Pastor's and Miscellaneous Travel	374.44
Office Supplies and Expenses	77.31
Clerical Help	540.40

Sisters' Quarterly Allowances	5,026.70
Sisters' Vacation Allowances	1,525.00
Sisters' Travel Allowances	876.03
Sisters' Hospital and Medical Expense	1,672.15
Sisters' Wearing Apparel	3,374.35
Telephone and Telegraph	230.84
Printing and Stationery	1,628.62
Postage	395.53
Audit	115.00
Water Rent, 1901 Thomas Avenue	76.80
Water Rent, 1905 Thomas Avenue	1,302.70
Incidentals	1,195.05
Household Wages	2,226.50
Household Food	4,947.18
Household Furnishings	389.17
Gas and Electric	812.10
Coal	1,112.18
Engineer	750.00
Helper	458.45
Grounds and Property	211.87
Insurance	365.72
Improvements and Repairs	1,745.89
Water Rent	45.32
Miscellaneous	48.04
Mary J. Drexel Home and Philadelphia Motherhouse of Deaconesses	2,525.00
Annuity Bond Interest	1,979.35
Funeral Expenses	102.30
Clerical Permits	155.00

Total Disbursements $41,658.86

Cash Balance, June 30, 1938 .... $965.78

CASH RECEIPTS AND DISBURSEMENTS—OTHER FUNDS

July 1, 1937 to June 30, 1938

	New Building Fund	Endowment Fund	Annuity Fund
Cash Balance, July 1, 1937	$1,193.43	$4,750.13	$1,389.97
RECEIPTS			
Interest on Deposits	$30.20	$66.19	$26.75
Distribution in Bank Reorganizations	7.92	16.30	
Securities Sold			3,000.00
Contributions	41.00		
Total Receipts	$79.12	$82.49	$3,026.75
	$1,272.55	$4,832.62	$4,416.72
PAYMENTS			
Cash Balances, June 30, 1938	$1,272.55	$4,832.62	$4,416.72

BALANCE SHEET

June 30, 1938

ASSETS

Cash in Banks and on Hand $11,487.67
Ground Rents Owned 21,333.33
Securities 8,261.38*
Real Estate and Equipment 318,816.15
Lorraine Park Burial Plot 600.00

Total Assets $360,498.53

FUNDS

General Fund $308,245.55
New Building Fund 7,409.78
Endowment Fund 7,332.62
Annuity Fund 37,510.58

Total Funds $360,498.53

*Market Value, June 30, 1938, $8,226.25.

SECURITIES OWNED

June 30, 1938

Par Value		Book Value June 30, 1938	Market Value June 30, 1938
$3,000.00	Washington County Maryland, 4½% School Bond, July 1, 1939	$3,161.25	$3,090.00
1,000.00	City of Frederick, Maryland, 4½%, May 1, 1939	1,040.00	1,020.00
2,000.00	United States Treasury Bond, 2½%, December 15, 1949-1953	2,000.00	2,038.75
2,000.00	United States Treasury Bond, 2⅞%, March 15, 1955-1960	2,060.13	2,077.50
546.48	York Ice Machinery Corporation, 3% Unsecured Note, due December 1, 1944		No Market

Shares			
2	Union Trust Company of Maryland		No Market
40	The Summers Fertilizer Company, 8% Cumulative Preferred Stock		No Market

Totals		$8,261.38	$8,226.25

GROUND RENTS OWNED

June 30, 1938

2002 East Twentieth Street $2,000.00
3007 Wayne Avenue 1,300.00

5301 Midwood Avenue	1,000.00
247 North Payson Street	1,000.00
3610 Plateau Avenue	1,400.00
819 South Elwood Avenue	600.00
2019 West North Avenue	1,333.33
4504 Wakefield Road	1,500.00
4506 Wakefield Road	1,500.00
4508 Wakefield Road	1,500.00
38 South Calverton Road	1,200.00
40 South Calverton Road	1,400.00
46 Prospect Avenue	1,500.00
53 Prospect Avenue	1,500.00
20 Prospect Avenue	1,400.00
1413 Longwood Street	1,200.00
Total Ground Rents Owned	$21,333.33

Respectfully submitted,

FREDERICK J. SINGLEY, *Treasurer.*

We have audited the books of account and have examined or satisfactorily accounted for the securities of the Board of Deaconess Work of the United Lutheran Church in America for the biennium beginning July 1, 1936 and ending June 30, 1938, and we hereby certify that the foregoing statements of Cash Receipts and Disbursements for the two years under audit, the Balance Sheet as of June 30, 1938, and the Schedules of Ground Rents and Securities Owned as of June 30, 1938, are in agreement with the books of account of that Board, and, in our opinion, are true and correct.

TAIT, WELLER AND BAKER,
Accountants and Auditors.

Dr. Hoover introduced the Rev. W. A. Wade, the first Executive Secretary of the Deaconess Work in the United Lutheran Church, filling the newly established office. Dr. Wade addressed the Convention.

The Rev. E. F. Bachmann, Pastor of the Philadelphia Motherhouse, was introduced and addressed the Convention.

Dr. Hoover introduced Sister Martha Hansen, directing sister of the Baltimore Motherhouse, and Sister Anna Ebert, directing sister of the Philadelphia Motherhouse, each of whom addressed the Convention.

The probationers, present at the Convention, were introduced.

Moved and carried that the Convention request the Board of Deaconess Work to establish at least biennial conferences with such pastors, whose churches make use of deaconesses, as may desire to confer with the Board.

It was moved and carried that this Convention express, through its President, a word of congratulation from this Convention to the Philadelphia Motherhouse at its coming Fiftieth Anniversary celebration.

On motion the report of the auditors was accepted.

Mr. Carl M. Distler, President, presented the report of the Inner Mission Board.

REPORT OF THE INNER MISSION BOARD

(For action on the recommendations in this report, see p. 386.)

Against a background of rapidly changing developments in the whole field of social welfare the Inner Mission task of the Church assumes increasing significance. The struggle for economic and social security, which dominates modern life, seriously affects the spiritual health of mankind. The entrance of governmental agencies into the field of social work demands important adjustments on the part of the agencies and institutions of the Church, as well as of other private organizations. New attitudes of mind and new methods of approach lead to new emphases in dealing with the social needs of individual souls. The Church must be alert to the changed conditions it faces and recognize its increasing opportunities for Inner Mission service.

Conscious of its grave responsibility in the face of these modern conditions, the Inner Mission Board humbly and gratefully submits its report to the Eleventh Biennial Convention of the United Lutheran Church in America. The Board is grateful for the privilege of service which has been placed in its hands. It is humble before the tremendous responsibilities of the task, and trusts only in the all powerful Head of the Church to give that supply of grace of which we all ever stand in need. Our sufficiency is in Him "Who doeth all things well."

ADVANCE IN TWENTY YEARS

A glance backward over the twenty years of Inner Mission service of The United Lutheran Church in America reveals interesting and significant growth. That the Church has kept pace with the changing human needs of the age is apparent from the records.

Institutionally the Church was fairly well equipped at the beginning of 1918. Yet even here we find a steady growth in these twenty years. Seven new Homes for the Aged have come into existence to make a present total of twenty such institutions, serving wholly or in part the constituency of the United Lutheran Church in America. Two Lutheran hospitals have been established to make a total of seventeen general hospitals. Four new homes for children bring the total up to twenty-one. Six of the eleven hospices which the Church helps to maintain have been established within the last twenty years.

But more significant is the record of growth in agency development. This is in line with the trend of the times and the needs of our people. A little more than half of the thirty Inner Mission Societies serving the needs for Christian work in larger metropolitan areas have been organized since 1918, sixteen to be exact. Of a total of seven settlements and neighborhood houses, five have been established, most of them in the last eight years. Of even greater significance are these records: Six fresh air homes for underprivileged children have come into being, one mission for the deaf, one for the blind, one industrial mission caring for homeless men, and one child-placing agency have been organized since 1920.

Although all of these new institutions and agencies have been organized under sectional or local auspices, the impetus which helped to create them was due in part to the efforts of your Board in stimulating an Inner Mission spirit in the congregations of the Church. This has been done through Synodical Inner Mission Committees, of which there are now thirty-one in the thirty-four Synods; through literature which has been prepared and distributed; and through conferences and institutes which have been conducted by the Board. *Inner Mission Work,* a quarterly of Inner Mission methods and information, has been developed and distributed freely during the last five years to 700 Inner Mission leaders.

The Board in 1925, organized a Department of Immigrant and Seamen's Work which had a full-time Secretary, the Rev. E. A. Sievert, until 1932. Since that time, due to the decrease in immigration, Pastor Sievert has been employed only part time. A full-time worker has been maintained at Ellis Island, New York, and grants in aid have been given to the two Canadian Synods, to help maintain immigrant missionaries in Montreal and Winnipeg, Canada.

The Board has also entered the field of work for the physically handicapped, helping to maintain a Missionary to the Deaf who works in the territory of four states and three synods. A service to the Blind has been undertaken, to supply "Talking Books" for the blind and to publish Lutheran literature in Braille and on Talking Book records.

"A Message for the Day" for shut-ins and shut-outs has been continuously supplied to the Church at a cost far from self maintenance, throughout the twenty years.

REPORT FOR THE BIENNIUM

I.   Organization

During the last biennium, the Board has met regularly in semi-annual meetings in New York City. The Executive Committee has met, in the interim, on an average of six times each year to supervise the work and to plan for its advance.

The officers and personnel of the Board during the last two years were:

Officers:

President: Carl M. Distler, Esq., 401 American Building, Baltimore, Md.

Vice-president: The Rev. G. H. Bechtold, D.D., 1228 Spruce St., Philadelphia, Pa.

Secretary: The Rev. Harold S. Miller, 5313 Fourth Ave., Brooklyn, N. Y.

Treasurer: Mr. L. Henry Lund, 39 E. 35th St., New York City (until December 31, 1937).

Treasurer: Mr. Carl H. Lammers, 39 East 35th St., New York City (since January 1, 1938).

Executive Secretary: The Rev. C. E. Krumbholz, D.D., 39 E. 35th St., New York City.

Secretary for Immigrant and Seamen's Work: The Rev. E. A. Sievert, 219 Seventh Ave., New York City (part time only).

Board Members:

Terms Expire in 1938

The Rev. H. E. Crowell, D.D., 838 Woodlawn Ave., Springfield, Ohio

The Rev. Harold S. Miller, 5313 Fourth Ave., Brooklyn, N. Y.

The Rev. J. L. Sieber, D.D., 352 Church Ave., S. W., Roanoke, Va.

H. C. Hoffman, M.D., 295 Wills Road, Connellsville, Pa.

Mr. L. Henry Lund, Westinghouse Electric, East Pittsburgh, Pa.

Terms Expire in 1940

The Rev. F. K. Fretz, Ph.D., D.D., 330 Ferry St., Easton, Pa.

The Rev. A. H. Keck, D.D., 1348 West Fifth Ave., Gary, Ind.

The Rev. R. E. Kern, 135 South Third St., Hamburg, Pa.

Mr. T. P. Hickman, 10th St. and Penna Ave., N. W., Washington, D. C.

Mr. H. E. Isenhour, Salisbury, N. C.

Terms Expire in 1942

The Rev. G. H. Bechtold, D.D., 1228 Spruce St., Philadelphia, Pa.

The Rev. Herman Brezing, D.D., Wartburg Orphans' Farm School, Mt. Vernon, N. Y.

The Rev. P. D. Brown, D.D., 1330 Laurel St., Columbia, S. C.

Mr. Carl M. Distler, 401 American Building, Baltimore, Md.

Mr. Peter P. Hagan, 1103 Prospect Ave., Philadelphia, Pa. (Resigned May 1938.)

Mr. Carl H. Lammers, 160 Arlington Ave., Brooklyn, N. Y. (Elected by the Executive Board to fill the unexpired term.)

Advisory Members (appointed by the Women's Missionary Society): Mrs. P. M. Rossman, 318 West 84th St., New York City (until December 1937).
Mrs. Walter Hanning, 723 W. 4th St., Williamsport, Pa. (since May 1938).
Mrs. Wm. A. Snyder, 476 Clinton Ave., Brooklyn, N. Y.

Of the Board members whose terms expire in 1938, all except Dr. H. C. Hoffman, who has served faithfully for two terms, are eligible for re-election to the Board. Mr. L. Henry Lund though eligible has asked that his name be not placed on the nomination list, due to his inability to attend Board meetings.

II. Departments
A. CONGREGATIONAL

1. *An Inner Mission Program for the Congregation.*
The stimulation of the congregation in Inner Mission activity continues to be an outstanding concern of the Board. During the biennium this has been given new impetus through the publication of a four-page leaflet, "A Call to Adventure." Here the congregational program is outlined in the briefest terms possible. The leaflet has had wide distribution through Synodical Inner Mission Committees, at Summer Schools and during Inner Mission Month in 1937. Numerous conferences and study courses have been made the occasion to explain and discuss this program. Fuller suggestions for a congregational and community survey have also been made available as has the pamphlet, "Saved to Serve," which contains many helpful suggestions of a practical nature.

2. *The Outline for a Preaching Mission.*
This has also been distributed widely and put into use in many congregations. The merger of the Board and the Commitee on Evangelism will doubtlessly give this program for preaching missions a new impetus. The plan is easily adaptable to an educational mission and is being so used in a number of congregations. It has proved to be a valued means of strengthening faith and winning new souls to the Saviour. It is conservative, Lutheran, and avoids many of the abuses of careless and ineffective methods of evangelism.

3. *Child Welfare.*
The rapidly growing needs of the child in the midst of a depression and post depression period are of great concern to governmental, secular and Church agencies. This applies to the home as well as the institutional and health needs of children. Unfortunately, little attention has been

given by those concerned, to the recommendation of the Board adopted at the Columbus Convention: "That the Church recommend to its constituent Synods and their officers and to Inner Mission Committees and Boards the study of the need of Lutheran Child Caring Agencies in each Synod."

In only a few cases has this important resolution borne fruit. It is anticipated that in one instance, however, a child caring agency on a Synod-wide basis will be organized. The grants of the Federal Government to States for the care of dependent children, for child health service and for service to crippled children is being constantly studied by the Board in relation to the Church institutions.

4. *Lutheran Nurses' Guild.*

In co-operation with the Board of Education, the Inner Mission Board is vitally interested in a service to Lutheran nurses and their spiritual welfare. This service is being pushed forward with new vigor. Nurses' Guilds are being organized, communion services for nurses are being held and study groups organized. While the Lutheran nurse is a member of a professional group, her ministry is very largely to the underprivileged and she is in need of the interest and support of her Church. An effort is now being made to make every parish aware of the presence of Lutheran nurses in community hospitals, public health services, and elsewhere.

5. *Community Survey Conducted.*

At the request of the Inner Mission Committee of the Ohio Synod, the Board conducted a community survey of a certain district of Cincinnati which presents an Inner Mission problem. As a result of the survey the Board counselled with the Synodical authorities and offered to assist in the development of an Inner Mission project. In co-operation with other Synodical Committees assistance was also given to the problems of churches in industrial areas.

B. INSTITUTIONAL DEPARTMENT

1. *Consultation Service.*

The Consultation Service which the Board maintains for the benefit of institutions and agencies emerges into great usefulness with the changing trends in social work. The social security programs of the Federal and State Governments are being closely followed in the interests and protection of Church institutions particularly those for the care of children and the aged. Visitation of institutions and advice and counsel with their Superintendents and Boards form no small part of the work of this department. A multitude of problems face our institutions and agencies. These problems call for the sympathetic co-operation of the Church in their solution. There is need for adequately trained staffs of workers, for administrative effectiveness, and often for the introduction of approved methods of treatment of those under care. These and other vital concerns often fail of accomplishment because of the lack of proper support and intelligent interest on the part of the constituency of the organizations.

The Board is studying the subject of the Training of Cottage Mothers and Institutional Group Workers. It is also striving for more effective interpretation of the institution to the Church and a closer relationship of the institution to the Church through its constituent synods.

2. New Organizations.

The Board is happy to announce the development of additional services by the Rochester, N. Y., Inner Mission Society through the purchase of a Neighborhood House, where group work activities for children and adults and an industrial department have been established; the purchase by the Dayton Inner Mission League of a Neighborhood House which had been formerly rented; the establishment of Haverford Center, a Settlement House ministering to colored people, by the Philadelphia Inner Mission Society; the organization of a state-wide Lutheran Welfare Society with child care in Wisconsin; the merger of the Milwaukee Inner Mission Society with this new state agency; the calling of an Institutional Chaplain by the Lutheran Charities of Detroit; the erection of new buildings at Lowman Home, White Rock, S. C., and Tabitha Home, Lincoln, Nebr.; the recent organization of Inner Mission service by the congregations of Columbia, S. C.; and proposed organizations in Indianapolis, Ind.; Gary, Ind.; and Buffalo, N. Y.

Through the effective activity of the Lutheran Welfare Council of New York City, the first official Lutheran Chaplain ever appointed by the City of New York is serving as full-time chaplain at the Queens County General Hospital in Jamaica. A temporary grant in aid from the Inner Mission Board helps to supplement the small stipend received from the City.

The Board has also advised a number of Lutheran communities with regard to the organization of new work.

3. Statistics.

It is the duty of the Board each year to gather and compile for publication in the Year Book the statistics of all Inner Mission agencies and institutions which congregations of the United Lutheran Church in America help to support. The co-operation of the organizations in supplying these statistics is gratefully acknowledged. The information service which the Board maintains is greatly enhanced by these statistics, which are called for by agencies in and outside of the Lutheran Church.

A list of the institutions and agencies and full statistics regarding their services will be found in the Year Book of the United Lutheran Church. We incorporate only a summary in this report. These figures are for the year 1937.

21 Children's Homes cared for 2,068 children, including orphans, half orphans and those from broken homes.

15 Summer Camps gave 3,893 boys and girls a summer outing with training. Average length of stay was two weeks.

20 Old People's Homes ministered to 719 aged persons.

17 Hospitals gave treatment to 34,854 patients. 80,330 Dispensary visits were made.

11 Hospices provided a "home away from home" for 3,044 young men and women.

7 Sanatoria and Special Homes took care of 910 patients.

3 Seamen's Missions served 15,013 seamen in a variety of ways.

5 Settlements provided group work for 121,177 persons, including men, women and children.

91 children were placed in foster homes by one child-placing agency, making a total of over 500 children under supervision in this one agency.

3,724 deaf and blind persons were spiritually cared for in worship services and pastoral care.

2,089 men received assistance toward self-support in two Industrial Missions.

702,444 persons were served through 30 Inner Mission Agencies, which conduct family and child welfare departments, employment bureaus, institutional ministrations, prison missions and other services.

138 Institutions use 2,045 paid workers and 1,467 volunteers in caring for 843,508 persons at an expense of $3,162,663.

C. EDUCATIONAL DEPARTMENT

1. *Publications.*

Upon this department falls the major responsibility for the Board's promotional efforts. The publication of *Inner Mission Work*, a quarterly review of activities and information, the issue of a Bi-Monthly News Service for Synodical Inner Mission Committees, the preparation of pamphlets on social problems, the publication of literature on the work of the other departments, the preparation of materials for Inner Mission Month and the preparation of a new series of "A Message for the Day" have taken much time.

During the biennium, the Board has published:

"A Call to Adventure"—(Congregational Program)
"A Stranger and Ye Took Me In"—(Immigrant and Seamen's Work)
"Inner Mission Work" (eight issues)
"A Tour Through Inner Mission Fields" (Institutional)

"Flood, Fire and Drought"—(Disaster Relief)
"Inner Mission Parish Bulletin Cover" (for use during Inner Mission
    Month)
New Series of "A Message for the Day"

The Board has under consideration the publication of additional
pamphlets on Temperance. There is an unquestioned increase in the use
of alchoholic beverages and narcotics, and a consequent increase in im-
morality and crime. New treatments are being sought by medical science
for the care and cure of addicts. But spiritual forces must be applied
not only to the cure but to the prevention of these evils. No mere con-
demnation of the evil is sufficient. Pronouncements against the liquor
and drug traffic are in themselves futile. The Church, the Synods and
most of all the congregation must strive by educational and by spiritual
means and methods to eradicate the evils of the liquor traffic and the use
of narcotics.

Gambling and its train of tragic consequences has also been a subject
of serious study during the biennium. A pamphlet on this subject is
soon to be ready for publication.

However, in view of the merger of the Inner Mission Board and the
Committees on Moral and Social Welfare and on Evangelism, publication
of pamphlets on these social questions has been postponed until the
new and enlarged Board comes into being at this Convention of the
Church. The Inner Mission Board shares with the whole Church the
expectation and determination that under this new merged board a
vigorous and thorough study of social evils and their Christian solution
will be undertaken. Motivated by a thorough going evangelism and implemented with loving service of congregations, institutions and agencies,
the Inner Mission of the Church will, under a compassionate Saviour,
be fulfilled.

2. *Inner Mission Month.*

Due to the change in the calendar of Special Days and Seasons adopted
by the Columbus Convention, Inner Mission Month has been observed
from October 15th to November 15th. This change proved to be advan-
tageous to the Board, coinciding as it does with the time of "The
Mobilization for Human Needs," conducted by national Community
Chests and Councils. It was found acceptable also to a growing number
of Inner Mission Agencies which are conducting their annual appeal
for support at that time.

The Board offered the Church for the observance of its special season,
a parish bulletin cover with an appropriate picture and information
concerning the program of the Board. In addition, several Educational
pamphlets and booklets were offered for distribution. The Synodical
Inner Mission Committees, the official Church papers, and the co-opera-

tion of pastors made Inner Mission Month in 1937 top all records for the number of pieces of literature requested and active interest aroused.

Requests for literature were received from 1,105 parishes in 38 states, the District of Columbia, and Canada. Requests were filled for 210,886 Parish Bulletin Covers, 109,108 Immigrant Work folders, 49,643 copies of "A Call to Adventure," 1,837 "Why I Believe in Temperance," various leaflets and other pieces of literature. In all over 400,000 pieces of literature were distributed to the congregations.

3. A Message for the Day.

During the biennium, a new series of "A Message for the Day" has been prepared for the next four years. This message, covering each Sunday and all major festivals of the Church Year, is issued in about sixty separate four-page leaflets for each year. Each leaflet contains the propria of the day, a sermonette, a prayer and a hymn. It is designed to meet the needs of those who are prevented from attending church worship by reason of illness, disability or occupation. The annual subscription price is a very modest one, the Board supplementing the cost. The messages are sent out in bulk to cover a two-month period. There are now 9,615 subscriptions on order, a substantial increase over the number reported for the previous biennium. Many high testimonials of the effectiveness of this Message have been received.

"Der Kranken Trost," a similar message in German published in Germany, is also available and has a subscription list to date of 226.

4. Summer School Courses.

Inner Mission Courses in Lutheran Summer Schools have been given each summer of the biennium. The courses afford an invaluable opportunity to interpret to the lay leadership of the Church the work of the Board and the various types of Inner Mission service. They also present an outstanding opportunity to win workers for congregational Inner Mission service. Six courses in as many Summer Schools have been conducted by the Executive Secretary during the biennium. Inner Mission leaders over the country have conducted other courses.

D. DEPARTMENT OF WORK FOR THE HANDICAPPED

This department at present serves two types of handicapped persons, the deaf and the blind.

1. The Deaf.

The work among the deaf is carried on through the Rev. Edward F. Kaercher, Missionary to the deaf in the Ministerium of Pennsylvania. The Board makes a grant in aid to the salary of Missionary Kaercher because of his activity in four states and three synods. Preaching points are maintained in twelve cities, and frequent visits are made to institutions and in private homes.

Reports over the past two years show that 193 meetings were held at the twelve preaching points with an attendance of 7,638. There were 641 individual visits, 48 visits to Torresdale Home, 31 to the Pennsylvania School at Mt. Airy, 14 to Gallaudet College, 13 to the Eastern State Penitentiary, 13 to the Farview State Hospital for the Criminal Insane, and one visit to the Fanwood School.

Holy Communion was administered to 1,337. There were 3 baptisms, 34 confirmations, 1 marriage, 4 private communions, 711 contacts with prospects, and 4 new members. The Tenth Anniversary of the Philadelphia Mission for the Deaf was observed on November 29, 1936.

As opportunity affords, Pastor Kaercher meets with groups of deaf people during the winter for an evening of Bible study.

Owing to the extent of the field to be covered, the Board has interested itself in the preparation for this special ministry of another young man, admirably suited in personal qualifications. During the past biennium, Mr. Louis B. Sorensen was granted a scholarship sufficient to enable him to finish his first year at the Philadelphia Seminary. In the summer of 1937, this student was employed to survey the field of possible work in New York City, Binghamton, Elmira, Endicott and Johnson City. The results revealed that there is a field of ministry among the deaf in the cities of the southern part of New York State. Services are being held in Binghamton as often as possible. Unfortunately Mr. Sorensen has been compelled to leave the Seminary for reasons beyond his control. It is hoped that he may again enter the seminary in the fall of 1938 to complete his course.

The work among the deaf is beset with many difficulties, rarely understood by hearing people. That the work is worth while is amply attested by the spiritual response of those to whom this ministry is extended.

2. *The Blind.*

The work among the blind takes two forms. One is the purchase and distribution among Inner Mission Agencies of the Talking Book for the Blind and the preparation of Lutheran records for this machine. The other is the publication in Braille of Lutheran literature.

The "Talking Book" is equipped with both radio and turntable for records. Both the radio dial and the records are equipped with Braille lettering so that the machine can be operated by a sightless person. The records are obtainable through the Library of Congress, which maintains the service through branches covering the country, through which loans of records are made, postage free.

Through a fund given to the Inner Mission Board by the Women's Missionary Society and designated for this purpose, the Board has purchased and loaned Talking Books to the following Inner Mission Societies:

Lutheran Inner Mission Society of Trenton, N. J.
Lutheran Inner Mission Society of North Dakota
Lutheran Inner Mission Society of Reading, Pa.
Lutheran Charities of Detroit, Mich.
Inner Mission Society of New York City (two machines)
Board of Inner Missions of the Ministerium of Pennsylvania
Lutheran Welfare Society of Tacoma, Wash.
Lutheran Inner Mission Society of Pittsburgh, Pa.
Lutheran Inner Mission League of Miami Valley, Dayton, Ohio
Lutheran Inner Mission Society, Springfield, Ohio

Semi-annual reports of the use of the machines are required and the machines remain the property of the Board.

By special arrangement with Missionary J. R. Fink, a Talking Book has been sent to Rentinchintala, India, where a Lutheran School for the blind is maintained.

Through the kindness of Mr. John H. Schell, a booklet of which he is the author has been recorded on a Talking Book record. Mr. Schell has contributed to the Board twenty-five copies of this recording. These have been distributed on loan to those who are using the machines. The book, "Lutheran Landmarks and Pioneers in America," by the Rev. Wm. J. Finck, D.D., is now being recorded on a Talking Book record.

Luther's Small Catechism and Explanation by Dr. Stump is being printed in Braille and will be ready for distribution in the fall of 1938.

The Board is in a position to supply the International Sunday School Lessons in Braille upon application to its Headquarters. The co-operation of the John Milton Foundation makes this possible.

E. Department of Immigrants' and Seamen's Work

The work of this department is under the care of a part-time Secretary for Immigrant Work, the Rev. E. A. Sievert.

1. *General.*

Active service is rendered the immigrant and emigrant in three centers, the Port of New York, the Port of Montreal, Quebec, Canada, and in Winnipeg, Manitoba, Canada. The Board maintains a full-time social service worker at Ellis Island, who is rendering most efficient service. Co-operation and most cordial relationships are maintained in the Port of New York with the Lutheran Emigrant House Association, the Lutheran Immigrant Society, the Lutheran Welfare Council, the German Society and with Government officials and other workers with immigrants.

In Canada, the Board co-operates with the Canada Synod and with the Manitoba Synod, giving grants in aid to both for the immigrant work done in Montreal and Winnipeg respectively.

2. *Statistics.*

The character of the work done at each of the immigrant stations differs from the other two. Hence, uniform statistics are difficult. Nevertheless, a uniform report blank has been developed and put into use during the biennium. The large number of immigrants are arriving in Canada; therefore of the 4,402 names of Lutheran persons sent to pastors, 2,884 arrived in Montreal and were first greeted by Dr. Otto Klaehn, the Immigrant Missionary of the Canada Synod. The 1,657 persons met on arriving and departing trains were also served in the Canadian cities of Montreal and Winnipeg, where the Rev. G. O. Juettner acts as Immigrant and City Missionary of the Manitoba Synod. The service rendered on the other hand to emigrants was largely done in the Port of New York where Miss Amanda Schneider is employed for full time by the Board. Under a variety of classifications 2,918 cases of emigrants were served. Our Immigrant Secretary, the Rev. E. A. Sievert, with the co-operation of the Emigrant House Association, has sent out the names of 1,366 immigrants to the pastors all over the United States.

The following statistics compiled from the monthly reports of the work done in New York, Montreal and Winnipeg for the biennium show the following interesting figures:

Hospital calls—2,993 on 1,823 patients
Other calls made in institutions (Homes for Aged, Prisons, etc.)—1,434
Office interviews including telephone interviews—5,129
Letters written—4,388
Employment secured for 330 persons
Relief given in cash, food, clothing to 550
Funds handled for those detained at Ellis Island—$1,213.90
Religious services held—132
Baptisms—10
Marriages—58
Funerals—11
Communion administered to—128

These are only a few of the figures culled from the reports. They do not begin to tell the story of a Christian work of mercy done among the strangers at our gates. The heartaches, the disillusionments, the intricate maze of laws and regulations, the sickness of body and soul, all these lie behind figures and are recorded only in the hearts of the missionaries and of the thousands who pass in and out of the stations maintained by the Church for their service and comfort.

3. *Contacts with Foreign Ports.*

The Board also maintains active contacts with European Lutheran workers. These contacts are valuable both from the standpoint of those who enter this country and Canada and also in the interests of those who are voluntarily or legally deported. The services to those who are in danger of deportation are many and require exact knowledge of the legal questions involved, as well as regular contacts with government officials.

The conditions in some of the countries from which Lutheran immigrants come has immeasurably added to the difficulties of our immigrant missionaries. To avoid hopeless confusion it is essential that there be one common Lutheran agency in this country to act particularly in the case of religious refugees. The Lutheran World Convention seems the logical organization to conduct this agency. (See Recommendation 3.)

4. *Survey of Port Work for Seamen.*

To assist in making effective the recommendation adopted at the Columbus Convention regarding the needs of Lutheran seamen, the Board has made a survey of seamen's work in ocean and lake ports in the United States and Canada. The Inner Mission Committees of those Synods on whose territory ports are located were asked to help in this survey. The Committees of ten synods responded. The work in twenty ocean and lake ports was thus surveyed. From the replies received, it is apparent that distinctly American work is done through the Y. M. C. A. The Church of England operates through Seamen's Institutes, while work which is nationalistic or linguistic in character is usually termed a Church Mission. Most agencies organized on the basis of national interests are Lutheran. In twelve cities the Lutheran Church does a distinctive work, and in eight others it co-operates with other Churches.

The situation in the city of Mobile is to be further investigated with a view to establish the need for work to be built on a former service which is now inoperative.

As a result of the survey we believe that Synodical Inner Mission Committees and congregations in port cities should interest themselves in a four-fold program of work among Lutheran seamen:

1. To create library facilities and to contribute books and magazines.
2. To provide spiritual services in the churches and pastoral care for our own seamen.
3. To provide helpful social contacts for seamen through proper entertainments and outings.
4. To care spiritually for seamen who are sick in hospitals.

F. DISASTER RELIEF

At the Columbus Convention, the Church took action authorizing this Board to develop an adequate organization and program to cope with disaster emergencies that may affect the Church on any part of its territory. During the biennium three such disasters occurred and disaster relief work became a reality.

Inasmuch as the full story of the work of Disaster Relief appears in pamphlet form at this convention it will not be necessary to rehearse it here. For the sake of the record, only a brief report is therefore made.

During the last week of January 1937, the Ohio River Valley was visited with the worst flood of its history. Devastation and ruin were widespread. Twenty-two of the congregations of the United Lutheran churches were seriously affected either by damage to church properties or losses in the homes of the members or both.

The Disaster Relief Committee outlined a four-fold program which it immediately put into effect.

Emergency relief was made available to the pastors and people of the stricken area. Four clothing centers were opened at strategic points as soon as transportation facilities were available. With Dayton, Ohio, as temporary relief headquarters, clothing, bedding, food and furniture were sent into the affected areas.

As soon as possible visits were made to each of the churches which had suffered. Pastors who had sustained losses in their own homes were quickly rehabilitated so that they could serve their people. Co-operation was eagerly offered by all concerned, and the dire needs of the first pressing necessity were relieved.

The rehabilitation of Church properties was a more serious matter. Expert opinion was sought and readily given by other Boards and Committees of the Church. Thirteen church properties were repaired or restored through grants in aid from the funds gathered by special appeal, authorized by the officers of the Church. Amounts were given according to the need and the ability of the congregation to bear some of the loss.

Family rehabilitation was also undertaken where and when necessary, the pastors co-operating with the Committee. It was more than a year after the flood before the last church was rededicated and the disaster relief closed in the Ohio River Valley.

The Hindenberg disaster occurred early in May 1937. Representatives of the Inner Mission Board arrived on the scene within a few hours after the disaster. Pastoral ministrations were offered to the victims, many of whom were Lutheran brethren. Dr. G. H. Bechtold and the Rev. Carl H. Miller attended Captain Lehmann and ministered to him at his death. Regular visits were made for weeks after the disaster to four hospitals in which the victims were cared for. Funerals were held for those who died and their families were comforted.

The drought in the Saskatchewan province of Western Canada brought an appeal from the Manitoba Synod to the Board for assistance. Investigation by the Board's representative revealed that here, too, was a disaster of no small import.

Again the utmost care was given to insure the wisest use of the funds of the Church. Clothing collections in the states nearest the border were made and arrangements were effected for transportation to strategic points in Canada. Sixteen pastors were given grants to take the place of salaries which could not be paid because the crops had failed, in many places for five to seven successive years. These grants are being paid quarterly extending over the year from November, 1937, to September, 1938, when it is hoped a new harvest can be gathered.

The Church has responded generously to the appeal for the relief of its stricken brethren. Funds were carefully administered at the point of greatest need.

The Inner Mission Board is grateful for the opportunity to serve the Church in these disasters. A permanent organization is being perfected through Synodical Inner Mission Committees so that the whole Church will be covered and disasters dealt with promptly when and where they occur. The Board submits the full report of this department of its work in booklet form as a part of this report.

III.   General Matters

1. *Synodical Committees.*

During the biennium definite efforts have been made to make the work of Synodical Inner Mission Committees more effective. One-day conferences with the Chairmen and members of these committees have been made in twenty Synods. It is important that the personnel of these committees be continued over a period of years so that more effective work can be done. The Synodical Committees have co-operated to a marked degree with the Board in Disaster Relief work, Inner Mission Month, and in securing information of the Inner Mission activities of congregations and pastors. The congregational program is being promoted and institutional ministrations are widespread.

2. *Placement Bureau.*

The Board has received during the biennium a large number of applications from individuals seeking service in the Inner Mission field. A small number of these have been placed in positions, for which they are qualified to serve. The problem of trained workers for agencies and institutions is a major one today. The Church must keep pace with the standards of work set by secular and governmental agencies. To do this trained workers are required who can be accredited and recognized as leaders in their field.

The Board is developing a placement bureau through which applicants can be placed in Inner Mission agencies and institutions where vacancies occur. This placement bureau will also advise those who apply of the requirements for service in Inner Mission work. It is hoped that our organizations will co-operate with this Bureau when they have vacancies in their staffs.

3. *The National Lutheran Inner Mission Conference.*

The Board has always had a deep interest in this conference which brings together in annual convention Inner Mission workers from all

Lutheran bodies, save one. The Conference is for free discussion, with no administrative functions for the organizations which are members. It deals with techniques close to the operations of Inner Mission work, but it is evolving through the years a philosophy of Church social work. It is also establishing standards for all phases of the activities represented.

4. *Other Activities.*

In addition to other services, the Board has seized every opportunity to present its work to Synods, conferences and other groups. Addresses and sermons were delivered, institutions and agencies were officially visited and counselled, courses in summer schools were held and the student bodies of seminaries were counselled concerning Inner Mission work in their future pastorates.

Individual conferences in the office and in the field were held. The administration of the Board's headquarters and its many interests have been cared for by the Board's three full-time workers and a part-time secretary for Immigrant work.

RECOMMENDATIONS
(For action, see p. 386.)

1. We recommend that the Church approve as a general principle that constituent synods seek such relationship with non-synodical inner mission agencies and institutions on their respective territories as shall give the latter recognition as official church organizations.

2. In keeping with the high ideals underlying all Christian work we recommend that all inner mission institutions and agencies of the Church keep all records, books and accounts in strict conformity with the highest standards approved by Federal and State agencies.

3. We recommend that the Inner Mission Board be authorized to co-operate with the Lutheran World Convention in caring for religious refugees who come to the United States and Canada.

Respectfully submitted,

FOR THE INNER MISSION BOARD,
CARL M. DISTLER, *President.*
C. E. KRUMBHOLZ, *Executive Secretary.*

REPORT OF THE TREASURER OF THE INNER MISSION BOARD

CASH RECEIPTS AND DISBURSEMENTS—GENERAL FUND
July 1, 1936 to June 30, 1937

Balance, July 1, 1936 .... $ 5,307.42
RECEIPTS
Apportionment $16,150.00
Sales "Message for the Day".. 1,074.95

Sales, Other Literature......................................	33.00	
Contributions	567.30	
Refunds and Miscellaneous.............................	437.43	
United Lutheran Publication House........................	1,806.20	
		20,068.88
Total Receipts		$25,376.30

DISBURSEMENTS

Executive:		
Secretary Salary	$3,166.60	
Secretary Travel	684.21	
Board Meetings	1,377.27	
Committee Meetings	325.22	
		$ 5,553.30
Administrative:		
Office Salary	$1,590.00	
Extra Help	120.60	
Supplies	145.41	
Expense	194.78	
Maintenance	656.16	
Postage	100.46	
Insurance and Miscellaneous..................	260.25	
Audit	100.00	
		3,167.66
Promotion:		
Literature and Printing.............................	$ 495.64	
Postage	200.00	
		695.64
"Message for the Day":		
Postage	$ 200.00	
Printing	1,464.32	
		1,664.32
Immigrant and Seaman's Work:		
Expenses	$ 270.07	
Secretary Salary	600.00	
Worker's Salary	1,351.00	
		2,221.07
Deaf and Blind Work:		
Expense	$ 1.64	
Talking Machines Bought........................	234.76	
Scholarships	250.00	
Surveys	200.00	
		686.40
Grants in Aid:		
Ellis Island	$ 60.00	
Canada Synod	240.00	
Manitoba Synod	699.96	
Ministerium of Pennsylvania,		
Deaf Work	900.00	
Williams-Henson Homes	349.92	
		2,249.88
Total Disbursements		16,238.27
Cash in Bank, June 30, 1937...		$ 9,138.03

CASH RECEIPTS AND DISBURSEMENTS—DISASTER RELIEF

July 1, 1936 to June 30, 1937

RECEIPTS

Dr. E. C. Miller... $39,000.00

DISBURSEMENTS

Office and Clerical...	$ 145.75
Travel	501.95
Literature and Printing.......................................	715.18
Office Expense	168.42
Office Postage	208.39
Property Rehabilitation	28,800.80
Miscellaneous Flood Relief.................................	8,073.02

Total Disbursements 38,613.51

Cash in Bank, June 30, 1937... $ 386.49

CASH RECEIPTS AND DISBURSEMENTS—GENERAL FUND

July 1, 1937 to June 30, 1938

Cash in Bank, July 1, 1937.. $ 9,138.03

RECEIPTS

Apportionment	$17,170.00	
Contributions:		
Women's Missionary Society	500.00	
German Society of New York.....................................	360.00	
Bequest, Bauer Estate..	256.32	
Miscellaneous	488.34	
Sales, "Message for the Day".....................................	1,120.23	
Accrual, "Message for the Day"..............................	2,699.96	
Sales, "Der Kranke Trost" and other literature	37.15	
Interest on Savings Accounts.....................................	32.85	
Refund, Cincinnati Survey...	133.18	
		22,798.03

Total Receipts $31,936.06

DISBURSEMENTS

Executive:		
Secretary Salary	$3,900.00	
Secretary Travel	660.72	
Board Meetings	632.46	
Committee Meetings	146.65	
		$ 5,339.83
Administrative:		
Office Salary	$1,590.00	
Extra Help	355.93	
Supplies	138.44	
Expense	151.49	
Maintenance	1,024.76	

Postage	158.26	
Insurance and Miscellaneous..................	155.95	
Audit	100.00	
Furniture	25.00	
		3,699.83

Promotion:

Office Library	$ 24.56	
Literature and Printing............................	2,622.55	
Regional Conferences	47.80	
Committee of Executive Secretaries......	144.50	
Postage	400.00	
		3,239.41

"Message for the Day":

Accrual	$2,699.96	
Postage	250.00	
Printing	1,508.83	
		4,458.79

Immigrant and Seaman's Work:

Expenses	$ 153.99	
Secretary Salary	600.00	
Workers' Salary	1,351.50	
		2,105.49

Deaf and Blind Work:

Survey	$ 100.00	
Literature Published	275.00	
John Milton Society....................................	25.00	
		400.00

Grants in Aid:

Ellis Island Relief.......................................	$ 90.00	
Canada Synod	456.60	
Manitoba Synod	699.96	
Ministerium of Pennsylvania,		
Deaf Work	900.00	
Williams-Henson Home	349.92	
Queens Chaplain	300.00	
	2,796.48	
Bond Purchased	262.50	

Total Disbursements	22,302.33
Cash in Bank, June 30, 1938..	$ 9,633.73

CASH RECEIPTS AND DISBURSEMENTS—DISASTER RELIEF

July 1, 1937 to June 30, 1938

Cash in Bank, July 1, 1937..	$ 386.49

Dr. E. C. Miller	$26,000.00
Contributions	952.15
Total Receipts	$26,952.15
	$27,338.64

DISBURSEMENTS

Flood Relief	$20,671.66
Canadian Relief	6,241.66
Total Disbursements	$26,913.32
Cash in Bank, June 30, 1938	$ 425.32

BALANCE SHEET

June 30, 1938

ASSETS

	General Fund	Disaster Relief
Cash in Banks:		
Fifth Avenue Bank	$ 5,881.07	
Fifth Avenue Bank	250.00	$ 425.32
Bowery Savings Bank, "Message for the Day"	3,072.19	
Bowery Savings Bank, Women's Missionary Fund	430.47	
Total Cash in Banks	$ 9,633.73	$ 425.32
United States Savings Bonds	262.50	
Petty Cash	50.00	
Furniture and Fixtures	100.00	
Talking Book Machines	300.00	
Travel Expense Fund	100.00	
Total Assets	$10,446.23	$ 425.32

FUNDS

General Fund	$10,446.23	
Disaster Relief		$ 425.32

Respectfully submitted,
CARL H. LAMMERS, *Treasurer.*

We have audited the books of account of the Treasurer and examined the securities of the Inner Mission Board of the United Lutheran Church in America for the biennium beginning July 1, 1936 and ending June 30, 1938, and we hereby certify that, in our opinion, the foregoing statements of Cash Receipts and Disbursements for the years ended June 30, 1937 and June 30, 1938, and the Balance Sheet as of June 30, 1938, are in accordance with the books of account, and are true and correct.

TAIT, WELLER AND BAKER,
Accountants and Auditors.

Mr. Distler introduced the Rev. Harold S. Miller, Chairman of the Educational Department, who spoke on the work of that department; the Rev. F. K. Fretz, Chairman of the Institutional Department, who spoke on that work; and the Rev. G. H. Bechtold, Chairman of the Congregational Department and the Department of Disaster Relief, who spoke especially of the service of relief in the flood area of the middle west and in the needy areas of northwest Canada, making reference also to Pastor Carl H. Miller in his service given in special cases.

Mr. Distler also introduced the Rev. C. E. Krumbholz who spoke of his work as Executive Secretary.

The recommendations of the Inner Mission Board were considered and 1, 2 and 3 were adopted.

On motion the report of the auditors was accepted.

As an item of unfinished business, Item V, 2, of the report of the Executive Board, concerning the Budget of the United Lutheran Church, for 1940 and 1941, was considered. (For other references, see pp. 88, 481, 482.)

The Rev. Carl W. Nutzhorn presented the following as a substitute for that which appears under V, 2, of the report of the Executive Board:

That the total budget for 1940 and 1941 be set at $1,100,000, which is an increase of slightly more than ten per cent over the total disbursements of 1937-1938, the receipts to be divided on the percentage basis stated in the recommended budget, V, 2.

	Percentage	Amount	1938 Disbursement	Proposed Budget
Foreign Missions...............	30.00	$330,000	$303,000	$600,000
American Missions..........	38.57	424,270	389,557	771,400
Education	9.00	99,000	90,900	180,000
Social Missions	1.82	20,200	19,404*	36,400
Ministerial Pen. & Rel...	11.75	129,250	118,675	235,000
Deaconess Work.............	2.00	22,000	20,200	40,000
Parish & Church School	1.22	13,420	11,830	24,400
National Luth. Council	1.15	12,650	11,615	23,000
Amer. Bible Society	.25	2,750	2,525	5,000
U. L. C. A. Treasury....	4.24	46,690	42,824	84,800
	100.00	$1,100,230	$1,010,530	$2,000,000

* Note: This amount is composed of the following items: Inner Mission Board $17,170; Tabitha Home $1,420; Lowman Home $284; Total $19,404.

The substitute was seconded. (For further action, see pp. 481, 482.)

A motion to adjourn was made and carried.

The Rev. John C. Mattes, Chairman of the Committee of Reference and Counsel, announced the deaths of the Rev. George W. Fritch, Sr., and the Rev. August Pohlman.

At twelve o'clock the Convention adjourned with prayer by the Rev. M. Koolen.

SEVENTH SESSION

LORD BALTIMORE HOTEL
Baltimore, Maryland
Monday, October 10, 1938, 2.00 P. M.

Devotions were conducted by the Rev. C. S. Simonton, and the President called the Convention to order.

The Secretary presented the report concerning the roll of the Convention as follows:

> Number of delegates elected:
> Clergymen, 278; Laymen, 272; Total—550
>
> Number of delegates in attendance:
> Clergymen, 277; Laymen, 264; Total—541
>
> Upon the reception of the Central Pennsylvania Synod, one clerical and one lay delegate were dropped from the combined delegation.
>
> Twenty-five synods have one hundred per cent attendance of their delegations.
>
> Seven laymen are absent. Five synods have one delegate absent; one synod has two delegates absent.
>
> Two delegates from the Andhra Evangelical Lutheran Church, and one delegate and one visitor from the Evangelical Lutheran Church in Japan are present.

The Special Committee on Minutes reported that they had examined the Minutes of the Third, Fourth and Fifth Sessions and, finding them correct, moved their approval. The motion was carried and the President declared the Minutes of those sessions approved.

The Rev. J. C. Mattes, Chairman, presented the following report of the Committee of Reference and Counsel.

REPORT OF THE COMMITTEE OF REFERENCE AND COUNSEL

1. We recommend that the special representatives present be heard at the conclusion of this report and be given three minutes each:

> Rev. George William Brown, American Bible Society
> H. P. Caemmerer, Secretary of the National Commission of Fine Arts
> Rev. John Hall, Chaplain
> Rev. S. O. Thorlaksson of the Icelandic Synod, bringing the greetings of that body

2. We recommend that the President convey the greetings and best wishes of the Convention to Dr. Uhl.

3. We propose that the matter referred to us by Mrs. W. N. Schnure be referred to the Executive Board for disposition.

4. Presented by the Rev. Carl H. Hirzel—"Resolved, that the question of corporate communion by auxiliaries of the Church be studied by the Executive Board." Recommended for adoption.

5. Presented by the Rev. Horace S. Mann—"Resolved, that the United Lutheran Church investigate the feasibility of forming a holding company in which boards and congregations may invest endowments, and from which congregations could borrow for building purposes." We recommend that this be referred to the Executive Board.

6. We recommend that the Convention approve the following:

> Whereas the Executive Board of the Golden Gate International Exposition has offered to set apart a day, or a series of days, which will be devoted to Lutheran use; and

> Whereas the congregations of The United Lutheran Church in America in the San Francisco area have made a request for such participation, and all other Lutheran bodies will be referred to them in the event that they wish to sponsor such a day or days;

> Resolved, that The United Lutheran Church in America endorse such a day, the exact day or dates to be determined by the local committee in consultation with the Executive Board of The United Lutheran Church in America.

7. We recommend that the report of the Special Committee of Nine on theological education be made a special order immediately following the report of the Committee on Title of Bishop and that thirty minutes be assigned for such presentation.

8. We recommend that the Publicity Committee be given three minutes for an announcement concerning special envelopes, etc., directly after the special representatives have been heard.

9. In view of the fact that today is the Canadian National Thanksgiving Day, we suggest that the President extend the felicitations of the Convention to the Church in Canada.

10. The following greetings have been received:

"Japan Mission looks confidently to Baltimore Convention."

"May the spirit of God guide your Convention to know and to do His Will. Greetings with Isaiah 40: 9. T. O. Burntvedt, President, Lutheran Free Church."

"I regret that I was not able to arrange my Eastern trip in such a way as to make it possible for me to attend your Church Convention at Baltimore. Neither was it possible to send some other pastor as my representative.

"However, by means of this letter I wish to express my sincere greetings and wishes for God's richest blessing on the Convention and your work. I also hope that the friendly spirit and mutual understanding between our Synod and your Church body will continue in increasing measure. A. Haapanen, President, The Finnish Evangelical Lutheran Church."

1. Adopted.

2. Adopted.

3. Adopted.

4. Adopted.

5. Adopted.

6. Adopted.

7. Adopted.

8. Adopted.

9. Adopted. The President carried out this instruction by addressing the representatives of the Church in Canada, present as delegates to the Convention.

10. The greetings were received and responses provided for.

The report of the Representative of the U. L. C. A. on the Advisory Council of the American Bible Society was presented by the Rev. H. C. Alleman.

REPORT OF REPRESENTATIVE IN THE ADVISORY COUNCIL OF THE AMERICAN BIBLE SOCIETY

(For action on the recommendations in this report, see p. 391.)

Your representative in the Advisory Council of the American Bible Society herewith submits his ninth biennial report.

Two meetings of the Council were held during our biennium. Your representative was present at the first meeting; his place was taken at the second meeting by Dr. E. B. Burgess. It was again gratifying to your representatives to find, among the more than thirty ecclesiastical bodies represented, that five of them were Lutheran, namely, the Augustana Synod, the Norwegian Lutheran Church, the American Lutheran Church, the United Lutheran Church and, unofficially, the Missouri Synod. Dr. Bersell was chosen as chairman of the 1937 meeting.

The chief function of the Council is to secure a closer relation between the churches and the Society. The Council sits with the Secretaries and the Treasurer in making the budget for the ensuing year and with the Board of Managers when the budget is adopted. The general work of the society, including its missionary activities and its financial operations, is thus intimately laid before the representatives of the churches. Recommendations from the Council are sought and welcomed.

Since the depression of 1929 the Society has been operating on a curtailed budget of less than a million dollars. The sale of Scriptures has yielded about a quarter of that amount, the income from invested funds another quarter, all other sources another quarter. For the balance it must look to the churches. In 1937 the churches contributed $117,354. Our own United Lutheran Church led the Lutheran groups with $3,266.

The Society is able to announce a matter of world-wide interest, namely, the fact that the number of languages in which the Scriptures have been published has passed the one thousand mark. The Society has therefore adopted as the theme for Bible Sunday this year "And Now—One Thousand Tongues." Material, including a new stereopticon lecture, will be furnished on request to pastors as usual. At the end of 1937 the whole Bible had been published in 179 languages, the New Testament in 213, portions or selections in 616 more, making a total of 1,008 languages and dialects.

In the most important of its activities the Society's total circulation in 1937 fell somewhat below the previous year due chiefly to the state of war in China and a combination of circumstances in Japan. In spite of handicaps in these two great mission fields a grand total of more than seven and one-third million copies of Bibles, Testaments, Gospels and Portions were distributed throughout the world.

A decided increase in Latin America of more than twenty per cent would have been even greater had it not been that inadequate funds stood in the way. In Brazil once again more Scriptures were put in circulation than in any year since the Society began its work there more than fifty years ago. In the Philippine Islands and Siam there were also encouraging increases. In the Near East and in China united operations were effectively carried on with the British and Foreign Bible Society resulting in a greater simplicity of administration and in a reduction in expenses.

In the United States the circulation was appreciably above that of the year before there being a very noticeable increase in the number of New

Testaments distributed. The Ohio Valley flood emergency early in the year, met by a special appeal, required nearly ten thousand Bibles and more than fifty thousand Testaments and Portions for churches, individuals, and refugee camps. Slightly over forty-one thousand New Testaments were furnished free to the young men in the CCC camps, and federal institutions, hospitals, orphanages, and other agencies were supplied with generous grants. Nearly thirty-five hundred embossed volumes were furnished in Braille and other systems to the blind at a moderate cost, or when appropriate, as outright grants.

The American Bible Society is therefore a great missionary institution, continually aiding the churches in their work of extending the Kingdom of God at home and abroad, being particularly the invaluable handmaid of the foreign missionary enterprise.

Your representative recommends: (For action, see p. 391.)

1. That this body endorse the observance of Universal Bible Sunday by our churches;

2. That we endorse the work of the Society in its program of extend-. ing the circulation of the Holy Scriptures in the languages of the world;

3. And that the United Lutheran Church continue its representation in the advisory council of the American Bible Society.

Respectfully submitted,

HERBERT C. ALLEMAN.

Dr. Alleman introduced Dr. George William Brown, Secretary of the American Bible Society, who emphasized the work done by that great institution in a concrete way, holding before the eyes of the Convention a copy of the Gospel according to St. John as it has recently been translated into the one thousandth language.

The recommendations of the representative on the Advisory Council of the American Bible Society were considered and 1, 2 and 3 were adopted.

The President conveyed the best wishes of the Convention to Dr. Uhl, age 91, who appeared in person and addressed the Convention briefly.

Mr. Belding B. Slifer, President, introduced Mr. Harry Hodges, Executive Secretary, who presented the report of the Board of Ministerial Pensions and Relief.

REPORT OF THE BOARD OF MINISTERIAL
PENSIONS AND RELIEF

(For action on the resolution in this report, see p. 415.)

Someone has said and well said, that birthday anniversaries are the milestones in life's journey and as the United Lutheran Church celebrates the twentieth of these its anniversary landmarks, the Board of Ministerial Pensions and Relief congratulates it on having traveled thus far successfully on and expresses the hope that as it goes from milestone to milestone, it may go from strength to strength, and from grace to grace.

During seven of these twenty years, this Board has served in the Church as a Board of Relief and for thirteen years as a Board of Pensions and Relief. Not until the scroll of time is unrolled will the blessings of its ministrations be manifest.

At the beginning of its career its family was constituted as follows:

Retired Ministers	165
Disabled Ministers	25
Widows	313
Children	73
Total	576

Today its family is constituted as follows:

Retired Ministers	347
Disabled Ministers	55
Widows	568
Children	157
Missionaries (Women)	6
Total	1,133

Its family has increased 97%. Its income from the Church has decreased 30%. See the appended graph.

It is only in the past twenty years that the Evangelical Churches in the United States and Canada have taken up seriously the God-given duty of providing a regular and adequate support for ministers after they have retired from service. Before that the Church leaders on this side of the Atlantic Ocean acted as though their responsibility extended no farther than giving alms to such of the old workers or their families as might be in actual want. It had long been recognized that God's command to care for them in a stated and sufficient manner was explicit, and many were determined to undertake the task in earnest.

At first it was believed that large endowments would furnish the necessary money. More careful study showed that this method would never be equal to the task. The Protestant Episcopal Church collected a prior service fund of about $8,000,000 and then set up an actuarial annuity fund in 1918. Its success and adequacy in a brief time was such that all the leading American churches (the Universalists and ourselves being the exceptions) have followed the model and are now establishing contributory annuity funds.

Twenty-six strong communions have funds that are giving present relief to ministers who have already grown old and are building up strong reserves to pay virtual retirement salaries in the future. They are making annual payments of $10,411,436 today to 37,419 persons and have 21,555 members participating in the reserve funds for future annuities. It has been said that this is the greatest movement in recent years to correct the shortcomings of the Church in the past.

During the past biennium, the question has been asked of the Board repeatedly: "Why have we heard nothing concerning the new pension plan?" The Board has remained silent on the subject and makes no reference to the plan in this report because the Columbus Convention took it from the Board and placed it with a Committee, who will report to this Convention.

May we state in passing, that this Convention must either adopt a contributory pension plan or grant the Board more money as it cannot continue indefinitely to pile up a deficit, which today amounts to $85,811.18. The Pension Roll grows annually but the income does not. We pay $1,000 more in pensions per month than we did one year ago.

At the Columbus Convention you privileged the Board to continue to pay pensions at the present rate, in spite of the fact that there was a continuous accumulating deficit.

There has been no money borrowed. The deficit represents moneys belonging in the endowment fund. There is a note in the endowment fund for the amount. At this Convention we ask you to take definite action with a resolution at the end of the report.

Employees of religious organizations are not included in the provisions of the Social Security Act. The Pension Boards of other Communions have made provision for their lay employees. Your Board raises the question has the time come for the United Lutheran Church to follow suit.

From a perusal of the financial report, it will be noted that the Board is a good steward, the income from the endowment is good; but it is equally manifest that the Church is a poor steward, the income from the apportionment is not good. Owing to the persistent low rate of interest on all invested money and the necessity of purchasing the highest grade of bonds, the average interest earned is 4% net, which we all know is a very good average under present-day conditions.

It is easily seen that if a rate of interest in the amount of six per cent per annum were obtained on the entire fund of the Board, the total income would only be increased $68,129.23 yearly, which, if added to the present income, would still fall very short of the amount needed to pay pensions, even at the present rate of but $300 per year for ministers and $200 for widows.

The various accounts are watched continually to see that as much money as possible may be kept earning interest.

The negotiable securities are kept in a custodian account with one of the best banks in Philadelphia.

The Finance Committee, composed of men of financial, insurance and real estate experience, gives considerable time each month studying the real estate problems and makes every effort to hold down the cost of maintenance and upkeep. The maintenance of our real estate, exclusive of the Beury Building, in 1937 amounted to $14,867.50 or 21.5% of the gross income. The maintenance of the Beury Building amounted to $37,148.48 or 61.3% of the gross income. Our real estate at all times has been kept in very good physical condition.

THE CAMPAIGN FUND

The total subscription was $4,175,065. At this date (June 30, 1938) there has been paid $3,235,346.86 or 77%. Of this amount there has been paid during the past biennium $7,897.20. 665 churches have paid their subscriptions in full. 421 churches paid nothing.

STATISTICS

Since the last report the following additions and deductions have been made in the roll: .

Additions:

Retired and Disabled Ministers, 107; Widows, 68; Children, 55; Missionaries, 1.

Deductions:

Retired and Disabled Ministers, 51; Widows, 76; Children, 39; Missionaries, none.

During the biennium 78 special grants were made amounting to $3,675. The Roll by Synods is as follows:

Synod	Retired	Dis-abled	Widows	Chil-dren	Mission-aries	Pension	Relief
Alleghany	10		9			$ 4,800	$ 100
California	16	2	13	1		8,050	300
Canada	12	1	16	3		7,250	100
East Pennsylvania	17	2	34*	1		12,550	100
Florida	3	2	1	3		1,850	
Georgia-Alabama	1		6			1,500	60
Illinois	10	3	28****	17		10,350	700
Indiana	10		11	1		5,250	160
Iowa	2	1	5	3		2,050	
Kansas	3	1	8	2		2,900	
Kentucky-Tennesse			5			1,000	
Manitoba	4	7	5	15		5,050	280

Maryland	23	1	29			13,000	600
Michigan			8	1		1,650	
Midwest	17	2	15	10		9,200	
Mississippi		1		1		350	
Nebraska	3	1	10			3,200.00	100
New York	31	4	79*	17		27,150	480
North Carolina	11		28	5		9,150	340
Northwest	1		10	5		2,550	
Nova Scotia		2	1	2		900	
Ohio	33	3	47	12	1	21,100	760
Pacific	6		5			2,800	100
Pennsylvania Min.	42	6	64	15		27,950	560
Pittsburgh	26	4	43*	7	2	18,550	380
Rocky Mountain	4		4			2,000	200
Slovak Zion		3	1	7		1,450	
South Carolina	3	4	13	6		5,000	360
Susquehanna	11		13	2		6,000	200
Texas	5		3	2		2,200	220
Virginia	20	1	14	6		9,400	
Wartburg	5	3	9*			4,200	100
West Pennsylvania	15	1	26	9		10,450	250
West Virginia	2		4	4		1,600	
Specials	1		1		3	1,400	
TOTAL 1938	347	55	568	157	6	$243,850	$6,450
TOTAL 1936	292	51	582	145	5	228,050	7,830

NOTE: * Includes Unmarried Daughter of Clergyman.

AMENDED RULES

During the past biennium two rules were amended with the approval of the Executive Board.

1. Widows engaged in full-time remunerative employment were removed from the roll at a saving of $5,400 per annum.

2. Children born after the parents become beneficiaries of the Board were declared ineligible for pensions.

WOMEN'S MISSIONARY SOCIETY

The Board voices its high appreciation of their appropriation of $7,980 during the past biennium. The Board is now pensioning six women missionaries.

ANNUITY BONDS AND BEQUESTS

During the biennium seven annuity bonds have been sold amounting to $11,100.

Eight annuitants have died releasing to the Board $9,500, and one annuitant has canceled his bond, releasing $2,000.

Two bequests have been reported amounting to $5,250. Thirteen bequests have been paid amounting to $32,782.22.

NOMINATIONS

At this Convention the terms of the following members expire:

G. Harry Ditter   Belding B. Slifer
Francis Seiberling   Daniel F. Yost

There is one vacancy.

The Board places in nomination the following:

G. Harry Ditter   Belding B. Slifer
Francis Seiberling   Daniel F. Yost
                Ralph L. Smith

RESOLUTION

(For action, see p. 415.)

As hereinbefore mentioned we submit a resolution for formal action by the Church:

BE IT RESOLVED THAT

The Board of Ministerial Pensions and Relief shall, regardless of an accumulating deficit, continue to make payments of pensions and relief, to such classes of persons and in such amounts as heretofore, these payments to continue until such time as the United Lutheran Church shall declare to the contrary.

Respectfully submitted,

HARRY HODGES, *Executive Secretary.*

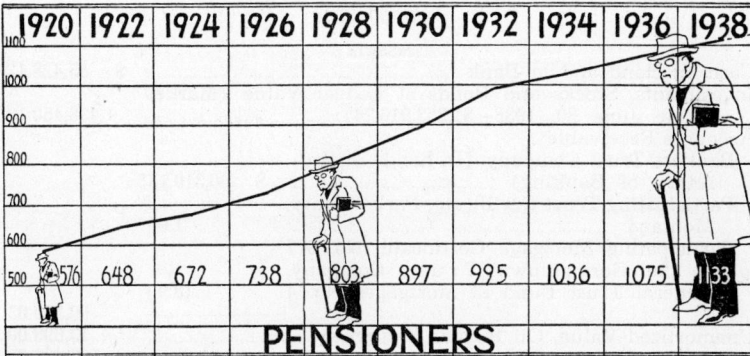

1920	1922	1924	1926	1928	1930	1932	1934	1936	1938
576	648	672	738	803	897	995	1036	1075	1133

PENSIONERS

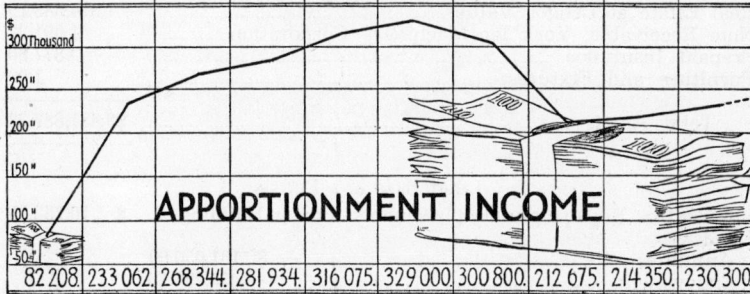

APPORTIONMENT INCOME

82 208.	233 062.	268 344.	281 934.	316 075.	329 000.	300 800.	212 675.	214 350.	230 300.

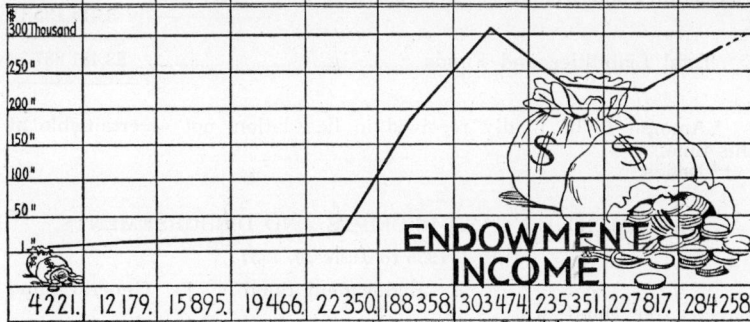

ENDOWMENT INCOME

4221.	12 179.	15 895.	19 466.	22 350.	188 358.	303 474.	235 351.	227 817.	284 258.

REPORT OF THE TREASURER OF THE BOARD OF MINISTERIAL PENSIONS AND RELIEF

BALANCE SHEET
June 30, 1938

ASSETS

Cash on Hand and in Bank		$ 55,428.12
Investments, Stocks and Bonds at Ledger Value (Market Value June 30, 1938—$1,253,916.24)		1,438,450.12
Accounts Receivable:		
Bankers Trust Company (In hands of Secretary of Banking)	$ 60,319.13*	
Participating Trust Certificate, Park County, Montana	1.00	
Participating Mortgage Certificate, No. 977 of the Germantown Trust Company, General Trust Fund of Mortgages No. 4	18.90	
		60,339.03
Unamortized Value, Oil Burner Equipment		13,693.00
Mortgages		597,423.65
Real Estate at Ledger Values		1,314,583.19
Note Receivable, York Ice Machinery Corporation		1,091.32
Prepaid Insurance		877.80
Furniture and Fixtures		1.00
Total Assets		$3,481,887.23

LIABILITIES AND FUNDS

Reserve for Repairs and Replacements, Beury Building		$ 10,752.05
Funds:		
Annuities	$ 101,650.00	
Endowment	3,455,296.36	
General Fund Deficit	85,811.18**	
		3,471,135.18
Total Liabilities and Funds		$3,481,887.23

* Amount to be finally received in liquidation, not ascertainable at this time.
** Deficit

STATEMENT OF CASH RECEIPTS AND DISBURSEMENTS
July 1, 1936 to June 30, 1937

	Endowment Fund	General Fund
Balance on Hand—July 1, 1936	$124,137.49	$81,819.27*
RECEIPTS		
Campaign for Endowment Fund	$ 3,918.65	

Bequests	6,205.38		
Donations — Pensions, General		$ 2,488.66	
Annuity Contracts Sold..	4,000.00		
Mortgages paid in full or on account	56,052.20		
Securities Called or Sold	81,637.59		
Proceeds from sale of Real Estate	11,326.99		
Tax Refund	12.94		
Amortization — Mrs. Hoppe Pension	200.00		
United Lutheran Church —Apportionment		124,109.06	
Women's Missionary Society		3,990.00	
Donations — General Relief		2,955.26	
Interest and Dividend: Interest on Mortgages		42,394.07	
Interest on Bonds........ Dividends on Stocks....		58,985..	
Rents Collected: Beury Building		54,123.06	
Other Real Estate........		66,570.18	
Discount earned on payment of real estate taxes		823.72	
Collected on Accounts Receivable		1,276.19	
Office Equipment Sold....		5.00	
Total Receipts		163,353.75	357,718.77
		$287,491.24	$275,899.50

DISBURSEMENTS

Expense in connectio. with Real Estate Sales	$ 804.50	
Real Estate Foreclosure Costs	2,926.85	
Improvements to Buildings	3,736.66	
Securities Purchased......	135,249.75	
Mortgages Purchased......	1,000.00	
Campaign for Endowment Expense (war service certificate)........	121.50	
Real Estate Purchased....	5,561.75	
Pensions: Retired Ministers		$ 91,150.00
Disabled Ministers		15,570.00
Widows of Ministers....		116,846.61

Children of Ministers..	7,259.40	
Missionaries	1,650.00	
	$232,476.01	
Relief:		
Ministers	$ 5,745.28	
Widows of Ministers....	3,680.00	
	$ 9,425.28	
Annuity Interest Paid......	$ 6,402.07	
		$248,303.36
Salaries:		
Executive Secretary....	$ 3,600.00	
Office Employees..........	3,683.33	
Total Salaries............	$ 7,283.33	
Traveling Expenses of Executive Secretary....	201.30	
Expenses of Board Members	178.65	
Promotion Expenses.......	929.00	
Treasurer's Fidelity Bond	62.50	
Auditing	700.00	
Postage	426.09	
Office Supplies and Expense	581.91	
Rental of Office................	701.25	
Actuarial Expenses..........	100.00	
Interest paid on Money Borrowed	2.33	
Fees paid for collection of Bond Interest and Dividend on Stock........	1,192.43	
Total Expenses	$ 5,075.46	
Total Administrative Salaries and Expenses		12,358.79
Real Estate Expenses (Properties other than Beury Building):		
Real Estate Agents' Fees	$ 4,000.00	
Legal Fees.....................	1,666.67	
Real Estate Agents' Fidelity Bond............	200.00	
Other Real Estate Agents' Expenses......	97.02	
		5,963.69
Real Estate Property Expenses:		
Plumbing and Heating	$ 3,303.59	

Papering	1,618.91
Painting	901.12
Roofing	1,871.10
General Repairs	5,289.78
Taxes	16,008.66
Water Rent	1,548.39

Total Real Estate Property Expenses	$ 30,541.55

Insurance:

Fire Insurance	$ 325.12
Vandalism	132.06
Plate Glass	243.79
Public Liability and Compensation	323.55

Total Insurance	$ 1,024.52

Heat, Light and Power:

Electric Power	$ 190.65
Gas	117.61
Coal and Oil	1,350.78
Total Heat, Light and Power	$ 1,659.04

Janitor Services	$ 1,035.00

Miscellaneous Expenses	$* 143.06

Total Expenses of Real Estate other than Beury Building		34,403.17
Real Estate Expenses (Beury Building):		
Repairs	$ 6,343.18	
Taxes and Water Rent	14,012.27	
Insurance	1,357.99	
Heat, Light and Power	6,851.15	
Janitor Supplies	682.50	
Labor	18,388.60	
Elevator Service	1,554.00	
Commissions Paid on Rent Collections	1,647.68	
Miscellaneous Expenses	1,474.26	
		$ 52,311.63
Beury Building Oil Burner, Purchase and Installation	$ 15,063.39	
Less Provision for Amortization during period	563.39	
		14,500.00

5528 Wayne Avenue (Apartment) Oil Burner, Purchase and Installation........ $ 1,978.00
Less Provision for Amortization during period 205.00
1,773.00
Deposit on Water Cooler 60.50
Office Equipment Purchased 170.52
Taxes advanced for account of mortgagors.... 911.20

Total Disbursements.... $149,401.01 $370,755.86
Balance—June 30, 1937 138,090.23
Overdraft—June 30, 1937 94,856.36*

$287,491.24 $275,899.50

SUMMARY:
Cash Balance—Endowment Fund, June 30, 1937 .... $138,090.23
Cash Overdraft—General Fund, June 30, 1937.... 94,856.36*

$ 43,233.87

Cash on Hand in Office $ 25.00
Cash in Checking Account, Fidelity Philadelphia Trust Co......... 43,005.87
Cash in Investment Fund, Fidelity Philadelphia Trust Co......... 3.00
Cash in hands of Lehman and Snyder.......... 200.00

$ 43,233.87

* Deficit.

STATEMENT OF CASH RECEIPTS AND DISBURSEMENTS
July 1, 1937 to June 30, 1938

	Endowment Fund	General Fund
Balance on Hand, July 1, 1937	$138,087.23	$ 95,081.36*

RECEIPTS

Campaign for Endowment Fund	$ 4,208.16	
Bequests	25,644.47	
Donations for Pensions..		$ 2,716.03

Annuity Contracts Sold..	7,000.00		
Mortgages Paid in Full or on Account..............	33,256.10		
Securities Called or Sold	105,589.75		
Proceeds from Sale of Real Estate:			
Cash	22,744.68		
Purchase Money Mortgage	22,000.00		
Accounts Receivable (Fidelity-Philadelphia Trust Company, Principal Account)..............	105,586.75		
Amortization — Mrs. Hoppe Pension..............	200.00		
Matured Annuities Transferred to Endowment Fund	4,500.00		
United Lutheran Church in America—Apportionment		118,675.00	
Increase in Depreciation Fund		3,480.00	
Women's Missionary Society		3,990.00	
Donations for General Relief		4,829.28	
Interest and Dividends:			
Interest on Mortgages		34,905.74	
Interest on Bonds........		61,735.85	
Dividends on Stocks....		369.25	
Rents Collected:			
Beury Building..............		60,603.11	
Other Real Estate........		69,292.93	
Discount Earned on Payment of Real Estate Taxes		855.47	
Advance for Mortgagors, Returned..........		260.79	
Office Equipment Sold....		40.00	
Water Cooler in Beury Building		220.00	
Recovery of Loss Sustained by Fire..............	515.54		
Refunds of Interest and Taxes	127.26		
Total Receipts............		331,372.71	361,973.45
		$469,459.94	$266,892.09

DISBURSEMENTS

Accounts Receivable (Fidelity-Philadelphia Trust Company, Principal Account)..............	$105,583.75

Expense in Connection with Real Estate Sales	2,163.25		
Real Estate Foreclosure Costs	3,100.30		
Securities Purchased	174,459.31		
Mortgages Purchased	22,000.00		
Campaign for Endowment Fund Expense	108.11		
Annuities of Deceased Donors Transferred to Endowment Fund	4,500.00		
Interest and Taxes Paid for Mortgagors	127.26		
Replacement of Property Damaged by Fire	515.54		
Pensions:			
Retired Ministers		$ 98,650.00	
Disabled Ministers		16,125.00	
Widows of Ministers		118,303.56	
Children of Ministers		8,205.68	
Missionaries		1,800.00	
		$243,084.24	
Relief:			
Ministers		$ 5,565.00	
Widows of Ministers		3,441.00	
		$ 9,006.00	
		$ 6,275.95	
Annuity Interest Paid			
Total Pensions, Relief and Annuity Payments			$258,366.19
Salaries:			
Executive Secretary		$ 3,600.00	
Office Employees		3,800.00	
Total Salaries		$ 7,400.00	
Traveling Expenses of Executive Secretary		$ 446.55	
Expenses of Board Members		254.15	
Promotion Expenses		1,078.89	
Treasurer's Fidelity Bond		62.50	
Auditing		700.00	
Postage		550.41	
Office Supplies and Expense		579.24	
Rental of Office		701.25	
Actuarial Expenses		322.50	
Interest Paid on Overdraft (Fidelity-Philadelphia Trust Co., Principal Account)		23.26	

Fees Paid for Collection of Bond Interest and Dividends on Stocks....	1,283.16	
Office Equipment Purchased	30.00	
Plate Glass Insurance Deferred Account........	877.80	
Total Expenses	$ 6,909.71	
Total Administrative Salaries and Expenses		14,309.71
Real Estate Expenses (Properties Other Than Beury Building):		
Real Estate Agents' Fees for Collecting Rents	$ 2,593.20	
Real Estate Agents' Fees for Collecting Mortgage Interest....	1,406.80	
Legal Fees in Connection with Real Estate	600.00	
Legal Fees in Connection with Mortgages	600.00	
Real Estate Agents' Fidelity Bonds..........	200.00	
Other Real Estate Expenses	174.91	
		5,574.91
Real Estate Property Expenses:		
Plumbing and heating	$ 3,995.84	
Papering	1,316.25	
Painting	3,796.67	
Roofing	1,515.21	
General Repairs............	1,837.58	
Taxes	16,634.36	
Water Rent....................	1,346.63	
Total Real Estate Property Expenses..	$ 30,442.54	
Insurance:		
Fire Insurance................	$ 1,873.90	
Vandalism	442.37	
Plate Glass....................	114.74	
Public Liability and Compensation	290.52	
Total Insurance..............	$ 2,721.53	

Heat, Light and Power:

Electric Power	$ 201.52	
Gas	69.48	
Coal and Oil	1,563.28	
Total Heat, Light and Power	$ 1,834.28	
Janitor Services	$ 571.67	
Sundry and Legal	$ 173.66	
Total Expenses of Real Estate Other than Beury Building		35,743.63

Real Estate Expense (Beury Building):

Repairs	$ 6,354.80	
Taxes and Water Rent	13,762.49	
Insurance	742.67	
Heat, Light and Power	7,571.60	
Janitor Supplies	705.31	
Labor	19,459.68	
Elevator Service	1,584.00	
Commission on Rentals Paid to Lehman and Snyder	1,841.74	
Miscellaneous Expenses	1,674.61	
Oil Burner Equipment	900.00	
		54,596.90
Total Disbursements	$312,557.52	$368,591.39
Balance, June 30, 1938	156,902.42	
Overdraft, June 30, 1938		101,699.30*
	$469,459.94	$266,892.09

SUMMARY:

Cash Balance—Endowment Fund, June 30, 1938	$156,902.42	
Cash Overdraft—General Fund, June 30, 1938	101,699.30*	
		$ 55,203.12
Cash on Hand in Office	$ 25.00	
Cash Checking Account —Fidelity Phila. Trust Company	54,978.12	
Cash in Hands of Lehman and Snyder	200.00	
		$ 55,203.12

* Deficit.

INVESTMENTS

June 30, 1938

Par Value	Railroad Bonds	Book Value			Market Value as of June 30, 1938
$ 50,000.00	Atchison, Topeka and Santa Fe, General Mortgage 4s, due 1995	$ 48,321.25	@	102¾	$ 51,375.00
25,000.00	Baltimore and Ohio, Refunding and General Mortgage 5s, due 1995	25,515.00	@	24½	6,125.00
50,000.00	Buffalo, Rochester and Pittsburgh, Consolidated Mortgage 4½s, due 1957	47,250.00	@	23	11,500.00
25,000.00	Canadian Pacific Railway Company, Equipment Trust 5s, due 1944	25,375.00	@	111½	27,875.00
10,000.00	Canadian, Pacific Railway Company, Consolidated 4s, Perpetual	9,427.25	@	79	7,900.00
25,000.00	Chesapeake and Ohio Railroad Co., Equipment Trust 4½s, due 1940	24,900.33	@	104¼	26,062.50
25,000.00	Chesapeake and Ohio Railroad Co., General Mortgage 4½s, due 1992	26,312.50	@	116	29,000.00
6,000.00	Chicago, Indianapolis and Louisville, First and General Mortgage "A" 5s, due 1966	6,000.00	@	4	240.00
25,000.00	Chicago and Northwestern, Convertible Series "A" 4¾s, due 1949	24,925.00	@	5¾	1,437.50
10,000.00	Chicago and Western Indiana Railroad Co., First and Refunding, Series "D" 4¼s, due 1962	10,162.50	@	84	8,400.00
25,000.00	Cincinnati Union Terminal Co., First Mortgage "C" 5s, due 1957	27,291.20	@	108¾	27,187.50
1,000.00	Des Moines Railway Co., 20-year Income Bonds, 5s, due 1955	950.00	@	14	140.00
10,000.00	Great Northern Railway Co., Series "E," General Mortgage 4½s, due 1977	10,122.51	@	76½	7,650.00
25,000.00	Harbour Commission of Montreal, First Mortgage Guaranteed 5s, due 1969	25,412.50	@	119	29,750.00
25,000.00	Kansas City Terminal Railway Co., First Mortgage 4s, due 1960	22,156.25	@	105⅜	26,343.75
15,000.00	Lehigh Valley Harbor Terminal Co., First Mortgage 5s, due 1954	15,690.35	@	35	5,250.00

5,000.00	Lehigh Valley Railroad Co., General Consolidated Mortgage 5s, due 2003........	5,110.00 @ 26	1,300.00
5,000.00	Lehigh Valley Terminal Railway Co., First Mortgage 5s, due 1941...............	5,313.13 @ 50	2,500.00
5,000.00	Louisville and Nashville Railroad, First and Refunding Series "E" 3¾s, due 2003	4,831.25 @ 74	3,700.00
25,000.00	Milwaukee Electric Railway and Light Co., First Mortgage 5s, due 1971...............	25,471.66 @ 101	25,250.00
50,000.00	New York Central Railway Co., Refunding and Improvement Series "A" 4½s, due 2013	49,531.25 @ 55⅛	27,562.50
50,000.00	New York, Chicago and St. Louis, Refunding Mortgage Series "C" 4½s, due 1978	48,870.00 @ 36½	18,250.00
25,000.00	New York Connecting Railroad Co., First Guaranteed Mortgage Series "A" 4½s, due 1953......................	25,784.61 @ 99	24,750.00
10,000.00	New York, Lackawanna and Western Railway Co., 1st and Refunding Series "B" 4½s, due 1973......................	10,594.65 @ 52	5,200.00
35,000.00	Pennsylvania Company, Secured 4s, due 1963...............	35,000.00 @ 89	31,150.00
25,000.00	Pennsylvania Railroad, Debentures 4½s, due 1970....	23,812.50 @ 82	20,500.00
5,000.00	Pennsylvania Railroad, General Mortgage Series "A" 4½s, due 1965......................	5,000.00 @ 94	4,700.00
25,000.00	Pere Marquette Railway Co., Equipment Trust, 4½s, due 1942	24,885.22 @ 102	25,500.00
25,000.00	Pere Marquette Railway Co., Series "C" First Mortgage 4½s, due 1980......................	24,937.50 @ 58	14,500.00
5,000.00	Pittsburgh, Cincinnati, Chicago and St. Louis Railroad, General Mortgage Series "B" 5s, due 1975......	4,985.00 @ 98	4,900.00
25,000.00	Southern Pacific Railroad Co., 4½s, due 1969	24,281.25 @ 43¼	10,812.50
25,000.00	Southern Pacific Railroad, Oregon Lines, First Mortgage Series "A" 4½s, due 1977	24,375.00 @ 49	12,250.00
10,000.00	Southern Railway Company, First Consolidated Mortgage 5s, due 1994...............	10,876.50 @ 65	6,500.00

15,000.00	Terminal Railroad Association of St. Louis, General Refunding Mortgage 4s, due 1953	15,039.21 @ 101¼	15,187.50
$722,000.00		$718,510.37	$520,748.75

Public Utility Bonds

$ 25,000.00	American Telephone and Telegraph Co., Sinking Fund Debenture 5½s, due 1943	$ 27,312.50 @ 112¾	$ 28,187.50
10,000.00	Bell Telephone Co. of Pennsylvania, First and Refunding Mortgage Series "C" 5s, due 1960	10,373.13 @ 128⅜	12,837.50
10,000.00	Brooklyn Union Gas Co., First Consolidated Mortgage 5s, due 1945	10,126.09 @ 105½	10,550.00
25,000.00	Carolina Power and Light Co., First and Refunding 5s, due 1956	25,175.00 @ 92½	23,125.00
25,000.00	Delaware Power and Light Co., First Mortgage 4½s, due 1971	27,003.54 @ 108½	27,125.00
25,000.00	Detroit Edison Co., General and Refunding Mortgage Series "D" 4½s, due 1961	23,997.50 @ 113½	28,375.00
50,000.00	Georgia Power Co., First and Refunding Mortgage 5s, due 1967	49,987.50 @ 91¾	45,875.00
25,000.00	Harrisburg Gas Co., First Mortgage 5s, due 1970	26,957.50 @ 107	26,750.00
10,000.00	Kansas Power and Light, First Mortgage 4½s, due 1965	10,301.65 @ 109¼	10,925.00
25,000.00	Monongahela West Penn Public Service Co., First and General 4½s, due 1960	25,000.00 @ 105½	26,375.00
15,000.00	New York Steam Co., First Mortgage 5s, due 1951	15,872.25 @ 105⅞	15,881.25
5,000.00	New York Water Service, First Mortgage Series "A" 5s, due 1951	5,062.50 @ 91¼	4,562.50
10,000.00	Pacific Gas and Electric Co., First and Refunding Series "G" 4s, due 1964	10,200.00 @ 110¼	11,025.00
25,000.00	Pennsylvania Power and Light Co., First Mortgage Guaranteed 4½s, due 1981	26,517.80 @ 98¾	24,687.50
25,000.00	Philadelphia Co., Series "A" 5s, due 1967	24,675.00 @ 93	23,250.00
50,000.00	Philadelphia Electric Power Co., First Mortgage 5½s, due 1972	51,547.77 @ 112	56,000.00

24,500.00	Philadelphia R a p i d Transit Co., First Mortgage 6s, due 1944	24,500.00 @	79	19,355.00
5,000.00	Scranton Gas and Water Co., First Mortgage 4½s, due 1958	5,050.00 @	99	4,950.00
2,000.00	Tennessee P o w e r Co., First Mortgage 5s, due 1962	1,600.00 @	84½	1,690.00
25,000.00	Toledo E d i s o n Co., First Mortgage 5s, due 1962	26,986.40 @	105⅞	26,468.75
5,000.00	West Virginia Water Service, First Mortgage 4s, due 1961	5,000.00 @	100	5,000.00
5,000.00	Wisconsin Public S e r v i c e Co., F i r s t Mortgage 4s, due 1961	5,231.25 @	106¼	5,312.50
5,000.00	Yadkin River Power Company, 30-year First Mortgage 5s, due 1941	5,094.65 @	101	5,050.00
$431,500.00		**$443,572.03**		**$443,357.50**

Governmental and Municipal Bonds

$ 10,000.00	City of Ottawa, Debenture, 4½s, due 1954	$ 9,309.96 @	113	$ 11,300.00
10,000.00	City of Philadelphia 4s, due 1947	8,456.81 @	106	10,600.00
15,000.00	City of Philadelphia 4s, due 1953	12,174.90 @	108½	16,275.00
75,000.00	City of Philadelphia 4¼s, due 1977	67,296.87 @	107½	80,625.00
25,000.00	City of Philadelphia 4¼s, due 1978	20,112.71 @	108¼	27,062.50
10,000.00	Montreal Metropolitan Commission, Sinking Fund 4½s, due 1953	9,262.50 @	100	10,000.00
25,000.00	New York City, Corporation Stock, Issue of 1911, 4¼s, due 1960	23,250.00 @	113	28,250.00
20,000.00	Province of Alberta, Canada, Debenture 5s, due 1959	19,775.00 @	56	11,200.00
10,000.00	Province of Manitoba, Canada, Debenture 5s, due 1959	9,937.50 @	92	9,200.00
25,000.00	Province of Ontario, Canada, Debenture 5s, due 1960	25,750.00 @	122	30,500.00
25,000.00	P r o v i n c e of Saskatchewan, Canada, Debenture 5s, due 1959	25,112.50 @	83	20,750.00
$250,000.00		**$230,438.75**		**$255,762.50**

Industrial and Miscellaneous Bonds

$ 5,000.00	The Fred W. Albrecht Grocery Company, 15-year Debentures, 5s, due 1953....	$ 5,000.00 @ 95	$ 4,750.00
1,000.00	Howard Gas and Coal Co., 20-year Sinking Fund 6s, due 1961 (Certificate of Deposit)	1,000.00 @ 10	100.00
10,000.00	National Dairy Products (W. W.) Debenture 3¾s, due 1951	10,413.58 @ 101½	10,150.00
7,984.20	Walnut Street Trust Building, First Mortgage 6s, due 1932	7,984.20 @ 8	638.74
20,000.00	York Ice Machinery Corporation, First Mortgage Sinking Fund 6s, due 1947........	20,000.00 @ 90	18,000.00
$ 43,984.20		$ 44,397.78	$ 33,638.74

Shares   Miscellaneous Stock

17	Pennsylvania Railroad Company....	$ 531.19 @ 18¾	$ 318.75
10	Philadelphia Dairy Products Corporation $4.00 Non-Cumulative, Second Preferred	1,000.00 @ 9	90.00
		$ 1,531.19	$ 408.75

SUMMARY

Railroad Bonds	$ 718,510.37	$ 520,748.75
Public Utility Bonds..	443,572.03	443,357.50
Government and Municipal Bonds..................	230,438.75	255,762.50
Industrial and Miscellaneous Bonds..............	44,397.78	33,638.74
Miscellaneous Stocks	1,531.19	408.75
	$1,438,450.12	$1,253,916.24

MORTGAGES
June 30, 1938

Fund	Property	Net Amount of Mortgage June 30, 1938	Rate of Interest	Classification of Mortgage	Appraised Value June 30, 1938	Assessed Value
189	5901 Belden St., Phila., Pa.......$	9,000.00	5½%	AY	$ 9,500.00	$ 7,200.00
109	5345 Belfield Ave., Phila., Pa.	2,900.00	5%	B	2,500.00	3,300.00
307	5917 North Bingham Street, Phila., Pa.	2,850.00	5%	A	3,100.00	3,500.00
306	5923 North Bingham Street, Phila., Pa.	2,850.00	5%	A	3,100.00	3,500.00
334	5961 North Bingham Street, Phila., Pa.	2,625.00	6%	A	3,100.00	3,500.00
253	616 E. Brill St., Phila., Pa........	3,000.00	6%	A	2,800.00	3,200.00
227	622 E. Brill St., Phila., Pa........	3,000.00	6%	A	2,800.00	3,500.00
263	626 E. Brill St., Phila., Pa........	2,425.00	6%	A	2,800.00	3,200.00
328	1310 Butler St.. Phila.. Pa.......	4,000.00	6%	C	3,200.00	4,200.00
190	S. E. cor. Buxmont and Overhill Road, Somerton Gardens, Pa.	6,000.00	5%	A	7,000.00	4,400.00

Fund	Property	Net Amount of Mortgage June 30, 1938	Rate of Interest	Classifica-tion of Mort-gage	Appraised Value June 30, 1938	Assessed Value
316	N. W. cor. Buxmont and Over-hill Road, Somerton Gardens, Pa.	4,500.00	5%	A	6,000.00	5,200.00
72	8130 Cadwallader Ave., Elkins Park, Pa.	11,850.00	6%	AS	17,000.00	6,500.00
261	3228 N. Carlisle St., Phila., Pa.	1,900.00	5%	B	3,000.00	3,300.00
53	312 Chandler St., Phila., Pa.	4,000.00	5%	A	4,200.00	5,000.00
37	1407 W. Chelten Ave., Phila., Pa.	4,850.00	6%	BY	5,500.00	5,500.00
12	599 East Cheltenham Avenue, Phila., Pa.	3,825.00	6%	A	4,200.00	5,500.00
342	4614 Chester Ave., Phila., Pa.	5,000.00	5%	A	7,500.00	8,900.00
270	6631 Chew St., Phila., Pa.	4,275.00	5%	BY	5,500.00	6,200.00
271	6633 Chew St., Phila., Pa.	4,000.00	6%	BY	6,200.00	5,800.00
336	213 Church Road Elkins Park, Pa.	4,500.00	5%	BS	6,000.00	3,000.00
289	535 East Church Road, Elkins Park, Pa.	6,750.00	6%	AS	10,000.00	4,500.00
290	537 East Church Road, Elkins Park, Pa.	9,076.57	5%	AS	10,000.00	4,500.00
22	7530 Claridge St., Phila., Pa.	3,200.00	6%	A	3,800.00	4,000.00
96	305 Corinthian Ave., Willow Grove, Pa.	2,812.50	6%	AS	4,500.00	3,200.00
331	4221 Cottman St., Phila., Pa.	3,062.50	6%	A	4,600.00	5,000.00
326	4225 Cottman St., Phila., Pa.	3,106.25	6%	A	4,600.00	5,000.00
304	4235 Cottman St., Phila., Pa.	3,500.00	6%	A	4,600.00	5,000.00
303	4237 Cottman St., Phila., Pa.	3,650.00	6%	A	4,600.00	5,000.00
302	4239 Cottman St., Phila., Pa.	3,125.00	6%	A	4,600.00	5,000.00
329	231-233 Coulter St., Phila., Pa.	11,625.00	5%	CY	10,000.00	15,200.00
29	104 Cypress Avenue, Jenkin-town Manor, Pa.	8,900.00	5%	AS	7,500.00	4,500.00
226	2605 N. Douglas St., Phila., Pa.	2,050.00	6%	C	1,800.00	1,700.00
33	300-304 S. Easton Road, Wil-low Grove, Pa.	3,325.00	5%	CYS	7,500.00	7,000.00
192	2505 N. 18th St., Phila., Pa.	2,850.00	5%	C	2,400.00	3,900.00
218	5952 Elsinore St., Phila., Pa.	2,700.00	5%	B	2,700.00	3,000.00
344	6524 Elmwood Ave., Phila., Pa.	1,300.00	6%	A	2,600.00	3,800.00
129	1622 W. Erie Ave., Phila., Pa.	9,550.00	6%	BY	9,500.00	10,400.00
310	213 Evergreen Road, Jenkin-town Manor, Pa.	9,975.00	6%	AS	10,500.00	5,800.00
32	1133 Faunce St., Phila., Pa.	1,998.00	6%	B	2,500.00	4,000.00
92	6053-55 N. Fifth St., Phila., Pa.	9,300.00	6%	AY	22,000.00	17,800.00
130	184 W. Fern St., Phila., Pa.	3,000.00	5%	A	2,400.00	2,400.00
332	4630 N. Fifth St., Phila., Pa.	8,775.00	5%	BY	9,000.00	9,000.00
105	6041 N. Fifth St., Phila., Pa.	6,000.00	5%	AY	11,000.00	11,000.00
102	7214 Frankford Ave., Phila., Pa.	7,747.73	6%	AY	9,000.00	9,000.00
235	2642 Germantown Ave., Phila. Pa.	15,000.00	6%	BY	15,000.00	12,600.00
309	5340 Germantown Ave., Phila., Pa.	17,220.00	4%	CY	10,000.00	13,200.00
104	148-150 W. Girard Ave., Phila., Pa.	10,808.74	5%	BY	8,500.00	9,200.00
279	461-463 E. Girard Ave., Phila., Pa.	2,500.00	6%	CY	2,700.00	4,000.00
1	522 E. Godfrey Ave., Phila., Pa.	1,800.00	6%	A	3,200.00	4,000.00
2	528 E. Godfrey Ave., Phila., Pa.	2,312.50	6%	A	3,200.00	4,000.00
4	538 E. Godfrey Ave., Phila., Pa.	2,875.00	6%	A	3,200.00	4,000.00
5	542 E. Godfrey Ave., Phila., Pa.	1,800.00	6%	A	3,200.00	4,000.00
134	609 E. Godfrey Ave., Phila., Pa.	2,900.00	5%	A	3,000.00	3,700.00
136	613 E. Godfrey Ave., Phila., Pa.	3,205.00	6%	A	3,000.00	3,700.00
137	615 E. Godfrey Ave., Phila., Pa.	2,900.00	5%	A	3,000.00	3,700.00
139	619 E. Godfrey Ave., Phila., Pa.	3,340.00	6%	A	3,000.00	3,700.00
145	631 E. Godfrey Ave., Phila., Pa.	3,100.00	6%	A	3,000.00	3,700.00
337	755 E. Herkness St., Phila., Pa.	3,800.00	5%	A	3,800.00	4,000.00
34	8317 High School Road, Elkins Park, Pa.	8,325.00	5%	AS	11,000.00	4,500.00
54	8431 High School Road, Elkins Park, Pa.	2,850.00	5%	AS	3,200.00	1,900.00
55	8435 High School Road, Elkins Park, Pa.	436.20*	5%	AS	3,200.00	1,900.00

Fund	Property	Net Amount of Mortgage June 30, 1938	Rate of Interest	Classification of Mortgage	Appraised Value June 30, 1938	Assessed Value
97	S. W. cor. Jenkintown and Evergreen Roads, Jenkintown Manor, Pa.	9,500.00	5%	AS	13,000.00	6,500.00
229	6429 Lawndale Ave., Phila., Pa.	762.50	6%	A	4,200.00	4,700.00
180	4704 N. Lawrence St., Phila., Pa.	2,925.00	6%	A	3,200.00	3,300.00
186	622 Levick St., Phila., Pa.	4,825.00	5%	AY	5,200.00	6,000.00
27	1210 Limekiln Pike, North Hills, Pa.	6,250.00	5%	BS	8,500.00	5,200.00
185	208 W. Linton St., Phila., Pa.	2,395.00	5%	A	2,700.00	2,600.00
168	230 W. Linton St., Phila., Pa.	1,500.00	6%	A	2,700.00	2,500.00
100	8237 Manor Road	4,875.00	5%	BS	8,000.00	3,500.00
295	3430 Midvale Ave., Phila., Pa.	5,005.00	5%	A	5,200.00	6,000.00
291	308 Marvin Road, Phila., Pa.	10,400.00	5%	AS	12,500.00	5,000.00
338	1551 McKean St., Phila., Pa.	7,500.00	5%	CY	5,000.00	6,800.00
220	2009 Norris St., Phila., Pa.	2,400.00	5%	C	2,000.00	3,500.00
107	7215 Oak Ave., Phila., Pa.	2,370.00	6%	C	2,200.00	1,800.00
314	2853-55 W. Oakdale St., Phila., Pa.	6,780.00	6%	CY	6,000.00	5,900.00
293	6167 Oakly St., Phila., Pa.	3,000.00	6%	A	6,200.00	5,500.00
311	8240 Ogontz Ave. (Brookside Ave.), Phila., Pa.	9,000.00	6%	AS	7,100.00	3,200.00
179	22 and 24 Park Ave., Upper Darby, Pa.	20,000.00	4%	CYS	12,000.00	6,000.00
181	6032 N. Philip St., Phila., Pa.	2,812.50	5%	A	2,800.00	3,000.00
256	1031 Pleasant St., Phila., Pa.	400.00	6%	AS	1,600.00	1,600.00
259	3425 Princeton Ave., Phila., Pa.	3,600.00	6%	A	3,900.00	4,600.00
257	3427 Princeton Ave., Phila., Pa.	3,900.00	6%	A	3,900.00	4,600.00
282	3435 Princeton Ave., Phila., Pa.	3,700.00	6%	A	3,900.00	4,600.00
320	3443 Princeton Ave., Phila., Pa.	3,328.47	5%	A	3,900.00	4,600.00
276	3451 Princeton Ave., Phila., Pa.	3,844.19	6%	A	3,900.00	4,600.00
101	3459 Princeton Ave., Phila., Pa.	250.00	6%	A	3,900.00	4,600.00
251	Rhawn and Ridgeway Streets, Phila., Pa.	4,230.00	6%	A	5,400.00	5,200.00
165	6529 Rising Sun Ave., Phila., Pa.	7,125.00	5%	AY	8,000.00	9,500.00
260	36 Robbins Ave., Rockledge, Pa.	3,500.00	6%	B	3,500.00	4,000.00
343	1623 Ruscomb St., Phila., Pa.	1,750.00	5½%	A	4,000.00	4,900.00
62	1222 St. Vincent St., Phila., Pa.	1,325.00	5%	C	2,600.00	2,500.00
95	3337 St. Vincent St., Phila., Pa.	3,500.00	5%	A	3,900.00	4,400.00
188	3353 St. Vincent St., Phila., Pa.	3,600.00	6%	A	3,900.00	4,400.00
35	3357 St. Vincent St., Phila., Pa.	2,000.00	6%	A	3,900.00	4,400.00
274	5127 Sheldon St., Phila., Pa.	1,975.00	6%	C	1,900.00	2,700.00
90	3401 N. 16th St., Phila., Pa.	18,250.00	5%	BY	15,000.00	14,000.00
292	6520 N. 16th St., Phila., Pa.	5,500.00	5%	A	4,800.00	5,000.00
173	2514 W. Somerset St., Phila., Pa.	2,925.00	6%	C	2,800.00	3,400.00
224	2862 N. Stillman St., Phila., Pa.	1,400.00	6%	C	2,000.00	2,200.00
341	4209 Stirling St., Phila., Pa.	1,000.00	6%	A	3,400.00	3,600.00
339	4217 Stirling St., Phila., Pa.	2,900.00	5%	A	3,400.00	3,600.00
69	7248 Tabor St., Phila., Pa.	3,375.00	5%	A	3,400.00	3,300.00
275	7526 Tabor Road, Phila., Pa.	2,500.00	6%	A	7,200.00	7,500.00
197	4010 E. Teesdale St., Phila., Pa.	3,100.00	5%	A	3,000.00	3,500.00
199	4014 E. Teesdale St., Phila., Pa.	2,850.00	6%	A	3,000.00	3,300.00
112	4015 E. Teesdale St., Phila., Pa.	3,200.00	6%	A	3,000.00	3,300.00
116	4037 E. Teesdale St., Phila., Pa.	3,100.00	5%	A	3,000.00	3,300.00
205	4044 E. Teesdale St., Phila., Pa.	3,100.00	5%	A	3,000.00	3,300.00
122	4047 E. Teesdale St., Phila., Pa.	3,100.00	5%	A	3,000.00	3,300.00
207	4048 E. Teesdale St., Phila., Pa.	3,100.00	5%	A	3,000.00	3,300.00
123	4049 E. Teesdale St., Phila., Pa.	3,100.00	5%	A	3,000.00	3,300.00
208	4050 E. Teesdale St., Phila., Pa.	3,100.00	5%	A	3,000.00	3,300.00
124	4051 E. Teesdale St., Phila., Pa.	3,100.00	5%	A	3,000.00	3,300.00
127	4057 E. Teesdale St., Phila., Pa.	3,100.00	5%	A	3,000.00	3,300.00
195	4058 E. Teesdale St., Phila., Pa.	3,040.00	5%	A	3,000.00	3,300.00
345	3743 N. 10th St., Phila., Pa.	800.00	6%	A	2,400.00	2,600.00
330	2226 N. 13th St., Phila., Pa.	4,500.00	6%	CY	3,500.00	5,200.00
335	5900 N. 21st St., Phila., Pa.	7,500.00	5½%	AY	6,500.00	6,000.00
277	2764 N. 22d St., Phila., Pa.	500.00	6%	C	2,800.00	4,300.00
175	2915 N. 22d St., Phila., Pa.	6,875.00	6%	AY	8,000.00	7,900.00
50	2836 N. 27th St., Phila., Pa.	1,000.00	6%	A	3,000.00	3,600.00
178	7611 Veree Ave., Phila., Pa.	3,500.00	6%	A	3,900.00	4,500.00
28	5708 Virginian Rd., Phila., Pa.	6,000.00	6%	A	5,500.00	5,600.00

Fund	Property	Net Amount of Mortgage June 30, 1938	Rate of Interest	Classification of Mortgage	Appraised Value June 30, 1938	Assessed Value
234	5300 Wayne Ave., Phila., Pa.....	17,550.00	5%	BY	12,000.00	12,900.00
79	6908 Weisel Road, Warrington Township, Pennsylvania	3,000.00	6%	CYS	5,500.00	5,600.00
65	1421 W. Westmoreland Street, Phila., Pa.	7,775.00	5%	BY	8,200.00	8,600.00
132	223 W. Widener St., Phila., Pa.	2,880.00	6%	A	2,600.00	2,500.00
183	240 W. Widener St., Phila., Pa.	2,925.00	6%	A	2,800.00	2,900.00
169	243 W. Widener St., Phila., Pa.	2,900.00	6%	A	2,600.00	2,500.00
315	600 E. Woodlawn Ave., Phila., Pa.	4,650.00	6%	BY	5,000.00	5,400.00
		$597,423.65			$674,800.00	$644,600.00

Summary	Total Number of Mortgages	Total Amount of Mortgage	Appraised Value	Assessed Value
A	84	$306,699.18	$373,600.00	$342,200.00
AY	8	58,372.73	79,200.00	74,400.00
B	8	28,623.00	36,700.00	29,300.00
BY	11	105,483.74	99,400.00	99,600.00
C	10	21,795.00	23,700.00	30,200.00
CY	9	76,450.00	62,200.00	68,900.00
	130	$597,423.65	$674,800.00	$644,600.00

* Under and Subject to First Mortgage of $2,944.80.

SUMMARY OF REAL ESTATE OWNED

June 30, 1938

No. of Properties	Book Value	Assessed Value	Appraised Value
140	$ 809,350.86	$ 616,550.00	$ 559,000.00
Beury Building......	505,232.33	517,000.00	615,000.00
141	$1,314,583.19	$1,133,550.00	$1,174,000.00

Respectfully submitted,

WILLIAM G. SEMISCH, Treasurer.

We have audited the books of account of the Treasurer of the Board of Ministerial Pensions and Relief of The United Lutheran Church in America for the biennium beginning July 1, 1936 and ending June 30, 1938; we have examined the Mortgages, Deeds and Securities held by this Board as of June 30, 1938, and we hereby certify that the foregoing statements:

Balance Sheet as of June 30, 1938

Statement of Receipts and Disbursements for the year ending June 30, 1937

Statement of Receipts and Disbursements for the year ending June 30, 1938

Investments as of June 30, 1938

Mortgages owned as of June 30, 1938

Summary of Real Estate Owned as of June 30, 1938

are in accordance with the books of account and, in our opinion, are true and correct.

TAIT, WELLER AND BAKER,
Accountants and Auditors.

Mr. Hodges gave a clear exposition of the various parts of the report, and Mr. Slifer gave full statement concerning all investment interests.

·A vote of appreciation and confidence in the work of the Board of Ministerial Pensions and Relief was given a hearty voice.

The report presented one resolution which was adopted.

The report of the Committee on New Pension Plan was presented by Dr. E. Clarence Miller, Chairman.

REPORT OF COMMITTEE ON NEW PENSION PLAN

(For action on the recommendations in this report, see pp. 424, 425.)

The Committee to which was referred the Contributory Pension Plan submitted at the Columbus Convention for study and report, has held two meetings.

After fully considering the plan, two changes seemed desirable:

1. The dividing of the ten per cent contribution equally between the pastor and the congregation.

2. The employment of less technical language in the plan.

The Chairman of the Committee visited the Conference of Synodical Presidents, who unanimously agreed with the Committee on the two points mentioned.

The Board of Ministerial Pensions and Relief were then asked to submit a simplified plan embodying these two points.

They have done so and we append it to this report together with a series of questions and answers bearing on the plan which they also submit.

Your Committee believes that the present plan is inadequate as a proper pension for our pastors and their dependents and with a steadily increasing roll without increasing income, no material improvement is in sight, therefore it would recommend: (For action, see pp. 424, 425.)

1. That the amended plan be approved by the Church in Convention.

2. That the Board of Ministerial Pensions and Relief be authorized to put it into operation when in their judgment the time is propitious

and when not less than five hundred congregations and their pastors have agreed to accept its provisions and operate under it.

3. That as soon as the new contributory plan has been decreed operative no pastors shall be entitled to participate in the benefits of the present plan in addition to those now on the rolls of the United Lutheran Church in America except to make up any difference between the amount received by him under the new plan and what would have been forthcoming under the old.

PROPOSED CONTRIBUTORY PENSION PLAN OF THE UNITED LUTHERAN CHURCH IN AMERICA

CONTRIBUTION OF THE MEMBER

The contribution of each member would be at the rate of five per cent of his salary basis, the salary basis to include the cash salary with a fifteen per cent addition where free rent of a home is furnished.

CONTRIBUTION OF THE CHURCH

The contribution of each local congregation or other salary-paying organization would be an amount equivalent to the five per cent contribution of the member, serving such congregation or other organization.

AGE RETIREMENT PENSION

Upon retirement, after attaining the minimum retirement age of sixty-five, the entire accumulations to the credit of the member out of his own contributions and his church's contributions, together with interest additions, shall be applied towards providing an annuity for the member of which sixty per cent would continue as a widow's annuity should his wife survive him, if their marriage took place before entering upon the age annuity.

DISABILITY PENSION

In the event of total and permanent disability before entering upon an age retirement annuity, a disability pension would be provided from the entire accumulations to the credit of the member out of his own contributions and his church's contributions, together with interest additions.

WIDOWS' AND MINOR ORPHANS' PENSIONS

In the event of death before entering upon an age retirement annuity, a widow's pension would be provided from the entire accumulations to the credit of the member out of his own contributions and his church's contributions, together with interest additions.

WITHDRAWAL BENEFITS

A member terminating service with the United Lutheran Church otherwise than through disability or age retirement shall withdraw the accumulations of his own five (5) per cent contributions together with interest additions but without further claim on the Contributory Pension Fund.

TIME OF PAYMENTS

All contributions of the member and his church or other salary-paying organization shall be paid into the Contributory Pension Fund monthly, quarterly, semi-annually, or annually in advance and shall be regarded as a matter of current expense and not of benevolence.

INTEREST CREDITS

Interest credits will be allowed at a net rate to be determined annually by the Board.

ADDITIONAL CONTRIBUTIONS

The member has the privilege of paying into the Fund amounts additional to his regular contributions. Such additional amounts would be applied towards providing annuity benefits additional to those provided through the regular contributions, with the right of the member to withdraw such additional contributions.

CONTINGENT FUND

A Contingent Fund will be maintained to which would be credited gifts, contributions, legacies and other available income, all for the purpose of providing benefits additional to those provided through the regular contributions of the member and his churches.

COMMENCEMENT OF OPERATION OF FUND

It is hoped that the proposed Contributory Pension Plan will receive the approval of the Church and that it will go into effect at an early date.

NOTE: The above is a popular statement of the proposed Contributory Pension Plan, and therefore, does not give in detail the rules and regulations under which the Plan will be administered.

UNITED LUTHERAN CHURCH PENSION PLAN

Illustrations of Application of Accumulations of $100 a year to provide a disability annuity, in the event of the disability of a member during the accumulation period.

AT END OF YEARS INDICATED

Age at Entry	5	10	15	20	25	30	35
25	$25	$59	$104	$165	$251	$373	$552
30	27	63	113	182	282	427	
35	29	68	124	204	322		
40	31	76	139	234			
45	35	85	160				
50	39	97					

BASIS: Interest at 3½%, compounded at end of each year. Annuities payable in installments at end of each month.

UNITED LUTHERAN CHURCH PENSION PLAN

Annuity provided upon retirement at age 68 by deposits of $100 a year on both the single-life basis and the joint life and survivor (60% to widow) basis for a man and wife of the same age.

Entry Age	Number Years to Age 68	Accumulation of $100 Per Year at age 68	Single-life Annuity	Joint-life and Survivor Annuity
25	43	$9,685	$1,042	$846
26	42	9,261	996	809
27	41	8,851	952	773
28	40	8,455	910	739
29	39	8,072	868	705
30	38	7,703	829	673
31	37	7,346	790	642
32	36	7,001	753	612
33	35	6,667	717	582
34	34	6,345	683	554
35	33	6,034	649	527
36	32	5,733	617	501
37	31	5,443	586	476
38	30	5,162	555	451
39	29	4,891	526	427
40	28	4,629	498	404
41	27	4,376	471	382
42	26	4,131	444	361
43	25	3,895	419	340
44	24	3,667	394	320
45	23	3,446	371	301
46	22	3,233	348	282
47	21	3,027	326	264
48	20	2,828	304	247
49	19	2,636	284	230
50	18	2,450	264	214
51	17	2,271	244	198
52	16	2,097	226	183
53	15	1,930	206	169
54	14	1,768	190	154
55	13	1,611	173	141
56	12	1,460	157	128
57	11	1,314	141	115
58	10	1,173	126	102
59	9	1,037	112	91
60	8	905	97	79
61	7	778	84	68
62	6	655	70	57
63	5	536	58	47
64	4	421	45	37
65	3	311	33	27
66	2	204	22	18
67	1	100	11	9

BASIS: Interest at 3½% compounded at end of each year. Annuities payable in installments at end of each month.

UNITED LUTHERAN CHURCH PENSION PLAN

Illustrations of application of accumulations of $100 a year to provide an annuity for a widow, in the event of the death of her husband during the accumulation period.

AT END OF YEARS INDICATED

Age at Entry	5	10	15	20	25	30	35
25	$24	$56	$ 98	$154	$231	$340	$494
30	26	59	105	168	256	383	
35	27	64	115	186	289		
40	29	70	127	210			
45	32	77	143				
50	35	87					

BASIS: Age of Wife—same as husband's. Interest at 3½%, compounded at end of each year. Annuities payable in installments at end of each month.

UNITED LUTHERAN CHURCH PENSION PLAN

Annuity provided upon retirement by deposits of $100 a year on both the single-life basis and the joint-life and survivor (60% to widow) basis for a man and wife of the same age.

Age at Entry	Age at Retirement					
	65	66	67	68	69	70
			SINGLE LIFE			
25	$819	$887	$961	$1,042	$1,130	$1,227
30	646	701	762	829	901	981
35	500	545	595	649	708	773
40	377	414	454	498	546	599
45	274	303	335	371	409	452
50	187	210	236	264	294	328
55	114	132	152	173	197	224
60	52	66	81	97	116	136
			JOINT LIFE AND SURVIVOR			
25	674	727	784	846	913	987
30	532	575	622	673	728	789
35	412	447	485	527	573	622
40	311	339	370	404	441	482
45	225	249	274	301	331	363
50	154	172	192	214	238	264
55	94	108	124	141	159	180
60	43	54	66	79	94	109

BASIS: Interest at 3½% compounded at end of each year. Annuities payable in installments at end of each month.

PROPOSED CONTRIBUTORY PENSION PLAN OF THE UNITED LUTHERAN CHURCH IN AMERICA

QUESTIONS AND ANSWERS

1. What is the Contributory Pension Plan of the United Lutheran Church?

    A scientific, contributory plan, in accord with modern pension systems, by which a clergyman or other eligible worker of the United Lutheran Church may safeguard the period of old age, also with benefits for himself in case of disability and for his family in the event of his death, and through which the Church may pay its sacred debt.

2. What is meant by "scientific"?

    That the Plan is wrought out in accordance with the science of modern pension systems.

3. What is meant by "contributory" as used in connection with the proposed Pension Plan?

    That the clergyman himself, according to the best practice in modern pension systems, shall make payments toward his own age annuity, in addition to the payments made by his church or other employer.

4. Why ask the clergyman thus to contribute?

    His payment (1) promotes self-respect, since his age annuity is thus in part the result of his own initiative; (2) it expresses his willingness to co-operate with his Church and its whole ministry in safeguarding him against some of the major contingencies of life; (3) regular payments by the member, accumulated at compound interest, are an important element in securing larger benefits for himself and family; (4) it helps bring more system into his personal finances; (5) it safeguards and multiplies his savings.

5. What are the benefits of the Contributory Pension Plan of the United Lutheran Church.

    It contemplates a pension for each clergyman and missionary, in the service of the Church. This pension will be provided by annual payments equivalent to ten (10) per cent of the salary of the clergyman and missionary. It is hoped and expected that the pensions provided through the regular contributions will be increased when possible and as the available resources justify, out of the receipts of other available funds. In addition to the age retirement benefits, pensions are provided upon total and permanent disability and provision is also made for pension benefits for the widows and minor orphans.

6. What is the minimum retirement age?

    The minimum retirement age is sixty-five (65) years.

7. Who are eligible for membership in the Contributory Pension Plan?

(a) Clergymen who are members of the Church serving as pastors of congregations; (b) Clergymen who are members of the Church, serving at institutions or churches that are owned, controlled or served by the Church or who are in the service of the Church in some other capacity; (c) Foreign missionaries commissioned by the home Church; (d) such other persons or groups of persons as may be declared eligible from time to time by the Board, subject to the approval of the Church.

8. What is the basic principle of the Contributory Pension Plan?

That, in recognition of sacrificial service, it is the duty of the Church to provide an effective life support for the clergymen, including those who are retired, in accordance with the teachings of Jesus that "the laborer is worthy of his hire" and the statement of Paul: "Even so hath the Lord ordained that they who preach the gospel should live of the gospel"; principles which are embodied in the conviction that the right to an effective support inheres in the gospel ministry. Money did not and cannot buy this right. The price paid is sacrificial service.

9. How is the age retirement pension to be calculated?

The amount of the age retirement pension will be determined by the entire accumulations to the credit of the member at the time of retirement out of his own contributions and his churches' contributions, together with interest additions.

10. What is the widow's pension?

The widow's pension is sixty (60) per cent of her husband's pension, or in the event of his death before entering upon a retirement pension, the amount of the widow's pension is related to the accumulations to the credit of the member at the date of death.

11. What other death benefits are provided?

In the event of the death of the member before entering upon an age or disability retirement annuity leaving no widow but a minor child or children surviving, the entire accumulations to the credit of the member out of his own contributions and his churches' contributions, together with interest additions, shall be applied by the Board for the benefit of such minor child or children, during minority. However, if after making reasonable provision for such child or children during minority there remains any balance of such accumulation, an amount equivalent to such balance, at the option of the Board, may be paid to a dependent or to the legal representative, or to the next of kin of the deceased member.

In the event of the death of the member before entering upon an age or disability retirement annuity leaving no widow and no minor child or children surviving, the Board may pay at its own option to a dependent or to the legal representative, or to the next of kin of the deceased member, an amount equivalent to the accumulation to the credit of the member out of his own contributions. In such event any balance remaining to the credit of the member shall be transferred to the Contingent Fund.

12. What is meant by "disability"?

Such as would totally and presumably permanently prevent the member from performing the duties of a United Lutheran clergyman.

13. What pension will come to a man who is disabled before attaining the minimum retirement age?

In the event of total and presumably permanent disability, the amount of the annuity will be such as may be provided from the entire accumulations to the credit of the member out of his own contributions and his churches' contributions, together with interest additions.

14. How may larger pensions be secured?

By paying into the Contributory Pension Fund such additional amounts as the member may elect, all to be increased by interest additions for the purpose of providing annuity benefits additional to those otherwise provided through the regular payments into the Fund.

15. What benefits will a member receive if he makes his regular contributions for a number of years and then withdraws from the ministry of the United Lutheran Church?

The member shall withdraw the accumulations of his own five (5) per cent contributions together with interest additions but without further claim on the Contributory Pension Fund.

16. How is the member's account kept?

As an individual account; wholly separate from all other accounts.

17. What advantage to the member is secured by this method?

The member receives an annuity based upon the accumulations to his credit supplemented by annuity credits from the churches' contributions.

18. What is the part of the local church?

The church or organization employing the clergyman or other worker is to pay into the Fund during each year of the service of the member an amount equivalent to five (5) per cent of the total salary basis as a regular contribution.

19. What does "the total salary" include?

The cash received from the church or other salary-paying organization, plus fifteen (15) per cent of the salary in case a home is provided free.

20. How is this fifteen (15) per cent reckoned?

This will be clear from the following example:

Suppose a clergyman receives a salary of $2,000 and a home. His total salary basis would be:

Cash	$2,000
Home, 15 per cent of $2,000..	300
Total	$2,300

21. Why is a uniform rate of rental used?

The Pension Board cannot enter into the question of the exact value of the free rental of the home, with widely variant conditions in different communities.

22. Why should the local church co-operate in the Contributory Pension Plan?

The Contributory Pension Plan offers a privilege which any church may well covet for itself and its clergymen. At the minimum cost and the maximum security, it makes provision for age or disability and protects the family in case of the clergyman's untimely death. This plan has the highest commendation of pension actuaries.

23. Is the local church's participation temporary?

No. The church is not entering the Contributory Pension Plan merely for the benefit of the man who happens to be its clergyman at the moment. It is the office that the Plan seeks to protect. Of course, if the church fails to adopt the Plan, it will thus seriously handicap its clergyman in his desire to enter the Plan, and will assume the entire responsibility for providing for his disability or age.

24. When will the church's and member's contributions to the Plan begin?

These payments to the Plan begin when the Contributory Pension Plan is declared operative.

25. If a church fails to make its contributions, what then?

It will thereby penalize its clergyman and force him to lose pension credit for that year.

26. How should the church take action towards participation in the Contributory Pension Plan?

It is suggested that the following resolution be adopted by the proper authorities of the local church:

....
(Name of church or other organization)

hereby agrees to participate in the Contributory Pension Plan of the United Lutheran Church, when put into operation by paying to the Plan each year, in monthly installments, a sum equivalent to five (5) per cent of the total salary basis or bases of the clergyman rendering service, as a regular contribution.

....

Per ....

Address ....

Date ....

27. How shall the church provide for its contributions in its financial budget?

The regular (5) per cent should be placed in the congregational expense fund of the local church along with such items as salaries, light, heat, water, music, etc.

28. What is the part of the clergyman?

The clergyman is to pay five (5) per cent of his salary to the Contributory Pension Plan as his share of the cost of the pension benefits.

29. When should a clergyman become a member of the Contributory Pension Plan?

As soon as the Contributory Pension Plan is put into operation, and in the case of later ordination or transfer in ministerial standing to the United Lutheran Church, as soon as such ordination or transfer may be completed.

30. Why should a clergyman's wife be interested?

The purpose of the Plan is to help clergymen and their wives in the event of death, disability or age. Should the clergyman meet with a serious accident or incapacitating disease, the disability retirement allowance would surely be appreciated by the wife. In inactive years, the regular monthly checks will relieve anxiety and need. In case of the clergyman's death, monthly payments continue to the widow.

31. Is it permissible for a member to discontinue the payment of dues and withdraw his accumulations from the Pension Fund?

A member remaining in the service of the United Lutheran Church may discontinue the payment of dues but may not withdraw his accumulated contributions. If, however, the member is withdrawing from the service of the United Lutheran Church, then he may withdraw his own accumulations.

32. What is the provision for administrative expenses?

Insofar as possible, the Board of Ministerial Pensions and Relief will provide administrative expenses out of such funds as may be available but the Board reserves the right to draw upon the churches' contributions to the Contributory Pension Fund to help meet its administrative expenses in an amount not to exceed one-half of one (0.5) per cent out of the five (5) per cent contributions.

E. CLARENCE MILLER, *Chairman.*

Moved and seconded to adopt recommendation 1.

After prolonged discussion, which brought out opinions upon almost every phase of the question, including a number of motions to refer or modify the report, the prevailing sentiment of the Convention became apparent and the Convention disposed of the report as a whole by the adoption of the following motion:

Moved and carried that we refer the entire report back to the Committee with instructions that it prepare a plan whereby there would be a payment of equal pension to all, placing the plan before the constituent synods, if possible, before their 1939 meetings.

On motion the report of the auditors for the Board of Ministerial Pensions and Relief was accepted.

The Convention adjourned at 5.00 P. M. Prayer led by the Rev. E. R. Hauser.

Monday Evening

Great interest was manifested in the observance of the Fiftieth Anniversary of the adoption of the Common Service, which observance was most fittingly provided for by the Common Service Book Committee, and the meeting was largely attended in the Lord Baltimore Hotel.

EIGHTH SESSION

Lord Baltimore Hotel
Baltimore, Maryland
Tuesday, October 11, 1938, 8.45 A. M.

Matins were conducted by the Rev. Hermann F. Miller.

The President called the Convention to order.

The President announced that it seemed necessary to provide for an evening session. It was therefore moved and carried that the hours for this day's sessions be as follows: 8.45 A. M. to 12.00 noon; 1.45 P. M. to 5.00 P. M.; 7.30 P. M. until adjournment.

There being no objection, the reports of the Committees of Tellers were heard at this time.

Mr. William H. Menges, Chairman, reported for the Committee of Tellers No. 1, as follows:

For the *Executive Board,* each of the following received a majority of the votes cast for the term expiring 1944:

Rev. Paul H. Krauss   Claude T. Reno

The President declared them elected.

For the *Commission of Adjudication,* each of the following received a majority of the votes cast for the term expiring 1944:

Rev. P. W. H. Frederick   F. Wm. Cappelmann

The President declared them elected.

For the *Committee on Church Papers,* each of the following received a majority of the votes cast for the term expiring 1944:

Rev. John W. Horine   E. F. Eilert

The President declared them elected.

For the *Executive Committee of the Laymen's Movement,* Mr. E. G. Hoover received a majority of the votes cast for the term expiring 1940. The President declared him elected.

Mr. Alvin R. Nissly, Chairman, reported for Committee of Tellers No. 2, as follows:

For the *Board of Foreign Missions,* each of the following received a majority of the votes cast for the term expiring 1944:

Rev. J. Harold Mumper   John C. Korn

The President declared them elected.

For the *Board of American Missions* and the *West Indies Mission Board,* the Rev. George W. Miley received a majority of the votes cast for the term expiring 1944. The President declared him elected.

For the *Board of Education,* each of the following received a majority of the votes cast for the term expiring 1944:

Rev. C. F. Koch   H. S. Bechtolt
                                   J. Conrad Seegers

The President declared them elected.

For the *Board of Social Missions*, each of the following received a majority of the votes cast:

Term expiring 1944:

Rev. C. B. Foelsch   Harry C. Hoffman
Rev. Franklin Clark Fry
Rev. Harold S. Miller

The President declared them elected.

Term expiring 1942:

Rev. E. E. Flack   J. W. Jouno
Rev. F. K. Fretz
Rev. F. W. Otterbein

The President declared them elected.

Term expiring 1940:

Rev. R. E. Kern   John G. Kurzenknabe
Rev. G. Morris Smith

The President declared them elected.

For the *Board of Publication*, each of the following received a majority of the votes cast for the term expiring 1944:

Rev. Joseph Sittler, Sr.   Clarence C. Dittmer

The President declared them elected.

For the *Board of Ministerial Pensions and Relief*, Ralph L. Smith received a majority of the votes cast for the term expiring 1944. The President declared him elected.

For the *Parish and Church School Board*, each of the following received a majority of the votes cast for the term expiring 1944:

Rev. Earl S. Rudisill   W. E. Tilberg

The President declared them elected.

For the *Board of Deaconess Work*, each of the following received a majority of the votes cast for the term expiring 1944:

Rev. Lewis A. Speaker   Mrs. George H. Haase

The President declared them elected.

By general consent, the Rev. H. A. Bosch presented the following resolution which was adopted:

> Resolved, that the matter of eligibility to the boards of the Church be referred to the Executive Board, with special reference to those who might be connected with the institutions and agencies of the Church which are the beneficiaries of said boards.

Mr. J. Milton Deck, President, presented the report of the Lutheran Brotherhood.

REPORT OF THE BROTHERHOOD

A DUAL ANNIVERSARY

The Brotherhood and the United Lutheran Church in America are celebrating their Twentieth Anniversaries in 1938. We rejoice in the fact that the Brotherhood's existence parallels that of the U. L. C. A., and while much has been said in recent months, this convention will further emphasize the Twentieth Anniversary of the organization of the U. L. C. A.

The Monday evening session of the Brotherhood Convention will be the occasion for a fitting celebration of two decades of service, by the Brotherhood and the U. L. C. A.

Although the Brotherhood is the youngest auxiliary of our Church, it will attain its majority during the coming year. The succeeding paragraphs contain a brief outline of the biennium's activities of this virile organization of men in our great Church.

THE SPRINGFIELD CONVENTION

The Springfield Convention will always be remembered as the time when the Brotherhood faced a grave crisis. Viewed from any angle, this Convention was the turning point in our Brotherhood history. If the story is ever told, of the heroic sacrifices by the small group of Brotherhood officers who dedicated themselves and their resources to saving the Brotherhood, it will constitute a shining example of Christian service; worthy of admiration by our Lutheran Church.

Our prayers were answered when the Convention adopted the new plan for financial support. When we contemplate the momentous decisions that were made at our Springfield Convention, we are convinced that we were frustrated in our attempts to secure a large attendance, so that with a smaller, more wieldy group, we could give prayerful consideration to the rebuilding of our Brotherhood structure, and lay our plans for the future.

Those of us who arrived at Springfield with grim determination to *Pray* our way through, and then *Pay* our way through, left for Columbus, with a certain conviction that "A new day had dawned for the Brotherhood."

EDUCATIONAL PROGRAM

Stewardship. The Brotherhood has always laid special emphasis on the value of adult Christian Education. During the past biennium we have made considerable progress in educating our men's organizations to recognize the definite spiritual motive that underlies true Christian Stewardship. We have supplemented the work of the *Lutheran Laymen's Movement for Stewardship,* by means of group discussions on Christian Stewardship at our conventions and rallies.

Through the courtesy of Mr. Arthur P. Black, Executive Secretary of the Laymen's Movement for Stewardship, we distributed many pieces of Stewardship literature, including thousands of copies of *"The Uniform Stewardship Program for Lutheran Brotherhoods,"* which was approved by the Savannah Convention of the U. L. C. A. in 1934.

"Lutheran Men" is the official publication of the Brotherhood and contains a co-ordinated program of Educational and Inspirational "Topics" arranged for discussion at the monthly Brotherhood meetings. These "Topics" have taken a new form and increased importance, by reason of the gracious offer of the *Parish and Church School Board* to undertake their preparation. This new series of "Topics" was inaugurated in January, 1938, and has resulted in a valuable contribution to our Brotherhood program. The popularity of these new "Topics" is attested by the fact that many additional Brotherhoods have adopted our monthly "Topic" program in recent months.

The Parish and Church School Board will prepare a three-year course of "Topics," with the first-year series dealing almost exclusively with the objectives of the various U. L. C. A. Boards established under the "Calendar of Special Days and Seasons."

"LUTHERAN MEN" TOPICS

First Year—*Christian Attitudes*
1938

January—The Christian Man's Attitude toward Foreign Missions
February—The Christian Man's Attitude toward Women's Work in the Church
March—The Christian Man's Attitude toward the Unchurched in the Community
April—The Christian Man's Attitude toward Jesus Christ
May—The Christian Man's Attitude toward Church Colleges
June—The Christian Man's Attitude toward World Lutheranism
July—The Christian Man's Attitude toward Government
August—The Christian Man's Attitude toward Daily Work
September—The Christian Man's Attitude toward the Christian Education of Children

October—The Christian Man's Attitude toward Works of Mercy
November—The Christian Man's Attitude toward Church Appeals
December—The Christian Man's Attitude toward the Pastor

Second Year—*Questions of Interest to Men*
1939
January—Is Our Brotherhood Really Worth While?
February—What May Our Congregation Rightfully Expect of Us Men?
March—What Obligations Have We Men to the United Lutheran Church
in America?
April—What Obligations Have Church Men to Their Local Community?
May—Are Jesus' Teachings Practicable for Our Day?
June—Should the Church Work for Social Betterment?
July—What is the Christian Attitude toward Political "Isms"—Socialism,
Communism, Fascism?
August—Should all Lutheran Church Bodies in America Unite?
September—What May Our Sunday School Rightfully Expect of Us Men?
October—What Are Our Congregation's Greatest Needs?
November—What Can We Men Do to Re-establish Religious Life in
Our Homes?
December—Does Jesus Christ Really Figure in Our Daily Life?

Third Year—*Christian Contributions*
1940
January—What Can Christian Men Contribute to Better Race Relations?
February—What Can Christian Men Contribute to a Higher Regard for
Womanhood?
March—What Can Christian Men Contribute to Church Expansion?
April—What Can Christian Men Contribute to Making Christ Supreme
in Life?
May—What Can Christian Men Contribute to the Christian Training of
Youth?
June—What Can Christian Men Contribute to the Creation of a Chris-
tian World?
July—What Can Christian Men Contribute to the Purification of Politics?
August—What Can Christian Men Contribute to the Beneficial Use of
Leisure?
September—What Can Christian Men Contribute to the Local Educa-
tional Program?
October—What Can Christian Men Contribute to Social Progress?
November—What Can Christian Men Contribute to the Advancement
of Christian Stewardship?
December—What Can Christian Men Contribute to World Peace?

Through the medium of these "Topics" and the use of the "Six Objectives" of the Brotherhood, as a plan for practical application, it will be only a matter of time, until our laymen will develop their latent abilities, and prepare themselves for efficient and consecrated service in their congregations.

The Six Objectives—

1. Win the Unsaved for Christ.
2. Bring Back the Lapsed Member.
3. Develop the Church Life of Our Youth.
4. Increase the Attendance of Men at the Service of Worship.
5. Practice and Promote Christian Citizenship.
6. Meet the Congregational Apportionment in Full.

BROTHERHOOD SUNDAY

The third Sunday in October is observed throughout the Lutheran Church as "Brotherhood Sunday." *Brotherhood Sunday* can be made a significant occasion to strengthen the Kingdom of God in the local congregation. We recognize the Brotherhood Sunday Service as an opportunity to enlist the manpower of the congregation for a new year of service, and to stimulate our laymen to a greater degree of Stewardship in placing themselves and their means at the disposal of the Church.

With the Brotherhood's emphasis on the *Annual Every Member Visitation,* it is impossible to evaluate the benefits that Brotherhood Sunday affords in providing an impetus to awaken the dormant laymen from their lethargy. Brotherhood Sunday offers a valid reason for visiting our laymen who are indifferent or irregular in their church attendance.

We plead for the earnest co-operation of our pastors in arranging a Brotherhood Sunday Service, in which their laymen will participate.

CO-OPERATION WITH THE U. L. C. A., BOARDS AND AUXILIARIES

The Columbus Convention

The Columbus Convention of the U. L. C. A. adjusted the work of the auxiliaries. It specifically instructed the Brotherhood and other auxiliaries to "include in their spheres of interest, the Whole Program of the Whole Church, as formulated by the Church through its official action." The resolution adopted by the Columbus Convention further states, "That the program of the Brotherhood shall include:

"(a) The stimulation of congregations to meet apportionments in full.

"(b) The assumption of definite responsibility for designated projects properly authorized by the Church."

In carrying out the above instructions, the Brotherhood has prepared literature, and published special articles in *Lutheran Men* to promote the objectives of the various Boards of the U. L. C. A. The monthly "Topics" for 1938 were prepared for study in keeping with "The Calendar of Special Days and Seasons" of the Church Year.

Sixth Objective

The Springfield Convention of the Brotherhood adopted the following as the sixth and latest objective of the Brotherhood: "The stimulation of the congregation, through educational, inspirational, and promotional efforts, to meet, *as a minimum* the apportionment of the Church in full." This was approved by the Columbus Convention, and has become one of the foremost tasks of the Brotherhood.

We will continue our efforts to educate our congregations to "The Tragedy of Deficits," and work even harder during the coming biennum for a minimum of a 100 per cent apportionment paid in each congregation of the U. L. C. A.

PLAN OF PROMOTION

The participation of the auxiliaries in the Plan of Promotion (Part Three) as adopted by the Columbus Convention, is a matter of vital concern to the Brotherhood.

President Knubel very wisely delayed action on this phase of the Plan for Promotion, in order to establish committees for the effective application of the first two "objectives" of the promotional plan.

Early in the spring of this year, President Knubel called a meeting of the representatives of the auxiliaries of the U. L. C. A., and plans were laid to insure a better understanding of the work and purpose, of the auxiliary organizations in the local congregation. Dr. Knubel in a clarifying statement illustrated the influence of the congregation as "A vital force; *Centrifugal,* Radiating out; — . — . — . and *Centripetal,* Expanding within."

The Committee on Promotion of the auxiliaries has completed the first part of their work, and will issue an interesting tract entitled, "The Ideal Congregation" for distribution at the Baltimore Conventions. It is hoped that this piece of literature will portray the need for the three auxiliaries in each congregation of the U. L. C. A., and indicate how the congregational program of Missions, Education, Evangelism and Stewardship will be advanced through the medium of these organizations.

The place of the auxiliaries in "The Ideal Congregation" will be visually demonstrated by the use of "Public Conversation" groups representing the church council, the Sunday school, the Women's Missionary Society, the Luther League and the Brotherhood, at a special meeting of each congregation in the U. L. C. A. The exact time of the meeting will be left to the discretion of the pastor, but it is hoped that the meeting will be held sometime during the months of January or February 1939. A sufficient number of copies of the dialogue and suggested hymns will be sent to each pastor.

GROUP MEETINGS

The Brotherhood takes pride in the fact the *Group Meetings* sponsored by "Group One" of the Plan for Promotion were very well attended by our laymen. We made a special effort to get our men out to these meetings, and feel well repaid for the effort.

THE ANNIVERSARY APPEAL

In the spring of 1938 the Brotherhood was given an opportunity to share in the *Twentieth Anniversary Appeal of the Board of American Missions.* By means of letters and through the columns of *Lutheran Men* we urged our laymen to co-operate in the campaign of Evangelism, and recently we have given our best efforts to promote the financial objective. We are pleased to note that many of our Brotherhood officers are serving as synodical and conference committee chairmen for the Anniversary Appeal.

THE IRON MOUNTAIN BOYS' SCHOOL

The Iron Mountain Boys' School Campaign was officially terminated on December 31, 1937. We are truly grateful to Almighty God for the generous contributions received for this most worthy cause. To everyone who contributed their time or means, in the Iron Mountain School Campaign we extend a hearty, "Thank you."

A detailed report of receipts by synods will be found on page 379.

THE BALTIMORE CONVENTION

Our opening statement called attention to the dual anniversaries of the U. L. C. A. and the Brotherhood. With this thought in mind the Operating Committee of the Brotherhood decided to accept the invitation of the Baltimore Brotherhoods, and the Maryland Synodical Brotherhood to hold our Eleventh Biennial Convention, immediately preceding the U. L. C. A. Convention. Accordingly, this convention is being conducted in the Lord Baltimore Hotel, Baltimore, Md., from October 2 to 4, 1938.

In arranging the program for the *Baltimore Convention,* our committee recognized its responsibility to develop a forward-looking program to mark the Brotherhood's entrance into a new decade of service to the Church.

Keeping in mind the importance of selecting experienced men to present practical methods, we are assured of outstanding Brotherhood men and educators who are specialists in their field, in addition to the officers of the U. L. C. A. appearing on our Convention program.

We extend a cordial invitation to the *Delegates* of the *U. L. C. A. Convention* to attend the Brotherhood Convention. Your interest in the welfare of your official men's organization will be deeply appreciated.

The Brotherhood operates on a strictly "pay as you go" basis. Nowa-days, the stewardship of funds is oft-times lightly regarded. The officers of the Brotherhood have stretched the dollars to the limit in order that we might continue our essential functions, in spite of inadequate funds.

The solving of the Brotherhood financial problem is primarily its own affair, but indirectly it affects our service to each layman and congre-gation of the U. L. C. A., and becomes a matter of vital concern to the U. L. C. A. as a whole.

It should not be any more necessary for Brotherhood Headquarters to "pass the hat" for operating funds than for any other board or agency of our Church, to do the same. Likewise, it should not expect the loyal servants of the Brotherhood to bear the brunt of "Budget Balancing" at the close of each biennium. We question the ethics of a procedure that virtually demands that "you must go out and collect your salary or else forget about it."

This is no exaggeration, but the simple truth that is everyone's busi-ness. The uncertainty of financial income seriously hampers the morale and efficiency of those who have been employed in full-time service.

It is ridiculous, but only too true, that we sometimes hear people say, "We will not give anything for the support of the Brotherhood, until they prove themselves a success." It must be borne in mind that the Brother-hood is a "Promotional and Educational" agency of our Church, and as such must spend its time and funds in non-profit enterprises.

New Dues Plan

In casting about for a system of dues that would meet the needs of the Brotherhood without placing a financial burden upon any church group, the Springfield Convention adopted a schedule of dues based on active membership, as follows:

(Resolution): "Each congregational Brotherhood existing in synods affiliated with the United Lutheran Church in America shall make an annual contribution to defray the operating and administrative expenses of the Brotherhood of the United Lutheran Church in America.

"This shall consist of membership dues, payable annually (or semi-annually, if preferred), and is based on their membership."

A Brotherhood having 10 member or less, the dues per annum...... $ 3.00
  11 to 25 members.. 5.00
  26 to 50 members.. 7.50
  51 to 100 members.. 10.00
  101 members, and over.. 12.50

Nearly 350 Brotherhoods have remitted their 1938 annual dues, and we are hoping that many additional organizations will enroll as "active" members of the Brotherhood in the coming biennium.

A plan for the collection of the U. L. C. A. and synodical Brotherhood dues has been given a trial in the East Pennsylvania, and Ministerium of Pennsylvania Brotherhoods. Although it is too early to make a prediction, we believe this method will aid in solving the problem of adequate financial support.

MISCELLANEOUS

A New Constitution

A Committee has been hard at work drafting a new Brotherhood Constitution, which will be presented to the Baltimore Convention.

Literature Secretaries

We have noted the valuable tracts prepared by our Church boards and agencies that lie around in church vestibules, and eventually are consigned to the waste basket. We are urging the appointment of Literature Secretaries in each Brotherhood, to insure an efficient distribution of literature in each congregation. The Literature Secretaries will also serve to promote the circulation of *Lutheran Men.*

AN APPRECIATION

The officers of the Brotherhood express their sincere appreciation for the fine co-operation received from our synodical presidents and the officers of the U. L. C. A.

We are especially indebted to the Parish and Church School Board for their kindness in preparing a new series of *Lutheran Men* Topics.

Our hearty thanks is extended to the secretaries of our boards and agencies, for their many courtesies. We again express our gratitude to the many individuals who have shown their interest in our work, by their prayers and contributions. We will endeavor to merit their confidence and continued support in the coming biennium.

LOOKING AHEAD

We have been reading of the falling away of the men from certain groups in other denominations. One has had 300,000 lapses in membership. In another instance the Brotherhood was absorbed by the Board of Education, after its financial obligations became too burdensome.

The Brotherhood will shortly celebrate its twenty-first anniversary, and no longer ask ourselves the question, "Will we fail?" The Brotherhood is engaged in the greatest enterprise that can be given to the hands of men. If we remain true to our original purpose, "Organization for Service," we cannot fail, for by "Service We Grow."

We face the future with optimism, in the knowledge that the day of the Brotherhood is at hand, and with the help of God we are going to have an even larger part in promoting the program of the whole Church. The call of Christ demands, *"The Church must be planted," . . . "The Brotherhood must also be planted"—NOW.*

Respectfully submitted,

EARLE W. BADER, *Executive Secretary.*

OFFICERS AND EXECUTIVE COMMITTEE
Biennium—1936-1938

President—J. Milton Deck, 6008 Nassau Road, Philadelphia, Pa.
First Vice-president—Alfred Arnesen, 3837 N. Monticello St., Chicago, Ill.
Second Vice-president—Lawrence F. Speckman, Esq., 404 Urban Bldg.,
    Louisville, Ky.
Third Vice-president—Oliver C. C. Fetta, 1306 Linden St., Indianapolis,
    Ind.
Secretary—O. Roy Frankenfield, 4911 N. 12th St., Philadelphia, Pa.
Treasurer—Harry A. Fritsch, care of Lehigh Valley Oil Co., 12th and
    Walnut Sts., Allentown, Pa.

EXECUTIVE COMMITTEE
Term Expires 1938:
P. L. Wahlberg, P. O. Box 2098, Houston, Texas.
Heiby W. Ungerer, Esq., 1014 Union Trust Bldg., Rochester, N. Y.
Francis K. Ford, 45 Falls St., Niagara Falls, N. Y.

Term Expires 1940:
Henry Miller, Riverview Route 9, Station F, Milwaukee, Wis.
William Schnellhardt, 4229 Latona Ave., Seattle, Wash.
William Rahn, Elmira, Ontario, Canada.

Term Expires 1942:
H. E. Isenhour, 120 W. Innes St., Salisbury, N. C.
Fred Wessels, 19 E. Bay St., Savannah, Ga.
Rev. Charles F. Brobst, Telford, Pa.

List of Meetings Held by the EXECUTIVE and OPERATING COMMITTEE

		Met at
November 28, 1936	Operating Committee	Brotherhood Headquarters
January 16, 1937	Operating Committee	Brotherhood Headquarters
March 13, 1937	Operating Committee	Philadelphia Theological Seminary, Mt. Airy, Philadelphia, Pa.
June 26, 1937	Executive Committee	Muhlenberg Building, Philadelphia, Pa.
December 4, 1937	Operating Committee	Brotherhood Headquarters
January 29, 1938	Operating Committee	Philadelphia Theological Seminary, Mt. Airy, Philadelphia, Pa.
February 26, 1938	Operating Committee	Home of Rev. Brobst, Telford, Pa.
April 2, 1938	Operating Committee	Brotherhood Headquarters
June 4, 1938	Operating Committee	Philadelphia Theological Seminary, Mt. Airy, Philadelphia, Pa.
June 11, 1938	Operating Committee	Brotherhood Headquarters

STANDING COMMITTEES
Biennium—1936-1938

Finance—Harry A. Fritsch, Allentown, Pa.; O. Roy Frankenfield, Philadelphia, Pa.; Fred Wessels, Savannah, Ga.

Constitution—H. E. Isenhour, Salisbury, N. C.; L. F. Speckman, Esq., Louisville, Ky.; Heiby W. Ungerer, Rochester, N. Y.; Harry A. Fritsch, Allentown, Pa.

Operating Committee—J. Milton Deck, Philadelphia, Pa.; Harry A. Fritsch, Allentown, Pa.; Francis K. Ford, Niagara Falls, N. Y.; O. Roy Frankenfield, Philadelphia, Pa.; Rev. Charles F. Brobst, Telford, Pa.; Earle W. Bader, Bethlehem, Pa. (ex-officio).

To Arrange Closer Relations with Laymens' Movement—J. Milton Deck, Philadelphia, Pa.; Harry A. Fritsch, Allentown, Pa.; John Greiner, Jr., Scranton, Pa.; H. Torrey Walker, Collingswood, N. J.

REPORT OF THE IRON MOUNTAIN BOYS' SCHOOL CAMPAIGN

Total Receipts from I. M. S. Campaign—May 1936 to July 1, 1938	$17,333.66	
Balance, May 1, 1936	111.73	
Advance from Board of American Missions	402.92	
Total Income		$17,848.31
Remitted to Board of American Missions	$13,466.40	
Campaign Expenses	4,343.40	
Total Disbursements		$17,809.80
Balance, July 1, 1938		$ 38.51

N. B.—The above figures do not include amounts forwarded direct to the Board of American Missions.

In accordance with your request, I have reviewed your cash receipts records for the account of Iron Mountain Lutheran Boys' School from May 1, 1936 to December 31, 1937.

I hereby certify that, in my opinion, the cash receipts as shown in your monthly reports are correct.

WALLACE L. DAVIS, *Auditor.*

SYNODICAL REPORTS AS OF JULY 1, 1938

Synod	Men's Organizations	Membership Dues 1937 Dues No.	Membership Dues 1937 Dues Amount	Iron Mountain School 1938 Dues No.	Iron Mountain School 1938 Dues Amount	Campaign Receipts
Alleghany	39	3	$ 20.00	2	$ 12.50	$ 240.00
California	19			1	5.00	39.50
Canada	21	7	30.50	8	43.00	15.00
East Pennsylvania	123	12	79.00	27	163.50	1,759.31
Florida	4	1	3.00	2	10.50	21.00
Georgia-Alabama	8	1	5.00	1	5.00	60.00
Illinois	98	20	118.50	28	173.50	494.51
Indiana	33	5	27.50	10	46.00	81.50
Iowa	18	1	10.00	2	17.50	32.09
Kansas	17	4	22.50	5	32.50	121.00
Kentucky-Tennessee	19	3	17.50	4	20.50	150.00
Manitoba	5					
Maryland	57	8	43.50	23	140.50	1,674.39
Midwest	6	1	5.00	2	10.00	12.00
Michigan	14	2	12.50	3	15.50	12.50

Ministerium of Penna..........	342	54	320.50	66	415.00	4,977.60
Mississippi	11					
Nebraska	21	7	45.00	8	51.50	334.63
New York	297	12	80.50	26	181.00	2,340.16
North Carolina	54	21	117.50	23	137.50	597.87
Northwest	88	6	33.50	11	65.50	107.25
Nova Scotia	1			1	2.50	
Ohio	140	13	73.50	19	108.00	369.40
Pacific	14	4	18.00	4	22.50	45.00
Pittsburgh	155	17	107.50	24	146.75	1,062.68
Rocky Mountain	11	2	10.00	2	10.00	12.00
Slovak Zion	2					
South Carolina	35	2	10.00	7	35.50	204.38
Susquehanna	45			1	7.50	267.59
Texas	11	9	51.00	8	50.25	629.26
Virginia	24	1	5.00	2	10.00	877.75
Wartburg	19	2	12.50	1	5.00	
West Pennsylvania	38			4	30.50	142.50
West Virginia	13	5	30.00	8	47.50	652.79
Total	1,802	223	$1,309.00	333	$2,022.00	$17,333.66

Mr. Deck introduced the Rev. Amos J. Traver, the newly elected editor of *Lutheran Men*. Dr. Traver addressed the Convention concerning that publication.

Several questions were asked concerning the work of the Brotherhood, which questions were answered by certain members of the Brotherhood who are delegates.

Mr. Deck next introduced Mr. Earle W. Bader, Executive Secretary, who addressed the Convention.

Due to the illness of Mrs. C. E. Gardner, President, Mrs. Oscar C. Schmidt, Vice-president, presented the report of the Women's Missionary Society.

REPORT OF THE WOMEN'S MISSIONARY SOCIETY

True to its purpose of missionary education and inspiration and assisting in the support of the whole work of our Church, the Women's Missionary Society has continued its program during the past biennium through all of its regularly established departments. In general there has been progress, although no new work of any great magnitude has been undertaken.

For the first time, in 1937, the Society held a triennial convention in October in Buffalo, New York. Previous to this, conventions from the time of the merger, were held biennially.

AUGMENTING THE WORK OF THE BOARDS OF THE CHURCH

As an authorized auxiliary of the Church, the Women's Missionary Society carries on its program educationally and financially through the Boards of the Church. Naturally, being a missionary organization, most of this support goes through the Board of Foreign Missions and the Board of American Missions. Again, because all women missionaries are supported by this organization, and because by the nature of their work there are more women missionaries in service in the Church abroad than at home, the appropriation to the Board of Foreign Missions is larger than that to the Board of American Missions. Approximately one-fourth of the work done through the Board of Foreign Missions is made possible by the Women's Missionary Society. About one-tenth of the total budget of the Board of American Missions is made up of the contributions of the Women's Missionary Society.

Through the Board of Foreign Missions

Under the Board of Foreign Missions the society supports fifty-nine missionaries in five foreign fields and the institutions in which they serve. The present list is as follows: In India, 33; in Liberia, Africa, 7; in Japan, 11; in China, 7; in South America, 1.

During the biennium, upon recommendation of the Executive Board of the Women's Missionary Society the Board of Foreign Missions called and commissioned the following women missionaries:

Miss Myrtle A. Onsrud, India
Miss Virginia Aderholt, Japan
Miss Selma M. Bergner, Japan
Mrs. J. W. Miller, Liberia
Miss Elsie Otto, Liberia

Mrs. J. W. Miller as Miriam Treon, served as a missionary in Liberia prior to her marriage in 1926 to Mr. J. W. Miller. After his death she reapplied and was returned to this mission field.

Miss Elsie Otto was reappointed to Liberia after spending five years in America.

Two missionaries are under appointment at the present time,—Miss Hazel Naugle to India and Miss Hazel Biederbeck to Liberia.

Women missionaries supported by individual congregations of the United Lutheran Church are listed in the report of the Board of Foreign Missions.

It is with deep regret that we report the resignation of Dr. Arlene M. Beal, missionary in India on account of health; an enforced leave of absence from the field in the case of Dr. Grace Moyer who is ill. With regret and at the same time with our wishes for happiness, we record the loss from the staff of single women missionaries of Miss Frances Segner and Dr. Gladys Morgan, both of whom were married in India.

Misfortune came to mission property in India during the cyclone in October 1936. Immediately the Women's Missionary Society responded with a gift of $5,000 to meet the emergency. Recently damage came to the buildings in the Tsimo School compound in China when Japanese bombs were dropped into the compound.

To assist in the China relief program in our mission, the Women's Missionary Society voted $2,000 toward the Epiphany Appeal of the Board of Foreign Missions this year.

Through the Board of American Missions

To this Board the society makes an annual appropriation of $70,639. In Church extension loans the Board administers $8,280 in Women's Missionary Society funds.

Four women missionaries are supported entirely, and approximately forty home mission pastors wholly or in part. The maintenance of the Rocky Boy Mission, and the support of the Konnarock Training School in Konnarock, Virginia, are the responsibility of the society.

It is with genuine regret and appreciation for her services that the resignation of Miss Helen Dyer, principal of the Konnarock School, is reported.

In loyalty to the Anniversary Appeal an appropriation of $2,000 was made to the Board of American Missions.

Through the Board of Inner Missions

Inner Mission projects which are in so many instances local or synodical receive the services and support of members of our organization through many channels which are not reported for our records. Recognizing the importance of this phase of work of our Church the Board of Inner Missions was included in the annual budget of the society for a contribution of $1,000 beginning in 1938.

Through the Board of Education

The Women's Missionary Society appreciates the privilege of co-operating with the Board in several ways. The student department through which the student census is taken is one of its regular departments. Dr. Mary E. Markley and Miss Mildred E. Winston, together with synodical secretaries give to the Church this valuable service. These secretaries of the Board of Education assist in many other ways the work of the organization, especially in their contacts with student groups and in the cultivation of missionary candidates. Dr. Markley served the organization from 1922 to 1938 as chairman of the Personnel Committee. In this capacity she rendered the organization an invaluable service. During her chairmanship a number of helpful policies and procedures have been evolved for dealing with missionary candidates.

The annual financial contribution to this Board is $2,250.

Through the Deaconess Board

The deaconess cause is promoted also through a special department of the Women's Missionary Society. Our co-operation, therefore, with this Board has been largely educational and promotional. A request from the Board for an annual appropriation is to receive the attention of the Executive Board at its October meeting.

Through the Board of Ministerial Pensions and Relief

An annual financial appropriation of $3,990 is made to this Board. Five women missionaries are receiving assistance from this Board at the present time.

Through the Parish and Church School Board

A small annual appropriation of $100 was voted to this Board for the Leadership Training School at Nawakwa. Contributions of missionary books have been made annually to the missionary library at Nawakwa.

Representatives to Boards

To all of the boards mentioned above the Women's Missionary Society has the privilege of sending two representatives to serve in an advisory capacity. On three of the regular boards, the Board of Education, the Deaconess Board and the Parish and Church School Board the women who are voting members are at the same time actively associated with the work of the Women's Missionary Society.

The present advisers to the boards are the following: To the Board of Foreign Missions, Mrs. C. E. Gardner and Miss A. Barbara Wiegand; to the Board of American Missions, Mrs. Oscar C. Schmidt and Miss Flora Prince; to the Board of Inner Missions, Mrs. W. A. Snyder and Mrs. W. C. Hanning; to the Board of Education, Mrs. Merle Cain; to the Board of Deaconess Work, Mrs. W. P. M. Braun and Mrs. John M. Cook; to the Board of Ministerial Pensions and Relief, Mrs. H. C. Reller and Mrs. D. Burt Smith; to the Parish and Church School Board, Mrs. J. J. Neudoerffer and Mrs. W. F. Morehead.

INTERDENOMINATIONAL CO-OPERATION

The Women's Missionary Society co-operates with the Foreign Missions Conference of North America, the Council of Women for Home Missions and the Missionary Education Movement. By election in the Foreign Missions Conference Miss A. Barbara Wiegand serves as a member of the Committee of Reference and Counsel. On the Executive Committee of the Council of Women for Home Missions are Mrs. P. M. Rossman and Mrs. W. F. Morehead. The Missionary Education Movement publishes missionary books for different age groups. Numerous uses are made of these materials in our own educational program. Mrs. W. F. Morehead serves the Movement as a member of the Adult Committee and also as a member of the Board of Managers. Miss Nona M. Diehl serves as chairman of the Home Mission Section of the Youth Committee; Miss Jane Gilbert serves on the Children's Committee.

Mrs. D. Burt Smith is the chairman of the standing committee on interdenominational relationships of our own organization.

GROWTH IN TWENTY YEARS

Since the organization of the Women's Missionary Society in 1918 five presidents have served the society. All of these continue active members. They are Mrs. J. G. Traver, Mrs. S. R. Kepner, Mrs. W. F. Morehead, Miss Flora Prince, and Mrs. C. E. Gardner.

When the women of three former missionary bodies merged to form the present society they came together in faith but at the same time with due deliberation. They did not hope for the impossible. Nevertheless their fondest dreams have in many respects been more than realized.

The first budget committee after making what they considered careful and conservative estimates on membership and income concluded that the combined membership by the end of the first biennium might reach 81,000 and that they ought to be assured of $162,000. The first statistical report showed the membership estimate a bit too high, but the income figure much too low. The following is the record for the twenty years.

	Membership	Receipts
1920	79,134	$ 251,597.21
1922	101,367	611,324.49
1924	102,646	890,288.02
1926	110,411	875,156.38
1928	117,996	997,771.10
1930	116,663	1,080,469.15
1932	113,300	888,578.71
1934	109,819	709,946.34
1936	112,715	683,347.54
1938	111,296	747,013.37
		$7,735,492.31

Receipts for first decade	$3,626,137.20
Receipts for second decade	4,109,355.11
	$7,735,492.31

The values and the spiritual blessings which came to the women and young women and children whose prayers and consecrated service, went into the work represented by these figures, can, of course, not be measured.

New Projects During the Twenty Years

A glimpse at the fields around the world would show also a number of institutions and projects which were not in existence at the time of the merger. Among these we mention as outstanding illustrations an additional school for girls in India,—the Iowa Girls' School at Repalle, a memorial to Mrs. Beegle, the first executive secretary of the united society; a hospital at Bhimavaram, made possible by the Augustana Women's Missionary Society, which organization co-operates so effectively with ours in India; the Virginia Boyer Memorial Hall at the Kodaikanal School in India; the Janice James School, and the Colony of Mercy in Japan, as well as other projects carried on by women missionaries; two interior stations in Liberia, which have the services of women missionaries; a well-established school in Buenos Aires; a missionary's residence in Puerto Rico; the Konnarock Training School in Virginia; the development of work in the Watauga Parish, Boone, North Carolina, and the responsibility for the maintenance of the Rocky Boy Mission in Montana.

To assist in the purchase of the China Mission in 1925, the Women's Missionary Society gave $35,000. Here in addition to work begun by the Berlin Missionary Society a hospital has been opened which is served by women missionaries. A Bible School and a School for Girls—now co-educational—are projects supported in this field by the Women's Missionary Society.

MISSIONARIES THEN AND NOW

At the time of the merger there were 35 women missionaries on the foreign fields. Today that number is 59, with two under appointment. In the twenty years since the merger 80 women have been sent to the different fields. Of the original 35, 15 are still in active service on the fields, and 3 are retired. Two more will retire during the coming biennium.

ADVANCE IN CHRISTIAN STEWARDSHIP

The above brief glance backward over twenty years would lead to the conclusion that the organization has advanced in stewardship. Realizing the need for a continued emphasis on spiritual advancement which will express itself in renewed consecration to the whole program of Christian living, the special objective for the present triennium is "Advancing in Christian Stewardship." Following the past triennium when our special emphasis was educational—"Missionary Advance"—there is as a part of the present objective an opportunity for an expression in financial gifts. The principle involved in this emphasis is a basic one and needs to be courageously promoted in the Church. If even that one-fifth of the Church's women belonging to the Women's Missionary Society acquire a renewed sense of Christian stewardship, it will be felt throughout the Church and find expression in its missionary work. The Triennial Special Fund has come into being because of aroused interest in meeting the pressing needs on home and foreign mission fields. After years of service, buildings are in need of repair. Some must be rebuilt entirely. Salaries of national workers must be restored, and there are always new urgent needs to be met. These needs are being listed and are being assumed by synodical societies and other groups as they desire to have the privilege of assisting.

Examples of some of the items already assumed in connection with this program are the following: The rebuilding of the Samalkot Girls' School in India; extensive repairs to the Central Girls' School in Rajahmundry; the opening of a secondary teacher training department in the Stall School in Guntur, India; repairs to the Phoebe Hospital in Liberia; a contribution of $1,500 toward the emergency fund for the support of Gossner Mission in India; and other similar requests.

It is our hope that this objective will bring blessings to our fellow Christians in all fields, to the Church at home, and to our own membership.

Mrs. H. C. Michael is serving as the chairman of this stewardship program.

ADMINISTRATION

The officers, board members and staff elected in October 1937 for the present triennium are the following:

President..Mrs. C. E. Gardner
Vice-president..Mrs. Oscar C. Schmidt
Recording Secretary...Miss A. Barbara Wiegand
Statistical Secretary..Mrs. J. M. Cook
Treasurer and Treasurer of the Board of Trustees....Miss Flora Prince

SYNODICAL REPRESENTATIVES

*Alleghany..Mrs. H. C. Michael
California..Mrs. J. E. Hoick
Canada..Mrs. J. R. Collins
East Pennsylvania..Mrs. D. Burt Smith
Florida..Mrs. W. E. Pugh
*Illinois...Mrs. O. A. Sardeson
Indiana...Mrs. A. H. Keck
Iowa..Mrs. M. E. Redeen
Kansas..Mrs. J. P. Jensen
Maryland..Mrs. Merle Cain
Michigan..Mrs. F. M. Keller
Mississippi...Mrs. John W. Mangum
Nebraska..Mrs. J. Lad Skocpol
*New York..Mrs. W. A. Snyder
North Carolina..Mrs. J. L. Morgan
Northwest..Mrs. A. E. Birch
Ohio..Mrs. C. S. Stroup
*Pennsylvania Ministerium...............................Mrs. J. J. Neudoerffer
Pittsburgh..Mrs. H. C. Reller.
South Carolina..Mrs. J. H. Summer
Susquehanna...Mrs. W. C. Hanning
Texas...Mrs. C. Zirjacks
Virginia..Mrs. J. L. Almond, Jr.
Wartburg..Mrs. R. E. Belter
West Pennsylvania ....Mrs. H. D. Hoover

* Members of Administrative Committee.

STAFF

Executive Secretary..Miss Nona M. Diehl
Executive Secretary, Education Department......Mrs. W. F. Morehead
Secretary for Light Brigades................................Mrs. Alfred J. Fenner

It was with genuine regret that the resignations of two staff members were accepted during the biennium. Mrs. Julius F. Seebach, editor of *Lutheran Woman's Work*, had served in this capacity for twenty-one years beginning her services before the merger. Miss Amelia D. Kemp served the society as executive secretary from 1924 to 1937. The Women's Missionary Society appreciates the contributions made by these two women and regrets their withdrawal from their official connection with the organization.

EDUCATION AND PROMOTION

Through the Education Department the society makes its many and varied contacts with the local groups and with the entire Church. Monthly programs studied by congregational groups, materials for mission study classes, books, and pamphlets of all kinds written, printed, and distributed by this department make possible a program of missionary education which is being extended increasingly into all phases of the work of our Church.

Important also in the promotion of the organization and of missions in general is the monthly magazine, *Lutheran Woman's Work*. The present number of subscriptions is 36,170. This figure shows a gain of 3,000 subscriptions during the past biennium. The editing of this periodical is carried at the present time in the Education Department with a staff, Mrs. W. F. Morehead, editor-in-chief, Miss Jane Gilbert, and Miss Nona M. Diehl.

The September issue for this year is a special twentieth anniversary number.

THE PROGRAM FOR THE CHILDREN OF THE CHURCH

The Church has asked the Women's Missionary Society to be the promotional agency for the new children's organization which beginning in 1939 will take the place of all present Junior Luther Leagues and Light Brigades.

Following the action of the Church at its Convention in 1936, the Committee authorized to draw up plans for this organization made its report to the Executive Board of the United Lutheran Church in America. The report accepted by the Executive Board on January 4, 1938, provided "That the Women's Missionary Society be designated as the agency to carry on this work in all congregations of the Church."

This report provided further for the final planning of the program to be the work of a committee of nine of which three were to be appointed by the Women's Missionary Society. Mrs. Merle Cain, Mrs. A. J. Fenner and the Executive Secretary have been serving on this committee. From the report of this committee we quote the following:

Promotion

To be conducted by the Women's Missionary Society as one of the regular departments of its work.

The head of this department to be a full-time, salaried worker to be known as the Secretary of *The Children of the Church,* and to be appointed by the Women's Missionary Society in consultation with the Committee on Program for The Children of the Church.

The Women's Missionary Society, in carrying on this work, to use as synodical secretaries, leaders to be known as synodical secretaries for *The Children of the Church.* These synodical secretaries to be appointed by the Committee on Parish Education of each synod, in consultation with the officers of the synodical Women's Missionary Society and Luther League.

The Administrative Committee of the Women's Missionary Society at its meeting on May 4, 1938, voted to approve the report submitted to it together with the obligations involved. A contribution of $2,500 has been given by the Women's Missionary Society to finance the work for the first six montns according to a budget submitted by the Committee on Program for The Children of the Church. The office for The Children of the Church was opened in Room 713 of the Muhlenberg Building in Philadelphia on August 1. The Secretary for The Children of the Church is Mrs. A. J. Fenner and the Associate Secretary, Miss Brenda Melhouse.

The Women's Missionary Society recognizes its responsibility in this important work as that of promotion. We have agreed furthermore to carry on the work requested of us as one of the departments of our organization, even though the procedure outlined is different from that followed in any of our regular departments. We desire to co-operate so that we may render the Church the service it is asking of us. The spirit of a recent editorial in *Lutheran Woman's Work* we believe to be the spirit of our entire organization.

"The best of plans need the loyal co-operation of all to realize their best accomplishment. No time to speak of preference for this name or that. There is one overwhelming necessity, one paramount challenge— the child, his need today of whatever we can do to further his growth in the life that has at its heart allegiance to Christ, and the living of His way."

YOUNG WOMEN

A significant part of the work of the Women's Missionary Society is accomplished by young women. These groups have always been an integral part of the organization, never functioning independently either synodically or nationally. At the present time there are more than 12,000 members in more than 600 groups in this department. During the past biennium the young women have contributed more than $70,000 toward the budget of the organization. The Sixth Young Women's Congress, a part of the Buffalo convention program, was a great inspiration to the large number who came to hear and to meet the missionaries and missionary leaders of our Church.

There is no age limit to missionary interest or enthusiasm. The challenging missionary program of our United Lutheran Church in all of its fields attracts old and young alike. Friendships are formed between young people of our churches in the East and the West which become cherished spiritual treasures. As members of one great Church we wish to co-operate in every way possible in carrying on an adequate program of education for all age groups. We hope these spiritual blessings which come from continued study and prayer and fellowship with our worldwide church will continue.

Promotion of Auxiliaries

The Women's Missionary Society is participating in the preparation for the part the auxiliaries are to have in the general plan for promotion throughout the Church. Serving on this committee during the past year have been Mrs. W. F. Morehead and Miss Nona M. Diehl. It is our hope that when the Luther League, the Brotherhood, and the Women's Missionary Society come before each congregation with a joint program in January or February of 1939, the Church will welcome the opportunity, and that mutually good results to the Church and to the auxiliaries will lead to advance in the program of the entire Church.

In Looking Ahead

All the hopes of the Women's Missionary Society can be summed up in the common prayer that every one of its members may be an acceptable servant in the eyes of the Master and in the Church at large, and that the organization may prove a worthy power for increasing good in the advancement of our own great Church and in the Kingdom of God.

Anna S. Gardner, *President.*

Nona M. Diehl, *Executive Secretary.*

GENERAL TREASURER'S ACCOUNTS

STATEMENT OF CASH RECEIPTS AND DISBURSEMENTS

July 1, 1937 to June 30, 1938

Receipts

General Accounts:
General Fund	$80,050.23
Advance in Christian Stewardship	5,027.66
Thank Offering	90,214.87
Christmas Offering	7,568.40
Life Memberships	21,420.00
In Memoriams	6,455.00

Contributions to Home Fields		2,809.12
Contributions to Foreign Fields		1,787.46
Support of Missionaries		21,096.50
Support of Native Teachers and Bible Women		10,642.34
Scholarships		6,175.98
Synodical Specials		17,213.18
Visitation Department		656.86
Cut Fees, Life Membership Department		165.00
Interdenominational		312.07
Emergency Scholarship Fund		302.12
Telephone Refunds		77.35
Miscellaneous Refunds		694.28
Transfers from Treasurer, Board of Trustees—Matured Annuities for:		
Board of Foreign Missions	$200.00	
Africa	5,000.00	
India	500.00	
American Missions	200.00	
General Fund	2,400.00	
		8,300.00
Income from Investments:		
Annuity Funds	$12,051.13	
Cronk Memorial Fund	1,041.62	
Mehring Legacy	1,045.85	
Dr. Luther A. Kuhlman Fund	60.00	
Other Trust Funds	6,023.55	
		20,222.15
Total General Accounts		**$301,190.57**

Special Accounts:		
Bequests and Legacies	$2,471.60	
Annuities	800.00	
India Lace Industry	22,670.00	
Box Work	3,741.66	
Triennial Convention	5,612.08	
Week of Prayer Offering	7,524.98	
Total Special Accounts		**42,820.32**

Designated Gifts:		
American Missions	$2,084.72	
Inner Missions	148.50	
Africa	70.43	
China	478.59	
India	9,872.01	
Japan	51.00	
South America	2.95	
Miscellaneous	1,087.33	
Rajahmundry Land	749.82	
Cyclone Relief	92.87	
Light Brigade International Toy Shop Project	678.46	
Total Designated Gifts		**15,316.68**
Total Receipts		**$359,327.57**

DISBURSEMENTS

General Accounts:

Board of American Missions	$68,784.12

Board of Foreign Missions:

For Epiphany Appeal	2,000.00
Africa	14,679.15
China	12,955.35
India	96,838.71
Japan	36,201.40
South America	7,660.00
Board of Education	2,250.00
Board of Ministerial Pensions and Relief	3,990.00
Inner Mission Board	500.00
Parish and Church School Board	100.00
Interdenominational	3,776.85
Quarterly Gifts to Retired Missionaries	800.00
Missionaries Outfit Allowances	450.00
Medical and Clinical Expenses	949.85
Scholarships	300.00
Education Department Budget	8,061.02
Payments to Annuitants	13,530.77
Furniture and Equipment	81.75
National Lutheran Council for Gossner Mission	1,500.00
General Fund Miscellaneous	708.74

$276,117.71

Administration:

Salaries:

Executive Secretary (Miss A. D. Kemp)	750.00
Executive Secretary (Miss N. M. Diehl)	1,600.00
General Treasurer (Mrs. J. M. Cook)	600.00
Treasurer, Board of Trustees (Miss F. Prince)	450.00
Education Department Secretary, (Mrs. W. F. Morehead)	1,900.04
Young Women's Secretary (Miss N. M. Diehl)	600.00
Light Brigade Secretary (Mrs. A. J. Fenner)	1,200.00
Editor Lutheran Woman's Work (Mrs. M. R. Seebach)	450.00
Business Manager, India Lace Department (Mrs. Wm. Jaxheimer)	1,500.00
Office Salaries	3,599.10
President's Allowance	150.00
Education Department Salaries and Wages	8,427.26
Expenses of Executive Board and Committee Meetings	2,314.43
Expenses of Representatives at Meetings	399.96
Office Supplies and Expenses	249.63
General Treasurer's Office Expense	197.44
Executive Office Expense	364.02
Young Women's Office Expense	52.09
Light Brigade Department Expense	68.59
Life Membership Department Expense	3,776.92
Rent	4,314.75
Telephone	294.62

Accounting and Auditing	660.00	
Treasurer's Bonds	63.44	
Field Travel	200.00	
Total Administration		34,182.29

Designated Gifts:

American Missions	$1,876.22	
Inner Missions	244.33	
Africa	116.42	
China	390.30	
India	8,188.23	
Japan	1,061.04	
South America	2.95	
Cyclone Relief	1,327.25	
Miscellaneous	1,146.14	
Light Brigade International Toy Shop Project	790.00	
Total Designated Gifts		15,142.88

Special Accounts:

Transferred to Treasurer, Board of Trustees:

Annuities	$800.00	

Bequests and Legacies Transmitted to:
Board of Foreign Missions:

China	$2,383.85	
Japan	2,383.85	
		4,767.70

Matured Annuities Transmitted to:

Board of Foreign Missions	$200.00	
Board of Foregin Missions for:		
Africa	5,000.00	
India	500.00	
Board of American Missions	200.00	
		5,900.00
India Lace Industry	5,073.78	
Box Work	3,960.95	
West Indies Industries	5.00	
Cronk Memorial Scholarship Fund	900.00	
Mehring Legacy Scholarship Fund	600.00	
Triennial Convention Expense	10,932.64	
Week of Prayer Offering	120.80	
Loan to Education Department	2,000.00	
Total Special Accounts		35,060.87
Total Disbursements		$360,503.75

SUMMARY

Cash Balance, July 1, 1937		$162,178.50
Receipts		359,327.57
		$521,506.07
Disbursements		360,503.75
Cash Balance, June 30, 1938		$161,002.32

General Fund Cash Balance $130,743.56
Designated Gifts and Other Fund Cash Balances........................... 15,940.45
Rajahmundry Land Fund, Cash Balance 14,318.31

$161,002.32

Mrs. Schmidt read the message from Mrs. Gardner to the Convention.

Mrs. Schmidt introduced Miss Nona M. Diehl, Executive Secretary of the Women's Missionary Society, who addressed the Convention.

It was agreed that the greetings of the Convention be sent to Mrs. Gardner praying for her speedy recovery. The President asked Mrs. Schmidt to convey these greetings.

Mr. John George Kurzenknabe, President, presented the report of the Luther League.

REPORT OF THE LUTHER LEAGUE OF AMERICA

Life is not made up of things we omit, but of the things we do. Training youth: to obtain a clearer consciousness of Christian faith, for a life of active personal service in the Church, and to become a true witness for Christ, is the important task that the Luther League endeavors to accomplish.

We realize that far too many of our young people are lost to our congregations and to the Church at large every year. There are many contributing causes. It has been correctly said "every influence in the world is against the sermon preached on Sunday."

These tremendous losses present a tremendous challenge. The problem that faces us is to be found in the changed conditions in which we live. The increased facilities for social intercourse, of communication and transportation have placed temptations in the way of present-day youth which were almost unknown to the former generation.

There is no more important work for the Church at the present time than that of conserving youth. The duty of the Church has always been soul-saving and soul-keeping. And it is especially with the young people that her greatest efforts in soul-keeping must be expended at the present time. The Church can survive only if it recognizes youth, not merely as a grave problem, but also and above all, as its very valuable possession

The Church of today and tomorrow needs these energetic young people with their boundless vitality, their fresh courage, their consecrated daring. The world is seeking to enlist their interests and their powers. From all over the world there comes the flashing news of various governments organizing live, pulsating movements, appealing for the strength, the optimism, the courage and idealism of youth, imposing upon them a physical and mental discipline in order to train them for the furtherance of their cause. Our youth movement towers far above these as the soul towers above the body. The Church of Christ has prime claim on both body and soul of our youth. We shall be able to keep them with Christ only as we keep them busy for Christ.

Our objective is to bring our present-day Christian youth face to face with the challenging task of the Church and help to find its place in this century by adopting in word and deed a Christian philosophy of life. Especially is it our purpose to reach into the lives of these young people who are on the fringe of our churches and whose lives are not centered in Christ.

In this biennium the Luther League of America has endeavored through its representatives on various committees to co-operate in every possible way with the actions of the Church and its Executive Board in matters in which it was vitally concerned.

The Luther League of America, again during the past two years, has helped with its program and suggestions to bring to thousands of our young people opportunities for knowledge and service both in the local congregation and the Church at large. Certainly there was no sense of failure or spirit of defeatism in the hundreds of young men and women who met in conventions. That spirit will continue to dominate the thinking of the Luther League of America as we realize there is more to be done in the future than in the past. Youth never looks back. We may see in the present a number of problems in our own Church that cry for solution. We may become depressed by the coldness and indifference of so many within the visible Church to the heart-searching challenge of the eternal Redeemer in a new day and a new world. We may be confronted by the dismaying decay of the religious life in America and the collapse of the entire philosophy of life whose heart has the lust for gold. But we turn from the wrecks of human hopes and ambitions to a calm consideration of the ways and means through which to bring to the service of our Church the conquering power of youth.

One of the high privileges of the past biennium was our close contact with a number of our District, State and Synodical Leagues. In this contact we learned to know more of their problems and recognized their devoted efforts of co-operation with the Luther League of America.

One outstanding feature of the past biennium has been the appreciable growth in things spiritual. We have noted with pleasure the increasing desire to make our Luther League devotional meetings, conventions and rallies outstandingly spiritual. As a result of these the gatherings have been better attended and made more helpful to our Leaguers. We believe that the success of our other activities is due to the fact that we have placed an increased emphasis on the spiritual side of our program.

PERSONNEL

Officers and Executive Committee for 1937-1939 are as follows: Honorary Members: Rev. L. M. Kuhns, D.D., Litt.D.; Hon. E. F. Eilert, C.S.D.; Mr. Harry Hodges; Rev. A. J. Traver, D.D. Officers: President, Mr. John G. Kurzenknabe; vice-president, Mr. Alvin H. Schaediger; second vice-president, Mr. J. W. Cobb; recording secretary, Miss Gladys Broeker; treasurer, Mr. Charles W. Fuhr; executive secretary, Rev. Paul M. Kinports, D.D.; intermediate secretary, Rev. R. J. Wolf; junior secretary, Miss Brenda L. Mehlhouse; educational secretary, Rev. C. P. Harry, D.D.; missionary secretary, Miss J. Dorothy Borgstede; Life Service secretary, Rev. A. J. Beil. Members at Large: Miss Mildred Gartelmann, Mr. John Lauman, Rev. Wm. J. Ducker, Rev. J. W. Frease, Mr. Robert Ray Inslee, Mr. Howard Logan, and Rev. F. H. Bloch.

AGE DEPARTMENTS

The Luther League is divided into three departments: Junior (8-12 years) with supplementary program for little Leaguers under eight; Intermediate (13-16), and Senior (17 plus). Throughout these three departments the program of Education, Missions and Life Service has a unique place and value.

The Intermediate Department is seeking to satisfy some of the many interests and activities peculiar to the teen age. Rev. R. J. Wolf, secretary of this department, says:

"Feeling the palpitating pulse of youth between the ages of 12 to 16 and feeding into their spiritual and mental and physical blood stream the requisite nourishment to keep them actively 'tied in loyalty' to the Church, has been our concern for these thirteen years. Within that time 828 congregations of the Church have registered their teen-age youth with the Intermediate Department of the Luther League. Many other congregations, due to having a limited number of youth of all ages and for a variety of other reasons, have been compelled to foster a single mass youth program, thus depriving the Intermediate Department of direct claim to a larger membership.

"Intermediate Leagues come and go—then frequently come back again. We are truly a fluctuating flock. However, several hundred churches have solidly maintained their Intermediate Leagues since first registering same.

"With a program covering sixteen specific lines of activity, inclusive of a well-rounded set-up for teen-agers, we are able to report 300 Leagues in on ten or more of the points for the year 1937.

"These organized bands of early adolescents do things when efficiently and intelligently guided. To enumerate all they do is voided by lack of space. Let's touch a few high spots of accomplishment, however. With dues at ten cents a member the percentage of payment for the past four years averaged 97 per cent. In addition to dues the sum of $2,556 was given into the Sustaining Membership Fund in a ten-year period. A total of $3,521 has been contributed to the several missionary objectives of the Luther League. There is almost a hundred per cent study given the weekly devotional topics. Daily Bible reading, church and Sunday school attendance, and individual participation in local church activity, are a few of the interests by which the boys and girls of our organization are trained, and to which they noticeably respond. Actually thousands of dollars are contributed annually by Intermediate Leagues to local and benevolent interests other than prescribed for them by their own organization.

"Other phases of teen-age interest and activity have received their relative attention in so far as time, talent and the treasury have permitted."

The Junior Department in caring for the children under the direction of Miss Brenda Mehlhouse reports that "The Junior Department has been practically 'marking time' during the past biennium, pending the disposition of children's work; but despite this fact it has grown materially in numbers, service and contributions.

"It now numbers about 1,100 groups of Juniors and 150 of Little Leaguers, with approximately 20,000 children enrolled, in the United States, Canada, Puerto Rico, South America, and India.

"During the biennium we observed our fortieth anniversary. Grace, N. S., Pittsburgh, Pa., the first Junior League to be organized, celebrated its fortieth anniversary in October 1937, with a record of forty years of continuous existence, under the leadership of Mr. Charles W. Fuhr, Treasurer of the Luther League of America. In May of this year Grace, Reading, Pa., celebrated its fortieth birthday.

"At the Springfield Convention of the Luther League of America there was a large exhibit, a presentation of the Juniors' share in our Education, Missions, and Life Service Departments, a Doll Show, a Christmas Party and a Toy Shower for the Juniors of the Oesterlen Orphans' Home, a fine Junior Rally, a Fortieth Birthday Party Luncheon, and a presentation before the convention.

"The three-fold objective of the League—Education, Missions and Life Service—has been carried on in the Junior Department, and first steps in training given there.

"The children have been trained through *weekly* meetings, with study programs, where they have learned the program of the Church.

"The topics arranged for the past two years have been on the general theme, 'Guiding Juniors in Daily Christian Living,' and through units of study on Religion and the Church, the Home, School, Health, Play, Art, Citizenship, Vocations, Friendship, the Neighborhood, we have endeavored to reach down into every part of the child's life and to have the Church help build Christian character in all his experiences.

"In addition, there are available units of study on our United Lutheran Church, the Bible (in various aspects), Christmas, Easter, Lent, Prayer, Worship, Recreation, and other phases of Christian activity, to the number of twenty-five—an abundant store of permanent material for the leader.

"Through yearly Reading Courses the Juniors have been trained to read the best books.

"The Good Neighbor Club has provided the means of helping our Juniors in institutions and mission fields.

"A Twelve-point Program with a yearly Honor Roll has helped to stimulate a well-rounded cycle of activities.

"Rallies, conventions—with the Juniors themselves in charge, have developed leadership.

" 'Nation-wide Junior Rally Day' observed each year with simultaneous rallies, using the same program, has stimulated the work.

"The leaders themselves have been helped through conferences, training classes of various sorts, and institutes. An annual yearly National Institute—during the biennium the twelfth and thirteenth were held—has proved most successful.

"Missionary training and the development of a spirit of world friendship has been promoted through (1) monthly missionary programs, (2) Junior mission study classes—two each year, home and foreign, and (3) missionary service and giving. The Juniors have contributed to every cause of our United Lutheran Church. The Juniors of Pennsylvania alone in addition to their gifts to various Luther League specials, contributed in one year $1,126 to local needs and $1,083 to benevolence.

"The Life Service Department finds its beginnings with the children. Through programs, exercises, rallies, and the stories of our church and missionary heroes, a vision of full-time service is given. These children are the future church, the church in training, and here we have been developing the future pastors, deaconesses, missionaries, the future workers of the church. Many are being claimed for future leadership.

"At the Columbus Convention the merging of the Junior Luther League and the Light Brigade, and the further extension of organized children's work was authorized, and a Committee charged with the same.

"At this writing (August 1) this Committee is functioning and the new organization—The Children of the Church—is being promoted.

"The Junior Secretary after nineteen years of work automatically relinquishes her position January 1.

"She has been called to the office of Associate Secretary of The Children of the Church.

"It is her one concern that not one bit of the splendid work of the Junior Department be lost, but that the efforts, the training, the cooperation, and the work done, be carried on into and become part of the new organization."

EXTENSION

Efforts are being made through the various State and synodical Luther Leagues to contact pastors and young people in the interests of our organization and its program. A considerable number of the 3,961 congregations in the United Lutheran Church have no young people's organizations. Reports from the various extension committees show successful results from our efforts, and a number of new Leagues have been organized.

MEMBERSHIP

The steady growth of the League membership indicates an interest in the League and its program by the youth of the Church. Comparative statistics reveal a decided increase in organizations and membership.

	1936	1937	1936	1937
	Organizations		Membership	
Senior	1,375	1,475	26,957	30,742
Intermediate	492	540	8,170	10,424
Junior	807	978	20,702	22,943

THE PROGRAM

Education—The educational program has been promoted through: topics discussion, reading course, Pocket Testament League, and the publications represented in the distribution per month of the *Luther League Review,* 6,000 copies; *Topics Quarterly,* 10,000 copies per quarter; *Intermediate Helps,* 3,000 copies per quarter; *Junior Topics Booklets,* 2,000 copies per year; and hundreds of promotional pamphlets.

The Pocket Testament League which endeavors to encourage daily Bible reading has a membership of 6,402.

Missions—The Luther League is decidedly interested in the missionary program of the Church. It has manifested this interest from year to year by encouraging the youth of the Church to give liberally to the apportionment of the Church and also to establish a special objective in the support of the missionary work of the Church.

In July 1937 the League completed its China Objective and contributed $11,349 for the erection of a Church with a social center consisting of a kindergarten, dispensary and equipment for Christian education in Tai Tung Chen, China.

The League in convention assembled at Springfield, Ohio, July 1937, at the suggestion of the American Mission Board and the approval of the Executive Board of the United Lutheran Church, decided to forward a financial missionary objective to be administered through the Board of American Missions the sum of $10,000. This project is in the southern mountains to be known as the Konnarock Medical Center. The League hopes to complete this objective in July 1939. On August 1, 1938, $6,762.59 has already been contributed.

Life Service—Through the Life Service Department, the League is endeavoring to encourage youth to realize their desire to render some distinctive service to the Church and to participate in the activities of the local congregation.

CO-OPERATION WITH OTHER LUTHERAN YOUTH ORGANIZATIONS

At the Charleston Convention in July 1935 a resolution was adopted:

"That the Luther League of America request the Youth Commission of the American Lutheran Conference to recommend that duly appointed representatives of the constituent Luther Leagues of the American Lutheran Conference meet the duly appointed representatives of the Luther League of America at a date and place to be set by mutual agreement to discuss closer co-operation."

The Executive Committee at its meeting in January 1936 adopted the following resolution:

"That we ask the Executive Board of the United Lutheran Church in America for permission to send representatives to meet with duly appointed representatives of youth groups of the constituents of the American Lutheran Youth Conference to discuss closer co-operation.'

At the meeting of the Executive Board of the United Lutheran Church in America held April 8, 1936, the following action was taken: "That this request is in harmony with other external relationships of similar nature, approved by the United Lutheran Church and that this request be granted."

Contacts with the Youth Commission of the American Lutheran Conference in the interests of the program for the youth of the Church have been made and the Luther League of America is urging all local, district, State and synodical Leagues to cultivate friendship and understanding, and, so far as possible, co-operate with young people's groups of other synodical bodies to seek a closer co-operation in our youth activities.

CONVENTIONS

The twenty-first Biennial Convention was held in Springfield, Ohio, July 5-9, 1937. With a splendid convention program and a delightful host, the convention was most successful. The total registration was 639.

The twenty-second Biennial Convention will be held in Long Beach, California, July 6-10, 1939. Plans for the convention are under way and it is hoped that a large delegation will participate in this convention.

FINANCES

The League continues to function under a slight deficit due to a decrease in income from dues and Sustaining Membership Fund. Only 80 per cent of the budget expenditures is raised through dues and the appropriation from the United Lutheran Church. The other 20 per cent is contributed by members and friends of the League.

Herewith we submit the report of the Treasurer and auditors:

FINANCIAL REPORT

June 1, 1935 to May 31, 1937

RECEIPTS

Balance, June 1, 1935.. $ 2,015.85

Dues	Senior	Intermediate	
1935—June-December	$ 2,630.00	$ 210.19	
1936—January-December	6,265.36	777.90	
1937—January-May	4,275.87	648.04	
	$13,171.23	$1,636.13	14,807.36

United Lutheran Church Appropriation		
1935—June-December	$ 3,000.00	
1936—January-December	6,000.00	
1937—January-May	1,500.00	
		10,500.00

Sustaining Membership Fund
1935—June-December	$ 1,492.31	
1936—January-December	2,375.25	
1937—January-May	1,970.00	
		5,837.56
Literature Sales		1,274.70

Review, Topic and Helps Receipts
For Review	$10,445.91	
For Topics	2,976.20	
For Helps	773.33	
Advertising in Review and Topics	1,005.50	
		15,200.94
Charleston Convention Registration Fees		1,009.00
Charleston Convention Offerings		318.93
Miscellaneous		29.79
		$50,994.13

EXPENDITURES

Salaries
Executive Secretary	$ 7,999.84	
Intermediate Secretary	6,399.92	
Junior Secretary	4,399.84	
Office Secretary	2,288.33	
Office Secretary	2,199.92	
India Secretary	25.00	
		23,312.85

Travel Expenses
Executive Secretary	840.00	
Intermediate Secretary	334.25	
Junior Secretary	150.00	
		1,324.25
Executive Committee		1,285.30
Ways and Means Committee	124.02	
Educational Committee	112.28	
Others	281.53	
		517.83

Printing of Literature
Senior	590.75	
Intermediate	104.67	
Junior	983.75	
Missionary	63.38	
Life Service	53.75	
Sustaining Membership	339.00	
Annual Church Booklet	169.91	
		2,305.21
President's Expense		97.50

Office Administration Expenses
Rent	1,402.50	
Postage	1,167.29	
Miscellaneous Office Expense	854.05	
		3,423.84
Canadian Exchange		2.08
Charleston Convention Expense		1,746.97

Springfield Convention Expense, to date....................		197.25
Printing Review, Topics and Helps		
Review	11,344.79	
Topics	2,079.25	
Helps	1,098.83	
Bulk Postage ....:......	795.07	
Cuts	345.73	
Addressograph Plates	34.90	
		15,698.57
		$49,911.65

RECAPITULATION

Receipts	$50,994.13	
Expenditures	49,911.65	
Balance, May 31, 1937, in bank............................	1,082.48	
Balance in Convention Reserve............................	902.75	
Balance, May 31, 1937...	$ 179.73	

Outstanding Bills—$1,714.93.

CHARLES W. FUHR, Treasurer.

CERTIFICATE OF AUDIT

We have audited the books of the Treasurer of the Luther League of America over the period extending from June 1, 1935 to May 31, 1937, and have found the same to be correct.

Respectfully submitted,
HARRY HODGES,
WILLIAM H. PATRICK, JR.,
Auditing Committee.

ACKNOWLEDGMENT

The Luther League expresses its deep appreciation and hearty thanks to the United Lutheran Church for the support given during the past biennium to carry on an enlarged program in an ever extending field of service.

Pastors and church workers, the Luther League has proven its practical value in the local congregation and Church at large. What the League shall be and do in the future depends in no small measure upon us. The League needs your help, guidance, co-operation and prayers.

Respectfully submitted,
PAUL M. KINPORTS, <i>Executive Secretary.</i></div>

Mr. Kurzenknabe introduced the Rev. Paul M. Kinports, Executive Secretary, who addressed the Convention.

Mr. Kurzenknabe next introduced Miss Brenda L. Mehl-house, Junior Secretary, and the Rev. R. J. Wolf, Intermediate Secretary, each of whom addressed the Convention.

Mr. Kurzenknabe expressed the appreciation of the Luther League for the financial assistance given by the Church.

The Rev. H. E. Turney, a member of the Commission, presented the report of the Commission concerning the Title of "Bishop."

REPORT OF COMMISSION CONCERNING TITLE OF "BISHOP"

(For action on the recommendations in this report, see p. 464.)

At the Columbus Convention of the U. L. C. A., in connection with the consideration of a memorial from the Texas Synod (Minutes, p. 358), the following resolution was adopted (Minutes, p. 359):

> Resolved, That a special commission of seven be appointed by the President of the Church to study the whole matter of the title "Bishop" in The United Lutheran Church in America and to report to the next convention of the Church concerning its consonance with Scripture, its historical implications, its desirability and feasibility among us, and the changes in constitution and practice that would be necessitated by its introduction among us.

By appointment of the President, the commission was established as follows: Rev. Rees Edgar Tulloss, convener; Rev. H. J. Pflum, Rev. A. G. Weng, Rev. H. E. Turney, Rev. W. C. Waltemyer, Rev. Fred W. Kern, Mr. Harry Hodges, and Mr. Carl Distler.

In the interest of economy, no meeting of the commission was held, but a considerable amount of correspondence has been carried on, and conferences among various members of the commission have been held as opportunities were presented during the biennium. A number of conferences were held also with officers and members of other Lutheran bodies, in which it appears interest in the problem has developed.

Strong representations have come to the commission, both from within and without the United Lutheran Church, with the spirit of which representations the members of your commission are inclined to agree, to the effect that the matter is one with reference to which a degree of uniformity of practice among all Lutheran bodies in America is desirable, and that therefore the problems involved are such as to call for a common study and, if possible, a common final decision.

At a meeting of the National Lutheran Council, held in Detroit, Mich., January 26 and 27, 1938, the matter received attention. The following is an excerpt from the minutes of that meeting (pages 9 and 10):

"The Executive Committee presented the following recommendation:

"'Whereas the Lutheran Church is conscious of the need of more clearly defining its polity and whereas the problem of Church administration has more recently invariably led to a discussion of the pros and cons of the bishopric as an administrative office with larger pastoral implications, whereas we believe the problem to be one which concerns the whole Lutheran Church in America rather than its district synods,

"'Therefore, we recommend that the National Lutheran Council provide an opportunity and a time for the discussion of this question.'

"The recommendation was adopted and a lengthy discussion followed.

"It was moved by P. O. Bersell, seconded and carried that

"'Whereas the question of the timeliness of establishing the episcopacy in the Lutheran Church in America, and related questions of church polity, are matters of common interest and whereas the National Lutheran Council recognizes the importance of these questions to the Lutheran Church, but has no mandate from its co-operating bodies to take the matter under consideration,

"'Be it resolved that the National Lutheran Council appreciates the desirability of the consideration of these questions in joint meetings of committees appointed by the co-operating bodies for this purpose.'"

In view of the above, your commission has hesitated to prepare and present the general study suggested in the action of the Columbus Convention, believing that a wiser procedure would be to encourage, and to co-operate in, the study suggested by the action of the National Lutheran Council. Our recommendations, therefore, look in that direction.

It is our desire, however, to the end of providing some added basis for thought and discussion regarding the matter under consideration, to indicate something of the varied views and desires of those who have suggested the change and those who oppose it, and to indicate something of the complexity of the general problem, particularly from the viewpoint of a consideration of the practical problems which are involved.

Roughly classified, those who have expressed their interest in the matter may be divided into two groups.

I

There are those who suggest no change in the present policy of administration of the synods or the general church, or in our present procedures as to election or tenure, but who desire merely a change in the title of the executive officer from "president" to "bishop." These urge that the title "president" is a secular term, that it is without scriptural foundation, that it is without good precedent in ecclesiastical history, and that it carries no special prestige in the popular mind. It is suggested that the adoption of the title of "bishop" would be pleasing to many of our people, that it would bring greater prestige to the executive office, that it would have distinct publicity value, that it would secure greater respect for officially-expressed opinions and pronouncements, and that it would tend to secure increased recognition for the Lutheran Church. Reference is made to the values along these lines which are said to have accrued to other church bodies following such practice, especially the Roman Catholic, Episcopal, and Methodist Episcopal churches.

It is suggested, in opposition to such proposal, that a mere change of title, without change of policy, would be unjustified by the arguments advanced, that it would in all probability fail to produce the results hoped for by its proponents, and that the action proposed would be undesirable on the ground of seeking the "shadow without the substance."

It is further urged that the election of bishops inevitably implies either (a) life-tenure in office, or (b) a removal of the title when the term of office is ended, or (c) the acceptance of a situation in which we shall have an increasing number of "bishops" who are no longer filling the office of a bishop. Attention is called to the recent two-to-one vote in one of our large synods against the proposed establishment of life tenure for the president; to the incongruity of removing the title after it has once been bestowed; and on the other hand to the undesirability of continuing such a title beyond the occupancy of the office. It is suggested that it may be better to have no bishops in the church than to have too many!

II

There are those who, in their support of the proposed change, are influenced by a recognition of certain defects of our present congregational form of church government, especially in the matter of the placement and change of pastors, and who seek, along with the adoption of the title of "bishop," the granting of much greater authority to executive officers. It is said: "It is not the name we want, it is the results in effective church administration."

In this group, there is a wide variety of opinion as to the extent of change of our polity which would be involved, and as to the degree of centralization of authority which may be desirable.

Emphasis seems to be placed upon the particular problem of placement of pastors. It is contended that in this matter, the hands of our synodical presidents are tied by an ineffective system. Illustrations are given of changes in pastoral relationships urgently desirable from the standpoint of both pastor and congregation, which cannot be brought about; of unwise choices of pastors made by congregations whose thoughtlessness, indifference or neglect deprive them of the guidance which might be given them by a wise synodical executive clothed with some real authority; of young pastors achieving an advancement too rapid for their own good or the good of congregations calling them; of questionable methods of seeking pastors and pastorates; of capable and faithful pastors without fields of service.

Attention is called to the advantages of the system of placement in vogue in certain episcopally governed churches. We are told that this system insures a field of work to every pastor desiring work, a reasonable program of promotion, a recognition of faithful service, and a means of terminating a pastorate when conditions indicate the need for a change.

It is urged that the introduction of the title of bishop, and a change of our policy to one in harmony with the practice of the episcopal churches, would produce prompt, far-reaching, and highly desirable results. The practice of the European Lutheran bodies is presented as not only good precedent but good practice.

On the other hand, it is contended that the advantages claimed for a Lutheran episcopacy in America would be more than offset by the loss of values inherent in our present system; that in a democratic country, a democratic church government is most likely to function well; that a placement system in which pastors are *assigned* rather than *chosen* is not without its serious disadvantages; that even in episcopally governed bodies there is a tendency toward greater congregational and pastoral voice in the establishment and continuance of pastoral relationships; that dissatisfaction with the evils of our present policy should not lead us to "fly to others that we know not of"; that the existent evils may at least in part be corrected by a more careful regard for existing constitutional requirements, by a fuller use of procedures already available, and by the development of a practice of closer co-operation between synodical presidents, pastors and congregations (see the statement regarding the "Call" on pages 41 to 49 of this bulletin); that the adoption of an effective episcopal control in the field of placement carries with it implications of a control in other fields which our Church would be slow to accept; and that there is a deep-seated love of democracy in our Church which would oppose the centralization of authority which would inevitably be a concomitant of episcopacy.

From all of the above it appears (a) that there are wide divergencies of opinion within the United Lutheran Church as to what is meant by, and what would be involved in, the adoption of the title of "bishop"; (b) that there are wide differences of opinion as to the feasibility and desirability of such change of polity as would be involved in any material measure of episcopal government; and (c) that in all probability some time must elapse and much discussion take place, before any unanimity of opinion favoring the proposed change will exist within our general body.

RECOMMENDATIONS
(For action, see p. 464.)

Your commission presents the following resolutions for the consideration of the convention, and recommends their adoption:

Resolved (1) that in view of the action of the National Lutheran Council above referred to, the United Lutheran Church in America request the National Lutheran Council to seek the co-operation of all general Lutheran bodies in America in arranging for a joint committee to be made up of representatives of all bodies desiring to participate, said joint committee to engage in a study of the historical, theological and practical questions which are involved in the use of the title of "bishop," and to report its findings, through the Council, to all participating bodies; and (2) that the President of the U. L. C. A. be authorized, in case of favorable response of the National Lutheran Council to this request, to appoint representatives of this body upon such proposed joint committee.

Signed, for the commission,

REES EDGAR TULLOSS, *Convener.*

The two recommendations from the Commission were presented and it was moved and seconded to adopt recommendation (1).

After discussion the motion was put and *lost.* The President stated that therefore resolution (2) could not be considered because it depended upon (1).

Having reached the time of the Special Order, the Rev. Alvin E. Bell, Chairman, presented the following report of the Special Committee of Nine on theological education under U. L. C. A. control. (For other references, see pp. 61, 107, 184, 465, 483, 484.)

REPORT OF SPECIAL COMMITTEE OF NINE

WHEREAS there has been persistent unrest in the Church in relation to the control of theological education of The United Lutheran Church in America, as evidenced in repeated memorials from constituent synods pertaining to this matter, and

WHEREAS this condition of unrest is detrimental to the best interests of our institutions of theological education, your Committee is unanimous in its feeling that it will be beneficial to the interests concerned to have the Church declare its mind in this important matter, and to facilitate this clarification, submits to this Convention the following resolutions pertaining thereto, viz:

RESOLVED:

1. That the principle of U. L. C. A. control of theological education be adopted.

2. That the President appoint a committee of seven members to seek ways and means for realizing this principle, including the proper wording of amendments to the Constitution, and to report to the next Convention.

(Substitute adopted, see pp. 465, 483.)

(Signed)   F. R. KNUBEL,
WILLIAM H. HAGER,
W. H. MENGES,
A. J. TRAVER,
F. W. KERN,
HENRY J. PFLUM,
L. W. STRICKLER,
R. H. GERBERDING,
ALVIN E. BELL.

It was moved and seconded to adopt the report and recommendations of the Special Committee of Nine, as a substitute for that which appears under II, 16 of the report of the Executive Board and attached items.

Division of the consideration of the recommendations was called for.

Resolution 1. It was moved and seconded to adopt resolution 1.

It was moved and seconded that debate be limited and that a vote be taken at 11.55 A. M. This motion was adopted by a two-thirds vote.

At 11.55 A. M. a vote was taken, and by a vote of 203 to 187, resolution 1, of the report of the Special Committee of Nine, was adopted.

It was moved and seconded to adopt resolution 2.

The time for adjournment having been reached, this item became a matter of unfinished business.

At twelve o'clock the Convention adjourned with prayer by the Rev. I. S. Sassaman.

NINTH SESSION

LORD BALTIMORE HOTEL
Baltimore, Maryland
Tuesday, October 11, 1938, 2.00 P. M.

Devotions were conducted by the Rev. Wm. F. Sunday, and the President called the Convention to order.

The Special Committee on Minutes reported that they had examined the Minutes of the Sixth and Seventh Sessions and finding them correct, moved their approval. The motion was carried and the President declared the Minutes of those sessions approved.

The Rev. J. C. Mattes, Chairman, presented the following report of the Committee of Reference and Counsel, which was adopted:

REPORT OF COMMITTEE OF REFERENCE AND COUNSEL

Resolved, That the Convention express its appreciation of the efforts of the local committees and of the various local agencies who contributed to the comfort of the delegates and provided special facilities for the conduct of the business of the Convention; that special note be made of the installation of the organ through the kindness of Mr. M. P. Moller, Jr., and of the pageant, the music festival, and the service in Druid Hill Park, and that those who contributed to the success of these occasions be commended for their services.

Dr. Mattes then recommended that Dr. Evald Lawson, representative of the Augustana Synod, the Rev. S. O. Thorlaksson, and Mr. H. B. Caemmerer be heard at this time. The recommendation was adopted.

Dr. Evald Lawson was introduced and addressed the Convention as the official representative of the Augustana Synod. At the request of the President, the Rev. J. J. Scherer, Jr., President of the Virginia Synod, replied to the greetings from the Augustana Synod.

The Rev. S. O. Thorlaksson, representative of the Icelandic Synod, and also one of the U. L. C. A. missionaries to Japan, brought the greetings from the Icelandic Synod, to which he had previously extended the greetings of the U. L. C. A. by official appointment.

The Rev. J. J. Scherer, Jr., introduced Mr. H. B. Caemmerer, Secretary of the National Commission of Fine Arts, who, for the Federal Government, will be in charge of the erection of the monument for which the Federal Government has made an appropriation to honor the Rev. John Peter Gabriel Muhlenberg at Woodstock, Va. The brief address of Mr. Caemmerer was appreciated.

The following resolution was adopted:

Resolved, that, having heard with genuine gratitude of the effort now being put forth by the Virginia Synod to reproduce a replica of the Lutheran Church at Woodstock, Virginia, we commend this project to the members of the United Lutheran Church, hoping that historically minded individuals may be prompted to assist in the worthy completion of this laudable purpose.

The next order of business being the report of the Commission on Relationships to American Lutheran Church Bodies, the President announced that that report had been previously committed to a special committee composed of all theological professors registered as delegates to the Convention. (For report of Committee, and action thereon, see pp. 472, 474, 475.)

REPORT OF COMMISSION ON RELATIONSHIPS TO AMERICAN LUTHERAN CHURCH BODIES

Inasmuch as this commission made a report to the convention of the Church in 1936, this report should be received as a continuation thereof.

I. Meetings

Four meetings of our commission itself have been held since 1936, namely, November 23, 1936, in Detroit; June 9, 1937, in Philadelphia; February 25, 1938, in Pittsburgh; June 28, 1938, in Philadelphia. The first joint conferences were held with a commission of the Synod of Missouri, Ohio and Other States at Detroit on November 23 and 24, 1936, and at Pittsburgh on February 25 and 26, 1938. In continuation of the two conferences with the commission of the American Lutheran Church during the previous biennium, a third conference occurred on March 11, 1938, in Columbus, Ohio.

II. Meetings with the Missouri Synod

The first meeting was significant chiefly because it was the first time that representatives of the two bodies had met officially. Two topics were discussed: (1) "The Need for Lutheran Solidarity," introduced by Dr. Knubel; (2) "The Scriptures and Their Inspiration," presented by Drs. Arndt and Engelder on the basis of the pertinent sections of "The Brief Statement of the Doctrinal Position of the Missouri Synod," and by Dr. Jacobs on the basis of his paper, "The Word of God and the Scriptures." The net result was to clarify the points of difference between the Missouri Synod and the U. L. C. A., though there was no attempt to formulate either the agreements or disagreements that were discovered. The spirit of the discussions was cordial, even when differences of opinion were frankly stated.

Regarding the second meeting, the following was agreed upon as a satisfactory joint report:

"The doctrines discussed were 'Conversion and the Election of Grace,' on the basis of the Brief Statement of the Missouri Synod, and 'The Word of God and the Scriptures,' on the basis of a paper presented by the commission of the United Lutheran Church.

"While on the presentation of the doctrine of 'Conversion and the Election of Grace' there was general agreement among the commissioners, a point of serious difference concerned the definition of inspiration, particularly the presentation of verbal inspiration as given in the Brief Statement of the Missouri Synod."

The above-mentioned presentation of verbal inspiration in the Brief Statement is as follows: "We teach also that the verbal inspiration of the Scriptures is not a so-called 'theological deduction,' but that it is taught by direct statements of the Scriptures, II Tim. 3: 16; John 10: 35; Rom. 3: 2; I Cor. 2: 13. Since the Holy Scriptures are the Word of God, it goes without saying that they contain no errors or contradictions, but that they are in all their parts and words the infallible truth, also in those parts which treat of historical, geographical, and other secular matter, John 10: 35."

Our commission was unable to accept the statement of the Missouri Synod that the Scriptures are the infallible truth "also in those parts which treat of historical, geographical and other secular matters." We find the words quoted not in accordance with our Lutheran Confessions (see Formula of Concord, Epitome, Introd.), nor with the Scriptures themselves.

This second meeting was saddened by the sudden illness of Dr. Jacobs, an illness which as is now known resulted finally in his death.

III.   Meeting with the American Lutheran Church

At the meeting with the commission from this body the third point mentioned in our report of 1936, namely, the Scriptures and particularly their inspiration, occupied the entire time. The agreed report of this meeting says that "satisfactory progress was made toward an understanding of this question." It was, however, also agreed that the two commissions would report to their respective bodies the exact situation in the discussion, revealing the one sentence concerning which agreement could not be reached. In all other portions of the following statement there was agreement.

1. "The Bible (that is, the canonical books of the Old and New Testaments) is primarily not a code of doctrines, still less a code of morals, but the history of God's revelation, for the salvation of mankind, and of man's reaction to it. It preserves for all generations and presents, ever anew, this revelation of God, which culminated and centers in Christ, the Crucified and Risen One. It is itself the Word of God, His permanent revelation, aside from which, until Christ's return in glory, no other is to be expected.

2. "The Bible consists of a number of separate books, written at various times, on various occasions, and for various purposes. Their authors were living, thinking personalities, each endowed by the Creator with an individuality of his own, and each having his peculiar style, his own manner of presentation, even at times using such sources of information as were at hand.

(AMERICAN LUTHERAN CHURCH)	(UNITED LUTHERAN CHURCH)
"Nevertheless, by v i r t u e of a unique operation of the Holy Spirit (II Tim. 3: 16; II Peter 1: 21) by which He supplied to the Holy Writers content and fitting word (II Peter 1: 21; I Cor. 2: 12, 13) the separate books of the Bible are related to one another, and, taken together, constitute **one o r g a n i c whole without contradiction and error** (John 10: 35).	"Nevertheless, by v i r t u e of a unique operation of the Holy Spirit (II Tim. 3: 16; II Peter 1: 21) by which He supplied to the Holy Writers content and fitting Word (II Peter 1: 21; I Cor. 2: 12, 13), the separate books of the Bible are related to one another, and, taken together, constitute **a c o m p l e t e, p e r f e c t, unbreakable whole of which Christ is the center** (John 10: 35).

"They are rightly called the Word of God. This unique operation of the Holy Spirit upon the writers is named inspiration. We do not venture to define its mode, or manner, but accept it as a fact.

3. "Believing, therefore, that the Bible came into existence by this unique co-operation of the Holy Spirit and the human writers, we accept it (as a whole and in all its parts) as the permanent divine revelation, as the Word of God, the only source, rule, and norm for faith and life, and as the ever fresh and inexhaustible fountain of all comfort, strength, wisdom, and guidance for all mankind."

IV.   Recommendations

The record of our meetings with the commissions of both the American Lutheran Church and the Missouri Synod serves to indicate the great extent of agreement and the slight extent of disagreement. The disagreement relates furthermore to a matter of theological interpretation which in addition applies only to a non-existent original text of the Scriptures. In itself it is not a sufficient warrant to keep the various Lutheran bodies apart, especially as Lutheranism faces the conditions which were declared at length in our Savannah Convention when this commission was appointed. It is not our judgment that we can regard their views as outside of a Lutheran conception of the Scriptures, much less that they can so regard our views. We therefore recommend to the United Lutheran Church in America:

1. That this Commission on Relationships to American Lutheran Church Bodies be continued, to deal with and confer with similar commissions from other Lutheran Church bodies upon all matters that may lead to closer relations and organic union.

It will be noted that in those conferences the discussion finally centered around the Word of God and the Scriptures. In view of the desperate need in the world today of a faithful and intelligent witness to the Truth as revealed in Christ, and particularly in view of the need for a clear statement on this topic, as manifested in the differences of definition that arose in these inter-Lutheran conferences, your commission submits the following declaration. It is a paper mentioned above in our reports as having been prepared by Dr. C. M. Jacobs. It was, however, in course of constant revision by him and by the commission as a whole. A further revision was contemplated by him before his death. This revision was undertaken by Dr. H. Offermann and finally completed by the commission. It has further been submitted to the Executive Board of the Church for their advice. We recommend:

2. That the United Lutheran Church in America adopt the following declaration— (For amended Declaration, see pp. 472-474.)

The Word of God and the Scriptures

(In order that all misunderstandings and misconceptions of this declaration, or of any of its parts, may be avoided, the United Lutheran Church in America declares in advance that it does not regard the statements therein contained as altering or amending the Confessions of the Church in any particular, or as changing the doctrinal basis of the United Lutheran Church, set forth in Article II of the Constitution. On the contrary it considers this declaration to be nothing more than a desirable statement at the present time of beliefs which are in full harmony with the Scriptures and the Confessions.) (For substitute, see p. 472.)

I. We believe that "the only rule and standard, according to which all dogmas and teachers are to be esteemed and judged, are nothing else than the prophetic and apostolic Scriptures of the Old and of the New Testaments" (Formula of Concord, *Epitome*, Intro., I, cf. *Sol. Dec.*, Comp. Summary, 1). We also accept the teaching of the whole Lutheran Church that the Scriptures have this unique authority, because they are the Word of God.

II. Both in the Scriptures and in the Confessions of the Church, this term "Word of God" is used in more than one sense. For this reason it is important that we should understand what these different senses are and what we mean when we call the Scriptures by this name.

III. We believe that, in its most real sense, the Word of God is the Gospel, *i. e.*, the message concerning Jesus Christ, His life, His work, His teaching, His sufferings and death, His resurrection and ascension for our sakes, and the saving love of God thus made manifest in Him.
We believe that in and through this Gospel the Holy Spirit comes to men, awakening and strengthening their faith, and leading them into lives of holiness. (cf. Explanation of the Third Article in Luther's Small Catechism.) For this reason we call the Word of God, or the Gospel, a means of grace (AC, Arts. V, XX; FC, *Epitome*, Ch. II, 4-6, 19.)

IV. We believe that, in a wider sense, the Word of God is that revelation of Himself which began at the beginning of human history, continued throughout the ages, and reached its fullness and completion in the life and work of Jesus Christ our Lord (Gal. 4: 4; Heb. 1: 1ff).
We believe that this revelation was given to men chosen and inspired by God Himself to interpret the historical events in which God made Himself known, and that this history of His revelation also belongs to the Word of God in this wider sense. (Amended, see p. 473.)

V. We believe that the whole revelation of God to men, which reached completion in Christ, the crucified and risen Saviour, is faithfully recorded and preserved in the Holy Scriptures, through which alone it comes to us. We therefore accept the Scriptures as the infallible truth of God in all matters that pertain to His revelation and our salvation.

We also believe that the Scriptures are now, and will be for all time to come, God's revelation of Himself. And because He continues to make Himself known through them, we believe that the Scriptures also are the Word of God, and this is the third sense in which that term is used.

VI. We believe that, as God's revelation is one and has its center in Jesus Christ, so the Scriptures also are a unity, centering in the same Lord and Christ. Therefore we believe that the whole body of the Scriptures in all its parts is the Word of God.

This should not be understood to mean that we place all parts of the Scriptures on one plane. They have their more important and their less important parts, and the measure of their importance must always be the closeness of their relation to Christ, our Lord, and to the Gospel which is the Word of God in the most real sense (see above, No. III). (Amended, see p. 473.)

We believe that there is a difference between the Scriptures of the Old Testament and of the New Testament. The Old Testament is chiefly prophecy; the New Testament, fulfillment of this prophecy. The Scriptures of the Old Testament testify of the Christ Who was to come (John 5: 39; Luke 4: 21; Luke 24: 27; II Cor. 1: 20). The Scriptures of the New Testament are God's testimony to the Incarnate Son of God, our Lord and Saviour Jesus Christ, Who by His suffering, death, and resurrection has reconciled us to God, and has committed unto us the word of reconciliation (II Cor. 5: 19). Nevertheless, every portion of the Scriptures has its own place in God's total revelation of Himself.

We believe that the canonical Scriptures of the Old Testament have been sanctioned by the Lord Jesus Himself and His apostles (Matt. 5: 17f; John 10: 35; Rom. 1: 2; I Cor. 15: 3, etc.) We also believe that the Scriptures of the New Testament were accepted as canonical by the Christian Church under the guidance of the same Spirit of truth of Whom the Lord Jesus said to His disciples, "He shall guide you into all truth" (John 16: 13).

VII. We believe that the whole body of the Scriptures is inspired by God.

God's saving truth, which comes to us through the Scriptures, and not otherwise, is God's own revelation of Himself. The writers of the Scriptures have been His agents in its transmission. The power to receive and record it has been bestowed by Him. The act of God, by which this power was conferred, we call by the Scriptural name of inspiration (II Tim. 3: 16).

We do not venture to define the mode or manner of this inspiration, since God's ways of using human instruments are past our finding out. But we accept the inspiration of the Scriptures as a fact of which our faith in God, through Christ, assures us, and this assurance is supported by words of Scripture in which the fact of inspiration is asserted or implied (I Cor. 2: 12; II Tim. 3: 16; II Peter 1: 21).

The Scriptures are God's testimony to His Son, Who is their center (see above, No. V). They are God's Word, the means through which God leads us to faith in Christ (see above, No. III), and in our faith we see their testimony as God's own. Thus we know that they come from Him, are inspired by Him, and are God's Word.

VIII. Holding these things to be true, we believe that the Scriptures are:

1. The spring from which the saving power of God continuously flows into the lives of men;

2. The only source of truly Christian doctrine; and

3. The only rule and norm for Christian faith and life.

Respectfully submitted,

F. H. KNUBEL,   E. F. EILERT,

HENRY H. BAGGER,   J. K. JENSEN,

PAUL H. KRAUSS,   E. CLARENCE MILLER,

H. OFFERMANN,   EDWARD RINDERKNECHT.

The Rev. H. Offermann, Chairman, was called upon to speak on the report of the Special Committee of Theological Professors, of which Committee the Rev. B. H. Pershing was the Secretary.

The Committee presented the following report:

REPORT OF THE SPECIAL COMMITTEE OF THEOLOGICAL PROFESSORS

(For action on this report, see pp. 474, 475.)

The Committee on Report of Commission on Relations to American Lutheran Church Bodies, composed of Professors H. Offermann, H. C. Alleman, F. B. Clausen, Emil E. Fischer, P. W. H. Frederick, H. B. Reed, Luther D. Reed, Thomas D. Rinde, M. L. Stirewalt, N. Willison, and B H. Pershing, held four sessions. Organization was effected by the election of Dr. Offermann as chairman and Dr. Pershing as secretary. The members of the Commission were invited to attend the sessions if they so desired.

The Committee was unanimously of the opinion that Sections I, II, III, and under Section IV the first paragraph leading to the first recommendation, and also the second paragraph leading to the second recommendation, are presented as historical material which is to be received as such. This reception in no way is an expression of the judgment of this Convention on any statement included in these Sections.

The Committee recommends that the first recommendation in Section IV be approved by this Convention.

The Committee recommends that the Convention approve the second recommendation in Section IV amended as follows:

That The United Lutheran Church in America, in view of the need of the world today for a clear testimony to the saving truth of God in Christ and in the belief that this clear testimony can be given by a statement concerning the Word of God and the Scriptures, adopt the following declaration which it holds to be in harmony with the teaching of the Scriptures as interpreted in our Confessions:

THE WORD OF GOD AND THE SCRIPTURES

I. We believe that "the only rule and standard, according to which all dogmas and teachers are to be esteemed and judged, are nothing else than the prophetic and apostolic Scriptures of the Old and of the New Testaments" (Formula of Concord, *Epitome,* Intro., I, cf. *Sol. Dec.,* Comp. Summary, 1). We also accept the teaching of the whole Lutheran Church that the Scriptures have this unique authority, because they are the Word of God.

II. Both in the Scriptures and in the Confessions of the Church, this term "Word of God" is used in more than one sense. For this reason it is important that we should understand what these different senses are and what we mean when we call the Scriptures by this name.

III. We believe that, in its most real sense, the Word of God is the Gospel, *i. e.,* the message concerning Jesus Christ, His life, His work, His teaching, His sufferings and death, His resurrection and ascension for our sakes, and the saving love of God thus made manifest in Him.

We believe that in and through this Gospel the Holy Spirit comes to men, awakening and strengthening their faith, and leading them into lives of holiness. (Cf. Explanation of the Third Article in Luther's Small Catechism.) For this reason we call the Word of God, or the Gospel, a means of grace (AC, Arts. V. XX; FC, *Epitome,* Ch. II, 4-6, 19).

IV. We believe that, in a wider sense, the Word of God is that revelation of Himself which began at the beginning of human history, continued throughout the ages, and reached its fullness and completion in the life and work of Jesus Christ our Lord (Gal. 4: 4; Heb. 1: 1ff).

We believe that this revelation was given to men chosen and inspired by God Himself to interpret the historical events in which God made Himself known.

V. We believe that the whole revelation of God to men which reached completion in Christ, the crucified and risen Saviour, is faithfully recorded and preserved in the Holy Scriptures, through which alone it comes to us. We therefore accept the Scriptures as the infallible truth of God in all matters that pertain to His revelation and our salvation.

We also believe that the Scriptures are now, and will be for all time to come, God's revelation of Himself. And because He continues to make Himself known through them, we believe that the Scriptures also are the Word of God, and this is the third sense in which that term is used.

VI. We believe that, as God's revelation is one and has its center in Jesus Christ, so the Scriptures also are a unity, centering in the same Lord and Christ. Therefore we believe that the whole body of the Scriptures in all its parts is the Word of God.

The Scriptures have their more important and their less important parts, and the measure of their importance must always be the closeness of their relation to Christ, our Lord, and to the Gospel, which is the Word of God in the most real sense (see above, No. III).

We believe that there is a difference between the Scriptures of the Old Testament and of the New Testament. The Old Testament is chiefly prophecy; the New Testament fulfillment of this prophecy. The Scriptures of the Old Testament testify of the Christ Who was to come (John 5: 39; Luke 4: 21; Luke 24: 27; II Cor. 1: 20). The Scriptures of the

New Testament are God's testimony to the Incarnate Son of God, our Lord and Saviour Jesus Christ, Who by His suffering, death, and resurrection has reconciled us to God, and has committed unto us the word of reconciliation (II Cor. 5: 19). Nevertheless, every portion of the Scriptures has its own place in God's total revelation of Himself.

We believe that the canonical Scriptures of the Old Testament have been sanctioned by the Lord Jesus Himself and His apostles (Matt. 5: 17f; John 10: 35; Rom. 1: 2; I Cor. 15: 3, etc.) We also believe that the Scriptures of the New Testament were accepted as canonical by the Christian Church under the guidance of the same Spirit of truth of Whom the Lord Jesus said to His disciples, "He shall guide you into all truth" (John 16: 13).

VII. We believe that the whole body of the Scriptures is inspired by God.

God's saving truth, which comes to us through the Scriptures, and not otherwise, is God's own revelation of Himself. The writers of the Scriptures have been His agents in its transmission. The power to receive and record it has been bestowed by Him. The act of God, by which this power was conferred, we call by the Scriptural name of inspiration (II Tim. 3: 16).

We do not venture to define the mode or manner of this inspiration, since God's ways of using human instruments are past our finding out. But we accept the inspiration of the Scriptures as a fact of which our faith in God, through Christ, assures us, and this assurance is supported by words of Scripture in which the fact of inspiration is asserted or implied (I Cor. 2: 12; II Tim. 3: 16; II Peter 1: 21).

The Scriptures are God's testimony to His Son, Who is their center (see above, No. V). They are God's Word, the means through which God leads us to faith in Christ (see above, No. III), and in our faith we see their testimony as God's own. Thus we know that they come from Him, are inspired by Him, and are God's Word.

VIII. Holding these things to be true, we believe that the Scriptures are:

1. The spring from which the saving power of God continuously flows into the lives of men;

2. The only source of truly Christian doctrine; and

3. The only rule and norm for Christian faith and life.

Signed:

H. OFFERMANN, *Chairman;*	H. B. REED,
B. H. PERSHING, *Secretary;*	N. WILLISON,
F. B. CLAUSEN,	E. E. FISCHER,
M. L. STIREWALT,	HERBERT C. ALLEMAN,
P. W. H. FREDERICK,	THOMAS D. RINDE,

LUTHER D. REED.

Moved and seconded to adopt the recommendations of the Special Committee of Theological Professors as a whole.

The President declared that the whole report was open for free discussion and for the proposal of such changes as might be desired. After two full hours of general discussion, during which numerous amendments were proposed and voted on, all of which were lost, the original motion for adoption as a whole was carried.

By general consent, the time of the session was extended in order to hear the Rev. Ralph H. Long, Executive Director of the National Lutheran Council, in connection with the consideration of the report of the Commissioners of the United Lutheran Church to the National Lutheran Council.

REPORT OF THE COMMISSIONERS TO THE NATIONAL LUTHERAN COUNCIL

September 6, 1938, marks the twentieth anniversary of the organization of the National Lutheran Council. Many changes have taken place in these twenty years and many blessings have been experienced. Since regular reports were submitted at the biennial conventions, no attempt will be made here to summarize the record of twenty years' service, except to say that it has been a large and useful ministry which has been rendered by this common agency.

Death has been exceedingly active in the last biennium. It is with profound sorrow that we have to record the deaths of the Rev. George Linn Kieffer, D.D., Litt.D., April 25, 1937; the Rev. Carl Christian Hein, D.D., April 30, 1937; the Rev. John Augustus William Haas, D.D., LL.D., July 22, 1937; the Rev. Paul Warren Koller, D.D., November 11, 1937; and the Rev. Lloyd W. Steckel, D.D., March 20, 1938. We desire to record the high esteem and affectionate regard in which these co-laborers are held in memory.

There are now eight Lutheran bodies co-operating in the National Lutheran Council, the Danish Evangelical Lutheran Church in America having been received at the annual meeting, January 27 and 28, 1937, upon its application. A resolution was passed at the 1938 meeting instructing the President and Executive Director to approach other general Lutheran bodies with a view to effecting closer co-operation.

Representation among the co-operating churches, as well as among other religious organizations, as required, was conducted by the Executive Director. Through him, as an advisory member of the General Committee on Army and Navy Chaplains, the general interests of the Lutheran Church in this form of service have been represented. By resolution of the Council a special committee was appointed, consisting of Drs. Peter Peterson, Emil H. Rausch, and L. W. Steckel, to make a study of the position of the National Lutheran Council in the Matter of Chaplains for the Army and Navy. This study was presented at the

1938 meeting and approved with some minor revisions. In continuation of the established practice, the Executive Director also represented Lutheran interests in the "Church of the Air" of the Columbia Broadcasting System and in a number of other religious and musical broadcasts. Eight services per year are now assigned to the Lutherans, assignments being made through the National Lutheran Council.

The eighth edition of the Lutheran World Almanac appeared about September 1, 1937, after having been delayed several months, due to the illness and death of Dr. Kieffer, its editor. An edition of 5,000 was printed instead of 3,000 as in previous editions, and the price was reduced to $1.25 per copy. Special efforts have been made, with varying success, to have copies of the Lutheran World Almanac placed in libraries by local congregations or one of the organizations within the congregation. A survey of the number of Lutheran books in public libraries reveals the fact that there are very few Lutheran books in public libraries.

Pursuant to the request of a group of Stewardship Secretaries and the authorization of the Council, a Stewardship Conference was held at Toledo, Ohio, September 28 and 29, 1937. All who were present manifested a deep interest in the Conference and expressed themselves enthusiastically in favor of holding these Conferences every two years. Approximately one thousand copies of the addresses and proceedings of the Conference were made available by the National Lutheran Council and distributed among the delegates and other persons interested in Stewardship in the participating bodies. The Conference passed a resolution petitioning the National Lutheran Council to take under advisement the possibility of publishing a suitable textbook on Stewardship for use in Sunday schools, confirmation classes, Luther Leagues, and other Church organizations, also, to consider the advisability of issuing posters, films, and other helps for furthering the idea of Christian Stewardship. The request was granted by the National Lutheran Council and a Committee appointed to consider the matter.

The matter of a Lutheran delegate from America to the International Missionary Conference which was to have been held at Hangchow, but which now has been transferred to Madras, India, having been referred to the National Lutheran Council by the Executive Secretaries of the respective Foreign Mission Boards, it was unanimously resolved that Professor A. R. Wentz, D.D., Ph.D., of Gettysburg, Pa., be the first choice and Professor Paul Buehring, D.D., of Capital University, Columbus, Ohio, the second choice for recommendation to the Executive Committee of the International Missionary Council.

Under the sponsorship of the National Lutheran Council, as has been previously reported, Harper & Brothers published "The Quest for Holiness" which is the English edition of Koeberle's "Rechtfertigung und Heiligung." In November 1937 the publishers advised that the first edition was completely sold out and arrangements have since been made with the Augsburg Publishing House to issue a re-print. Meanwhile, the translation and publication of the second book which has been selected by the Committee of the National Lutheran Council has been completed. Professor Sasse's "Was heisst Lutherisch?", translated by Professor Theodore G. Tappert, appeared late in April 1938, under the title, "Here We Stand, the Nature and Character of the Lutheran Faith." The prospects are that there will be a greater demand for this book than for the first one that was published. The Committee is arranging the translation and publication of a third book, the selection of which has not yet been definitely announced.

In preparation for a suitable Lutheran exhibit at the New York World's Fair, 1939, a Committee appointed by the National Lutheran Council was organized into a Joint Committee representing all Lutherans in the Metropolitan Area. Considerable effort and energy were expended in negotiating with the Fair Authorities for suitable space on which to erect a building in which the exhibit was to have been housed. Early in 1938 the committee was advised that all religious exhibits would be excluded from the New York World's Fair, 1939, and instead a temple of religious freedom would be erected by a special committee on a piece of ground donated by the Fair Authorities. This temple of religious freedom will be a tower with a large auditorium in which there will be a pipe organ. It can be used for religious programs and musical concerts, but not for specifically religious services.

Dr. Isaac Cannaday was appointed a Trustee of the property of the Gossner Mission for the National Lutheran Council to succeed Dr. R. Dunkelberger who served in this capacity during Dr. Cannaday's furlough in America.

During the biennium studies were made by the Committee on Social Trends on the questions of Marriage and Divorce, Communism and the Church, Gambling, and Boys' Work. On the basis of a rather comprehensive study of the Problem of Divorce submitted by Dr. G. M. Bruce, the Committee recommended that the principles and practices outlined in this study be submitted to the various co-operating bodies for consideration and action in order to bring about, as far as possible, unity of views and practices with respect to the matter of marriage and divorce within the Lutheran churches of America. This recommendation was approved by the Council and the principles have been submitted to the co-operating churches. Although it may be expecting too much to find a general unanimous agreement on these principles, the Committee believes that if sufficiently clear statements of objection and suggestion are made, it will be possible to arrive at a common denominator which will express the united position of the Lutherans of America on this question. During the year 1938 the Committee will devote its attention to a study of the subject, "The Duty of the Church in Its Social Relations." The Committee is inviting a number of outstanding Lutherans throughout the nation to co-operate in this study, and hopes in this way to prepare a symposium which will be a real contribution in this matter.

On the basis of the recommendation which the special Committee on Inner Mission Survey made, that a Department be established by the National Lutheran Council to act as a clearing house and co-ordinating agency, action was taken at the 1938 meeting, authorizing the establishment of such a Department, to be known as the Department of National Lutheran Welfare. It is understood that this department shall not be administrative in function, but shall seek to co-ordinate the welfare work of the co-operating bodies. The functions and purposes of this department were outlined by a special committee appointed by the National Lutheran Inner Mission Conference, and include among other things, grouping organization of Lutheran Welfare agencies according to states and regions, representation of Lutheran Welfare work before general and governmental agencies, co-ordination of effort in meeting common needs in time of general disaster, assistance in establishment of standards, and the organization and conduct of a general conference of Lutheran Charities. The Council instructed its Executive Committee to work out the details and to select a secretary to head up the Department.

In the interest of a larger program and wider dissemination of Lutheran information the Council authorized its Executive Committee to inaugurate a Motion Picture Service as soon as possible. The plan is to assemble a library of Lutheran films which can be used throughout the Church for general information; also to add such religious films as shall be suitable in the program of visual religious education. It is also proposed, when the department is once firmly established, to engage in the production of films which will depict the history and development of the Lutheran Church in America.

The Council endorsed the action of the Electoral Conference which was held in Washington in January 1938, in naming Dr. F. H. Knubel as the representative of the Lutherans of America to the meeting of the Provisional Conference of Sixty, to be held in Utrecht, Holland, in May 1938, in preparation for the World Council of Churches.

It is the unanimous opinion of the commissioners of the Council that a complete and adequate story of the development of the Lutheran Church in America in the last quarter century ought to be prepared while many of the men who participated in the various movements are still with us. This story will include the record of the Lutheran Church during the World War, the organization and activity of the National Lutheran Commission for Soldiers' and Sailors' Welfare, the observance of the Quadricentennial of the Reformation, the mergers of the Norwegian Lutheran Church, the United Lutheran Church, the American Lutheran Church, and the formation of the American Lutheran Conference, the organization and activities of the National Lutheran Council, the formation of the Lutheran World Convention, and many other events of notable interest. This matter was referred to a special committee consisting of Drs. F. H. Knubel, Peter Peterson, A. T. Dorf, W. E. Schuette, and L. W. Boe.

In the field of statistics Dr. Kieffer continued to function up until the time of his death, April 25, 1937, for the National Lutheran Council. Since that time the most necessary services of the department have been maintained by the personnel of the staff under the direction of the Executive Director. This also applies to the Reference Library. In view of the proposed inauguration of a new Department of National Lutheran Welfare and the setting up of a Motion Picture Library, a successor to Dr. Kieffer has not yet been named, pending the necessary adjustments in the development of the larger program. The question of a larger and more useful program was thoroughly discussed in the annual meeting of 1937, as a result of which, authorization was given to develop the services of this common agency in several respects, particularly in the field of publicity and promotion.

In accordance with the enabling resolution, Mr. Osborne Hauge was selected to become the full-time secretary of the Department of Publicity and News. For a number of years this work was capably and efficiently performed by the Rev. C. K. Fegley, pastor of the Lutheran Church of the Good Shepherd, Weehawken, New Jersey, on a part-time basis. Mr. Hauge assumed his duties July 1, 1937, and immediately did the preliminary groundwork necessary to orientate himself. He has outlined a program which, when in full operation, will constitute a comprehensive and complete publicity service in behalf of the Lutheran Church in America.

Dr. E. F. Eilert, Treasurer, reports that, including the balance from the previous year, refunds, and income, there was available for the operating expenses of the National Lutheran Council in the year 1936, $28,308.95. The total expenses, including special items of publicity and flood relief, amounted to $26,240.01, leaving a balance of $2,068.94, cash on hand, December 31, 1936. For the year 1937 the total amount available, including balances, refunds, and receipts from the Lutheran World Almanac, was $32,905.68. Total expenditures were $30,736.47, leaving a balance on hand of $2,169.21, December 31, 1937. The contributions of the co-operating churches for 1936 and 1937 are as follows:

	1936	1937
United Lutheran Church	$10,350.00	$11,615.00
American Lutheran Church	5,479.23	4,666.71
Norwegian Lutheran Church	4,000.00	4,000.00
Augustana Synod	3,600.00	3,600.00
Lutheran Free Church	285.00	300.00
United Danish Church	269.85	390.00

Danish Evangelical Lutheran Church..................
Icelandic Synod...
Miscellaneous **83.50**   **20.28**

$24,067.58 $24,591.99

The budget adopted for 1938 amounts to $26,530.

The officers of the Council are: President, Dr. Ellis B. Burgess; vice-president, Dr. T. O. Burntvedt; secretary, Dr. Peter Peterson; treasurer, Dr. E. F. Eilert; members of the Executive Committee, Dr. L. W. Boe, Dr. N. C. Carlsen, Dr. A. T. Dorf, Dr. E. P. Pfatteicher, Dr. E. Poppen.

E. P. PFATTEICHER, *Chairman.*
ELLIS B. BURGESS.
REES EDGAR TULLOSS.

Dr. Long was presented by the Rev. E. B. Burgess, President of the National Lutheran Council and member of the U. L. C. A. Commission. Dr. Long spoke reassuringly of the co-operative work being done through the National Lutheran Council for all of the Bodies connected therewith.

The Rev. E. B. Burgess, by a special privilege, presented the following action taken by members of the United Synod of New York, who were in attendance upon the Convention:

"The undersigned members of The United Lutheran Synod of New York have attended the Eleventh Convention of The United Lutheran Church in the city of Baltimore, October 5-12, 1938.

"We are impressed with the substantial organization that has been set up under the leadership of Doctor Frederick Herman Knubel, and are convinced that the future Evangelical Lutheran Church in America will profit for many years from his fine leadership.

"We have seen the progress of our Church tested through twenty years of service, and reaffirm our confidence in its value.

"As a special recognition of the favor of God upon us during these twenty years, we unite in an appeal to all pastors and congregations of The United Lutheran Synod of New York for a distinct advance in benevolence during the coming year."

Signed by Clergy

Ellis B. Burgess	Oliver W. Powers
Paul C. White	Frederick Noeldeke
Walter Krumwiede	Charles A. Davis
J. Henry Meyer	Robert Barkley
Carl H. Hirzel	Paul Y. Livingston
Arnold F. Keller	Yost Brandt
John H. Sprock	Paul E. Scherer
George R. F. Tamke	Henry C. Wasmund
Martin J. Lorenz	Edmund A. Steimle
Carl W. Nutzhorn	Arthur M. Schroeder

C. Reinhold Tappert
Dorr E. Fritts
Carl H. Miller
Herbert A. Bosch
Paul Andrew Kirsch
Henry H. Wahl
Howard R. Gold
David G. Jaxheimer
Clifford E. Eichner
J. Christian Krahmer

Herman F. Vesper
Robert J. Van Deusen
Luther F. Gerhart
William C. J. Weidt
Cyrus M. Wallick
Henry J. Pflum
Clarence E. Krumbholz
Frederick R. Knubel
Oscar V. Werner
William F. Sunday

Signed by Laity
Henry G. Pfeil
Louis A. Wilke
Ulysses G. Van Hoesen
Howard L. Logan
Adolf Nutzhorn
Martin Neumann
Herman T. Erhardt
John Holzkamp
Ray W. Doell
William Eck
J. H. Flathmann
O. K. Edelmann
Ellsworth A. Miller
Wilmer T. Hartwig
Ehrhardt G. Schubert
Henry Lang
Clinton Eany
Otto H. Reisch

Philip H. Ketterer
Charles H. Dahmer
Christine Jaxheimer
Frederick C. Schaefer
Paul C. Buhl
Harold I. Stewart
Ross E. Smith
John H. Bahrenburg
F. S. Kiesel
William Blohm, Jr.
John Mayer
O. R. Brandenberger
H. Frank Wiegand
S. F. Telleen
Joseph M. Lotsch
G. Peter Nuss
Henry Beisler
Fred C. Schaefer

Dr. Knubel expressed his deep appreciation of the action of the members from his own Synod and referred to the fact that his entire ministry had been spent without a change of synodical connection.

At 5.15 P. M., the Convention adjourned with prayer by the Rev. E. W. Harner.

TENTH SESSION

LORD BALTIMORE HOTEL
Baltimore, Maryland
Tuesday, October 11, 1938, 7.30 P. M.

Devotions were conducted by the Rev. F. B. Clausen, and the President called the Convention to order.

As the first item of unfinished business, the President stated that Item V, 2, of the Report of the Executive Board, concerning the Budget, as well as the motion to adopt the substitute presented by the Rev. Carl W. Nutzhorn, was before the Convention. (For other references, see pp. 88, 386.)

After much discussion, the previous question was moved and carried.

The motion to adopt the substitute was put and *lost.*

The original motion to adopt the budget of the U. L. C. A. for 1940 and 1941, as given under V, 2, of the Report of the Executive Board, was adopted.

Mr. W. H. Hager presented the following which was adopted:

> Be it resolved, that the Laymen's Movement for Stewardship ask this Convention of the United Lutheran Church to urge the agreement of all the synodical bodies to institute a campaign among its congregations for the years 1939 and 1940, to raise 100% of their apportionment, with the conviction that the accomplishment of this purpose, and the realization of the immense values which will be secured thereby, for all the operations of the United Lutheran Church, will convince synods and congregations that this annual objective, the two million dollar apportionment, can and should be regularly attained.
>
> Also, be it resolved, that the Laymen's Movement for Stewardship pledge its utmost assistance in the successful carrying forward of such a campaign.
>
> Also, be it resolved, that it is our well considered opinion that such action by this Eleventh Biennial Convention of the United Lutheran Church does fittingly mark the Twentieth Anniversary of the United Lutheran Church.

The Rev. E. W. Harner presented the following resolution which was adopted:

> That the Executive Board be directed to make a restudy of the distribution of the apportionment to the boards.

Items of unfinished business, from the report of the Executive Board, were as follows:

Item VII, Department of National Lutheran Welfare of the National Lutheran Council, page 91. The recommendation of the Executive Board was adopted.

Item X, B, 3, regarding the appointment of a Commission on World Conference on Faith and Order, page 95. The recommendation was adopted.

Item X, C, 2, concerning participation in the World Council of Churches, page 98. The recommendation was adopted.

Item XI, 1, Social Security for Church Workers, page 101. The recommendations were, on motion, referred back to the Executive Board.

The President called for the matter concerning II, 16, Theological Education under control of the U. L. C. A.
(For other references, see pp. 61, 107, 184, 464, 465.)

The President stated that the motion to adopt the second resolution of the Special Committee of Nine was before the Convention for consideration.

It was moved and seconded to substitute recommendation (b) of the report of the Executive Board for resolution 2 of the report of the Special Committee of Nine.

The Rev. C. B. Foelsch gave notice that if this substitute was adopted, he had another to propose, and the privilege was assured him by the President.

The motion to substitute the recommendation (b) of the Report of the Executive Board for resolution 2 of the Special Committee of Nine was adopted.

The substitute report, as amended, was thereupon adopted. The report, as adopted, is as follows:

II, 16. Theological Education under Control of the U. L. C. A.:

Whereas, there has been persistent unrest in the Church in relation to the control of theological education of The United Lutheran Church in America, as evidenced in repeated memorials from constituent synods pertaining to this matter, and

Whereas, this condition of unrest is detrimental to the best interests of our institutions of theological education, your Committee is unanimous in its feeling that it will be beneficial to the interests concerned to have the Church declare its mind in this important matter, and to facilitate this clarification, submits to this Convention the following resolutions pertaining thereto, viz:

Resolved:

1. That the principle of U. L. C. A. control of theological education be adopted.

2. That the Executive Board of the U. L. C. A. shall appoint, from the Church at large, a commission of seven members on theological education.

The Rev. C. B. Foelsch presented the following, which was adopted.

Resolved, That we direct the new theological education commission to seek ways and means of realizing the principle of control (Resolution 1), but interpreting the word "control" as applying in the field of theological education curriculum content, academic standards and kindred matters, but specifically not in the field of seminary ownership or maintenance.

Mr. Arthur P. Black, Executive Secretary, presented the report of the Laymen's Movement for Stewardship, and addressed the Convention concerning the work of the biennium. He introduced Mr. Harry Hodges, who addressed the Convention concerning the pastors' institutes.

REPORT OF LUTHERAN LAYMEN'S MOVEMENT FOR STEWARDSHIP

(For action on the resolution in this report, see p. 488.)

At the Columbus Convention the Laymen's Movement summarized the results of the nine promotional activities that made up its program during the preceding biennium. In this report it notes with supreme satisfaction that during this biennium the Promotional Plan has put the whole church back of four of those nine activities in a sense never before true: (1) the Every Member Visitation; (2) the printing and distribution of special literature; (3) the Calendar of Causes; and (4) regional meetings for pastors and laymen. This co-operative effort, though still in the experimental stage, has already justified itself. The following three paragraphs deal specifically with such co-operative effort:

The Every Member Visitation

The Every Member Visitation was intentionally gloved in with the 260 Group Meetings throughout the church, under the Promotional Plan. Three major pieces of literature were used to promote both. Three additional pieces of literature were used in the promotion of the Group Meetings only. All literature, except the Every Member Visitation free-will-offering card, bore the imprint of the Board of Executive Secretaries, and all members of that Board co-operated in producing it. This was the first time in the twenty years' history of the United Lutheran Church in America *that* ever happened. More pastors ordered literature during the last quarter of 1937 than in any preceding similar period—

2,126, or four of every five pastors actually in charge of one or more congregations. The *gain* in the number of orders over the preceding year was 188, another all-time record. These gains undoubtedly contributed to the increase in free-will offerings for benevolences both for local causes and for the U. L. C. A. apportionment, as shown by the official records.

THE CALENDAR OF CAUSES

The Laymen's Movement made the Calendar of Causes one of its major activities during the biennium preceding the Columbus Convention. Regional meetings were held in a number of synods, supplemented by a considerable volume of correspondence, in a further effort to emphasize the spiritual and educational values of the Calendar of Causes to any congregation that would incorporate it in the regular congregational program. But it was not until the Promotional Plan put all the boards and agencies back of it that pastors and lay workers generally began to realize its tremendous possibilities. To help build up and sustain interest in the Calendar of Causes the Laymen's Movement since the spring of 1937 has been mailing a special information letter to more than four hundred key officials throughout the church, covering each Cause in its proper order on the Calendar. The practice will be continued during the coming biennium.

REGIONAL MEETING

Like the Calendar of Causes, the regional meetings for pastors and laymen, promoted by the Laymen's Movement as well as several of the boards for a number of years, needed the Promotional Plan to coordinate them on a church-wide basis in order to realize the best cooperative results. All pastors and lay workers know about the 260 Group Meetings held during the Fall of 1937. This Fall institutes for pastors only are being held throughout the church. Institutes for laymen only are being contemplated for the Fall of 1939. The Laymen's Movement deems it a privilege to contribute both service and money to the development of regional meetings, as well as the Every Member Visitation and special literature, under the Promotional Plan. It is our way of rendering an acceptable account of our stewardship.

UNITED STEWARDSHIP ENVELOPES

An added feature of the Laymen's Movement program this biennium has been the promotion of the use of the new United Lutheran Stewardship "Standard Form" Duplex Envelopes sponsored by our United Lutheran Publication House under the direction of Dr. Grant Hultberg. These new envelopes made their appearance January 1, 1937. Their distinguishing feature is their messages. They follow the Calendar of Causes, and thus fit in perfectly with the Promotional Plan. All the Board Secretaries have co-operated wholeheartedly with the Secretary of the Laymen's Movement in the preparation and assembling of the messages each year. There was a very substantial increase in the number of sets ordered for 1938 over the number ordered for 1937, and there has been a very substantial increase in the orders for 1939 over 1938.. Copy for the messages for 1940 will go to the printer the first of this coming November. These new envelopes, undoubtedly will appeal more and more to our pastors and their official personnel because their messages bear directly upon our United Lutheran Church in America program, and emphasize the stewardship of substance, service, and self.

SEMINARIES VISITED
Our annual contacts with seminarians become more and more worth while each year. It is planned to spend more time on this phase of our work during the coming biennium. To the extent the plan works (1) the development of the conference idea, (2) the imperative need for more co-operation in working out the congregational program, (3) methods of procedure in the solution of problems of administration, and (4) presentation of programs, can be given more attention. Annual visits twelve of the last thirteen years have been made to the following seminaries: Southern, Mt. Airy, Gettysburg, Hamma Divinity, Chicago, Northwestern, and Western. This biennium special emphasis was placed on the Calendar of Causes, which is basic in the Promotional Plan, and stewardship fundamentals.

SPECIAL HELPS FOR PASTORS AND LAY WORKERS
Between February 15 and May 15 this year all our pastors in charge of one or more congregations received a letter from our office with these inserts:

1. Comprehensive outline for a year round *congregational* setup under the Promotional Plan, based on (a) the folder, "Something Every Congregation Can Do: How to Do it"; and (b) actual programs that already were working successfully in congregations.
2. The official report of Chuch Treasurer, Dr. E. Clarence Miller, covering the calendar year 1937, by synods, showing (a) communing membership, (b) the budget apportionment, (c) the amount paid, (d) the per cent paid, and (e) the amount paid per capita.
3. Official report showing comparisons, by synods, for the years 1936 and 1937, of (a) amount of apportionment paid, (b) gains, and (c) losses.

This letter and outline carried suggestions, and the reports gave facts, that every pastor can use with telling effect to stimulate and encourage the members of his congregation to redouble their efforts to render a more acceptable account of their stewardship.

STUDENT AID : CIRCULATING LIBRARY : DEVOTIONAL BOOKLET
Seven student aid beneficiaries of the Laymen's Movement were graduated from our seminaries during the biennium. This brings the total number to 170, representing an investment of $167,402. Nine are on the

foreign field. The freshman of this wonderful group is Missionary George Flora who sailed for Africa, July 20, 1938. Missionary Flora is a native of Gurley, Nebraska.

We now have 300 volumes in our Circulating Library. They include books on stewardship, missions, evangelism, worship, church administration, and biography. An increasing number of pastors are making use of our library. The only cost to them is for postage when books are returned. Folder listing books available can be had for the asking. We have been operating our Library since 1933.

The promotion of the use of the devotional booklet, "Light for Today," authorized by the Savannah Convention and sponsored by our Common Service Book Committee; and weekly reading of The Lutheran, continue to be permanent features of our year around program. The Family Altar and the official church paper are indispensable aids to the Christian life in the home, and to intelligent and sustained promotion of the whole program of the whole church.

1918-1938 : A FEW COMPARISONS SHOWING PROGRESS

At the time of the Merger in 1918 the Laymen's Movement already was eleven years old, having been organized in 1907 in Sunbury, Pa., to help promote the benevolence program of the General Synod through the Every Member Visitation and its aids—the Budget, the Duplex Envelope, the Pledge Card, and the Quarterly Statement. In 1922 it was directed by the Buffalo Convention to add Christian Stewardship and Student Aid to its program. Twenty years after the Merger the following comparisons are submitted as information:

1918
No record of official recognition of Christian stewardship fundamentals by congregations, conferences, or synods.

No Student Aid Program.

No official records covering the Every Member Visitation prior to 1926. In that year 1,120 pastors ordered Every Member Visitation literature.

1938
Official recognition of Christian Stewardship fundamentals in practically all congregations, conferences and synods, with fine programs in many.

Since 1922 there have been 170 men helped into our U. L. C. A. ministry, representing an investment of $167,402. Nine of the number are serving our missions in India and Africa.

In 1937 the number of pastors who ordered literature totaled 2,126, representing four of five pastors actually in charge of a congregation. Every year but one since 1926 registered a gain.

1918	1938
Distribution of literature limited to General Board.	There have been requests for well over 2,000,000 copies of literature, annually, in recent years. Since 1930 a total of 15,780,910 pieces of literature have been printed. It includes six folders dealing exclusively with stewardship fundamentals.
Personal contacts with synods, conferences, summer schools, seminaries, and group meetings, the exception rather than the rule.	Such contacts have increased regularly every year since 1923.
Many pastors indifferent to or "cold" toward the Laymen's Movement program.	Many of the most ardent supporters of the Laymen's Movement program in recent years have been pastors and members of seminary faculties.

RECOMMENDATION

(For action, see p. 488.)

Since its major objectives are now included in the general Promotional Plan of the church, we recommend that the continued co-operative service of the Laymen's Movement in such relationship be approved, and that more intensive efforts be developed to make the individual church member stewardship-conscious.

Respectfully submitted,

J. L. CLARK, *President.*

ARTHUR P. BLACK, *Executive Secretary.*

The resolution of the Laymen's Movement for Stewardship was adopted.

The Rev. P. D. Brown, Chairman, presented the report of the Committee on Memorials from Constituent Synods.

REPORT OF THE COMMITTEE ON MEMORIALS FROM CONSTITUENT SYNODS

(For action on this report, see p. 493.)

1. RELATIONSHIP OF CHURCH AND STATE: *From the Pittsburgh Synod*

That the Pittsburgh Synod memorialize the United Lutheran Church to press for a definite statement from its Committee on Church and State concerning the relationship of Church and State.

Reply: In view of the proposed study of this subject by a special committee of the Lutheran World Convention in 1940, we recommend that the Committee on Church and State make a study of this committee's findings and report to the next convention of the U. L. C. A.

2. PROPOSED BOARD OF CO-ORDINATION: *From the Pittsburgh Synod*

That the Pittsburgh Synod memorialize The United Lutheran Church in America as follows:

a. It is the common experience of the congregations of our Church that, with rare exceptions, the individual parishioners are not adequately acquainted with the purposes, uses, authority, sphere of influence and operation of The United Lutheran Church in America.

b. Such report as comes to the parishioners of the activities of the church-at-large is commonly in the way of reports of various Boards of the Church which fail to give a true representation of the general purpose and activities of the church-at-large, being largely ex parte or fragmentary.

c. In the opinion of the Synod, if The United Lutheran Church in America is to accomplish its full purpose toward the individual parishioner and the separate congregations it must endeavor first to create in parishioners a consciousness of the whole value of Lutheranism, and must attempt to knit together and co-ordinate the general and various activities of the church-at-large and the interest and the action of the several congregations as far as possible.

d. In our opinion this can best be done by creating a Board of Co-ordination to be composed of representatives of the Church and to be staffed by first, a full-time, paid lay publicity director to be selected on his experience and, *secondly,* a staff of competent ministers familiar with and trained in the work of the church-at-large as well as in the work of synods and congregations, to include a director of church music, all of whom will expend all of their time in contacting the various congregations, not only by letter, but primarily in person, to explain and promote the work of the church-at-large and to co-ordinate the activities of the various synods and congregations; and that to this Board no member of the executive staff or any individual board of the church be eligible.

> Reply: Inasmuch as this memorial deals with promotion, and since such splendid results have been obtained under our present promotional plan, we recommend that this memorial be referred to the President of the U. L. C. A. and the Committee of Secretaries for consideration and report to the next convention of the U. L. C. A.

3. EDUCATIONAL AND ADMINISTRATIVE PROGRAMS: *From the Pittsburgh Synod*

That in the interest of greater efficiency on the foreign field, and a better comprehension at home of the whole foreign mission program, the Pittsburgh Synod memorialize The United Lutheran Church in America to appoint a special committee to study the work of its missionary agencies with a view to the unification of their educational and administrative programs.

> Reply: The exact meaning of this memorial is not clear, and we recommend that no action be taken.

4. LITERATURE ON MORAL, SOCIAL AND ECONOMIC ISSUES:
From the Synod of Ohio

Whereas, numerous conferences of student pastors convened within the United Lutheran Church in the year 1936 and 1937 have strongly indicated that the sphere of discussion among Christian students that is most alive with questions and confusions is the sphere of the application of the evangelical gospel to the pressing and critical moral, social, and economic issues of our time (*i. e.*, war, labor relationships, race relations, civil liberties, etc.) and,

Whereas, these student pastors are, and for years have been, embarrassed and trammeled in their ministry by the paucity of theological works in English relevant to these issues, and

Whereas, this paucity has forced the student pastors and student groups to seek out and use the productions of commissions and individuals whose theological position we do not share and whose demand for direct social action we believe to arise from superficial interpretation of the gospel ethical life, and

Whereas, this necessary reliance on non-Lutheran materials and programs has created in the minds of our young people serious wonderment as to the cause of our Church's silence, and

Whereas, evangelical theologians of other lands have produced profound, creative, and clear treatises precisely relevant to this aspect of the Gospel's operation in life, and

Whereas, there are within our Church in America men completely competent to translate into English these productions:

Therefore be it resolved, that this convention of the Synod of Ohio memorialize The United Lutheran Church in America to take such measures as shall encourage the creation and facilitate the publication of such materials for student group study by the competent men of our own church, and take such further measures as may be effective to mobilize the competence and will of our church toward the translation, publication and dissemination of recognized works in other languages.

> Reply: We recommend the approval of this memorial, and that the Board of Education and the Board of Publication be requested to provide the literature to meet the evident need as stated in this memorial.

5. POPULAR EDITION OF COMMON SERVICE BOOK: From the Nova Scotia Synod

Whereas, the Lutheran Church is a singing church, and,

Whereas, our liturgical service makes it essential that there be a liberal supply of books in the pews, and since the present editions make the maintaining of such a supply a burden to a small congregation, and,

Whereas, much of the material contained in the present editions could be eliminated from a pew edition, such as the written epistles and gospels, the occasional services, with the exception of the Confessional Service, the History of the Passion, and the general rubrics,

Be it therefore resolved, that we memorialize The United Lutheran Church in America to take under consideration the feasibility of preparing such an edition to sell, if possible, for fifty cents or thereabouts.

> Reply: We do not favor an abridgement of the Common Service Book. We recommend that this memorial be referred to the Board of Publication, urging that it furnish, if possible, the Common Service Book at a lower price.

6. COMPENSATION OF U. L. C. A. WORKERS: *From the West Pennsylvania Synod*

We, the West Pennsylvania Synod in session assembled, May 26th, 1937, at York, Pa., respectfully memorialize The United Lutheran Church in America:

a. First, to take action requiring all boards and auxiliary agencies of the Church to mention, in reports submitted to the Church, the names of all those who serve as executives, or board secretaries, or editors, or the like, and with each individual name to state the total of all appropriations, including salaries, bonuses, rental appropriations, and appropriations of any kind whatsoever; and

b. Second, to authorize the President, with the advice of the Executive Board, to appoint a special committee of five members whose duty it shall be to review all salaries and other appropriations made to those who serve all boards and auxiliary agencies of the United Lutheran Church as executives, or board secretaries, or editors, or the like, and to make a report concerning the desirability that the Church establish a minimum and a maximum salary.

> Reply: We recommend—
> 1. That item (a) be not approved. (Substitute adopted, see p. 493.)
> 2. That item (b) be approved.

7. LUTHER LEAGUE PROGRAM: *From the New York Synod*

Be it resolved, that the United Lutheran Synod of New York memorialize The United Lutheran Church in America to request the Luther League of America to study the matter of its organization so that it may correspond to the needs and natural groupings of our young people.

> Reply: Since the Luther League of America has already given this matter some consideration, we recommend that this memorial be referred to the Luther League of America for study.

8. SPECIAL COMMUNICATION: *From the Ministerium of Pennsylvania.*

Resolved, that the resolutions contained in the memorials of the Danville, Lancaster, Philadelphia, Reading, and Wilkes-Barre Conferences, concerning the Social Security Act, and Pension Plans for pastors, be noted by the Secretary of Synod and communicated to the United Lutheran Church, requesting that they be given consideration by a special committee appointed to study this matter.

DANVILLE CONFERENCE

Resolved, That the Conference go on record as favoring the plan for pastors to pay five per cent of their salaries and congregations to pay a like amount into the Pension Fund.

LANCASTER CONFERENCE

Resolved, That we do hereby petition the Ministerium of Pennsylvania and Adjacent States that it memorialize The United Lutheran Church in America, that it (the U. L. C.) petition the Federal Government to include clergymen in the provisions of the Social Security Act.

PHILADELPHIA CONFERENCE

Resolved, That we memorialize the Ministerium of Pennsylvania to petition the United Lutheran Church to investigate the advisability of petitioning our Federal Government to include clergymen and all church workers in the Social Security Act.

READING CONFERENCE

Resolved, That the Reading Conference memorialize the Ministerium of Pennsylvania to petition the United Lutheran Church to petition, in turn, the Federal Government to include clergymen, and all employees of congregations and church institutions, in the Social Security Act.

WILKES-BARRE CONFERENCE

We, the members of the Wilkes-Barre Conference of the Ministerium of Pennsylvania and Adjacent States, recommend, that the Ministerium of Pennsylvania petition The United Lutheran Church in America to in turn petition the Federal Government to include clergymen in the Social Security Act.

> Reply: Since the Committee on the New Pension Plan and the Executive Board have dealt sufficiently with these items, in reports to this Convention, we recommend that no additional action be taken.

9. *To the Representatives and Delegates of The United Lutheran Church in America, in Convention at Baltimore, Maryland:*

Dear Brethren in Christ:

The Evangelical Lutheran Ministerium of Pennsylvania and the Adjacent States, assembled in its 191st annual convention, May 23-26, 1938, at Allentown, Pennsylvania, looks unto Almighty God with a profound sense of thanksgiving at this close of the twentieth year of progress and achievement of The United Lutheran Church in America. Twenty years ago, those groups now united into this Church body sought, in the unity of their common confessions and Lutheran heritage to combine their endeavors, that there might result the Greater Glory of the Father of Our Lord, Jesus Christ, the deeper inspiration of their members through common worship and mutual edification and a more fruitful harvest in the great educational and missionary program of the Church. Subsequent developments have seemed to strengthen our conviction that the Guiding Hand of the Holy Spirit was clearly manifest in the formation of the U. L. C. A. We believe that these achievements of the past two decades are evidences of hopes realized—direct answers to our prayers. We rejoice not only in the efficiency of administration and the successful concentration of effort, but also in the visible proportions of the harvest of souls. We would, therefore, congratulate and felicitate the U. L. C. A. on this occasion, humbly mindful of the strength of God made perfect in our weakness, and confident of His continued guidance and blessing in future endeavor of His servants, united in this Church.

THE MINISTERIUM OF PENNSYLVANIA AND ADJACENT STATES.

We recommend that the Secretary of the U. L. C. A. be requested to acknowledge the receipt of the message of congratulations and felicitations from the Ministerium of Pennsylvania on the occasion of the twentieth anniversary of the U. L. C. A., and to express the grateful appreciation of the U. L. C. A. of the sentiments conveyed.

10. In order that the Committee on Memorials from Constituent Synods may be enabled to make the best possible recommendations to the Church on memorials, we recommend that constituent synods memorializing the U. L. C. A. be requested to attach to the memorial a written statement of the mind of the synod in the memorial proposed, such as the background and purpose of the memorial, and any other information as to the intent and content of the memorial that may be helpful to the Committee on Memorials.

Recommendations 1, 2, 3, 4, and 5 were adopted.

Recommendation 6 (b) was adopted.

Recommendation 6 (a). As a substitute for recommendation 6 (a), it was moved and carried that it be referred to the committee established under (b).

Recommendations 7, 8, 9 and 10 were adopted.

The Convention adjourned at 10 : 15 P. M., with prayer by the Rev. J. I. Meck.

ELEVENTH SESSION

LORD BALTIMORE HOTEL
Baltimore, Maryland
Wednesday, October 12, 1938, 8.45 A. M.

Matins were conducted by the Rev. W. E. Frey.

The President called the convention to order.

The Special Committee on Minutes reported that they had examined the Minutes of the Eighth, Ninth and Tenth Sessions and, finding them correct, moved their approval. The motion was carried and the President declared the Minutes of those sessions approved.

The Rev. J. C. Mattes, Chairman, presented the following resolution, from the Committee of Reference and Counsel, which was adopted:

> Resolved, That the Executive Board be given authority to reprint and distribute the Declaration on the Word of God and the Scriptures, and such other actions of this convention as it may deem desirable.

The Rev. J. D. Krout, Chairman, requested that the Rev. C. B. Foelsch, Secretary, present the Report of the Committee on President's Report.

REPORT OF THE COMMITTEE ON THE PRESIDENT'S REPORT
(For action on this report, see p. 495.)

Your Committee on the President's Report notes with gratitude to God the progress of the Church, and the stirring of its life in new confidence and zeal to the remotest confines of our beloved Lutheran Zion during the past biennium. We note with joy, and record with deep gratitude, that in His goodness God has given to our President continuing health and strength, amplified by the experience of these notable twenty years for the prosecution of his solemn and weighty responsibilities.

The Church today is fired with a confidence, empowered with plans, and is moving along the lines of those plans, with a courage which promises a harvest of blessing for the Kingdom of God and the souls of men.

At the convention of the Church in Columbus, Ohio, inspired by the conviction that the time was ripe for, and the condition of the world critically demanded, a new vigorous advance against the forces of secularism and materialism that threaten the soul of man today, it was voted to undertake a comprehensive plan for the promotion of the power of the Church against such forces of evil. That resolution placed the responsibility for organizing and implementing such a forward movement in the hands of the President of the United Lutheran Church, with the commitment of the whole power of the Church loyally to that end.

The following specific suggestions were made for the guidance of the President in the organizing of the work:

1. That a minimum of organization be set up as a standard;
2. That no new agencies be set up where existing agencies could effectively serve the new and larger purposes;
3. That existing agencies be reinforced and intensified.

Through our official publications, through the revised and renewed presentations of the work of the major boards, and particularly through the joint efforts of the Executive Secretaries led by the President in the publication of special promotional literature, and by means of promotional rallies at strategic centers, the clergy and laity have been educated and inspired to new courage and more effective service. We note with deep satisfaction the fine quality of that promotional literature. While the final objectives have by no means been obtained—perhaps to the distress of some who may have hoped for a quick harvest—we believe that such seed sowing of vital truth concerning the program of the whole church is bound to bear abundant fruitage in the coming years.

We concur, with specific approval, in the President's judgment that our plans must be laid for a long pull, and that care must be taken to avoid the exhaustion and inefficiency implicit in big, special, excited "drives." We further concur in, and would call the attention of the Church to, the wisdom that stresses the significance of the local congregation and the individual pastor as the key to any advance in the witness and work of the Church.

Therefore we recommend:

1. That this convention again herewith officially record its heartfelt thanks to God for the manifesting of His Spirit in the new life of the Church, especially in the leadership of the President of the United Lutheran Church and the operation of the promotional plan during the past biennium.

2. That if the Executive Board deem it desirable the President of the Church prepare for widespread distribution in abbreviated pamphlet form a graphic summary of the contents of this report that will be of inspirational value to the Church as a whole.

3. We heartily approve the President's specific recommendations and recommend their adoption as follows:

(1) Resolved, that this convention express its thankful joy over the unanimous co-operation which has characterized the promotional efforts of the past biennium.

(2) Resolved, that this convention approve in general the ideas and plans described in this report, and direct that they be continued in harmony with the arrangements adopted at the convention of 1936.

(3) Resolved, that the Executive Board be directed to continue the plans whereby it will send to each synodical meeting one representative of the Church as a whole, with all its causes.

(4) Resolved, that in repeating our recognition of the Luther League of America, the Women's Missionary Society, and the Lutheran Brotherhood as official auxiliaries of the Church, we request all congregations to consider the desirability of establishing congregational units of these auxiliaries within the congregational operations.

Respectfully submitted,
COMMITTEE ON PRESIDENT'S REPORT.

The recommendations of the Committee were considered, and recommendations 1, 2 and 3 were adopted.

By general consent, the Rev. F. Eppling Reinartz, recently appointed, spoke of his work in the newly created office of Promotional Editor.

The Rev. L. D. Reed, Chairman, presented the report of the Common Service Book Committee.

REPORT OF THE COMMON SERVICE BOOK COMMITTEE

(For action on the recommendations in this report, see p. 501.)

The Committee held two general meetings during the biennium, each continuing for three days. At the first meeting Dr. Luther D. Reed was elected chairman and Dr. Harvey D. Hoover secretary. Subcommittees held numerous meetings and prepared material for consideration by the full Committee.

The Committee lost two members by death during the biennium, Prof. E. H. Klotsche, Ph.D., D.D., and the Rev. August Steimle, D.D. Dr. Klotsche's connection with the Committee was very brief, and he did not attend the meetings. Dr. Steimle's service was outstanding and covered a long period of years. As a member of the Joint Committee which prepared the Common Service Book, he participated actively in the work of the subcommittees on the Liturgy and the music of the Book. During the past twenty years he attended practically every meeting of the general Committee. His broad scholarship, accurate knowledge of the Church, and excellent judgment enabled him to make significant contributions to the Committee's deliberations and decisions. With a deep sense of the loss which it has sustained by his death, the Committee gratefully records its high appreciation of Dr. Steimle's character, attainments and distinguished services.

SIGNIFICANT ANNIVERSARIES

This year marks the fiftieth anniversary of the Common Service and the twentieth anniversary of the Common Service Book. The adoption and widespread use of the Common Service represent one of the outstanding achievements of the Lutheran Church in this country. The preparation and general introduction of the Common Service Book advanced the standards of common life and worship throughout the United Lutheran Church and materially contributed to its unification and spiritual strength.

The Common Service of 1888 was an important expression of the historical, doctrinal and churchly revival of the nineteenth century. This revival grounded the Lutheran Church in America solidly upon the foundations laid by the Reformers of the sixteenth century in the classic confessions and liturgies of that time. It also established connections again with the deeper and older foundations of faith and worship represented in a consensus of historic Christianity.

The Rule under which the Common Service was prepared lifted the entire work above individual preference and taste, or the mere effort to reconcile imperfect and conflicting uses. The men who were active in its preparation cannot be held in too high honor. Particularly are to be remembered Beale M. Schmucker, George U. Wenner and Edward Traill Horn. These constituted the active subcommittee which determined the general plan, conducted the necessary researches and put the decisions of the larger Committee into final form. Their grasp of doctrinal and liturgical history and forms, their accurate scholarship and their sure command of pure and fitting English, enabled them to restore to the Church in this country in the language of the land, "the full Lutheran Service, with all its provisions, for all who wish to use it."

The Common Service soon proved to be an adequate expression of the living faith and devotion of our people and a bond and basis for a common churchly development which crossed all synodical boundaries. Its immediate acceptance by practically all Lutheran groups in America was a recognition of its representative character and quality. It was also an indication that the Church in this country was ready to employ again the rich and beautiful services which our fathers had used centuries ago, and which subsequent developments had obscured or destroyed. In addition to the three bodies which prepared it, the Iowa Synod, the Joint Synod of Ohio, the Missouri Synod, the Norwegian Church, and the Augustana Synod officially approved it for use in their English services. Translated in whole or in part into Telugu, Japanese, Spanish and Italian, it is used in the mission fields in many lands. Study and use of it have called forth a considerable literature in the field of Liturgics, Church music and Church art.

As we think of the preparation and adoption of the Common Service fifty years ago, and of its extensive use and influence since, we may well ask whether any other single achievement of our Church in this country during the past half century surpasses it in point of universal scope, spiritual power and practical churchmanship.

The desire for an even more complete agreement in liturgical and musical forms throughout the Church led to co-operative endeavors which resulted in the Common Service Book of 1918. A Joint Committee of more than thirty representative scholars labored for nearly ten years on the four major problems involved: the unification of the text of the Common Service itself; the preparation of a common Hymnal; the preparation of Orders for Occasional Services; and the adoption of complete musical settings for the Liturgy and Hymnal.

This new and larger work was in all respects simply an extension of the principles and forms represented in the Common Service. Exhaustive studies were made by subcommittees. The comparative usage of hymns and tunes throughout the English-speaking world was summarized. Much original work was contributed by the editors and others. A fine spirit of mutual co-operation and concession among the leaders, and an ever-strengthening Church consciousness among the people, carried the project to completion. When the United Lutheran Church was organized in New York City, November 14-18, 1918, the new body with its forty-five synods, had ready for immediate use a complete and carefully prepared Service Book and Hymnal representative of the highest standards of Lutheran worship. Its introduction brought order out of confusion, gave a new sense of the Church's historic continuity and of its potential strength, and elevated standards of practice and appreciation everywhere.

In the future the Common Service and the Common Service Book can confidently be expected to exert an even wider influence through the extension of their use, through increased understanding of our heritage in worship, and through improved standards in the observance of their provisions in the public worship of the Church.

LIGHT FOR TODAY

"Light for Today" has been published monthly since December 1935, under the editorial direction of a sub-committee, Dr. H. D. Hoover, chairman. The authors have been chosen to represent, so far as possible, the territory of the United Lutheran Church and the various district synods. The circulation has been stable from month to month, rising during the Lenten Season above the average. Many similar publications have been started since "Light for Today" first appeared.

"Light for Today" is used as a daily devotional guide by all classes of people. It has met the need and desire for guidance and the spiritual hunger of young and old. It has been found helpful for personal devotions, family worship and the worship services of groups, school assemblies, etc. It is being used in every continent of the world.

Helpful suggestions have come from those who have faithfully used this publication. A better publication can be issued when the circulation increases. A greater service can be rendered by a wider use. A large distribution is possible through personal, pastoral and group or society activities, the use of the mails and printed announcements. It can be distributed by personal correspondence. It is an appropriate birthday and anniversary gift. Church societies may assume the task of a wider distribution among Church members and people of the community. The sick and shut-in find it very helpful. There are a thousand and one ways of using this devotional guide. How many of them are you using? Are you using it yourself?

AN ORDER OF SERVICE FOR ROGATION-TIDE

In accordance with instructions of the Church at the Columbus Convention, 1936, the Committee prepared an Order of Service for the Blessing of the Fields. Services of this character originated in the early Church and soon became general, particularly in Western Europe. They were regularly held on Rogate Sunday and the three days following (Rogation Days) immediately preceding the Feast of the Ascension. Recent widespread observance of this Sunday as Rural Life Sunday by a number of communions perpetuates a distinctive and colorful feature of the historic Church Year and meets a definite need of the present day.

Copies of the Service for Rogation-tide will be submitted separately in connection with this report and copies in quantity for use by congregations may be purchased from the Publication House.

THE DAILY OFFICE BOOK

The Committee reports progress in its work upon the Daily Office Book, under the direction of a subcommittee of which Dr. Paul Z. Strodach is chairman. The purpose and plan of this book were described in the Committee's report to the Columbus Convention (Minutes 1936, p. 434ff). The general scheme and the material previously prepared have been carefully revised in the light of criticisms and suggestions received, in the desire to bring about simplification. It is now proposed to omit the Homily and to include a brief period for private Meditation and another for Personal Intercessions and Supplications in the Daily Office. This Daily Office will be a complete and individual Service for every day in the year, developed upon a plan which provides a different structure for the different days of the week. The following table shows the scheme of Offices for the week.

Daily Office	Sun.	Mon.	Tue.	Wed.	Thu.	Fri.	Sat.
Invocation	X	X	X	X	X	X	X
Versicle and Gloria	X	X	X		X	X	X
Psalm and Gloria		X	X or H	X			
Thanksgiving							X
Lesson or Capitulum	L	L	L	C	L	C	L
Respond	X	X	X	X	X	X	X
Responsory	X						
Meditation	X	X	X	X	X	X	X
Confession							X
Comfortable Words							X
Canticle or Hymn	C			C or H	Ps or H		
Kyrie	X		X	Preces		Litany	
Lord's Prayer	X		X				
Collect for Day	X	X	X		X		
Other Collects	X	X	X		X		
Intercessions	X	X	X		X		
Benedicamus	X	X	X	X	X	X	
Prayer of Preparation							X
Benediction or Commendation	X	X	X	X	X	X	X

Two brief invariable Services, the Mid-day Office and the Night Office, as originally reported, will also be included, as well as an invariable Lord's Day Office to be used when there is a celebration of the Holy Communion.

In addition to the changes in plan indicated above, much of the liturgical material already provided has been simplified without impairing variety or richness. Work has been completed from the first Sunday in Advent to Septuagesima Sunday.

In order to give the Church a clear idea of what is proposed and to have the benefit of further criticism and suggestion, the Publication House has co-operated most helpfully with the Committee and issued a proof copy. This contains the material for two weeks of the Advent and Christmas cycles. This proof copy will be distributed in connection with the presentation of this report.

In the Daily Office Book the Committee hopes to provide the Church with a representative book of private prayer for the clergy, particularly, incorporating in simplified and evangelical form the historic liturgical uses of the Western Church, and comparable in spirit and scope with the Church's official book of public prayer, the Common Service Book. The completion of this work is a task of the first magnitude. According to the present plan the complete work will probably be in two volumes of approximately 600 pages each. In view of the importance and scope of this undertaking, the Committee earnestly desires the mature judgment of the Church upon both the plan and the content of the work. It therefore requests careful study of the proof copy and the submission of constructive criticisms and suggestions by all interested before it proceeds farther with the project.

RECOMMENDATIONS ON VESTMENTS

The Executive Board of the Church, in response to requests from several synods, called upon the Common Service Book Committee to prepare a Statement on Vestments for the information and guidance of the Church. With full appreciation of the difficulties involved in a discussion of so controversial a subject, the Committee gave this request careful consideration and was pleased to submit a practically unanimous report with recommendations to the Executive Board.

MISCELLANEOUS

The Occasional Page in *The Lutheran* devoted to "Liturgical Life and Practice" and conducted by the Common Service Book Committee, has been continued as opportunity permitted. Dr. Strodach's column on the Collects has also been a regular feature of *The Lutheran* during the past year.

In order to keep abreast of conditions and developments in the field of Hymnody, a sub-committee consisting of Drs. Seltzer, Strodach, Stirewalt, Hoover and Reed, has been appointed. This committee will study important collections and all possible sources for hymns and translations of merit, both old and new, and will report to the general Committee. It may also issue occasional publications on the subject for the information of the Church.

RECOMMENDATIONS
(For action, see p. 501.)

The Committee offers the following recommendations:

1. That the Church at this Convention recognize with thanksgiving the fiftieth anniversary of the Common Service and the twentieth anniversary of the Common Service Book, and record its appreciation of the significant contributions made by these devotional works to the ordered life and worship of the Church, and to its spiritual development and inner unity and strength.

2. That the devotional pamphlet "Light for Today" be continued and commended to all pastors and congregations.

3. That the Order of Service for Rogation-tide be approved.

4. That the Committee be instructed to continue its work upon the Daily Office Book, giving careful consideration to such criticisms and suggestions as may be offered, and carrying the project to completion as speedily as circumstances permit.

Respectfully submitted,
LUTHER D. REED, *Chairman.*
HARVEY D. HOOVER, *Secretary.*

Dr. Reed introduced the Rev. H. D. Hoover, who spoke of the devotional booklet, "Light for Today."

Recommendations 1, 2, 3 and 4 were adopted.

The Rev. E. A. Trabert presented the following resolution, which was adopted:

Resolved, That the Committee be instructed to continue its study of the hymnody of the Church, its progress to be reported to the next convention.

The Rev. J. C. Mattes presented the following resolution, which was adopted:

Resolved, That the Common Service Book Committee be authorized to appoint a special sub-committee to engage in special liturgical and hymnological studies in conjunction with similar committees of other Lutheran bodies, should any choose to co-operate, and that an invitation to do so be extended to them to join in such an undertaking, with the understanding that such studies and conferences are for the purpose of mutual assistance and study, and for the publication of helpful information, but not for the issuance of authoritative documents.

Mr. J. Milton Deck presented the following:

Whereas, the United Lutheran Church formerly authorized and published a Service Book for use at meetings of the three auxiliaries of the Church, containing Prayers, Services, Hymns, Psalms, etc., which publication is now out of print; and

Whereas, there are frequent calls for such a Service Book which the auxiliaries can call their own, of smaller size than the usual hymnal and adapted to their needs, containing in addition to material in the former book, services for the opening and closing of conventions of Lay Organizations, installation of officers, suggestive Scriptural readings, etc.;

Therefore, be it resolved, that we instruct the Common Service Book Committee to study the matter, conferring with representatives of the auxiliaries and the Board of Publication, and prepare such a book during the next biennium with the consent of the Executive Board.

It was moved and carried that this resolution be referred to the Common Service Book Committee with power.

The Rev. J. C. Mattes, at the request of the Rev. Gomer C. Rees, Chairman, presented the Report of the Committee on Church Music.

REPORT OF THE COMMITTEE ON CHURCH MUSIC

The Committee on Church Music met in the Muhlenberg Building, Philadelphia, on April 27, 1938. The Rev. Gomer C. Rees, D.D., was elected chairman and the Rev. George R. Seltzer, Ph.D., secretary. Several members of the Committee were unable to be present but upon the request of the chairman had sent valuable suggestions which were carefully considered.

From the minutes of the meeting we present the following digest of the actions taken.

It was resolved that the Committee prepare a list of the easiest anthems for each Sunday and Festival of the Church Year; which list shall be made available in *The Lutheran,* and later in printed form.

The chairman was asked, with the help of the secretary, to communicate with members of the Committee, to carry out the above action. It was also moved that the final gathering and choice of suggestions be made by a sub-committee; and that the list be submitted to the whole Committee by mail.

The chairman was requested, with other suggested members of the Committee, to co-operate with Dr. Harry A. Sykes in the preparation of phonograph recordings of The Service.

Dr. Marks was asked to prepare an article for *The Lutheran* incorporating ideas expressed in his letter to the chairman (a service based on hymns sung by the choir and congregation, illustrated by hymn tune preludes).

Organist Seibert was requested to prepare an article for *The Lutheran* on the improvement of hymn singing in the congregation.

The chairman was asked to prepare the report of the Committee for the United Lutheran Church in America.

It was resolved that a subcommittee be appointed to gather and to list all available musical materials for a collection of Introits, Graduals, Psalms and Antiphons, Responsories and Versicles; and to prepare suggestions for publication; also, to prepare specimens of two or three of each of the Propers named; the subcommittee to present the same to the full Committee for consideration and action.

THE MUSICAL FEATURE OF THIS CONVENTION

On March 21, 1938, the chairman of the Committee upon the request of the Baltimore Committee arranging for this Convention of the United Lutheran Church, met with the local committee and the musical representatives of five colleges, namely, Gettysburg, Newberry, Susquehanna, Muhlenberg and Hartwick.

The purpose of the meeting was to arrange a program of Lutheran Church Music to be presented in the Peabody Auditorium, Baltimore, on Saturday evening, October 8, 1938. The following outline of the program was adopted:

Organ Recital—8:00-8:30 P. M.—by Mr. Henry F. Seibert, Organist of Trinity Church, New York City

"Wake, Awake for Night is Flying"—Melody by Philipp Nicolai, 1599 (Wachet auf, ruft uns die Stimme)............................Arranged by J. S. Bach
Massed Choirs
Old Lutheran Motets....................................by the Susquehanna Motet Choir
Pre-Bach Numbers.......................................by the Muhlenberg Chapel Choir
Bach Numbers..by the Hartwick College Choir

"O Sacred Head Now Wounded"..Christiansen
"Beautiful Saviour"..Christiansen
Massed Choirs
Organ Interlude..by Mr. Henry F. Seibert

Music of Nineteenth Century Period........by the Newberry College Choir
Contemporary Lutheran Church Music....by the Gettysburg College Choir

"Now Thank We All Our God"..Cruger, 1648
"A Mighty Fortress is Our God"..Luther, 1529
Massed Choirs
Organ Postlude................... ....by Mr. Henry F. Seibert

The chairman of the Music Committee was asked to prepare the program notes and comments.

Naturally, not all of our colleges were able to participate on account of the distances to be traveled but this co-operative effort is indicative of the great interest taken in church music at all of our institutions of learning and gives promise of even finer music in our churches in the future. The Committee on Church Music heartily commends all such activities for the advancement of greater excellency in this field of church life.

Concerning the above program, we congratulate the local Baltimore Committee for its initiative and wisdom in planning for it. We also desire to express our cordial thanks to all who shall participate in this presentation of Lutheran church music. Their willingness to co-operate is highly commendable. We feel sure their combined efforts will enhance the appreciation of everyone for the great resources of churchly music within the Lutheran Church.

THE YEAR BOOK ANTHEM LIST

In conformity with the plan of previous years the list of anthems for the Year Book has been prepared by different organists. For the year 1938 the list was compiled by Mr. Edgar B. Kocher, organist of Christ Church, Allentown, Pa., and for the year 1939 by Harry A. Sykes, Mus.D., organist of Trinity Church, Lancaster, Pa., and a member of this Committee. This plan of having many different church musicians prepare the list on successive years gives a very wide selection of proper anthems for the Church Year. We earnestly suggest that organists and choir leaders preserve these lists from year to year so that they may be able to build up an adequate repertoire of excellent anthems suitable to the abilities and needs of their respective choirs.

SYNODICAL COMMITTEES ON CHURCH MUSIC

The action of the United Lutheran Church at its last convention suggesting the appointment of Committees on Church Music by its constituent synods, has been carried into effect by a number of these synods. Inquiries have come to us from the chairmen of several such committees. We shall be pleased to co-operate with all such men in every way possible. We believe this co-operation to be most desirable, so that a unified purpose and practise may prevail in all our churches. Our mutual ideals and aims may thus be preserved and fostered for the best interests of the entire musical activities of the Church.

CONVOCATIONS

We desire to direct the attention of the Church to the desirability of holding Convocations of Church Musicians, Congregations and Pastors from time to time. These Convocations have proved their worth in the past and are highly educational, inspirational and practical in producing a fine understanding of true Christian worship. An outline of such Convocations has been presented in a former report, but, if it is not readily available, we shall be glad—when desired to do so—to co-operate in planning for such an occasion.

CONCLUSION

Encouraged by the advance of the Church in musical matters and realizing the great importance of good music in its lasting effects on Christian worship, we hold ourselves in readiness to do everything possible to enhance the glory of God and the adoration of our people that they may truly and joyfully "worship the Lord in the beauty of holiness."

Respectfully submitted,
GOMER C. REES, Chairman.

Dr. Mattes presented the following resolution, which was adopted:

> Resolved, That the work of the Committee on Church Music, looking towards the provision of musical settings for those portions of the Common Service Book not now provided with proper music, be commended, and that the Committee be encouraged to prosecute this work energetically in connection and co-operation with the Common Service Book Committee.

The Rev. L. D. Reed, Chairman, presented the report of the Committee on Church Architecture.

REPORT OF THE COMMITTEE ON CHURCH ARCHITECTURE

At its first meeting of the biennium the Committee organized by electing Dr. Luther D. Reed, chairman, and Mr. Charles A. Scheuringer, secretary.

CORRESPONDENCE, INTERVIEWS, ETC.

Between meetings of the general Committee the officers conferred frequently and conducted an extensive correspondence with pastors, architects and building committees. The secretary reports letters from twenty-two states and Canada; the chairman letters from twenty-five states, Canada and China.

Much of the correspondence had to do with requests for literature, information concerning architects, suggestions concerning minor alterations, etc. A number of larger projects involved extensions, rebuilding operations, chancel rearrangement, interior decoration, etc. In a dozen instances or more the secretary furnished sketches suggesting solutions of the problems submitted.

The officers also held a number of conferences with pastors and building committees in different localities.

During the first half of the biennium there was little activity apart from correspondence and conferences, as economic conditions prevented actual construction in many cases. During the past year greater activity has been evidenced.

The other members of the Committee also counselled with pastors and building committees as opportunity afforded.

GENERAL CONFERENCES ON CHURCH ARCHITECTURE

The officers of the Committee actively participated in several important general conferences on Church Architecture. The secretary attended the Conference conducted by the Home Missions Council in Asbury Park, N. J., January 10, 1937.

The chairman, as president of the Associated Departments on Church Architecture and Allied Arts, presided at two important National Conferences held at the Cathedral of St. John the Divine, New York City, October 6, 1936, and March 4, 1938.

At the request of the *Christian Herald* a plan for a small church and Sunday school building was designed by the secretary and described in the January 1937 issue of this magazine.

FIELD VISITS

An important service was rendered by the secretary in response to requests from the Board of American Missions and the Inner Mission Board. In connection with the relicf work undertaken by these Boards, Mr. Scheuringer made several field visits in March and June 1937 to report on church buildings damaged in the flooded areas near Louisville and Paducah, Ky., and Lawrenceville, Ind. He also visited the mission churches in Pontiac and Lansing, Mich., and the Iron Mountain School at Konnarock, Va. As a result of this visit sketches were prepared by Mr. Scheuringer for alterations to the girls' dormitory and the proposed Medical Centre Building.

MISSION CHURCHES FROM STANDARD PLANS

The following mission congregations erected church buildings during the biennium from standard plans prepared by the secretary and approved by the Committee. In a number of instances it was necessary to make adaptations to conform to local conditions. The cost of these buildings varied from $10,000 to $18,000.

Church of the Ascension, Pontiac, Mich., the Rev. Ewald G. Berger pastor.

St. Matthew's Church, Paducah, Ky., the Rev. Ivan Ross pastor.
Trinity Church, Rocky Mount, N. C., the Rev. C. R. Ritchie pastor.
St. Paul's Church, Linden, N. J., the Rev. George E. Heck pastor
Church of the Advent, Charleston, S. C., the Rev. Dermon A. Sox pastor.
Holy Trinity Church, Anderson, S. C., the Rev. Alton C. Clark pastor.
Church of the Redeemer, Flushing, L. I., the Rev. Walter J. Bielitz
pastor.

OTHER PLANS APPROVED

Plans for the following congregations were also approved by the
Committee:

Christ Church, Wantagh, N. Y., the Rev. W. S. Avery pastor. Cherry &
Matz architects.

Church of the Good Shepherd, Hightstown, N. J.

St. Peter's Church, Jamaica, N. Y., the Rev E. G. Schaertel pastor.
Cherry & Matz architects. A one-story and basement church in brick in
pleasing Colonial style.

Fayetteville Church, Fayetteville, N. C. R. L. Clemmer architect. A
small chapel in brick—English style. Design commended.

Woodale Lutheran Church, St. Louis Park, Minn., the Rev. D. H.
Jensen pastor. Bard and Vanderbilt architects.

St. James' Church, Stewart Manor, N. Y., the Rev. E. I. Morecraft
pastor. R. F. Schirmer architect.

St. James' Church, Ozone Park, N. Y., the Rev. H. J. Kreider pastor.
Office of Hobart Upjohn architects.

Church of the Messiah, Homestead Park, Pa. A. N. Steinmark architect.
A basement and one-story chapel in English style. Basement portion
only to be erected at present.

Church of the Epiphany, Denver, Colo. Jamieson Stiffler architects.

St. Andrew's Church, Brownville, Pa. G. E. Martsolf architect. Basement and one-story chapel in English design.

Auburn Church, Springfield, Ohio, the Rev. J. M. Warnes pastor. Lloyd
J. Zellar architect. A new church addition with alteration to an existing
building in Colonial style—design commended.

Church of the Redeemer, Maywood, N. J., the Rev. Cyrus M. Wallick,
pastor. Cherry and Matz, architects.

PUBLICATIONS

The Committee supplies the following pamphlets and other publications
without cost upon request:

"Church Principles in Church Architecture"—a 20-page pamphlet pre-
    pared by the chairman.

"Practical Suggestions for Building Committees"—an 8-page pamphlet
    prepared by the chairman.

"Space Requirements for Church Organs"—prepared by the Rev. Dr.
    J. F. Ohl.

"Architectural Leaflets" Nos. 1-6, a series of four-page folders with illustrations and descriptive write-ups of successful buildings. Leaflets 5 and 6 illustrate two designs of "Standard Plans," each with additional alternate exterior designs. These plans, designed by the secretary for mission congregations, have been approved by the Committee. Complete plans and specifications for the same can be secured by mission congregations at nominal cost.

The Committee has no recommendations.

Respectfully submitted,

LUTHER D. REED, Chairman.

CHARLES A. SCHEURINGER, Secretary.

The Rev. I. F. Frankenfield, Chairman, presented the report of the Statistical and Church Year Book Committee.

REPORT OF THE STATISTICAL AND CHURCH YEAR BOOK COMMITTEE

(For action on the recommendations in this report, see p. 519.)

This Committee has held one regular meeting, at the call of Dr. George L. Kieffer, convener, in Gettysburg, Pa., on April 15, 1937. All members were present. The Committee was organized by the election of Dr. George L. Kieffer as chairman, and Dr. W. H. Greever as secretary. Special consideration was given to the functions of the larger Committee, constituted by the advisory membership of all statistical secretaries of the Constituent Synods.

The principal item of business was the consideration of the Blank of the State of the Church. After much discussion and many amendments to the old blank, the matter was referred to the secretary of the Committee with instructions to include such amendments and consider additional suggestions in the preparation of a form to be submitted by mail to members of the Committee before being put into final form. Due to circumstances over which we had no control, the final form was delayed, and could not be gotten into hands of Synods and congregations in time as proposed.

The following important resolution was adopted with instructions to the secretary to send it to the statistical secretaries of all synods with the request that they present it to their synods for adoption:

Resolved, That this Synod instruct its officers to notify all pastors and congregations that they are required by synodical membership to make full and correct statistical reports annually, according to standard blank furnished by the Church, and that the statistical secretary of the synod is required to make a summary report from those parochial reports, to the United Lutheran Church in America, not later than March 1st each year. Therefore, these parochial reports should be in the hands of the statistical secretary not later than   of each year, and failure to comply with this requirement is subject to censure.

The secretary was instructed to investigate supplies of congregational record cards in stock by the Publication Board, and to provide such new forms as may be necessary to conform to the amended Parochial Blank.

The regular annual visitation of theological seminaries was made by members of the Committee. Seminaries provided for regular hours in the official schedule of the seminary work.

The Committee has given its approval to the Editorship of the Year Book and is co-operating on proposed improvements in future editions.

This year marks the Twentieth Anniversary of the United Lutheran Church in America. The statistical picture of her growth numerically and spiritually, the statistical picture of her development in functions of efficiency and practise, the statistical picture of her interpretations of values and usefulness, give occasion for us to rejoice as we look back over past achievements and forward to the unfinished task, pressing forward toward "the mark for the prize of the high calling of God in Christ Jesus." In no department, in spite of many obstacles and difficulties, has more progress been made than in the statistical department. In the twenty years of beginning, planning, formulating, unifying, completing, no one wielded a greater influence, no one had made a greater study of the field, no one was a greater storehouse of facts and information, no one was a more indefatigable worker, no one was more self-sacrificing for his Church and the love of his Lord and Master than *George Linn Kieffer, the great Statistician of the Lutheran Church.*

With the departure of our beloved chairman and co-worker, the Rev. George L. Kieffer, D.D., who passed into life eternal on Sunday afternoon, April 25, 1937, we have lost a most valuable and efficient member, and the Lutheran Church a great leader in the statistical world. He was born on a farm near Millersburg, Pa., November 25, 1883, graduated from Gettysburg College in 1909, and from Gettysburg Seminary in 1912, was licensed by the Synod of East Pennsylvania in 1911, and ordained by the same body, October 3, 1917, on receiving a call from Rosedale, Long Island. His ministerial life was crowded into twenty years, each one of which was rich in spiritual fruit. At the time of his death he was the Statistician and Reference Librarian of the National Lutheran Council, and president of the Association of Statisticians of Religious Bodies of America. Since the death of Dr. Carroll he served as the Statistician for the *Christian Herald.* He was one of the founders and builders of the American Lutheran Statistical Association of America, and one of its most ardent workers. His contribution to this general association of Lutherans of this country was surpassed by no one. As a servant of the whole church, he made and held many warm friends in every Lutheran Synod, and was able to foster fellowship movements among Lutherans whose wholesome effect upon church life will be felt for many years to come.

RECOMMENDATIONS

(For action, see p. 519.)

1. Your Committee, recognizing the importance of the Conference of Statistical Secretaries, recommends the holding of such Conference at the time of the meeting of the next Convention of the United Lutheran Church in America.

2. We recommend that all dates mentioned in former report on the Blank of the State of the Church be suspended and the Committee be instructed to complete this work as circumstances permit, and its deferred report be referred to the Executive Board, with power to approve and adopt.

3. We recommend that the tribute given to Dr. George L. Kieffer in this report be adopted by this Convention, and a copy of it be sent to Mrs. Kieffer through the Secretary of the Church.

IRA F. FRANKENFIELD,
W. H. GREEVER,
JOSEPH D. KROUT,
HARRY E. PUGH.

STATISTICAL REPORT OF THE UNITED LUTHERAN CHURCH IN AMERICA FOR THE YEAR 1936

Index No.	SYNOD	When Organized	Pastors	Parishes	Congregations	Baptized	Confirmed	Communing	Contributing	Non-member Adherents	Acc. Children Baptism	Acc. Children Otherwise	Acc. Adult Baptism	Acc. Adult Confirmation	Acc. Adult Certificate	Acc. Adult Otherwise	Losses Children Death	Losses Children Otherwise	Losses Adult Death	Losses Adult Certificate	Losses Adult Otherwise	Church Papers
1	Ministerium of Penna.	Aug. 15, 1748	498	392	593	308172	208691	148989	126617	15557	5944	2817	453	6976	2580	1612	364	2782	3463	1817	5175	5068
2	United Synod of N. Y.	Oct. 23, 1786	480	396	432	249180	164885	108932	82109	22512	4765	4482	401	5170	1633	2775	244	5277	5122	1105	6575	5321
3	United Synod of N. C.	May 2, 1803	114	160	160	39961	28532	20463	15669	1971	737	405	200	941	90	437	36	86	308	423	195	760
4	Maryland Synod	Oct. 11, 1820	143	139	139	75941	55707	32344	31049	9534	1444	450	194	1445	749	278	57	762	736	438	592	1610
5	Synod of S. Carolina	Jan. 14, 1824	77	112	112	29638	22400	15801	14027	1149	532	178	72	628	779	259	23	72	531	390	183	195
6	Synod of West Penna.	Sept. 5, 1825	130	66	158	66329	49893	35779	36431	2669	1127	467	263	1233	306	68	37	238	689	209	700	647
7	Synod of Virginia	Aug. 10, 1829	97	80	171	28260	22802	13307	13132	3670	414	81	243	382	68	686	10	68	313	751	120	1112
8	Synod of Ohio	Sept. 7, 1836	256	200	279	89154	63195	50023	34399	6905	1815	840	605	2030	1300	643	101	484	1002	652	1129	1217
9	East Penna. Synod	May 9, 1842	171	129	159	57870	57870	35101	27629	8856	1332	758	274	1505	990	119	77	613	809	286	1072	1688
10	Alleghany Synod	Sept. 2, 1842	85	85	145	43345	33624	20862	15521	1689	683	119	197	900	406	171	37	398	398	930	463	1417
11	Pittsburgh Synod	Jan. 15, 1845	275	212	306	130316	91685	56297	43586	6512	2439	1049	267	2625	1167	1212	143	1452	1028	191	2592	1181
12	Indiana Synod	Oct. 28, 1848	89	68	103	24051	18133	11900	8256	1976	412	215	149	441	335	154	58	324	335	324	632	1698
13	Illinois Synod	Sept. 8, 1851	155	122	141	68841	48008	32159	26373	11190	1509	1023	340	1829	672	887	48	1212	487	443	1194	693
14	Texas Synod	Nov. 10, 1851	23	81	30	6772	4951	4951	1896	3020	174	121	26	206	59	196	12	96	55	56	167	714
15	Susquehanna Synod	Feb. 25, 1855	112	81	161	53726	40306	25418	21591	2815	826	288	143	941	566	247	48	804	552	385	657	647
16	Mississippi Synod	July 25, 1855	7	5	12	1087	782	378	378	433	25	223	11	18	8		8		118	187	280	707
17	Synod of Iowa	July 20, 1860	34	30	33	21393	14387	8385	6471	1452	499	53	116	522	242	219	26	178	118	45	82	50
18	Georgia-Ala. Synod	July 21, 1861	19	19	31	6642	4287	3027	3083	433	81	53	9	77	69	18	5	52	75	134	508	217
19	Synod of Canada	Nov. 5, 1868	85	81	104	31568	21538	16162	12736	1963	669	166	16	680	188	261	33	265	134	113	246	239
20	Synod of Kansas	Sept. 1, 1871	39	36	43	12920	9636	5657	3883	2204	242	129	127	286	183	266	10	276	188	195	417	911
21	Synod of Nebraska	Sept. 1, 1875	60	48	52	25880	17888	11630	7606	1008	625	271	202	694	340	247	23	257	221	51	99	293
22	Wartburg Synod	July 24, 1890	57	43	46	24801	15972	11070	5918		516	459	19	602	104	427	18	218	131	40	175	234
23	Ger. Nebraska Synod	April 2, 1891	85	69	82	18741	13201	10411	3864	3872	421	201	69	520	277	227	23	211	103	118	723	280
24	Synod of California	May 6, 1891	64	37	37	10528	6821	4168	1597	1084	319	404	69	197	85	345	31	495	131	36	166	253
25	Rocky Mt. Synod	Sept. 23, 1891	28	14	14	4032	2903	1761	29471	4861	143	87	184	955	669	99	43	68	44	468	2244	275
26	Synod of the Northwest	July 16, 1897	104	89	99	58715	39586	29801		773	1366	1214	19	1955	66	1148	60	1361	280	102	257	126
27	Manitoba Synod	Sept. 26, 1901	63	55	132	19001	11086	6762	1812	775	617	302	36	387	130	311	5	211	71	243	76	632
28	Pacific Synod	July 10, 1903	38	26	26	6652	3863	2166	2706	242	157	177	13	146	101	102	7	38	58	14	100	474
29	Nova Scotia Synod	April 17, 1912	31	31	31	8231	3551	2250	2569	414	172	4	36	43	43		8	67	58	52	55	100
30	Synod of West Virginia	June 10, 1919	22	24	33	9006	5576	3475	2907	444	132	57	22	75	75	36	4	74	58	14	98	162
31	Slovak Zion Synod	June 10, 1920	26	23	31	11837	6305	4474	3488	613	163	45	54	176	56	24	181	24	58	86	4	190
32	Michigan Synod	Sept. 24, 1928	35	32	34	2488	8101	4530	995	428	315	276	13	359	206	191	2	21	77	366	366	160
33	Synod of Florida	June 6, 1934	18	14	14	2488	1824	1207	995	428	59	55	13	68	80	32	3	21	17	27	30	268
34	Kentucky-Tenn. Synod		19	26	26	7766	6278	3863	3337	507	136	92	48	159	184	157	3	68	75	80	145	81
35	Totals for U. S. and Canada		3520	2796	3969	1582090	1104474	742065	590728	121515	30810	17509	4898	34328	15860	13856	1563	18589	17439	10613	27417	29544
36	Totals Outside U. S. and Canada				1829	190182	90794	90311			3033		1516	77	9		16	204	34	180	408	
37	U. L. C. A. World Total		3520	2796	5798	1772272	1195268	832376	590728	121515	33843	17509	6414	34405	15869	13856	1579	18793	17473	10793	27825	29544

STATISTICAL REPORT OF THE UNITED LUTHERAN CHURCH IN AMERICA FOR THE YEAR 1936—Continued

INDEX NUMBER	PAROCHIAL — CHURCH SCHOOLS — SUNDAY Number	Officers and Teachers	Scholars	Home Dep't.	Cradle Roll	WEEKDAY Number	Teachers	Scholars	Catechetical Catechumens	STUDENTS Ministry	Diaconate	In Lutheran Institutions	In Non-Lutheran Institutions	CHURCH SOCIETIES — MEN'S Number	Members	WOMEN'S Number	Members	YOUNG P. Number	Members	FINANCIAL — VALUATION OF CHURCH PROPERTY Church Edifices	Parsonages	School and Parish Houses
1	590	13570	129911	3621	10310	163	1347	14469	9778	100	18	285	1763	342	14038	926	35277	882	26585	22681444	2133515	2504050
2	436	8234	67856	1796	8920	108	509	5545	8582	59	6	146	1573	297	12421	835	27838	873	21938	21742646	2441919	3297710
3	154	2386	26421	379	1142	89	522	7739	3102	27		128	300	53	1247	185	5129	236	6708	2803678	359059	201368
4	141	3829	36308	1525	3232	15	123	1138	2505	11		59	568	57	2444	251	9780	234	6928	6564402	702879	619225
5	109	1493	14700	178	708	68	572	7256	1392	29	2	136	215	35	1038	172	5000	199	5189	2258383	247190	225550
6	156	4423	46313	1269	3045	25	221	3332	3577			119	385	38	2230	258	9136	204	6616	5701500	563950	358250
7	282	1790	16770	432	978	71	300	4461	1145			61	225	24	739	184	4964	163	8577	1840260	334966	95690
8	157	5409	50027	1309	2979	36	220	2686	3625	8		282	829	140	5040	562	18633	379	3888	8169664	746600	339050
9	133	4368	40940	2820	3027	45	343	3698	3556	36		119	718	123	5673	349	12749	307	11210	7459642	903407	676110
10	298	2631	24610	76	1606	45	325	3653	1556	45		40	306	39	1590	170	4609	145	2126	3123050	401526	126900
11	103	5853	53390	1896	4799	59	360	3941	910	18	10	209	799	155	4962	603	18333	459	6742	9672176	1230237	450386
12	140	1630	11847	231	640	18	102	834	2713	3		21	236	33	1040	157	5370	104	902	2290495	170150	15100
13	31	3200	26881	385	2839	29	299	2018	302	21		131	547	98	3795	314	9748	289	4522	4601053	566278	300850
14	169	344	2585	202	179	20	20	110	1846	2		6	46	11	235	37	1121	45	114	135000	61350	35250
15	10	3466	33046	1258	2111	48	309	3425	35	23	3	73	380	45	2080	224	6413	170	4522	4294500	461100	155950
16	35	65	412		9	8		776	610	1		1	15		92	8	92			31300	10100	
17	26	719	6374	54	860	14	28	1159	208	7		23	205	18	601	97	2822	61	2082	1026383	134622	3500
18	96	373	2897		160	12	136	1083	982	1		13	91	18	164	41	1033	44	871	623475	39100	108050
19	42	1047	7293	8	1076	27	121	628	698	3		22	43	21	523	97	3562	106	2637	1164332	197450	83050
20	58	718	5684	118	575	4	35	349	753	12		7	157	21	592	111	2891	66	1563	1225009	166330	29600
21	46	983	8979	161	1126	21	23	1163	890	11	1	48	248	21	845	90	2988	90	2054	1297350	154600	18000
22	67	746	7438		478	8	131	153	740	8		23	80	19	94	80	3302	59	1715	1039710	158050	39800
23	38	505	4826	33	315	32	12	693	526	5	2	29	69	6	583	73	1984	42	1154	696300	218100	15250
24	13	550	4065	77	414	5	43	217	194			6	58	19	142	84	2152	74	1445	1273950	69000	33600
25	100	2076	16224	133	248	28	22	85	620	26		4	186	88	583	238	783	22	450	477450	38650	144800
26	115	2823	1677	113	2183	95	174	2723	3414		2	51	592	5	2548	37	7386	40	5549	3970478	326111	1800
27	21	258	2823		23	4	95	2354	251			6	11	10	127	37	698	32	852	308120	80925	14750
28	22	166	1930	2	239		39	563	173	5		5	67	1	208	43	975	16	514	368804	35809	3000
29	33	484	1386	50		11	62	806	296	4		11	13	12	40	24	666	44	360	196400	30000	2000
30	33	116	3616		267	16	19	517	374	3		5	79	14	262	50	1206	21	789	827200	166751	19000
31	33	557	1026	92	68	5	19	204	695	2		10	88	4	107	13	702	45	693	530200	79225	112300
32	33	150	4971	41	592	1	4	42	112			8	31	14	265	54	1618	21	783	894300	112250	8200
33	23	393	1184	27	38	17	20	174	266	3			77	19	67	21	546	21	351	342800	60000	31000
34			3763	103	174										511	67	1925	47	959	920500	102500	
35	3861	73002	668673	18397	55360	1136	6648	77994	60459	556	50	2099	11002	1783	66863	6491	211431	5756	149146	120555954	13503719	10069139
36	1147	2394	62427			1111		47232		127			9	760	20437	697	17904	42	1138	210445	50150	33650
37	5008	75396	731100	18397	55360	2247	6648	125226	60459	683	50	2099	11011	2543	87300	7188	229335	5798	150284	120766399	13553869	10102789

STATISTICAL REPORT OF THE UNITED LUTHERAN CHURCH IN AMERICA FOR THE YEAR 1936—Concluded

FINANCIAL

Index Number	Endowment	Other Property	Total Valuation	Indebtedness	Current (Cong. Exp.)	Unusual	Total	Apportioned Paid	Excess	Deficit	Education	Foreign Missions	Home Missions	Inner Missions	Other Benevolence	Total Unapportioned Benevolence	Total Benevolence	Total Expenditures
1	1572910	1033013	29924932	3664567	1575588	772226	2347814	278838	659	237641	14798	26133	9560	50366	38867	137724	418562	2766376
2	915503	1299911	29697689	4749982	1960851	301671	2262522	156035	787	271396	39819	16312	10406	51731	24470	142738	298773	2561295
3	23725	106707	3494537	260704	203236	98621	301857	42733		33557	11023	3431	4196	9460	12178	40288	83021	384878
4	200601	227683	8314790	1117904	514190	279633	793823	92453	1522	23557	2006	16729	6812	30202	13179	68928	161381	955204
5	16600	151678	2899401	228860	125636	57098	182734	24079	140	17014	16902	2607	2445	11093	12865	33848	57927	240661
6	353074	173508	7150282	513910	402082	126484	528566	98421	3569	35300	1436	15562	2789	9624	7425	43745	142166	670732
7	79456	144012	2494384	146079	152144	54308	206452	29992	53	23495	8147	1866	2168	14346	7629	29434	59426	265878
8	246618	253599	9755383	963849	674697	142629	817326	140366	488	69558	2820	23173	6720	27175	18860	53638	194001	1011330
9	315662	401751	9755572	1377778	637510	150183	787693	104545		44214	4762	13973	3639	4884	12988	74818	179363	967056
10	47985	129296	3828757	1930316	224089	57654	281743	49251		25659	2243	5451	2032	34891	6606	21216	70467	352210
11	214536	738356	12305691	429598	808249	275901	1084150	115642		25763	3380	12069	6184	11980	22242	78766	194408	1278558
12	37500	148276	2661521	1470299	174030	59565	233595	30359		66213	3118	1063	882	13355	3527	17570	47929	281524
13	68095	130308	5666584		446755	90282	537037	57091	30	8581	1379	6573	6729	596	8452	36488	93579	630616
14	275	13650	245525	244755	31673	14503	46176	3620	49	39891	122	420	235	5102	1213	2586	6206	52382
15	87534	117051	5116135	480216	313526	80452	393978	63030	792	601	986	5941	899		5443	18371	81401	475379
16		41400	41400	5323	3469	1662	5131	610	12	15496	111	13	8	62	128	322	932	6063
17	10833	40584	1215922	323693	122706	46083	168789	10773		4753	37	2536	635	1446	1601	6255	17028	185817
18	21095	69020	860740	158318	44940	29885	74825	9539	27	4024	1642	529	1120	2125	1752	7168	16707	91532
19	37816	71350	1553998	120106	145950	24316	170266	21231	569	11450	5677	1566	1929	3392	3388	15952	37183	207449
20	16150	16150	1463992	163399	97398	23653	121051	16263	8	12364	339	1583	994	2542	3589	9047	25310	146361
21	4035	127128	1601113	119981	109211	17221	126432	20519	10	568	548	1977	1793	2765	681	9778	30297	156729
22	1000	15320	1254240	161745	123412	21434	144846	7344	649	55428	66	746	149	1324	1516	2966	10310	155156
23	10500	19283	955470	40789	73398	10828	84226	6800		6090	79	841	167	1263	3407	4055	10855	95081
24	80000		1475833	162033	104120	162040	266160	8940	61	1473	124	310	248	1559	1619	6709	15649	281809
25	63		531133	200920	33660	12894	46554	5467	373		1583	5250	3350	485	10051	2786	8253	54807
26	17205	64925	4523519	1695941	375348	87526	462874	63354		2560	194	265	38	6175	164	26409	89763	552637
27	1450	12176	404471	50711	44134	20073	64207	5828		4915	326	329	507	98	995	759	6587	70794
28	640	14660	434663	187682	32012	9734	41746	4244	21	6217	592	125	37	570	434	2727	6971	48717
29	1000	6000	236400	16750	21736	2008	23744	1655			356	862	200	30	1418	1218	2873	26617
30	350	73220	1069521	187649	60245	10051	70296	7869	4	7029	20	75	130	569	699	3405	11271	81570
31	375	7000	635800	116072	34316	15031	49347	564		233	121	521	402	88	1414	1012	1576	50923
32		25483	1144333	464390	86212	15348	101560	12375	474		484	211	284	1544	552	4002	16377	117337
33		5600	416600	164790	21171	22422	43593	2554	17	3745	280	1627	528	548	1783	2079	4633	48226
34	18950	105961	1178911	174090	74145	39597	113742	14201						1482		5700	19901	133643
35	4401536	5780042	154310242	21978434	9851839	3133016	12984855	1506585	10983	1191368	122788	171946	78602	307341	233830	914507	2421092	15405947
36		2495256	2789501		3281		3281								241642	241642	241642	244923
37	4401536	8275298	157099743	21978434	9855120	3133016	12988136	1506585	10983	1191368	122788	171946	78602	307341	475472	1156149	2662734	15650370

U. L. C. A. STATISTICAL REPORT OF OTHER COUNTRIES OUTSIDE U. S. A. AND CANADA—1936
(Foreign Missions compiled by Board of Foreign Missions; American Missions by Board of American Missions)
PAROCHIAL

INDEX NUMBERS	COUNTRY	PROVINCE	WHEN ORGANIZED	PASTORS	Congregations	MEMBERSHIP			ACCESSIONS				LOSSES			CHURCH PAPERS
						Baptized	Confirmed	Communing	Net	CHILDREN & ADULT			CHILDREN & ADULT			No. S. S. Papers Distributed
										Baptism	Con-firmation	Certificate	Death	Certificate	Otherwise	
1	India	Madras	1842	Ord. Miss. 25, Nat. Workers 2848, Unord. men & women 36	1703	175000	85000	85000	3560							
2	Africa	Liberia	1860	Ord. Miss. 3, Nat. Workers 61, Unord. men & women 9.....	16	1055	410	410	79							
3	Japan	Kyushu-Hondo	1892	Ord. Miss. 11, Workers 70, Unord. men & women 11.....	31	4458	750	750	233							
4	China	Shantung	1898	Ord. Miss. 6, Unord. men & women 6....	36	3239	1502	1502	553							
5	Virgin Islands		1666	U. L. C. A. 3....	3	1110	790	440	4							
6	British Guiana	Berbice	1889	U. L. C. A. 2, Workers 12....	8	661	388	388								
7	Puerto Rico		1898	U. L. C. A. 9....	20	2957	876	743		103	77	9	35	150	550	
8	Argentina	Buenos Aires	1908	Ord. Miss. 2, Nat. Workers 27, Unord. men & women 1....	12	1702	1078	1078	17				15	30	62	
9	Totals Outside U. S. A. & Can.			Pastors 61, Workers 3018, Unord. 63.	1829	190182	90794	90311	4446	103	77	9	50	180	612	

U. L. C. A. STATISTICAL REPORT OF OTHER COUNTRIES OUTSIDE U. S. A. AND CANADA—1936 Concluded

PAROCHIAL

INDEX NUMBERS	CHURCH SCHOOLS						Inquirers	Catechu-mens (Catechetical)	STUDENTS		CHURCH SOCIETIES					
	SUNDAY			WEEKDAY					In Ministry	In Non-Luth. Institutions	MEN'S		WOMEN'S		YOUNG P.	
	Number	Officers and Teachers	Scholars	Number	Officers and Teachers	Scholars					Number	Members	Number	Members	Number	Members
1	1125	2225	55028	1044		43270	16278		100		760	20437	685	17644		
2			200	5		425	480									
3			3586	16		1528	400		14							
4			1000	28		1144	479		10							
5	5	70	335	4		6	94		1							
6			397	6		107	21		1							
7		99	1562	6		13	244			9			12	260	42	1138
8	17		319	6		739	100		1							
9	1147	2394	62427	1111		47232	18096		127	9	760	20437	697	17901	42	1138

FINANCIAL

INDEX NUMBERS	SUMMARY				VALUATION OF CHURCH PROPERTY				
	Total Expenditures	Benevolence	Field Contributions	Congregational Expenses	Total Valuation	Other Property	Schools and Parish Houses	Parsonages	Church Edifices
1	222370	25825	196545		1225000	1225000			
2	2227		2227		80000	80000			
3	7052		7052		690000	690000			
4	3960		3960		195000	195000			
5					156700	14200	20300	19200	103000
6	1723		1723		61000	61000			
7	3395	114		3281	151801	56	13350	30950	107445
8	4196		4196		230000	230000			
9	244923	25939	215703	3281	2789501	2495256	33650	50150	210445

STATISTICAL REPORT OF THE UNITED LUTHERAN CHURCH IN AMERICA FOR THE YEAR 1937

Index No.	SYNOD	When Organized	Pastors	Parishes	Congregations	Membership: Baptized	Confirmed	Communing	Contributing	Non-member Adherents	Paroch. Access. Children: Baptism	Otherwise	Adult: Baptism	Confirmation	Certificate	Otherwise	Losses Children: Death	Otherwise	Adult: Death	Certificate	Otherwise	Church Papers
1	Ministerium of Penna.	Aug. 15, 1748	510	398	595	309299	211712	151116	136406	18181	6084	3054	682	7052	2861	2278	267	3068	3478	1983	4837	4983
2	United Synod of N. Y.	Oct. 23, 1786	482	402	431	245408	166909	109233	91448	27941	4953	4467	433	5318	2114	2613	319	4658	2498	1070	4949	2660
3	United Synod of N. C.	May 9, 1803	118	93	160	41282	29595	20523	17639	2741	808	527	185	980	786	115	34	695	303	546	155	793
4	Maryland Synod	Oct. 11, 1820	144	99	139	76195	55808	33546	29029	10788	1433	527	105	1455	818	476	65	105	664	465	932	1591
5	Synod of S. Carolina	Jan. 14, 1824	84	66	112	30262	23126	16261	14868	1312	489	173	140	624	628	257	29	258	271	403	562	1166
6	Synod of West Penna.	Sept. 5, 1829	140	96	158	67236	50649	35994	37510	2819	1119	382	243	1216	664	833	63	226	634	442	1568	1076
7	Synod of Virginia	Aug. 10, 1829	99	80	167	28378	22912	13082	13388	2841	402	144	270	422	295	163	23	513	269	230	449	1758
8	Synod of Ohio	Nov. 7, 1836	265	194	158	91853	65354	50627	38965	9131	1801	679	270	1762	1105	833	93	516	963	823	1568	1408
9	East Penna. Synod	May 2, 1842	185	131	158	81741	58410	35227	30554	8452	1283	667	192	1461	1212	163	63	200	829	693	1158	689
10	Allegheny Synod	Sept. 9, 1842	84	66	145	43477	34030	20955	15122	5758	580	167	358	675	395	1522	32	1090	358	315	343	2042
11	Pittsburgh Synod	Jan. 15, 1845	270	213	305	132842	93520	58402	49240	11834	2545	1234	160	2772	1393	125	120	186	1213	1006	1991	488
12	Indiana Synod	Oct. 28, 1848	94	68	105	24629	18533	12298	9857	2227	455	224	28	650	334	1024	23	963	287	198	599	780
13	Illinois Synod	Sept. 8, 1851	150	124	143	70320	49355	32400	25578	591	1443	991	184	1778	723	92	43	74	472	504	1638	334
14	Texas Synod	Nov. 10, 1851	29	22	30	6993	5090	3597	2238	2816	147	89	2	169	93	328	5	891	46	77	87	708
15	Susquehanna Synod	Nov. 21, 1855	115	81	161	54807	40820	25786	25637	39	1008	317	395	985	749	749	67	374	581	481	813	39
16	Mississippi Synod	Feb. 25, 1855	6	4	11	979	772	316	305	2783	13	11	17	2	10	82	21	39	6	1	4	223
17	Synod of Iowa	July 3, 1855	33	33	31	21639	14666	8633	7079	421	419	230	26	569	271	24	21	300	133	206	714	267
18	Georgia-Ala. Synod	July 20, 1860	19	19	103	6672	4352	3099	3211	2386	69	53	96	75	116	340	30	145	40	67	71	1006
19	Synod of Canada	July 21, 1861	86	67	43	31916	21776	16273	13536	2093	636	266	203	699	195	136	4	247	316	167	749	240
20	Synod of Kansas	Nov. 5, 1868	36	36	48	13324	9953	5857	4339	2206	275	146	83	304	214	231	18	221	116	134	174	258
21	Synod of Nebraska	Sept. 1, 1871	61	51	82	26957	18648	11622	8191	1809	656	290	16	684	331	350	26	64	142	223	324	241
22	Wartburg Synod	July, 1875	59	4	63	24879	16191	11560	4089	639	526	492	139	636	88	448	17	275	255	53	237	142
23	Synod in the Midwest	July 24, 1890	79	69	36	20148	13824	10670	4265	3856	288	139	16	285	51	87	18	54	111	50	10	300
24	Synod of California	April 2, 1891	63	36	15	11083	7271	4265	1609	1609	304	349	43	345	353	74	84	275	79	148	534	107
25	Rocky Mt. Synod	May 6, 1891	23	15	101	4213	3044	1825	1825	6613	111	48	275	81	76	448	18	54	26	37	87	586
26	Synod of the Northwest	Sept. 23, 1891	104	91	144	19172	41269	31887	30929	686	1765	1377	53	1858	528	1791	28	1247	286	535	1972	469
27	Manitoba Synod	July 16, 1897	64	55	64	6553	11513	7241	3800	1050	337	250	29	343	93	206	13	162	56	95	97	102
28	Pacific Synod	Sept. 26, 1901	40	24	26	8323	4210	2243	1987	261	164	13	5	171	195	171	10	190	42	65	160	173
29	Nova Scotia Synod	July 10, 1903	12	8	30	6173	3582	2186	2719	190	119	36	29	85	33	43	13	14	38	21	31	230
30	Synod of West Virginia	April 17, 1912	23	24	33	8602	5760	3631	2579	428	123	27	3	178	99	37	8	20	65	51	43	140
31	Slovak Zion Synod	June 10, 1919	28	23	33	12047	6047	4394	3631	834	157	216	70	163	42	158	8	231	70	101	453	232
32	Michigan Synod	June 10, 1920	33	31	33	2529	1925	4764	2999	2265	54	43	3	348	182	39	11	31	77	20	59	79
33	Synod of Florida	Sept. 24, 1928	21	14	14	8228	4194	1194	1007	2265	295	31	63	63	88	39	11	31	17	20	59	79
34	Kentucky-Tenn. Synod	June 6, 1934	19	19	26	8154	6537	4107	4056	748	134	193	143	143	158	146	13	86	91	44	103	96
35	Totals for U. S. and Canada		3578	2756	3990	1599102	1125399	754814	658465	139860	30995	17908	5688	34351	17293	14977	1547	17275	14832	11262	26028	26099
36	Totals Outside U. S. and Canada				1970	197986	92533	92036			4063		2031	100		35	12	35	23	35	72	
37	U. L. C. A. World Total		3578	2756	5960	1797088	1217932	846850	658465	139860	35058	17908	7719	34451	17293	14977	1559	17310	14855	11297	26100	26099

STATISTICAL REPORT OF THE UNITED LUTHERAN CHURCH IN AMERICA FOR THE YEAR 1937—Continued

	PAROCHIAL																			FINANCIAL		
	CHURCH SCHOOLS								Catechetical Catechumens	STUDENTS				CHURCH SOCIETIES						VALUATION OF CHURCH PROPERTY		
	SUNDAY					WEEKDAY								MEN'S		WOMEN'S		YOUNG P.				
Index No.	Number	Officers and Teachers	Scholars	Home Dep't.	Cradle Roll	Number	Teachers	Scholars		Ministry	Diaconate	In Lutheran Institutions	In Non-Lutheran Institutions	Number	Members	Number	Members	Number	Members	Church Edifices	Parsonages	School and Parish Houses
1	593	13808	131219	4411	10125	161	1289	14167	10852	103	14	308	1836	337	13395	939	34952	890	26498	22891645	2183343	2658050
2	431	8149	66322	1717	8975	112	519	5723	8586	55	6	181	1645	290	12163	833	32184	884	21581	21959406	2432681	3293250
3	155	2397	26354	462	1118	105	607	9215	2356	34		158	336	49	1061	198	9879	245	6589	2875574	375328	214177
4	141	3619	34971	1540	3119	19	150	1681	2485	21		42	579	59	2346	253	5076	243	6631	6675852	700870	635441
5	111	1579	14968	153	848	73	613	7937	1425	8	2	134	260	28	687	175	9053	203	5048	1572583	264990	250300
6	158	4411	46340	1275	2986	22	244	3247	3228	25		121	411	41	2400	258	4552	213	6785	5788200	564776	280650
7	158	1853	16519	446	958	78	373	4139	1072	9	1	58	227	24	767	181	12370	162	3806	1860860	337566	100185
8	277	5310	49547	1159	2886	36	181	2535	3412	32	2	214	850	137	4974	568	19446	405	8830	8370104	749800	350750
9	155	4409	40631	2916	3113	50	353	3923	2470	48	4	144	758	129	5871	354	17853	320	3583	7456842	894575	672900
10	166	2197	21642	667	1331	40	424	4075	1371	15	1	46	266	40	1436	154	5535	141		3124700	397475	112300
11	298	5841	52146	1783	4852	67	88	4515	4957	30	4	188	845	159	5153	608	10415	442	11027	9891110	1224692	488436
12	105	1678	26587	258	2896	14	219	694	1134	2		23	214	35	1084	155	1183	102	2090	2421200	167350	16100
13	142	3143		558	277	26	1	2067	2622	24	1	127	616	95	3371	334	6536	245	6826	4735418	557411	242499
14	32	328		127	1994	1	290	308	364	4		11	42	54	227	35	118	38	894	109400	62855	32000
15	171	3486	32934	1200	10	40	15	3008	1822	25	1	76	385		2548	230	2931	183	5002	4307770	471650	180250
16	52	52	324		797		125	242	32	8			12	18	14	10	1088	5	74	30700		
17	33	912	6263	59	100	15	40	980	635	10	4	21	213	18	643	88	3619	73	2241	1022933	9500	3500
18	26	374	2870		987	13	181	1019	309	8		20	91	18	153	45	3074	45	915	715450	130350	117750
19	98	1069	7494	61	530	30	14	767	1052	5	1	17	35	18	514	102	3101	107	2692	1217196	38600	83925
20	40	714	5667	119	1050	8	20	376	633	6	1	10	192	14	518	100	3012	66	1559	1235688	212850	25650
21	56	1068	8691	126	486	23	17	167	981	7	1	42	264	20	463	111	1013	91	2241	1307535	163800	18000
22	43	733	7156	8		18	317	229	933		1	21	79	22	871	78	2336	65	1575	993010	159550	93800
23	40	293	2894		394	5	99	241	465	23		13	54	4	67	46	772	22	525	779550	243750	12600
24	38	575	4168	98	242	5	41	258	596	15		5	223	23	706	90	7564	69	1378	472300	225700	34100
25	14	234	1591	111	2230		2	3460	175	5			53	79	158	29	744	24	548	4020789	66300	4000
26	104	2033	15947	101	16	43	47	2495	3272	5		60	624	9	2545	240	1027	222	5281	319220	39850	175150
27	106	217	2866		227	105	17	279	676	6	3	14	15	9	62	37	610	40	935	366080	337642	1800
28	24	291	2251	71	35	1	23	50	326			110		13	208	44	1207	37	652	195700	83349	14750
29	22	177	1385		306	9	15	709	105			5	11	15	42	22	660	12	292	826500	22500	4000
30	33	483	3504	106	108	9	15	536	279	2	1	7	76	4	280	52	1663	32	665	480000	30000	
31	15	97	986		576	6		263	294			8	118	16	65	11	512	13	416	885800	160451	19500
32	30	590	4724	23	16	3		185	693			6	33		321	53	2163	52	952	353000	66250	111600
33	24	162	1203	28	115			130	106			4	77		73	23		19	300	929900	107150	6981
34	13	395	3798	43					320	2	1	12			439	73		48	1000		61000	30000
35	3860	72677	658776	19641	54602	1158	6753	80753	60048	539	48	2207	11461	1766	65625	6529	215935	5758	147420	121444972	13640954	10284394
36	22	169	60665			1097	19	52379		107			9			12	260	42	1138	210445	50150	33650
37	3882	72846	719441	19641	54602	2255	6772	133132	60038	646	48	2207	11470	1766	65625	6541	216195	5800	148558	121655417	13691104	10318044

STATISTICAL REPORT OF THE UNITED LUTHERAN CHURCH IN AMERICA FOR THE YEAR 1937—Concluded

FINANCIAL

INDEX NUMBER	Valuation of Church Property — Endowment	Other Property	Total Valuation	Indebtedness	Congregational Expenses — Current	Unusual	Total	Congregational Benevolence — Apportioned — Paid	Excess	Deficit	Unapportioned — Education	Foreign Missions	Home Missions	Inner Missions	Other Benevolence	Total Un-apportioned Benevolence	Summary — Total Benevolence	Total Expenditures
1	1580370	976085	30289493	3640294	1609934	959299	2569233	285536	585	227328	23929	26464	10206	60603	44271	165473	451009	3020242
2	926927	1277601	29989865	4661012	1971874	500914	2472788	164518	1149	293810	32278	16502	11777	60069	29692	150318	314836	2787624
3	22560	101371	3589010	265239	213468	170569	384037	45434		30586	3491	3891	5539	12788	14387	40096	85530	469567
4	161067	28788	8461113	1040692	517730	259591	777331	96096	2150	20186	2563	16297	7546	32311	17115	75832	171928	949249
5	17091	154117	2259081	225356	127680	87129	214809	25746	64	12843	9819	2487	3495	10862	8657	38034	63780	278589
6	405654	135034	7174314	460119	424128	144139	568267	102937	3998	32068	1386	16212	3801	11749	19260	51521	154458	722725
7	78034	137419	2511064	145583	156562	73900	230162	31180	124	22776	2559	1748	1966	11749	8451	26473	57653	288115
8	215049	272197	9957900	904130	670557	240999	911556	149368	1519	64581	1262	14515	3030	28580	22137	62003	211371	1122927
9	327218	411737	9762772	1314986	633927	177559	811486	100264	1046	40617	4687	23610	6638	5696	13706	77221	186485	997971
10	411737	106760	3778570	154300	208860	57499	266359	49490		74710	1386	4328	1683	13423	8005	21098	70588	336047
11	106760	734220	12525806	2026186	839327	306335	1145662	149690	68	16491	2154	10147	4708	26185	22758	65952	215612	1361304
12	187348	144801	2792226	412110	182917	74462	257379	32299	466	25509	47	7757	620	13423	7490	23480	55779	313158
13	42775	134430	5738302		464658	121864	586522	63801		61293	4239	106	3623	19660	10278	45557	109358	695880
14	68544	17685	221940	10966	33677	5950	39627	4038	1059	3397	710	6240	92	686	7491	1684	5722	45349
15		116338	5166064	456516	329420	98171	427594	65620	16	36921	561	17	1983	7087	23362	23362	88982	516576
16	88049	300	40500	4009	3746	1456	5202	682	7	837	60	1941	17	75	933	311	993	6195
17		39436	1207151	286889	127253	39438	166691	11704		15145	140	1941	221	2012	2727	7041	18715	185436
18	10932	19600	912405	153414	46598	40873	87171	10786	1030	3210	757	483	1836	2228	2307	7611	18397	105868
19	37729	72327	1624027	120106	155331	32389	187720	23336		2770	7538	1424	607	4139	3296	17001	39340	227060
20	8650	21441	1456129	142583	100104	24461	124565	17775	30	10390	3047	1395	1352	3771	3547	13112	30887	155452
21	4389	126452	1615926	118546	107790	29029	136819	19201		25639	1898	2031	278	1950	2797	13009	32210	169029
22	250	15930	1346740	147458	123388	24568	147956	8621	1013		187	608	278	6508	1586	4603	13230	161186
23	12325	14630	1044452	40789	56055	7129	63184	10332		5575	311	1645	528	1707	1147	10139	14757	77041
24	60000	27002	519901	162033	108721	33441	142162	5497	132	1625	1092	505	598	423	4894	8796	19128	161290
25	780	2987	4610535	208493	397119	120786	517905	69615	295		1929	198	534	7344	1340	2930	8427	66604
26	10521	66433	418880	1422378	28525	7294	35819	4012		2776	490	5464	2339	494	11768	28844	98459	616364
27	1500	13011	416794	58593	38947	14667	53614	5162	95	5184	291	97	63	524	34	827	4839	40658
28	616	12848	236700	161756	29979	14667	22925	1886		5667	34	387	395	191	1443	3239	8401	62015
29	1000	6000	1062601	14478	38947	14478	74482	8454	52			60	40	672	503	1085	2971	25896
30	450	75200	579218	187551	57619	16863	55220	13631	167	5977		213	199	882	1638	3532	11986	86468
31		13468	1130256	50750	84392	12172	105390	2861		429		190	190	91	116	644	1338	56548
32		25706	430031	445291	18856	9934	28700	14913	102	3665	132	403	402	2553	1936	5294	18925	124315
33	765	8285	430031	164790	18856	9934	28700	2861		429	132	138	204	645	1087	2206	5067	33857
34	17125	97545	1164570	164511	75819	49981	125800	14913	102	3665	288	1269	376	2633	1860	6426	21339	147139
35	4346148	5666279	155382747	21107095	10015254	3787740	13802994	1607787	15502	1052345	109938	171196	78824	366849	277956	1004763	2612550	16415544
36		14256	2878501		2913		2913								256020	256020	256020	258933
37	4346148	5680535	158261248	21107095	10018167	3787740	13805907	1607787	15502	1052345	109938	171196	78824	366849	533976	1260783	2868570	16674477

U. L. C. A. STATISTICAL REPORT OF OTHER COUNTRIES OUTSIDE U. S. A. AND CANADA—1937
(Foreign Missions compiled by Board of Foreign Missions; American Missions by Board of American Missions)

PAROCHIAL

Index Numbers	Country	Province	When Organized	Pastors	Congregations	Membership Baptized	Membership Confirmed	Membership Communing	Accessions Net	Accessions Children & Adult Baptism	Con-firmation	Certificate	Losses Children & Adult Death	Certificate	Otherwise	Church Papers No. S. S. Papers Distributed
1	India	Madras	1842	Ord. Miss. 24, Nat. Workers 2957, Unord. men & women 36	1820	181378	85817	85817	4962							
2	Africa	Liberia	1860	Ord. Miss. 3, Nat. Workers 43, Unord. men & women 8.....	32	1730	514	514	254							
3	Japan	Kyushu-Hondo	1892	Ord. Miss. 11, Workers 170, Unord. men & women 11...	43	4815	1662	1662	185							
4	China	Shantung	1898	Ord. Miss. 5, Unord. men & women 7, Nat. Workers 125.	40	3767	1546	1546	527	30	30		20	20	50	
5	Virgin Islands		1666	U. L. C. A. 3.........	3	1080	780	425								
6	British Guiana	Berbice	1889	Ord. Miss. 1, Workers 13.....	6	665	304	304	34							
7	Puerto Rico		1898	U. L. C. A. 11.........	14	2992	882	740		52	70		15	15	57	
8	Argentina	Buenos Aires	1908	Ord. Miss. 2, Nat. Workers 30, Unord. men & women 1....	12	1559	1028	1028	50							
9	Totals Outside U. S. A. & Can.			Pastors 60, Workers 3338, Unord. 63.	1970	197986	92533	92036	6012	82	100		35	35	107	

U. L. C. A. STATISTICAL REPORT OF OTHER COUNTRIES OUTSIDE U. S. A. AND CANADA—1937 Concluded

FINANCIAL

Index Numbers	Valuation of Church Property Church Edifices	Parsonages	Schools and Parish Houses	Other Property	Total Valuation	Congregational Expenses	Field Contributions	Benevolence	Summary Total Expenditures
1					1300000		239000		239000
2					80000		1007		1007
3					700000		7000		7000
4					200000		4000		4000
5	103000	19200	20300	14200	156700		1748		1748
6					60000				
7	107445	30950	13350	56	151801	2913		365	3278
8					230000		2900		2900
9	210445	50150	33650	14256	2878501	2913	255655	365	258933

PAROCHIAL

Index Numbers	Church Schools Sunday Numbers	Sunday Officers and Teachers	Sunday Scholars	Weekday Number	Weekday Officers and Teachers	Weekday Scholars	Inquirers	Catechu-mens	Students Ministry	Students In Non-Luth. Institutions	Men's Number	Men's Members	Women's Number	Women's Members	Young P. Number	Young P. Members
1			55617	1033		48168	18658		85							
2			250	5		366	900									
3			759	19		1719	200		12							
4	5	70	1000	21	6	995	449		8							
5			335	2		94										
6			381	4		125	27		1	9						
7	17	99	2043	6	13	244			1						42	1138
8			280	7		668							12	260		
9	22	169	60665	1097	19	52379	20234		107	9			12	260	42	1138

Rev. Frankenfield requested that the Rev. W. H. Greever address the convention with regard to his work as Statistical Secretary.

Recommendations 1 and 2 were adopted. Recommendation 3 was adopted by a rising vote.

The Report of the Committee on German Interests was presented.

REPORT OF THE COMMITTEE ON GERMAN INTERESTS

The Committee on German Interests reports with great satisfaction and sincere appreciation two outstanding developments in the life of the U. L. C. A. along the lines for which it was created.

The resolution adopted at the recent convention at Columbus, Ohio, to arrange for the exchange of qualified students with Germany to prepare them for German and German-English charges has been carried out with splendid results through the agency of the various boards. We feel confident that the encouraging results achieved will continue such an exchange in accordance with the needs within the life of our Church.

The arrangements and the convocations of the tenth German general conference of the U. L. C. at Edmonton, Alberta, July 30, 1937, engaged the attention of the committee for a considerable part of the past biennium.

The conference met on July 30 and 31, 1937, in the Hotel MacDonald at Edmonton, Alberta. The Rev. C. R. Tappert, D.D., was elected president; the Rev. R. H. Ischinger, vice-president; the Rev. W. Herrmann, secretary; and the Rev. Paul Schmeider, treasurer. Problems pertaining to our German and German-English work were discussed and the needs of the congregations voiced. The fraternization between the brethren of the East and West brought splendid results. There was a greater understanding of the common needs and an open discussion of the outstand-opportunities and requirements of our German Home Mission work in the West. It is to be noted especially that the attendance at this conference was considerably larger than at the Ninth General German Conference at Buffalo.

The Committee feels that it may report that its work has resulted in a far better understanding on the part of the Church and its various agencies of the needs of our German and German-English work, particularly also the Home Mission work; and that the results of the Edmonton Convention will make themselves felt for years to come in fruitful contacts formed between congregations on the mission field and established churches in the East. These have already culminated in considerable practical, especially also financial support to the needy churches in the far West.

The committee is grateful for the opportunity to serve the Church and looks forward confidently to ever-increasing results within its sphere of activities.

ROBERT H. ISCHINGER, *Secretary.*

The Rev. C. K. Fegley presented the report of the Committee on Publicity.

REPORT OF COMMITTEE ON PUBLICITY

During the biennium, the development of the Promotional Plan, and the questions which that plan raised in publicity for the Church as a whole, led the Publicity Committee to a re-study of its functions. Our Committee organized with the Rev. Charles K. Fegley as chairman and the Rev. L. W. Rupp as secretary.

Functioning directly, we believe the Committee has two major tasks: One is the provision of an efficient program and personnel for the handling of the news publicity of the biennial conventions of the United Lutheran Church. The other is the ad interim publicizing of all those general activities of the United Lutheran Church and of its boards, committees, auxiliaries and institutions, which may have a nation-wide, continent-wide, or world-wide significance.

Functioning indirectly, our committee's task lies in the creation and operation of such agencies and methods as will bring about the enlarged news-mindedness of every portion of the Church, and insure thorough news coverage of Church activities in all sections and localities where the Church is represented and is operating.

In the matter of our direct duties, we have provided for this convention a Press Room with the following personnel: General director, C. K. Fegley; Osborne Hauge, publicity director of the National Lutheran Council; L. W. Rupp and A. R. Naus. A considerable amount of pre-convention publicity has been promoted and all arrangements made for news coverage during the convention and subsequent to adjournment. The radio program is more elaborate than any attempted hitherto.

In the development of an adequate ad interim program of publicity education and organization, it was decided that this aim could best be attained in co-operation with the National Lutheran Council through its News Bureau's plan for the establishment of a regional staff set-up. Conferences, consultations, and investigations have been under way for some time. The plan is so vital a one and its importance so great that the old adage, "make haste slowly," has been followed. The expectation is that within the next biennium this regional set-up will be functioning effectively.

In respect to our organization within the United Lutheran Church, necessary for the best results in publicity, the Committee would suggest that the Conference of Presidents give this matter attention at its next meeting, considering the importance of seeking the best persons possible from the standpoint of interest, experience and ability, for appointment to the publicity committee of the respective synods, and considering as well the importance of making these appointments with a view to insuring continuity in the carrying out of the plans of the United Lutheran Church committee and of those of the synodical committee.

One thing to be borne in mind, however, is that no matter how thoroughly this general plan of organization and personnel in Church-wide publicity may be accomplished, the effective functioning of Church Publicity will not approach the best standards, nor reach its desirable proportions without the understanding and continual co-operation of our individual pastors and congregations. This is another sphere in which "The Whole Church" must function.

While none of the Church's money was spent for a clipping service, the co-operation of interested individuals throughout the Church has given to the office of the Secretary of Publicity a very definite conviction that sustained general United Lutheran Church publicity has had a wider spread and a larger volume in 1938 than at any previous time. Much was added to this volume by the publicity secured by the Board of American Missions in connection with the Anniversary Appeal.

C. K. FEGLEY,
W. H. GREEVER,
A. R. NAUS,
L. W. RUPP.

Rev. Fegley requested Dr. Greever to speak concerning the general plans of publicity.

Rev. Fegley introduced Mr. Osborne Hauge, the full-time Publicity Director of the National Lutheran Council, who spoke concerning the co-operative work of his bureau with the U. L. C. A. Committee.

Rev. Fegley presented a supplementary report, and the recommendation therein was adopted:

SUPPLEMENTARY REPORT OF THE PUBLICITY COMMITTEE

The committee begs leave to ask the convention to approve this opening paragraph expressing its sincere appreciation of service and news and radio courtesies extended to the convention by the persons and organizations herein mentioned:

The newspapers of Baltimore; the Baltimore offices of the wire services and of the telegraph companies; the New York *Times,* and the Chicago *Tribune,* who sent special correspondents; *Life Magazine,* which sent a staff photographer; the Baltimore radio stations, the Columbia and the National Broadcasting Companies; Delegates William Weidt, Mark Trexler, and Bruce Shaffer, who served at the press table; Pastors Cletus Senft, William Ducker, William Erhard, and G. F. Genszler, who also rendered press table service; Osborne Hauge, National Lutheran Council Publicity Director, and Carl Will, Publicity Director of the Board of American Missions, who rendered general assistance throughout the entire convention.

We are happy to report the evidences of the appreciation with which the radio broadcast program has been received over a wide territory, and will welcome any constructive criticism of this phase of our activity, should the delegates desire to offer them.

We call attention to the fact that our experience at this convention leads to the conclusion that news publicity for both the Brotherhood and the United Lutheran Church conventions would be secured and maintained more effectively were each convention to be held at a separate time and in a different city.

CHARLES K. FEGLEY,
ALFORD R. NAUS,
L. W. RUPP,
W. H. GREEVER.

REPORT OF THE COMMITTEE TO PREPARE A STATEMENT CONCERNING RELATIONS OF CHURCH AND STATE

No report.

The Rev. W. H. Greever stated that there was no report from the **Committee on Transportation.**

REPORT OF THE ARCHIVIST

The following accessions to the Archives of the U. L. C. A. were received during the biennium 1937-38:

Ordination certificate of Walter D. Sharritt (Michigan Synod) received from the President of Synod.

Official correspondence of President Knubel, 1933-34.

Official copy of minutes of the ninth biennial convention of the U. L. C. A. 1934.

Documents connected with the Investigation of Board of Ministerial Pensions and Relief.

Respectfully submitted,

LUTHER D. REED, *Archivist.*

Mr. H. Beisler, Chairman, presented the report of the Lutheran Laymen's Radio Committee.

REPORT OF THE LUTHERAN LAYMEN'S RADIO COMMITTEE

(For action on the recommendations in this report, see p. 524.)

Before the meeting of this convention the eighth season of Sunday Vespers, the radio program of our Church, will have been completed. Because of the date this report had to be ready, it covers mainly the seasons of 1936 and 1937.

In each of these years our season has covered four months, from June through September. In 1936 the total of co-operating radio stations was 51. In 1937 we had 71 continental stations and 3 short-wave stations which carried our Church's message across the seas. The number of stations has been increased every year since we went on the air. Dr. Paul Scherer has continued to be the preacher for most of the Sundays. Co-operating with him were Dr. Frederick H. Knubel, Dr. Harry F. Baughman, Dr. Oscar F. Blackwelder, and Dr. Gould Wickey. As heretofore, all have served without compensation.

In 1936 expenditures totaled $3,571.65 and in 1937 $3,119.24. These covered payments for the quartet, administration expenses, stationery, postage, printing, etc. A principal item of expense each season is the printing each week of the radio sermon and the subsequent cost of distributing the same. During the years covering our radio ministry, but not including this year, requests for 89,600 copies of these sermons came from men and women who represented, seemingly, almost all walks and conditions of life in our forty-eight states, in Canada and in many remote places of the world. These requests are eloquent testimony to the character of our Church's message and the need therefor.

No part of our expenses has been covered by payment from the treasury of the Church. In the first seven years of our Committee's existence the number of contributors totaled 1,212 but in no one year was the total that large. It does seem to our Committee that more laymen and men's organizations should want to have a share in this work, the importance of which we can appreciate only faintly.

As in previous years, the time we have been allotted on the air has been a gift from the National Broadcasting Company, which, in addition thereto, has contributed for other expenses a sum several times larger than that which we have been called upon to pay.

Our Committee recommends to this convention: (For action, see p. 524.)

First, that it express to Drs. Frederick H. Knubel, Paul Scherer, Harry F. Baughman, Oscar F. Blackwelder and Gould Wickey its appreciation of their contribution to the Church and to humanity through their radio ministry.

Second, that it express to the National Broadcasting Company its appreciation for the Company's great services to art, to education and, above all, to religion; that it express its admiration of the principles and policies the Company has followed in connection with religious broad- casting; and that it particularly express its gratitude for the facilities afforded us in the past eight years.

Third, that it commend the work of the Laymen's Radio Committee and invite laymen and men's organizations of the Church to support this exceptional method of spreading the gospel in circles untouched by our congregational activities.

HENRY BEISLER, *Chairman.*
FRANK C. GOODMAN, *Secretary.*
S. FREDERICK TELLEEN, *Treasurer.*

Mr. Beisler requested Mr. S. F. Telleen, Treasurer of the Committee, to address the convention on the finances of the Committee.

Recommendations 1, 2 and 3 were presented and adopted.

It was moved and carried that an offering be taken, immediately, for this work, which resulted in $314.18.

The Rev. C. E. Krumbholz, Secretary, presented the report of the Committee on Army and Navy Work.

REPORT OF THE COMMITTEE ON ARMY AND NAVY WORK

(For action on the recommendations in this report, see p. 526.)

Your Committee on Army and Navy Work submits the following report to the Eleventh Biennial Convention of the United Lutheran Church.

Because of the wide distances which separate the members of the Committee, and the expense involved in calling them together, your Committee has had no plenary session during the biennium. Its business is conducted through an executive committee composed of members in greater New York. The full membership, however, is consulted by mail to confirm any actions which are taken by vote in absentia. The Executive Committee is composed of the Rev. Charles D. Trexler, D.D., chairman; the Rev. C. E. Krumbholz, D.D., secretary; the Rev. Harold S. Miller and Mr. Charles H. Dahmer. The other members of the Committee appointed for the past biennium are the Rev. John F. Fedders, D.D., the Rev. R. H. Gerhart, Jr., D.D., the Rev. Henry Manken, Jr., and the Rev. Emil W. Weber.

Three meetings of the Executive Committee have been held in New York City. Fifteen applications for appointment to chaplaincies in the

THE UNITED LUTHERAN CHURCH IN AMERICA   525

Army and the Navy of the United States and in the Army and Navy Reserve Corps were received. These applications of United Lutheran Church pastors are received by your Committee through the General Committee on Army and Navy Chaplains. Each application carries full information of the qualifications of the applicant with his educational and pastoral background. Each application is supported by at least five letters of recommendation. The Committee reviews each application with the utmost care, in order to insure the best available men to represent the United Lutheran Church in this highly important service.

Of the fifteen applications received eleven were approved for Army Reserve Chaplaincies, one for the Naval Reserve Chaplaincy. Two men now in the Army Reserve Corps were approved for Naval Chaplaincies.

At Christmas during the past two years the Committee sent a personal letter of greeting to our Lutheran Chaplains, 18 in number. In 1937 a gift in the form of a copy of "America Awake," by P. W. Huntington, a former chaplain, was sent to each chaplain. This gift and the letters were highly appreciated as an evidence of the interest of the Church in the work our Chaplains are doing.

To inform the Church of the extent of the services rendered by our chaplains a questionnaire was addressed to our Chaplains asking for statistics of their services for the year 1937.

Fourteen replies have been received and compiled by the Committee. They show that 1,542 Sunday worship services were held at the Posts where these chaplains are stationed with a total attendance of 159,989. 605 weekday services with an aggregate attendance of 53,558 were held in addition. 431 Sunday school services were held with an attendance of 19,061. Other meetings of religious organizations totaled 181 with a total attendance of 16,330.

Official acts were performed as follows: Baptism: Adults, 9; children, 96; marriages, 30; funerals, 40; private communions, 52; public communion services, 480; communicants, 1,210.

Interviews for pastoral counsel were held in chaplain's offices to the number of 6,443 in addition to 6,158 held in other places. 147 Bibles, 2,127 Testaments, 1,803 Scripture portions and 7,053 Tracts were distributed.

Addresses other than sermons totaled 276 at Posts and 240 outside of the Posts. These fourteen chaplains presented their work 151 times, attended 119 meetings and held 240 conferences.

In addition to these activities, reports show that our chaplains are active in ministering to various types of hospitals and other institutions, in and outside of their Posts.

The Committee is happy to report these statistics as an evidence of the spiritual contribution our chaplains are making in the faithful discharge of their duties. In order that the Church may know the personnel of her representatives in the service of the chaplaincy the following list is herewith given:

Regular Army: J. H. A. Borleis, Captain; Joseph O. Ensrud, Captain; Luther W. Evans, Captain; John Hall, Lieutenant Colonel; F. H. Moehlmann, Captain; Herbert A. Rinard, Major; Peter C. Schroder, Captain.

Regular Navy: Frank H. Moyer, Lieutenant Commander.

Army Reserve: Earl R. Baublitz, Wayne M. Daubenspeck, F. C. Frommhagen, John W. Fry, Paul W. Hanshew, Walter D. Oberholtzer, Charles F. Steck, Jr., Herman Wennermark, John O. Woods, Loren H. Wyandt.

The Committee feels also that the Church is deeply interested in the work her servants in the Army and Navy are doing. To this end we have arranged for an exhibit of the work of the chaplaincy service at this convention. We trust it will receive the careful review of the delegates and visitors.

After careful study and with the full vote of the membership of the Committee we recommend: (For action, see p. 526.)

1. That the Church in Convention assembled, extend to its pastors who are serving as chaplains in the Army and Navy and their respective Reserve Corps its hearty greetings and express deep appreciation and interest in the important service being performd.

2. That the National Lutheran Council be requested to act as the representative of the Committee on Army and Navy Work in all contacts with the General Committee on Army and Navy Chaplains, or Government Departments.

3. That the Committee on Army and Navy Work of the United Lutheran Church in America receive from the National Lutheran Council, and recommend action upon, the applications of the United Lutheran Church pastors who desire to enter the service of the Army or Navy as chaplains and report such recommended action to the National Lutheran Council for transmittal to the proper authorities.

4. That, therefore, the Committee on Army and Navy Work be permitted to withdraw membership from the Committee on Chaplains of the Federal Council of Churches in America and from the General Committee on Army and Navy Chaplains.

Respectfully submitted,

Approved by the Committee,

C. D. TREXLER, *Chairman.*

Recommendations 1, 2, 3 and 4 were adopted.

The Rev. I. S. Sassaman, Chairman, presented the report of the Committee on Place of Next Convention:

REPORT OF COMMITTEE ON PLACE OF NEXT CONVENTION

Your Committee on Place of the Next Convention, with twenty-seven synodical presidents present, found it difficult to determine which of the four invitations ought to be recommended for acceptance of its

1940 convention. With invitations from Minneapolis-St. Paul., Minn., in the territory of the Synod of the Northwest; from Ft. Wayne, Indiana; from Omaha, Nebraska; and from New York City, all presented with a spirit of hearty welcome and with strong and logical reasons why the next convention should be held in those cities, it was very difficult for your committee to arrive at a conclusion.

Only after several ballots the following action was passed:

That we recommend that the 1940 convention of the United Lutheran Church be held in Omaha, Nebraska, on condition that, in the judgment of the Executive Board the facilities be found ample for the convention needs.

Respectfully submitted,

IRA S. SASSAMAN, *Chairman.*

After consideration and discussion, the recommendation of the Committee was adopted by a vote of 158 to 154.

It was moved and carried that a Committee be appointed by the President of the Church, to plan, in advance, for the placing of U. L. C. A. conventions, to secure full information concerning facilities, territorial needs and like matters, and to report these facts to the Committee on Place of Next Convention.

The Rev. C. B. Foelsch presented the report of the Committee on Moral and Social Welfare.

REPORT OF THE COMMITTEE ON MORAL AND SOCIAL WELFARE

The Committee has busied itself, during the past biennium, with the plans for the directed merger of the Inner Mission Board, the Committee on Evangelism, and the Committee on Moral and Social Welfare, and has concentrated its attention upon a most effective transfer of its responsibilities to the new Board when it shall have been instituted.

Among things to be transmitted to the new Board will be a summary account of work done by this committee during the past twenty years, including especially a list of literature and report documents.

WILLIAM H. HAGER,	E. E. FLACK,
W. A. SADTLER,	J. H. HARMS,
G. MORRIS SMITH,	N. WILLISON,
STANLEY BILLHEIMER,	W. C. ZIMMANN,
PAUL H. HEISEY,	CHARLES FOELSCH,
FRANK A. DRESSEL,	*Committee.*

Dr. Foelsch stated that, through the kindness of the Rev. H. Manken, Jr., of Washington, D. C., a photostatic copy of the original Bill of Rights, signed by Speaker Frederick Augustus Muhlenberg, and by the then Vice-President, John Adams, was presented for historical value. Dr. Knubel received it to be placed in the Church House.

REPORT OF AMERICAN MEMBERS OF THE EXECUTIVE COMMITTEE OF THE LUTHERAN WORLD CONVENTION

Two meetings of the Executive Committee were held in the last biennium, at Amsterdam, Holland, August 24-28, 1937, and at Uppsala, Sweden, May 21-25, 1938. Both of these meetings were concerned with the program of relief and assistance to the weaker and younger churches, gave consideration to the question of the revision of the Constitution of the Lutheran World Convention, and made the necessary preliminary plans for the Convention which is to be held in Philadelphia in 1940. Particular consideration was also given to the question of the relationship of the Lutheran Church to the Ecumenical Movements.

At the Amsterdam meeting, Dr. Wentz, who had been a delegate of the United Lutheran Church in America, to the Conference on Faith and Order in Edinburgh, gave a report of the proposal to organize a World Council of Churches, which should include also the Universal Christian Council for Life and Work and other ecumenical movements. It was the conviction of the Executive Committee that the attitude and approach of the Lutheran churches of the world to this ecumenical organization ought to be a united one. Furthermore, it was resolved to give expression to the conviction that representation in the proposed World Council should be on the basis of churches and confessions rather than according to territories and countries. Bishop Marahrens, president of the Executive Committee, was instructed to present these convictions to the Committee of Sixty to which he had been named as a member, at its meeting in Utrecht, in May, 1938. In his absence Dr. F. H. Knubel, first vice-president of the Executive Committee, presented these claims to the Provisional Committee of Sixty at Utrecht. The Provisional Committee did not see fit to adopt the recommendations, but made provisions in the proposed constitution whereby it can be accomplished without difficulty later on. Dr. Knubel gave a report of the proceedings at Utrecht to the Executive Committee at its meeting in Uppsala. As a result of the discussion the following resolution was adopted by the Executive Committee of the Lutheran World Convention:

"The Executive Committee has heard the report of two of its members who participated in the ecumenical meeting at Utrecht from the 9th to the 13th of May, and records with satisfaction that the confession of our Lord Jesus Christ as God and Saviour was unanimously adopted as the basis of the proposed World Council of Churches. We would emphatically state that thereby agreement in faith was acknowledged as the unavoidable requirement for a true unification of the churches. If Jesus Christ is confessed in the fullest sense as our God and Saviour, it involves that He is the only mediator between God and man and that we are justified before God only through faith in Him, the crucified and risen One. Only where the Gospel of Jesus Christ is rightly and purely taught and the Sacraments are administered according to the institution founded by Jesus will true church unity be maintained, according to the testimony of the New Testament as confessed by our church.

"In the organization of the World Council this principle was practically applied in the case of the Orthodox Church, which as such is to have special representation in the proposed new organization. This corresponds factually with the principle of confessional representation expressed in our Amsterdam resolution of 1937. Although this principle was carried through at Utrecht in the further arrangements for representation, we welcome the fact that the constitution provides for a possible change of the present territorial representation, and regard the present arrangement as only a temporary one, leading to such a change. The Lutheran World Convention believes that only on a confessional basis will participation in the work possess permanent and hopeful prospect."

THE 1940 CONVENTION

Since the 1940 convention is to be held in America, the Executive Committee at Amsterdam requested the American members to plan the program and make all necessary arrangements for the convention. A proposed program was submitted by the American members at the Uppsala meeting and accepted with minor changes. The program provides for the appointment of three commissions to prepare studies of three topics under the general theme, "The Lutheran Church Today." These commissions will consist of nine men each, six from each of the three groups with three others to collaborate. The German commission will prepare the study on "The Church, Word and Sacrament." The Scandinavian commission will prepare the study on "The Church and the Churches." The American commission is to make a study of the subject, "The Church and the World." The American commission which has been appointed consists of: the Rev. Dr. Walton H. Greever, New York City, secretary of The United Lutheran Church in America, chairman; the Rev. Dr. Conrad Bergendoff, president of Augustana College and Theological Seminary, Rock Island, Ill.; the Rev. Dr. Bernhard M. Christensen, president of Augsburg College and Seminary, Minneapolis, Minn.; the Rev. Dr. Thaddeus F. Gullixson, president of Luther Theological Seminary, St. Paul, Minn.; the Rev. Dr. Emil E. Fischer of Philadelphia Lutheran Theological Seminary, and the Rev. Prof. E. C. Fendt of Capital University, Columbus, Ohio. The Rev. Dr. Henry Offermann of the Philadelphia Lutheran Seminary, has been appointed

to collaborate with the German commission, and the Rev. Dr. M. Reu
of the Wartburg Theological Seminary, Dubuque, Iowa, has been named
as a member of the Scandinavian commission. The appointment of a
committee on arrangements and other necessary preliminary plans are
under way now. A request has also been made to the co-operating
churches in America to underwrite a fund of $15,000 which is to be
used for the necessary expenses of printing, publicity, and other in-
cidentals. Since the convention is to be held from May 24 to June 2,
1940, it is requested that all the co-operating Lutheran bodies in
America name their delegates to the convention as soon as possible.

RELIEF PROGRAM

Archbishop Eidem ably supported by Bishop Rohde and Professor
Wollmer, presented a strong plea for a more adequate support of the
Ukrainian Movement. The Swedish National Committee and the Martin
Luther Bund have been furnishing the major portion of the support
which has gone to the Ukranian Movement in the past several years.
Additional funds are necessary at this time if the work is to be continued
and developed. It was therefore resolved to make an earnest effort to
increase the support so that additional pastors can be called.

The question of relief for our brethren in Russia also came up for
serious discussion. It was reported that the support of one hundred
families of Lutheran pastors and other martyrs requires at least $26,000
per annum, and that there is a likelihood that the need will become
greater. It is still possible through trusted channels to administer relief.
Only by co-operation is it possible for the Lutherans of the world to
assist their breathren under persecution in Russia.

Since 1937, when it was agreed to assist the Gossner Mission in the
amount of $9,000 per annum, the situation has become more critical
because of a ruling that no funds can be sent from Germary to the
Gossner field since it is an autonomous church and no longer a German
mission. This makes it necessary to increase the support of this, the
second largest Lutheran mission in the world. Assistance must be given
also to the Breklum Mission in India and the Berlin Mission in China.

Among the minority churches there is also great need, and an item
has been included in the budget for this purpose. There is also an
item of $4,000 in the budget for assistance of individuals, which is used
largely in behalf of refugees. The budget for 1938, which was adopted
by the Executive Committee, is as follows:

The Lutheran Movement in the Ukraine	$14,000.00
Russian Relief	25,000.00
Younger Churches	21,000.00
Minority Churches	8,000.00

Suffering Individuals and Refugees 4,000.00
Administration 7,500.00

Total $79,500.00

This amount has been allocated to the respective churches in the various countries as follows:

Lutherans in America $26,000.00
            Germany 23,940.00
            Sweden 13,260.00
            Denmark 9,500.00
            Norway 5,300.00
            Finland 1,500.00

            Total $79,500.00

The distribution of the $26,000 which has been allocated to the Lutherans of America is as follows:

For the Ukraine $2,000.00
For Russian Relief 1,000.00
For Younger Churches 19,000.00
For Minority Churches 1,000.00
For Refugees 3,000.00

It should be noted in this connection that the major portion of the support for the Ukraine has been allocated to Sweden and Germany, whereas the major portion for the support of the mission churches has been allocated to the United States, and the major portion for Russian relief is carried by Germany and the Scandinavian countries. It should also be remembered that the $7,500 for administration is borne entirely by Germany. We respectively request the approval of this budget.

Honorable mention is due the women's missionary societies which so wholeheartedly responded to the request to assist in 1938 in the support of the Gossner mission. The women's organizations of the respective churches have contributed the following amounts:

United Lutheran Church $1,500.00
American Lutheran Church 900.00
Augustana Synod 600.00
United Danish Church 50.00

It is evident that if we are to raise the full amount that has been allocated to us in America we shall have to have a much wider co-operation on the part of local congregations than we have had in the past several years.

Respectfully submitted,
F. H. KNUBEL,
R. H. LONG,
A. R. WENTZ,
L. W. BOE.

It was moved and carried that the Executive Board be authorized to make the selection of delegates from the U. L. C. A. to the Lutheran World Convention.

Mr. Lawrence F. Speckman, of the Kentucky-Tennessee Synod delegation, presented the following testimonial to the Inner Mission Board for relief service rendered in connection with the 1937 flood:

> The Kentucky-Tennessee Synod offers the following resolutions of appreciation for the work of the Inner Mission Board and the Church during the flood of 1937:
> Whereas, during the months of January and February, 1937, the Ohio River Valley was visited by the worst flood in its history, bringing in its wake devastation and ruin not only to the homes of the people of our congregations, but also to a great number of the churches on its territory;
> And whereas, the prayers of our people for help were immediately answered by our loving Heavenly Father, and relief was directed through the instrumentality of our Inner Mission Board;
> And whereas, the appeals made by the Inner Mission Board were heard by our brethren throughout the United Lutheran Church, and most generous contributions were made of money and clothing—(how much was given and distributed is printed in the pamphlet entitled "Flood, Fire and Drought");
> And whereas, without this help some of our churches would probably not have been able to rehabilitate themselves, and would have been lost forever to our Church,
> Therefore, we the members of the Kentucky-Tennessee Synod, and on behalf of the congregations whom we represent, do hereby declare before this convention of The United Lutheran Church in America our gratitude and heartfelt thanks to our Heavenly Father, to the Inner Mission Board, and to the "Church that cared," for the spiritual and material gifts which have so graciously been bestowed upon us in our time of distress. The love of the brethren has been truly said to be real and tangible, of which we here bear witness.
>
> DAVID M. FUNK, *President of Synod,*
> CLAYTON A. ROBERTSON,
> JAMES M. WOOD,
> LAWRENCE F. SPECKMAN.

The Rev. S. W. Herman presented the report of the Lutheran Historical Society:

THE LUTHERAN HISTORICAL SOCIETY

The Historical Society of the United Lutheran Church, owing to the absence of its Curator, has postponed its meeting scheduled for this week, to next summer, to be held in connection with a meeting of seminary professors, when subjects of historical interest will be considered and important projects undertaken.

We would report that the work of the Curator during the past biennium has been largely the routine of filing papers and periodicals, getting minutes of Synods, binding pamphlets and magazines, and responding to requests for information. Requests for historical information have been received increasingly from individuals and congregations. Universities and the Library of Congress continue to refer their research students to our collection of materials.

We share our duplicates with Lutheran libraries and occasionally effect valuable exchange of materials. Hundreds of bound volumes of pamphlets and other materials have been made available through our own binding machinery.

Every effort continues to be made by our Curator to keep our collection as complete as possible, and he urges the co-operation of synodical secretaries and local historians in forwarding to our files any books or papers that might be used by Lutheran historians of the future— Synodical minutes, congregational histories, unpublished letters and manuscripts that treat of the life of Lutheran organizations or Lutheran personalities. Such materials, seemingly unimportant, sometimes become most important for a historian. Our shelves and vault are offered as a repository for all such material.

The resignation of Mr. J. Elmer Musselman, as Treasurer, has been received. Mr. I. C. Bucher of Gettysburg, has been appointed to that office.

The following are the officers:

President, Rev. S. W. Herman.
Vice Presidents, Rev. W. J. Finck, Rev. John C. Horine, Rev. O. F. Blackwelder, Mr. Addison A. Freeman.
Recording Secretary, Rev. Prof. H. C. Alleman.
Treasurer, Mr. I. C. Bucher.
Curator, Rev. Prof. A. R. Wentz.

Additional members of the Executive Committee: Rev. G. Morris Smith, and Rev. H. F. Baughman.

The Rev. G. H. Bechtold presented the report of the Lutheran Church Book and Literature Society:

THE LUTHERAN CHURCH BOOK AND LITERATURE SOCIETY

During the biennuim the Lutheran Church Book and Literature Society has continued the free distribution of literature of the United Lutheran Church. These gifts included Common Service Books, Parish and School Hymnals, Hymns and Prayers, Kirchenbuch, Luther's Small Catechism, Augsburg Sunday school quarterlies and tracts.

Donations were made to congregations scattered from Manitoba to South Carolina, to hospitals, public institutions, and to Lutheran army and navy chaplains.

Plans are under way for the wider distribution of Luther's Small Catechism, and the preparation of materials suitable for the use of shut-ins.

Greater service to the Church depends entirely on an increase in the number of members who will contribute one or more dollars per annum.

The officers, who serve without compensation, are Honorary President, Rev. F. H. Knubel, D.D.; President, Rev. P. Z. Strodach, D.D.; Secretary, Rev. G. H. Bechtold, D.D.; Treasurer, Mr. H. Torrey Walker.

The society wishes to express to the Church its appreciation of the co-operation of the Board of Publication and "The Lutheran."

Respectfully submitted,

G. H. BECHTOLD.

At the request of the Rev. Joseph Sittler, Jr., Chairman, the Rev. S. D. Sigler presented the report of the Committee on Leave of Absence.

REPORT OF COMMITTEE ON LEAVE OF ABSENCE

All of the 277 clerical delegates, elected to this Convention, were present, and out of the 271 lay delegates elected, 264 were present.

The following Synods have a perfect record of attendance, all delegates being registered and all present at all sessions: California, Illinois, Iowa, Kansas, Kentucky-Tennessee, Michigan, Nebraska, Nova Scotia, Slovak Zion, Texas, and Virginia.

Eighty-eight absences were excused, and twenty-two were unexcused.

Respectfully submitted,

JOSEPH SITTLER, JR., Chairman.

The report was received as information.

On motion the approval of the Minutes of the Eleventh Session, and the printing of the Minutes were referred to the Executive Board.

Dr. Knubel addressed the Convention in a personal strain, expressing appreciation of the honor and confidence manifested in connection with his service as President, and asked the privilege of paying tribute to his fellow workers, the Treasurer and the Secretary.

Following the personal address of Dr. Knubel, the Rev. E. A. Trabert presented the following, which was adopted by the Convention:

There has been one present at this Convention, as she has at many Conventions of The United Lutheran Church in America, seated between our honored President and Secretary. She has been responsible for much of the mechanical work of this body, and deserves our recognition and expression of gratitude. I refer to Miss Mabel Groneberg, the efficient private secretary of the Secretary of The United Lutheran Church in America, Dr. W. H. Greever.

At twelve o'clock, the Convention was closed with the Order for the Closing of Synods.

W. H. GREEVER, Secretary.

LIST OF BOARDS AND ELECTIVE COMMITTEES

1. Executive Board.
2. Commission of Adjudication.
3. Board of Foreign Missions.
4. Board of American Missions and West Indies Mission Board.
5. Board of Education.
6. Board of Social Missions.
7. Board of Publication.
8. Board of Ministerial Pensions and Relief.
9. Parish and Church School Board.
10. Board of Deaconess Work.
11. Committee on Church Papers.
12. Executive Committee of the Laymen's Movement.

LIST OF STANDING COMMITTEES, COMMISSIONS, ETC.

1. Statistical and Church Year Book Committee.
2. Committee on Common Service Book.
3. Committee on Church Music.
4. Committee on German Interests.
5. Committee on Army and Navy Work.
6. Committee on Church Architecture.
7. Committee on Publicity.
8. Committee on Transportation.
9. Necrologist.
10. Archivist.
11. Such other Standing Committees as may be provided for from time to time.

SPECIAL COMMITTEES

1. Committee to Conduct the Opening and Closing Services of Each Session.
2. Committee on Leave of Absence.
3. Committee on Memorials from Constituent Synods.
4. Committee of Reference and Counsel.
5. Committee to Nominate Executive Committee of Laymen's Movement.
6. Committee to Nominate Members of Boards.
7. Committee to Nominate Members of Executive Board and all Elective Commissions or Committees.
8. Committee of Tellers.
9. Committee on Place of Next Convention.
10. Convention Committee on Daily Minutes.

BOARDS AND ELECTIVE COMMITTEES

EXECUTIVE BOARD

President—Rev. F. H. Knubel, D.D., LL.D., S.T.D., Litt.D., 39
East 35th St., New York City.

Secretary—Rev. W. H. Greever, D.D., LL.D., 39 East 35th St.,
New York City.

Treasurer—E. Clarence Miller, LL.D., 1508 Walnut St., Philadelphia, Pa.

Term Expires 1942

Rev. Henry H. Bagger, D.D.; Rev. A. E. Bell, D.D.; Rev. Paul H.
Krauss, D.D.; Mr. J. K. Jensen; James C. Kinard, LL.D.; Hon.
Claude T. Reno.

Term Expires 1940

Rev. E. B. Burgess, D.D., LL.D.; Rev. H. W. A. Hanson, D.D.,
LL.D.; Rev. E. P. Pfatteicher, D.D., Ph.D., LL.D.; Mr. Robert F
Bowe; Robbin B. Wolf, LL.D.; Hon. John L. Zimmerman, LL.D.

COMMISSION OF ADJUDICATION

Vice-President—Rev. L. F. Gruber, D.D., LL.D., 1600 S. 11th
Ave., Maywood, Ill.

Secretary—Rev. George J. Gongaware, D.D., LL.D., 31 Pitt St.,
Charleston, S. C.

Clerk—Hon. James F. Henninger, 1649 Linden St., Allentown, Pa.

Term Expires 1944

Rev. B. H. Pershing, Ph.D., D.D.; Rev. P. W. H. Frederick, D.D.;
F. Wm. Cappelmann, Esq.

Term Expires 1942

Rev. Wm. E. Frey, D.D.; Rev. L. Franklin Gruber, D.D., LL.D.;
Hon. James F. Henninger.

Term Expires 1940

Rev. George J. Gongaware, D.D., LL.D.; Rev. Paul J. Hoh,
S.T.M.; Hon. John F. Kramer.

BOARD OF FOREIGN MISSIONS

President—Rev. G. A. Greiss, D.D., 38 S. Eighth St., Allentown, Pa.

Vice-President—Rev. Samuel Trexler, D.D., 1170 Fifth Ave.,
New York, N. Y.

Recording Secretary—Rev. George Drach, D.D., 18 E. Mt. Vernon
Place, Baltimore, Md.

Treasurer—Mr. George R. Weitzel, 18 E. Mt. Vernon Place, Baltimore, Md.

General Secretaries—Rev. George Drach, D.D.; Rev. M. Edwin Thomas, D.D.

Term Expires 1944

Rev. Joseph B. Baker, D.D.; Rev. Robert D. Clare, D.D.; Rev. J. Harold Mumper; Rev. F. Eppling Reinartz; Mr. John C. Korn; Mr. Claude L. Peterman; George S. Yost, Esq.

Term Expires 1942

Rev. P. O. Bersell, D.D.; Rev. H. H. Beidleman, D.D.; Rev. E. E. Fischer, D.D.; Rev. P. E. Monroe, D.D.; Mr. Warren M. Koons.

Term Expires 1940

Rev. H. C. Brillhart, D.D.; Rev. G. A. Greiss, D.D.; Rev. L. C. Manges, D.D.; Rev. Samuel Trexler, D.D.; Mr. M. P. Moller, Jr.; Mr. W. A. Rast; Mr. S. F. Telleen.

BOARD OF AMERICAN MISSIONS
and
West Indies Mission Board

President—Rev. H. J. Pflum, D.D., 247 Parkside Ave., Buffalo, N. Y.

Vice-President—Rev. J. J. Scherer, Jr., D.D., 1603 Monument Ave., Richmond, Va.

Secretary—Mr. A. H. Durboraw, 1228 Spruce St., Philadelphia, Pa.

Treasurer—Mr. H. Torrey Walker, 1228 Spruce St., Philadelphia, Pa.

Executive Secretary—Rev. Zenan M. Corbe, D.D., 39 East 35th St., New York City.

Assistant Executive Secretary—Rev. Paul Andrew Kirsch, 39 East 35th St., New York City.

Assistant General Superintendent—Rev. J. F. Seibert, D.D., 4137 N. Hamlin St., Chicago, Ill.

Divisional Secretary of English Missions—Rev. A. M. Knudsen, 860 N. Wabash Ave., Chicago, Ill.

Divisional Secretary, Linguistic Interests—Rev. E. A. Tappert, D.D., 39 East 35th St., New York City.

Departmental Secretary of Church Extension and Finance—Mr. H. Torrey Walker, 1228 Spruce St., Philadelphia, Pa.

Term Expires 1944

Rev. Robert H. Ischinger; Rev. George W. Miley, D.D.; Rev. Henry J. Pflum, D.D.; Rev. A. A. Zinck, D.D.; Mr. Philip Glatfelter; James C. Kinard, LL.D.; Elwood M. Rabenold, Esq.

Term Expires 1942

Rev. A. J. Holl, D.D.; Rev. John Schmieder; Rev. Chester S. Simonton, D.D.; Rev. Emil W. Weber, D.D.; A. S. Bauer, Esq.; Mr. Louis Hanson; Heiby W. Ungerer, Esq.

Term Expires 1940

Rev. O. Garfield Beckstrand, D.D.; Rev. Franklin C. Fry; Rev. J. Edward Harms, D.D.; Rev. J. J. Scherer, Jr., D.D.; Mr. Henry Beisler; Mr. A. H. Durboraw; Mr. Wm. Eck.

BOARD OF EDUCATION

President—Rev. Howard R. Gold, D.D., 15 Vaughn Ave., New Rochelle, N. Y.

Executive and Recording Secretary—Rev. Gould Wickey, Ph.D., D.D., 744 Jackson Place, N. W., Washington, D. C.

Treasurer—Mr. Thomas P. Hickman, 744 Jackson Place, N. W., Washington, D. C.

Secretaries:

Rev. Carolus P. Harry, D.D., 744 Jackson Place, N. W., Washington, D. C.

Miss Mary E. Markley, Litt.D., 744 Jackson Place, N. W., Washington, D. C.

Miss Mildred E. Winston, 744 Jackson Place, N. W., Washington, D. C.

Term Expires 1944

Rev. J. L. Deaton, D.D.; Rev. C. F. Koch, D.D.; Rev. Walter H. Traub, D.D., LL.D.; Rev. Abdel Ross Wentz, Ph.D., D.D.; Mr. Howard S. Bechtolt; J. Conrad Seegers, Ph.D.; Levering Tyson, Litt.D.

Term Expires 1942

Rev. Stanley Billheimer, D.D.; Rev. H. J. Black, D.D.; Rev. F. K. Fretz, Ph.D., D.D.; Rev. H. R. Gold, D.D.; Prof. O. F. H. Bert, Sc.D.; Mr. Frederick Henrich; Prof. R. J. Seeger, Ph.D.

Term Expires 1940

Rev. Henry H. Bagger, D.D.; Rev. E. C. Herman, D.D.; Rev. M. L. Stirewalt, D.D.; Rev. A. A. Zinck, D.D.; Mrs. Adelaide Burge; Miss Flora Prince; Hon. Charles Steele.

1Stop

BOARD OF SOCIAL MISSIONS

Executive Secretary—Rev. C. E. Krumbholz, D.D., 39 East 35th St., New York City.

Secretary for Immigrant Work—Rev. E. A. Sievert, 219 Seventh Ave., New York City.

Treasurer—Mr. Carl H. Lammers, 39 East 35th St., New York City.

Term Expires 1944

Rev. G. H. Bechtold, D.D.; Rev. C. B. Foelsch, Ph.D.; Rev. Franklin Clark Fry; Rev. Harold S. Miller; Carl M. Distler, Esq.; Mr. W. H. Hager; Harry C. Hoffman, M.D.

Term Expires 1942

Rev. H. Brezing, D.D.; Rev. E. E. Flack, Th.D., D.D., S.T.M.; Rev. F. K. Fretz, Ph.D., D.D.; Rev. F. W. Otterbein, D.D.; Mr. H. E. Isenhour; Mr. J. W. Jouno; Mr. L. Henry Lund.

Term Expires 1940

Rev. P. D. Brown, D.D.; Rev. P. H. Heisey, Ph.D., D.D.; Rev. R. E. Kern; Rev. G. Morris Smith, D.D.; Mr. T. P. Hickman; Mr. John George Kurzenknabe; Mr. Carl H. Lammers.

BOARD OF PUBLICATION

President—Rev. S. W. Herman, D.D., 121 State St., Harrisburg, Pa.

Vice-President—Mr. E. G. Hoover, 25 N. Third St., Harrisburg, Pa.

Secretary—Rev. J. Henry Harms, D.D., 2111 Sansom St., Philadelphia, Pa.

Treasurer and Business Manager—.., 1228 Spruce St., Philadelphia, Pa.

Term Expires 1944

Rev. H. F. Baughman, D.D.; Rev. Lloyd M. Keller; Rev. Joseph Sittler, Sr., D.D.; Rev. Russell D. Snyder, D.D.; F. Wm. Cappelmann, Esq.; Mr. Clarence C. Dittmer; Mr. H. F. Heuer.

Term Expires 1942

Rev. Oscar F. Blackwelder, D.D.; Rev. S. W. Herman, D.D.; Rev. J. J. Scherer, Jr., D.D.; L. Russell Alden, Esq.; Mr. Henry Beisler; Mr. James L. Fisher; Mr. E. G. Hoover.

Term Expires 1940

Rev. J. Aberly, D.D., LL.D.; Rev. J. Henry Harms, D.D.; Rev. George W. Nicely, D.D.; Mr. Robert D. Raeder; Mr. W. G. Semisch; J. Myron Shimer, Esq.

BOARD OF MINISTERIAL PENSIONS AND RELIEF

President—Mr. Belding B. Slifer, 236 Summit Ave., Jenkintown, Pa.

Vice-President—William H. Emhardt, Esq., 5521 Germantown Ave., Philadelphia, Pa.

Executive Secretary—Mr. Harry Hodges, 1228 Spruce St., Philadelphia, Pa.

Treasurer—Mr. W. G. Semisch, Integrity Trust Co., 16th and Walnut Sts., Philadelphia, Pa.

Term Expires 1944

Mr. G. Harry Ditter; Mr. Francis Seiberling; Mr. Belding B. Slifer; Mr. Ralph L. Smith; Mr. D. F. Yost.

Term Expires 1942

Rev. J. H. Reble, D.D.; William H. Emhardt, Esq.; William A. Granville, Ph.D., LL.D.; Mr. H. J. Herbst; W. T. Stauffer, Esq

Term Expires 1940

Rev. E. C. J. Kraeling, D.D.; Mr. J. Henry Frick; Mr. J. C. Rovensky; Mr. Edward Schoeppe; Mr. W. G. Semisch.

PARISH AND CHURCH SCHOOL BOARD

President—Rev. F. R. Knubel, D.D., 330 Barrington St., Rochester, N. Y.

Vice-President—Rev. Wm. C. Schaeffer, Jr., D.D., 18 S. 14th St., Allentown, Pa.

Secretary—Rev. D. Burt Smith, D.D., 1228 Spruce St., Philadelphia, Pa.

Treasurer—Rev. C. P. Wiles, D.D., 1228 Spruce St., Philadelphia, Pa.

Executive Secretary—Rev. S. White Rhyne, D.D., 1228 Spruce St., Philadelphia, Pa.

Associate Secretaries—

Field—Rev. C. H. B. Lewis, D.D., 748 E. Military Ave., Fremont, Nebr.

Leadership Education—Rev. Arthur H. Getz, 1228 Spruce St., Philadelphia, Pa.

Editors—

Rev. Chas. P. Wiles, D.D., 1228 Spruce St., Philadelphia, Pa.

Rev. D. Burt Smith, D.D., 1228 Spruce St., Philadelphia, Pa.

Rev. Theodore K. Finck, 1228 Spruce St., Philadelphia, Pa.

Assistant Editor—Miss Mabel Elsie Locker, 1228 Spruce St., Philadelphia, Pa.

Term Expires 1944

Rev. Paul J. Hoh, S.T.M.; Rev. Paul H. Krauss, D.D.; Rev. Earl S. Rudisill; W. E. Tilberg, Ph.D.

Term Expires 1942

Rev. R. Homer Anderson, D.D.; Rev. Paul H. Heisey, Ph.D., D.D.; Rev. Wm. C. Shaeffer, Jr., D.D.; Mr. Clarence C. Dittmer.

Term Expires 1940

Rev. P. D. Brown, D.D.; Rev. Carl C. Rasmussen, D.D.; Rev. Amos J. Traver, D.D.; Mrs. Virgil B. Sease.

BOARD OF DEACONESS WORK

President—Rev. H. D. Hoover, D.D., Ph.D., S.T.D., Litt.D., Gettysburg, Pa.

Vice-President—Rev. L. A. Thomas, D.D., Lincolnton, N. C.

Executive Secretary—Rev. William A. Wade, D.D., 1905 Thomas Ave., Baltimore, Md.

Treasurer—Frederick J. Singley, Esq., 215 N. Charles St., Baltimore, Md.

Term Expires 1944

Rev. P. S. Baringer; Rev. Lewis A. Speaker, D.D.; Mrs. George H. Haase; Mr. Harry R. Hagerty; Mrs. Orville A. Sardeson.

Term Expires 1942

Rev. J. J. Schindel, D.D.; Rev. Allen L. Benner, D.D.; Rev. L. A. Thomas, D.D.; Mr. E. S. Gerberich; Frederick J. Singley, Esq.

Term Expires 1940

Rev. H. D. Hoover, D.D., Ph.D., S.T.D., Litt.D.; Rev. U. S. G. Rupp, D.D.; Rev. W. C. Schaeffer, Jr., D.D.; Mrs. Elsie Singmaster Lewars; Mr. C. C. Stoughton.

COMMITTEE ON CHURCH PAPERS

Chairman—Rev. Hermann F. Miller, D.D., 527 Washington St., Reading, Pa.

Secretary—Rev. H. F. Baughman, D.D., 3123 Queen Lane, Philadelphia, Pa.

Term Expires 1944

Rev. Hermann F. Miller, D.D.; Rev. John W. Horine, D.D., LL.D.; Hon. E. F. Eilert, C.S.D.

Term Expires 1942

Rev. H. C. Alleman, D.D.; Rev. A. J. Holl, D.D.; C. G. Shatzer, Sc.D.

Term Expires 1940

Rev. Harry F. Baughman, D.D.; Rev. C. E. Gardner, D.D.; Rev. C. A. Linn, Ph.D.

EXECUTIVE COMMITTEE OF THE LAYMEN'S MOVEMENT

Chairman—Mr. J. L. Clark, Ashland, Ohio.

Executive Secretary—Mr. Arthur P. Black, 700 Chandler Bldg., 1427 Eye St., N. W., Washington, D. C.

Treasurer—Mr. Harold U. Landis, Palmyra, Pa.

Chairman of the Administrative Committee—Mr. William H. Hager, Lancaster, Pa.

H. J. Albrecht; J. L. Clark; P. H. Glatfelter; Peter P. Hagan; W. H. Hager; E. G. Hoover; E. Clarence Miller, LL.D.; M. P. Moller, Jr.; S. F. Telleen; Hon. Charles B. Zimmerman.

STANDING COMMITTEES

STATISTICAL AND CHURCH YEAR BOOK COMMITTEE

Secretary of The United Lutheran Church in America, ex-officio (Convener), 39 East 35th St., New York, N. Y.; Rev. Ira F. Frankenfield; Rev. J. D. Krout, D.D.; Mr. Harry E. Pugh; Rev. Edward T. Horn, III; Miss Mary E. Boozer.

Corresponding Members—The official statisticians of the Constituent Synods.

COMMITTEE ON COMMON SERVICE BOOK

Rev. L. D. Reed, D.D., A.E.D. (Convener), 7204 Boyer St., Mt. Airy, Philadelphia, Pa.; Rev. Robert D. Clare, D.D.; Rev. E. E. Fischer, D.D.; Rev. H. D. Hoover, Ph.D., D.D., S.T.D., Litt.D.; Rev. E. F. Keever, D.D.; Rev. Willard A. Allbeck, Ph.D.; Rev. J. F. Ohl, D.D., Mus.D.; Rev. H. J. Pflum, D.D.; Rev. Paul E. Scherer, D.D.; LL.D., Litt.D.; Rev. George R. Seltzer, S.T.M., Ph.D.; Rev. Carl R. Simon; Rev. M. L. Stirewalt, D.D.; Rev. P. Z. Strodach, D.D.; Rev. C. P. Swank, D.D., S.T.D.; Rev. W. R. Seaman, S.T.D.

COMMITTEE ON CHURCH MUSIC

Rev. G. C. Rees, D.D. (Convener), 211 South Main St., North Wales, Pa.; Rev. Paul M. Brosy, S.T.M.; Rev. H. Grady Davis; Rev. E. F. Krauss, D.D.; Rev. George R. Seltzer, S.T.M., Ph.D.; Rev. E. A. Trabert, D.D.; Mr. William Benbow; Ralph P. Lewars, Mus.D.; Harold K. Marks, Mus.D.; Rob Roy Peery, Mus.D.; Prof. Carl P. Pfatteicher, Th.D.; Henry F. Seibert, Mus. D.; Harry A. Sykes, Mus. D.; Prof. J. C. Williams.

COMMITTEE ON GERMAN INTERESTS

Rev. E. C. J. Kraeling, D.D. (Convener), 132 Henry St., Brooklyn, N. Y.; Rev. S. G. von Bosse; Rev. F. O. Evers; Rev. F. Flothmeier; Rev. L. A. Fritsch, D.D.; Rev. R. H. Ischinger; Rev. H. A. Kropp; Rev. Kurt E. B. Molzahn; Rev. J. L. Neve, D.D., D.Th.; Rev. T. O. Posselt, D.D.; Rev. J. H. Reble, D.D.; Rev. C. R. Tappert, D.D.; Rev. Theodore Buch, D.D.; Rev. Wm. F. Herrmann; Rev. Wilfried C. H. Tappert, Th.M.

Corresponding Members—The presidents of the Manitoba, Midwest, Texas, and Wartburg Synods.

COMMITTEE ON ARMY AND NAVY WORK

Rev. Charles Trexler, D.D. (Convener), 100-11 Herrick Ave., Forest Hills, N. Y.; Rev. J. F. Fedders, D.D.; Rev. R. H. Gearhart, Jr., D.D.; Rev. C. E. Krumbholz, D.D.; Rev. Henry Manken, Jr.; Rev. Harold S. Miller; Rev. Emil W. Weber, D.D.; Mr. Chas. H. Dahmer.

COMMITTEE ON CHURCH ARCHITECTURE

Rev. L. D. Reed, D.D., A.E.D. (Convener), 7204 Boyer St., Mt. Airy, Philadelphia, Pa.; Rev. Wm. H. Cooper; Rev. J. L. Deaton, D.D.; Rev. H. S. Kidd; Rev. E. F. Krauss, D.D.; Rev. G. H. Schnur, D.D.; Rev. Bela Shetlock; Rev. E. A. Trabert, D.D.; Mr. Frank P. Albright; Prof. Warren P. Laird, Sc.D., LL.D.; Mr. Luther M. Leisenring; Mr. Charles F. Obenhack; Mr. Charles A. Scheuringer; Rev. Ellerslie R. Lebo; Mr. Herbert E. Matz.

COMMITTEE ON PUBLICITY

Secretary of The United Lutheran Church in America, ex-officio (Convener); Rev. C. K. Fegley; Rev. A. R. Naus; Rev. L. W. Rupp.

Corresponding Members—The official publicity appointees of the constituent Synods.

COMMITTEE ON TRANSPORTATION

Rev. W. H. Greever, D.D., LL.D. (Convener), 39 East 35th St., New York, N. Y.; Rev. J. M. Bramkamp, D.D., 1901 S. 19th Ave., Maywood, Ill.; Mr. W. H. Patrick, 7000 Lincoln Parkway, Germantown, Philadelphia, Pa.

NECROLOGIST

Rev. James F. Lambert, D.D., 415 Howertown Ave., Catasauqua, Pa.

ARCHIVIST

Rev. L. D. Reed, D.D., A.E.D., 7204 Boyer St., Mt. Airy, Philadelphia, Pa.

COMMISSIONERS TO THE NATIONAL LUTHERAN COUNCIL

Rev. E. P. Pfatteicher, Ph.D., D.D., LL.D. (Convener), 1228 Spruce St., Philadelphia, Pa.; Rev. E. B. Burgess, D.D., LL.D.; Rev. M. R. Hamsher, D.D.; Rev. C. E. Krumbholz, D.D.; Hon. E. F. Eilert, C.S.D.; G. F. Greiner, Esq.; Rev. R. E. Tulloss, Ph.D., D.D., LL.D.; Rev. Armin George Weng, Ph.D.; Rev. P. D. Brown, D.D.; Rev. G. H. Bechtold, D.D.; Rev. A. A. Zinck, D.D., S.T.M.

REPRESENTATIVE ON THE ADVISORY COMMITTEE OF THE AMERICAN BIBLE SOCIETY

E. Clarence Miller, LL.D., 1508 Walnut St., Philadelphia, Pa.

CONSULTATIVE REPRESENTATIVES TO COMMISSIONS OF THE FEDERAL COUNCIL OF CHURCHES

Executive Committee: Rev. Zenan M. Corbe, D. D., Rev. C. E. Krumbholz, D.D., 39 E. 35th St., New York, N. Y.

Department of Social Service: Rev. W. H. Greever, D.D., LL.D., 39 E. 35th St., New York, N. Y.

Department of Radio: Rev. W. H. Greever, D.D., LL.D., 39 E. 35th St., New York, N. Y.

Committee on Worship: Rev. L. D. Reed, D.D., A.E.D., 7204 Boyer St., Mt. Airy, Philadelphia, Pa.

COMMITTEE TO PREPARE A STATEMENT CONCERNING RELATIONS OF CHURCH AND STATE

Rev. F. K. Fretz, Ph.D., D.D.; Rev. Abdel Ross Wentz, Ph.D., D.D.

COMMISSION ON WORLD CONFERENCE ON FAITH AND ORDER

Rev. John Aberly, D.D., LL.D. (Chairman), Gettysburg, Pa.; Rev. E. E. Flack, Th.D., D.D., S.T.M.; Rev. W. H. Greever, D.D., LL.D.; Rev. Abdel Ross Wentz, Ph.D., D.D.

COMMISSION ON INVESTMENTS

Chairman—Mr. Wm. H. Stackel, 103 East Main St., Rochester, N. Y.

Secretary—

Members elected by the Executive Board:

Mr. S. F. Telleen (term expires 1944); Rev. R. E. Tulloss, Ph.D., D.D., LL.D. (term expires 1943); Robbin B. Wolf, LL.D. (term expires 1942); Mr. Wm. H. Stackel (term expires 1941); Mr. W. G. Semisch (term expires 1940).

Members Ex-Officio:
President of The United Lutheran Church in America—Rev.
F. H. Knubel, D.D., LL.D., S.T.D., Litt.D.
Treasurer of The United Lutheran Church in America—E.
Clarence Miller, LL.D.
Members elected by their respective Board or Agency:
Miss Flora Prince, the Women's Missionary Society.
Mr. George R. Weitzel, the Board of Foreign Missions.
Mr. Heiby W. Ungerer, the Board of American Missions.
Hon. Charles Steele, the Board of Education.
Mr. Belding B. Slifer, the Board of Ministerial Pensions and
Relief.

SPECIAL COMMISSION ON RELATIONS TO AMERICAN LUTHERAN CHURCH BODIES

Rev. F. H. Knubel, D.D., LL.D., S.T.D., Litt.D. (Chairman),
39 East 35th St., New York, N. Y.; Rev. Henry H. Bagger, D.D.;
Rev. Paul H. Krauss, D.D.; Rev. H. Offermann, D.D.; Hon. E. F.
Eilert, C.S.D.; Mr. J. K. Jensen; E. Clarence Miller, LL.D.; Mr.
Edward Rinderknecht; Rev. Paul H. Roth, D.D.

COMMITTEE ON ORGANIZED WORK WITH CHILDREN

Rev. W. H. Greever, D.D., LL.D. (Chairman), 39 East 35th St.,
New York, N. Y.; Rev. Chester S. Simonton, D.D.; Mrs. A. J.
Fenner; Rev. Paul M. Kinports, D.D.; Rev. S. White Rhyne, D.D.

COMMITTEE FOR NEW PENSION PLAN

E. Clarence Miller, LL.D. (Chairman), 1508 Walnut St., Phila-
delphia, Pa.; Rev. J. Sittler, D.D.; Rev. William F. Buch, D.D.; Rev.
W. E. Frey, D.D.; Rev. Jacob Diehl, D.D., LL.D.; Mr. B. B. Slifer;
Mr. Arthur P. Black.

COMMITTEE ON CENTENNIAL TOUR TO INDIA

Rev. George A. Rupley (Convener), 314 Dewey Ave., Buffalo,
N. Y.; Rev. F. J. Fiedler; Rev. E. J. Mollenauer; Mr. M. P. Moller,
Jr.; Mr. Carl Schulz; Rev. C. C. Hine; Rev. Dallas C. Baer.

COMMITTEE TO DEFINE CHURCH PAPER POLICY

Rev. Hermann F. Miller, D.D. (Convener), 527 Washington St.,
Reading, Pa.; Mrs. C. E. Gardner; Mr. J. Milton Deck; Mr. John G.
Kurzenknabe; Rev. G. A. Greiss, D.D.; Rev. J. J. Scherer, Jr., D.D.;
Rev. H. F. Baughman, D.D.; Rev. S. White Rhyne, D.D.; Rev.
Charles A. Puls; Mr. Henry Beisler.

COMMITTEE ON INVITATIONS TO CONVENTIONS

Rev. Paul H. Krauss, D.D. (Convener), 405 W. Wayne St., Ft. Wayne, Ind.; Rev. Paul C. Empie; Rev. Russell F. Auman.

COMMISSION ON THEOLOGICAL EDUCATION

To be appointed by the Executive Board.

CORPORATE TITLES

The United Lutheran Church in America, 39 East 35th Street, New York City.

The Board of Foreign Missions of the United Lutheran Church in America, 18 East Mt. Vernon Place, Baltimore, Md.

The Board of American Missions of the United Lutheran Church in America, 39 East 35th St., New York City.

The Board of Education of the United Lutheran Church in America, 744 Jackson Pl., N. W., Washington, D. C.

The Board of Social Missions of the United Lutheran Church in America, 39 East 35th Street, New York City.

The Board of Publication of the United Lutheran Church in America, 1228 Spruce Street, Philadelphia, Pa.

Board of Ministerial Pensions and Relief of the United Lutheran Church in America, 1228 Spruce St., Philadelphia, Pa.

The Parish and Church School Board of the United Lutheran Church in America, 1228 Spruce St., Philadelphia, Pa.

The Board of Deaconess Work of the United Lutheran Church in America, 2500 W. North Avenue, Baltimore, Md.

The Women's Missionary Society of the United Lutheran Church in America, 1228 Spruce St., Philadelphia, Pa.

Evangelical Lutheran Seminary of Canada, Waterloo, Ontario, Canada.

The Theological Seminary of the Evangelical Lutheran Church at Chicago, Ill., 11th Avenue & Harrison Street, Maywood, Ill.

The Theological Seminary of the General Synod of the Evangelical Lutheran Church in the United States and of the United Lutheran Church in America, Gettysburg, Pa.

The Hartwick Seminary, 83 Christopher Street, New York, N. Y.

Northwestern Lutheran Theological Seminary, 1018 Nineteenth Ave., N. E., Minneapolis, Minn.

Pacific Theological Seminary of the Evangelical Lutheran Church, 4300 E. 45th St., Seattle, Wash.

The Lutheran Theological Seminary at Philadelphia, 7301 Germantown Ave., Mt. Airy, Philadelphia, Pa.

The Lutheran College and Seminary, Saskatoon, Sask., Canada.

Trustees of the Lutheran Theological Southern Seminary, at Columbia, S. C.

The Western Theological Seminary of the United Lutheran Church in America, Fremont, Nebr.

Carthage College, Carthage, Ill.

Gettysburg College, Gettysburg, Pa.

Lenoir-Rhyne College, Hickory, N. C.

Marion Female College (known as Marion Junior College), Marion, Va.

Midland College of the United Lutheran Church in America, Fremont, Nebr.

Muhlenberg College, Located at Allentown, Lehigh County, Pennsylvania.

Newberry College, Newberry, S. C.

The Trustees of Roanoke College, at Salem, Va.

Susquehanna University, Selinsgrove, Pa.

Trustees of Thiel College of the Evangelical Lutheran Church, Greenville, Pa.

Wagner Memorial Lutheran College, Staten Island, N. Y.

The Board of Directors of Wittenberg College, Springfield, Ohio.

Hartwick College, Oneonta, N. Y.

Hartwick Academy, Hartwick Seminary, N. Y.

Lutheran Orphans' Home in Berks County, Pennsylvania.

Tressler Orphans' Home of the Evangelical Lutheran Church of the General Synod in the United States of America, Loysville, Pa.

The Zelienople Orphans' Home Board of Directors of the Pittsburgh Synod of the Evangelical Lutheran Church, Zelienople, Pa.

The Oesterlen Orphans' Home of the United Lutheran Church of North America, located at Springfield, Ohio.

The Lutheran Orphan Home of the South, located at Salem, Va.

The Nachusa Lutheran Orphanage, Nachusa, Ill.

Wartburg Orphans' Farm School of the Evangelical Lutheran Church, in the State of New York, Mount Vernon, N. Y.

Evangelical Lutheran St. John's Orphan Home at Buffalo and Sulphur Springs, N. Y., "Station D," Buffalo, N. Y.

Old People's Home of the Pittsburgh Synod of the Evangelical Lutheran Church, at Zelienople, Pa.

Evangelical Lutheran Charities Society of Charleston, S. C. (for The Jacob Washington Franke Lutheran Hospital and Home), Charleston, S. C.

The Association of the Lutheran Church Home for the Aged and Infirm of Buffalo, N. Y.

The Lutheran Church Home for the Aged and Infirm of Central New York, Inc., Clinton, N. Y. (Office at Utica, N. Y.)

The National Lutheran Home for the Aged, Washington, D. C.

The Feghtly Lutheran Home, Tipp City, Ohio.

Lowman Home for the Aged and Helpless, White Rock, S. C.

Lutheran Home for the Aged, of Erie, Pennsylvania.

Lutheran Inner Mission Society of the State of Connecticut, Inc. Owner of "Lutheran Home for the Aged, Southbury, Conn."

Tabitha Home, Lincoln, Nebr.

Emaus Orphan House, Middletown, Pa.

Lutheran Home for Orphans and Aged at Germantown, 6950 Germantown Ave., Philadelphia, Pa.

The Good Shepherd Home, Allentown, Pa.

The Auxiliary Board of the Passavant Memorial Homes for the Care of Epileptics, Rochester, Pa.

Bethesda Home of the Pittsburgh Synod of the Evangelical Lutheran Church, Crawford Co., Pa.

APPENDIX

CONSTITUTION AND BY-LAWS

of

The United Lutheran Church
in America

REVISED TO 1938

The Constitution of The United Lutheran Church in America

PREAMBLE

In the Name of the Father, and of the Son, and of the Holy Spirit. Amen.

Having been called by the Gospel and made partakers of the grace of God, and, by faith, members of our Lord and Saviour Jesus Christ, and, through Him, of one another,

We, members of Evangelical Lutheran congregations in America, associated in Evangelical Lutheran Synods, recognizing our duty as people of God to make the inner unity which we have with one another manifest in the common confession, defense and maintenance of our faith, and in united efforts for the extension of the Kingdom of God at home and abroad; realizing the vastness of the field that God has assigned us for our labors in this Western world, and the greatness of the resources within our beloved Church which are only feebly employed for this purpose; conscious of our need of mutual assistance and encouragement; and relying upon the promise of the divine Word that He who hath begun this work will perfect it until the day of Christ Jesus,

Hereby unite, and now invite and until such end be attained continue to invite all Evangelical Lutheran congregations and synods in America, one with us in the faith, to unite with us, upon the terms of this Constitution, in one general organization, to be known as THE UNITED LUTHERAN CHURCH IN AMERICA.

CONSTITUTION

ARTICLE I

NAME

The name and title of the body organized under this Constitution shall be THE UNITED LUTHERAN CHURCH IN AMERICA.

ARTICLE II

DOCTRINAL BASIS

Section 1. The United Lutheran Church in America receives and holds the canonical Scriptures of the Old and New Testaments as the inspired Word of God, and as the only infallible rule and standard of faith and practice, according to which all doctrines and teachers are to be judged.

Section 2. The United Lutheran Church in America accepts the three ecumenical creeds: namely, the Apostles, the Nicene, and the Athanasian, as important testimonies drawn from the Holy Scriptures, and rejects all errors which they condemn.

Section 3. The United Lutheran Church in America receives and holds the Unaltered Augsburg Confession as a correct exhibition of the faith and doctrine of the Evangelical Lutheran Church, founded upon the Word of God; and acknowledges all churches that sincerely hold and faithfully confess the doctrines of the Unaltered Augsburg Confession to be entitled to the name of Evangelical Lutheran.

Section 4. The United Lutheran Church in America recognizes the Apology of the Augsburg Confession, the Smalkald Articles, the Large and Small Catechisms of Luther, and the Formula of Concord, as in the harmony of one and the same pure Scriptural faith.

ARTICLE III

PRINCIPLES OF ORGANIZATION

In accordance with the foregoing Doctrinal Basis, The United Lutheran Church in America sets forth and declares the following principles as fundamental to its organization:

Section 1. All power in the Church belongs primarily and exclusively to our Lord and Saviour Jesus Christ, the Head of the Church. This power is not delegated to any man or body of men.

Section 2. All just power exercised by the Church has been committed to her for the furtherance of the Gospel through the Word and sacraments, and is conditioned by this end and pertains to her as the servant of Jesus Christ. The Church, therefore, has no power to bind the conscience except as she teaches what her Lord teaches and faithfully commands what He has charged her to command.

Section 3. Congregations are the primary bodies through which power committed by Christ to the Church is normally exercised.

Section 4. In addition to the pastors of churches, who are *ex officio* representatives of their congregations, the people have the right to choose representatives from their own number to act for them under such constitutional limitations as the congregations may approve.

Section 5. The representatives of congregations convened in Synod and acting in accordance with their Constitution are, for the ends defined in it representatively the congregations themselves, and have the right to call and set apart ministers for the common work of all the congregations; whose representatives they thereby become, and as such also members of the Synod.

Section 6. Congregations representatively constituting the various Synods may elect delegates through those Synods to represent them in a general body, all decisions of which, when made in accordance with the Constitution, bind so far as the terms of mutual agreement make them binding, those congregations and Synods which consent to be represented in the general body.

Section 7. In the formation and administration of a general body, the Synods may know and deal with each other only as Synods. In all such cases, the official record is to be accepted as evidence of the doctrinal position of each Synod and of the principles for which alone the other Synods are responsible by connection with it.

ARTICLE IV

MEMBERSHIP

Section 1. The United Lutheran Church in America at its organization shall consist of the congregations that compose the Evangelical Lutheran Synods which have been in connection with the General Synod of the Evangelical Lutheran Church in the United States of America, the General Council of the Lutheran Church in North America, or the United

Synod of the Evangelical Lutheran Church in the South, and which accept this Constitution with its Doctrinal Basis as set forth in Article II.

Section 2. Any Evangelical Lutheran Synod applying for admission which has accepted this Constitution with its Doctrinal Basis as set forth in Article II, and whose Constitution has been approved by the Executive Board, may be received into membership by a majority vote at any regular Convention.

ARTICLE V

DELEGATES

Section 1. Each Synod connected with The United Lutheran Church in America shall be entitled to representation at its Conventions by one ordained minister and one layman for every ten pastoral charges or major fraction thereof, on its roll; provided, however, that each Synod shall be entitled to at least one ministerial and one lay delegate; and provided further that the delegates elected by the Synods to the last conventions of the general bodies to which they respectively belong held prior to the first convention hereunder, shall be and they are in the adoption hereof chosen by their respective Synods as their duly elected delegates to said first convention hereunder, irrespective of the basis of representation upon which they were chosen. The ratio of representation may be changed at any regular Convention of The United Lutheran Church in America by a two-thirds vote, provided that notice of the proposed change has been given at the preceding regular Convention.

Section 2. Each Synod shall choose its delegates in such manner as it may deem proper. The delegates from each Synod shall elect one of their own number as chairman unless the Synod itself has designated the chairman.

ARTICLE VI

OBJECTS

The objects of The United Lutheran Church in America are:

Section 1. To preserve and extend the pure teaching of the Gospel and the right administration of the sacraments. (Eph. 4 : 5, 6; The Augsburg Confession, Article VII.)

Section 2. To conserve the unity of the true faith (Eph. 4 : 3-16; I Cor. 1 : 10), to guard against any departure therefrom (Rom. 16 : 17), and to strengthen the Church in faith and confession.

Section 3. To express outwardly the spiritual unity of Lutheran congregations and synods, to cultivate co-operation among all Lutherans in the promotion of the general interests of the Church, to seek the unification of all Lutherans in one orthodox faith, and thus to develop and unfold the specific Lutheran principle and practice and make their strength effective.

Section 4. To awaken, co-ordinate and effectively direct the energies of the Church in such operations as the following:

(a). The training of ministers and teachers to be witnesses of the Word.

(b). The extension of the kingdom of God by Home, Foreign and Inner Missions.

(c). The proper regulation of the human externals of worship, that the same, in character and administration, may be in keeping with the New Testament and the liberty of the Church, and may edify the Body of Christ.

(d). The appointment of editorial committees or editors of Church papers and Sunday school literature.

(e). The preparation and publication of such literature as shall promote the dissemination of knowledge as to the doctrines, practice, progress, and needs of the Lutheran Church.

(f). The creation, organization and development, through Boards and Committees, of agencies to carry on all departments of work.

Section 5. To lay apportionments, and to solicit and disburse the funds necessary for these and other purposes defined in this Constitution.

Section 6. To foster and develop the work of Synods, to exercise a general supervision of the Church, and on appeal of Synods to give counsel and to adjudicate questions of doctrine, worship and discipline.

Section 7. To enter into relations with other bodies in the unity of the faith and to exchange official delegates with them.

ARTICLE VII
CONVENTIONS

Section 1. A Convention of the duly elected delegates of The United Lutheran Church in America shall be held at least once in every two years, at such time and place as may be determined by the preceding Convention of the body, or by the Executive Board.

Section 2. Special Conventions shall be called by the officers at the request of two-thirds of the members of the Executive Board, or at the request of the presidents of a majority of the Synods. The delegates shall be those who represented the Synods at the previous regular Convention, provided they have not been disqualified by removal or by the election of new delegates. Vacancies in delegations shall be filled according to the rules of the respective Synods.

Section 3. A majority of the delegates representing a majority of the Synods, shall constitute a quorum.

ARTICLE VIII
POWERS

Section 1. *As to External Relations.* The United Lutheran Church in America shall have power to form and dissolve relations with other general bodies, organizations and movements. To secure uniform and consistent practice no Synod, Conference or Board, or any official representative thereof, shall have power of independent affiliation with general organizations and movements.

Section 2. *As to Internal Relations.* The United Lutheran Church in America shall have power to deal with internal matters that affect all its constituent Synods or the activities of The United Lutheran Church as a whole, except that when the operation of such power takes place within the domain of any of the Synods their consent and co-operation must first be secured.

Section 3. *As to Intersynodical Dealings.* The United Lutheran Church in America shall have power to address and counsel its constituent Synods for the promotion of intersynodical harmony. Any question of interpretation of law, rights, or principle, that comes within its jurisdiction, or any proper cases referred to it on appeal of a Synod, shall be determined by a Commission of Adjudication hereinafter provided for.

Section 4. *As to Individual Synods and Specific Cases.* If Synods have had due and legal opportunity to be represented in the Conventions of The United Lutheran Church in America, they are bound by all resolutions that have been passed in accordance with this Constitution. But each Synod retains every power, right and jurisdiction in its own internal affairs not expressly delegated to The United Lutheran Church in America.

Section 5. *As to Doctrine and Conscience.* All matters of doctrine and conscience shall be decided according to the Word of God alone. If, on grounds of doctrine or conscience, the question be raised as to the binding character of any action, the said question shall be referred to the Commission of Adjudication. Under no circumstances shall the right of a minority be disregarded or the right to record an individual protest on the ground of conscience be refused.

Section 6. *As to the Maintenance of Principle and Practice.* The United Lutheran Church in America shall protect and enforce its Doctrinal Basis, secure pure preaching of the Word of God and the right administration of the sacraments in all its Synods and congregations. It shall also have the right, where it deems that loyalty to the Word of God requires it, to advise and admonish concerning association and affiliation with non-ecclesiastical and other organizations whose principles or practices appear to be inconsistent with full loyalty to the Christian Church, but the Synods alone shall have the power of discipline.

Section 7. *As to Books of Devotion and Instruction, etc.* The United Lutheran Church in America shall provide books of devotion and instruction, such as Liturgies, Hymn Books and Catechisms, and no Synod without its sanction shall publish or recommend books of this kind other than those provided by the general body.

Section 8. *As to Work and Administration.* The United Lutheran Church in America shall have the power to engage in the work described under "Objects" (see Article VI), to create and regulate Boards and Committees, to determine budgets, and to lay apportionments.

Section 9. The executive power of The United Lutheran Church in America shall be vested in the officers of the general body, in an Executive Board, and in various other Boards for special purposes, subject to this Constitution and the Conventions of the general body.

ARTICLE IX

OFFICERS

Section 1. The officers of The United Lutheran Church in America shall be a President, a Secretary and a Treasurer. The President shall be an ordained minister of the Church. The officers shall be elected by ballot at each regular Convention, but shall not take office until the first day of the third month after their election.

Section 2. The President shall preside at all sessions of the Convention, shall have the appointment of committees, unless The United Lutheran Church otherwise directs; shall see that the Constitution be observed and resolutions carried out; shall sign all official papers, and shall discharge such other duties as are delegated to him by the Convention.

Section 3. The Secretary shall keep a record of the proceedings, attest all documents of the body, and publish the time and place of the next meeting at least two months in advance. In case of a special meeting he shall give a written notice thereof to the President of each of the Synods immediately upon the issue of the call, and shall publish the same at least thirty days in advance of the meeting.

Section 4. The Treasurer shall receive and disburse all moneys, and keep an account of all his transactions and submit a report of the same at each regular Convention. He shall make disbursements only upon the order of the President, attested by the Secretary. He shall be required to give corporate surety in such amount as shall be determined by the Executive Board.

Section 5. In the event of the death, resignation or incapacity of any officer in the interim between Conventions, the Executive Board shall fill the vacancy.

ARTICLE X

INCORPORATION

The United Lutheran Church in America shall be incorporated.

ARTICLE XI

THE EXECUTIVE BOARD

Section 1. The Executive Board of The United Lutheran Church in America, which shall also be its Board of Trustees, shall consist of the President, the Secretary, and the Treasurer of the general body who shall also be the officers of the Executive Board, together with six ministerial and six lay members who shall be elected by the general body for a term of four years.

Section 2. At the first election three ministerial and three lay members shall be elected to serve four years, and three ministerial and three lay members to serve two years. Thereafter three ministerial and three lay members shall be elected at each regular Convention to serve four years.

Section 3. The Executive Board shall meet at stated times. It shall be the duty of the Executive Board to represent The United Lutheran Church in America and to carry out its resolutions and attend to its business during the interim; it shall co-ordinate the work of the executive departments, receive reports as to the work and needs of the several Boards, present a budget to the Conventions with apportionments, fill vacancies not otherwise provided for, and perform such other work as may be delegated to it by the general body, to which it shall make full report of its acts.

ARTICLE XII

COMMISSION OF ADJUDICATION

Section 1. A Commission of Adjudication shall be established to which shall be referred, for interpretation and decision, all disputed questions of doctrine and practice, and this Commission shall constitute a court for the decision of all questions of principle or action arising within The United Lutheran Church in America, and which have been properly referred to it by resolution or by appeal of any of the Synods.

Section 2. This Commission of Adjudication shall consist of nine members, six ministers and three laymen, learned in the doctrine, the law and the practice of the Church. All of the members of this Commission shall be elected at the first Convention of The United Lutheran Church in America, two ministers and one layman for a period of six years, two ministers and one layman for a period of four years, and two ministers and one layman for a period of two years. As their terms expire their successors shall be elected at each Convention for a term of six years.

Section 3. The Commission shall elect its own officers, and shall meet at least semi-annually for the transaction of business. When it holds meetings, or renders decisions, due notice of the time and place of meeting shall be given by its secretary to all persons interested, and a standing notice of the time and place of its regular meetings shall be published in the Church papers.

Section 4. The consent of at least six members shall always be necessary for a decision.

Section 5. The Commission shall render a written report of all its actions and decisions to the next regular Convention, but the right of appeal from its decisions shall always be recognized.

ARTICLE XIII

BOARDS

Section 1. The United Lutheran Church in America shall determine the number of members in the several Boards which it shall create, and these Boards shall always be amenable to it.

Section 2. All members of Boards shall be elected by The United Lutheran Church in America. Vacancies occurring in any Board ad interim shall be filled by the Executive Board of the Church on nomination of the Board in which the vacancy exists. No person shall be a member of more than one board at one and the same time. No member of any Board, including the Executive Board, shall be a member of the Commission of Adjudication; but the President of The United Lutheran Church shall at all times have a seat and a voice in all the Boards and in the Commission of Adjudication.

Section 3. These Boards, upon the determination of the general body, shall secure articles of incorporation which must be in harmony with the purposes of The United Lutheran Church in America; but no Board shall apply for incorporation until its proposed charter shall have received the approval of the general body in Convention, or, in the interim, of the Executive Board.

Section 4. The Boards, unless otherwise provided, shall have power to elect their own officers and employees, and to carry on their work in accordance with the design of their appointment. No member of a Board shall be a salaried employee thereof.

Section 5. The Boards shall require corporate surety from their respective treasurers. At each regular Convention of The United Lutheran Church in America, they shall render full and accurate reports of their work during the preceding biennium.

Section 6. The Woman's Missionary Society, as auxiliary to Boards of The United Lutheran Church in America, shall have the right to appoint two women as advisory members of each of the missionary and benevolent Boards to the support of whose work they regularly or officially contribute.

ARTICLE XIV

SYNODS

Section 1. No Synod in connection with The United Lutheran Church in America shall alter its geographical boundaries without the permission of the general body.

Section 2. Synods shall give advice to their ministers and congregations concerning doctrine, life and administration, and shall exercise such disciplinary measures as may be necessary.

Section 3. The Presidents of Synods shall exercise an oversight of the pastors and congregations composing their respective Synods, and shall be charged with the duty of carrying out the rules and regulations adopted by the Synods. When requested by the Executive Board they shall appear before it to represent their Synods. They may also make suggestions to the Executive Board, or seek its advice, with respect to the conditions and work in their Synods.

Section 4. Should any Synod in connection with The United Lutheran Church in America desire to continue its established lines of work for reasons satisfactory to the general body, such privilege may be granted.

ARTICLE XV

COMMITTEES, BY-LAWS AND AMENDMENTS

Section 1. The United Lutheran Church in America may appoint special and standing committees. It may adopt By-Laws for the transaction of its business, provided that they do not conflict with this Constitution. These By-Laws may be suspended or amended at any Convention by a two-thirds vote.

Section 2. Amendments to this Constitution must be presented in writing at a regular Convention of The United Lutheran Church in America, which shall decide by a two-thirds vote whether and in what form they shall be submitted to the Synods. An exact copy of proposed amendments shall be transmitted by the Secretary to the Presidents of the Synods for submission to their respective bodies. If at a subsequent Convention two-thirds of the Synods shall report their approval of the amendments proposed they shall be declared adopted.

BY-LAWS

SECTION I

MEETINGS

Item 1. Arrangements for the Conventions of The United Lutheran Church in America shall be made by the officers acting in conjunction with the pastor loci or a local committee appointed for the purpose.

Item 2. Every Convention shall begin with The Service. The sermon shall be preached by the President or someone appointed by him. The first business session shall be opened by the use of the prescribed order.

Item 3. A tentative order of business shall be prepared by the Executive Board. Boards and other representatives of causes desiring to hold meetings in the interest of their specific work shall make request to the Executive Board for a place on the program of the Convention at least two months before the regular meeting. All appointments for religious services and public meetings in the interest of specific causes shall be left with the President.

SECTION II

DELEGATES

Item 1. A roll of the delegates of the Convention of The United Lutheran Church in America shall be prepared by the Secretary prior to each meeting. To facilitate his work each President of a Synod in connection with The United Lutheran Church in America shall forward a list of delegates elected by his Synod to the President and Secretary of the General Body at least 30 days before the meeting, signed by the President and Secretary of the Synod.

Item 2. No changes shall be made in the roll of delegates unless such change is duly authorized by the Synod concerned.

Item 3. In the absence of a quorum the delegates present may adjourn from time to time and postpone the session of the Convention until a quorum shall appear.

Item 4. Delegates, Commissions or representatives from other Lutheran Bodies not in union with The United Lutheran Church in America may be given a voice and a seat, but no vote, in the Convention by a majority vote of the delegates at any meeting.

Item 5. The mileage of all delegates shall be paid from the treasury of The United Lutheran Church, and the apportionment for the treasury shall be made sufficient to cover this expense. Other necessary expenses of delegates shall be provided for as the Synods may determine.

Item 6. Delegates shall not absent themselves from the sessions of the Convention without valid excuse, which shall be presented to the Committee on Leave of Absence. Said committee shall make a final report at the closing session of the Convention. Delegates absenting themselves without being excused shall forfeit their mileage.

SECTION III
RECEPTION OF SYNODS

Item 1. The application of a Synod desiring to be received into The United Lutheran Church in America shall be presented to the Executive Board together with a copy of the Synod's Constitution. Upon recommendation of the Executive Board the Synod may be received in accordance with the Constitution, Article IV, Section 2. The delegates of such Synod upon the approval of their credentials shall at once be seated in the Convention and their names entered upon the roll.

SECTION IV
ELECTIONS

Item 1. At the beginning of every biennial Convention the President shall appoint tellers to conduct the election of officers and Boards in accordance with rules and regulations adopted by the General Body.

Item 2. Election of officers, members of the Executive Board and of the other Boards, including the Commission of Adjudication and all elective Committees, shall be by ballot. The Secretary shall prepare printed ballots for the use of voters in the Convention.

Item 3. In the election of a President, the following rules shall obtain: On the first ballot, three-fourths of all the votes cast shall be necessary to an election. On the second ballot, two-thirds of all the votes cast shall be necessary to an election. If two ballots fail to result in an election, the third ballot shall be confined to the two persons who in the second ballot receive the highest number of votes and no vote cast for any other shall be counted. In the third ballot a majority of the votes shall elect.

Item 4. In the election of the Secretary, Treasurer and members of regular Boards and elective Committees, a majority of the votes cast shall be necessary for an election.

Item 5. The result of each ballot shall be announced by the tellers to the Convention.

SECTION V
BOARDS AND COMMITTEES
A. List of Boards and Elective Committees
There shall be:
1. An Executive Board.
2. A Commission of Adjudication.
3. A Foreign Mission Board.
4. A Board of American Missions.
5. A Board of Northwestern Missions.
6. An Immigrants Mission Board.
7. A West Indies Board.
8. A Board of Education.
9. An Inner Mission Board.
10. A Board of Publication.
11. A Board of Ministerial Pensions and Relief.
12. A Parish and Church School Board.
13. A Board of Deaconess Work.
14. A Committee on Church Papers.
15. An Executive Committee of the Laymen's Movement.

B. Nominations and Appointments
Item 1. In the first Convention the Boards which shall agree to merge their interests in a common Board shall jointly nominate members for such Board. An equal number may be nominated from the floor. In either case the term of each person placed in nomination shall be indicated so that one-third of the members shall serve for two years, one-third for four years and one-third for six years.

Item 2. Thereafter beginning with the second biennial Convention of The United Lutheran Church in America, the term of each regularly elected member shall be six years. Nominations for membership shall be made as follows:

A committee appointed by the President shall nominate a number equal to the number of vacancies on each Board. The Board itself may also nominate a number equal to twice the number of vacancies. If any Board shall fail to make such nominations, the Nominating Committee shall present a sufficient number of nominations so as to present a total equalling three times as many as are to be elected. Nominations may also be made from the floor. Nominations shall not be so construed as to confine voting to the nominees.

Item 3. The membership of Boards of The United Lutheran Church in America shall consist of not less than nine, or more than twenty-one members.

Item 4. No member of any Board shall be eligible for election for more than two successive terms.

Item 5. Early in the session of each Convention of The United Lutheran Church the President shall appoint:

(1). A Nominating Committee of nine ministers and nine laymen to make the nominations necessary to fill all vacancies on the several benevolent Boards. Nominations made by the Boards themselves shall be referred to this Committee as soon as appointed.

(2). A Nominating Committee of nine ministers and nine laymen, to make nominations necessary to fill all vacancies on the Executive Board and on all Commissions and Committees that are to be elected by the Convention.

These Committees shall report at such time as the Convention may designate.

Item 6. A Standing Committee on Church Papers to consist of nine members shall be elected by The United Lutheran Church.

At the first Convention three shall be elected for two years, three for four years and three for six years. Beginning with the second biennium the term for the newly elected members shall be six years.

It shall be the duty of this Committee to select editors of such Church Papers as The United Lutheran Church may recognize, authorize or found. The selection of these editors shall be made, if possible, before or during the Conventions of The United Lutheran Church, and subject to its ratification. If, however, it be impossible to make the selection at the time named the Committee shall have full power to act *ad interim*. The salaries of the editors shall be determined by the Committee and the Board of Publication jointly.

This Committee shall also be charged with the general oversight of the Church Papers whose editors shall be responsible to the said Committee. The Committee shall see that the papers are conducted in accordance with the spirit and intent of the Constitution, in the interest of The United Lutheran Church and for the edification of the people.

Item 7. The President shall appoint a Standing Committee consisting of fifteen members, known as the Common Service Book Committee, to whom shall be referred all matters pertaining to the worship of the Church.

This Committee shall be responsible for the Common Service Book, with respect to text and form in all editions; it shall prepare forms and manuals of worship and devotion authorized by the Church; and shall consider such other matters as may be referred to it by the Church.

Item 8. The President shall appoint a Committee of three ministers and four laymen to nominate a Standing Committee of ten laymen which shall be known as the Executive Committee of the Laymen's Movement and shall have charge of its development and administration. It shall have power to increase its membership as deemed expedient.

Item 9. No person shall be a member of more than two appointive standing committees at one and the same time.

C. Powers and Duties

Item 1. Inasmuch as the Boards and Committees are representatives of The United Lutheran Church in America, and of its work, the general policies of all Boards and Committees shall be decided by the Church, and it shall be the duty of Boards to refer all questions affecting the principles, practice and policy of the Church as a whole, to The United Lutheran Church for decision. It shall be the duty of the Boards to carry out and administer these principles and policies thus decided; and when changes seem advisable they may suggest any changes to the Church for its approval, after which only they shall become operative.

Item 2. No official relationship with any other ecclesiastical bodies or their agencies shall be entered into by any Board or Committee of The United Lutheran Church in America without the approval of the Church. See Constitution, Art. VIII, Sec. 1.

Item 3. All Boards, Standing Committees and Commissions after each meeting shall furnish the Executive Board with a copy of their proceedings that said Executive Board may be thoroughly informed and qualified to co-ordinate the work of the entire body. Boards which seek appropriations or apportionments shall present their request for the amount desired together with a statement of financial operations to the Executive Board not less than three months before each regular Convention, to enable the Board to prepare its budget.

Item 4. No Board shall have the right to inaugurate a propaganda for the raising of funds, outside of its regular budget, without the consent of the Executive Board of The United Lutheran Church.

Item 5. The financial accounts of the several Boards and Commissions shall be submitted for audit to an accredited accountant. In connection with its report each Board shall present to the Convention the report of the Treasurer certified by said accountant. The fiscal year of all Boards shall close on the last day of the fourth month preceding the one in which the Convention of the United Lutheran Church shall meet.

Item 6. All reports of Boards and Standing Committees, with recommendations, shall be sent to the Secretary of The United Lutheran Church at least sixty days before each Convention. The Secretary shall send out a Bulletin containing reports ten days in advance of the Convention.

Item 7. All reports of Boards shall be regularly signed by their officers. All reports of Committees shall be signed by a majority of the members thereof.

Item 8. Special and institutional reports shall, as far as possible, be incorporated into the report of the Board or Committee dealing with the general subject, and where this cannot be done, shall be heard only in connection with the consideration of that report, and shall be edited before printing.

Item 9. The person first named on a temporary Committee shall act as its Chairman. Standing Committees shall be convened by the person first named, and shall elect their own officers.

Item 10. When, besides the report of the majority of a Committee, there is also a report of a minority, the former shall be read first.

Item 11. In all cases of appeal from any decision of the Commission of Adjudication rendered within the interim between Conventions of The United Lutheran Church in America, Notice of Intention to Appeal shall be given in writing to the President of the Commission at least ten days prior to the first day of the Convention following: Provided, however, that when decisions have been rendered at any Convention, or within thirty days prior thereto, appeal may be made during the Convention upon consent obtained by a two-thirds' vote of the delegates present. The Convention shall thereupon fix a time when the appeal shall be made a special order of the Convention.

Item 12. An appeal from any decision of the Commission of Adjudication can be made only at the Convention of the United Lutheran Church at which such decision has been reported, and can be entertained only when Item 11 above has been fully complied with and the appeal shall have been submitted in writing by five delegates to said Convention. After the submission and argument of the appeal it shall not be voted upon until the succeeding day, unless by reason of limited time, the Convention, by two-thirds' vote, shall decide to adjudicate the appeal on the same day. To sustain the appeal and reverse the decision from which the appeal is made, a two-thirds' vote of the members present and voting shall be necessary. In the discussion of any such appeal, the Commission of Adjudication shall be fully heard through any of its members whom it may designate, whether they be or be not delegates to the Convention.

SECTION VI

CONCERNING THE PRESIDENT

Item 1. The President shall conduct all business according to the Constitution, By-Laws, and Order of Procedure of The United Lutheran

Church, and insist upon the observance of the same on the part of every member. He shall appoint all committees unless otherwise provided for.

Item 2. Robert's Rules of Order Revised shall be the governing parliamentary law except where not in harmony with the Constitution and By-Laws.

Item 3. He shall prepare a biennial report which shall briefly summarize the general conditions in the Church and his own work during the biennium and which shall be presented and assigned to Committees prior to the Convention's entering into the election of a successor.

SECTION VII

COMMITTEES

A. Special Committees

The following special Committees shall be appointed by the President at the first session of each Convention of The United Lutheran Church in America:

1. Committee to conduct the opening and closing services of each session.
2. Committee on Leave of Absence.
3. Committee on Memorials from Constituent Synods.
4. Committee of Reference and Counsel. (Its duties shall include the consideration of all general resolutions before they are submitted to the Convention, arrangements with the President for the hearing of representatives sent to the Conventions, and general assistance to the President in the daily program.)
5. Committee to Nominate Executive Committee of Laymen's Movement.
6. Committee to Nominate Members of Boards.
7. Committee to Nominate Members of Executive Board, and all elective Commissions or Committees.
8. Committee of Tellers.
9. Committee on Place of Next Convention.
10. Convention Committee on Daily Minutes.

B. Standing Committees

The following Standing Committees shall be appointed by the President:

1. Statistical and Church Year Book Committee.
2. Committee on Common Service Book.
3. Committee on Church Music.
4. Committee on German Interests.

(It shall arrange, in conference with the Executive Board, for any meetings of a German Conference required. It shall also be a place of counsel for any agencies of the Church when they are dealing with matters which concern especially the German-speaking portions of the Church. It shall, furthermore, have the privilege to approach any agency of the Church upon matters which are for the interest of that portion of the Church.)

5. Committee on Army and Navy Work.
6. Committee on Moral and Social Welfare.
7. Committee on Evangelism.
8. Committee on Church Architecture.
9. Committee on Publicity.

10. Committee on Transportation. (Its duties shall include all transportation interests, including the mileage and transportation arrangements for the Conventions.)

11. A Necrologist.

12. An Archivist.

13. Such other Standing Committees as may be provided for from time to time.

SECTION VIII

AMENDMENT

These By-Laws may be suspended or amended at any Convention by a two-thirds vote of the members present and voting; provided that due notice of the amendment proposed shall have been given on the preceding day.

Declaration of Principles Concerning the Church and Its External Relationships

ADOPTED AT
THE SECOND CONVENTION OF THE UNITED
LUTHERAN CHURCH IN AMERICA

AT

WASHINGTON, D. C.

OCTOBER 26, 1920

DECLARATION OF PRINCIPLES

CONCERNING

The Church and Its External Relationships

WHEREAS, During the past two years the Executive Board has been asked repeatedly to define the attitude of The United Lutheran Church in America toward co-operative movements, both within and without the Lutheran Church, toward movements of various kinds looking in the direction of church union, and toward organizations, tendencies and movements, some of them within and some of them without the organized Church: and

WHEREAS, The Constitution of The United Lutheran Church in America (Art. VIII, Sec. 1) and its By-Laws (Sec. 5, Div. C. Items 1 and 2) require that the forming and dissolving of "relations with other bodies, organizations and movements" lies within the power of The United Lutheran Church alone and that "all questions affecting the principles, practice and policy of the Church as a whole" shall be referred to the Church for decision: therefore,

The Executive Board submits to The United Lutheran Church the following DECLARATION OF PRINCIPLES CONCERNING THE CHURCH AND ITS EXTERNAL RELATIONSHIPS, and recommends it for adoption.

In order that all misunderstandings and misconstructions of this Declaration, or of any of its parts, may be avoided, The United Lutheran Church in America declares in advance that it does not regard the statements therein contained as altering or amending the Confessions of the Church in any particular, or as changing the doctrinal basis of The United Lutheran Church, set forth in Article II of the Constitution. On the contrary, it considers this Declaration nothing more than the application to present conditions of doctrines already contained in the Confessions.

A. CONCERNING THE CATHOLIC SPIRIT IN THE CHURCH

I. In its Confessions the Evangelical Lutheran Church declares its belief that there is "one holy Church," which "will continue forever." It defines this Church as the "congregation of saints and true believers." (Augs. Conf., VII and VIII.)

II. This one holy Church performs its earthly functions and makes its presence known among men through groups of men who profess to be believers in Jesus Christ. In these groups the Word of God is preached and the Sacraments are administered. To such groups also the name "Church" is given in the New Testament and in the Confessions of our Church.

III. The existence of the one, holy Church is not capable of demonstration. It is a "mystery" that can be apprehended only by faith. To the eyes of men it appears that there is not one Church, but only many churches; nevertheless, we believe that there is but one Church of Jesus Christ. This conviction rests upon our belief in the continued life of Christ in all His Christians, binding them together into one spiritual body, of which He is the Head, and building them up into one spiritual Temple, of which He is the Cornerstone; and upon our belief in the efficacy of the Word of God and the Sacraments as Means of Grace (A. C., V). We believe that wherever the Word of God is preached nd the Sacraments are administered, the Holy Spirit works faith in Christ. In every such place, therefore, there are believers in Jesus Christ, and wherever there are believers, there the one holy Church is present. For this reason we call the Word and the Sacraments "marks" or "signs" of the one holy Church. Therefore the Augsburg Confession adds to its definition of the Church the words, "in which the Gospel is rightly taught and the Sacraments are rightly administered."

IV. In the Nicene Creed we confess our belief that this Church is "one, holy, catholic and apostolic."

1. We believe that this Church is one, because we believe that there cannot be more than one "congregation of saints and true believers," or more than one spiritual Body of which Christ is the Head, or more than one spiritual Temple of which He is the Cornerstone.

2. We believe that this Church is holy, because we believe that to all believers the righteousness of Christ is given, with the forgiveness of their sins, for which reason true believers are called "saints" in the New Testament and in the Confessions of our Church. Moreover, the Holy Spirit, through the Word and the Sacraments preached and administered in the churches, does progressively create holiness of life and will and purpose in all those who believe, and progressively unites their lives with the continued life of Christ.

3. We believe that this one holy Church is catholic, because we believe that, since there is but one "congregation of saints and true believers," it must include all the saints and true believers, of every time and place (Apol., Chap. IV). By the term "catholic," therefore, we describe that quality of universality which belongs to the Church as a spiritual reality, or object of faith (Cf. III, above), and raises it above all local and temporal forms of expression in organization, rite and ceremony.

4. We believe that this one, holy, catholic Church is also apostolic, not because of the union of its members in any one organization which claims to possess external, historical connection with the apostles, but because we believe that the faith in Jesus Christ, which all the members of the one, holy catholic Church have in common, is the same faith that was in the hearts and lives of the apostles of Jesus Christ; and because we believe that this faith has been and still is perpetuated by the unbroken testimony of believers, through all the centuries of Christian history, from the days of the apostles to the present day; and because we believe that in the Holy Scriptures we have a permanent and authoritative record of that apostolic truth which is the ground of Christian faith.

V. Every group of professing Christians calling itself a Church will seek to express in its own life the attributes of the one, holy, catholic and apostolic Church. This it does:

1. By professing faith in Jesus Christ. Faith in Christ, as the Saviour of the world and the Revealer of the will and love of God the Father, is necessary to the existence of the Church. Therefore, no group of men, however organized, which does not exist as a congregation of professed believers in Jesus Christ, may claim the name of Church; for it is Christ Himself, living, by the Holy Spirit, in believing Christians, Who makes the Church one and holy.

2. By preaching the Word and administering the Sacraments. Every group calling itself a Church must preach the Word and administer the Sacraments, for these are the means through which the Holy Spirit works faith, and thus creates and perpetuates the one holy Church. Therefore, the Word and the Sacraments are properly called "marks" of the Church (Cf. III, above), for where they are present the Church is; where they are absent the Church is not and cannot be.

In the preaching of the Word and the administration of the Sacraments every group of Christians seeks to express the apostolic character of the one holy Church. Every such group bases its preaching and teaching upon the Scriptures, and endeavors to proclaim what it has learned from them. Believing that it has correctly ascertained this truth, it becomes its duty to teach, preach and confess it fully, freely and courageously. Christians must not only profess their faith in Christ, but must also confess and publicly declare what they believe about Christ and His Gospel; this duty of every Christian is the imperative duty of every group of Christians calling itself a Church.

3. By works of serving love. The ideals of love and service which Christ has taught as the true ideals of the individual Christian life, must also be the ideals of any group calling itself a Church. The love of Christians for God and His Christ, for one another and their fellow men, is a motive strong enough to drive them to works of service, and this love, itself a creation of God the Holy Spirit within the hearts of

men, sets tasks for every group that calls itself a Church. They are
tasks of service, not of government; of love, not of law (Cf. D, IV, 3,
below). These works of love and service are a witness to the faith
that lives in the whole group and an evidence of the presence of the
living Christ, and are in themselves a proclamation of the Gospel. In
outward form they may appear to be merely humanitarian and altruistic;
in motive they are Christian, born of the love of Christ, and performed
in His name and in obedience to His command.

4. By the attempt to secure universal acceptance of the truth which
it holds and confesses. Such an attempt need not be accompanied by
the effort to enlarge its own external organization by drawing into its
membership Christians of other organizations, for the aim of a Church
should be not to make proselytes, but to spread the truth of the Gospel.
To this end it will constantly bear witness to the truth which it believes,
and by this testimony, and by the cultivation of sympathy with all those
who hold the same truth, every group will seek to attain universality,
and thus express completely the holy Church's attribute of catholicity.

5. To accomplish these purposes (Nos. 1-4 above) every such group
will maintain the office of the ministry, commanded and instituted by
Christ. For the sake of good order and efficiency, further organization is
also necessary, but the forms which the organization takes will vary
with circumstances of time and place, and are, in themselves, matters
of expediency.

VI. Every group of professing Christians in which the Word of God
is so preached and the Sacraments are so administered that men are
saved therein is truly, partial and imperfect, as it may be, an expression
of the one holy Church (Cf. II, above), inasmuch as it displays the
marks of the Church (Cf. III and V, 2, above). Therefore, no one group
can rightfully claim that it is the one, holy, catholic and apostolic
Church in the sense in which these terms have been defined above
(No. IV).

We believe, however, that distinctions must be recognized between one
group and another. In making these distinctions, we believe that those
groups in which the Word of God is most purely preached and confessed,
according to the Holy Scriptures, and in which the Sacraments are
administered in the closest conformity to the institution of Christ, will
be the most complete expression of the one, holy Church. For this
reason it is necessary that, when occasion arises, any such group of
Christians shall define its relationship to other groups which also claim
the name of Church, as well as to other groups and organizations which
do not bear that name.

VII. This definition of relationships should be framed in the spirit
of catholicity. Moved by that spirit, a Church will always be ready:

1. To declare unequivocally what it believes concerning Christ and
His Gospel, and to endeavor to show that it has placed the true inter-

pretation upon that Gospel (Cf. V, 2 and 4, above), and to testify definitely and frankly against error.

2. To approach others without hostility, jealousy, suspicion or pride, in the sincere and humble desire to give and receive Christian service.

3. To grant cordial recognition to all agreements which are discovered between its own interpretation of the Gospel and that which others hold.

4. To co-operate with other Christians in works of serving love (Cf. V, 3, above) in so far as this can be done without surrender of its interpretation of the Gospel, without denial of conviction, and without suppression of its testimony as to what it holds to be the truth.

B. Concerning the Relation of the Evangelical Lutheran Church Bodies to One Another

In the case of those Church Bodies calling themselves Evangelical Lutheran, and subscribing the Confessions which have always been regarded as the standards of Evangelical Lutheran doctrine, The United Lutheran Church in America recognizes no doctrinal reasons against complete co-operation and organic union with such bodies.

C. Concerning the Organic Union of Protestant Churches

In view of the widespread discussion concerning the organic union of the Protestant Churches in America, we declare:

I. That we hold the union of Christians in a single organization to be of less importance than the agreement of Christians in the proclamation of the Gospel. We believe that the one, holy, catholic and apostolic Church exists through and under divergent forms of external organization. Union of organization we hold, therefore, to be a matter of expediency; agreement in testimony to be a matter of principle.

II. That holding the preaching of the Gospel and the administration of the Sacraments to be the primary function of every Church, we believe that a clear definition of what is meant by "Gospel" and "Sacrament" must precede any organic union of the Churches. We believe that a permanent and valid union of Churches must be based upon positive agreements concerning the truth for which the united Church Body is to stand. The Churches cannot unite as mere protestants, but only as confessors. (Cf. A, V, 2; VII, 4.)

III. That as a necessary step toward a genuine organic union, we believe that the Protestant Church Bodies in America should endeavor to set forth, definitely and positively, the views of Christian truth for which each of them does now actually stand, in order that by their clear and unequivocal testimony to what they hold to be the truth, the nature and extent of their agreements and disagreements may become apparent.

IV. That we recognize the obligation which rests upon us to make a clear and full declaration concerning the truth which we hold, and are therefore ready, as opportunity offers, to give answer concerning our reasons for accepting and maintaining the doctrines and principles set forth in the Confessions of the Evangelical Lutheran Church.

V. That until a more complete unity of confession is attained than now exists, The United Lutheran Church in America is bound in duty and in conscience to maintain its separate identity as a witness to the truth which it knows; and its members, its ministers, its pulpits, its fonts and its altars must testify only to that truth.

D. Concerning Co-operative Movements Among the Protestant Churches

In view of the many proposals for co-operation of the Protestant Churches in various departments of practical activity, and in view of the many organizations already formed, and in process of formation, for the carrying on of such co-operative work, we declare

I. That it is our earnest desire to co-operate with other Church Bodies in all such works as can be regarded as works of serving love, through which the faith of Christians finds expression; provided, that such co-operation does not involve the surrender of our interpretation of the Gospel, the denial of conviction, or the suppression of our testimony to what we hold to be the truth. (Cf. A, V, 4; VII, 3, above.) In this connection, however, we call attention to the Constitution of The United Lutheran Church in America, Article VIII, Section 1, "No Synod, Conference or Board, or any official representative thereof, shall have the power of independent affiliation with general organizations and movements," and also to the By-Laws, Article V, Division C, Item 2, "No official relationship with any other ecclesiastical bodies or their agencies shall be entered into by any Board or Committee of The United Lutheran Church in America, without the approval of the Church."

II. That we cannot give general approval to all co-operative movements and organizations of the Churches, since we hold that co-operation is not an end in itself, but merely a means to an end. Our attitude toward any such organization or movement must be determined by a consideration of

(a) The purposes which it seeks to accomplish.

(b) The principles on which it rests.

(c) The effect which our participation will produce upon the independent position of our Church as a witness to the truth of the Gospel which we confess. (Cf. C, VII, above.)

III. That, holding the following doctrines and principles, derived from the Holy Scriptures, to be fundamental to the Christian message, we propose them as a positive basis of practical co-operation among the Protestant Churches. To avoid all possible misunderstandings or misconstructions of these statements, we declare that we do not regard them as a summary of Lutheran doctrine, or as an addition to, a substitute for, or a modification of the Confessions of our Church; nor do we propose them as an adequate basis for an organic union of the Churches, but merely as a criterion by which it may be possible for us to determine our attitude toward proposed movements of co-operation.

1. The Fatherhood of God, revealed in His Son Jesus Christ, and the sonship bestowed by God, through Christ, upon all who believe in Him.

2. The true Godhead of Jesus Christ, and His redemption of the world by His life and death and resurrection; and His living presence in His Church.

3. The continued activity of God the Holy Spirit among men, calling them into the fellowship of Jesus Christ, and enlightening and sanctifying them through the gifts of His grace.

4. The supreme importance of the Word of God and the Sacraments of Baptism and the Lord's Supper, as the means through which the Holy Spirit testifies of Christ and thus creates and strengthens faith. (In common with the whole Evangelical Lutheran Church, we confess the mystery of the Real Presence in the Sacrament of the Lord's Supper, and we invite all Christians to a renewed study of the teachings of the Holy Scriptures concerning this Sacrament, and the Sacrament of Holy Baptism.)

5. The authority of the prophetic and apostolic Scriptures of the Old and New Testaments, as the only rule and standard by which all doctrines and teachers are to be judged.

6. The reality and universality of sin, and the inability of men, because of sin, to attain righteousness or earn salvation through their own character or works.

7. The love, and the righteousness, of God, Who for Christ's sake bestows forgiveness and righteousness upon all who believe in Christ.

8. The present existence upon earth of the kingdom of God, founded by His Son Jesus Christ, not as an external organization, but as a spiritual reality and an object of faith.

9. The hope of Christ's second coming, to be the Judge of the living and the dead, and to complete the kingdom of God.

IV. That, in view of the above statements, our attitude toward proposed co-operative movements and organizations, already defined in principle in Section A, VII and D, I, above, must be subject to the following limitations:

1. We cannot enter into any co-operative movement or organization which denies any of the doctrines or principles set forth in III, above.

2. We cannot enter into any organization or movement which limits the co-operating Churches in their confession of the truth or their testimony against error. In all co-operative movements we claim the right, and regard it as a duty, to testify freely to the truth as it is set forth in the Confessions of our Church, and we believe that the same

right must be guaranteed to every participating Church. All such testimony should receive a courteous and respectful hearing.

3. We cannot enter into co-operative movements or organizations whose purposes lie outside the proper sphere of Church activity. In determining what that sphere is, we must be guided by the fundamental principle that the functions of the Church are the preaching of the Word, the administration of the Sacraments, and the performance of works of love (Cf. A, V, above). We hold that the use of the Church organization as an agency for securing the enactment and enforcement of law, or for the application of other methods of external force, is foreign to the true purpose for which the Church exists.

V. That there are organizations and movements into which we cannot enter as a Church, in regard to which, however, the Church may definitely declare itself and which it may heartily commend to the pastors and members of its congregations as important spheres of activity for Christians, such as movements and organizations for social and political reform, the enforcement of law and order, the settlement of industrial conflicts, the improvement of the material environments of life, and the like.

E. Concerning Movements and Organizations Injurious to the Christian Faith

In view of the prevalence throughout our land of doctrines which are subversive of the Christian faith; and in view of the indifference manifested by many Christian people to the doctrines and principles of the teachers, sects and organizations which seek their adherence and support; and in view of the fact that through the acceptance of religious and other teachings which contradict the Gospel of Christ, the faith of Christians is endangered; we declare

I. That we solemnly warn all our pastors and the members of our congregations against all teachers, sects and organizations of any kind, whose doctrines and principles contradict the truths set forth in Section D, III, of this Declaration, or which limit their adherents or members in a free confession of their Christian faith (Cf. A, V, 3, above.)

II. That we warn them especially against all teachers, sects and societies whose doctrines and principles deny the reality of sin, the personality of God, the full and complete Godhead of our Lord Jesus Christ, and His redemption of the world by His sufferings and death, and the truth and authority of the Holy Scriptures; as well as against all teachers, sects and societies which teach that men can be saved from sin, or can become righteous before God, by their own works or by any other means than the grace and mercy of God in Jesus Christ. We believe that such doctrines are not only not Christian, but are anti-Christian and destructive of true Christian faith and life.

III. That inasmuch as these and other false and dangerous doctrines are widely spread, not only by the activity of individual teachers, but also by the dissemination of literature and through the agency of societies and other organizations, calling themselves by various names which oftentimes conceal the real nature of the doctrines and principles for which they stand; we therefore lay it upon the consciences of the pastors and of the members of all our congregations to scrutinize with the utmost care the doctrines and principles of all teachers, sects, organizations and societies of every sort which seek their adherence and support, and to refuse such adherence and support in all cases of conflict or possible contradiction between these principles and doctrines and those set forth in Holy Scripture and in the Confessions of the Church. In the application of this principle the Church should always appeal to a conscience which it is her sacred duty to enlighten, patiently and persistently, from the Word of God. (Cf., also Constitution of The United Lutheran Church in America, Art. VIII, Sec. 6.)

INDEX

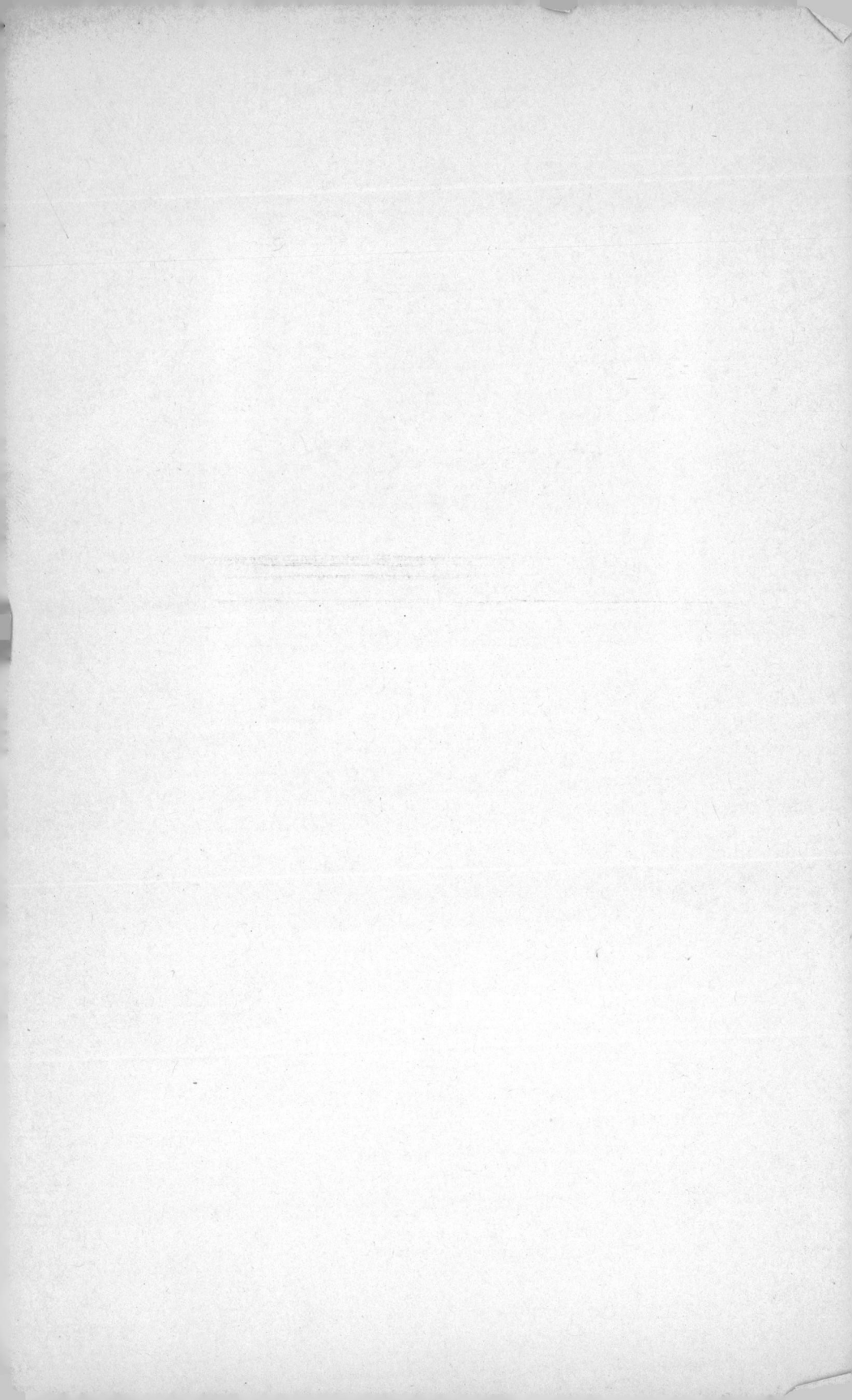